# The UNIX and X Command Compendium

## A Dictionary for High-Level Computing

# The UNIX and X Command Compendium

## A Dictionary for High-Level Computing

**Alan Southerton**
**Edwin C. Perkins, Jr.**

JOHN WILEY & SONS, INC.
New York • Chichester • Brisbane • Toronto • Singapore

*Library of Congress Cataloging-in-Publication Data*

Southerton, Alan.
    The UNIX and X command compendium : a dictionary for high level computing
/ Alan Southerton, Edwin C. Perkins, Jr.
      p.    cm.
    Includes bibliographical references.
    ISBN 0-471-01281-5 (alk. paper). — ISBN 0-471-30982-6 (pbk.)
    1. UNIX (Computer file) 2. X Window System (Computer system)
I. Perkins, Edwin C., 1970– . II. Title.
QA76.76.O6S656   1994
005.4'3—dc20

93-48628
CIP

Printed in the United States of America
10 9 8 7 6 5 4 3 2 1

*This book is dedicated to my sons, Thomas James Southerton, William McLean Southerton, and Edward Alan Southerton, whom I love and cherish.*
—Alan Southerton

*This book is dedicated to my parents, Edwin and Joyce Perkins, for their support and understanding.*
—Edwin C. Perkins, Jr.

# About the Authors

**Alan Southerton** is the president of Newline Computer Services, Inc., a firm specializing in UNIX and X Window System development, consulting, and benchmarking. Current products available from the firm are Button Manager, Xterm Manager, and Resource Manager.

Mr. Southerton has also written six other computer books, including one on UNIX and one on the X Window System and Motif. He is also one of the fouding editors of *SCO World Magazine*, which specializes in UNIX topics, and a columnist for the *X Journal*. Formerly, Mr. Southerton was Product Reviews Editor at *UNIXWORLD Magazine* (now *Open Systems Magazine*) and was associated with that publication for seven years. In his dark past, Mr. Southerton edited the complete set of UNIX documentation for a major hardware and software systems vendor.

**Edwin C. Perkins, Jr.** is the Lab Director of *SCO World Magazine* and has written articles and reviews for other publications. Mr. Perkins holds a degree in Electrical Engineering from Rensselaer Polytechnic Institute and is currently a Development Manager at Newline Computer Services, Inc. Formerly, Mr. Perkins was a consultant with the Information Systems department at the Massachusetts Institute of Technology.

# Preface

In the ever-changing computer industry, one thing has remained consistent for more than 20 years: the commands and utilities associated with the UNIX operating system.

This book represents a massive effort by several people to compile a dictionary-like reference to the UNIX commands. It is different from all other books because its sole intention is to deliver real examples. In other words, you don't have to search for examples because the book is a compilation of examples, arranged in alphabetical order.

*The UNIX and X Command Compendium* provides a quick reference for UNIX users. The book spans all topics related to state-of-the-art UNIX, including networking, email, shell script programming, the Internet, the X Window system, and graphical user interfaces. By providing more than 2,000 examples, the book has the potential of delivering more information in shorter periods of time than traditional computer books. The book's ultimate goal is to reduce the UNIX learning curve by months, if not years.

The authors, persons who have tested the commands in the book, and numerous administrative personnel have sought to make *The UNIX and X Command Compendium* as comprehensive as possible. We have tested commands on many versions of UNIX, including SunOS, SCO, System V, IBM AIX, and the MKS toolkit for MS-DOS systems.

In developing the book, the authors looked at UNIX through the eyes of both BSD and System V users. While recognizing that

BSD is the most loved of the two versions, we also recognize the ever continuing push toward re-unification of UNIX under the System V banner, as well as the involvement of other operating systems with the UNIX commands, and so we have attempted to treat the MKS toolkit for MS-DOS and Windows/NT on a par with other versions of UNIX.

We intend that *The UNIX and X Command Compendium* be a living document. Please send any corrections or additions to **book@newl.com**. If you do not have email, call Newline Computer Services, Inc., at (508) 921-4458. For your efforts, we will provide you through email a current list of corrections and additional commands.

## Acknowledgments

We are indebted to numerous persons for their assistance on *The UNIX and X Command Compendium*. We would like to pay special thanks to Emily Dawkins, research assistant at Newline Computer, Inc., who helped us with administrative and editorial matters throughout the project. We would also like to thank other Newline associates, including Pat Capobianco, Steven Goldberg, and Robert Landau. We would also like to thank Diane Cerra, our editor at John Wiley & Sons, and her assistant, Tammy Boyd, for their support. Much thanks also goes to Frank Grazioli, our production manager at Wiley, for his superlative approach to quality control, despite the often beleaguered manuscript pages we submitted.

*Sadly, on May 20, 1994, Alan Southerton passed away. Unfortunately, he was not able to see the publication of this treatise. As it now appears in print, I believe that he would have been pleased with the book on which we worked together for so long. He will be sorely missed.*

*Edwin C. Perkins, Jr.*
*Essex, Massachusetts*

# Contents

# Introduction

There are two ways to look at commands and utilities in the UNIX operating system. The first way is to consider them as standalone programs that perform a function. This is fine, so long as all you need to do is perform a single purpose operation, such as list a directory with **ls** or read a file with **more**.

If this is your approach to commands, you can make do with the UNIX manual pages and perhaps a reference book or two that describe the abstract use of commands. For many people, however, learning the abstract is a noble exercise, but one better left to users with more time on their hands.

In writing this book, we used the same perspective that any lexicographer would take: namely, we wanted to provide a comprehensive compendium of words in popular usage. Our words, however, are spoken in the following environments: the UNIX operating system, the X Window System, the Network Files System (NFS), and the Internet and other TCP/IP networks.

This marks a different approach to presenting a UNIX book or any computer book for that matter. We can safely say that we are the first authors who have devised and compiled a computer book founded on what we believe to be some basic facts of computing:

- The commands used to interact with operating systems and environments fit the classical description of a language.

- Traditional command references present a command in its abstract form. The equivalent in an English-language dictionary would be to present words as root words only.

- Beginning in the early 1980s, computing emerged as a global and egalitarian part of society. This phenomenon is a polar opposite to the abstract approach—and the doctrine that the most efficient and logical way of executing a command is the right way, versus other ways, which also execute correctly, but take one or two seconds longer to do so.

This brings us to another way of looking at UNIX commands. Instead of standalone programs, UNIX commands can be freely mixed with one another to create solutions to your computing problems. Unfortunately, to use the commands to solve problems, you still need to learn the abstract theory—unless, that is, you have purchased a copy of *The UNIX and X Command Compendium*, which does much of the work for you.

*The UNIX and X Command Compendium* is structured like a dictionary. Command examples appear alphabetically. Per command, the reader can find anywhere from 1 to 50 examples. For instance, the find command has 28 entries, each with a unique example that solves a specific problem. In a traditional UNIX reference, the find command has one entry, a text section, an options listing, and maybe a few examples. This leaves you to piece things together. In *The UNIX and X Command Compendium*, there is little piecing together: even with commands that have multiple examples, the reader can easily decide by reading the brief description whether to read the rest of the entry.

The design of *The UNIX and X Command Compendium* caters to the reading habits of computer users, most of whom are disinterested, concerned only with seeking the answer to a problem. As a result, computer users scan, flip through pages, and read books back-to- front. The graphic design of the entries in *The UNIX and X Command Compendium* capitalize on this in several ways:

- Examples are set in 13-point boldface text.

- Descriptive text is concise, taking up about a sixth of a page on average.

- An optional reference table, which is used for ancillary material such as configuration files, is concise.

- An optional command output section (if required for the reader to understand the command) is again concise.

- The status bars serve well if you are merely interested in scanning the book for items of interest.

Subjects covered in *The UNIX and X Command Compendium* include most of the UNIX commands, File Transfer Protocol (ftp), Telnet, the Network File System (NFS), and programs and utilities in the X Window System, OSF/Motif, Sun OpenWindows, and SVR4.2's Open Look. Operating system variants include SunOS (a.k.a. Solaris), IBM AIX, SCO UNIX, SVR4.2, and BSD as incarnated on NeXT and OSF/1 systems. The book also provides entries for important configuration files. Further, in each entry, the status line notes one of the following user categories: end, script, power, and sysadm.

Because many of the keyword entries in *The UNIX and X Command Compendium* have numerous pointers, as in the example, the entries serve both the novice and experienced user. They serve the novice because they note the most appropriate reference first. They serve the experienced user and system administrator because they provide a summary of all related commands covered in *The UNIX and X Command Compendium*. What is more, the experienced user does not despise the mere presence of the more simplified commands—that is, no more so than a dictionary reader despises the presence of words he or she already knows.

## Organization

*The UNIX and X Command Compendium* is about learning versus doing, and about learning from theory versus learning by doing. It is also about giving new, seasoned, and even expert UNIX users an ultimate way to solve problems using the UNIX operating system.

The standout feature of *The UNIX and X Command Compendium* is its dictionary approach to commands. Unlike other books that describe commands in alphabetical order, however, *The Command Compendium* lists and describes actual examples. As a result, any single entry might actually contain several commands, because in UNIX, you often use multiple commands at the same time to solve a problem. Here is an example:

calendar | grep `date +"%m/%d"`

This example uses the **calendar** program to access your personal database of reminders. More than this, however, it also uses the

**grep** utility to filter the reminders, and is therefore typical of many of the compound commands found in the book (although the example is one of the more basic commands in the book). So here is an example of a more complex command:

ps -e | awk '/xterm/ && ! /awk/ {print $1}'

This command lets you extract the job id from a **ps** listing. The **ps** command is designed to list information about running programs and processes that are active. By filtering the output into **ps**, using the pipe symbol, you let **awk** do the dirty work of finding what you want. (This is an extremely powerful compound command, given that after you obtain a job id, you can manipulate the running program or process).

All commands appear in alphabetical order in *The Command Compendium*. This makes it easy for you to look up a command when you have an idea of what the command is. Each entry comes with additional information, including the type of user the command is designed for. The following excerpt shows a typical entry in *The Command Compendium*:

### acctmerg -vt < *.acct

| ALL | SVR4 OSF AIX | SYSADM |
|-----|--------------|--------|

This command accumulates totals from one or more accounting files. The **-v** option specifies ASCII output. The **-t** option specifies a single record totalling all input.

**Keyword:**   system information, security

**Files:**   /etc/passwd, /usr/lib/acct, /var/adm/pacct, /var/adm/wtmp

**See Also:**   acctcms, acctcom, acctcon, acctprc, runacct

As the example shows, UNIX lends itself to *The Command Compendium's* approach. UNIX commands are rich with options, and flexible when combined with other commands. The result is often a unique function —a command unto itself. The pedagogical alternative would have been to group commands by keyword, and then alphabetize the book by keyword. In practice, however, computer users remember functionality by the command name, not by a generic heading arrived at by the authors.

Complementing these features is a thorough index. Instead of a last minute project, the index in *The UNIX and X Command Compendium* is the result of daily work and the coordination of command databases developed by the authors. The index is useful for associating generic names with commands, but it is further useful in associating naming conventions that *The UNIX and X Command Compendium* would not otherwise address. For example, an OpenWindows user can look up "Text Editor" in the index and be referred to "textedit," the actual command name.

## Using the Compendium

To use *The UNIX and X Command Compendium* to its fullest, you need to understand the different parts of each entry. The first thing to look for is the *category* to which the command belongs. There are four categories of users:

- Enduser: someone experienced with another operating system, but beginning to use UNIX for the first time. In addition to the extensive index, the new user should pay attention to the icons representing user categories.

- Shell Script Writer: someone interested in writing shell scripts, primarily to increase productivity in manipulating files and data.

- Power User: someone experienced in UNIX and networking.

- System Administrator: although not a guide to system administration, *The UNIX and X Command Compendium* offers hundreds of commands that system administrators can use to reduce their workload.

The actual design of *The UNIX and X Command Compendium* caters to the reading habits of computer users, most of whom are disinterested, concerned only with seeking the answer to a problem. As a result, computer users scan, flip through pages, and read books back-to- front. The graphic design of the entries in *The UNIX and X Command Compendium* cater to this reading style.

## accept myprinter

ALL  SVR4  SYSADM

This command provides access for print requests to either a printer or class of printers. The opposite command, **reject**, restricts access to a printer or class of printers.

**Keyword:**  printing

**See Also:**  lpadmin, lpsched, enable, lp, lpstat

## acct

ALL  SVR4  SYSADM
     OSF
     AIX

If the UNIX accounting utilities had a snazzier name, maybe more people would know about them. They have nothing to do with financial accounting. Instead, they provide tools for monitoring what happens on the system. Included under SVR4 are: **acctdisk**, which creates accounting records from user information; **acct-dusg**, which calculates disk usage; and **acctwtmp**, which records events on the system. *The UNIX and X Command Compendium* provides coverage of the SVR4 and SCO accounting utilities. Because different vendors implement entirely different suites of utilities, however, it is not practical to document each suite.

**Keyword:**  system information, security

**Files:**  /etc/passwd, /usr/lib/acct, /var/adm/pacct, /var/adm/wtmp

**See Also:**  acctcms, acctcom, acctcon, acctmerg, acctprc, runacct

## acctcms -a -c local.acct

ALL  SVR4  SYSADM
     OSF
     AIX

The **acctcms** utility evaluates commands and tracks any process that has executed a command while the command was running as the result of another process previously executing it. The **-a** option specifies ASCII output. The **-c** option specifies sorting by total CPU time.

**Keyword:**  system information, security

**Files:**  /etc/passwd, /usr/lib/acct, /var/adm/pacct, /var/adm/wtmp

**See Also:**  acctcom, acctcon, acctmerg, acctprc, runacct

## acctcom -b local.acct

ALL  SVR4  SYSADM
     OSF
     AIX

The **acctcom** utility searches the specified accounting file and displays process, user, and device information for previously executed commands. The **-b** option in the example causes **acctcom** to search backwards and display most recent commands first.

**Keyword:** system information, security

**Files:** /etc/passwd, /usr/lib/acct, /var/adm/pacct, /var/adm/wtmp

**See Also:** acctcms, acctcon, acctmerg, acctprc, runacct

## acctcon -l dialup.acct -o init.acct < /var/adm/wtmp

| | | |
|---|---|---|
| ALL | SVR4 OSF AIX | SYSADM |

The **acctcon** command tracks login usage. The **-l** option in the example writes line usage statistics to **dialup.acct** (an arbitrary filename). The **-o** option writes startup information to **init.acct** (also arbitrary). The **/var/adm/wtmp** file supplies the initial information. The **acctcon** utility has two aliases: **acctcon1**, which converts login records; and **acctcon**, which converts them to **tacct** format, which is used by the various accounting utilities.

**Keyword:** system information, security

**Files:** /etc/passwd, /usr/lib/acct, /var/adm/pacct, /var/adm/wtmp

**See Also:** acctcms, acctcom, acctmerg, acctprc, runacct

## acctmerg -vt < *.acct

| | | |
|---|---|---|
| ALL | SVR4 OSF AIX | SYSADM |

This command accumulates totals from one or more accounting files. The **-v** option specifies ASCII output. The **-t** option specifies a single record totalling all input.

**Keyword:** system information, security

**Files:** /etc/passwd, /usr/lib/acct, /var/adm/pacct, /var/adm/wtmp

**See Also:** acctcms, acctcom, acctcon, acctprc, runacct

## acctprc < /var/adm/pacct > process.acct

| | | |
|---|---|---|
| ALL | SVR4 OSF AIX | SYSADM |

The **acctprc** command totals information on processes, including mean memory statistics. There are two aliases: **acctprc1**, which converts input in the accounting utilities **tacct** format; and **acctprc2**, which reads and writes the output from **acctprc1**.

**Keyword:** system information, security

**Files:** /etc/passwd, /usr/lib/acct, /var/adm/pacct, /var/adm/wtmp

**See Also:** acctcms, acctcom, acctcon, acctmrg, runacct

## addbib report.bib

ALL  SunOS  POWER

This interactive program is used to create and maintain a bibliography. In this example, *The UNIX and X Command Compendium* was added to the **report.bib** file.

```
      Author:    Ed Perkins
       Title:    The UNIX and X Command Compendium
     Journal:
      Volume:
       Pages:    512
   Publisher:    John Wiley and Sons
        City:    New York
        Date:    7/26/93
       Other:
    Keywords:
    Abstract:
^D
   Continue? n
```

**Keyword:**   text handling

**See Also:**   vi, ed, sed, emacs

## alias a alias

CSH  ALL  ALL

This is perhaps one of the most common aliases in existence. It simply aliases the **alias** command to **a**. It's common to see this command in a **.cshrc** file as the first alias listed.

**Keyword:**   keyboard shortcuts

**Files:**   $HOME/.cshrc

**See Also:**   csh

## alias CAT ´cat !* | tr "[a-z]" "[A-Z]"´

CSH  ALL  END
SCRIPT

Perhaps everyone won't like this alias, but users who like uppercase letters might. By using **cat** to pipe all the files on the command line (represented by **!***) into **tr**, all lowercase letters are converted into uppercase letters. Note that some UNIX variants don't use brackets with **tr**; instead, they use only double quotes around the letter ranges.

**Keyword:**   text display

**Files:**   $HOME/.cshrc

**See Also:**   cat, tr

| CSH | ALL | END SCRIPT |
|-----|-----|------------|

## alias cd ´cd \!*; set prompt="[`hostname`]<$cwd> "´

A common practice among shell users is to alias the **cd** command to the **set prompt** command. The result is a command line prompt that displays the current path at all times. In this command, the alias also includes the **hostname** command, which combined with the **$cwd** variable (the system variable that holds the value of the current directory), produces a prompt similar to the following:

```
[alpha]</usr/lib/X11>
```

This alias is an excellent candidate for the C shell's **.cshrc** startup file. If you use it there, you also need to enter the following:

```
set prompt="[`hostname`]<$cwd> "
```

This takes care of initializing the prompt when you first start a version of the shell. The **cd** alias only begins to work the first time you use the **cd** command.

**Keyword:**   user environment

**Files:**   $HOME/.cshrc

**See Also:**   cd, hostname, prompt, set

| CSH | ALL | END SCRIPT |
|-----|-----|------------|

## alias census ´who | wc -l´

This alias gives you a quick way to determine how many users are currently working on the system. The **who** command lists users by default (one per line), and the **wc -l** counts the lines and displays the result.

**Keyword:**   keyboard shortcuts

**Files:**   $HOME/.cshrc

**See Also:**   wc, who

| CSH | ALL | END SCRIPT |
|-----|-----|------------|

## alias day date +"%A"

Maybe you don't know what day of the week it is. Or maybe you want a command to output the date to a log or note file. This alias does the trick, using the **%A** function to the **date** command.

**Keyword:**   time

**Files:**   $HOME/.cshrc

**See Also:**   cal, calendar, date

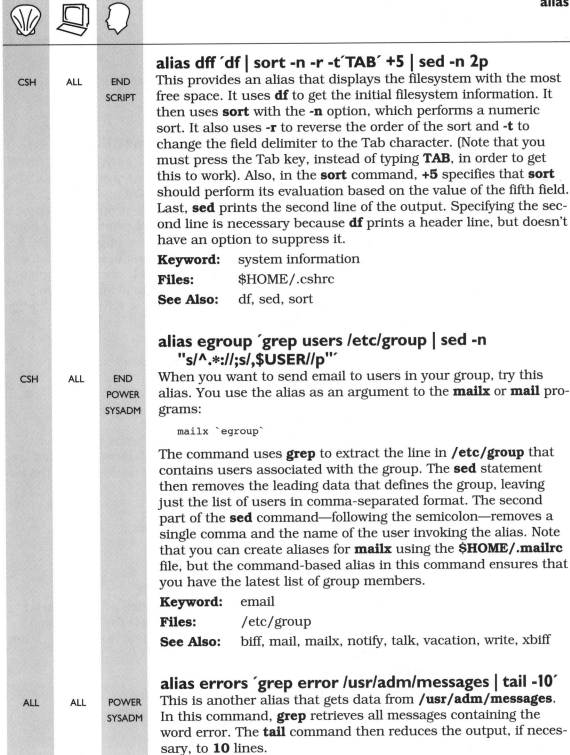

| CSH | ALL | END<br>SCRIPT |

## alias dff ´df | sort -n -r -t´TAB´ +5 | sed -n 2p

This provides an alias that displays the filesystem with the most free space. It uses **df** to get the initial filesystem information. It then uses **sort** with the **-n** option, which performs a numeric sort. It also uses **-r** to reverse the order of the sort and **-t** to change the field delimiter to the Tab character. (Note that you must press the Tab key, instead of typing **TAB**, in order to get this to work). Also, in the **sort** command, **+5** specifies that **sort** should perform its evaluation based on the value of the fifth field. Last, **sed** prints the second line of the output. Specifying the second line is necessary because **df** prints a header line, but doesn't have an option to suppress it.

**Keyword:**   system information

**Files:**   $HOME/.cshrc

**See Also:**   df, sed, sort

| CSH | ALL | END<br>POWER<br>SYSADM |

## alias egroup ´grep users /etc/group | sed -n "s/^.*://;s/,$USER//p"´

When you want to send email to users in your group, try this alias. You use the alias as an argument to the **mailx** or **mail** programs:

```
mailx `egroup`
```

The command uses **grep** to extract the line in **/etc/group** that contains users associated with the group. The **sed** statement then removes the leading data that defines the group, leaving just the list of users in comma-separated format. The second part of the **sed** command—following the semicolon—removes a single comma and the name of the user invoking the alias. Note that you can create aliases for **mailx** using the **$HOME/.mailrc** file, but the command-based alias in this command ensures that you have the latest list of group members.

**Keyword:**   email

**Files:**   /etc/group

**See Also:**   biff, mail, mailx, notify, talk, vacation, write, xbiff

| ALL | ALL | POWER<br>SYSADM |

## alias errors ´grep error /usr/adm/messages | tail -10´

This is another alias that gets data from **/usr/adm/messages**. In this command, **grep** retrieves all messages containing the word error. The **tail** command then reduces the output, if necessary, to **10** lines.

**Keyword:**  system information
**Files:**  $HOME/.cshrc, /usr/adm/messages
**See Also:**  grep, tail

### alias ethernet ´sed -n ´\´´s/^.*\(Ethernet\)/\1/p´\´´ /usr/adm/messages | uniq´

ALL  ALL  POWER
SYSADM

On some UNIX systems there is no ready-made command to tell you the Ethernet hardware address. Using **sed** and **uniq** in an alias that reads the **/usr/adm/messages** file is one way to provide such a command. In this command, **sed** prints the line containing **Ethernet**, stripping away any text that appears before it on the line. The **uniq** command is used to produce a single line of text. The **/usr/adm/messages** file probably contains numerous identical commands. As an alternative to using **uniq**, you can use a **sed** address with the **q** command to have **sed** quit after finding the first instance.

**Keyword:**  networking
**Files:**  $HOME/.cshrc, /usr/adm/messages
**See Also:**  uniq, sed

### alias ff grep \!$ /usr/phone/phone.dir

CSH  ALL  POWER

This example creates an alias in the C shell using parameter substitution. Note that the bang character (**!**) must be quoted for the shell to interpret it correctly. (Korn shell users refer to the following example.)

**Keyword:**  text search, text handling
**Files:**  $HOME/.cshrc, a phone data file
**See Also:**  grep

### alias ff=´grep $1 /usr/phone/phone.dir´

KSH  ALL  ALL

This is used to create an alias in the Korn shell with parameter substitution. Unlike the C shell, you must use the equals sign to set a Korn shell alias. Also use single quotation marks, which are necessary.

**Keyword:**  printing
**Files:**  $HOME/.kshrc, a phone data file
**See Also:**  grep

| | | |
|---|---|---|
| ALL | ALL | END SCRIPT |

## alias grope ´more `grep -l \!:1 \!:2`´

With this alias, you can specify a search string for **grep** and one or more filenames. In return, you get a full display of all files that contain the search string. Command substitution is used to feed the output from **grep** to **more**. The **-l** flag to **grep** specifies that the output should be just the associated filenames.

| | |
|---|---|
| **Keyword:** | text search |
| **Files:** | $HOME/.cshrc |
| **See Also:** | grep, more |

| | | |
|---|---|---|
| ALL | ALL | END SCRIPT |

## alias grub ´pr -t -o6 `grep -l \!:1 \!:2` | sed´\´´s/ \(.*\)\!:1\(.*\)$/ \*\*\* \1\!:1\2 \*\*\*/´\´´ | more´

This alias finds a word or phrase and marks the line containing the string with asterisks in the left and right margins. The **grep** command is used initially to match files containing the search string. The **pr** command is used to format the files for display. You execute the alias by entering **grub UNIX os.doc**. In this example, **UNIX** could be any string of text. The one drawback to the alias is that it finds parts of words if you use a small search string.

| | |
|---|---|
| **Keyword:** | text search |
| **Files:** | $HOME/.cshrc |
| **See Also:** | grep, more, pr, sed |

| | | |
|---|---|---|
| ALL | ALL | POWER |

## alias h history

The **h** alias is probably the second most common alias among C shell users after the **a** alias. As the example shows, the **h** alias executes the **history** mechanism.

| | |
|---|---|
| **Keyword:** | user environment |
| **Files:** | $HOME/.cshrc |
| **See Also:** | history |

| | | |
|---|---|---|
| ALL | ALL | USER |

## alias H: ´cd /usr/H:´

Assuming you work in a mixed UNIX and DOS environment, you might like to implement this alias. As a result, any time that a DOS user—while working in a UNIX session—types **H:**, the aliased command changes to the **/usr/H:** directory. The alias assumes that the DOS users have a UNIX filesystem mounted to their PCs. In DOS, you must reference the filesystem as a logical

7

drive (D–Z). Also, in DOS, users move between drives by entering the drive letter followed by a colon.

**Keyword:**    filesystem, directories

**Files:**        $HOME/.cshrc

**See Also:**   history

### alias H:=´cd /usr/H:´

ALL    ALL    USER

This command is the Korn shell version of the previous command. Note that the only difference is the use of the equals sign. This is typical of many simple aliases in the two shells.

**Keyword:**    filesystem, directories

**Files:**        $HOME/.cshrc

**See Also:**   history

### alias h=history

ALL    ALL    POWER

The Korn shell requires an equals sign between **h** and **history** to make the alias take effect. See the equivalent C shell example for a comparison.

**Keyword:**    user environment

**Files:**        $HOME/.kshrc

**See Also:**   history

### alias kill ´/bin/kill \!*´

CSH    ALL    END
SYSADM

If you prefer **/bin/kill** to the C shell's version of **kill**, which is a built-in and handles job IDs as well as process IDs, you should consider this alias. It simply aliases an existing command to another command, which is quite common in aliasing. All arguments from the command line, thanks to the **\!*** sequence, are passed to the aliased command.

**Keyword:**    job control

**Files:**        $HOME/.cshrc

**See Also:**   kill

### alias ll ´ls -ltF !* | head -15´

ALL    ALL    ALL

This is an alias for the **ls** command. The **-ltF** options combine to display a long listing with the most recently created files at the top of the list. The **-F** option places a slash next to directory names and an * next to executable filenames. (If you want to list dot files as well, include the **-a** option.) The last thing that happens in the alias is that **head** reduces the output to **15** lines.

**Keyword:** file display

**Files:** $HOME/.cshrc

**See Also:** head, ls

### alias ls ls -aF

This creates an alias for an existing command. It can be a strategy for providing new users with a consistent interface. The drawback is that users cannot implement different options with the given command.

**Keyword:** file handling

**Files:** $HOME/.cshrc

**See Also:** ls

### alias lss ´file * | grep ´/bin/sh´ | awk -F: ´\´{print $1}´\´´

If you're not necessarily the most organized user, and sometimes leave scripts in the same directory as documents and binary files, you can use this alias to output a listing of scripts. The **file** command is key here; it determines whether a file is a script. The **awk** command cleans up the output.

**Keyword:** file display

**Files:** /etc/magic

**See Also:** awk, file, grep

### alias lsub ´ls -lF | grep \/$´

In cases when you just want to list subdirectories, use **lsub** or even type the command out if you're a fast typist. The entry uses **grep** to filter out directories. It does this by searching for the **/** character at the end of each line of output. The **-F** option to **ls** is reponsible for appending **/** to the end of each line.

**Keyword:** directories

**Files:** $HOME/.cshrc

**See Also:** grep, ls

CSH ALL ALL

CSH ALL END SYSADM

CSH ALL END SYSADM

| | | |
|---|---|---|
| CSH | ALL | END SYSADM |

### alias lup ´ls -ls `ls -A1F | sed -n ´\´´/^[.A-Z]*[0-9A-Z] *[\/0-9A-Z]$/p´\´~´

Users who started in a mainframe or VMS environment like capital letters. With the **lup** alias in this command, you can view files with all uppercase letters. The regular expression in the **sed** command takes into account different types of files that might be all uppercase letters, including those beginning with a dot, single-letter filenames, and directories. You execute **lup** in the directory that you want to list. If a directory is included in the output to **ls -ls**, as is **ADIR2** in the example, the files in that directory are listed, but not in uppercase. All files in the current directory do meet the regular expression criteria. To specify the same criteria for additional subdirectories would require a lot of recursion, to say the least. Note that when you use **lup**, if none of the files in the current directory meet the criteria for uppercase letters, **lup** displays all files in the directory (excluding dot files).

**Keyword:** file handling

**Files:** $HOME/.cshrc

**See Also:** ls, sed

| | | |
|---|---|---|
| ALL | ALL | END SCRIPT |

### alias mail /bin/mailx

Many **mailx** users are accustomed to typing **mail** instead of **mailx**, and many of these users don't even know about **mail**, the original but generally unused UNIX mail program. So, if your site does not use the original **mail** program, consider using this alias.

**Keyword:** email

**Files:** $HOME/.cshrc

**See Also:** mail, mailx

| | | |
|---|---|---|
| ALL | ALL | POWER |

### alias mailx ´/bin/mailx -n -F \!* -f mail/mbox´

It is convenient to alias **mailx** itself. The **-n** option lets you bypass systemwide **mailx** settings made in the **Mail.rc** file. This is necessary if you want your **$HOME/.mailrc** file to fully define your mail environment. The **-F** option causes outgoing messages to be saved in your home directory under the name of the first recipient in your mail address. You can also use the **record** variable in **.mailrc** to specify this feature.

**Keyword:** email

**Files:** $HOME/.cshrc, Mail.rc, .mailrc

**See Also:** mailx

## alias mailx ´sed ´\´´s#set prompt.*$#XaX#´\´´ $HOME/.mailrc | sed "s#XaX#set prompt=[$cwd]#" > /tmp/m$$; mv /tmp/m$$ $HOME/.mailrc; /bin/mailx -n \!*´

This alias is complicated by the fact that **sed** refuses to accept the C shell **$cwd** environment variable at the same time as the **$** to indicate the end of a line. Thus, two **sed** statements are used to update the prompt value in **$HOME/.mailrc**. The result is the current directory in your **mailx** prompt.

**Keyword:** email

**Files:** $HOME/.cshrc, .mailrc

**See Also:** mailx, prompt, set

---

ALL ALL END SCRIPT

## alias mem ´sed -n ´\´´s/^.*\(able memory\)/\1/p´\´´ /usr/adm/messages | head -2´

One way to find out how much memory is available for your system is to peek in the **/usr/adm/messages** file. This example uses **sed** to cut the appropriate text from **/usr/adm/messages** and **head** to limit the output. You could use **sed** for the entire sequence, if you specified **able memory** as a **sed** address and used the **q** command.

**Keyword:** system information

**Files:** $HOME/.cshrc, /usr/adm/messages

**See Also:** head, sed

---

ALL ALL POWER SYSADM

## alias mop ´find $HOME \( -type f -a -name "\!:1" \) -ok rm {} \;´

If you are are in the habit of creating temporary files that you later have to purge from the system—or any other set of files that you need to search the disk for a remove—you'll like this alias. It runs **find** in interactive mode using the **-ok** option, which executes the **rm** command. The **find** command also specifies that the type of file is a plain file using **-type f**. The **-name** option should be familiar to anyone who has ever used **find**. The alias works by accepting a filename or filename specification (meaning you can use wildcards). The command searches the directory hierarchy beginning with **$HOME**.

**Keyword:** file handling

**Files:** $HOME/.cshrc

**See Also:** find, rm

---

CSH ALL END SCRIPT

### alias mv mv -i

CSH ALL ALL

This alias displays a confirmation prompt before the user can overwrite an existing file. If a file of the same name does not exist, the **-i** option does not display a prompt.

**Keyword:** file handling

**Files:** $HOME/.cshrc

**See Also:** mv

### alias nopass ´awk -F: ´\´´length($2)==0 {print}´\´´ /etc/passwd´

ALL ALL SYSADM

This is an alias for system adminstrators. It gives you a quick command to verify whether all users on the system have passwords. If a user does not have a password, the command prints the user's entry from the **/etc/passwd** file. The alias requires no option arguments.

**Keyword:** user environment

**Files:** $HOME/.cshrc, /etc/passwd

**See Also:** awk

### alias path ´echo $PATH | awk -F: ´\´´{for(i=1; i<=NF; ++i) {print $i}}´\´´ | nl´

ALL ALL END SCRIPT

Because the usual horizontal display of the system path—when you use either **echo** or **set**—is hard to read when there are many directories in the path, this alias has potential. It uses **awk** to break the path listing up into lines, and **nl** to number the lines. As for the name of the alias, no standard UNIXes have a **path** command, so it's okay to use.

**Keyword:** user environment

**Files:** $HOME/.cshrc

**See Also:** awk, nl

### alias print ´pr \!* | lpr´

CSH ALL ALL

This example creates an alias to handle all parameters. The **\!*** sequence, like parameter substitution in the C shell, handles all parameters on the command line. Note that the bang character (**!**) must be escaped.

**Keyword:** printing

**Files:** $HOME/.cshrc

**See Also:** lpr, pr

## alias pwd ´echo $cwd´

You'll run across this alias a lot. The **/bin/pwd** command, because it is an external command, is slower executing than **echo $cwd**. Both **echo** and **$cwd** are C shell built-in commands. On newer workstations, however, you'll be hard pressed to measure the performance difference.

| | |
|---|---|
| **Keyword:** | user environment |
| **Files:** | $HOME/.cshrc |
| **See Also:** | echo, pwd |

## alias rgo ´rlogin \!:1 -l \!:2´

The **rgo** alias makes logging into a remote system a little easier. The alias requires two arguments: the remote system name and the name of the user that you want to log in as. This is convenient for adminstrators who must log into different systems as different users. Without the **-l** option, **rlogin** assumes you want to log in under your current identity.

| | |
|---|---|
| **Keyword:** | networking |
| **Files:** | $HOME/.cshrc |
| **See Also:** | rlogin, telnet |

## alias rm rm -i

This is a common alias to safeguard file removal and is a must for new users. When the **rm** command is used, the **-i** option causes a confirmation prompt to appear before the file is removed.

| | |
|---|---|
| **Keyword:** | file handling |
| **Files:** | $HOME/.cshrc |
| **See Also:** | rm |

## alias rs ´set noglob; eval `resize`; unset noglob´

This alias allows C shell users to transparently use the **resize** command in the X Window System. The command is used with windows that cannot inform associated processes of the fact that the window has been resized. You may find that this happens frequently when using an Xterm window to log in via a modem to another system. Note that some versions of the C shell do not support **eval.**

| | |
|---|---|
| **Keyword:** | window handling |

The table on the left margin:

| | | |
|---|---|---|
| ALL | ALL | END SCRIPT |
| ALL | ALL | END SCRIPT |
| CSH | ALL | ALL |
| CSH | XWIN | ALL |

**Files:** $HOME/.cshrc
**See Also:** eval, set, unset

### alias scsi ´grep unit /usr/adm/messages | cut -d: -f4 | uniq | sort -n +4´

ALL  ALL  POWER SYSADM

In this example, **grep** extracts all lines containing **unit** with the ultimate goal of producing a list of SCSI devices attached to the system. The **cut** command is then used to extract the relevant data. Using **cut**, however, is dependent on the format of **/usr/adm/messages** on your system. Here is output from an OSF system:

```
rz0 at asc0 unit 0 (RZ56)
rz1 at asc0 unit 1 (RZ56)
```

The **uniq** command in the example reduces the output to a single line for each SCSI device. The **sort** command orders the output by SCSI number. Check your **/usr/adm/messages** file for a unique search word, such as **unit** in the example.

**Keyword:** system information
**Files:** $HOME/.cshrc, /usr/adm/messages
**See Also:** cut, grep, uniq, sort

### alias td ´( echo;  date +" %b %d %r"; cal | tail -7 )´

CSH  ALL  END SCRIPT

This alias changes the display of the system **cal** utility. Instead of displaying the month in the first line, it displays the output from the **date** command:

```
 Sep 11 05:31:45 PM
Su Mo Tu We Th Fr Sa
          1  2  3  4
 5  6  7  8  9 10 11
12 13 14 15 16 17 18
19 20 21 22 23 24 25
26 27 28 29 30
```

**Keyword:** time
**Files:** $HOME/.cshrc
**See Also:** cal, date, echo, tail

### alias topnote ´cat - \!:1 > /tmp/.$$.; mv /tmp/.$$. \!:1´

CSH  ALL  END SCRIPT

This alias lets you add a note to the top of an existing file. You run the alias by specifying an existing filename, as in **topnote**

**march.rep**. The example uses **\!:1** to represent the first command line argument, or **march.rep**. The - construct tells **cat** to accept input from the keyboard before the alias processes **\!:1**. The combined output from the keyboard and **\!:1** are stored in a temporary file. The semicolon then ends the command, closing **\!:1**. Finally, the second command does a simple **mv** and **\!:1** is updated.

| | |
|---|---|
| **Keyword:** | text handling |
| **Files:** | $HOME/.cshrc |
| **See Also:** | cat, mv |

### alias tyme date +"%r"

CSH ALL END SCRIPT

This is a simple alias that displays the time in AM and PM format (which is the function of **%r**). Note the apparent misspelling. The reason for this is the UNIX **time** command, which *times* the performance of an executable file.

| | |
|---|---|
| **Keyword:** | time |
| **Files:** | $HOME/.cshrc |
| **See Also:** | date |

### alias vib ´cp \!:1 \!:1.bak; vi \!:1´

CSH ALL END SCRIPT

If you use **vi** for editing—or any other editor or program that modifies files—you might want to create an alias that automatically makes a backup file. In the example, **vib** is aliased to a combination of the **cp** command and **vi**. First, the **cp** command makes a copy of the file and adds a **.bak** extension. Then **vi** loads the file. If you don't want to make a backup copy—for instance, you might want to preserve the previous backup copy—you can always use the original command (in this case **vi**).

| | |
|---|---|
| **Keyword:** | file handling |
| **Files:** | $HOME/.cshrc |
| **See Also:** | cp, vi |

### alias waste ´mv !* $HOME/wastebasket´

CSH ALL ALL

This alias places deleted files in **wastebasket**. Intended as a simple method of removing but not deleting files, the command requires that you have a directory called **wastebasket** in **$HOME**. One limitation of this approach is that you cannot recursively remove directories.

| | |
|---|---|
| **Keyword:** | file handling |

**Files:**      $HOME/.cshrc, a trash directory

**See Also:**   mv

## alias xt ´xterm -bg #000000 -fg #00ea0b -fn "*fix*bold*140*75*" &´

CSH  XWIN  ALL

Loading an Xterm window from the command line can be tedious. With an alias, it is as easy as two letters. The example aliases **xt** to **xterm**, which has the foreground set to **#000000** (black) and **#00ea0b**, a medium-shade green (not in the standard X11 **rgb.txt** file). The **-fn** option specifies a fixed bold 14-point font from the X11 font database.

**Keyword:**    window handling

**See Also:**   xfd, xfontsel, xterm

## alias xtn ´xterm -bg #000000 -fg #00ea0b -fn "*fix*bold*140*75*" -name \!:1 &´

CSH  XWIN  ALL

This command lets you specify a resource name at the command line. You execute **xtn** with a single argument: a name such as one contained in **$HOME/.Xdefaults**, **$XAPPLRESDIR/XTerm**, or **$HOME/XTerm**. If you do not specify a name, the alias produces an error.

**Keyword:**    window handling, X resources

**Files:**      $HOME/.cshrc

**See Also:**   xfd, xfontsel, xterm

## alloc

ALL  ALL  POWER
          SYSADM

This C shell built-in displays statistics on dynamic memory used by the system. If you supply a memory address argument (8 or any increment thereof), **alloc** shows you the status (busy or in use) of each memory block.

**Keyword:**    system information

**See Also:**   dmesg, ps

## apply ´ln %1 /usr/bin/X11´ *

ALL  OSF  POWER
          SYSADM

This command is used to link all of the files in the current directory to the **/usr/bin/X11** directory.

**Keyword:**    file handling

**See Also:**   find, ln, ls

| | | |
|---|---|---|
| ALL | XWIN | ALL |

## appres

Without any arguments, the **appres** client program lists any general resources that are in effect in your X Window System session. The following commands show you how to use **appres** when you want to know the resources for specific client programs.

**Keyword:**   X resources

**See Also:**   editres, listres, viewres, xrdb

| | | |
|---|---|---|
| ALL | XWIN | ALL |

## appres Wp wp

You can use **appres** for any X client. Commercial applications should have both a class and an instance name. The example displays the resources that the WordPerfect word processor loads.

**Keyword:**   X resources

**See Also:**   editres, listres, viewres, xrdb

| | | |
|---|---|---|
| ALL | XWIN | ALL |

## appres XTerm

The **appres** program is a convenient way for X customizers and programmers to determine what resources an application loads. In the example, the **XTerm** class name is supplied to **appres**. The output shows the relevant resources, including those specifically for **XTerm** as well as general resources, such as **\*Foreground** and **\*font**.

**Keyword:**   X resources

**See Also:**   editres, listres, viewres, xrdb

| | | |
|---|---|---|
| ALL | XWIN | ALL |

## appres XTerm editor

In this command, the **appres** program lists resources that specifically apply to a named instance of an Xterm window. The named instance here is **editor**, which presumably is a special set of Xterm resources designed for use with **vi**, **emacs**, or another editor. The example shows you both specific resources and general resources.

**Keyword:**   X resources

**See Also:**   editres, listres, viewres, xrdb

| | | |
|---|---|---|
| ALL | ALL | POWER |

## apropos editor

This command finds all the **man pages** that have **editor** listed in the **Name** line. This is useful if you don't know the exact com-

mand you want to find. This command is the same as **man -k**.
Example output on a SunOS system looks like this:

```
$ apropos editor
  bitmap, bmtoa, atobm (1)  - bitmap editor and converter
                              utilities for X
  textedit  (1)             - XView window- and mouse-based text
                              editor
  xedit (1)                 - simple text editor for X
```

**Keyword:**  documentation

**Files:**  /usr/share/man/whatis

**See Also:**  man, whatis, catman

### ar -rv archive arlist.a

ALL    ALL    POWER

The **ar** command lets you create a file containing information
about archived files. All **ar** requires is that the first line of an
archive file be ASCII text, so it can read it and add information to
the output file. In the example, the **-r** tells **ar** to replace the
named file in the archive; the **-v** option tells it to give a file-by-file
description of the update process. The SVR4 and BSD versions of
this command are significantly different, but the present command works in both cases. Note, however, that the BSD version
may not recognize the - sign preceding the options.

**Keyword:**  archiving

**See Also:**  ld, ranlib

### ar ruv myXm.a getcash.o

ALL    ALL    ALL

This command stores the **getcash.o** object routine in the archive
directory specified by **myXm**.

**Keyword:**  programming

**See Also:**  ld, ranlib

### arch

ALL    ALL    ALL

The **arch** command displays the architecture of the host system.
Most users should already know the architecture of their own
system, but in a network environment, users and administrators
may need to query the architecture in order to know whether an
application can run on a given system.

**Keyword:**  system information

**See Also:**  hostname, mach, machid

| | | |
|---|---|---|
| ALL | SunOS | ALL |

## arch -k

On SunOS systems only, the **-k** option displays the architecture of the kernel. For example, this command might output **sun4**, which represents older RISC-based Sun servers; and **sun4c**, which represents newer RISC-based SPARCstations.

**Keyword:**  system information

**See Also:**  hostname, mach, machid

| | | |
|---|---|---|
| CSH | SunOS | SCRIPT POWER |

## argv

The C shell's **argv** feature gives shell scripters a lot more flexibility manipulating positional parameters than you can find in the Bourne and Korn shells. The C shell still supports the standard positional parameters, namely **$1-$9**, but **argv** handles many times more arguments without requiring a shift mechanism. Here is an example:

```
if( -e $argv[i] ) then
    more $argv[i]
else
    echo "$argv[i] not found!"
endif
```

**Keyword:**  programming

**See Also:**  getopt, getopts, shift

| | | |
|---|---|---|
| ALL | SVR4 | POWER |

## as -o myprog.o myprog.asmi

This command creates an object file from an assembly file.

**Keyword:**  programming

**See Also:**  cc, dbx, make

| | | |
|---|---|---|
| ALL | SCO | POWER SYSADM |

## assign

When you invoke the SCO **assign** command without options, the command displays a list of assignable devices. If any devices are currently assigned, the list includes the name of the user who has it assigned.

**Keyword:**  devices

**Files:**  /etc/atab, /dev/asglock

**See Also:**  deassign, tar

### assign /dev/fd

ALL  SCO  POWER SYSADM

The main purpose of the SCO **assign** command is to assign a device to the current user. If the specified device is already assigned, the command fails. In the example, **/dev/fd** specifies the default diskette drive. To glean information on available devices, see **/etc/atab**.

**Keyword:** devices

**Files:** /etc/atab, /dev/asglock

**See Also:** deassign, tar

### at -l

ALL  ALL  POWER

The **-l** option displays jobs queued by the **at** command. The display shows the username, job number, and the specified queue. If no queue is specified, the **a** queue is used. The **c** queue is reserved for **cron**. You can name any other queue corresponding to a letter in the alphabet. A typical **-l** display looks like the following:

```
root.745124400.a      Wed Aug 11 23:00:00 1993
root.745160400.a      Thu Aug 12 09:00:00 1993
```

**Keyword:** background processing

**See Also:** atrm, atq, at, cron, fg, bg

### at -m 12:30pm $HOME/atlunch

ALL  ALL  POWER

This example executes the commands in the file **atlunch** at 12:30 PM and sends mail notifying you that the job has completed. The main output looks like this:

```
Date: Tue, 10 Aug 93 12:53:01 EDT
From: root (Operator)
Message-Id: <9308101653.AA00491@unix_world.matherland>
To: root
Subject: Output from "at" job
Status: R

Your "at" job "3694" completed.
```

**Keyword:** background processing

**See Also:** atrm, atq, at, fg, bg

### at -r 3695

ALL  ALL  POWER

The **-r** option removes a job from the **at** queue. In order to use the **-r** option, you must supply the job number. You can obtain this by using the **-l** option to **at**.

**Keyword:** background processing
**See Also:** atrm, atq, at, cron, fg, bg

### at 17:00 fri

When only a time and date are specified, the **at** command begins an interactive session. If you wanted to write a week-ending message to your screen and remove core files, you might have a session such as the following:

```
at> banner TGIF > /dev/ttyp1
at> find ~ -name core -exec rm {} \;
at> Ctrl-D
```

**Keyword:** background processing
**See Also:** atrm, atq, at, cron, fg, bg

### at 8pm fri $HOME/onfriday

This command executes the **atfile** called **onfriday** at 8 PM on Friday. The **atfile** contains commands that are load-intensive or simply better executed during off-hours. An **atfile** contains commands like a script file:

```
# Example atfile called onfriday
  rm $HOME/trash
  find ~ -name core -exec rm {} \;
```

**Keyword:** background processing
**Files:** /usr/spool/cron/atjobs
**See Also:** atrm, atq, at, cron, fg, bg

### at now + 5 min

The **at** command comes with the handy **now** option. It lets you schedule a job even if you don't know the current time. This is especially useful if you are on a remote system and want to have a job execute after you log out.

**Keyword:** background processing, job control
**Files:** /usr/spool/cron/atjobs
**See Also:** atrm, atq, at, bg, cron, fg

### atobm -chars @$ tree.txt > tree.xbm

If you need to change the default ASCII characters used by **atobm**, you can do it with the **-chars** option. The example

ALL    ALL    POWER

ALL    ALL    POWER

ALL    ALL    POWER

ALL    XWIN    ALL

changes the default characters to the @ and **$** characters. Note that the first character represents a blank space (the 0 bit), and the second character represents a filled-in space (the 1 bit).

**Keyword:**    graphics files

**See Also:**    bitmap, bmtoa, iconedit

### atobm tree.txt > tree.xbm

**ALL    XWIN    ALL**

The **atobm** program is an X Window System command that converts ASCII files into bitmaps. The ASCII files must be formatted with characters acceptable to **atobm**. By default, valid characters are the hyphen character (-) and number sign (#). Here are a few example lines from an ASCII file that **atobm** can convert:

```
--######-######-------#------#------#--#
---------##---###-----###-----#----##--#
#-#-#---#####--###------###---#---##---#
```

**Keyword:**    graphics files

**See Also:**    bitmap, bmtoa, iconedit

### atq -c

**ALL    ALL    POWER**

This command prints the queue of jobs waiting to be run, sorting the queue by the time the **at** command is issued.

**Keyword:**    background processing

**See Also:**    atrm, at, cron, bg, fg

### atq -n

**ALL    ALL    POWER**

This command prints only the number of files currently in the queue, waiting to be run.

**Keyword:**    background processing

**See Also:**    atrm, at, cron, bg, fg

### atq perkie

**ALL    ALL    POWER**

This command prints all the jobs that user **perkie** has waiting to be run.

**Keyword:**    background processing

**See Also:**    atrm, at, cron, bg, fg

### atrm -a perkie

| | | |
|---|---|---|
| ALL | ALL | POWER |

This command removes all the jobs that user **perkie** created with **at** command. This command is the same as the one above, except that it removes *all* queued commands rather than just one.

**Keyword:** program execution

**See Also:** at, atq, batch, cron

### atrm -f perkie

| | | |
|---|---|---|
| ALL | ALL | POWER |

This command removes all the jobs that user **perkie** created with the **at** command. It differs from **atrm -a perkie** in that it shows no information about the jobs.

**Keyword:** program execution

**See Also:** at, atq, batch, cron

### atrm -i -a perkie

| | | |
|---|---|---|
| ALL | ALL | POWER |

This is the same as **atrm -a perkie** except that user **perkie** will be prompted before each command is removed from the queue.

**Keyword:** program execution

**See Also:** at, atq, batch, cron

### atrm perkie.1993.a

| | | |
|---|---|---|
| ALL | ALL | POWER |

This command removes the job **1993.a** created by user **perkie** with the **at** command. This is for queuing commands to be run at a certain time. If you have put a job in the queue, and then decide you don't want to run it, use this command.

**Keyword:** program execution

**See Also:** at, atq, batch, cron

### awk '! /returns/' sales.rep

| | | |
|---|---|---|
| ALL | ALL | POWER |

Another simple **awk** example, this command imitates the **grep -v** command. By using the **!** operator to indicate a logical OR, the command extracts all lines in the file except those containing the word **returns**. Note the whitespace after the **!** operator; it is necessary.

**Keyword:** text handling

**See Also:** cut, grep, sed

| | | |
|---|---|---|
| ALL | ALL | POWER |

## awk ´/gold/ {print FILENAME": "$0}´ cash.db

This command first extracts all lines containing the word **gold**. It then prints the filename and complete line for each line extracted. The **awk** command's built-in **FILENAME** variable is used without a dollar sign in front of it. The **$0** requires the dollar sign, however, because it references all fields in the record (much as **$0** references all arguments in a shell command line.)

**Keyword:** text handling

**See Also:** cut, fold, sed, grep, ed

| | | |
|---|---|---|
| ALL | ALL | POWER |

## awk ´/Jill/ {print $2, $1, $3}´ people.db

This **awk** command combines pattern matching and string manipulation. First, it extracts all lines from the file **people.db** that contain the name **Jill**, which is in field **1**. It then prints them out as fields **2**, **1**, and **3**. Output might look like this:

```
Carter Jill 011-84-1234
Smith Jill 032-28-3485
```

**Keyword:** text handling

**See Also:** cut, fold, sed, grep, ed

| | | |
|---|---|---|
| ALL | ALL | POWER |

## awk ´/JUNE/,/AUGUST/´ sales.rep

This convenient **awk** command displays all text in **sales.rep** that occurs between the words **JUNE** and **AUGUST**. Assuming you are consistent with your capitalization when writing documents, you can use this entry as a routine text extraction tool.

**Keyword:** text handling

**See Also:** cut, grep, sed

| | | |
|---|---|---|
| ALL | ALL | SCRIPT |
| | | POWER |
| | | SYSADM |

## awk ´index($1,"awk") == 1 {print $1}´ cmds.txt

The **index** function returns the position of a substring within a string. You can hardcode a substring, as demonstrated in the example, or you can specify another variable known to **awk**. If **cmds.txt** contained a list of command descriptions, and **$1** equaled the command name, you could use this to extract **awk** examples. If the database contained **gawk** and **nawk** examples, these would not be output.

**Keyword:** text handling

**See Also:** cut, fold, sed, grep, ed

| | | |
|---|---|---|
| ALL | ALL | POWER |

## awk ´July sales´ sales.rep

One of the more straightforward **awk** statements, this command imitates a basic **grep** statement. In other words, it extracts all lines containing **July sales** from **sales.rep**.

**Keyword:**   text handling

**See Also:**   cut, grep, sed

| | | |
|---|---|---|
| ALL | ALL | POWER |

## awk ´length > 14´ table.txt

The **length** function is built into **awk**. With it, you can test for line lengths in a document. The example does this, and as a result, outputs only those lines longer than **14** columns. Note that this is the behavior of **length** when no argument is given to it. You can give **length** an argument in the form **length(expr)**.

**Keyword:**   text handling

**See Also:**   cut, fold, sed, grep, ed

| | | |
|---|---|---|
| ALL | ALL | POWER |

## awk ´NF == 5 {print $1}´ people.db

Another interesting twist to the **NF** variable is that you can reset it in order to limit which lines are output. In the example, **NF** equals 5, which means that lines with only five fields are considered by **awk**. The **print** command then tells **awk** just to print field **1** from its already narrowed list. Viewed this way, **NF** operates similar to an **if** statement: When there are five fields in the record, **print** field **1**.

**Keyword:**   text handling

**See Also:**   cut, fold, sed, grep, ed

| | | |
|---|---|---|
| ALL | ALL | POWER |

## awk ´NR >= 430 && NR <= 500´ db

The **&&** operator allows you to specify a range of line values for **awk**. In the command, lines **430** through **500** (inclusive) are printed.

**Keyword:**   text handling

**See Also:**   cut, fold, sed, grep, ed

| | | |
|---|---|---|
| ALL | ALL | END SCRIPT |

## awk ´NR%2 == 0´ lineup.lst

This **awk** entry is a quick way to display the even-numbered lines in a file. The modulus operator, **%**, is used to determine even-numbered lines. As a result, **awk** displays only those lines that have a remainder of zero; in other words, the even-numbered

lines. To display odd-numbered lines only, change **==** to **!=** as in:
**awk 'NR&2 !=' lineup.lst**.

**Keyword:**   file display

**See Also:**   cat, pr, sed

### awk ´{for(i=0; i<=NF; ++i) t += $i} END{print t}´ ledger

ALL    ALL    POWER

The **for** statement gives you even more power to accumulate totals from a file. Although more suited to script use, the **for** statement serves some purposes in single-line **awk** commands. In the example, it lets you accumulate the values from all fields in **ledger**. It then prints them as a single value, thanks to the **END** statement.

**Keyword:**   text handling, math

**See Also:**   cut, fold, sed, grep, ed, expr, bc, dc

### awk ´{if ($5>=30 && $7>10) {print $0}}´ db

ALL    ALL    END SCRIPT

This **awk** command evaluates a compound **if** statement, and prints any lines matching the criteria. The **&&** operator tells **awk** that both sides of the **if** statement must be true. In other words, it performs a logical AND operation. In the example, all lines having a fifth field greater than or equal to **30** and a seventh field greater than **10** are displayed.

**Keyword:**   text handling

**See Also:**   cut, fold, grep, sed

### awk ´{if ($5>=30) {print $0}}´ people.db

ALL    ALL    END SCRIPT

This command demonstrates how to create an **if** statement in **awk**. Although you might have more occasion to use **if** in **awk** scripts, it's still a relatively short command to type at the command line. The **if** occurs immediately after the opening curly bracket, followed by a necessary whitespace, which is then followed by the **if** comparison, enclosed in parentheses. To add a **print** statement, you must enclose it in another set of curly braces. In the example, all lines having a fifth field greater than or equal to **30** are displayed.

**Keyword:**   text handling

**See Also:**   cut, fold, grep, sed

## awk ´{print $0, " ("NF")"}´ people.db

ALL    ALL    POWER

This example is similar to the last one. The only difference is that the value of **NF** is intermixed with a text string, which is enclosed in double quotation marks. It looks like **NF** itself is quoted, but it is not. Instead, the whitespace and parentheses are quoted separately.

**Keyword:**    text handling

**See Also:**    cut, fold, sed, grep, ed

## awk ´{print $0, NF}´ people.db

ALL    ALL    POWER

This **awk** command prints the number of fields in each record at the end of each line. The **NF** operator (which stands for *number of fields*) needs no special adornment when used this way.

**Keyword:**    text handling

**See Also:**    cut, fold, sed, grep, ed

## awk ´{print $1, $2 VAR}´ VAR=", please call HQ" people.db

ALL    ALL    POWER

This command shows how you can insert a user-defined variable into an **awk** command line. The **VAR** variable could have been any name; you choose it. The variable is defined outside the single quotes surrounding the **print** command.

**Keyword:**    text handling

**See Also:**    cut, fold, sed, grep, ed

## awk ´{print $1, length($1)}´ people.db

ALL    ALL    SCRIPT POWER SYSADM

The **length** function can take an argument and be used within a **print** statement. Note that **length**, and other functions, do not require a preceding dollar sign.

**Keyword:**    text handling

**See Also:**    cut, fold, sed, grep, ed

## awk ´{print $1; print $3; print $5}´

ALL    ALL    POWER

The **awk** command prints each field on its own line. Assume you have a four-field file; fields **1** and **3** print correctly, but there is no field **5**. Here, **awk** prints a blank line, which in this case is the desired effect. But you might not want to deal with such a clunky mechanism, so read the next several entries about **printf**.

**27**

awk

**Keyword:**   text handling
**See Also:**   cut, fold, sed, grep, ed

### awk ´{print $3 + $4, subtotal += $3 + $4}´ cash.db

As this example shows, you can do more than just add two fields. Using the C language increment operator, you can accumulate a subtotal. As the command processes each line, it increments the value of **subtotal** by the value of **$3 + $4**. For example:

```
20  20
12  32
50  82
```

**Keyword:**   text handling, math
**See Also:**   cut, fold, sed, grep, ed, expr, bc, dc

### awk ´{print $3 + $4}´ cash.db

This command adds the values from fields **3** and **4** in the file. The output is a single column of numbers, each one representing the total of fields **3** and **4** for the given line in the file. The full set of match operators used by **awk** includes +, -, *, /, %, and the C language operators ++, --, +=, -=, *=, /=, and %=. Valid variables are fields (as in the example), integers, floating point numbers, variables defined in the **awk** statement, and arrays (usually used only in **awk** scripts).

**Keyword:**   text handling, math
**See Also:**   cut, fold, sed, grep, ed, expr, bc, dc

### awk ´{print $NF, $1}´ people.db

Compare the way the **NF** variable is written in this example to the way it is written in the previous one. With a leading dollar sign to indicate it is a variable, the **NF** operator represents the final field in the record. Thus, the command prints out the last and first fields from the file.

**Keyword:**   text handling
**See Also:**   cut, fold, sed, grep, ed

### awk ´{print int($5)}´ db

The **int** function, like other math functions in **awk**, returns a numeric value. Specifically, **int** extracts the integer portion of a floating point number. If **$5** equaled **10.5**, **int** would return **10**.

Here are the other built-in math functions:

```
cos(expr)    cosine
exp(expr)    exponent
log(expr)    logarithm
sin(expr)    cosine
sqrt(expr)   square root
```

**Keyword:**    math
**See Also:**    expr, bc, dc

### awk ´{print NR, $1, $3, $5}´ people.db

This command takes advantage of the **NR** variable and uses it to number each line, which otherwise displays the values of fields **1**, **3**, and **5**.

**Keyword:**    text handling
**See Also:**    cut, fold, sed, grep, ed

### awk ´{print substr($1,1,1)"."., $2}´ people.db

With the **substr** function, you can extract part of a string from an **awk** variable. The first argument to **substr** is the actual string; the second argument is the length of the string you want to extract; the third argument tells **awk** that, to be considered, the string must be at least this many characters in length. In the example, **substr** extracts the first letter of the string. If field 1 and field 2 looked like this:

```
Donna Blake
```

The output would look like this:

```
D. Blake
```

**Keyword:**    text handling
**See Also:**    cut, fold, sed, grep, ed

### awk ´{printf("%s",$1)}´

The example demonstrates the **printf** command, which **awk** borrows from the C programming language. Unlike **print**, the **printf** command lets you do extensive formatting to text strings. If you run this example, however, you see that all instances of field **1** stream together, without any formatting at all. This is the default behavior of **printf**. There might be a

ALL    ALL    POWER

ALL    ALL    SCRIPT
              POWER
              SYSADM

ALL    ALL    SCRIPT
              POWER

time you need this effect, but most other times you'll want to use format specifiers:

```
c    Single ASCII character
d    Decimal integer
e    Floating point (exponent)
f    Floating point (decimal)
g    Same as e or f, but no trailing zeros
o    Octal value (unsigned)
s    Text string
x    Hexadecimal number (unsigned)
```

A format specifier appears in double quotation marks, and a percent sign always precedes it. If you want to display a percent, precede it by a percent sign. A comma separates the quotes and the set of variable values that follow. Variables sequentially pair to format specifiers.

**Keyword:**   text handling

**See Also:**   cut, fold, sed, grep, ed

## awk ´{printf("%s\n%s\n\n",$1,$2)}´

ALL   ALL   POWER

This command makes printing multiple blank lines easy. The **\n** sequence tells **printf** to start a new line. The successive **\n** sequences create the blank lines between records.

**Keyword:**   text handling

**See Also:**   cut, fold, sed, grep, ed

## awk ´{total += $5 + $6} END{print total}´ cash.db

ALL   ALL   POWER

If you need a single-number total, you can borrow a statement used only in **awk** scripts and use it in the command line—namely, you can use **END** to indicate the end of normal processing. Thus, in the example, the values in fields **5** and **6** are accumulated, but **awk** doesn't print anything until after the **END** statement. At this point, **total** equals a single number.

**Keyword:**   text handling, math

**See Also:**   cut, fold, sed, grep, ed, expr, bc, dc

## awk -F"\t" ´{print $3}´ people.db

ALL   ALL   POWER

This **awk** command prints the third column of a file with columns delimited by tabs. The point to note here is the argument to -**F**, the **\t** sequence, which changes the delimiter to the Tab character.

**Keyword:** text handling
**See Also:** cut, fold, sed, grep, ed

### awk -F# ´NF == 2 {print $2}´ people.db

This command is a variation of the earlier use of **NF** to narrow the number of lines considered by **awk**. The **NF** variable acts as a test mechanism, because it instructs **awk** to display only lines with five fields. What's unique about this command is the field separator has been changed. This means you can put different types of data in the same file and selectively extract it.

**Keyword:** text handling
**See Also:** cut, fold, sed, grep, ed

### awk -F´#´ ´$2 ~ /DEC/ {print $2, $1}´ /etc/hosts

This command uses the "contains" operator, which is the ~ symbol. The example tells **awk** that if field **2** contains the name DEC, print field **2** followed by field **1**. The **-F** option changes the delimiter character to the **#** comment symbol. It is traditional to add a comment describing the hardware to the end of each line in **/etc/hosts**, so the entry yields system types.

**Keyword:** text handling
**See Also:** cut, fold, sed, grep, ed

### awk -F: ´$7 ~ /csh/ {print $1}´ /etc/passwd

Similar to the previous entry, this **awk** command displays all lines in which field **7** contains **csh**. If you are interested in who your fellow C shell users are, use this command.

**Keyword:** text handling
**See Also:** cut, fold, sed, grep, ed

### awk -F: ´{ for (i=NF; i>0; --i) print $i }´ people.db

By taking advantage of the **for** command in **awk**, you can open the door to many possibilities. In the example, the **for** loop uses the **NF** value (the total number of fields in the file) to print all fields in reverse order. The **i=NF** sequence sets this value; **i>0** performs the test if **i** each time through the loop; and **--i** decrements the value of **i**.

**Keyword:** text handling
**See Also:** cut, fold, sed, grep, ed

ALL ALL POWER

| | | |
|---|---|---|
| ALL | ALL | POWER |

## awk -F: ´{print "User: "$1,"; Other: ",$5}´ /etc/passwd

This is a simple example to illustrate that you can insert a text string anywhere in an **awk** print command. All you have to do is remember to surround it with double quotation marks. Sample output from the entry looks like this:

```
User: alans; Other: UNIX-to-UNIX Copy
```

**Keyword:**  text handling
**See Also:**  cut, fold, sed, grep, ed

| | | |
|---|---|---|
| ALL | ALL | POWER |

## awk -F: ´{print $1, $5}´ OFS=´^I´ /etc/passwd

You know that the **-F** option changes the delimiter that **awk** uses to parse a string. Now, here is **OFS**, which lets you specify a field separator for output (either to the terminal or a file). In the example, **OFS** is set to a tab. The **^I** sequence is just symbolic. When you enter this, or a similar command, press the Tab key.

**Keyword:**  text handling
**See Also:**  cut, fold, sed, grep, ed

| | | |
|---|---|---|
| ALL | ALL | POWER |

## awk -F: ´{print $1}´ /etc/passwd

Using **awk** to extract data from system files is a time-honored tradition. In the example, **awk** resets the delimiter with the **-F** option and then parses **/etc/passwd**. The username is always the first field in **/etc/passwd**, so the entry is a quick tool to list users and processes that have login status.

**Keyword:**  text handling
**See Also:**  cut, fold, sed, grep, ed

| | | |
|---|---|---|
| ALL | ALL | POWER |

## awk -F: ´{print $4}´ /etc/inittab | grep -v ´^$´

You can pipe the results of **awk** into other commands if you find it necessary. The idea of the example is to list all the processes started in the **/etc/inittab** file, with the exception of **init** itself. In the example, the output is piped in **grep -v** to get rid of blank lines. The problem could have been handled with a more complete **awk** command. For example:

```
awk -F: 'NF == 4 {print $NF}' /etc/inittab
```

This produces almost the same results as the **grep -v** approach. The one difference is a blank line at the top of the output, representing the record containing **initdefault**, which appears in the third field on some systems.

**Keyword:**     text handling

**See Also:**     cut, fold, sed, grep, ed

### awk -F buttons %HOME/.mwmrc

ALL     ALL     POWER

This is an example of using **awk** with a command script. The command here calls a script arbitrarily named **buttons**. The **-F** option specifies the filename. The following script extracts buttons defined in the motif **.mwmrc** file.

```
BEGIN {FS = ">"}
/Buttons/,/}/\
{print $1}
```

**Keyword:**     text handling

**See Also:**     cut, fold, grep, sed

### backup -c -t -d /dev/rmt/ctape1

ALL     SVR4     SYSADM

This command makes a master backup of the entire system, or an incremental backup if a master backup already exists. The **-c** argument specifies a complete backup, **-t** specifies that the output device is a tape, and **-d** specifies the type of tape.

**Keyword:**     backup and restore

**See Also:**     cp, cpio, dd, dump, mount, restore, smit, sysadm, sysadmsh, tar, umount

### backup -t -u "all" -d /dev/rmt/ctape1

ALL     SVR4     POWER

This command backs up the home directories of every user on the system. It will write its output to the tape **/dev/rmt/ctape1**.

**Keyword:**     backup and restore

**See Also:**     cp, cpio, dd, dump, mount, restore, smit, sysadm, sysadmsh, tar, umount

### backup -t -u perkie -d /dev/rmt/ctape1

ALL     SVR4     POWER

This command makes a backup of user **perkie**'s home directory. Every file in the directory, and all subdirectories are backed up.

**Keyword:**     backup and restore

**See Also:**     cp, cpio, dd, dump, mount, restore, smit, sysadm, sysadmsh, tar, umount

| | | |
|---|---|---|

### banner "This is a" Test!

ALL    ALL    END

The **banner** command prints the specified message in large letters to standard output. Each line in the **banner** output may be up to 10 uppercase or lowercase characters long. On output, all characters appear in uppercase, and the lowercase input characters appear smaller than the uppercase input characters. If you want words to stay on the same line, enclose them in quotes, as in the example.

**Keyword:**    text display

**See Also:**    echo

### banner HELLO | sed ´s/ /-/g´ | atobm > hello.xbm

ALL    XWIN    ALL

Combining the commands in this example allows you to automatically create a bitmap from the command line. This is a useful trick if you want to create small pieces of text for a bitmap. It can also be turned into a root window message system if you want to create a script command based on this approach.

**Keyword:**    X graphics

**See Also:**    bmtoa, echo, iconedit, sed

### banner HELLO | write perkie@megasun

ALL    ALL    ALL

This command is a real attention getter. By piping the output of **banner** into the **write** command, the user on the receiving end gets quite a greeting.

**Keyword:**    text display

**See Also:**    echo, write

### basename $SHELL

ALL    ALL    END SCRIPT

The command **basename** gives the base filename in a string, stripping everything from the first **/** to the last **/**. In the example, **basename** returns the type of shell you are using.

**Keyword:**    data extraction

**See Also:**    awk, cut, sed

### basename ape.txt .txt

ALL    ALL    SCRIPT POWER

This use of the **basename** command lets you strip off a trailing section of the filename. It is usually used with file extensions, as in the example.

**Keyword:**    text handling

**See Also:**    awk, cut, sed

ALL   ALL   POWER

## batch

The **batch** command lets you run jobs at another time when the system load is not high. An interactive session begins when you enter **batch**. Here is an example:

```
cc myprogram.c
<Ctrl-d>
```

**Keyword:** background processing

**See Also:** at, atrm, atq, cron

ALL   ALL   POWER

## bc

The **bc** command is an interactive program that provides unlimited precision arithmetic. It is a preprocessor for the **dc** command. Here is an example session:

```
5+7    Simply add two numbers
12     Get the result

6-9    Subtraction
-3

4*3    Multiplication
12

67/8 Division
8      Notice that the result doesn't include the remainder

67%8 Divide and then output just the remainder
3
```

**Keyword:** math

**See Also:** awk, dc, expr

ALL   ALL   POWER

## bc

The **bc** program lets you do higher-level math, such as working in different base number systems, obtaining the square root of a number, and increasing a number to a power. Here are examples:

```
obase = 16      Output numbers in base 16
255
FF              The output is hex
ibase = 16      Input the numbers in hexadecimal
obase = 10      Output numbers in base 10
FF
255

sqrt(25)        Obtain the square root
```

```
5
sqrt(32)
5

scale = 13        Keep precision to 13 decimal places
sqrt(32)
5.6568542494923

5.656 ^ 2         Square a number
31.990336
2 ^ 8             Increase by a power of 8
256
```

**Keyword:**  math

**See Also:**  awk, dc, expr

## bc -l myprog.bc

ALL    ALL    POWER

The **bc** program lets you write simple C-like programs, such as the following:

```
myprog.bc
    /* compute the factorial of n */

    define f(n) {
        auto i, r;

        r = 1;
        for (i=2; i<=n; i++) r =* i;
        return (r);
    }

bc -l myprog.bc
        f(5)    /*  5 factorial */
        120

        f(10)
        3628800
```

**Keyword:**  math

**See Also:**  awk, dc, expr

## bdftopcf -o courb.pcf courb.bdf

ALL    XWIN    POWER
              SYSADM

This command compiles fonts **courb.bdf** into Portable Compiled Format fonts for the X Window System (if you have X11R5 on your system). This allows your machine to read the fonts quickly; another unlike machine can still read them, just more slowly. The **-o** argument specifies the output filename; otherwise, the output would go to standard output.

**Keyword:** fonts
**See Also:** Xset

### bdiff -s book1.txt book2.txt

This command compares **book1.txt** to **book2.txt** and outputs every line that is different. The **bdiff** command is similar to **diff** except that it can handle much larger files by splitting the files and sending the parts to **diff**. The **-s** argument is used to suppress error messages.

**Keyword:** text comparison
**See Also:** diff

### bfs book.txt

This command will invoke the **bfs** interactive line editor on the file **book.txt**. It uses all of the same commands as **ed**, but it doesn't use a buffer. The lack of a buffer allows **bfs** to search much larger files than **ed**, and search them more efficiently. After entering **bfs** you can type **P** to be given a prompt; otherwise, the prompt is simply a blank line.

**Keyword:** text handling
**See Also:** ed, emacs, vi

### bg

This command executes the last stopped job in the background. It will work in **sh**, **csh**, and **ksh**. With the C shell, jobs are most often stopped with Ctrl-Z, as they are with the Korn and Bourne shells; however, the job number is not displayed.

**Keyword:** job control
**See Also:** fg, csh, ksh, sh

### bg %

This command executes the current job in the background. It is similar to the previous command, except that it works in the C shell only.

**Keyword:** job control
**See Also:** csh, ksh, sh, fg

ALL ALL POWER

ALL ALL POWER

ALL ALL POWER

CSH ALL POWER

| | | |
|---|---|---|
| CSH | ALL | POWER |

## bg %1

This command executes job **1** in the background in the C shell.

**Keyword:**   job control

**See Also:**   csh, ksh, sh, fg

| | | |
|---|---|---|
| SH KSH | ALL | POWER |

## bg 1

This command executes the stopped job **1** in the background. The job number is displayed when you stop the job. With the Korn or Bourne shell, you typically stop a job with Ctrl-Z.

**Keyword:**   job control

**See Also:**   csh, ksh, sh, fg

| | | |
|---|---|---|
| ALL | PD | POWER |

## bggen -w 8 -b 8  0 0 0  0 0 255 | xv -root -quit -best24 -

This command makes your screen black at the top and light blue at the bottom; all the colors in between are interpolated between black (0,0,0) and blue (0,0,255). The **bggen** is piped to **xv**, a public domain graphics program for the X Window System, because it generates a portable pixmap file, which **xv** displays. The **-w 8** option is used to set the width of the line, and **-b 8** is used to limit the colors to 8-bit, or 256 total colors.

**Keyword:**   graphics display

**See Also:**   xwd, xwud, xpr

| | | |
|---|---|---|
| ALL | PD | POWER |

## bggen -w 8 -b 8  0 0 255  0 255 0  255 0 0 | xv -root -quit -best24 -

This command draws a blue, green, and red rainbow on the root window.

**Keyword:**   graphics display

**See Also:**   xwd, xwud, xpr

| | | |
|---|---|---|
| ALL | PD | POWER |

## bggen -w 8 -b 8 -s 200  0 0 0  100 0 100  0 0 0 | xv -root -quit -best24 -

This command makes dark purple, horizontal cylinders on your screen. The **-s 200** option is used to set the screen size to 200 pixels. Because the screen is larger than this, it will repeat itself, making the cylinders.

**Keyword:**   graphics display

**See Also:**   xwd, xwud, xpr

| ALL | PD | POWER |
|-----|-----|-----|

### bggen -w 8 -b 8 0 0 255  0 255 255  0 255 0  255 255 0  255 0 0 | xv -root -quit -best24 -

This command makes a complete rainbow on your screen, starting with blue at the top and ending with red at the bottom.

**Keyword:**   graphics display

**See Also:**   xwd, xwud, xpr

| ALL | ALL | ALL |
|-----|-----|-----|

### biff n

The opposite of **biff y**, this tells the computer *not* to inform you if new mail arrives.  **biff y** is often a popular command among new users. When large amounts of email start coming in, however, it can get annoying, and **biff n** is a nice way to keep from being interrupted.

**Keyword:**   email

**See Also:**   mail, mailx, xbiff

| ALL | ALL | ALL |
|-----|-----|-----|

### biff y

This command tells the computer to inform you when new mail arrives during the current terminal session. It will output a message similar to this:

```
New mail for perkie@mit.edu has arrived:
----
From: Alan Southerton <alans@newl.com>
This is a test of the mail system.

----
```

This message will appear on your terminal screen.

**Keyword:**   email

**See Also:**   mail, mailx, xbiff

| ALL | ALL | ALL |
|-----|-----|-----|

### binmail

This is another name for the **mail** program. It has the same options and is, in fact, the same code. Since **mail** is less typing, we recommend using that, or using the more advanced **mailx** program.

**Keyword:**   email

**See Also:**   mail, mailx, biff, xbiff

## biod 8

ALL  SVR4  SYSADM

This is an NFS daemon that starts asynchronous block I/O dae-mons. In this example, **8** asynchronous block I/O daemons are started. These are normally invoked in run level **3**.

**Keyword:** networking

**See Also:** ftp, rcp, rlogin, telnet

## Bitmap

ALL  XWIN  ALL

This is the resource filename for the **bitmap** client program. A client's resource file can be located in any of several resource locations. The order of precedence of these locations is **$XENVI-RONMENT**, **$HOME/.Xdefaults-*hostname***, **$XAPPLRESDIR**, **$HOME/*app-file***, **$HOME/.Xdefaults**, **/usr/lib/X11/app-defaults/Xdefaults**, and **/usr/lib/X11/app-defaults/app-name**. Note that **.Xdefaults** is a customary name, not mandatory.

**Keyword:** X resources

**See Also:** xrdb

## bitmap -grid tree.xbm

ALL  XWIN  ALL

The **bitmap** client program changed with the X11R5 release of the X Window System. You no longer have to specify the size of the bitmap on the command line, for example. There are other additional features, such as the ability to turn off the grid (as shown in the example).

**Keyword:** X graphics

**See Also:** atobm, bmtoa, iconedit

## bitmap -size 50x50

ALL  XWIN  ALL

The **bitmap** program is an interactive X application that is used to edit **bitmap**. All of the standard X Toolkit command line argu-ments are supported by **bitmap**.

**Keyword:** graphics files

**See Also:** atobm, bmtoa, iconedit

## bkexcept -a */trash

ALL  SVR4  SYSADM

This command adds all files on the system that are named **trash** to the list of files that are not to be included in incremental back-ups, using the **incfile** command.

**Keyword:** backup and restore

**See Also:** backup, restore, sysadm

### bkexcept -d trash

This outputs */trash. The **-d** argument to **bkexcept** causes it to display all the items that have trash in them that are not going to be backed up with the **incfile** command.

**Keyword:** backup and restore

**See Also:** backup, restore, sysadm

### bkexcept -r */trash

This is the opposite of **bkexcept -a */trash** in that it removes all the trash files from the list of files not to be backed up by the **incfile** command.

**Keyword:** backup and restore

**See Also:** backup, restore, sysadm

### bkhistory

This command displays the contents of the **/etc/bkup/bkhist.tab** file. This file contains a log of information about successfully completed backups, using the **backup** command or the **incfile** command.

**Keyword:** backup and restore

**See Also:** backup, restore, sysadm

### bkhistory -h -l -d "0823,0916"

This command outputs a listing of all the files that were backed up on August 23 and September 16 of the current year. The **-h** argument eliminates the printing of header information, and the **-l** argument formats the output to be the same as the **ls -l** command.

**Keyword:** backup and restore

**See Also:** backup, restore, sysadm

### bkhistory -l -o /u1

This command displays a listing in the same format as **ls -l** of all the files that have been backed up in the **/u1** directory.

**Keyword:** backup and restore

**See Also:** backup, restore, sysadm

ALL SVR4 POWER

## bkhistory -p 6

ALL SVR4 POWER

This command deletes all backup history logs in the file **/etc/bkup/bkhist.tab** that are older than six weeks.

**Keyword:** backup and restore

**See Also:** backup, restore, sysadm

## bkoper

ALL SVR4 POWER

This is an interactive program used to service media insertion during backup operations. The available commands are as follows:

```
!<cmd>      The *!* escapes to the Bourne Shell to
            execute a command.
=           This ouputs the current backup operation
            number.
?           Outputs a summary of commands.
h           Outputs the list of backup operations.
t<n>        Interacts with the backup operation associated
            with the <n>th header.
```

**Keyword:** backup and restore

**See Also:** backup, restore, sysadm

## bkreg -A

ALL SVR4 POWER

This command outputs a record of all fields that are currently in the backup register.

**Keyword:** backup and restore

**See Also:** backup, restore, sysadm

## bkreg -p 4 -w 4

ALL SVR4 POWER

This command is used to view or edit the contents of a backup register, which contains descriptions of all the backups that are taken, or to be taken, off the system. The **-p** argument sets the rotation period; in this example, it is set to four weeks. The **-w** argument sets the current week to the fourth week of the rotation period.

**Keyword:** backup and restore

**See Also:** backup, restore, sysadm

## bkstatus

ALL SVR4 POWER

This command outputs the status of all system backup operations that are in progress.

**Keyword:** backup and restore

**See Also:** backup, restore, sysadm

### bkstatus -a

This command outputs all backup operations that have taken place in the current rotation period. The **-a** argument tells **bkstatus** to display both failed and completed backup operations, along with operations that are in progress.

**Keyword:** backup and restore

**See Also:** backup, restore, sysadm

### bkstatus -a -h

This command outputs all backup operations that have taken place in the current rotation period, but without header information. The header information is not displayed because of the **-h** argument.

**Keyword:** backup and restore

**See Also:** backup, restore, sysadm

### bkstatus -a -j back-726,back-892

This command shows a status report for backup jobs **back-726** and **back-892** whether they have completed successfully or failed.

**Keyword:** backup and restore

**See Also:** backup, restore, sysadm

### bkstatus -p 8

This command tells the system to save backup status information for the past eight weeks. Once it ages more than eight weeks, it is deleted from the system.

**Keyword:** backup and restore

**See Also:** backup, restore, sysadm

### bkstatus -s f

This command displays a report of all the backup operations in the current rotation period that have failed. Other options to the **-s** argument include **a** for active and **p** for pending.

**Keyword:** backup and restore

**See Also:** backup, restore, sysadm

ALL  SVR4  POWER

### bkstatus -u perkie

ALL | SVR4 | POWER

This limits the information displayed by **bkstatus** to just backup operations started by user **perkie**.

**Keyword:** backup and restore

**See Also:** backup, restore, sysadm

### bmtoa -chars @$ tree.txt > tree.xbm

ALL | XWIN | ALL

As with its counterpart command, **atobm**, the **bmtoa** command lets you specify which characters to use in the ASCII file. In the example, the @ character represents the 0 bit and the $ character represents the 1 bit. The hyphen (-) and number sign (#) are the default characters.

**Keyword:** X graphics

**See Also:** atobm, bitmap, iconedit

### bmtoa tree.xbm > tree.txt

ALL | XWIN | ALL

If you have reason to convert a bitmap file into an ASCII file, the **bmtoa** command does the trick. Without a doubt, the **bmtoa** command is useful if you frequently edit bitmaps as ASCII files. The ability to convert backward gives you the chance to view a bitmap and then edit it.

**Keyword:** X graphics

**See Also:** atobm, bitmap, iconedit

### break

SH
KSH | ALL | SCRIPT

This is a shell script command. When you place **break** inside a control loop, the script exits the loop if it encounters the command. Usually, **break** is combined with some test condition.

**Keyword:** programming

**See Also:** if, for, while

### break

CSH | ALL | SCRIPT

This command is used to exit a **while** or **foreach** loop, and then continue script execution after the **end** command. This is generally used if some criterion in the script has been met in a C shell script.

**Keyword:** programming

**See Also:** if, foreach, while

| | | |
|---|---|---|
| CSH | ALL | SCRIPT |

## breaksw

In a C shell script that has a **switch** statement, **breaksw** breaks execution, but resumes after the **endsw** command. This is often used for writing menus.

**Keyword:** programming

**See Also:** endsw, switch, case

| | | |
|---|---|---|
| ALL | ALL | ALL |

## cal

This command prints out an ASCII rendition of the calendar for the current month. Here is an example:

```
    August 1993
Su Mo Tu We Th Fr Sa
 1  2  3  4  5  6  7
 8  9 10 11 12 13 14
15 16 17 18 19 20 21
22 23 24 25 26 27 28
29 30 31
```

**Keyword:** time

**See Also:** calendar, date

| | | |
|---|---|---|
| ALL | ALL | ALL |

## cal 1995

This command prints out an ASCII rendition of the calendar for the specified year.

**Keyword:** time

**See Also:** calendar, date

| | | |
|---|---|---|
| ALL | ALL | ALL |

## cal 8 1995

This command prints out an ASCII rendition of the calendar for the specified month and year. Note that you cannot simply specify the month.

**Keyword:** time

**See Also:** calendar, date

| | | |
|---|---|---|
| ALL | ALL | ALL |

## cal 9 1752

This command outputs a calender for September 1752. Eleven days have been skipped to make up for no leap year adjustments:

```
   September 1752
Su Mo Tu We Th Fr Sa
       1  2 14 15 16
```

**cal**

```
17 18 19 20 21 22 23
24 25 26 27 28 29 30
```

**Keyword:**   time

**See Also:**   calendar, date

## cal `date +%Y`

ALL   ALL   SCRIPT

This command is good for scripts that span years. This example uses the **date** command and its **%Y** option to feed the current year to **cal**.

**Keyword:**   time

**See Also:**   calendar, date

## cal;date

ALL   ALL   ALL

The combination of **cal** and **date** work nicely together, especially if you need to know what the date is—which would probably mean you didn't know what the day of the week was, which would mean you were in sad shape.

**Keyword:**   time

**See Also:**   calendar, date

## calendar

ALL   ALL   ALL

This command prints out dates and reminders from the **$HOME/calendar** file. During the business week, **calendar** displays items for the current and next day. On Fridays and Saturdays, **calendar** displays items through Monday. On Sunday, it displays items for Sunday and Monday. In the **$HOME/calendar** file, you must keep your reminders to one line in length, and each line must have a reference to the date. You can reference dates in a number of ways, including 8/14, August 14, and 8/14/93. If you put an asterisk (*) in the month position, such as **\*/14**, the associated reminder is displayed on that day each month.

**Keyword:**   time

**Files:**   $HOME/calendar

**See Also:**   cal, date

## calendar -

ALL   ALL   SYSADM

This is a command for the superuser. The - tells **calendar** to send reminder items for today and tomorrow to all users on the system, via email.

**Keyword:** time
**Files:** $HOME/calendar
**See Also:** at, cal, crontab, date, mail, mailx

### calendar | grep `date +"%m/%d"`

**ALL   ALL   POWER**

If you want to filter **calendar** so that it prints only the current day's reminders, you can pipe it into **grep**. Using command substitution and the **date** command, you can obtain a date format similar to the one you use in your **$HOME/calendar** file. Be sure to use leading zeros when necessary, such as 01/11 and 21/05.

**Keyword:** time
**Files:** $HOME/calendar
**See Also:** at, cal, crontab, date, grep, mail, mailx

### calendar | mail -s "What's Up Doc" $USER

**ALL   ALL   POWER**

You can add this generic command to your shell startup file if your system does not otherwise automatically deliver your **calendar** items. This approach assumes you don't mind getting **calendar** messages each time you log in. However, if you log in and out a lot, use the following line in your **crontab** file:

```
1 0 * * * calendar | mail -s "What's Up Doc" $USER
```

**Keyword:** time
**Files:** $HOME/calendar
**See Also:** at, cal, crontab, date, mail, mailx

### cancel 8

**ALL   ALL   END
            SYSADM**

This command deletes print request number **8** on the default printer.

**Keyword:** printing
**Files:** /etc/printcap, /var/spool/*
**See Also:** lp, lpq, lpr, lprm

### captoinfo -v myterm.terminfo

**ALL   SVR4   SYSADM**

The **captoinfo** command converts a **termcap** description into a **terminfo** file on SVR4 systems. The **-v** option prints errors to the standard output. At some point, the **termcap** database is likely to be withdrawn from various versions of UNIX, so **captoinfo** serves as a bridge between the different ways of storing terminal definition information. Other options include **-**, which prints **termcap** fields on a single line, and **-w**, which lets you set the width of a line.

**Keyword:**    terminal settings

**See Also:**    curses, infocmp, terminfo, tic

## case

SH KSH    ALL    SCRIPT

The **case** statement is a shell script construct that lets you efficiently parse the value of one or more variables. In the Bourne and Korn shells, **case** begins the conditional statement:

```
#!/bin/sh/doit
option=$1; file=$2
case $option in
   -p) lpr $file ;;
   -d) more $file ;;
   -c) wc $file ;;
esac
```

This small script should demonstrate the conciseness of **case**. Doing the same thing with **if** statements would make the script longer and harder to read.

**Keyword:**    programming

**See Also:**    esac, if

## case

CSH    ALL    SCRIPT

In the C shell, **case** is a *label* for the **switch** statement. The **switch** statement is similar to the **case** statement in the Bourne and Korn shells. The C shell scripting language borrows the use of **switch** and **case** directly from C programming language. Here is the basic form:

```
#!/bin/csh/doit
set option=$1; set file=$2
switch ( $option )
   case -p: lpr $file
           breaksw
   case -d: more $file
           breaksw
   case -w: wc $file
           breaksw
endsw
```

**Keyword:**    programming

**See Also:**    switch

### cat - > /dev/ttyp7

This command is one way to send text to another terminal, Xterm window, or a remote system that has logged into your system. When you enter this on the command line, you can begin typing text on the next line. Each time you press Enter, the current line of text is sent to the other terminal. Press Ctrl-D to end the link. Note that the other terminal cannot respond, as it could if you were using the **talk** or **write** utilities.

**Keyword:**   user communication

**See Also:**   talk, write

ALL   ALL   END
SCRIPT

### cat - names.db > names.tmp

This is another way to add input to an existing file. The - construct looks for input from the keyboard, so you can type it in and press Ctrl-D to end the input. Note that you must redirect output to a new file (or you could use **>>** to add the output to an existing file, but not one already named as input in the command). See **alias topnote** for a one-step solution.

**Keyword:**   text handling

**See Also:**   ed, emacs, vi

ALL   ALL   END
SCRIPT

### cat -e -t -v old.wp

Using the **-e**, **-t**, and **-v** options together gives you the most possible information about a binary file. Not only does the **-t** option print nonprintable characters, the **-e** option adds a **$** to the ends of lines, and the **-v** option prints tabs as **^I**.

**Keyword:**   text handling

**See Also:**   od

ALL   ALL   SCRIPT
POWER
SYSADM

### cat -e r.txt | cat -e | sed ´s/^\$\$/\[PARA\]/p´ > r.tmp

This command inserts **$$** at the end of each line in the file, so that you can distinguish where blank lines in the file occur. The **sed** statement does this for you by replacing **$$** with **[PARA]**.

**Keyword:**   text handling

**See Also:**   awk, sed

ALL   ALL   SCRIPT
SYSADM

### cat -e r.txt | cat -e | sed ´s/^\$\$/\[PARA\]/p´ | sed ´s/\$\$//p´ > r.new

To extend the pipeline from the previous example further, this command removes any remaining instances of **$$**. The end

ALL   ALL   SCRIPT
SYSADM

**cat**

result is an ASCII text file containing **[PARA]** on every blank line. Of course, you could do the whole operation with **sed**, but if you need to involve other users in this special type of file conversion, explaining **cat -e** is much easier than explaining **sed**.

**Keyword:**     text handling
**See Also:**     awk, sed

### cat -e report | cat -e > tmp

Sometimes, when transferring or converting a document, you might like to ensure that line endings are properly denoted. The **-e** entry to **cat** can help. It inserts a **$** at the end of each line. By running the output through a pipe into **cat -e** a second time, you get **$$** at the end of each line. This is eminently more suitable for search and replace operations later. The last step in the entry redirects the output to a file.

**Keyword:**     text handling
**See Also:**     awk, sed

### cat -n bigscript > bigscript.num

This command simply numbers the lines in the file. For script writers, it is often convenient to number lines for documentation purposes. Note that **cat** automatically prepends up to six white-spaces before the line number, and appends a Tab character after the line number.

**Keyword:**     text handling
**See Also:**     awk, ln, pr

### cat -n book.txt | grep ´^ *[24].TAB´

This command uses the **-n** option to **cat** to number lines. It then uses **grep** to extract the lines that fall between 20 to 29 and 40 to 49. The regular expression in the **grep** command looks for lines that begin with any number of whitespaces, followed by the number **2** or **4**, followed by any character, followed by a tab. Note that **TAB** represents an actual keypress. On many UNIX systems, you cannot symbolically represent the Tab character as a regular expression.

**Keyword:**     text handling
**See Also:**     awk, ln, pr

ALL     ALL     END
SCRIPT
SYSADM

ALL     ALL     END
SCRIPT

ALL     ALL     END
SCRIPT

## cat -s long.txt > shorter.txt

ALL   ALL   SCRIPT POWER

The **-s** option to **cat** is a quick way to reduce the number of blank lines in a file. The option causes **cat** to remove multiple blank lines and replace them with a single blank line.

**Keyword:**   text handling

**See Also:**   awk, sed

## cat -t scores.dat

ALL   ALL   SCRIPT POWER SYSADM

The **t** option to **cat** strips tabs from a file and represents them as **^I**. A column of baseball scores would look like this:

```
Boston 10 ^INew York 9
Baltimore 2 ^IToronto 0
Milwaukee 8 ^ICleveland 0
```

**Keyword:**   text handling

**See Also:**   awk, sed, tr

## cat -v bigscript.Z

ALL   ALL   SCRIPT POWER SYSADM

If you need to examine a binary file for some reason, the **-v** option to **cat** serves as a rudimentary method. The **-v** option prints all characters that don't normally print, with the exception of tabs, newlines, and formfeeds. The option causes ASCII controls (octal 000 - 037) to be printed as **^n**, where **^n** is the corresponding octal character in the range octal 100 to 137. The **DEL** character is printed as **^?**. Other characters not in the octal range 100 to 137 are printed as **M-x**, where **x** is the ASCII character corresponding to the lower 7 bits of the octal number. As for the example, the first few lines of the compressed file might look like this:

```
^_M-^]M-^P!@49S^FM-^DM-^T2s^TM-^Q3&^LM-^H)tBH!S^G^Ni
^H#iX8T^@BA@&e\T^AafM-^M^\^Ppd$i#1^OM-^H;i\M-^Pysg
M-^N^K^PTP$M-^Y^C"MHM-^Qa`@)#M-^Qg^]4!AdQ^Hb^LM-^[4i
```

**Keyword:**   text handling

**See Also:**   od

## cat /dev/null > fresh.txt

ALL   ALL   SCRIPT POWER SYSADM

This is one way to empty a file of its contents, without removing the file altogether. The **/dev/null** file is a system file that is 0 bytes in size and more frequently used to absorb unwanted output (via redirection). Note that you can also use **cp** with **/dev/null** to create an empty file. In the Bourne shell, you can also create an empty file by entering **> fresh.txt**.

**Keyword:** file handling

**See Also:** cp

### cat /etc/passwd

The **cat** command is a quick way to display the contents of a file to the screen. If the file is short, as some **/etc/passwd** files are, **cat** serves perfectly well. For longer files, **more** or **pg** are more appropriate because they stop the display after each screen of data.

**Keyword:** text display

**See Also:** more, pg

### cat > mynotes

Using **cat** with the redirection operator before a filename causes **cat** to take input from the keyboard and direct it to the specified file. In "interactive" mode, **cat** lets you use basic editing keys, but you cannot reedit a previous line. To end the session, press Ctrl-D.

**Keyword:** file handling

**See Also:** ed, emacs, vi

### cat >> $HOME/calendar

This is a handy way to add one or more lines of text to any file. Similar to using a single redirection symbol (as in **cat >**), which creates a new file, this example appends text to an existing file when you use it with **cat**. For fast typists, it's a two-second procedure to update the **calendar** file. The **cat >>**, as with **cat >**, causes the shell to look for input from the keyboard. At the cursor, you type what you want, on as many lines as you want. You end the command by pressing Ctrl-D. Here is a sample session:

```
$ cat >> $HOME/calendar
July 10   Last day before vacation
July 31   Meeting with staff and consultant
<Ctrl-D>
$
```

**Keyword:** text handling

**See Also:** ed, emacs, vi

ALL ALL ALL

ALL ALL ALL

ALL ALL ALL

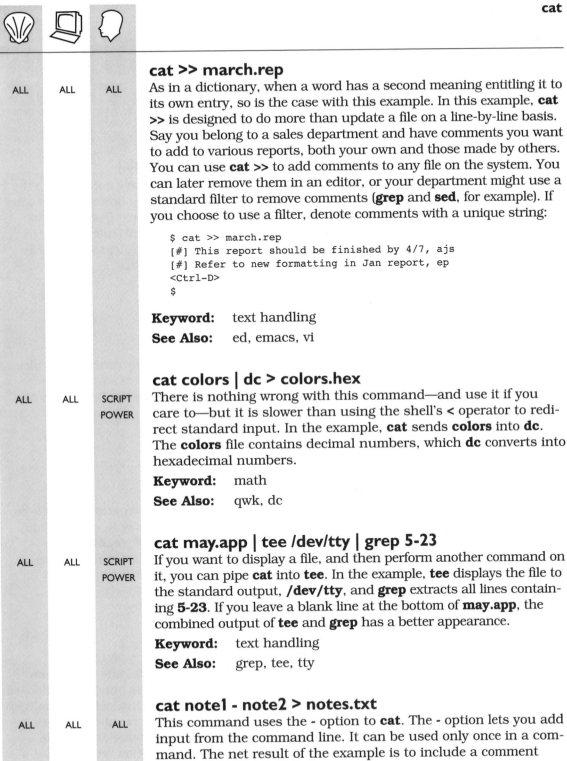

## cat >> march.rep

As in a dictionary, when a word has a second meaning entitling it to its own entry, so is the case with this example. In this example, **cat >>** is designed to do more than update a file on a line-by-line basis. Say you belong to a sales department and have comments you want to add to various reports, both your own and those made by others. You can use **cat >>** to add comments to any file on the system. You can later remove them in an editor, or your department might use a standard filter to remove comments (**grep** and **sed**, for example). If you choose to use a filter, denote comments with a unique string:

```
$ cat >> march.rep
[#] This report should be finished by 4/7, ajs
[#] Refer to new formatting in Jan report, ep
<Ctrl-D>
$
```

**Keyword:**    text handling

**See Also:**    ed, emacs, vi

## cat colors | dc > colors.hex

There is nothing wrong with this command—and use it if you care to—but it is slower than using the shell's **<** operator to redirect standard input. In the example, **cat** sends **colors** into **dc**. The **colors** file contains decimal numbers, which **dc** converts into hexadecimal numbers.

**Keyword:**    math

**See Also:**    qwk, dc

## cat may.app | tee /dev/tty | grep 5-23

If you want to display a file, and then perform another command on it, you can pipe **cat** into **tee**. In the example, **tee** displays the file to the standard output, **/dev/tty**, and **grep** extracts all lines containing **5-23**. If you leave a blank line at the bottom of **may.app**, the combined output of **tee** and **grep** has a better appearance.

**Keyword:**    text handling

**See Also:**    grep, tee, tty

## cat note1 - note2 > notes.txt

This command uses the - option to **cat**. The - option lets you add input from the command line. It can be used only once in a command. The net result of the example is to include a comment from the keyboard to separate the two files. After you type the comment, press Ctrl-D.

**Keyword:**    file handling

**See Also:**    ed, emacs, vi

### cat note1 - | mail -s "My Notes" emilyd

| | | |
|---|---|---|
| ALL | ALL | SCRIPT POWER |

This command illustrates one way to send an existing file to the **mail** program. In addition to sending the file, however, the - after the filename tells **cat** that you want to add text from the keyboard. You can add as much text as you want, just be sure to press Ctrl-D after completing the new text. Note, too, that this works with other mail programs such as **mailx**.

**Keyword:**    file handling, text handling

**See Also:**    mail, mailx

### cat report*.txt > report.txt

| | | |
|---|---|---|
| ALL | ALL | ALL |

With shell wildcard characters, you can easily concatenate files with **cat** and the redirection operator. In the example, all files that begin with **report** and end with **.txt** are combined into one file, **report.txt**.

**Keyword:**    file handling

**See Also:**    ed, emacs, vi

### cat report.txt >> year.txt

| | | |
|---|---|---|
| ALL | ALL | ALL |

With **cat** and the **>>** append operator, you can attach one file to the end of another file. This is the primary way to concatenate files in UNIX. You can also use the **>**, but **cat report.txt > year.txt** overwrites the original file; it is no different from **cp report.txt year.txt**.

**Keyword:**    file handling

**See Also:**    cp, join

### cat sales[4-6].rep > sales.q2

| | | |
|---|---|---|
| ALL | ALL | END SCRIPT |

Using this form of regular expression provides one way to concatenate a group of similarly named files. The bracketed wildcard tells **cat** to print **sales4.rep**, **sales5.rep**, and **sales6.rep** to a new files called **sales.q2**. You can also use other numbers, letters, and punctuation in bracketed wildcard ranges. For example, **[0-9]**, **[a-Z]**, and **[A-Z]** are valid. For punctuation, you can use a range, but you will probably want to group specifically targeted punctuation marks and special characters, such as **[=+-*/]**.

**Keyword:** file handling

**See Also:** cp

ALL ALL ALL

## cat sales[456].rep > sales.q2

This command concatenates **sales4.rep**, **sales5.rep**, and **sales6.rep**, in this order, to **sales.q2**. You don't use **>>** to append the files; you use a single **>** as if you were redirecting a single file.

**Keyword:** file handling

**See Also:** cp

ALL ALL SCRIPT POWER

## cat sales[456].rep >! sales.q2

If you're running the C shell, you probably have the **noclobber** variable set. The **noclobber** variable prevents you from overwriting a file when you are using redirection. Following the redirection symbol with an exclamation mark lets you override **noclobber**—which is to say that it lets you *clobber* the file.

**Keyword:** file handling

**See Also:** cp

ALL ALL ALL

## cat sales[654].rep > sales.q2

This command does not do what it appears to do. If you thought it would print **sales6**, **sales5**, and **sales4**, in that order, you were wrong. The shell prevents this by its adherence to its universal default condition of treating files alphabetically. Therefore, it prints **sales4**, **sales5**, and then **sales6**.

**Keyword:** file handling

**See Also:** cp

ALL ALL ALL

## (cat note1; ls; cat note2) > dir.txt

The command grouping feature of the shell lets you intermix output from some other command between two **cat** commands. The net result of the example is a single file, containing a note, directory listing, and another note. When using command grouping, be sure that you have a space after each semicolon.

**Keyword:** text display

**See Also:** less, more, pg

ALL ALL SYSADM

## catman -M /usr/local/man:/usr/share/man

This command updates **man** pages that do not meet with the current level of formatting. This could occur if you have added **man** pages for public domain or other software. If **catman** does find **man** pages that need reformatting, it also updates the **whatis** file. In the example, the -**M** option is used to specify the path(s) for the **man** pages.

**Keyword:** documentation

**See Also:** man, nroff, troff, whatis

ALL ALL SYSADM

## catman -w

This command updates the **whatis** database. It works by reading through the **man** pages and adding references for any new **man** pages to the **whatis** file. You should run **catman -w** whenever you add new **man** pages to the system.

**Keyword:** documentation

**See Also:** man, nroff, troff, whatis

ALL ALL END

## cb cars.c > cars.txt

This command converts the C program **cars.c** into a more readable form, and outputs it to **cars.txt**.

**Keyword:** programming

**See Also:** cat, less, more, pg

ALL ALL SCRIPT POWER SYSADM

## cc myprog.c

This is the simplest command you can use for the **cc** compiler, which compiles C source code into an executable file. By default, when you use a command like the example, an executable file called **a.out** is produced. There are numerous options with **cc**, however. Here are a few of the more important ones:

```
-c    create an object file, but no a.out file
-E    expand macros and print C code on standard output
-o    specify an output filename for the executable
-O    try to optimize the source code
-s    create an .s file containing assembly language
```

**Keyword:** programming

**See Also:** dbx, make

### cd

ALL ALL ALL

Used without any arguments, the **cd** command changes directories to the user's home directory. Using either **cd $HOME** or **cd ~** is redundant and unnecessary.

**Keyword:** directories

**See Also:** chdir, chmod, dirs, du, find, ln, ls, popd, pushd, pwd

### cd $HOME/docs

ALL ALL ALL

This is one way to change directories into subdirectories in your home directory. It works from anywhere on the system.

**Keyword:** directories

**See Also:** chdir, chmod, dirs, du, find, ln, ls, popd, pushd, pwd

### cd $XAPPLRESDIR

ALL XWIN ALL

The **cd** command works with environment variables that represent directories. In the example, the **cd** command changes to a directory in which you can store resource files for the X Window System.

**Keyword:** directories

**See Also:** pwd, XAPPLRESDIR

### cd ..

ALL ALL ALL

The double-dot symbol represents the parent directory. Using it with the **cd** command changes the current directory to the parent directory, unless of course you're in the root directory, which has no parent.

**Keyword:** directories

**See Also:** chdir, chmod, dirs, du, find, ln, ls, popd, pushd, pwd

### cd /home/DEC*/bin

ALL ALL ALL

You can use the wildcard characters **?** and **\*** with the **cd** command. In the example, the **\*** character completes the directory name beginning with **DEC**. The only thing you have to be wary of is ambiguous references. If two directories began with **DEC**, **cd** would refuse to work.

**Keyword:** directories

**See Also:** chdir, chmod, dirs, du, find, ln, ls, popd, pushd, pwd

### cd /usr/bin

With a directory argument, **cd** changes into the specified directory. Note that the example uses an absolute path. From the root directory, **usr/bin** is the equivalent relative address.

**Keyword:** directories

**See Also:** chdir, chmod, dirs, du, find, ln, ls, popd, pushd, pwd

### cd /usr; tar cf /house/usrtar . | (cd /house; tar xfBp -)

This command copies a filesystem into a **tar** file on a second filesystem. The first **cd** is grouped using the semicolon only. The second **cd** is grouped using the semicolon inside parentheses because of the open pipe.

**Keyword:** backup and restore

**See Also:** backup, cp, cpio, dd, dump, mount, restore, smit, sysadm, sysadmsh, tar, umount

### (cd /home/reports; ls > dir.lst; more dir.lst *.rep)

The **cd** command is frequently used as the first command in a command grouping. The shell recognizes a command grouping when all commands are contained inside parentheses and separated by semicolons (a space must follow each semicolon). In the example, the command changes into the **/home/reports** directory, executes the **ls** command and redirects its output into a file, and then executes **more**, which displays **dir.lst** as well as any files with a **.rep** extension.

**Keyword:** directories, file handling

**See Also:** chdir, chmod, dirs, du, find, ln, ls, popd, pushd, pwd

### CDPATH

In the Bourne and Korn shells, **CDPATH** is the search path that the **cd** command checks during execution. Usually defined in **.profile**, the **CDPATH** contains shorthand names for commonly accessed directories.

**Keyword:** directories

**Files:** $HOME/.profile

**See Also:** cd, chdir, chmod, dirs, du, find, ln, ls, popd, pushd, pwd

The leftmost columns indicate:

ALL ALL ALL

ALL ALL SYSADM

ALL ALL POWER

SH KSH | ALL | ALL

### cdpath

CSH | ALL | ALL

The C shell's **cdpath** variable specifies a list of alternate directories in which the **cd** and **chdir** commands can find subdirectories.

**Keyword:** directories

**Files:** $HOME/.cshrc, $HOME/.login

**See Also:** cd, chdir, chmod, dirs, du, find, ln, ls, popd, pushd, pwd

### chdir /usr/bin/X11

CSH | ALL | ALL

The C shell's built-in **chdir** command operates identically to the **cd** command. In fact, the **cd** command is a built-in alias to the **chdir** command. If you alias **cd** in your command line prompt, avoid using the **chdir** command unless you alias it as well. In the example, **chdir** makes **/usr/bin/X11** the current directory. The default behavior of **chdir**—that is, the behavior when you enter **chdir** without any arguments—is to make your home directory the current directory.

**Keyword:** directories

**See Also:** cd, chmod, dirs, du, find, ln, ls, popd, pushd, pwd

### chfn perkie

ALL | OSF | END SYSADM

This command changes password file information for the user **perkie**. Typical information that is changed with **chfn** is the user's full name, phone number, and address.

**Keyword:** user environment

**Files:** /etc/passwd

**See Also:** passwd

### chgrp -h mktg homelink

ALL | SVR4 | SYSADM

This command changes the group ownership of a symbolic link. If you do not use this option, the group ownership of the symbolic link is not changed, although the group of ownership of the file referenced by the link is changed.

**Keyword:** file ownership

**See Also:** chmod, chown, id, passwd

## chgrp -R mktg /home/proplan

ALL ALL SYSADM

This command changes the ownership of files in the specified directory and any subdirectories in it. In BSD versions, the group ownership of symbolic links is changed, but the link is not traversed. In SVR4 versions, you must use the **-h** option to change the group ownership of symbolic links, but the BSD version of **-R** does traverse symbolic links.

**Keyword:**   file ownership

**See Also:**   chmod, chown, id, passwd

## chgrp mktg rnotes

ALL ALL POWER SYSADM

The **chgrp** command changes the group ownership of a file. You must either own the file or be the superuser in order to use the command. BSD versions of the command permit the group ownership of symbolic links to be changed as you would change any other file. SVR4 versions require the **-h** option to change group ownership of symbolic links.

**Keyword:**   file ownership

**See Also:**   chmod, chown, id, passwd

## chkey

ALL SVR4 ALL

This changes the encryption key used to encipher and decipher encrypted files. Each user has a unique encryption key stored in the **publickey** database.

**Keyword:**   security

**Files:**   publickey

**See Also:**   encrypt, decrypt

## chmod +l findtxt

ALL SVR4 POWER SYSADM

This command adds file locking to the file. This means one process cannot access the file if another process is reading, writing, or executing the file. Further, to access the file, the group ID of the user must be the same as the group ID of the file. This is an SVR4-only feature.

**Keyword:**   file permissions

**See Also:**   chgrp, chown, ls, umask

| | | |
|---|---|---|
| ALL | ALL | END SYSADM |

### chmod +s findtxt

This command sets the group ID for the file and restricts access to that group. BSD and SVR4 automatically set the group, but in different ways. BSD sets the group according to the group of the current directory; SVR4 sets the group to that of the owner of the file.

**Keyword:**    file permissions

**See Also:**    chgrp, chown, ls, umask

| | | |
|---|---|---|
| ALL | ALL | SYSADM |

### chmod +t findtxt

This command sets the UNIX sticky bit, which restricts who can move and delete files in the directory. Anyone can create files in the directory, but only the superuser, owner of the directory, and the owner of a given file can move and delete a file.

**Keyword:**    file permissions

**See Also:**    chgrp, chown, ls, umask

| | | |
|---|---|---|
| ALL | ALL | ALL |

### chmod +x findtxt

To add execute permissions to all users, use the **+x** sequence. You can add any permission using the **+** symbol and delete any permission using the **-** symbol. If a file looked like this:

```
46 -rw-r--r--   1 alans    system    46818 Aug 11 10:50 findtxt
```

using the **+x** sequence with **chmod** would change the file to this:

```
46 -rwxr-xr-x   1 alans    system    46818 Aug 11 10:50 findtxt
```

**Keyword:**    file permissions

**See Also:**    chgrp, chown, ls, umask

| | | |
|---|---|---|
| ALL | SVR4 | POWER SYSADM |

### chmod -R 777 /home/docs/

This command changes file and directory permissions beginning with **/home/docs** and continuing through all files and subdirectories of **/home/docs**. The **-R** option causes **chmod** to leave the permissions on symbolic links intact, but the link is traversed and permissions on subsequent files and directories are changed. This **ls** display for the **docs** directory looks like this:

```
drwxrwxrwx   3 alans    users       512 Aug 11 12:34 docs
```

**Keyword:**    file permissions

**See Also:**    chgrp, chown, ls, umask

ALL    BSD    POWER
SYSADM

## chmod -R ugo=rw,+X /home/docs

This command changes file and directory permissions, but preserves the executable status of directories and any other file that has execute permission. The **+X** syntax is only available on BSD systems. The **-R** option causes **chmod** to recursively go through directories beginning with **/home/docs**. Note that the **-R** option on BSD systems does not change permissions of symbolic links, nor does it traverse links.

**Keyword:**    file permissions

**See Also:**    chgrp, chown, ls, umask

ALL    ALL    POWER
SYSADM

## chmod 1777 /home/templates

The **1777** value changes the permissions on the directory to read, write, and execute for all users. It also activates the UNIX sticky bit, which restricts who can move and delete files in the directory. Anyone can create files in the directory, but only the superuser, owner of the directory, and the owner of a given file can move and delete a file. The **ls -ls** display looks like this:

```
drwxrwxrwt   3 alans     users      512 Aug 11 12:34 templates
```

**Keyword:**    file permissions, security

**See Also:**    chgrp, chown, ls, umask

ALL    ALL    SYSADM

## chmod 2777 /home/scripts

The **2777** value changes the permissions of the directory to read, write, and execute for all users. It also activates the group ID bit. The group ID is set according to the group of the user making the change. When it is set, only members of the group can access the file. The **ls -ls** display looks like this:

```
drwxrwsrwx   3 alans     users      512 Aug 11 12:34 scripts
```

**Keyword:**    file permissions, file ownership

**See Also:**    chgrp, chown, ls, umask

ALL    ALL    END
SYSADM

## chmod 400 chkbook.wp1

The **400** octal value with **chmod** makes a file readable only to the owner. By restricting access to read, you can prevent your files from being accidentally overwritten. The superuser still has full access, however. The **ls -ls** display looks like this:

```
48 -r--------   1 root      system    49081 Aug 11 11:41 chkbook.wp1
```

ALL    ALL    SYSADM

**Keyword:**    file permissions, security
**See Also:**    chgrp, chown, ls, umask

### chmod 4000 findtxt

This **4000** value sets the user ID of the file and is relevant for executable files. When another user executes a *set user ID* (SUID) file, the user has the permissions of the file's owner. This technique is often used to provide root permissions to users executing a program, but for security reasons, you should avoid the technique whenever possible.

**Keyword:**    file permissions, file ownership
**See Also:**    chgrp, chown, ls, umask

ALL    ALL    END
SYSADM

### chmod 444 security.doc

The **444** octal value with **chmod** makes the file readable only. As a result, only the superuser can make changes to the file. The **ls -ls** display looks like this:

```
15 -r--r--r--    1 root      system      14931 Aug 11 11:36 security.doc
```

**Keyword:**    file permissions, security
**See Also:**    chgrp, chown, ls, umask

ALL    ALL    END
SYSADM

### chmod 600 secrets.doc

Using **600** changes the permissions on the file to read and write for the owner. It is important to note that the superuser can still read and write to the file, but **600** ensures that nonprivileged users will stay out. The **ls -ls** display looks like this:

```
2 -rw-------    1 alans     system      1091 Aug 11 11:30 secrets.doc
```

**Keyword:**    file permissions, security
**See Also:**    chgrp, chown, ls, umask

ALL    ALL    END
SYSADM

### chmod 644 help.doc

Using **644** with **chmod** changes the permissions on the file to read and write for the owner, read for the group, and read for others. The **ls -ls** display looks like this:

```
50 -rw-r--r--    1 alans     system      50632 Aug 11 11:28 help.doc
```

**Keyword:**    file permissions
**See Also:**    chgrp, chown, ls, umask

| | | |
|---|---|---|
| ALL | ALL | END SYSADM |

# chmod 700 .cshrc

The **700** octal number allows you to prevent all other users, except the superuser, from accessing a file. It is feasible that you would use **700** with **chmod** on shell startup files. Most shell startup files are usually executable. Some X Window System startup files need not be executable. Here is the **ls -ls** display for the entry:

```
2 -rwx------   1 alans    users     1057 Aug 10 07:24 .cshrc
```

**Keyword:**  file permissions

**See Also:**  chgrp, chown, ls, umask

# chmod 711 findtxt

Using **711** with **chmod** changes the permissions on the file to read, write, and execute for the owner; execute for the group; and execute for the public (others). The **ls -ls** display looks like this:

```
46 -rwx--x--x   1 alans    system    46818 Aug 11 10:50 findtxt
```

**Keyword:**  file permissions

**See Also:**  chgrp, chown, ls, umask

# chmod 755 findtxt

Using **755** with **chmod** changes the permissions on the file to read, write, and execute for the owner; read, write, and execute for the group; and read and execute for the public (others). The **ls -ls** display looks like this:

```
46 -rwxr-xr-x   1 alans    system    46818 Aug 11 10:50 findtxt
```

**Keyword:**  file permissions

**See Also:**  chgrp, chown, ls, umask

# chmod 774 findtxt

Using **774** with **chmod** changes the permissions on the file to read, write, and execute for the owner; read, write, and execute for the group; and read for the public (others). The **ls -ls** display looks like this:

```
46 -rwxrwxr--   1 alans    system    46818 Aug 11 10:50 findtxt
```

**Keyword:**  file permissions

**See Also:**  chgrp, chown, ls, umask

### chmod 775 findtxt

Using **775** with **chmod** changes the permissions on the file to read, write, and execute for the owner; read and write for the group; and execute for the public (others). The **ls -ls** display looks like this:

```
46 -rwxrwxr-x   1 alans    system    46818 Aug 11 10:50 findtxt
```

**Keyword:**    file permissions
**See Also:**    chgrp, chown, ls, umask

### chmod 777 findtxt

The **chmod** command changes the read, write, and execute permissions on files and directories, according to three main categories of file access: access by owner, access by group, and access by the public (others). In order to use the **chmod** command on a file or directory, you must be the owner or the superuser. The entry presumes that **findtxt** is a shell script and that it is permissible for all users to read, write, and execute it. Typically, **chmod** is used to grant selective access to files based on the category to which a user belongs. There are three categories of users: owner, group, and public. In the example, **777** is an octal number that corresponds to a file's permissions, as shown with the **ls -ls** command:

```
46 -rwxrwxrwx   1 alans    system    46818 Aug 11 10:50 findtxt
```

The following **chmod** entries use octal numbers to specify directories. Not all possibilities are included. Subsequent **chmod** entries list the symbolic equivalent of using octal numbers.

**Keyword:**    file permissions
**See Also:**    chgrp, chown, ls, umask

### chmod =rwx findtxt

This is yet another way to give read, write, and execute permissions to all users. Note that you can precede any combination of permissions with any of the three **chmod** operators: **=**, **-**, and **+**.

**Keyword:**    file permissions
**See Also:**    chgrp, chown, ls, umask

ALL    ALL    END
                SYSADM

**65**

### chmod a-x findtxt

| | | |
|---|---|---|
| ALL | ALL | END SYSADM |

The **a-x** sequence denies execute permissions to everyone. You might use this command if you were in the middle of editing a shell script and didn't want anyone to execute it.

**Keyword:**  file permissions

**See Also:**  chgrp, chown, ls, umask

### chmod go-x findtxt

| | | |
|---|---|---|
| ALL | ALL | END SYSADM |

This command removes execute permissions from the group and others (public). Note that you can combine **g** and **o**, or **u** for that matter, with any of the **chmod** operators.

**Keyword:**  file permissions

**See Also:**  chgrp, chown, ls, umask

### chmod u+s findtxt

| | | |
|---|---|---|
| ALL | ALL | SYSADM |

This command sets the user ID of the file and is relevant for executable files. When another user executes a *set user ID* (SUID) file, the user has the permissions of the file's owner. This technique is often used to provide root permissions to users executing a program, but for security reasons, you should avoid the technique whenever possible.

**Keyword:**  file permissions

**See Also:**  chgrp, chown, ls, umask

### chmod u+x findtxt

| | | |
|---|---|---|
| ALL | ALL | END SYSADM |

To give execute permissions to the owner of the file only, use the **u+x** sequence. This technique works for all three categories of user and can be combined with other syntax. For example, you could modify the entry to read **chmod u+x,go= findtxt**.

**Keyword:**  file permissions

**See Also:**  chgrp, chown, ls, umask

### chmod u=rw,go=r findtxt

| | | |
|---|---|---|
| ALL | ALL | ALL |

This command changes the permissions on the file to read and write for the owner, and read for the group. The **ls -ls** display looks like this:

```
50 -rw-r--r--   1 alans    system    50632 Aug 11 11:28 help.doc
```

**Keyword:**  file permissions

**See Also:**  chgrp, chown, ls, umask

### chmod u=rwx,go= findtxt

This command allows you to prevent all other users, except the superuser, from accessing a file. Note that setting **go** equal to nothing removes all permissions from the group and other (public) categories. The original state of a file's permissions depends on the **umask** value. Here is the **ls -ls** display for the file:

```
 2 -rwx------   1 alans     users        1057 Aug 10 07:24 .cshrc
```

**Keyword:** file permissions
**See Also:** chgrp, chown, ls, umask

### chmod u=rwx,go=x findtxt

This command changes the permissions on the file to read, write, and execute for the owner; execute for the group; and execute for the public (others). The **ls -ls** display looks like this:

```
46 -rwx--x--x   1 alans     system      46818 Aug 11 10:50 findtxt
```

**Keyword:** file permissions
**See Also:** chgrp, chown, ls, umask

### chmod ug=rwx,o=r findtxt

This command changes the permissions on the file to read, write, and execute for the owner; read, write, and execute for the group; and read for the public (others). The **ls -ls** display looks like this:

```
46 -rwxrwxr--   1 alans     system      46818 Aug 11 10:50 findtxt
```

**Keyword:** file permissions
**See Also:** chgrp, chown, ls, umask

### chmod ug=rwx,o=rx findtxt

This command changes the permissions on the file to read, write, and execute for the owner; read, write, and execute for the group; and read and execute for the public (others). The **ls -ls** display looks like this:

```
46 -rwxrwxr-x   1 alans     system      46818 Aug 11 10:50 findtxt
```

**Keyword:** file permissions
**See Also:** chgrp, chown, ls, umask

ALL ALL ALL

ALL ALL ALL

ALL ALL ALL

ALL ALL ALL

## chmod ugo=rwx findtxt

This **chmod** command uses the symbolic method of setting permissions. The example produces the same results as if you had used **chmod 777**. When using the symbolic method, you can specify **u** for user, **g** for group, or **o** for others (public). Permissions are set using **r** for read, **w** for write, **x** for execute, **s** for set user or group ID, and **t** for setting the sticky bit. On SVR4 systems, you can also use **l** to set lock access, which prevents a process from accessing a file if the file is being accessed by another process. The **ls -ls** display for the file looks like this:

```
46 -rwxrwxrwx   1 alans     system    46818 Aug 11 10:50 findtxt
```

**Keyword:**  file permissions, file locking

**See Also:**  chgrp, chown, ls, umask

## chown -h -R root /usr/scripts

This command recursively goes through a directory hierarchy and changes the ownership of all directories, files, and links. The **-h** option causes **chown** to change the ownership of links.

**Keyword:**  file permissions

**See Also:**  chgrp, chmod, ls, umask

## chown -R root /usr/scripts

This **chown** command recursively descends through directories and changes the ownership of directories and files. On BSD systems, the ownership of symbolic links is changed, but the links are not traversed. On SVR4 systems, the ownership is not changed, but the links are traversed.

**Keyword:**  file permissions

**See Also:**  chgrp, chmod, ls, umask

## chown -R root:system /usr/menus/*

This entry changes both the owner and the group for the specified list of files. The **-R** option performs the task recursively for all files in the directory hierarchy.

**Keyword:**  file permissions

**See Also:**  chgrp, chmod, ls, umask

| | | |
|---|---|---|
| ALL | ALL | ALL |
| ALL | ALL | SYSADM |
| ALL | ALL | SYSADM |
| ALL | ALL | SYSADM |

| | | |
|---|---|---|
| ALL | ALL | SYSADM |

### chown donna notes.txt

The **chown** command changes the owner of a file. In order to use **chown** on a file, you must be the owner of the file or the super-user. If an ordinary user makes the change, the user ID is cleared.

**Keyword:** file permissions

**See Also:** chgrp, chmod, ls, umask

| | | |
|---|---|---|
| ALL | OSF SVR4 | SYSADM |

### chroot /dev/ra1a /bin/sh

The **chroot** command is reserved for the superuser. It lets the root user set in effect a new filesystem and run a command in that filesystem. One typical command to run is a shell, as in the example. You can exit the shell by entering the **exit** command or pressing Ctrl-D. Note that in the entry, **/dev/ra1a** is an example of a special file referencing a hard disk.

**Keyword:** program execution

**See Also:** cd

| | | |
|---|---|---|
| ALL | OSF SVR4 | SYSADM |

### chroot /SCO4 /bin/ksh

Here, the **chroot** command is used to change the root filesystem to a mounted filesystem. It is typical to use system names when an entire filesystem from another platform is mounted. Thus, SCO4 is the same filesystem you would find if you sat down to that machine. With **chroot**, all system defaults, such as the system path and environment variables, are in effect.

**Keyword:** program execution

**See Also:** cd, mount

| | | |
|---|---|---|
| ALL | OSF | ALL |

### chsh alans

The **chsh** command changes the login shell of your username or of the specified username. Entering **chsh** without a username causes **chsh** to enter interactive mode and prompt you for a new shell for the current user.

**Keyword:** terminals

**Files:** /etc/passwd

**See Also:** passwd

## clear

**ALL · ALL · POWER**

This command simply clears the active terminal screen. If you have problems with this command, check the definition for the terminal. You may have an inaccurate **$TERM** environment variable, or a mistake in the **terminfo** database (SVR4) or **termcap\*** database (BSD).

**Keyword:**   terminals

**See Also:**   setenv

## clear_colormap

**ALL · SunOS · ALL**

On SunOS systems, this command clears the colormap. In a standard character mode session, the command makes any obscured text visible again. In an X Window System session, the command reinitializes the colormap, but you must also subsequently refresh the screen using a window manager command.

**Keyword:**   open look

**Files:**   /usr/openwin/lib/rgb.txt, /usr/lib/X11/rgb.txt

**See Also:**   xsetroot

## click

**ALL · SunOS · ALL**

On SunOS systems, the **click** command controls the keyboard click. The entry, with no arguments, disables the click. To reactivate the click, you can use the **click -y** command.

**Keyword:**   open look

**See Also:**   xset

## Clock

**ALL · XWIN · ALL**

This is the resource filename for the **oclock** client program. A client's resource file can be located in any of several resource locations. The order of precedence of these locations is **$XENVI-RONMENT, $HOME/.Xdefaults**-hostname, **$XAPPLRESDIR, $HOME/app-file, $HOME/.Xdefaults, /usr/lib/X11/app-defaults/Xdefaults**, and **/usr/lib/X11/app-defaults/app-name**. Note that **.Xdefaults** is a customary name, not mandatory.

**Keyword:**   X resources

**See Also:**   xrdb

| | | |
|---|---|---|
| ALL | SunOS | END |

## clock

On SunOS systems, the **clock** command displays a clock under an X Window session. The **clock** program is written in Open Look, which makes it suitable for Sun's OpenWindows. But you can also run it with third-party implementations of the Motif window manager for Sun.

**Keyword:** Open Look

**See Also:** xclock, date

| | | |
|---|---|---|
| ALL | OSF | ALL |

## cmdedit

This is a special version of the C shell created by Digital Equipment Corp. Its main feature is the addition of command line editing. To activate command line editing, you must set the **$editmode** variable in **$HOME/.cshrc**.

**Keyword:** user environment

**Files:** $HOME/.cshrc

**See Also:** csh, ksh, sh

| | | |
|---|---|---|
| ALL | SunOS | END |

## cmdtool -C &

This example starts a command tool window under Sun's Open-Windows. The **cmdtool** program is similar to the Xterm terminal emulator under the X Window System. The **-C** option starts **cmdtool** as a console monitor, allowing it to intercept system messages. The **&** operator executes the command in the background, so as not to tie up the terminal emulator window from which the command is typed.

**Keyword:** Open Look

**See Also:** xterm

| | | |
|---|---|---|
| ALL | SunOS | END |

## cmdtool -fn ´-adobe-helvetica-bold-r-normal--18-180-75-75-p-103-iso8859-1´ &

This example uses a font from the X Window System's standard fonts with a **cmdtool**. It ensures that the font string is complete—it uses cut and paste to obtain a string after running **xlsfonts**—and encloses the strings in quotes. The **-fn** option controls fonts for **cmdtool**.

**Keyword:** Open Look

**See Also:** xterm

### cmdtool -fn terminal-bold

ALL   SunOS   END

This example uses a font alias instead of an X Window System font string to specify the font in a **cmdtool** window. Some font aliases are standard with SunOS, and **terminal-bold** is one of these. Aliases under SunOS are defined in the files **Compat.lst** and **Synonyms.list**.

**Keyword:**   Open Look

**See Also:**   xterm

### cmdtool -Wp 20 780 &

ALL   SunOS   END

This starts Sun's **cmdtool** terminal emulator in the lower left-hand section of the screen. The **-Wp** option specifies screen location. The **&** operator executes **cmdtool** in the background.

**Keyword:**   Open Look

**See Also:**   xterm

### cmdtool -Wp 50 50 -Ws 600 100 &

ALL   SunOS   END

This starts Sun's **cmdtool** terminal emulator in the upper left-hand section of the screen and specifies its size as 600 pixels wide by 100 pixels high. The **-Wp** option specifies screen location; the **-Ws** option specifies window size. The **&** operator executes **cmdtool** in the background.

**Keyword:**   open look

**See Also:**   xterm

### cmp -l doc1.txt doc2.txt

ALL   ALL   END

Using the **-l** option with **cmp** compares two files by displaying the byte number (in decimal) and the different bytes in octal. For example, if bytes 15, 22, and 45 were different in **doc1.txt** and **doc2.txt**, the entry would produce the following:

```
 9 102 164
10 102 170
11 102  61
cmp: EOF on doc2.txt
```

**Keyword:**   text handling

**See Also:**   comm, diff

## cmp -s march.txt march.doc && rm march..doc

ALL   ALL   END SCRIPT

The shell's AND operator, **&&**, lets you execute a command if the first command returns a successful status code. In the example, if **cmp** finds that the two files are identical, the **rm** command removes the second file. If the two files were not identical, the **&&** operator would not pass control to the **rm** command. The **-s** option to **cmp** suppresses normal output.

**Keyword:**  file handling

**See Also:**  awk cat, chmod, cp, cpio, du, find, join, ln, ls, mv, pr, tar, touch, tr

## cmp -s phone.db phone.bak || cp phone.db phone.bak

ALL   ALL   END SCRIPT

The shell's OR operator, **||**, adds some extra power to **cmp** in this entry. First, the **-s** tells **cmp** not to display any output, so **cmp** just returns its status code, indicating whether the operation was successful. The OR operator keys in on this code. In the example, if the test is unsuccessful, **cp** copies **phone.db** to **phone.bak**. If the files had been the same, the OR operator would not have passed control to **cp**.

**Keyword:**  text handling

**See Also:**  ln, pr

## cmp doc1.txt doc2.txt

ALL   ALL   END

The **cmp** command compares the contents of two files. With no options, the command tells you at what point—or more specifically, at what byte offset—the files begin to differ. If two files differ altogether, the output of **cmd** resembles the following:

```
doc1.txt doc2.txt differ: byte 1, line 1
```

For shell script writers, **cmp** can be useful if you check for its exit status: If it is 0, the compared files are the same; if 1, the files are different; and if 2, **cmp** encountered an error.

**Keyword:**  text handling

**See Also:**  comm, diff

## col -b < any.man | sed ´s/[01]m//gp´ > any.txt

ALL   ALL   END POWER

This use of the **col** command assumes that you first redirect the output of the **man** command to a file. For example, **ls.man** could replace **any.man** in the example. The use of **col** to filter **man** page formatting is convenient, because it would take a more complicated **sed** command to do the additional removal of backspaces.

**Keyword:**    text display

**See Also:**    nroff, sed, tbl

### col -b `nroff report.nrf` > report.txt

The **col** command can be used to strip embedded backspace characters and other escape sequences from a document. The **col** program interprets character streams as would a printer or other device. When it encounters the backspace and a subsequent character, the **-b** option causes **col** to delete the second character.

**Keyword:**    text display

**See Also:**    nroff, tbl

ALL    ALL    END
POWER

### colrm 5 85 updates | more

This command outputs all the characters in the **updates** file between column **5** and column **85**. The command is piped through the **more** command to make the output easily readable.

**Keyword:**    text display, text handling

**See Also:**    cat, less, more, pg

ALL    OSF    END

### COLUMNS

This is an environment variable that defines window widths in editing and printing.

**Keyword:**    terminals

**See Also:**    nroff, sed, tbl

KSH    ALL    SCRIPT

### comm -12 list1 list2 > newlist

Here, the **comm** command is used to output only those items common to **list1** and **list2**. The **-12** syntax tells **comm** not to print columns one and two in its output. You can use any combination of 1,2,3 in removing lines.

**Keyword:**    text handling

**See Also:**    cmp, diff, sort, uniq

ALL    ALL    POWER

### comm -23 reps.93 reps.95 > reps.former

ALL ALL POWER

If you maintain sorted ASCII files of information that changes over time—such as the roll call in the House of Representatives—you can use **comm** to provide quick intelligence on former members. For instance, the example produces a list of House members who retired or were not reelected in 1992.

**Keyword:**   text handling

**See Also:**   cmp, diff, sort, uniq

### comm list1 list2

ALL ALL POWER

The **comm** command compares files. It places unique items from **list1** in column one of the output; unique items from **list2** in column two of the output; and common, or intersecting, items in column three. The **comm** command is convenient for working with lists and columns of numbers.

**Keyword:**   text handling

**See Also:**   cmp, diff, sort, uniq

### compress -c loadscript > loadscript.Z

ALL ALL END

The **-c** option prints the compressed file to standard output. As a result, you must redirect it to a file. The advantage of this approach to **compress** is that the original version of the file is not removed. You might use this command if you need to compress a file and send it to an associate. The behavior of **compress -c** is identical to that of **zcat**.

**Keyword:**   file handling

**See Also:**   pack, ar, tar, cat, uncompress, zcat

### compress -c plans.txt | crypt > plans.let

ALL ALL END

Use **compress** to enhance the security of an encrypted file. The **crypt** command appears on many UNIX systems, but public domain software programs can easily decrypt its output. Compressing a file before encrypting it adds a level of security, but skilled crackers can probably decrypt the file by trial and error interpretation of the **compress**.

**Keyword:**   file handling

**See Also:**   crypt, pack, ar, tar, cat, find, uncompress

### compress -d loadscript

ALL    ALL    END

The **-d** option to **compress** restores a compressed file. This is the same as using the **uncompress** command.

**Keyword:**    file handling

**See Also:**    pack, ar, tar, cat, uncompress

### compress -F `find $HOME -name "*.doc" -print`

ALL    ALL    END

If you put a premium on saving hard disk space, but you are not necessarily archiving your work regularly enough, you might like this command. Use it, or a similar command, when you want to compress a set of files. The command compresses all **.doc** files in **$HOME** and its subdirectories. Command substitution with **find** provides **compress** with the list of files.

**Keyword:**    file handling

**See Also:**    pack, ar, tar, cat, find, uncompress

### compress -F `find $HOME/wastebasket -type f -print`

ALL    ALL    END

If you have a **wastebasket** directory, or any other directory that you would like to compress regularly, this command suits the purpose. The **-F** option causes **compress** to compress all files, even those that won't necessarily decrease in size. The command output from **find** yields all files of type **f**—in other words, all regular files.

**Keyword:**    file handling

**See Also:**    pack, ar, tar, cat, find, uncompress

### compress -fF loadscript

ALL    ALL    END

The **-f** option tells **compress** to overwrite any previously compressed file of the same name. The **-F** option tells **compress** to go ahead and create a **.Z** file even if the compression operation would not decrease the size of the file.

**Keyword:**    file handling

**See Also:**    pack, ar, tar, cat, uncompress

### compress -vF loadscript

ALL    ALL    END

The options here do two things: **-v** tells **compress** to print an operational message after the compression finishes, and the **-F** option tells **compress** to go ahead and create a **.Z** file even if the compression operation would not decrease the size of the file. The message you would get from running this command would be similar to the following:

```
loadscript: Compression: 68.65% -- replaced with loadscript.Z
```

**Keyword:** file handling

**See Also:** pack, ar, tar, cat, uncompress

### compress loadscript

ALL ALL END

The indispensable **compress** command can save you diskette and tape space, and let you email files and pass fewer bytes along the wire. With no options, **compress** removes the original file and turns it into a compressed file with a **.Z** extension. For example, the **ls** display of **loadscript** might look like this before compression:

```
49 -rw-r--r--   1 alans     users      49173 Aug 12 18:02 test1
```

After using **compress**, **loadscript** would look like this:

```
16 -rw-r--r--   1 alans     users      15415 Aug 12 18:02 test1.Z
```

To restore a compressed file, use **compress -d** or **uncompress**.

**Keyword:** file handling

**See Also:** pack, ar, tar, cat, uncompress

### continue

ALL ALL END

In the Bourne and Korn shells, the **continue** command resumes the next iteration of the loop in which the **continue** statement is located. In the C shell, it resumes the next iteration only when used with **while** and **foreach** statements.

**Keyword:** shell programming

**See Also:** break

### continue 2

KSH ALL END

This command resumes the next iteration of a shell script loop at the second outer loop relative to the location of the statement. This, for example, would continue processing one loop above the loop in which the statement is located. The C shell does not support this feature.

**Keyword:** shell programming

**See Also:** break

| | | |
|---|---|---|
| ALL | ALL | END |

### cp *.sales /usr/reports

This command copies all files with the **.sales** extension into the specified directory. Various shell wildcard characters can be used with the **cp** command, including:

```
*        any string of characters, including no characters
?        any single character, but not a period
[...]    characters designated with the brackets
[a-z]    all lowercase letters
[A-Z]    all uppercase letter
[0-9]    all numbers
```

When using brackets, you can use any range of characters. For example, **[a-Z]** and **[0-Z]** are valid ranges.

**Keyword:**    file handling

**See Also:**    cp, cpio, find, mv, rcp, tar

| | | |
|---|---|---|
| ALL | ALL | END SCRIPT |

### cp -- system.txt -system.txt

The -- option in **cp** lets you copy a file to a file with a filename that begins with a minus sign. You can get a directory listing of filenames that begin with minus signs by executing **ls -- -\***.

**Keyword:**    file handling

**See Also:**    cpio, mv, tar

| | | |
|---|---|---|
| ALL | ALL | END |

### cp -i jan.sales /usr/reports

The **-i** option to **cp** prompts you to confirm your copy operation if you are about to overwrite an existing file. The prompt looks like this:

```
overwrite /usr/reports/july.sales?
```

At this point, you can answer **y** or **n**. On many systems, system administrators create shell functions or aliases to impose the **cp** **-i** behavior on new users.

**Keyword:**    file handling

**See Also:**    cp, cpio, find, mv, rcp, tar

| | | |
|---|---|---|
| ALL | ALL | END |

### cp -p july.sales /usr/reports

The **-p** option causes the copy of the file to have the modification time of the original file, as well as the same file permissions.

**Keyword:**    file handling

**See Also:**    cp, cpio, find, mv, rcp, tar

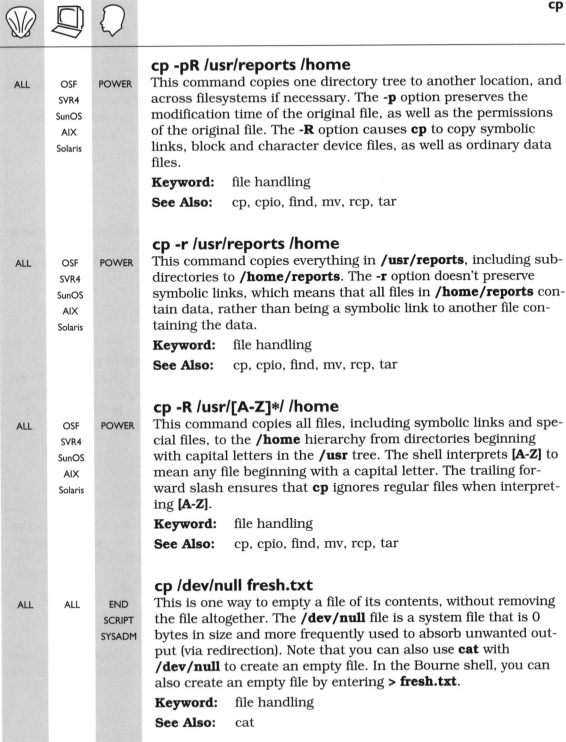

| ALL | OSF SVR4 SunOS AIX Solaris | POWER |
|---|---|---|

### cp -pR /usr/reports /home

This command copies one directory tree to another location, and across filesystems if necessary. The **-p** option preserves the modification time of the original file, as well as the permissions of the original file. The **-R** option causes **cp** to copy symbolic links, block and character device files, as well as ordinary data files.

**Keyword:**    file handling

**See Also:**    cp, cpio, find, mv, rcp, tar

### cp -r /usr/reports /home

This command copies everything in **/usr/reports**, including sub-directories to **/home/reports**. The **-r** option doesn't preserve symbolic links, which means that all files in **/home/reports** contain data, rather than being a symbolic link to another file containing the data.

**Keyword:**    file handling

**See Also:**    cp, cpio, find, mv, rcp, tar

### cp -R /usr/[A-Z]*/ /home

This command copies all files, including symbolic links and special files, to the **/home** hierarchy from directories beginning with capital letters in the **/usr** tree. The shell interprets **[A-Z]** to mean any file beginning with a capital letter. The trailing forward slash ensures that **cp** ignores regular files when interpreting **[A-Z]**.

**Keyword:**    file handling

**See Also:**    cp, cpio, find, mv, rcp, tar

### cp /dev/null fresh.txt

This is one way to empty a file of its contents, without removing the file altogether. The **/dev/null** file is a system file that is 0 bytes in size and more frequently used to absorb unwanted output (via redirection). Note that you can also use **cat** with **/dev/null** to create an empty file. In the Bourne shell, you can also create an empty file by entering **> fresh.txt**.

**Keyword:**    file handling

**See Also:**    cat

## cp /usr/march/* $HOME/work

| | | |
|---|---|---|
| ALL | ALL | END SCRIPT |

This **cp** command copies all the files in the directory **/usr/march** into the directory **$HOME/work**. Note that the wildcard is required: Simply trying to copy the directory causes **cp** to exit with an error.

**Keyword:**   file handling

**See Also:**   cpio, mv, tar

## cp city.txt ~/db/denver.txt

| | | |
|---|---|---|
| ALL | ALL | END |

This command copies a file from the current directory—whatever it may be—to the **db** subdirectory in the user's home directory. The file is also renamed in the process. Note that the ~ symbol denotes the home directory.

**Keyword:**   file handling

**See Also:**   cp, cpio, find, mv, rcp, tar

## cp jan.sales jan.costs jan.leads /usr/reports

| | | |
|---|---|---|
| ALL | ALL | END |

As long as you specify a target directory as the last argument to **cp**, you can copy multiple files to the directory. You can also use shell wildcard characters as shown in the next example. This example ensures that you copy just the specified files and no others.

**Keyword:**   file handling

**See Also:**   cp, cpio, find, mv, rcp, tar

## cp notice.txt /dev/ttyp1

| | | |
|---|---|---|
| ALL | ALL | END SCRIPT |

This command copies a file to an Xterm window. You can use **cp** to copy a file to most devices in with a file in the **/dev/** directory. In UNIX, device drivers are designed to be part of the filesystem.

**Keyword:**   file handling

**See Also:**   cpio, mv, tar

## cp update.ajs /usr/news

| | | |
|---|---|---|
| ALL | SVR4 Solaris SCO OSF AIX | END |

The **cp** command is probably the easiest way to update your contributions to the local newscast. Just copy a text file of interest to **/usr/news**.

**Keyword:**   user communication

**Files:**   /usr/news/*

**See Also:**   news

### cp `find /usr/docs -mtime -7 -print` $HOME/docs

ALL ALL END

Combined with the **find** command, **cp** can be used intelligently to copy files based on different criteria. In the example, the **-mtime** option to **find** feeds **cp** with the names of all files that have been modified within the last seven days.

**Keyword:** file handling

**See Also:** cp, cpio, find, mv, rcp, tar

### cpio -idv < /dev/rst0

ALL ALL POWER SYSADM

This command restores the entire contents of the tape archive and creates any directories as required. The **-d** option is responsible for creating the directories on the filesystem. The **-i** option indicates an **input** operation, and the **-v** option tells **cpio** to list filenames as it copies them.

**Keyword:** file handling

**See Also:** ls, find, tar, TAPE

### cpio -itv /dev/rst0

ALL ALL POWER SYSADM

To list the contents of a tape archive, use the **-t** option with the **cpio** command. The **-i** option indicates an **input** operation, and the **-v** option tells **cpio** to list filenames.

**Keyword:** file handling

**See Also:** ls, find, tar, TAPE

### cpio -iv "*.doc" < /dev/rst0

ALL ALL POWER SYSADM

The **cpio** command copies files to a tape drive. Although not as popular as **tar**, the **cpio** command still serves some older UNIX systems. The entry restores all **.doc** files from a tape archive and places them in the current directory on the hard disk. In the example, the **-i** option indicates an **input** operation, and the **-v** option tells **cpio** to list filenames as it copies them.

**Keyword:** file handling

**See Also:** ls, find, tar, TAPE

### cpio -iv /usr/reports < /dev/rst0

ALL ALL POWER SYSADM

This command restores a directory hiearchy from a tape archive using the **cpio** command. Files are restored to the current directory of the hard disk. The **-i** option indicates an **input** operation, and the **-v** option tells **cpio** to list filenames as it copies them.

**Keyword:** file handling
**See Also:** ls, find, tar, TAPE

## cpp

ALL    ALL    END

The **cpp** program is the C language preprocessor. It is normally invoked during the compilation process via **make** files. The **cpp** program works by parsing a source code file for directives such as **#include** and **#define**, and expands these directions. In most cases, **cpp** can also be used with other, non-C compilers. Using it as a macro processor, however, is not recommended.

**Keyword:** C programming
**See Also:** cc

## crash

ALL    SVR4    SYSADM

This SVR4 command examines the system memory image. It can read either a dump file or the current image of a running system. Its output shows control structures, tables, and other information. Command line options are: **-d**, dumpfile; **-n**, namelist; and **-w**, outputfile.

**Keyword:** system information
**See Also:** ldsysdump

## cron

ALL    ALL    POWER SYSADM

The **cron** daemon is responsible for executing commands at specified dates and times. Typically, **cron** is started automatically from a system startup file, and it exits only when the system comes down. At startup, **cron** reads commands contained in **crontab** and **at** files, and schedules these commands for execution. If a change is made to a **crontab** or **at** file, **cron** reads the file again and schedules any new commands included in these files. Unlike **at**, the **cron** program should be used for jobs that need to occur on a regular basis, rather than only one or two times.

**Keyword:** program execution
**Files:** /usr/spool/cron/crontabs
**See Also:** at, crontab

## crontab -e

ALL    ALL    POWER SYSADM

The **-e** option to **crontab** lets the current user edit the **crontab** file. By default, the editor invoked is determined by the value of the **$VISUAL** environment variable. If this variable is null, **crontab** invokes the editor defined by **$EDITOR**. If this is null, **ed** is used.

**Keyword:**    program execution

**Files:**        /usr/spool/cron/crontabs

**See Also:**    at, cron

### crontab -e -u alans

ALL   ALL   POWER SYSADM

A privileged user can edit, display, and remove another user's **crontab** file by using the **-u** option. In the example, a privileged user edits the **crontab** file belonging to **alans**. Note that on some systems, it is advisable to **su** to another user account in order to remove that user's **crontab**. Check your **man** pages.

**Keyword:**    program execution

**Files:**        /usr/spool/cron/crontab

**See Also:**    at, cron

### crontab -l

ALL   ALL   POWER SYSADM

The **-l** option to **crontab** displays the current user's **crontab** file. If you were the root user, entries in the **crontab** file might look something like this:

```
15 4 * * * find /var/preserve -mtime +7 -type f -exec rm -f {} \;
20 4 * * * find /tmp  -type f -atime +2 -exec rm -f {} \;
30 4 * * * find /var/tmp -type f -atime +7 -exec rm -f {} \;
40 4 * * * find /var/adm/syslog.dated -depth -type d -ctime +5
-exec rm -rf {} \;
```

There are six distinct fields in a **crontab** entry. The last field contains the actual command. The first five fields specify the time of execution in the following order: minute (0–59), hour (0–23), day of the month (1–31), month of the year (1–12), and day of the week (0–6; 0=Sunday). You don't have to fill all fields, but empty fields require an asterisk. You can also include comments in a **crontab** file by preceding comments with the **#** character.

**Keyword:**    program execution

**Files:**        /usr/spool/cron/crontabs

**See Also:**    at, cron

### crontab -r

ALL   ALL   POWER SYSADM

The **-r** option to **crontab** removes the current user's **crontab** file.

**Keyword:**   program execution
**Files:**       /usr/spool/cron/crontabs
**See Also:**   at, cron

ALL   ALL   POWER   SYSADM

### crypt < dir.tar.Z .cr | uncompress | tar xfvp -

This is a common use of the **crypt** command when dealing with compressed and tarred files. The command actually unwinds the following:

```
tar cvf - . | compress | crypt | uuencode dir.tar.Z .cr | mail alans.
```

**Keyword:**   security, text handling
**Files:**       /dev/tty
**See Also:**   makekey, more, pg, stty, vi

ALL   ALL   POWER   SYSADM

### crypt < secret.enc | more

This command reads an encrypted file. Because no password is supplied on the command line, **crypt** prompts for a password, which has to exactly match the password used when the file was encrypted.

**Keyword:**   security
**See Also:**   more

ALL   ALL   POWER   SYSADM

### crypt < secret.txt > secret.enc

The **crypt** command is available on many UNIX systems, but only those in the United States. The command encrypts a file using a password. In the example, the password has not been included, so **crypt** prompts for the password.

**Keyword:**   security
**See Also:**   des

ALL   ALL   POWER   SYSADM

### crypt NtXszBa < secret.enc

This example incorporates the password into the **crypt** command line. You can choose this method for both encrypting and decrypting files. The drawback to this method is that other users might be able to learn your passwords via the **ps** command, or by obtaining your C or Korn shell history files.

**Keyword:**   security
**See Also:**   ps

## csh

ALL    ALL    POWER

The C shell has been the favorite shell of power users ever since it was developed at the University of California (Berkeley) during 1979 through 1981. Of note, the C shell includes a symbolic language to address previous commands that you enter at the command line. This is complemented by a history mechanism to recall commands. The C shell's alias feature is also powerful. New users should note that when you execute **csh** at the command line, as in the example, a new instance of the C shell executes—even if you execute it from the Bourne or Korn shells.

**Keyword:**    user environment

**Files:**    $HOME/.cshrc, $HOME/.login, $HOME/.logout

**See Also:**    alias, history, ksh, sh

## csh -c mycmd

ALL    ALL    SCRIPT

Using the **-c** option to **csh** lets you run a command, script, or program. This is one way to guarantee that a shell script using the **csh** language is executed properly.

**Keyword:**    user environment

**Files:**    $HOME/.cshrc

**See Also:**    ksh, sh

## csh -f cscript

ALL    ALL    SCRIPT

The **-f** option to **csh** prevents the shell from executing **$HOME/.cshrc**. In the example, the **-f** option ensures that **cscript** is executed as fast as possible.

**Keyword:**    user environment

**Files:**    $HOME/.cshrc

**See Also:**    ksh, sh

## csh -n myscript

ALL    ALL    SCRIPT

The **-n** option to **csh** turns on debugging. Although **-n** doesn't help **csh** catch all errors, it does a fairly good job, catching things such as missing parentheses and mismatched **end** and **endif** statements.

**Keyword:**    user environment

**Files:**    $HOME/.cshrc

**See Also:**    ksh, sh

| | | |
|---|---|---|
| ALL | ALL | SCRIPT |

### csh -nv herscript

Add the **-v** option to the **-n** option and you get enhanced debugging in the C shell. The **-v** option causes **csh** to display each line in a C shell script as the script is being parsed.

**Keyword:**   user environment

**Files:**   $HOME/.cshrc

**See Also:**   ksh, sh

| | | |
|---|---|---|
| ALL | ALL | SCRIPT |

### csh -V anyscript

Similar to its lowercase namesake, the **-V** option displays commands in **$HOME/.cshrc** as well as the specified file.

**Keyword:**   user environment

**Files:**   $HOME/.cshrc

**See Also:**   ksh, sh

| | | |
|---|---|---|
| ALL | ALL | SCRIPT |

### csh -vxf ourscript

Add the **-x** option to the **-v** and **-f** options and you get more debugging in the C shell. The **-x** option prints each line in the specified script (**ourscript** in the example) after all substitutions are made, but before execution.

**Keyword:**   user environment

**Files:**   $HOME/.cshrc

**See Also:**   ksh, sh

| | | |
|---|---|---|
| ALL | ALL | SCRIPT |

### csh -X lastone

Also like its lowercase namesake, the **-X** option displays all commands in the script after substitutions have been made. And, like **-V**, it does the same thing for commands in **$HOME/.cshrc**.

**Keyword:**   user environment

**Files:**   $HOME/.cshrc

**See Also:**   ksh, sh

| | | |
|---|---|---|
| ALL | ALL | SCRIPT |

### csh_builtins

This not a command you will find on your system—unless you create a simple script file as we did. When you create the script, you also have to make it executable (**chmod +x** does the trick). Here is the script:

```
#!/bin/sh
```

```
echo '
csh, %, @, alias, bg, break, breaksw, case, continue, default,
dirs, else, end, endif, endsw, eval, exec, exit, fg, foreach,
glob, goto, hashstat, history, if, jobs, label, limit, logout,
notify, onintr, popd, pushd, rehash, repeat, set, setenv, shift,
source,  stop, suspend, switch, then, umask, unalias, unhash,
unlimit, unset, unsetenv, while  '
```

**Keyword:** help

**See Also:** ksh, ksh_builtins, sh, sh_builtins

### csplit -s -f sect. report "/^Section *[0-8]/" "{7}"

This **csplit** command uses the two options to control output. First, the **-s** option tells **csplit** not to display character counts as it processes. Second, the **-f** option lets you specify a filename prefix for each file that **csplit** produces. For example, the first three filenames would be **sect.00**, **sect.01**, and **sect.03**.

**Keyword:** text handling

**See Also:** cut, sed, split

### csplit -s -f weather. report /^FOG/ /^DRIZZLE/ /^RAIN/

You do not have to use shell wildcards with **csplit**, especially if there are well-defined headings in the original file. This example searches for three headings—**FOG**, **DRIZZLE**, and **RAIN**—and produces four split files. The four files are **weather.00**, **weather.01**, **weather.02**, and **weather.03**. The first file, **weather.00**, contains any matter that occurs in the file before **FOG**.

**Keyword:** text handling

**See Also:** cut, sed, split

### csplit report "/^Section *[0-8]/" "{7}"

The **csplit** command lets you split files by context. With **csplit**, you can specify a pattern that appears repeatedly throughout a file and have **csplit** create a file corresponding to the occurrence of the pattern. Using shell wildcard characters, you can narrow your specification to avoid miscellaneous occurrences of the pattern. In the example, **report** is the original file; "/^Section *[0-8]/" is the pattern; and {7} is the number of times the pattern occurs, minus one. It is necessary to subtract one, because **csplit** produces one file by default. Thus, {7} represents the number of times that **csplit** must repeat the default action. Note

ALL ALL END

ALL ALL END

ALL ALL END

that **csplit** produces an **xx00** file containing all matter that occurs before the first pattern match in the original file.

**Keyword:** text handling

**See Also:** cut, sed, split

## csplit report 100 {99}

ALL ALL END

This is a simple way to use **csplit**. The command divides the orginal file into files of 100 lines up to 10,000 lines. If there are more than 10,000 lines in the file, the last file contains the additional lines.

**Keyword:** file handling

**See Also:** cut, sed, split

## ct -s9600 -w1 1-555-1234

ALL OSF ALL

This command dials from an OSF system and issues a login prompt on a dumb terminal over a telephone line attached to a modem at each end of the connection. The phone number of the OSF system is **1-555-1234**, and the connection speed is set to **9600** baud. The computer is set to wait one minute for the dial tone.

**Keyword:** modem communications

**See Also:** cu, stty, uucp

## ctags *.c

ALL ALL POWER

The **ctags** command extracts function and type definitions from a C language source file and automatically places them in a file it creates called **tags**. The **tags** file is a standard ASCII text file and can be accessed as you would any other file. The **vi** and **ed** editors also use a special command, **tag**, to access a tag file's function and definitions on a by-name basis.

**Keyword:** C programming

**See Also:** ed, vi

## ctags -f menus.ctags m*.c

ALL ALL POWER

This version of the **ctags** commands shows you how to specify a filename, instead of settling for the default output filename of **tags**. If you use the **-f** option with other options, ensure that **-f** has its own leading minus sign.

**Keyword:** C programming

**See Also:** ed, vi

### ctags -x *.c > new.ctags

ALL ALL POWER

The **-x** option prints directly to standard output, so you must redirect the output to a file in order to retain it permanently. The special feature of the **-x** option is that it indexes function definitions. The index contains the line number and filename for each function.

**Keyword:** C programming

**See Also:** ed, vi

### cu -s 2400 -1 /dev/tty00 5551234

ALL ALL END

This command calls the remote computer system at the phone number **555-1234**, at a speed of **2400** baud, with the modem attached to the serial port **/dev/tty00**.

**Keyword:** modem communications, UUCP

**Files:** /usr/lib/uucp/Devices, /usr/lib/uucp/Systems

**See Also:** ct, cu, ps, stty, uucico, uucleanup, uucp, uusched, uucp, uustat, uutry, uuto, uux, uulog

### custom

ALL SCO SYSADM

This command is interactive, and is used to install packaged software on SCO systems. Both the operating system vendor (the Santa Cruz Operation of Santa Cruz, CA) and third-party vendors make use of the **custom** command.

**Keyword:** system setup

**See Also:** pkgadd

### cut -c25-30,45-60 ledger.dat

ALL ALL ALL

The **-c** option to **cut** lets you cut multiple column ranges just by separating them with a comma. The entry cuts two ranges, **25-30** and **45-60**.

**Keyword:** text handling

**See Also:** awk, sed, ed, grep

### cut -c45- ledger.dat

ALL ALL ALL

When you leave the **-c** option open-ended, as in the example, the **cut** command cuts all columns from the number specified through the end of the line. If **ledger.dat** consisted of 70 columns per line, the example would extract columns 45 through 70.

cut

**Keyword:** text handling

**See Also:** awk, sed, ed, grep

### cut -c45-60 ledger.dat

ALL ALL ALL

The **cut** command gives you numerous ways to extract columns of text from files and data streams from pipes. In the example, the **-c** option lets you specify precise columns to cut from the file.

**Keyword:** text handling

**See Also:** awk, sed, ed, grep

### cut -d: -f2-

ALL ALL ALL

This command is useful if you want to remove part of the output of a file. This example cuts the first column of data from the resulting display. The - after the **f2** tells **cut** to display all subsequent columns.

**Keyword:** text handling

**See Also:** more, less, head, tail

### cut -d: -f6 /etc/passwd

ALL ALL ALL

This command lists the usernames of every account on the system. It does this by reading the **/etc/passwd** file:

```
alans:9cMe0V6YYGXuQ:7:1:alans:/usr/users/alans:/bin/csh
```

and outputting the sixth field:

```
/usr/users/alans
```

Note that if the separating character is a space, you must place a space in single quotation marks following the **-d** option.

**Keyword:** system information

**See Also:** awk, sed, ed, grep, w, who

### cut -f1,3-5,7 ledger.dat

ALL ALL ALL

As with the **-c** option, the **-f** option works with one or more column ranges. This example displays columns associated with fields **1**, **3**, **4**, **5**, and **7**.

**Keyword:** text handling

**See Also:** awk, sed, ed, grep

### cut -f5 ledger.dat

ALL ALL ALL

The **-f** option followed by a field number extracts the column of data associated with the field. By default, **cut** expects the Tab character to separate fields. If you tried the command in the example on a file that used spaces as separators, **cut** would return no information.

**Keyword:**   text handling

**See Also:**   awk, sed, ed, grep

### cut -s -f1,3 ledger.dat

ALL ALL ALL

By default, **cut** extracts columnar data from all lines in a file. This means that it displays any blank lines or miscellaneous text in table footnotes and the like. The **-s** option helps offset this: It extracts only lines that contain no instances of the delimiter character.

**Keyword:**   text handling

**See Also:**   awk, sed, ed, grep, w, who

### cwd

CSH ALL SCRIPT

This internal C shell variable is the symbolic representation of the current directory in full-path format.

**Keyword:**   file display

**See Also:**   pwd

### date

ALL ALL POWER

This command outputs the local date and time as **Sat Aug 14 17:34:13 EDT 1993**.

**Keyword:**   system information

**See Also:**   time

### date "+%I %S" | awk ´{print $1 + $2}´

ALL ALL POWER

This command generates a random number between 0 and 72, using the current date as the seed. This is done because the **date "+%I %S"** outputs the hour, a space, and the second. Then **awk** takes these output numbers and adds them. Since the hour has to be between 0 and 12, and the seconds between 0 and 60, the total is between 0 and 72.

**Keyword:**   system information

**See Also:**   time

## date +"%B %d, %Y"

This command would output the date as **August 14, 1993**. The following format options are supported by **date**, and can be invoked as above.

```
a    Displays the locale's abbreviated weekday name.
A    Displays the locale's full weekday name.
b    Displays the locale's abbreviated month name.
B    Displays the locale's full month name.
c    Displays the locale's appropriate time and date representation.
C    Displays the locale's century.
d    Displays the day of the month as a number.
D    Displays the date in the format mm/dd/yy.
h    A synonym for %b.
H    Displays the hour from (00 to 24).
I    Displays the hour from (00 to 12).
j    Displays the day of year as a number.
m    Displays the month of year as a number.
M    Displays the minute as a number.
n    Inserts a newline character.
p    Displays the locale's equivalent of either AM or PM.
r    Displays the time using AM/PM notation.
S    Displays the second as a number.
t    Inserts a tab character.
T    Displays the time in 24-hour clock format.
U    Displays the week number of the year.
w    Displays the day of the week as a number.
W    Displays the week number of the year.
x    Displays the locale's appropriate date representation.
X    Displays the locale's appropriate time representation.
y    Displays the last two numbers of the year.
Y    Displays the full year as a decimal number.
Z    Displays the time zone name.
%%   Inserts a % character.
```

**Keyword:**    system information

**See Also:**    time

## date +"The date is: %A, %B %d, %Y%nThe time is: %I:%M:%S:%p"

This command would output:

```
The date is: Saturday, August 14, 1993
The time is: 05:54:36:PM
```

**Keyword:**    system information

**See Also:**    time

### date -u

ALL  ALL  POWER

This outputs the current date and time in Greenwich mean time.

**Keyword:**    system information

**See Also:**    time

### date 08141734.13

ALL  ALL  SYSADM

If you are a superuser, this will set the system date and time to:

```
Sat Aug 14 17:34:13 EDT 1993
```

**Keyword:**    system information

**See Also:**    time

### dbx a.out

ALL  ALL  POWER

This command will invoke **dbx**, an interactive source-level debugger, on the executable file **a.out**.

**Keyword:**    C programming

**See Also:**    cc

### dc

ALL  ALL  END

The **dc** command is an interactive calculator that works with Reverse Polish Notation. It is also summoned by **bc** to perform calculations.

```
4 6 * p
24
c
2
4
8
*
p
32
f
32
2
Ctrl-D
```

**Keyword:**    math

**See Also:**    awk, bc, expr, xcalc

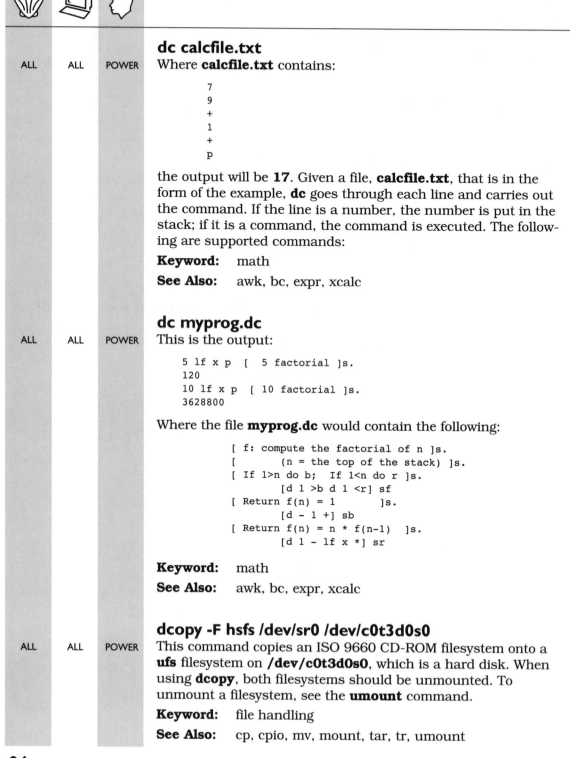

**dc**

ALL   ALL   POWER

## dc calcfile.txt

Where **calcfile.txt** contains:

```
7
9
+
1
+
p
```

the output will be **17**. Given a file, **calcfile.txt**, that is in the form of the example, **dc** goes through each line and carries out the command. If the line is a number, the number is put in the stack; if it is a command, the command is executed. The following are supported commands:

**Keyword:**   math

**See Also:**   awk, bc, expr, xcalc

## dc myprog.dc

ALL   ALL   POWER

This is the output:

```
5 lf x p  [  5 factorial ]s.
120
10 lf x p  [ 10 factorial ]s.
3628800
```

Where the file **myprog.dc** would contain the following:

```
[ f: compute the factorial of n ]s.
[        (n = the top of the stack) ]s.
[ If 1>n do b;  If 1<n do r ]s.
        [d 1 >b d 1 <r] sf
[ Return f(n) = 1          ]s.
        [d - 1 +] sb
[ Return f(n) = n * f(n-1)  ]s.
        [d 1 - lf x *] sr
```

**Keyword:**   math

**See Also:**   awk, bc, expr, xcalc

## dcopy -F hsfs /dev/sr0 /dev/c0t3d0s0

ALL   ALL   POWER

This command copies an ISO 9660 CD-ROM filesystem onto a **ufs** filesystem on **/dev/c0t3d0s0**, which is a hard disk. When using **dcopy**, both filesystems should be unmounted. To unmount a filesystem, see the **umount** command.

**Keyword:**   file handling

**See Also:**   cp, cpio, mv, mount, tar, tr, umount

### dd if=/dev/rmt0 of=tape.out ibs=800 cbs=80 conv=ascii,lcase

| | | |
|---|---|---|
| ALL | ALL | POWER |

This example reads an EBCDIC tape that is blocked ten 80-byte EBCDIC card images per record into the ASCII file **tape.out**.

**Keyword:**   file handling

**See Also:**   cp, cpio, tar, tr

### dd if=/dev/rmt0a of=/u1/perkie/data ibs=1024 obs=512

| | | |
|---|---|---|
| ALL | ALL | POWER |

This command reads input from a tape with 1024 byte blocks, and puts the data into a file called **data** that is written with 512 byte blocks. This command is useful for reading or writing to physical I/O because both the input and ouput block sizes can be changed.

**Keyword:**   file handling

**See Also:**   cp, cpio, tar, tr

### dd if=text.ascii of=text.ebcdic conv=ebcdic

| | | |
|---|---|---|
| ALL | ALL | POWER |

This command converts the ASCII file **text.ascii** to an EBCDIC file called **text.ebcdic**.

**Keyword:**   file handling

**See Also:**   cp, cpio, tar, tr

### dd if=text.doc of=text.bak

| | | |
|---|---|---|
| ALL | ALL | POWER |

This command copies the file **text.doc** to a new file called **text.bak**.

**Keyword:**   file handling

**See Also:**   cp, cpio, tar, tr

### ddefs -d /etc/dskdefs -e /dev/rsdk/c0t3d0s0

| | | |
|---|---|---|
| ALL | SVR4 | SYSADM |

This command edits the existing disk definition for the disk that is specified by **c0t3d0s0**, interactively.

**Keyword:**   system information

**See Also:**   format

### ddefs -d /etc/dskdefs -p /dev/rsdk/c0t3d0s0

| | | |
|---|---|---|
| ALL | SVR4 | SYSADM |

This command outputs the existing disk definition for the disk that is specified by **c0t3d0s0**.

| | | |
|---|---|---|

**Keyword:** system information
**See Also:** format

## deassign /dev/fd

ALL  SCO  POWER SYSADM

The SCO **deassign** command lifts the assignment restriction on the specified device, including removing the device lock file, which is **/dev/asglock**. In the example, **/dev/fd** specifies the default diskette drive.

**Keyword:** devices
**Files:** /etc/atab, /dev/asglock
**See Also:** assign, tar

## default

ALL  ALL  SCRIPT

This C shell script-only command labels the **default** case in a switch statement. The default usually follows all **case** labels.

**Keyword:** programming
**See Also:** case (csh), switch

## delsysadm -r main

ALL  SVR4  SYSADM

This command deletes everything from the **sysadm** menu, so that it is a useless program. Although we recommend not running this example, it is illustrative of the **-r** argument to **delsysadm**. It works the same as the **-r** argument to the **rm** command.

**Keyword:** system information
**See Also:** sysadm

## delsysadm main:applications:ndevices:nformat

ALL  SVR4  SYSADM

This command removes the **nformat** task from the **sysadm** menu structure.

**Keyword:** system information
**See Also:** sysadm

## deroff -i /usr/man/man1/xterm.1

ALL  ALL  POWER

This command will read in the file **xterm.1** and remove all **nroff**, **troff**, macro calls, backslash constructs, **eqn** constructs (between **.EQ** and **.EN** lines and between delimiters), and **tbl** descriptions, replacing many of them with spaces or blank lines;

it also writes the remainder of **xterm.1** to standard output. The
**-i** option suppresses processing of included files (**.so** and **.nx**).
This command also eliminates most formatting.

**Keyword:**    text handling

**See Also:**    nroff, troff, tbl

### des -b -e book.txt book.de

ALL    SunOS    POWER
       Solaris

This command encrypts **book.txt** using ECB encryption mode. It
encrypts 8 bytes at a time.

**Keyword:**    security

**See Also:**    crypt

### des -d book.des

ALL    SunOS    POWER
       Solaris

This command will decrypt the file **book.des** and output the contents to the computer terminal.

**Keyword:**    security

**See Also:**    crypt

### des -e -k ´dog´ book.txt book.des

ALL    SunOS    POWER
       Solaris

This encrypts the file **book.txt**, and the encrypted file is created
as **book.des**. The **-k** argument is used to set an encryption key,
in this case **dog**.

**Keyword:**    security

**See Also:**    crypt

### des -e book.txt book.des

ALL    SunOS    POWER
       Solaris

This command encrypts the file **book.txt**, and the encrypted file
is created as **book.des**. The encryption method is the NBS Data
Encryption Standard algorithm.

**Keyword:**    security

**See Also:**    crypt

### des -s -e book.txt book.de

ALL    SunOS    POWER
       Solaris

This command encrypts **book.txt** using software only. By
default, if your computer has an encryption chip installed, **des**
uses it. The **-s** argument tells **des** to use only software in doing
the encryption. This is about 50 times slower on a SPARCsta-
tion2 than using hardware.

**Keyword:** security
**See Also:** crypt

## devattr -v /dev/rdiskette

ALL   SVR4   POWER

This command lists all of the attributes of the diskette drive and exactly what those attributes are, such as **alias='diskette1'**.

**Keyword:** system information
**See Also:** df

## devattr /dev/dsk/c0t3d0s7

ALL   SVR4   POWER

This lists the properties of the device given. In this case, it indicates that **/dev/dsk/c0t3d0s7** is a disk that is formatted as a filesystem and where is it mounted. It also gives the total number of blocks on the disk.

**Keyword:** system information
**See Also:** df, mount

## devfree $MOUNTPID

ALL   SVR4   SYSADM

This command will free the device that was mounted by the **mount** command process identification number that is stored in **$MOUNTPID**. The **$MOUNTPID** variable has to be set specifically, because it isn't done by default.

**Keyword:** system information
**See Also:** df

## devinfo -i /dev/rsdk/c0t3d0s0

ALL   SVR4   POWER

This command outputs the device name, drive ID number, device blocks per cylinder, device bytes per block, and the number of device partitions.

**Keyword:** system information
**See Also:** df

## devinfo -p /dev/rsdk/c0t3d0s0

ALL   SVR4   POWER

This command outputs the device name, device major and minor numbers, partition start block, number of blocks allocated to the partition, partition flag, and partition tag.

**Keyword:** system information
**See Also:** df

### devnm /usr

ALL    SVR4    POWER

This outputs the device that is attached to the **/usr** mount point. It will give something like:

```
/dev/dsk/c0t3d0s6          /usr
```

**Keyword:**    system information
**See Also:**    df

### devreserv

ALL    SVR4    POWER

This will output a list of all the devices that have been reserved with the **devreserv $key** command, where **$key** is a process identification number.

**Keyword:**    system information
**See Also:**    df

### devreserv $MOUNTPID

ALL    SVR4    POWER

This is the opposite of **devfree**. It reserves devices for exclusive use. The device mounted with the **mount** command that has the process identification number stored in **$MOUNTPID** cannot be accessed by another process.

**Keyword:**    system information
**See Also:**    df

### df

ALL    BSD    POWER

The BSD version of **df** outputs a listing of all mounted filesystems, the total kilobytes each filesystem has, the KB used, KB available, percent of the filesystem used, and where the filesystem is mounted. This is useful for seeing where to install large programs.

**Keyword:**    system information
**See Also:**    devnm

### df

ALL    SVR4    POWER
       SCO
       OSF

The system V version of **df** outputs all of the mounted filesystems, the number of blocks free on these filesystems, and the total number of free inodes on them. The device entry is enclosed in parentheses, after the listing for the mount point.

**Keyword:**    system information
**See Also:**    devnm

| | | |
|---|---|---|
| ALL | SVR4 Solaris SCO OSF | POWER |

## df -k

On SVR4 systems, this command produces the same results as the unadorned use of **df** on BSD systems.

**Keyword:** system information

**See Also:** devnm

| | | |
|---|---|---|
| ALL | SVR4 Solaris SCO OSF | POWER |

## df -k | grep -v ´Filesystem´ | awk ´{print $6," ",$4}´

This command outputs how much space, in kilobytes, is left in each mounted filesystem.

**Keyword:** system information

**See Also:** devnm

| | | |
|---|---|---|
| ALL | SVR4 Solaris SCO OSF | POWER |

## df -k | grep -v ´Filesystem´ | awk ´{s += $3} END {print "Total disk space used is:", s/1024, "MB"}´

This command outputs the space that has been used on all of the mounted filesystems. The disk space is reported in megabytes, because the **-k** argument to **df** causes **df** to report space in kilobytes, and the **s/1024** in the **awk** command divides the total kilobytes by 1024, resulting in ouput that is listed as megabytes.

**Keyword:** system information

**See Also:** ls

| | | |
|---|---|---|
| ALL | SVR4 Solaris SCO OSF | POWER |

## df -k | grep -v ´Filesystem´ | awk ´{s += $4} END {print "Total disk space available is:", s, "KB"}´

This command adds up the amount of free space on each mounted filesystem, and outputs the total. This result is in kilo-bytes because of the **-k** argument to **df**.

**Keyword:** system information

**See Also:** ls

| | | |
|---|---|---|
| ALL | SVR4 Solaris SCO OSF | POWER |

## df -t

This command outputs a listing of all the mounted filesystems, the number of free blocks and inodes, and the total number of blocks and inodes. This command gives a good idea of how full each filesystem is.

**Keyword:** system information

**See Also:** devnm

## df | lpr

**ALL   ALL   POWER**

This command shows how much space is available in each filesystem on the computer, and prints out the information on the default printer.

**Keyword:**   system information
**See Also:**   devnm

## dfmount | lpr -Pmccpr

**ALL   SVR4   POWER**

This command prints out all the remote filesystems that are mounted on the local system to the default printer.

**Keyword:**   system information
**See Also:**   df, mount

## dfmounts

**ALL   SVR4   POWER**

This command shows all the remote filesystems that are mounted on the local system.

**Keyword:**   system information
**See Also:**   df, mount

## dfmounts -F nfs

**ALL   SVR4   POWER**

This command outputs all of the NFS remote filesystems that are mounted on the local system.

**Keyword:**   system information
**See Also:**   df, mount

## dfmounts -F nfs -h

**ALL   SVR4   POWER**

This command also outputs all of the NFS remote filesystems that are mounted on the local system, but it doesn't display header information. The **-h** argument suppresses the header information from being displayed.

**Keyword:**   system information
**See Also:**   df, mount

## dfmounts -F nfs -h alpha

**ALL   SVR4   POWER**

This command displays all of the NFS filesystems that are currently mounted on the local system, from the file server **alpha**.

**Keyword:**   system information
**See Also:**   df, mount

## dfshares

ALL  SVR4  POWER

This command shows all of the filesystems shared on the local system, regardless of the type of filesystem.

**Keyword:** system information

**See Also:** df, mount

## dfshares -F nfs

ALL  SVR4  POWER

This command shows all of the NFS filesystems shared on the local system.

**Keyword:** system information

**See Also:** df, mount

## dfshares -F nfs -h

ALL  SVR4  POWER

As in the **dfmounts** command, the **-h** argument to **dfshares** suppresses header information. This command shows all of the NFS filesystems shared on the local system, without any header information.

**Keyword:** system information

**See Also:** df, mount

## dfshares -F nfs -h alpha

ALL  SVR4  POWER

This command shows which filesystems are available on the system **alpha** to be mounted on the local system.

**Keyword:** system information

**See Also:** df, mount

## diction book.txt

ALL  OSF  END

Need to improve your writing? Use the **diction** command, which is available on OSF versions of the operating system. The **diction** program stands up against some aftermarket products that do the same thing. Among other English language miscues, it identifies passive voice. All identified language errors appear in square brackets when **diction** prints the file to standard output.

**Keyword:** text handling

**Files:** /usr/lbin/dict.d

**See Also:** explain

| | | |
|---|---|---|

### diff -b doc.txt doc2.txt

ALL   ALL   POWER

This command ignores trailing spaces, tabs (blanks), and other strings of spaces and tabs to be considered identical by **diff**.

**Keyword:**   text handling

**See Also:**   bdiff, cmp, comm, diff3, ed

### diff -e doc.txt doc2.txt > newdoc.txt

ALL   ALL   POWER

This produces a script of commands for the editor **ed**, which can re-create **doc.txt** from **doc2.txt**.

**Keyword:**   text handling

**See Also:**   bdiff, cmp, comm, diff3, ed

### diff -i doc.txt doc2.txt

ALL   ALL   POWER

This command compares **doc.txt** and **doc2.txt** and outputs all of the lines that don't match exactly; however, it ignores the case of the characters in the comparison.

**Keyword:**   text handling

**See Also:**   bdiff, cmp, comm, diff3, ed

### diff -l doc.txt doc2.txt

ALL   ALL   POWER

This command is the same as **diff doc.txt doc2.txt** except that it paginates the differences that are found between the two files.

**Keyword:**   text handling

**See Also:**   bdiff, cmp, comm, diff3, ed

### diff doc.txt doc2.txt

ALL   ALL   POWER

This command compares **doc.txt** and **doc2.txt** and outputs all of the lines that don't match exactly to standard output.

**Keyword:**   text handling

**See Also:**   bdiff, cmp, comm, diff3, ed

### diff3 doc.txt doc2.txt doc3.txt

ALL   ALL   POWER

This command is the same as **diff doc.txt doc2.txt** except that it also compares a third file, **doc3.txt**. This is useful for comparing three different files, rather than just two.

**Keyword:**   text handling

**See Also:**   bdiff, cmp, comm, diff3, ed

## diffmk -b -cb´.mc $´ -ab´.mc >´ -ae´.mc <´ -ce´.mc !´ -db´.mc (´ -de´.mc )´ book1.txt book2.txt >> book.nroff

ALL    ALL    POWER

This command compares the files **book1.txt** and **book2.txt** and creates a file that contains **nroff** change mark requests, called **book.nroff**. This puts an embedded command where changed lines begin with a **$**, added lines begin with a **>** and end with a **<**, changed lines end with a **!**, and deleted lines begin with a **(** and end with a **)**.

**Keyword:**    text handling

**See Also:**    nroff, troff, diff

## diffmk book1.txt book2.txt >> book.mc

ALL    ALL    POWER

This command compares **book1.txt** to **book2.txt**, and then it creates a file called **book.mc** that contains **nroff** change mark requests.

**Keyword:**    text handling

**See Also:**    nroff, troff, diff

## dinit -b /usr/lib/boot.bak

ALL    SVR4    SYSADM

This command tells the system to use the file **/usr/lib/boot.bak** as the bootloader program.

**Keyword:**    system information

**See Also:**    format

## dinit -f -t /badtracklist mfuj2624 /dev/rdsk/c0t3d0s0

ALL    SVR4    SYSADM

This command formats a disk, but instead of interactively asking the user to input the bad track numbers, it takes them from the file **/badtracklist**.

**Keyword:**    system information

**See Also:**    format

## dinit -f mfuj2624 /dev/rdsk/c0t3d0s0

ALL    SVR4    SYSADM

This command formats the disk as a FUJITSU 525MB hard disk. If you run this command on an unformatted disk, it will give two read errors, because the system is trying to read configuration information that isn't there. These two errors can be ignored.

**Keyword:**    system information

**See Also:**    format

## dinit -r -a /dev/rdsk/c0t3d0s0

ALL  SVR4  SYSADM

This command prints out the alternate defect list of the specified disk.

**Keyword:** system information

**See Also:** format

## dinit -r -x /dev/rdsk/c0t3d0s0

ALL  SVR4  SYSADM

This command outputs the defect list of the specified disk in hexadecimal.

**Keyword:** system information

**See Also:** format

## dinit -r /dev/rdsk/c0t3d0s | lp

ALL  SVR4  SYSADM

This command prints out the defect list of the specified disk to the default printer.

**Keyword:** system information

**See Also:** format

## dinit -R /dev/rdsk/c0t3d0s0

ALL  SVR4  SYSADM

This command with the **-R** argument is similar to the one with the **-r** argument, except it displays the manufacturer's defect list. This list is the one that comes with the drive.

**Keyword:** system information

**See Also:** format

## dinit -r /dev/rdsk/c0t3d0s0

ALL  SVR4  SYSADM

This command prints out the defect list of the specified disk; in this example, it is **/dev/rdsk/c0t3d0s0**.

**Keyword:** system information

**See Also:** format

## dinit -v 0 mfuj2624 /dev/rdsk/c0t3d0s0

ALL  SVR4  SYSADM

This command formats a disk as a FUJITSU 525MB hard disk. The **-v** argument specifies the level of disk surface verification. The **0** after the **-v** disables the verification.

**Keyword:** system information

**See Also:** format

### dinit -v 4 mfuj2624 /dev/rdsk/c0t3d0s0

ALL   SVR4   SYSADM

This command will format a hard disk as a FUJITSU 525MB disk, but it will also check the surface of the disk and verify the sectors.

**Keyword:**   system information

**See Also:**   format

### dircmp -d /usr/users/perkie /usr/users/alans

ALL   ALL   POWER

This command displays, for each common filename, the differing contents of the two files, if any. The display format is the same as that of the **diff** command.

**Keyword:**   file handling

**See Also:**   bdiff, cmp, comm, diff3, ed

### dircmp -s /usr/users/perkie /usr/users/alans

ALL   ALL   POWER

This command is the same as **dircmp /usr/users/perkie /back_up/usr/users/perkie** except that it doesn't display the names of identical files.

**Keyword:**   file handling

**See Also:**   bdiff, cmp, comm, diff3, ed

### dircmp /usr/users/perkie /back_up/usr/users/perkie

ALL   ALL   POWER

First, **dircmp** compares the filenames in each directory. When the same filename appears in both, **dircmp** compares the contents of the two files. In this example, it would compare how close **/usr/users/perkie** is to its backup **/back_up/usr/users/perkie** and output any differences.

**Keyword:**   file handling

**See Also:**   bdiff, cmp, comm, diff3, ed

### dirname $HOME

ALL   ALL   POWER

This command will return the parent directory of your home directory. The **dirname** command reads the string specified on the command line, deletes from the last **/** to the end of the line, and writes the remaining pathname to standard output.

**Keyword:**   file display

**See Also:**   basename, pwd

### dirs

CSH ALL POWER

This lists the current working directory in the C shell. If you are in your home directory, it will output a ~. All subdirectories of your home directory will be listed in the manner of **~/book/proposal**.

**Keyword:** file display

**See Also:** pwd

### dirs -l

CSH ALL POWER

This C shell command produces the same ouput as **dirs** with no arguments, if you are not in your home directory. The **-l** argument suppresses the ~ notation for directories. **dirs -l** executed from your home directory would look like this: **/home/perkie**.

**Keyword:** file display

**See Also:** pwd

### dis -h a.out

ALL ALL POWER

This is the same as **dis a.out**, except that the general register names are printed instead of the software register names. This is helpful in debugging.

**Keyword:** programming

**See Also:** cc

### dis -S a.out

ALL ALL POWER

This command displays the source listings in addition to the machine instructions. The argument **-a** is often useful, because with it you can see exactly which lines of source code generate which lines of machine code.

**Keyword:** programming

**See Also:** cc

### dis a.out

ALL ALL POWER

This command will disassemble the object file **a.out** into machine instructions. After compiling a C program, the compiler generates an executable file called **a.out**. It is useful at times to see exactly the machine code that is generated by the compiler; **dis** does this.

**Keyword:** programming

**See Also:** cc

## disgid | wc -l

ALL    SVR4    POWER SYSADM

This command displays the total number of groups on the system.

**Keyword:**    system information

**See Also:**    chgrp

## diskadd /dev/rdsk/c4t0d0s0

ALL    SVR4    SYSADM

This is an interactive command used to set up new disks on the system. In this example, **/dev/rdsk/c4t0d0s0** is the character special file pointing to the disk you want to add.

**Keyword:**    system setup

**See Also:**    mkdev

## dispadmin -c RT -g -r 1000000

ALL    SVR4    SYSADM

This command retrieves the current scheduler parameters from kernel memory and outputs them. The **-c** argument is for specifying the class whose parameters should be displayed. **RT** is for real-time, and **TS** is for time-sharing. The **-g** argument gets the parameters for the specified class and outputs them. The **-r** option sets the resolution for outputting time values in milliseconds.

**Keyword:**    system information

**See Also:**    ps

## dispadmin -c RT -s schedpara.cfg

ALL    SVR4    SYSADM

This command overwrites the current schedular parameters for the real-time class. The **-s** argument sets the scheduler parameters for the specified class using values from the file **schedpara.cfg**.

**Keyword:**    system information

**See Also:**    ps

## dispadmin -l

ALL    SVR4    SYSADM

This command lists the process schedular classes that are currently set up for the system.

**Keyword:**    system information

**See Also:**    ps

### dispgid

| | | |
|---|---|---|
| ALL | SVR4 | POWER SYSADM |

This command displays a list of all the group names that are on the system.

**Keyword:** system information

**See Also:** chgrp

### dispgid | lpr

| | | |
|---|---|---|
| ALL | SVR4 | POWER SYSADM |

This command will print out a list of all the group names that are on the system to the default printer.

**Keyword:** system information

**See Also:** chgrp

### DISPLAY=megasun:0; export DISPLAY

| | | |
|---|---|---|
| ALL | XWIN | ALL |

This command sets the **$DISPLAY** variable used by the X server to know which system and screen on which it should run client programs. If you are using the C shell, use the **setenv** command to set environment variables. If you just want to set the **DISPLAY** for a single X program, try using the program's **-display** option.

**Keyword:** X resources

**See Also:** hostname, xprop, xwininfo

### dispuid

| | | |
|---|---|---|
| ALL | SVR4 | POWER SYSADM |

This command displays a list of all the usernames on the system.

**Keyword:** system information

**Files:** /etc/passwd

**See Also:** passwd

### dispuid | lpr

| | | |
|---|---|---|
| ALL | SVR4 | POWER SYSADM |

This command prints out a list of all the usernames on the system to the default printer.

**Keyword:** system information

**Files:** /etc/passwd

**See Also:** passwd

### dispuid | wc -l

| | | |
|---|---|---|
| ALL | SVR4 | POWER SYSADM |

This command lists the total number of user accounts on the system.

**Keyword:**   system information
**Files:**   /etc/passwd
**See Also:**   passwd

### divvy

ALL   SCO   SYSADM

The **divvy** command divides hard disk partitions into divisions, which are identified by unique major and minor device numbers. You can also create and remove filesystems with **divvy**. In addition, **divvy** can serve as a tool to isolate bad spots on hard disks. The default device is **/dev/hd0a**. Entering **divvy** without options, as in the example, yields the following menu:

```
n[ame]      Name or rename a division.
c[reate]    Create a new filesystem on this division.
t[ype]      Select or change filesystem type on new filesystems.
p[revent]   Prevent a new filesystem from being created on this
            division.
s[tart]     Start a division on a different block.
e[nd]       End a division on a different block.
r[estore]   Restore the original division table.

Enter your choice or q to quit:
```

**Keyword:**   filesystem, devices
**See Also:**   fdisk, fsck, mkdev, mkfs, mknod, sysadmsh

### domainname

ALL   ALL   POWER

This command, without a domain name given, displays what the current NIS domain name is set to.

**Keyword:**   networking
**See Also:**   ypfiles, ypsetup

### domainname newl.com

ALL   ALL   POWER

This command will set the NIS domain for your system to **newl.com**. The Network Information Service is useful for administering small to midsize networks.

**Keyword:**   networking
**See Also:**   ypfiles, ypsetup

### dos2unix book.txt > book.asc

ALL   SVR4   ALL
     Solaris

This command strips out the Ctrl-M at the end of each line of an MS-DOS text file to make it compatible with a UNIX text file. The

SCO
SunOS

output of **dos2unix** goes directly to standard output, so it must be redirected into a file.

**Keyword:**   DOS

**See Also:**   tr, sed, unix2dos

### doscat -c c:/windows/word/example.txt

ALL   SCO   POWER

This command outputs the contents of **/windows/word/example.txt**, which is a DOS-formatted file on the system. If this disk is mounted, the operation halts immediately because of the **-c** argument. This is a good option to use, because accessing mounted DOS filesystems can cause the system to crash hard. DOS filesystems should be either mounted or accessed via DOS utilities, but not both.

**Keyword:**   DOS

**See Also:**   cat

### doscat -c c:/windows/word/example.txt | more

ALL   SCO   POWER

This command uses **more** to format the output to appear one screenful at a time. The contents of **example.txt** are displayed one screen at a time.

**Keyword:**   DOS

**See Also:**   cat

### doscat -r /dev/fd0:/ed/book.doc

ALL   SCO   POWER

This outputs the contents of the file **/ed/book.doc** that is on a DOS diskette. It will not perform newline conversions because of the **-r** argument. This would result in a **^M** at the end of each line.

**Keyword:**   DOS

**See Also:**   cat

### doscp -c /dev/fd0:/ed/book.doc /home/perkie/book/

ALL   SCO   POWER

This command is the same as the UNIX **cp** except that it works between MS-DOS filesystems and the UNIX filesystem. This will copy the file **book.doc** from an MS-DOS-formatted disk to the UNIX filesystem **/home/perkie/book/book.doc**.

**Keyword:**   DOS

**See Also:**   cp, mv

### dosdir -c b:

| | | |
|---|---|---|
| ALL | SCO | POWER |

The **dosdir** command gives a directory listing of the contents of the second installed diskette on the computer. The format of the output is the same as that of the DOS command **dir**, not the UNIX command **ls**.

**Keyword:** DOS

**See Also:** ls

### dosformat -f /dev/fd0

| | | |
|---|---|---|
| ALL | SCO | POWER |

This formats the disk in the first installed floppy drive on the computer as an MS-DOS version 2.0 disk. The command is not interactive because of the **-f** argument.

**Keyword:** DOS

**See Also:** fdformat

### dosformat -q a:

| | | |
|---|---|---|
| ALL | SCO | POWER |

This formats the disk in the first installed floppy drive on the computer as an MS-DOS version 2.0 disk. The normal output of this command is suppressed because of the **-q** argument.

**Keyword:** DOS

**See Also:** fdformat

### dosformat -v /dev/fd1

| | | |
|---|---|---|
| ALL | SCO | POWER |

This command formats the disk in the second installed floppy drive on the computer as an MS-DOS version 2.0 disk. After the format is complete, the computer prompts for a volume name because of the **-v** argument.

**Keyword:** DOS

**See Also:** fdformat

### dosls -c /dev/fd1

| | | |
|---|---|---|
| ALL | SCO | POWER |

This command is similar to **dosdir**, except that the format of **dosls** is the same as the UNIX **ls** command, rather than the MS-DOS command **dir**. This command lists the contents of the disk in the second installed diskette on the computer. As with the other MS-DOS commands, the **-c** argument causes the command to halt execution immediately if a file on a mounted filesystem is encountered.

**Keyword:** DOS

**See Also:** ls, l, lc, lr, ls, lx

| | | |
|---|---|---|
| ALL | SCO | POWER |

## dosmkdir -c a:/ed/book

This command creates the subdirectory **book** on the second installed diskette in the **ed** parent directory. This is the same as the UNIX **mkdir** command, except that it works on MS-DOS filesystems.

**Keyword:** DOS

**See Also:** mkdir

| | | |
|---|---|---|
| ALL | SCO | POWER |

## dosrm -c c:/ed/test.doc

This command deletes the file **test.doc** that is on an MS-DOS-formatted disk. This is the same as the UNIX command **rm**, except that it works with MS-DOS filesystems.

**Keyword:** DOS

**See Also:** cp, mv, rm

| | | |
|---|---|---|
| ALL | SCO | POWER |

## dosrmdir -c a:/ed/book

This is the opposite of **dosmkdir -c a:/ed/book**. It removes the **book** subdirectory from the parent directory **ed** on the MS-DOS-formatted diskette. This is the same as the UNIX command **rmdir**.

**Keyword:** DOS

**See Also:** rm, rmdir

| | | |
|---|---|---|
| SH KSH | ALL | END |

## . (dot command)

In the Bourne and Korn shells you can use the **dot** command—which is represented by the period, or dot, character—to run commands in a file and load environment information. A typical example is:

```
. .profile
```

This command loads all information contained in the **.profile** file, so the current shell references it. You also might run across the following:

```
. ./.profile
```

This statement again loads the information in **.profile**. The additional **./** notation is required to execute when the directory containing **.profile** is not in the user's path.

**Keyword:** user environment

**See Also:** source

| | | |
|---|---|---|
| ALL | SVR4 | POWER |

## download -p mccpr -m mccpr/maps

This command downloads the PostScript fonts listed in the file maps to the printer named **mccpr**.

**Keyword:** printing

**See Also:** lp, lpr

| | | |
|---|---|---|
| ALL | SVR4 | ALL |

## dpost -c 3 text.troff | lpr

This command prints three copies of each page of **text.troff** on the default printer.

**Keyword:** printing

**See Also:** lp, lpr, pr

| | | |
|---|---|---|
| ALL | SVR4 | ALL |

## dpost -e 2 text.troff | lpr

This command uses the **-e** argument to speed up the translation of the **troff** file to a PostScript file. It sets the encoding level to 2, which is about 20 percent faster than encoding level 0, which is the default.

**Keyword:** printing

**See Also:** lp, lpr, pr

| | | |
|---|---|---|
| ALL | SVR4 | ALL |

## dpost -m 2 text.troff | lpr

This command magnifies each page to twice its normal size because of the **-m** argument.

**Keyword:** printing

**See Also:** lp, lpr, pr

| | | |
|---|---|---|
| ALL | SVR4 | ALL |

## dpost -n 4 text.troff | lpr

This command prints four logical pages on each actual page of text that comes out of the default printer.

**Keyword:** printing

**See Also:** lp, lpr, pr

| | | |
|---|---|---|
| ALL | SVR4 | ALL |

## dpost -o 6 text.troff | lpr

This command prints out just page 6 of the file **text.troff** onto the default printer.

**Keyword:** printing

**See Also:** lp, lpr, pr

| | | |
|---|---|---|
| ALL | SVR4 | ALL |

## dpost -p l text.troff | lpr

This command prints out the **troff** file **text.troff** to the default PostScript printer in landscape mode.

**Keyword:**   printing

**See Also:**   lp, lpr, pr

| | | |
|---|---|---|
| ALL | SVR4 | POWER |

## dpost text.troff | lpr

This command will translate the **troff** file **text.troff** to a PostScript file. It will then print out on the default printer.

**Keyword:**   printing

**See Also:**   lp, lpr

| | | |
|---|---|---|
| ALL | SCO | POWER |

## dtox book.txt book.asc

This command reads in the MS-DOS text file **book.txt** and creates a new file, **book.asc**, that is a UNIX text file. The conversion removes the Ctrl-M that MS-DOS puts at the end of each line of a text file.

**Keyword:**   DOS

**See Also:**   doscp

| | | |
|---|---|---|
| ALL | ALL | ALL |

## du

The **du** command displays the number of blocks used in all subdirectories of the current directory. This can help to determine where, exactly, all of your disk space has gone.

**Keyword:**   filesystem

**See Also:**   df, diskadd, fsck, mount, mkfs, mknod, mountall, mountfsys, umount mkdev, newfs, smit, sysadmin, sysadmsh

| | | |
|---|---|---|
| ALL | ALL | ALL |

## du -a

This command reports the number of blocks used by files in addition to directories.

**Keyword:**   filesystem

**See Also:**   df, diskadd, du, fsck, mount, mkfs, mknod, mountall, mountfsys, umount mkdev, newfs, smit, sysadmin, sysadmsh

**du**

## du -as /

ALL   ALL   SYSADM

This command displays the total number of blocks used by every mounted filesystem on your computer. It also shows the number of blocks used by each file and directory.

**Keyword:** filesystem

**See Also:** df, diskadd, fsck, mount, mkfs, mknod, mountall, mountfsys, umount mkdev, newfs, smit, sysadmin, sysadmsh

## du -as /usr/perkie/book | sort -rn

ALL   ALL   POWER SYSADM

This outputs the number of blocks used by **/usr/perkie/book** and all files and subdirectories in **/usr/perkie/book**. It lists the largest files and subdirectories first.

**Keyword:** filesystem

**See Also:** df, diskadd, fsck, mount, mkfs, mknod, mountall, mountfsys, umount mkdev, newfs, smit, sysadmin, sysadmsh

## du -as | awk ´{ s += $1} END {printf("%s %f%s", "Directory uses", s/2048, "Mb\n")}´

ALL   ALL   POWER SYSADM

This command takes the output of **du -as**, adds it up, and prints it out. The resulting output tells how many megabytes of disk space is taken up by the current directory and all of its subdirectories.

**Keyword:** filesystem

**See Also:** df, diskadd, fsck, mount, mkfs, mknod, mountall, mountfsys, umount mkdev, newfs, smit, sysadmin, sysadmsh

## du -as | lpr

ALL   ALL   POWER SYSADM

This command is an excellent way to waste a large amount of paper, because it prints out the name and path of every file on the system. If this is your intention, however, the command is a time-saver.

**Keyword:** filesystem

**See Also:** df, diskadd, du, fsck, mount, mkfs, mknod, mountall, mountfsys, umount mkdev, newfs, smit, sysadmin, sysadmsh

### du -l

This command allocates blocks evenly among the links in files with multiple links. By default, a file with two or more links is counted only once.

**Keyword:** filesystem

**See Also:** df, diskadd, fsck, mount, mkfs, mknod, mountall, mountfsys, umount mkdev, newfs, smit, sysadmin, sysadmsh

### du -r

This is the same as **du** except that when it encounters an inaccessible directory, it outputs an error message.

**Keyword:** filesystem

**See Also:** df, diskadd, fsck, mount, mkfs, mknod, mountall, mountfsys, umount mkdev, newfs, smit, sysadmin, sysadmsh

### du -s /usr/reports

This command lists the number of blocks used by **/usr/reports**. The **-s** option tells **du** to handle both files and directories.

**Keyword:** filesystem

**See Also:** df, diskadd, fsck, mount, mkfs, mknod, mountall, mountfsys, umount mkdev, newfs, smit, sysadmin, sysadmsh

### dump -0 -f /dev/rmt0a /u1

This command copies the entire **/u1** filesystem to the tape specified as **rmt0a**. The **-0** argument specifies that all files be backed up to the tape. The **-f** argument is used to specify the output device; in this case, it is **/dev/rmt0a**.

**Keyword:** backup and restore

**See Also:** cpio, restore, tar

### dump -0 -f alpha:/dev/rmt0a /u1

This command backs up all the files on the **/u1** filesystem to a remote tape drive that is on the computer named **alpha**.

**Keyword:** backup and restore

**See Also:** cpio, restore, tar

## dump -0 -n -f /dev/rmt0a /u1

| ALL | BSD SunOS OSF | SYSADM |

This command backs up the entire **/u1** filesystem to tape; and, when a tape needs to be changed, it updates all users in the operator group by using the **wall** command.

**Keyword:**    backup and restore

**See Also:**    cpio, restore, tar

## dump -0 -u -f /dev/rmt0a /u1

| ALL | BSD SunOS OSF | SYSADM |

This command backs up the entire **/u1** filesystem, and writes the time of the beginning of the dump as the timestamp entry in the **/etc/dumpdates** file.

**Keyword:**    backup and restore

**See Also:**    cpio, restore, tar

## dump -3 -w

| ALL | BSD SunOS OSF | SYSADM |

This command tells the operators which files need to be backed up. It gets the information from the **/etc/dumpdates** and **/etc/fstab** files. All files are given a dump level; if the dump level is less than the one specified on the command line, it needs to be backed up again. The **-w** argument is used to inform the operator of the files to be backed up.

**Keyword:**    backup and restore

**See Also:**    cpio, restore, tar

## dump -3 -w | lpr

| ALL | BSD SunOS OSF | SYSADM |

This command tells the operator which files need to be backed up. It outputs the information to the default printer, rather than the terminal, however.

**Keyword:**    backup and restore

**See Also:**    cpio, restore, tar

## dump -a a.out

| ALL | SVR4 | SYSADM |

This command outputs the archive header of each member of an archive that is linked into the object file **a.out**.

**Keyword:**    backup and restore

**See Also:**    cpio, restore, tar

### dump -C a.out

This command outputs decoded C++ symbol table names from the file **a.out**.

**Keyword:** backup and restore

**See Also:** cpio, restore, tar

### dump -c a.out

This command outputs the string tables of the file **a.out**.

**Keyword:** backup and restore

**See Also:** cpio, restore, tar

### dump -D a.out

This command outputs the debugging information that is encoded into the object file **a.out**.

**Keyword:** backup and restore

**See Also:** cpio, restore, tar

### dump -f a.out

This command outputs all of the file header information that is encoded into the **a.out** object file.

**Keyword:** backup and restore

**See Also:** cpio, restore, tar

### dump -h a.out

This command outputs the section headers included in the **a.out** object file.

**Keyword:** backup and restore

**See Also:** cpio, restore, tar

### dump -L a.out

This command shows the dynamic linking information and static shared library information that is in **a.out**.

**Keyword:** backup and restore

**See Also:** cpio, restore, tar

### dump -o a.out

ALL    SVR4    SYSADM

This command outputs the program execution header in the **a.out** object file.

**Keyword:** backup and restore

**See Also:** cpio, restore, tar

### dump -r a.out

ALL    SVR4    SYSADM

This command outputs relocation information that is in the **a.out** object file.

**Keyword:** backup and restore

**See Also:** cpio, restore, tar

### dump -t a.out

ALL    SVR4    SYSADM

This command outputs the symbol table entries in the **a.out** object file.

**Keyword:** backup and restore

**See Also:** cpio, restore, tar

### dump -V a.out

ALL    SVR4    SYSADM

This command outputs the version information included in the **a.out** object file.

**Keyword:** backup and restore

**See Also:** cpio, restore, tar

### e notes.txt

ALL    ALL    ALL

The **e** command is a system-level alias for **ed**, which is a line editor included on all UNIX systems.

**Keyword:** text handling

**See Also:** ed, edit, emacs, vi, xedit

### e report.txt

ALL    AIX    ALL

On IBM UNIX systems, **e** is the command to invoke **INed**, an alternative editor available as part of the AIX software. Many users will find that **INed** is a more typical editor than **vi**. IBM's documentation interestingly points out that you "enter subcommands by command keys rather than on a command line." Other high points of **INed** are that it supports multiwindow editing and has a built-in file manager.

**Keyword:** text handling
**See Also:** ed, edit, emacs, vi, xedit

### echo !! >> $HOME/history.txt

CSH   ALL   POWER

This is a C shell method of recalling the previous command and storing it in a file. Single quotes are not required as in the next command. A suggested alias is **hbang**. The **!!** sequence is referred to as "bang, bang" by C shell users.

**Keyword:** programming
**See Also:** history

### echo !* >> deleted.log

CSH   ALL   POWER

This command is a handy way to track various files and other items in the C shell. The **!*** represents all arguments to the previous command. The example implies that the previous command deleted one or more files, so **echo !*** appends these filenames to the specified file, which serves as log of deleted files.

**Keyword:** programming
**See Also:** history

### echo "\07"

ALL   ALL   POWER

The external **echo** command supports functions and special characters associated with octal numbers. The octal number in this example rings the system bell.

**Keyword:** programming
**See Also:** od

### echo "\nType pin number below\nPIN: \c"

ALL   ALL   SCRIPT

This is another example of **/bin/echo**. The external **echo** command, as opposed to the shell built-in echo, resides in either **/bin** or **/usr/ucb**, or both on some systems. The external **echo** uses special characters to format output (see table). The example adds two line returns with the **\n** character, and suppresses the final line return with the **\c** character.

```
\b insert backspace          \c suppress newline
\f insert formfeed           \n insert newline
\r insert carriage return    \t insert tab
\v insert vertical tab        \\ insert backslash
```

**Keyword:**    programming
**See Also:**   echo (internal), read

### echo "`tty`:`date`" > $HOME/.logfile

| | | |
|---|---|---|
| ALL | ALL | POWER |

This command is designed for a startup file such as **.profile** in the Bourne and Korn shells. If you insert it near the beginning of the file, it allows you to keep track of the time, days, and terminals associated with your sessions on the system.

**Keyword:**    text display, system information, time
**See Also:**   date, tty

### echo $* > /$HOME/job.tmp

| | | |
|---|---|---|
| ALL | ALL | SCRIPT |

This stores command line arguments in a temporary file for later use within a shell script. There are many reasons to store arguments in this manner, including printing a list of arguments or using the arguments in another shell script. For example, a second shell script might use a **for** loop to process the arguments after extracting them from the file.

**Keyword:**    programming
**See Also:**   for, foreach (csh), until, while

### echo $PATH

| | | |
|---|---|---|
| ALL | ALL | ALL |

This command displays the current value of the path variable. You can use **echo** to display the value of any environment variable.

**Keyword:**    system information, text display
**See Also:**   env, set, setenv (csh)

### echo '!77' >> $HOME/.history.txt

| | | |
|---|---|---|
| CSH | ALL | POWER |

This is a C shell method of recalling a command that occurred earlier in the current command history. The C shell file **$HOME/.history** contains the current history. You can set the C shell variable **history** in your **.cshrc** file to increase or decrease the number of commands remembered in **history**.

**Keyword:**    programming
**See Also:**   history

## echo + | awk ´{printf("\n%50s", "Press any key to continue")}´

ALL    ALL    POWER

You can use **echo** as a front end to **awk** to format strings. Using **awk** makes for portability between systems and lets you easily add spaces to strings. The catch is that you must know the inner workings of the **printf** statement in **awk**. Also, note that the **+** sign is used arbitrarily; you can use any character you like to set the pipe in motion.

**Keyword:**   programming

**See Also:**   awk

## echo -n Please Enter Input:

ALL    ALL    SCRIPT

This command is commonly referred to as **/bin/echo**. It displays text on-screen and suppresses the line return that occurs when you use **echo** in its basic form. Although it is used by all three shells, it is most appropriate in shell scripts and C shell aliases. In both, it is frequently used with the **read** command, which obtains input from the user.

**Keyword:**   programming

**See Also:**   awk (print, printf), echo (internal), read

## echo .*

ALL    ALL    ALL

This lists all dot files in the current directory. Each file is separated by one space. This command is similar to **ls -a**, but the output is not as clean.

**Keyword:**   file handling, file listing

**See Also:**   ls

## echo accomodate | spell

ALL    ALL    ALL

Do you want to know if you have spelled a single word correctly? In most cases, the UNIX **spell** command can tell you. However, **spell** doesn't accept a single word from the command line; it only accepts files as input. As a result, you have to use **echo** to get **spell** to act on a single word. If the word is misspelled, **spell** redisplays the misspelled word. If it is not misspelled, you simply get the command prompt back.

**Keyword:**   writing

**See Also:**   look

| | | |
|---|---|---|
| ALL | ALL | ALL |

### echo esoteric | hashmake /usr/lib/spell/hlista

This command pipes the word **esoteric** into **hashmake**, which then adds it to the **hlista** file. Note that you can have two files: **hlista** and **hlistb**. On OSF systems, a similar command is called **spellout**.

**Keyword:**   writing

**Files:**   /usr/lbin/spell/hlistab, /usr/lib/spell/spellhist

**See Also:**   spell, spellin

| | | |
|---|---|---|
| ALL | OSF | ALL |

### echo esoteric | spellin /usr/lbin/spell/hlista > bizlist

This command pipes the word **esoteric** into **spellout**—an alias of **spell** on some systems—and adds it to the user's personal spelling list.

**Keyword:**   writing

**Files:**   /usr/lbin/spell/hlistab, /usr/lib/spell/spellhist

**See Also:**   spell, spellin

| | | |
|---|---|---|
| ALL | ALL | POWER |

### echo grep ´$1´ $filename >> config.script

This command determines the manner in which you use **echo** to create command lines in a secondary script. In the example, the word **grep** is echoed; the characters **$1** are echoed, not the value of the **$1** because of the single quotes; and the value of **$filename** is echoed, because it is not quoted.

**Keyword:**   programming

**See Also:**   getopt, getopts

| | | |
|---|---|---|
| ALL | XWIN | POWER SYSADM |

### echo pid=`ps -e | awk ´/mwm/ && ! /awk/ {print $1}´`

This is an example of using **echo** to test a command that you are going to use in a script.

**Keyword:**   job control

**See Also:**   awk, mwm, ps

| | | |
|---|---|---|
| ALL | ALL | END SCRIPT |

### echo \?

This command uses **echo** to display a single special character. If you did not precede the **?** with a **\**, **echo** would display any one-letter filenames in the current directory. When displaying more than one special character with **echo**, it is easier to use single quotes.

**Keyword:** text display, programming
**See Also:** read

## echo `ls` > /tmp/job.$$

ALL · ALL · POWER

This command creates a stream output of filenames from the current directory and puts them in the specified file. The output is not separated by commas as in the **ls -m** command.

**Keyword:** programming
**See Also:** ls

## echo `{ date +"%D"; who; tty; hostname; }`

SH KSH · ALL · END SCRIPT

You can create your own **who**-like commands by using **echo** and shell's {} command grouping operators. This example produces the following output: **09/10/93 alans /dev/ttyp0 digital2**.

**Keyword:** text display, programming
**See Also:** date, hostname, tty, who

## ed notes.txt

ALL · ALL · ALL

The **ed** editor handles text on a line-by-line basis. On some UNIX systems, **ed** is the only editor available in limited-access situations. Supported options include **-p**, which sets the prompt string, and **-**, which suppresses character counts.

**Keyword:** text handling
**See Also:** e, edit, emacs, vi, xedit

## EDITOR

ALL · ALL · ALL

This is an environment variable used to specify the default text editor for the system. Many UNIX utilities check to see if it is set. Shell scripts often include the {**EDITOR:=vi**} construct to set the system editor to **vi** if the user has not set the **EDITOR** variable.

**Keyword:** text handling
**See Also:** e, ed, emacs, vi, xedit, view

## Editres

ALL · XWIN · ALL

This is the resource filename for the **editres** client program. A client's resource file can be located in any of several resource locations. The order of precedence of these locations is **$XENVI-RONMENT**, **$HOME/.Xdefaults-*hostname***, **$XAPPLRESDIR**,

$HOME/*app-file*, $HOME/.Xdefaults, /usr/lib/X11/app-defaults/Xdefaults, and **/usr/lib/X11/app-defaults/app-name**. Note that **.Xdefaults** is a customary name, not mandatory.

**Keyword:**   X resources

**See Also:**   xrdb

### editres &

**ALL   XWIN   ALL**

The **editres** client is known as a programmer's tool, but it can come in handy for anyone who customizes windows with resources. To use **editres**, invoke it from the command line and, when it displays, choose the **Get the Widget Tree** item from the Commands menu. At this point, the mouse pointer changes to a cross-hair. Use it to select the window for which you want to display resource information. The **editres** program has several other options, including the ability to save resources to a file. A graphical tree view of resources also helps you understand an application's resource structure.

**Keyword:**   X resources

**See Also:**   appres, editres, listres, viewres, xrdb

### edsymsadm

**ALL   SVR4   SYSADM**

The **esymsadm** command runs an interactive system adminstration program under SVR4. The program lets you change menu and task definitions in the **sysadm** interface. It also lets you specify whether to make the changes specific to a given platform, or incorporate them in the master copy of **sysadm**.

**Keyword:**   system setup

**See Also:**   sysadm

### egrep "(MA|Mass\.|Massachusetts)[,.?: ]" history.txt

**ALL   ALL   SCRIPT   POWER**

This command uses the OR operator (|) to test for the different ways of writing **Massachusetts**. Note that you do not need the trailing **?** or **+** when you use the OR operator in parentheses.

**Keyword:**   text handling, programming

**See Also:**   awk, fgrep, grep, sed

### egrep "Bill |William " names.db

**ALL   ALL   END   SCRIPT**

This command depicts one of the simplest uses of **egrep**. It finds occurrences of both **Bill** and **William**, thanks to the logical OR operator, a feature that **grep** lacks. The example assumes that a space follows either of the two names.

**Keyword:**   text handling

**See Also:**   awk, fgrep, grep, sed

### egrep -i "Ma(ss)?(\.)?(achusetts)?[,.?: ]" history.txt

ALL   ALL   SCRIPT POWER

What if you need to search for the traditional abbreviation, **Mass** with a trailing period, as well as **MA** and **Massachusetts**. The command does this with a series of parenthetical tests followed by the **?** character. Example output could resemble the following:

```
Massachusetts, the full name
Mass., the traditional abbreviation
MA, the postal abbreviation
```

The command would ignore other text, such as **ss.** and **achusetts**, if for some reason these odd strings existed.

**Keyword:**   text handling, programming

**See Also:**   awd, fgrep, grep, sed

### egrep -i "Ma(ssachusetts)?[,.?: ]" history.txt

ALL   ALL   SCRIPT POWER

The **?** operator becomes more powerful when you group a regular expression in parentheses. In the example, **egrep** matches all instances of **MA** and **Massachusetts** and also displays the corresponding lines. The **-i** option makes **egrep** ignore the difference between uppercase and lowercase letters. The **[,.?: ]** wildcard expression ensures that **MA**—the only likely pattern to be part of another word—is not part of another word. This strategy is necessary, because unlike **grep**, **egrep** has no option to limit its search to a precise word.

**Keyword:**   text handling, programming

**See Also:**   awk, fgrep, grep, sed

### egrep Julie[t]+ plays.txt

ALL   ALL   END SCRIPT

The **+** operator, in its simplest form, acts on the previous character. When you make the previous character a wildcard, the **+** operator tells **egrep** to match one or more occurrences of the full regular expression. For instance, if the example parsed the following three lines,

```
Romeo and Juliet went astray
Julie stayed home all day.
And Juliet died in the fray
```

**egrep** would print out lines one and three. But why not just specify **Juliet** in the first place? The main reason perhaps is that the **+** operator is a toggle for the **?** operator, which does the reverse of the **+** operator (see the next command). At most, this is a shell script consideration and not likely something you will get into the habit of typing.

**Keyword:** text handling, programming

**See Also:** awk, fgrep, grep, sed

## egrep Julie[t]? plays.txt

ALL | ALL | END SCRIPT

The **?** operator tells **egrep** to match zero or more occurrences of the regular expression. Zero in this case is **Julie,** while more is **Juliet**.

**Keyword:** text handling, programming

**See Also:** awk, fgrep, grep, sed

## eject /dev/fd0

ALL | SunOS Solaris | ALL

On Sun workstations, this command ejects a diskette from the default diskette drive if a diskette is present.

**Keyword:** devices

**See Also:** mount, umount

## eject /dev/sr0

ALL | SunOS Solaris | ALL

On Sun workstations, this command ejects the CD-ROM disk if it is loaded.

**Keyword:** devices

**See Also:** mount, umount

## else

ALL | ALL | SCRIPT

Essentially implemented the same way in all three shells, this script language construct lets you program a conditional statement within an **if** statement.

**Keyword:** programming

**See Also:** if (sh), if (csh)

## emacs

ALL | ALL | ALL

The GNU **emacs** editor is the public domain program originally written by Richard Stallman for the DEC PDP-10. Its features can be customized and expanded through Lisp scripts. **Emacs** has an extensive interactive help module. To use it, you must know how to manipulate **emacs** windows and buffers. Ctrl-H enters the help module. PostScript files of the **emacs** manual are located in **/usr/lib/emacs/doc**. You can order printed copies of the *GNU Emacs Manual* from the Free Software Foundation, 675 Massachusetts Ave., Cambridge, MA 02139.

**Keyword:**   text handling

**See Also:**   e, ed, edit, vi, xedit

### enable postscript4

ALL   SVR4   ALL

This command enables a disabled printer on SVR4 systems. If the printer is remote, **enable** only activates the local queue to the printer, and you have to run **enable** on the remote system if you want the queue to be processed. The **lpstat -p** command displays the status of printers known to a UNIX system.

**Keyword:**   printing

**See Also:**   lp, lpstat

### end

CSHL   ALL   SCRIPT

This C shell construct terminates a **foreach** loop. Note that **end** must occur on a line by itself.

**Keyword:**   programming

**See Also:**   foreach

### endif

CSH   ALL   SCRIPT

Another C shell construct, **endif** does exactly as its name says: It ends an **if** statement. In the Bourne and Korn shells, use **fi**. The C language does not require a similar statement for single-line conditionals, but requires enclosing brackets ({}) for multiline line conditionals.

**Keyword:**   programming

**See Also:**   if

### ENV

KSH   ALL   POWER   SYSADM

This is an environment variable that contains a file to be executed upon entry to the shell. The file usually contains aliases and shell functions.

**Keyword:**   user environment

**See Also:**   env, printenv, set

| | | |
|---|---|---|
| ALL | ALL | ALL |

## env

This displays the current shell environment, including system path, environment variables, and terminal definition.

**Keyword:** system information

**See Also:** printenv, set, setenv

| | | |
|---|---|---|
| ALL | ALL | SCRIPT POWER |

## env - PATH=$PATH TERM=xterm HOME=$HOME sh

The - option to **env** ignores the current environment and only sets items defined on the command line. In the example, the system path is retained, but any environment variables and other information are ignored.

**Keyword:** user environment

**See Also:** printenv, set, setenv (csh)

| | | |
|---|---|---|
| ALL | ALL | SCRIPT POWER |

## env HOME=/usr/users/alans2 csh

You can use **env** to set a new system value before executing a subshell, or any other program, for that matter. In the example, the user's home directory is set to an alternative directory before **env** executes **csh**.

**Keyword:** user environment

**See Also:** printenv, set, setenv (csh)

| | | |
|---|---|---|
| ALL | ALL | SCRIPT POWER |

## env PATH=$ALTPATH /bin/csh

This command changes the path altogether to an alternate path. The example presumes that **$ALTPATH** has been defined in a startup file. The technique works with all three shells, even though **csh** is used.

**Keyword:** user environment

**See Also:** printenv, set, setenv (csh)

| | | |
|---|---|---|
| ALL | ALL | SCRIPT POWER |

## env PATH=$DBPATH startdb

This example redefines the path to an alternate path. The purpose of this example is to point out that **env** offers a very convenient way to provide applications with their own special paths. The benefit, if you start applications like this, is that the standard system path does not become cluttered.

**Keyword:** user environment

**See Also:** printenv, set, setenv (csh)

### env PATH=$PATH:/usr/users/alans sh

The command adds a directory to the existing path before executing the subshell. This is a handy way to create a modified environment for testing scripts and programs, without modifying any shell startup files.

**Keyword:**   user environment

**See Also:**   printenv, set

### env PATH=${PATH}:/usr/users/alans csh

The C shell requires curly braces around the **$PATH** environment variable in order for you to run **env** and modify the path.

**Keyword:**   user environment

**See Also:**   printenv, set, setenv (csh)

### env | grep ^X

This is a quick way to find out which environment variables are in effect for the X Window System. By convention, X environment variables begin with the letter X.

**Keyword:**   user environment

**See Also:**   printenv, set, setenv (csh)

### env | wc -c

This command is for environment space worrywarts. If you fall into this category, you will find the command invaluable. The output of the command is in bytes, as specified by the **-c** option to **wc**.

**Keyword:**   system information

**See Also:**   set

### ERRNO

This is an environment variable that is set to the value of the error generated by the most recent system failure.

**Keyword:**   user environment, system information

**See Also:**   echo

### eval $pointer

Because of its ability to perform a double pass, **eval** can be enlisted to create pointers in shell scripts. Here is a short example:

The left margin contains the following indicator columns:

| | | |
|---|---|---|
| SH KSH | ALL | SCRIPT POWER |
| CSH | ALL | END SCRIPT POWER SYSADM |
| ALL | ALL | END SCRIPT |
| ALL | ALL | POWER SYSADM |
| KSH | ALL | SCRIPT |
| ALL | ALL | SCRIPT |

```
#/bin/sh
item1=12; item2=24
pointer=item1
eval $pointer=$item2
echo $item1
```

The output is **24**, the value of **item2**. The reason is that the **eval $pointer** construct is the actual memory space in which **item1** has been stored. Thus, at the end of the script, **$pointer** does not equal **item1**; it equals the contents of **item1**, which have been changed by the **eval $pointer=$item2** statement.

**Keyword:**    programming

**See Also:**    exec

## eval $window

In shell scripts, when a variable has gone through various manipulations, you need to make a double pass to decipher it so that the shell can execute it properly. This is often true when a variable contains other variables or there are quotation marks within quotation marks in the variable. With **eval**, additional layers are stripped away and arguments look like arguments and options look like options.

**Keyword:**    program execution, programming

**See Also:**    exec

## eval `tset - -m dialup:ansi`

The **eval** command reads arguments as input to the shell. It then executes the command. Most often, **eval** is used in command substitution. The example obtains the terminal definition through **tset**, and the definition is executed as a result of the **eval** command.

**Keyword:**    program execution, programming

**See Also:**    exec, tset

## ex

The **ex** command is the underlying layer to **vi**. It is a line editor and is basically a superset of the **ed** line editor. In addition to **vi**, **ex** is integral to the **e**, **edit**, **vedit**, and **view** programs. In line editor mode, **ex** shares many of the terminal-based editing features of **vi**.

**Keyword:**    text editing

ALL  ALL  SCRIPT
            POWER

ALL  ALL  SCRIPT
            POWER

ALL  ALL  ALL

**Files:**      $HOME/.exrc

**See Also:**   e, ed, edit, emacs, vedit, vi, view, xedit

### ex -r work.txt

The **-r** option to **ex** is an important one. It lets you recover files that have been apparently lost as the result of a system crash or some other system problem.

**Keyword:**    text editing

**Files:**      $HOME/.exrc

**See Also:**   e, ed, edit, emacs, vedit, vi, view, xedit

### ex -v work.txt

More a note of interest than a practical command, the **-v** option executes the **vi** version of **ex**. It is exactly the same thing as loading **vi** itself.

**Keyword:**    text editing

**Files:**      $HOME/.exrc

**See Also:**   e, ed, edit, emacs, vedit, vi, view, xedit

### exec $HOME/.desktop

The **exec** command is a handy way to execute a file that itself is not executable. In the example, **exec** executes **$HOME/.desktop**, which is likely a file containing X clients. The only proviso using **exec** this way is that you want the existing shell to disappear. Otherwise, you should use the **.** command in the Bourne and Korn shells, or the **source** command in the C shell.

**Keyword:**    program execution

**See Also:**   dot command, eval, source

### exec $HOME/.xexec

Sometimes it is critical to limit end-user access to a special configuration file, such as the **.xexec** file that might be used in the X Window System. This command does the trick. It is appended to an existing startup file (but one that the end user can't touch) and executed as the last command. From there, the system executes the commands contained in **.xexec**.

**Keyword:**    user environment

**See Also:**   eval

ALL   ALL   ALL

ALL   ALL   ALL

ALL   ALL   SCRIPT

ALL   ALL   ALL

## exec 1<&-

| | | |
|---|---|---|
| ALL | ALL | SCRIPT |
| | | POWER |

The **exec** command is often used to control input/output redirection. One of the things it can control are file descriptors. As the entry shows, **exec** can even close the file descriptor for standard input. It doesn't lock out the keyboard, but if you type the example, you'll find that the shell ignores any command that you subsequently type.

**Keyword:**  redirection

**See Also:**  dot command, eval, source

## exec < cmdfile

| | | |
|---|---|---|
| SH | ALL | SCRIPT |
| KSH | | POWER |

This example ignores input from the keyboard, but does read the commands in **cmdfile**. After the commands are completed, the shell in which you executed **exec** terminates. Try this out in a subshell, but don't run it in an Xterm window unless you want the window to disappear.

**Keyword:**  redirection

**See Also:**  dot command, eval, source

## exec < cmdfile 2>errorfile

| | | |
|---|---|---|
| SH | ALL | SCRIPT |
| KSH | | SYSADM |

You can use **exec** to redirect all session errors to an **errorfile**. Here, the **cmdfile** is executed, and any errors that occur are recorded to **errorfile**.

**Keyword:**  program execution, redirection

**See Also:**  dot command, eval, source

## exec csh

| | | |
|---|---|---|
| ALL | ALL | SCRIPT |
| | | POWER |

The **exec** command terminates the current shell and executes the specified command. This is a good way to avoid running subshells, if indeed that's what you want to do. Try the command in an Xterm window. When you are in your new shell, press Ctrl-D and the window should disappear—just as if you had pressed Ctrl-D from your original shell.

**Keyword:**  program execution

**See Also:**  eval

## exit

| | | |
|---|---|---|
| ALL | ALL | END |
| | | SCRIPT |

The **exit** command is a shell built-in that terminates the current process and returns control to the previous shell. In the X Window System, entering **exit** in an Xterm window terminates the associated shell and closes the window. In a shell script, **exit** terminates the script.

**Keyword:**    program execution

**See Also:**    logout (csh)

### exit 0

ALL    ALL    SCRIPT

The **0** argument to **exit** is used in shell scripts to indicate that the script has completed successfully. This is an important technique if you have another script waiting to poll the exit status.

**Keyword:**    program execution

**See Also:**    logout (csh)

### exit 1

ALL    ALL    SCRIPT

The **1** argument to **exit** is used in shell scripts to indicate that the script has not completed successfully. This is an important technique if you have another script waiting to poll the exit status.

**Keyword:**    program execution

**See Also:**    logout (csh)

### expand -15,30,45 july.rep > july.txt

ALL    ALL    END SCRIPT

By listing a series of ascending numbers after **expand**, you can set the tab stops for columns. The entry sets the **tab** option to **-15,30,45**. The first column with a tab before it is equivalent to **15**. If your first column in the file begins a line, it is not affected because it doesn't have a tab before it.

**Keyword:**    text handling

**See Also:**    awk, sed, vi, unexpand

### expand -6 july.rep > july.txt

ALL    ALL    END SCRIPT

By specifying a number as an option to the **expand** command, you can change the width of the whitespace between columns in a text file. The example changes the number of whitespaces per tab to six; the default is eight. Note that any existing columns formatted with whitespace are unaffected.

**Keyword:**    text handling

**See Also:**    awk, sed, vi, unexpand

ALL ALL SCRIPT

## expand work.fmt > work.txt

The **expand** command is a BSD command that converts spaces into tabs. The method it uses fills the entire tabbed area with spaces. The contents of files look the same when **expand** finishes. To reverse the process, use the **unexpand** command.

**Keyword:**  text handling

**See Also:**  awk, sed, vi, unexpand

ALL OSF END

## explain

This interactive command looks up the words and phrases in a thesaurus file and displays synonyms. You can use the command interactively or with the output from the **diction** command.

**Keyword:**  text handling

**Files:**  /usr/lbin/explain.d

**See Also:**  diction, suggest

SH
KSH ALL ALL

## export DISPLAY

The **export** command is a shell built-in in the Bourne and Korn shells. **export** lets you make the shell aware of a new environment setting. Usually, **export** is written on the same line as the setting:

```
DISPLAY=sparky:0.0; export DISPLAY
```

The equivalent is the C shell is:

```
setenv DISPLAY sparky:0.0
```

**Keyword:**  user environment

**See Also:**  env, printenv, set, setenv

ALL ALL SCRIPT

## expr "$title" : ´[a-zA-Z]*´

This command lets you define name as:

```
name="Gone with the Window"
```

and **\*expr** returns a value of **4**. In other words, it stops counting characters as soon as it encounters the first whitespace in the title. The fix is to include the whitespace in the regular expression: **[a-zA-Z ]**. Note, too, that you must quote a variable—in this case, **$title**—when it contains whitespaces.

**Keyword:**  math, text handling

**See Also:**  awk, bc, dc, xcalc

**136**

### expr "$title" : ´\(.*d\)´

ALL   ALL   SCRIPT

By enclosing the regular expression in parentheses (the right-hand side of the equation), you can extract the matching string. Applied to "Gone with the Window," the example returns "Gone with the Wind."

**Keyword:**   math, text handling

**See Also:**   awk, bc, dc, xcalc

### expr "$title" : ´\(.................\)´

ALL   ALL   SCRIPT

This form of **expr** works because you match dots to the number of letters that you want to extract. It is convenient for smaller strings, but "Gone with the Wind" makes for a lot of dots.

**Keyword:**   math, text handling

**See Also:**   awk, bc, dc, xcalc

### expr $a + $b \> $c

ALL   ALL   END SCRIPT

If the equation is true—that is, if the left-hand side is greater than the right-hand side—**expr** returns a value of one. If it is false, expression returns zero. Here is the complete set of the **expr** comparison operators, which can be used on both integers and text strings:

```
=       equal
\>      greater than
|>=     greater than or equal
\<      less than
\<=     less than or equal
!=      not equal
```

Note that you must always escape the **<** and **>** operators, but you should not escape the **=** and **!=** operators.

**Keyword:**   math

**See Also:**   awk, bc, dc, xcalc

### expr $color \& $default

ALL   ALL   END SCRIPT

The logical AND operator is used here to tell **expr** to return the left-hand value if both sides of the equation are greater than zero (and not null). If this condition is not met, **expr** returns zero.

**Keyword:**   math

**See Also:**   awk, bc, dc, xcalc

### expr $color \| $default

ALL   ALL   END
SCRIPT

The logical OR operator is used here to tell **expr** to return the left-hand value if it is not null or zero. If it is null or zero, the right-hand value is returned.

**Keyword:**   math

**See Also:**   awk, bc, dc, xcalc

### expr $i + 1

ALL   ALL   END
SCRIPT

This example is designed for a shell script. It allows you to set up a loop counter, which is an invaluable programming tool. In an actual script, you would set **i** equal to the **expr** statement:

```
i=`expr $i + 1`
```

Command substitution causes **i** to be incremented by one. You can also use this technique to decrement a variable:

```
i=`expr $i - 1`
```

Be conservative in using **expr** for counters. Each time you use **expr**, the shell executes a process, unlike a programming language, which simply increments or decrements an internal counter.

**Keyword:**   math

**See Also:**   awk, bc, dc, xcalc

### expr $name : ´.*´

ALL   ALL   SCRIPT

This uses the **expr** "matching" operator for regular expressions. The : operator compares the first argument against the second argument. The output is the number of characters matched. In shell scripts, you might use a command like the example in order to check the string length of data entered via the **read** command. Or you might use it if you need to pad numbers with leading zeros. Here is an example of the latter:

```
while [ `expr $num : '.*'` -ne `expr $LEN : '.*'` ]
do
    num=0$num
done
```

**Keyword:**   math, text handling

**See Also:**   awk, bc, dc, xcalc

### expr $num : ´[0-9,\.]*´

ALL   ALL   SCRIPT

This command returns the length of a numerical string. If the string contains commas and/or periods, these are included in the string length. If you define **$num** as **1,234.56**, **expr** returns a value of **8**. If you do not include the comma and period in the regular expression (say you use just **[0-9]**), yet try to parse a number such as **1,234.56**, **expr** returns the value of the number of digits up to the first comma or period.

**Keyword:**    math, text handling

**See Also:**    awk, bc, dc, xcalc

### expr $x + $y - $z \| 100

ALL    ALL    END
SCRIPT

This example shows that you can combine math and logical operators. Again, if the left-hand side of the equation is null or zero, the value of the right-hand side is output. If the value of the left-hand side is negative, the negative number is output.

**Keyword:**    math

**See Also:**    awk, bc, dc, xcalc

### expr //$bname : ´.*/\(.*\)´

ALL    ALL    SCRIPT

The SVR4 **man** page for **expr** presents this interesting example. It simulates the **basename** command. First, it makes things simple by escaping the division operator so that the shell recognizes for its normal meaning. It escapes it by placing a second forward slash in front of it. The regular expression on the right-hand side of the equation then extracts the final string falling after the last forward slash in the pathname. For example, **/usr/bin/ls** would be parsed to **ls**—which is what **basename** does for you.

**Keyword:**    math, text handling

**See Also:**    awk, bc, dc, xcalc

### expr 12 + 12

ALL    ALL    ALL

The **expr** command is primarily a shell script tool, but it can be used from the command line for quick calculations. The major limitation of **expr** is that it only handles integers, not floating point decimal numbers (for these, you must use **awk**). In the example, **expr** adds two numbers and outputs the result. Note that the spacing before and after the operator is mandatory.

**Keyword:**    math

**See Also:**    awk, bc, dc, xcalc

ALL  ALL  END
SCRIPT

## expr 12 - 6

This command subtracts one number from another and outputs
the results. In a shell script, you probably would set a variable
equal to the output:

```
ans=`expr $months - $contract`
echo $ans
```

The spacing before and after the operator is mandatory. Note
that subtraction and addition have low precedence when part of
a more complicated statement.

**Keyword:**     math

**See Also:**     awk, bc, dc, xcalc


ALL  ALL  ALL

## expr 12 / 2

This command shows an example of division. Both division and
multiplication have equal precedence. The forward-slash character does not need to be escaped.

**Keyword:**     math

**See Also:**     awk, bc, dc, xcalc


ALL  ALL  ALL

## expr 2 \* 6

This command shows an example of multiplication. Because the
* character has special meaning to the shell, you must escape it
with a backslash. Multiplication has a higher priority than addition and subtraction.

**Keyword:**     math

**See Also:**     awk, bc, dc


ALL  ALL  ALL

## expr 23 % 7

This example produces the modulus remainder of the equation. In
this case, the remainder is **2**. In scripts, obtaining the modulus
after a division operation is often necessary for reasons of accuracy. If you simply executed **expr 23 / 7**, the answer would be **3**.

**Keyword:**     math

**See Also:**     awk, bc, dc


ALL  ALL  SCRIPT

## expr index 1234.55

The undocumented **index** function returns the position of the
character or characters specified by the second expression in the

first expression. The output for the entry is **5**. Note that you can specify multiple characters for the second expression, and **index** returns the position for the first match. The **index** function, as well as the undocumented **expr** functions in the following examples, might not be available on all UNIX implementations, but they can be found on the ones covered in *The UNIX and X Command Compendium.*

**Keyword:**  math, text handling

**See Also:**  awk, bc, dc, xcalc

### expr length $pid

ALL  ALL  SCRIPT

The undocumented **length** function returns the number of digits in an integer value or a string. The **length** function, as well as the undocument **expr** functions in the following examples, might not be available on all UNIX implementations, but they can be found on the ones covered in *The UNIX and X Command Compendium.*

**Keyword:**  math, text handling

**See Also:**  awk, bc, dc, xcalc

### expr match $lotto $ticket

ALL  ALL  SCRIPT

The undocumented **match** function works identically to the **match** operator. The function compares the first argument against the second argument. The output is the number of characters matched. If **$lotto** equalled **9-6-14** and **$ticket** equalled **9-6-8**, the result would be **4**.

**Keyword:**  math

**See Also:**  awk, bc, dc, xcalc

### expr substr $lastname 1 7

ALL  ALL  SCRIPT

The undocumented **substr** function extracts part or all of the string specified as the first expression. The second expression specifies the beginning position of the substring. The third expression specifies the length of the substring. In the example, if **$lastname** equalled **Washington**, the output would be **Washing**.

**Keyword:**  math, text handling

**See Also:**  awk, bc, dc, xcalc

## expr \( 14 + 7 \) \* 10 / 5

ALL   ALL   ALL

This shows a more complex **expr** statement. The addition is performed first because it is contained in parentheses. The parentheses must be quoted because they have special meaning to the shell. After this, because multiplication and division have equal precedence, **expr** performs its calculations on a left-to-right basis.

**Keyword:** math

**See Also:** awk, bc, dc, xcalc

## f

ALL   ALL   END SCRIPT

This is a system alias for the **finger** command. With options, the command outputs a list of users currently logged into the system. Output is in this order: usernames, real names, TTY devices, how long they have been idle, when they logged in, and where their offices are.

**Keyword:** user environment, system information

**Files:** $HOME/.plan, $HOME/.project

**See Also:** finger, ps, w, who

## factor 58

ALL   SVR4   ALL

This command finds the prime factors of the number **58**.

**Keyword:** math

**See Also:** awk, bc, dc, expr, xcalc

## false

ALL   ALL   SCRIPT

This command is used to return an unsuccessful exit status from a shell script. It is used in the Bourne, Korn, and C shells.

**Keyword:** programming

**See Also:** true

## fastboot

ALL   ALL   SYSADM

The fastboot command will reboot the system. It writes a file called **fastboot**, then runs the program reboot. When the system comes back up, it sees the **fastboot** file and omits running **fsck**.

**Keyword:** startup

**See Also:** fasthalt, reboot, shutdown, fsck, halt, init, sync

### fastboot -l

| | | |
|---|---|---|
| ALL | ALL | SYSADM |

This command does not log the reboot, nor does it place a record of the shutdown in the accounting file.

**Keyword:**  startup

**See Also:**  fasthalt, reboot, shutdown, fsck, halt, init, sync

### fastboot -n

| | | |
|---|---|---|
| ALL | ALL | SYSADM |

This is the same as **fastboot**, except that it does not sync the disks prior to shutdown, nor does it keep a log of the reboot.

**Keyword:**  startup

**See Also:**  fasthalt, reboot, shutdown, fsck, halt, init, sync

### fastboot -q

| | | |
|---|---|---|
| ALL | ALL | SYSADM |

This is the same as **fastboot**, except that it doesn't kill all of the running processes before rebooting the system. It also does not log the reboot.

**Keyword:**  startup

**See Also:**  kill, ps, fasthalt, reboot, shutdown, fsck, halt, init, sync

### fasthalt

| | | |
|---|---|---|
| ALL | ALL | SYSADM |

This command performs exactly the same as **fastboot**, except that the system is halted rather than rebooted. All of the options behave the same as with **fastboot**.

**Keyword:**  shutdown

**See Also:**  fastboot, reboot, shutdown, fsck, halt, init, sync

### fc -e vi 8 14

| | | |
|---|---|---|
| ALL | ALL | END |

This command lets you use **vi** to edit commands **8** through **14** and then execute them. The command ignores the value of **$FCEDIT**.

**Keyword:**  program execution

**Files:**  $HOME/.sh_history

**See Also:**  history, FCEDIT

## fc 20 24

**ALL** **ALL** **END**

The **fc** command is a Korn shell built-in. It lets you edit one or more commands and then execute them. The example specifies commands **20** to **24**, inclusive. The Korn shell uses the editor specified by **$FCEDIT**.

| | |
|---|---|
| **Keyword:** | keyboard shortcuts |
| **Files:** | $HOME/.sh_history |
| **See Also:** | csh, fignore, history, ksh |

## FCEDIT

**KSH** **ALL** **SCRIPT**

This is an environmental parameter containing the default editor name for the **fc** command. Most UNIX systems have this defined as **emacs** or **vi**.

| | |
|---|---|
| **Keyword:** | user environment |
| **See Also:** | emacs, fc, vi |

## fdetach /u1/test/document.txt

**ALL** **SVR4** **POWER**

This command detaches the **STREAMS**-based file descriptor from **/u1/test/document.txt**. After executing this command, all subsequent operations on **/u1/test/document.txt** will not be on the **STREAMS** file, but on **/u1/test/document.txt** directly.

| | |
|---|---|
| **Keyword:** | devices |
| **See Also:** | df, diskadd, du, fsck, mount, mkfs, mknod, mountall, mountsys, umount, mkdev, newfs, sysadm |

## fdformat -d /dev/rfd0c

**ALL** **Solaris** **ALL**

This command is used to format a diskette, and to install the MS-DOS filesystem and boot sector on it. This is equivalent to the MS-DOS command **format /s a:**.

| | |
|---|---|
| **Keyword:** | devices, DOS, filesystem |
| **Files:** | /dev/rfd0c, /dev/fd0c, /dev/diskette, /dev/rdiskette |
| **See Also:** | dosformat, format, newfs |

## fdformat -e /dev/rfd0c

**ALL** **Solaris** **ALL**

This command simply formats a diskette to 1.44 MB, and then ejects it from the disk drive.

| | |
|---|---|
| **Keyword:** | devices, DOS, filesystem |

**Files:** /dev/rfd0c, /dev/fd0c, /dev/diskette, /dev/rdiskette

**See Also:** dosformat, format, newfs

### fdformat -f /dev/rfd0c

| | | |
|---|---|---|
| ALL | Solaris | ALL |

By default, the computer will ask you to insert a diskette before beginning the format. The **-f** argument to **fdformat** causes the computer to begin the format immediately, without asking the user to insert the disk.

**Keyword:** devices, DOS, filesystem

**Files:** /dev/rfd0c, /dev/fd0c, /dev/diskette, /dev/rdiskette

**See Also:** dosformat, format, newfs

### fdformat -l /dev/rfd0c

| | | |
|---|---|---|
| ALL | Solaris | ALL |

Rather than formatting diskettes as high density (1.44 MB), this command formats diskettes as 720 KB, double density.

**Keyword:** devices, DOS, filesystem

**Files:** /dev/rfd0c, /dev/fd0c, /dev/diskette, /dev/rdiskette

**See Also:** dosformat, format, newfs

### fdformat -m -t nec /dev/rfd2c

| | | |
|---|---|---|
| ALL | Solaris 2.x | ALL |

This command is used only if you have a 5.25-inch diskette drive. It is used to format a 5.25-inch diskette as 1.2 MB.

**Keyword:** devices, DOS, filesystem

**Files:** /dev/rfd0c, /dev/fd0c, /dev/diskette, /dev/rdiskette

**See Also:** dosformat, format, newfs

### fdformat -t dos /dev/rfd0c

| | | |
|---|---|---|
| ALL | Solaris 2.x | ALL |

This command is exactly the same as the **-d** argument to **fdformat**. It formats a 3.5-inch diskette to 1.44 MB and puts the MS-DOS filesystem and boot sector on the diskette.

**Keyword:** devices, DOS, filesystem

**Files:** /dev/rfd0c, /dev/fd0c, /dev/diskette, /dev/rdiskette

**See Also:** dosformat, format, newfs

### fdformat -v /dev/rfd0c

| | | |
|---|---|---|
| ALL | Solaris | END POWER |

This command verifies that the diskette is okay after the system completes the format.

**Keyword:** devices, filesystem
**Files:** /dev/rfd0c, /dev/fd0c, /dev/diskette, /dev/rdiskette
**See Also:** dosformat, format, newfs

### fdformat /dev/rfd0c

ALL    Solaris    ALL

This command formats a diskette for use with a UNIX system.
The format in the example specifies high-density disks (1.44 MB).

**Keyword:** devices, filesystem
**Files:** /dev/rfd0c, /dev/fd0c, /dev/diskette, /dev/rdiskette
**See Also:** dosformat, format, newfs

### fdformat /dev/rfd0c; newfs /dev/rfd0c

ALL    Solaris    . END
POWER

This command creates a UNIX **ufs** filesystem on a diskette. It can
be used with unformatted disks, because the disk is formatted
before the filesystem is put on it.

**Keyword:** devices, filesystem
**Files:** /dev/rfd0c, /dev/fd0c, /dev/diskette, /dev/rdiskette
**See Also:** dosformat, format, newfs

### fdformat /dev/rfd0c; newfs /dev/rfd0c; mkdir /dk; mount /dev/rfd0c /dk

ALL    Solaris    SYSADM

This command mounts the diskette after it formats it to the
directory **/dk**. Only the superuser can execute this command.

**Keyword:** devices, filesystem
**Files:** /dev/rfd0c, /dev/fd0c, /dev/diskette, /dev/rdiskette
**See Also:** dosformat, format, newfs

### fdisk

ALL    SCO    SYSADM

The **fdisk** command lets you create and delete disk partitions,
view information about existing partitions, and select a single
partition as the active partition. The SCO version of **fdisk** is an
extended version of **FDISK** in the DOS environment. The two
products were originally developed in tandem by Microsoft Corp.
when it marketed Xenix. When you enter **fdisk** without options,
you get the following menu:

```
1. Display Partition Table
2. Use Entire Disk for UNIX
3. Use Rest of Disk for UNIX
```

```
4. Create UNIX Partition
5. Activate Partition
6. Delete Partition

Enter your choice or q to quit: q
```

**Keyword:**   filesystem, devices

**See Also:**   fdisk, fsck, mkdev, mkfs, mknod, sysadmsh

### ff -F hsfs /dev/rsd0

ALL   SVR4   SYSADM

This command displays information on the high-speed filesystem. Also, **/etc/vfstab** is not consulted.

**Keyword:**   devices, filesystem

**See Also:**   find, ncheck, stat

### ff -V /dev/rsd0

ALL   SVR4   SYSADM

This command echoes the command line but does not execute it. It is useful for verifying the options used and the contents of the **/etc/vfstab** file.

**Keyword:**   filesystem

**Files:**   /etc/vfstab

**See Also:**   find, ncheck, stat

### ff /dev/rsd0

ALL   SVR4   SYSADM

This command outputs the pathname and inode numbers of files in the **rsd0** filesystem. The filesystem type is determined by the file **/etc/vfstab**.

**Keyword:**   filesystem

**Files:**   /etc/vfstab

**See Also:**   find, ncheck, stat

### fg %1

CSH   ALL   POWER

This command brings the specified job into the foreground.

**Keyword:**   background processing, job control

**See Also:**   atrm, at, atq, cron, bg

### fgrep ´dog and cat´ pets.txt

ALL   ALL   END SCRIPT

This command outputs all lines containing **dog and cat** in the **pets.txt** file. Use **fgrep** when you only need to search for literal text patterns. Because **fgrep** doesn't support regular expressions, it is often faster than **grep**.

**Keyword:**   text display, text search

**See Also:**   grep, egrep, ed, sed, gres

### fgrep ´See Also:´ book.txt | awk ´{s+=1} END {print "commands=", s}´

This command can also be used to keep track of the number of commands completed. It uses **awk** to count the number of **See Also:** lines that **fgrep** outputs. It then stores that number in the variable **s**; then it just prints out a message, with **s** in it.

**Keyword:**   text display, text handling

**See Also:**   awk, egrep, fmlgrep, grep

### fgrep ´See Also:´ book.txt | wc -l | awk ´{print "commands=", $1}´

We used this command to keep track of the number of commands we had written so far. We used the **See Also:** as our search key for **fgrep**; then the command **wc -l** counted the number of lines that **fgrep** reported. We used **awk** to format the output.

**Keyword:**   text display, text handling

**See Also:**   awk, wc

### fgrep ´system´ /etc/group | awk -F: ´{print $4}´

This command outputs the usernames of everyone who has system privileges on the computer.

**Keyword:**   system information

**See Also:**   users, who

### fgrep -b ´icecream´ desserts.txt

This command puts a block number at the beginning of every line of output.

**Keyword:**   text display, text search

**See Also:**   grep, egrep, ed, sed, gres

### fgrep -c ´dog and cat´ pets.txt

This command outputs the number of lines that matched the search criteria, not the actual lines.

ALL  ALL  POWER

ALL  ALL  POWER

ALL  ALL  POWER
         SYSADM

ALL  ALL  END
         SCRIPT

ALL  ALL  END
         SCRIPT

**Keyword:** text display, text search

**See Also:** grep, egrep, ed, sed, gres

### fgrep -c ´See Also:´ book.txt

| | | |
|---|---|---|
| ALL | ALL | POWER |

This is the simplest way to find the number of **See Also:** in the **book.txt** file. The output isn't formatted.

**Keyword:** text handling, text search

**See Also:** awk, egrep, fmlgrep, grep

### fgrep -e ´-10´ temperature.txt

| | | |
|---|---|---|
| ALL | ALL | END SCRIPT |

The **-e** option should precede any pattern that begins with a **-**. In this example, the search pattern is **-10**, so the **-e** is added. This will output all the lines in the **temperature.txt** file that have a **-10** in them.

**Keyword:** text display, text search

**See Also:** grep, egrep, ed, sed, gres

### fgrep -f search data.txt

| | | |
|---|---|---|
| ALL | ALL | END SCRIPT |

The **-f** option causes **fgrep** to source the specified file for search patterns.

**Keyword:** text display, text search

**See Also:** egrep, sed

### fgrep -h dog *

| | | |
|---|---|---|
| ALL | SVR4 | END SCRIPT |

This command prints all the lines that have **dog** in them, checking every file in the current directory. The **-h** option causes **fgrep** to suppress filenames.

**Keyword:** text display, text search

**See Also:** grep, egrep, ed, sed, find, gres

### fgrep -i thomas phone.dir

| | | |
|---|---|---|
| ALL | ALL | END SCRIPT |

This command outputs all the lines that contain **Thomas** in the **phone.dir** file, regardless of the case of **thomas**. This can be convenient in a shell script used as:

```
fgrep -i $1 phone.book
```

where the input to the script is a search string.

**Keyword:** text display, text search

**See Also:** grep, egrep, ed, sed, find, gres

### fgrep -l dog *

ALL ALL END SCRIPT

This command prints the names of all the files that have **dog** in them, checking the current directory. It will *not* ouput the lines that have **dog** in them, however.

**Keyword:**   text display, text search

**See Also:**   grep, egrep, ed, sed, gres

### fgrep -n ´fork(´ mycode.c

ALL ALL END SCRIPT

This command outputs all the lines and line numbers in **mycode.c** that contain the word **fork** followed by a left parenthesis.

**Keyword:**   text display, text search

**See Also:**   grep, egrep, ed, sed, gres

### fgrep -v ´;´ mycode.c

ALL ALL END SCRIPT

This displays all the lines in **mycode.c** that do *not* have a semi-colon in them.

**Keyword:**   text display, text search

**See Also:**   grep, egrep, ed, sed, gres

### fgrep -x ´if(x < 2)´ mycode.c

ALL ALL END SCRIPT

This command outputs lines that have **if(x < 2)** as the entire line in **mycode.c**.

**Keyword:**   text display, text search

**See Also:**   grep, egrep, ed, sed, gres

### fignore

CSH ALL SCRIPT

This C shell environment variable outputs a list containing file suffixes. The C shell ignores the specified suffixes when it performs filename completion.

**Keyword:**   file handling

**See Also:**   csh

### file *

ALL ALL POWER

If possible, the **file** command tells you the file type. Using the asterisk as in the example, it displays a brief two- to three-word description of each file in the current directory.

**Keyword:**   file handling

**Files:**     /etc/magic

**See Also:**  find, ls

### file -c

| | | |
|---|---|---|
| ALL | ALL | POWER |

This command checks the **/etc/magic** file for format errors. This isn't done by default, and when **-c** is used, file typing is not done. The **/etc/magic** file contains formatting information that helps the **file** command determine file types.

**Keyword:**   file handling

**Files:**     /etc/magic

**See Also:**  find, ls

### file -f list

| | | |
|---|---|---|
| ALL | ALL | POWER |

This command tries to determine what type of data is in every file listed in the **list** file.

**Keyword:**   file handling

**Files:**     /etc/magic

**See Also:**  find, ls

### file -L mypointer

| | | |
|---|---|---|
| ALL | ALL | POWER |

This command displays data on a linked file, not the link itself. We could have named the file anything, but we chose **mypointer** for mnemonic purposes.

**Keyword:**   file handling

**Files:**     /etc/magic

**See Also:**  find, ls

### file -m ~/my_magic mycode.c

| | | |
|---|---|---|
| ALL | ALL | POWER |

The **-m** option to **file** specifies an alternative **magic** file; otherwise, it works the same as when you use **file** with no options.

**Keyword:**   file handling

**Files:**     user-defined magic file

**See Also:**  find, ls

### filec

| | | |
|---|---|---|
| CSH | ALL | POWER |

This is a C shell environment variable that allows filename completion. When set, an input line followed by Ctrl-D prints all filenames that start with the contents of the line. Or, an input line followed by ESC replaces the line with the longest unambiguous extension.

**Keyword:** keyboard shortcuts

**Files:** .cshrc

**See Also:** csh, fignore

### finc -a -7 /dev/rdsk/c0t3d0s0 /dev/rSA/ctape1

ALL    SVR4    SYSADM

This command copies all the files that are in the filesystem **/c0t3d0s0**, and that have been accessed in the last week, to the tape **/dev/rSA/ctape1**. The tape must have been formatted with the **labelit** command.

**Keyword:** backup and restore

**See Also:** backup, restore, tar, cpio

### finc -c -1 /dev/rdsk/c0t3d0s0 /dev/rSA/ctape1

ALL    SVR4    SYSADM

This command copies all the files that are in the filesystem **/c0t3d0s0** to the tape **/dev/rSA/ctape1**, which has had the inode changed today. The tape must have been formatted with the **labelit** command.

**Keyword:** backup and restore

**See Also:** backup, cp, cpio, restore, tar

### finc -m -2 /dev/rdsk/c0t3d0s0 /dev/rSA/ctape1

ALL    SVR4    SYSADM

This command copies all the files that are in the filesystem **/c0t3d0s0**, and that have been modified in the last 48 hours, to the tape **/dev/rSA/ctape1**. The tape must have been formatted with the **labelit** command.

**Keyword:** backup and restore

**See Also:** backup, restore, tar, cpio, labelit

### finc -n /.lstbackup /dev/rdsk/c0t3d0s0 /dev/rSA/ctape1; touch /.lstbackup

ALL    SVR4    SYSADM

This command uses the **touch** command to copy all the files that have been modified more recently than the **/.lstbackup** file. After the command finishes, it updates the modification date on **/.lstbackup**.

**Keyword:** backup and restore

**See Also:** backup, cp, cpio, restore, tar

### finc -n /.lstbackup /dev/rdsk/c0t3d0s0 /dev/rSA/ctape1 > /.lstbackup

**ALL   SVR4   SYSADM**

This command copies all the files that have been modified more recently than the file **/.lstbackup**. After the command finishes, it updates the modification date on **/.lstbackup** to the current date. This is a simple way of keeping track of which files need to be backed up.

**Keyword:**   backup and restore

**See Also:**   backup, cp, cpio, restore, tar

### finc -n /vmunix /dev/rdsk/c0t3d0s0 /dev/rSA/ctape1

**ALL   SVR4   SYSADM**

This command copies all the files that are in the filesystem **/c0t3d0s0**, and that have been modified more recently than the file **/vmunix**, to the tape **/dev/rSA/ctape1**. The tape must have been formatted with the **labelit** command.

**Keyword:**   backup and restore

**See Also:**   backup, cp, cpio, restore, tar

### find . -exec grep -ls STRING {} \;

**ALL   ALL   POWER**

This command searches current directory for the specified string. The **-exec** option allows you to combine most any other command with **find**. Be sure that the {} operator is included and that the terminating semicolon is escaped. The **-l** option to **grep** causes **grep** to list the filename; the **-s** option suppresses error messages.

**Keyword:**   file handling, text search

**See Also:**   grep

### find . -print

**ALL   ALL   POWER**

This command uses the dot to represent the current directory. As a result, the command lists directories and their contents, beginning with the current directory and continuing through all subdirectories.

**Keyword:**   file handling

**See Also:**   ls

### find / -atime +45 -print

**ALL   ALL   POWER**

The **-atime** option to **find** lets you search for files based on time of last access. The + sign before the number **45** indicates that you are interested in files that *have been* accessed in the last 45 days. If you use a minus sign instead of a plus sign, it specifies files that *have not been* accessed in 45 days. Other options that deal with time include **-ctime**, **-mtime**, and **-newer**.

**Keyword:** file handling

**See Also:** ls

### find / -ctime +10 -print

This command outputs all of the files on the system that have not had their status updated in the past 10 days.

**Keyword:** file handling

**See Also:** ls

### { find . -exec grep -ls STR {} \; | xargs grep STR; }

This should be used when the search will find too many files for the shell environment space to handle. Curly brackets are used to group commands for the shell. Be sure that a whitespace occurs after each semicolon so that the shell recognizes when a command ends. The result of the **find** and **grep** tandem is fed into **xargs**, which runs **grep** again on the string in each filename supplied.

**Keyword:** file handling, text search

**See Also:** grep, xargs

### find / -exec grep -ls STRING {} \;

This command searches the entire disk for the specified string. The **-exec** option allows you to combine most any other command with **find**. Be sure that the {} operator is included and that the terminating semicolon is escaped. The **-l** option to **grep** causes **grep** to list the filename; the **-s** option suppresses error messages.

**Keyword:** file handling, text search

**See Also:** grep

### find / -local -name passwd -print

This command is extremely useful if your computer is an AFS (Andrew File System) client, on which you might have literally thousands of directories attached to your system. You would not want to search all of them for **passwd** because it would take hours, and because **find** would generate lots of errors from searching directories where you don't have read permission.

**Keyword:** file handling

**See Also:** ls, passwd

| | | |
|---|---|---|
| ALL | ALL | POWER |

### find / -print
This command begins at the root directory. It prints a list of all directories and files on the system, because only the **-print** option is specified.

**Keyword:** file handling

**See Also:** ls

| | | |
|---|---|---|
| ALL | ALL | POWER |

### find / -prune -name mercedes -print
The **-prune** option to **find** lets you limit a search to the local hard disk. This is a true power tool because it tells **find** not to search remote mounted filesystems.

**Keyword:** file handling

**See Also:** du, ls

| | | |
|---|---|---|
| ALL | ALL | POWER<br>SYSADM |

### find / -user edp -exec ls -l {} \; | awk ´{s+=$5} END {print $3, s/1024, "K"}´
This is a good command for system administrators. It will check the entire computer system and list the amount of disk space in kilobytes that user **edp** has consumed.

**Keyword:** system information

**See Also:** df, du, ls

| | | |
|---|---|---|
| ALL | ALL | POWER |

### find /home \( -name "*.txt" -a -name "*.doc" \) -print
This command finds files in the home hierarchy that match both criteria. The **-a** option represents the AND operator. Be sure to include whitespaces on both sides of the **-a** operator. Note also that the enclosing parentheses must be preceded by a backslash, the escape character.

**Keyword:** file handling

**See Also:** ls

| | | |
|---|---|---|
| ALL | ALL | POWER |

### find /u1/FTP/Public/Info -mtime +7 -exec touch {} \;
This command is very useful if you have to keep information up to date, and your boss only checks the dates of the files to see that they have been updated. This looks in the directory **/u1/FTP/Public/Info**, and if it sees any files that are older than one week, it runs the **touch** command, which sets the date and time on the files to the current date and time.

**Keyword:** file handling

**See Also:** ls, touch

### find /usr ! -name "*.txt" -print

This command finds all files in the **/usr/projects** hierarchy that do not match the file specification. In the example, all filenames other than those with a **.txt** extension would be displayed on the screen. Be sure to use whitespaces on both sides of the exclamation mark.

**Keyword:**   file handling

**See Also:**   ls

### find /usr -follow -name xterm -print

The **-follow** argument to **find** causes the search for **xterm** to be widened to look along symbolic links. This can be especially useful for the large-size X Window System, where it is likely that directories will be linked together.

**Keyword:**   file handling

**See Also:**   ls

### find /usr -inum 46112 -print

This command finds a file by its inode number and displays the file. Its use is suggested for programmers and system administrators involved in low-level disk concerns. The **ls -i** command displays a file's inode number.

**Keyword:**   file handling

**See Also:**   ls

### find /usr -mount -name xterm -print

This command searches for the program **xterm**, but it limits its search to only the current filesystem. If, for example, **xterm** is in the **bin** directory that is mounted using the **mount** command to **/usr/bin**, it would not be found with this command.

**Keyword:**   file handling

**See Also:**   ls, touch

### find /usr -name book.txt -exec ls -l {} \;

This finds a file in the **/usr** partition and executes the **ls -l** command on it. The output would look similar to this:

```
-rw-rw-rw-  1 root    system   14446 Jul 20 07:19 /usr/CmdCmp/book.txt
```

Note that when using the **-exec** option, you must use the {} \; sequence after the command you specify. There must spaces on

ALL   ALL   POWER

ALL   ALL   POWER SYSADM

ALL   ALL   POWER

ALL   ALL   POWER

ALL   ALL   POWER

either side of the curly braces, but no space between the slash and semicolon.

**Keyword:**    file handling

**See Also:**    ls

### find /usr/projects -name "*.txt" -print

ALL   ALL   POWER

This command finds all files in the **/usr/projects** hierarchy that have a **.txt** extension. The use of double quotes is necessary for wildcards, but you do not have to use quotes if you specify a full filename. The **-print** option is required to actually display the filenames and their locations to the screen.

**Keyword:**    file handling

**See Also:**    ls

### find book  -ctime +10 -exec ls -l {} \;

ALL   ALL   POWER

This command outputs all files that have not had their status updated in the last 10 days; however, the output is formatted by the **ls -l** command.

**Keyword:**    file handling

**See Also:**    ls

### find book  -ctime +10 -exec ls -l {} \; | lpr

ALL   ALL   POWER

This command outputs all files that have not had their status updated in the last 10 days; the output is formatted by the **ls -l** command and printed on the default printer.

**Keyword:**    file handling, printing

**See Also:**    lpr, ls

### find ~ -name core -exec rm {} \;

ALL   ALL   POWER

From **$HOME**, this command checks for core files and deletes them. A core file is created after a system problem, which is usually the result of an errant application or some misguided action by a user.

**Keyword:**    file handling

**See Also:**    rm

### find ~/ -perm -006 -print

ALL   ALL   POWER

This command shows a list of all the files in your home directory that can be read and changed by anyone with access to the system, either locally or over a network.

**find**

Keyword: file handling, file permissions
See Also: chmod, ls

### find ~/ -perm 777 -print

ALL   ALL   POWER

This useful command prints out a list of all the files in your home directory that have the permissions set to **777**. Note that in the context of **find**, **print** means sending output to **stdout**, which is usually the terminal screen.

Keyword: file handling, file permissions
See Also: chmod, ls

### find ~/ -size 512c -print

ALL   ALL   POWER

This command outputs a list of all the files in your home directory that are 512 bytes in size. It also searches subdirectories of your home directory. You will notice that mostly directory names are output, because 512 bytes is a typical size for directories.

Keyword: file handling
See Also: ls

### find ~/.trash -ctime +30 -exec rm -r {} \;

ALL   ALL   POWER
SYSADM

This deletes your old trash files, but instead of **find** asking for confirmation for each file, **rm** does it.

Keyword: file handling
See Also: rm

### find ~/.trash -ctime +30 -exec rm {} \;

ALL   ALL   POWER
SYSADM

This command searches the **.trash** subdirectory in your home directory and deletes all files that have not had their status updated in the last month. This is useful in conjunction with aliasing **rm** to move files that you want deleted to the **.trash** directory. If you then decide that you really do need that file you deleted last week, you can just **mv** it wherever you want. We decided to name this directory **.trash** so that it wouldn't show up under the **ls** command, without the **-a** argument. You could put this command in your **.login** or **.profile** file, so that it is executed every time you log in.

Keyword: file handling
See Also: rm

### find ~/.trash -ctime +30 -ok rm {} \;

ALL   ALL   POWER SYSADM

This command deletes files that are 30 or more days old, but it asks you to confirm the deletion for each file. This can be annoying, but it is a good safety measure.

**Keyword:**   file handling

**See Also:**   rm

### find ~/.trash -exec ls -l {} \; | awk ´{ s += $5 } END { print "Your trash directory has", s / 1024, "KB of files in it."}´

ALL   ALL   POWER SYSADM

This command goes along with having a **trash** directory. It keeps track of the amount of space taken up by your trash, and tells you. This is useful in an environment where disk space is strictly controlled.

**Keyword:**   file handling

**See Also:**   awk, ls

### finger

ALL   ALL   END POWER SYSADM

This command outputs a list of users currently logged into the system, in this order: usernames, real names, TTY devices, how long they have been idle, when they logged in, and where their offices are.

**Keyword:**   system information, user environment

**Files:**   $HOME/.plan, $HOME/.project

**See Also:**   hostname, users, who

### finger -b perkie

ALL   ALL   END POWER SYSADM

This is the same as the regular **finger** command, except that it doesn't output the user's shell and home directory. It does give you the login name, real name, office and home phone, how long the user has been logged into the system, and user plan file.

**Keyword:**   system information, user environment

**Files:**   $HOME/.plan, $HOME/.project

**See Also:**   hostname, users, who

### finger -f

ALL   ALL   POWER SYSADM

This is the same as plain **finger**, except that it doesn't output a header for the information. Order of display is: usernames, real names, TTY devices, how long they have been idle, when they logged in, and where their offices are. None of this information will be preceded by a header saying what it is, unlike **finger** with no options.

**Keyword:**   system information, user environment

**Files:**      $HOME/.plan, $HOME/.project

**See Also:**   hostname, users, who

### finger -f | awk ´{print $1}´

This command just ouputs a list of the usernames of everyone currently logged into the system.

**Keyword:**   system information, user environment

**Files:**      $HOME/.plan, $HOME/.project

**See Also:**   awk, hostname, users, who

### finger -f | awk ´{print $2}´

This command outputs the first name of all the users currently logged into the system.

**Keyword:**   system information, user environment

**Files:**      $HOME/.plan, $HOME/.project

**See Also:**   awk, hostname, users, who

### finger -h Perkins

This is the same as **finger perkie**, except that it will not output the contents of your **.project** file.

**Keyword:**   system information, user environment

**Files:**      $HOME/.plan, $HOME/.project

**See Also:**   hostname, users, who

### finger -i

This command outputs usernames, TTY, when users logged into the system, and how long they have been idle, for all the users that are currently on the system.

**Keyword:**   system information, user environment

**Files:**      $HOME/.plan, $HOME/.project

**See Also:**   hostname, users, who

ALL   ALL   POWER SYSADM

### finger -l

This is the same as **finger *username*** in the format of its output; however, it lists all the users current logged into the system.

**Keyword:**   system information, user environment

**Files:**        $HOME/.plan, $HOME/.project

**See Also:**   hostname, users, who

### finger -m perkie

The **-m** argument to **finger** causes **finger** to look at only the username, not the person's real name, when conducting its search. In this example, on our system, we would get valid output from this command. If we tried **finger -m Perkins**, we would not find anyone, because there is no username of **Perkins** on the system.

**Keyword:**   system information, user environment

**Files:**        $HOME/.plan, $HOME/.project

**See Also:**   hostname, users, who

### finger -p perkie

This command outputs everything that **finger perkie** does, but the contents of **perkie**'s **.plan** file will not be shown.

**Keyword:**   system information, user environment

**Files:**        $HOME/.plan, $HOME/.project

**See Also:**   hostname, users, who

### finger -q

This command is the same as **finger -s**, but it doesn't output the user's real name, office, or how long the user has been idle. It does output the username, TTY, and when the user logged in.

**Keyword:**   system information, user environment

**Files:**        $HOME/.plan, $HOME/.project

**See Also:**   hostname, users, who

### finger -q -f | awk ´{print "User", $1, "is logged in on TTY:", $2}´

This command shows the usernames of everyone logged into the system and which TTY ports they are logged into.

ALL   ALL   POWER SYSADM

ALL   ALL   POWER SYSADM

ALL   ALL   POWER SYSADM

ALL   ALL   END POWER SYSADM

ALL   ALL   POWER SYSADM

**Keyword:** system information, user environment
**Files:** $HOME/.plan, $HOME/.project
**See Also:** awk, hostname, users, who

### finger -s

ALL    ALL    POWER SYSADM

This is similar to **finger -q**, but it also outputs the user's real name. The output generated consists of username, real name, TTY, how long the user has been idle, when the user logged in, and the user's office. This is the same output as the **finger** command with no options or arguments given to it.

**Keyword:** system information, user environment
**Files:** $HOME/.plan, $HOME/.project
**See Also:** hostname, users, who

### finger -w

ALL    ALL    END POWER SYSADM

This command lists the usernames of all the users currently logged into the system, TTY devices, how long they have been idle, and when they logged in.

**Keyword:** system information, user environment
**Files:** $HOME/.plan, $HOME/.project
**See Also:** hostname, users, who

### finger perkie | grep -v Directory

ALL    ALL    END POWER SYSADM

This command outputs everything **finger** does, except the user's home directory and login shell.

**Keyword:** system information, user environment
**Files:** $HOME/.plan, $HOME/.project
**See Also:** hostname, users, who

### finger perkie@alexei.mit.edu

ALL    ALL    END POWER SYSADM

This command displays information about user **perkie** on the computer **alexei** at MIT. It will display the login name, **perkie**; which terminal **perkie** is on, if currently logged in; and the write status. It will also display **perkie**'s full name, office number, and home phone number (if known); the user's home directory and login shell; idle time; any plan that the user has placed in the **.plan** file in the user's home directory; and the project on which the user is working from the **.project** file in the home directory. The **-b** option produces a briefer version of long format output. The **-f** option suppresses the display of a header line.

**Keyword:** system information, user environment

**Files:** $HOME/.plan, $HOME/.project

**See Also:** who, users, hostname

### finger Perkins | grep -v Project:

This is another way to prevent the contents of the **.project** file from being output by the **finger** command. All of the other information that **finger *username*** normally displays is still output.

**Keyword:** system information, user environment

**Files:** $HOME/.plan, $HOME/.project

**See Also:** hostname, users, who

### fixperm -c -s -dRTS /etc/perms/*

This command creates all the device nodes in the run time system, such as **/dev/console**, **/dev/null**, and **/dev/tty1a**.

**Keyword:** devices

**See Also:** custom

### fixperm -dRTS -dSER1 -dSER2 -dSER3 -dSER4 -dFD48 -dFD96 -dHD1 -dLPR -c -s /etc/perms/inst

This command creates all the device nodes on the system, provided no third-party device drivers are installed.

**Keyword:** devices

**See Also:** custom

### fmlcut -c10- ~/data/times.dat

This command shows all the columns of characters in the **times.dat** file, excluding the first nine. The **-c** argument to **fmlcut** is open-ended. In the example, the **fmlcut** command cuts all columns from the number specified through the end of the line.

**Keyword:** text handling

**See Also:** awk, cut, grep, sed

| | | |
|---|---|---|
| ALL | ALL | POWER SYSADM |
| ALL | SCO SVR4 | SYSADM |
| ALL | SCO SVR4 | SYSADM |
| ALL | SVR4 | POWER |

### fmlcut -c25-30,45-60 ~/data/times.dat

ALL    SVR4    POWER

The **-c** option to **fmlcut** lets you cut multiple column ranges just by separating them with a comma. The example cuts two ranges, **25-30** and **45-60**.

**Keyword:**   text handling

**See Also:**   awk, cut, grep, sed

### fmlcut -c3,5,10- ~/data/times.dat

ALL    SVR4    POWER

In this command, columns **3**, **5**, and **10** through the end in the **times.dat** file are output. The **-c** option to **cut** lets you cut multiple column ranges just by separating them with a comma.

**Keyword:**   text handling

**See Also:**   awk, cut, grep, sed

### fmlcut -d: -f1,5 /etc/passwd

ALL    SVR4    END POWER

This command extracts all of the system's usernames and real names from the file **/etc/passwd**.

**Keyword:**   text handling

**See Also:**   awk, cut, grep, sed

### fmlcut -f4,8-40,79

ALL    SVR4    END POWER

As with the **-c** option, the **-f** option works with one or more column ranges. The command displays columns associated with fields **4**, **8-40**, and column **79** last.

**Keyword:**   text handling

**See Also:**   awk, cut, grep, sed

### fmlcut -f8 ~/data/times.dat

ALL    SVR4    POWER

The **-f** option followed by a field number extracts the column of data associated with the field. By default, **fmlcut** expects the Tab character to separate fields. If you tried the command in the example on a file that used spaces as separators, **fmlcut** would return no information.

**Keyword:**   text handling

**See Also:**   awk, cut, grep, sed

### fmlexpr $DISPLAY : .*

ALL    SVR4    POWER

This command outputs the number of characters stored in the **$DISPLAY** variable.

**Keyword:** math
**See Also:** awk, expr, bc, dc

## fmlexpr ´9 + 8´

ALL SVR4 END POWER

Like the **expr** command, **fmlexpr** is primarily a shell script tool, but it can be used from the command line for quick calculations. In this example, the result would, of course, be **17**.
**Keyword:** math
**See Also:** awk, expr, bc, dc

## fmlexpr ´9 - 1´

ALL SVR4 POWER

This command subtracts **1** from **9**, outputting a result of **8**.
**Keyword:** math
**See Also:** awk, expr, bc, dc

## fmlexpr //$HZ : .*/\(.*\)

ALL SVR4 POWER

This command doubles the value of the variable **HZ**.
**Keyword:** math
**See Also:** awk, expr, bc, dc

## fmlexpr $HZ \* 2 | set -l HZ`

ALL SVR4 POWER

This command doubles the value of the variable **HZ**.
**Keyword:** math
**See Also:** awk, expr, bc, dc

## fmlgrep ´battleships´ warships.txt

ALL SVR4 POWER

This command finds all the lines in the **warships.txt** file with **battleships** in them, and outputs them.
**Keyword:** text display, text search
**See Also:** awk, egrep, fgrep, grep, gres, sed

## fmlgrep -b ´See Also:´ book.txt

ALL SVR4 POWER

This command puts a block number at the beginning of every line that has **See Also:** in it, in the **book.txt** file.
**Keyword:** text display, text search
**See Also:** awk, egrep, fgrep, grep, gres, sed

| | | |
|---|---|---|
| ALL | SVR4 | POWER |

## fmlgrep -b ´See Also:´ book.txt | awk ´{s+=$1} END {print "blocks=", s}´

This command tallies the number of blocks use by **See Also:** in the **book.txt** file, and outputs the result.

**Keyword:**   text display, text search

**See Also:**   awk, egrep, fgrep, grep, gres, sed

| | | |
|---|---|---|
| ALL | SVR4 | POWER |

## fmlgrep -c ´dog and cat´ pets.txt

This command outputs the number of lines in the **pets.txt** file that have **dog and cat** in them.

**Keyword:**   text display, text search

**See Also:**   awk, egrep, fgrep, grep, gres, sed

| | | |
|---|---|---|
| ALL | SVR4 | POWER |

## fmlgrep -i ´mcpherson´ names.txt

This command searches for all the lines in the **names.txt** file containing **mcpherson**. The argument **-i** tells **fmlgrep** to ignore the case of the letters as it conducts the search.

**Keyword:**   text display, text search

**See Also:**   awk, egrep, fgrep, grep, gres, sed

| | | |
|---|---|---|
| ALL | SVR4 | POWER |

## fmlgrep -i -n ´mcpherson´ names.txt

This command searches **names.txt** for **mcpherson**. It outputs the line number of each line that contains **mcpherson**, then it outputs the line of text itself.

**Keyword:**   text display, text search

**See Also:**   awk, egrep, fgrep, grep, gres, sed

| | | |
|---|---|---|
| ALL | SVR4 | POWER |

## fmlgrep -l ´Strategies´ *

This command searches all the files in the current directory for the word **Strategies**, and outputs a list of their names.

**Keyword:**   text display, text search

**See Also:**   awk, egrep, fgrep, grep, gres, sed

| | | |
|---|---|---|
| ALL | SVR4 | POWER |

## fmlgrep -s -l ´Strategies´ *

This command searches all the files in the current directory for the word **Strategies**, and outputs a list of their names. The **-s** argument tells **fmlgrep** not to display error messages. This is useful if you do not have read permission for all the files in the directory.

**Keyword:**    text display, text search
**See Also:**    awk, egrep, fgrep, grep, gres, sed

## fmlgrep -v -i ´mcpherson´ names.txt
This command outputs all the lines in the **names.txt** file that do not have **mcpherson** in them.
**Keyword:**    text display, text search
**See Also:**    awk, egrep, fgrep, grep, gres, sed

## fmli -i init.biz Menu.start
This command starts the Form and Menu Language Interpreter and opens the **Text.fml** frame file. It uses **init.biz** as the initialization file.
**Keyword:**    user interface
**See Also:**    fmlcut, fmlexpr, fmlgrep

## fmli Text.start
This command starts the Form and Menu Language Interpreter and opens the **Text.fml** frame file. After this has been invoked, you can use the commands **fmlcut**, **fmlexpr**, and **fmlgrep**, listed above.
**Keyword:**    user interface
**See Also:**    fmlcut, fmlexpr, fmlgrep

## fmt -80 document.txt > doc80col.txt
This command is the same as **fmt -w 80 document.txt > doc80col.txt**, except that it works for BSD UNIX, as opposed to SVR4. This command takes the **document.txt** file and formats the text to be 80 columns; the output is then written to a new file called **doc80col.txt**.
**Keyword:**    text handling
**See Also:**    awk, pr, sed

## fmt -c -w 80 document.txt > doc80col.txt
This command, with the argument **-c**, formats **document.txt** to have 80 columns of text, but also Crown margins. This is used to preserve the indentation of the first two lines of a paragraph. It then matches the left margin of each following line of the paragraph to the second line.
**Keyword:**    text handling
**See Also:**    awk, pr, sed

ALL   SVR4   END
SCRIPT

## fmt -w 80 -s myprog.c >> report.txt

This command makes each line of code in the **myprog.c** file 80 characters, if they are greater than 80. If the lines have fewer than 80 characters, it leaves them alone. After the formatting is complete, **fmt** appends the formatted text to the end of the **report.txt** file.

**Keyword:**   text handling

**See Also:**   awk, pr, sed

ALL   SVR4   END
SCRIPT

## fmt -w 80 document.txt > doc80col.txt

This command takes the **document.txt** file and formats the text to be 80 columns. The output is then written to a new file called **doc80col.txt**.

**Keyword:**   text handling

**See Also:**   awk, pr, sed

ALL   SVR4   SYSADM

## fmtmsg -c hard -u opsys,nrecov,print,console -l rootuser -s halt -t testmessage -a "reboot system" "system crash"

This command sends a message to either **stderr**, the system console, or both. The **-c** argument is used for specifying what caused the message to be sent. The **-u** argument gives more specific details as to the condition of the problem. The **-l** argument is used to tell the message receiver where the message came from. The **-s** argument specifies how severe the problem is. The **-t** option is used to specify an identifier for the message. The **-a** argument to **fmtmsg** is used to tell what action should be taken to correct the problem. The final field is used for a string to explain in better detail the exact problem.

**Keyword:**   system information

**See Also:**   ps

ALL   ALL   POWER

## fold -65 book.txt > book65.txt

This command breaks all lines in the **book.txt** file that are more than 65 characters long. It will write the output to a file called **book65.txt**, and all the lines in that file will be fewer than or equal to 65 characters long.

**Keyword:**   text handling

**See Also:**   cut, paste, expand, unexpand

### foreach file ( *.txt ) mv $file old/ end

ALL ALL SCRIPT

This short C-shell script moves all the text files in the current directory to the subdirectory **old**. Note that the **end** construct must appear on a line by itself.

**Keyword:** programming

**See Also:** mv, end

### FPATH

KSH ALL SCRIPT

This environment variable specifies search paths for function definitions. These are searched after the PATH list.

**Keyword:** user environment

**See Also:** PATH

### frec -f please.recover /dev/rmt/ctape1

ALL SVR4 SYSADM

This command retrieves all the files that are specified in the **please.recover** file from the tape **/dev/rmt/ctape1**. The **please.recover** file must be in the format:

```
12345:book1.txt
7890:book2.txt
1234:recovered
```

where the numbers are the file i_numbers and the text is the name of the recovered file.

**Keyword:** backup and restore

**See Also:** backup, cp, cpio, dd, dump, mount, restore, smit, sysadm, sysadmsh, tar, umount

### frec -p /u1/perkie/book /dev/rmt/ctape0 12345:book1.txt 7890:book2.txt 4567:/demo/alans/xshell/.Xdefaults

ALL SVR4 SYSADM

This command recovers the files with i_numbers **12345**, **7890**, and **4567**, and it puts them in files called **/u1/perkie/book/book1.txt**, **/u1/perkie/book/book2.txt**, and **/demo/alans/xshell/.Xdefaults**, respectively. The files are retrieved from the tape **/dev/rmt/ctape0**.

**Keyword:** backup and restore

**See Also:** backup, cp, cpio, dd, dump, mount, restore, smit, sysadm, sysadmsh, tar, umount

### frec /dev/rmt/ctape0 1234:recovered

ALL   SVR4   SYSADM

This command recovers a file from a backup tape in
**/dev/rmt/ctape0**. The i_number of the file is **1234**, and the filename **recovered** is restored.

**Keyword:**   backup and restore

**See Also:**   backup, cp, cpio, dd, dump, mount, restore, smit,
sysadm, sysadmsh, tar, umount

### fsck -b 32 /dev/rz1c

ALL   ALL   SYSADM

This command uses block number **32** as the super block for the
filesystem.

**Keyword:**   devices, filesystem

**See Also:**   newfs, diskadd, mkdev, sysadmsh, sysadmin

### fsck -c /dev/rz1c

ALL   ALL   SYSADM

This is a toggle switch between new and old filesystems, and will
switch **/dev/rz1c** to whichever system it currently is not.

**Keyword:**   devices, filesystem

**See Also:**   newfs, diskadd, mkdev, sysadmsh, sysadmin

### fsck -F ufs

ALL   ALL   ALL

This command specifies the **ufs -FSType** filesystem on SVR4.

**Keyword:**   devices, filesystems

**See Also:**   newfs, diskadd, mkdev, sysadmsh, sysadmin

### fsck -l 5

ALL   ALL   SYSADM

This command limits the number of parallel checks of filesystems
to five; otherwise, it is the same as **fsck** with no options.

**Keyword:**   devices, filesystem

**See Also:**   newfs, diskadd, mkdev, sysadmsh, sysadmin

### fsck -n /dev/rz1c

ALL   ALL   SYSADM

This is the same as **fsck** with no options, except that it answers
**no** to any prompts, and doesn't write to the **lost+found** file in the
filesystem. This is the default if you don't have write permission
on the filesystem.

**Keyword:**   devices, filesystem

**See Also:**   newfs, diskadd, mkdev, sysadmsh, sysadmin

### fsck -o /dev/rz1c

ALL   ALL   SYSADM

This command unconditionally checks the filesystem even if the filesystem's clean byte is set.

**Keyword:**   devices, filesystem

**See Also:**   newfs, diskadd, mkdev, sysadmsh, sysadmin

### fsck -p /dev/rz1c

ALL   ALL   SYSADM

This command noninteractively corrects inconsistencies on the **/dev/rz1c** filesystem.

**Keyword:**   devices, filesystem

**See Also:**   newfs, diskadd, mkdev, sysadmsh, sysadmin

### fsck -y /dev/rz1c

ALL   ALL   SYSADM

This command is the same as **fsck -n** except that it answers **yes** instead of **no**.

**Keyword:**   devices, filesystem

**See Also:**   newfs, diskadd, mkdev, sysadmsh, sysadmin

### fsck /dev/rz1c

ALL   ALL   SYSADM

This example of the **fsck** command interactively checks the **/dev/rz1c** filesystem for blocks claimed by more than one inode or the free list; blocks claimed by an inode outside the range of the filesystem; incorrect link counts; size checks: directory size not of proper format, partially truncated file, bad inode format; blocks not accounted for anywhere; directory checks, super block checks, bad free block format, and total free block and/or free inode count incorrect; unreferenced inodes, link counts in inodes that are too large, missing blocks in the free map, blocks in the free map that are also in files, and wrong counts in the super block.

**Keyword:**   devices, filesystem

**See Also:**   newfs, diskadd, mkdev, sysadmsh, sysadmin

### fstype -v /dev/rdsk/c0t3d0s0

ALL   SVR4   SYSADM

This command determines the filesystem type of the unmounted filesystem **/dev/rdsk/c0t3d0s0**. The **-v** option to **fstype** causes the command to output more detailed information than it does by default.

**Keyword:**   devices, filesystem

**See Also:**   diskadd, fsck, mkdev, newfs, sysadmin, sysadmsh

## fstype /dev/rdsk/c0t3d0s0

ALL   SVR4   SYSADM

This command determines the filesystem type of the specified unmounted filesystem.

**Keyword:**   devices, filesystem

**See Also:**   diskadd, fsck, mkdev, newfs, sysadmin, sysadmsh

## ftp -i newl.com

ALL   ALL   ALL

The **-i** option to **ftp** disables prompts, such as those that appear when you perform a wildcard send (**mput**) or receive (**mget**) operation.

**Keyword:**   Internet, networking

**Files:**   $HOME/.netrc

**See Also:**   hostid, hostname, ping, finger, rcp, rlogin, telnet, rcmd (SCO), rsh, rwho, xhost

## ftp digital2

ALL   ALL   ALL

This command initiates an **ftp** (file transfer protocol) session with a system named **digital2**. Once the network connection is made, a login prompt is displayed. Here is an example for a username **billw**:

```
ftp digital2
Connected to digital2.
220 digital2 FTP server (OSF Version 5.60) ready.
Name (digital2:billw):
331 Password required for billw.
Password:
230 User billw logged in.
Remote system type is UNIX.
Using binary mode to transfer files.
ftp> cd /usr/projects
250 CWD command successful.
ftp> send project8.txt
226 ASCII Transfer Complete
ftp> quit
221 Goodbye
```

In all, there are five prompts in this example. The first two are for the username and password. If the login defaults to the user that you want, just press Return. Next, supply the password, which is not echoed to the screen; then, perform **ftp** commands. In the example, the **cd** command is used to change to the target directory. The **send** command is then used to transfer a file. Finally, the **quit** command exits the **ftp** session.

**Keyword:**   Internet, networking

**Files:** $HOME/.netrc

**See Also:** rcp, rlogin, telnet

## ftp>

This is the standard **ftp** prompt. At the prompt, you can enter commands recognized by **ftp**. These commands do not work at the UNIX prompt. The following entries provide a well-rounded sampler.

**Keyword:** Internet, modem communications, networking

**Files:** $HOME/.netrc

**See Also:** rcp, rlogin, telnet

## ftp> binary

The **binary** command tells **ftp** to process all subsequent transfers as **binary** transfers. On UNIX systems, **binary** is usually set by default. On PCs running **ftp** software, this may not be the case.

**Keyword:** Internet, modem communications, networking

**Files:** $HOME/.netrc

**See Also:** rcp, rlogin, telnet

## ftp> cd /usr/info

The **cd** command inside **ftp** lets you change directories that reside on the remote system.

**Keyword:** Internet, modem communications, networking

**Files:** $HOME/.netrc

**See Also:** rcp, rlogin, telnet

## ftp> cdup

This command changes directories on the remote system to the parent directory of the current directory.

**Keyword:** Internet, modem communications, networking

**Files:** $HOME/.netrc

**See Also:** rcp, rlogin, telnet

## ftp> close

The **close** command inside **ftp** exits the remote system, but does not exit the **ftp** software. You can use this command if you want to initiate a subsequent remote session by using the **open** command.

# ftp

**Keyword:**     Internet, modem communications, networking
**Files:**         $HOME/.netrc
**See Also:**   rcp, rlogin, telnet

## ftp> delete oldstuff.txt

ALL   ALL   ALL

The **delete** command inside **ftp** lets you remove a file on the remote system. This is handy if you need to clean up your leftovers.

**Keyword:**     Internet, modem communications, networking
**Files:**         $HOME/.netrc
**See Also:**   rcp, rlogin, telnet

## ftp> get sales.dat

ALL   ALL   ALL

Using the **get** command at the **ftp>** prompt enables you to download a file from the remote system to the local system.

**Keyword:**     Internet, modem communications, networking
**Files:**         $HOME/.netrc
**See Also:**   rcp, rlogin, telnet

## ftp> lcd /wp50/docs

ALL   ALL   ALL

The **lcd** command inside **ftp** lets you change directories that reside on the local system. With a directory name like **/wp50/docs**, you know the local system is DOS-based.

**Keyword:**     Internet, modem communications, networking
**Files:**         $HOME/.netrc
**See Also:**   rcp, rlogin, telnet

## ftp> ls

ALL   ALL   ALL

The **ls** command inside **ftp** displays the contents of the remote directory. (On some systems, the **dir** command does the same thing.)

**Keyword:**     Internet, modem communications, networking
**Files:**         $HOME/.netrc
**See Also:**   rcp, rlogin, telnet

## ftp> ls remote.files

ALL   ALL   ALL

By specifying a filename as an argument to **ls** inside **ftp**, you get a file containing the listing of the directory on the remote system. The listing file is automatically transferred to the local system.

**Keyword:**   Internet, modem communications, networking

**Files:**       $HOME/.netrc

**See Also:**   rcp, rlogin, telnet

### ftp> mget *.doc

**ALL   ALL   ALL**

The **mget** command lets you obtain multiple files from the remote system with one command. Note that the **-g** command line option to **ftp** disables this feature.

**Keyword:**   Internet, modem communications, networking

**Files:**       $HOME/.netrc

**See Also:**   rcp, rlogin, telnet

### ftp> mput *.doc

**ALL   ALL   ALL**

The **mput** command lets you send multiple files to the remote system with one command. Note that the **-g** command line option to **ftp** disables this feature.

**Keyword:**   Internet, modem communications, networking

**Files:**       $HOME/.netrc

**See Also:**   rcp, rlogin, telnet

### ftp> open newl

**ALL   ALL   ALL**

If you are already inside the **ftp** program, the **open** command lets you initiate a connection. Presumably, you would use this after leaving a system with the **close** command.

**Keyword:**   Internet, modem communications, networking

**Files:**       $HOME/.netrc

**See Also:**   rcp, rlogin, telnet

### ftp> pwd

**ALL   ALL   ALL**

If you don't know the name of the current directory, the **pwd** command inside **ftp** tells you—just like the UNIX **pwd** command.

**Keyword:**   Internet, modem communications, networking

**Files:**       $HOME/.netrc

**See Also:**   rcp, rlogin, telnet

| | | |
|---|---|---|
| ALL | ALL | ALL |

## ftp> quit

The **quit** command exits the **ftp** software. Alternatively, if you do not want to leave **ftp**, but do want to exit a session with a remote system, you can use the **close** command. Note, too, that on most implementations of **ftp**, the **bye** command does the same thing as **quit**.

**Keyword:**  Internet, modem communications, networking
**Files:**  $HOME/.netrc
**See Also:**  rcp, rlogin, telnet

| | | |
|---|---|---|
| ALL | ALL | ALL |

## ftp> send report.doc

Using the **send** command at the **ftp>** prompt enables you to transfer a file from the local system to the remote system.

**Keyword:**  Internet, modem communications, networking
**Files:**  $HOME/.netrc
**See Also:**  rcp, rlogin, telnet

| | | |
|---|---|---|
| ALL | ALL | ALL |

## ftp> size

The **size** command inside **ftp** returns the size of a remote file. This is a handy command if you're cramped for space on the local system.

**Keyword:**  Internet, modem communications, networking
**Files:**  $HOME/.netrc
**See Also:**  rcp, rlogin, telnet

| | | |
|---|---|---|
| ALL | SVR4 | POWER SYSADM |

## fuser -c /u1

The **-c** argument to **fuser** is designed to work with mount points. In this example, all processes that are accessing anything in the **/u1** filesystem will have their process IDs displayed.

**Keyword:**  filesystem, networking
**See Also:**  chroot, kill, ps, mount, umount

| | | |
|---|---|---|
| ALL | SVR4 | POWER SYSADM |

## fuser -f /text.doc

This is the opposite of **fuser -c**, only the processes that are working with the named file, and not the filesystem, have their process IDs displayed.

**Keyword:**  job control, system information
**See Also:**  chroot, kill, ps, w, who

### fuser -k /dev/dsk/1s*

ALL   SVR4   POWER SYSADM

This command is similar to **fuser -kc /cdrom** in that it lets you run **umount** to unmount a disk, but in this case, it is a diskette that you are accessing directly from the device file, rather than the mount point.

**Keyword:**   devices, filesystem

**Files:**         /stand/unix

**See Also:**    mount, umount, chroot, kill, ps

### fuser -kc /cdrom

ALL   SVR4   POWER SYSADM

This is a useful command if you are trying to **umount** a CD-ROM disk, and you keep getting a device busy error. This will kill all the processes accessing the CD-ROM and allow you to then **umount** the disk.

**Keyword:**   devices, filesystem

**Files:**         /stand/unix

**See Also:**    mount, umount, chroot, kill, ps

### fuser -kc /cdrom -u /etc/passwd

ALL   SVR4   POWER SYSADM

This command kills all the processes accessing the CD-ROM and shows you who and what is accessing your **/etc/passwd** file.

**Keyword:**   job control, system information, user environment

**Files:**         /stand/unix

**See Also:**    mount, umount, chroot, kill, ps

### fuser -ku /etc/passwd

ALL   SVR4   POWER SYSADM

After you find someone running **crack** or **cracker** on your **/etc/passwd** file, you can use this command to stop them. It kills all the processes that are accessing the **/etc/passwd** file, and it displays those process IDs and the username of the person who was running them.

**Keyword:**   job control, security, system information

**Files:**         /stand/unix

**See Also:**    chroot, kill, ps, w, who

### fuser -u /etc/passwd

ALL   SVR4   POWER SYSADM

This is an excellent command for a system administrator to run frequently. It displays the process IDs of all processes that have the **/etc/passwd** file open. After the process IDs are displayed, the username of the person who is running the processes is also displayed. This shows you if someone is running **crack** or **cracker** on your **/etc/passwd** file and trying to break into your system.

**Keyword:**    job control, security, system information

**Files:**        /stand/unix

**See Also:**    chroot, kill, ps, w, who

### fuser book.txt

In this example, the process ID of **vi** is output, because **vi** has **book.txt** open. This command with no arguments outputs the process ID of programs that are accessing the file that is specified after **fuser**.

**Keyword:**    job control

**See Also:**    chroot, kill, ps, w, who

### fwtmp -ic < temp.record > /var/adm/wtmp

This command converts an ASCII record located in the **temp.record** file and outputs a binary accounting file called **/var/adm/wtmp**.

**Keyword:**    system information

**Files:**        /var/adm/wtmp

**See Also:**    acct

### fwtmp < /var/adm/wtmp > temp.record

This command takes the binary accounting record **/var/adm/wtmp** and converts it to an ASCII file called **temp.record** located in the current directory. The ASCII format allows you to fix bad records.

**Keyword:**    system information

**Files:**        /var/adm/wtmp

**See Also:**    acct

### gawk

The **gawk** command is from the Free Software Foundation and available as a standard command on some UNIX systems. The command adheres to the POSIX 1003.2 definition for the AWK language, which is based on the book titled *The AWK Programming Language* by Aho, Kernighan, and Weinberger, as well as

ALL    SVR4    POWER
SYSADM

ALL    SVR4    SYSADM

ALL    SVR4    SYSADM

ALL    FSF    POWER

additional features defined in SVR4. For examples, refer to the following examples and the examples for **awk**.

**Keyword:** text handling

**See Also:** awk, grep, nawk, sed

### gawk -F: ´{print $1}´ /etc/group

ALL  FSF  POWER

This command outputs a list of all the user groups on the system. The **-F** option specifies the colon character as the field delimiter.

**Keyword:** system information

**See Also:** awk, nawk

### getopt

ALL  ALL  SCRIPT

The traditional **getopt** command was superceded with the release of SVR4. On strict BSD systems, **getopt** is still used. It is also still supported on SVR4 systems, but the **intro(1)** section of the SVR4 documentation strongly suggests that you not use it. Even so, you will encounter it in old shell scripts, so an understanding of it will help you convert routines to the new **getopts** format. The basic difference between the two commands is that **getopt** requires the use of the **set** command and the **$\*** operator to interpret command line arguments. A concise **getopt** routine looks like this:

```
set -- opt=$1; OPTARG=$2 `getopt abc: $*`
while i in $*
do
  case $opt in
    a) size=$opt ;;
    b) color=$opt ;;
    c) style=$OPTARG
    --) shift; break ;;
  esac
done
```

The -- option indicates the end of command line arguments. If you don't include it in the **set** statement, **getopt** generates it automatically.

**Keyword:** programming

**See Also:** getopts

### getopts abc: x

SH
KSH  ALL  SCRIPT

The **getops** command is part of SVR4's attempt to enforce a consistent command line syntax. With **getopts**, which replaces the earlier **getopt** command, you can parse command options—and their

**179**

options, if necessary—in an easy-to-read format. A **while** loop is usually used:

```
while getopts abc: x
do
  case $opt in
    a) size=$opt ;;
    b) color=$opt ;;
    c) style=$OPTARG
    \?) echo $USAGE; exit 2 ;;
  esac
done
shift `expr $OPTIND - 1`
```

In essence, **getopts** sets variables as specified on the command line. For option **c**, an additional argument is required. This is stored by **getopts** in the shell variable **$OPTARG**. The number of total arguments is stored in **$OPTIND**, which is reset at the end of the routine.

**Keyword:**    programming

**See Also:**    getopt

## glob

SH    MKS    POWER

The **glob** program is an MKS-only facility that allows MKS commands to parse shell wildcard characters in keeping with UNIX shells. The full set of wildcards, or metacharacters, are supported. If you use the Korn shell under MKS, the shell obviates the need for **glob**.

**Keyword:**    file handling

**See Also:**    echo, ls

## glob `ls -1`

CSH    ALL    POWER

In the C shell, the built-in **glob** command acts somewhat like **echo**. It is designed to process a list of strings and delimit them only with a null character.

**Keyword:**    programming

**See Also:**    echo, ls

## grep "See Also:" *.txt | wc -l

ALL    ALL    SCRIPT
              POWER

This command is another way that we counted the entries in *The UNIX and X Command Compendium*. When files increase in number, passing them through the **wc -l** command makes sense, because you get a single total.

**Keyword:**   text display, text handling

**See Also:**   awk, egrep, fgrep, find, fmlgrep, gres, sed

### grep "[0-9a-z].*@[a-z]" mbox

ALL   ALL   SCRIPT POWER

This command combines number and character ranges with square brackets. The full regular expression matches email addresses that use the domain format. The metacharacter expression following the domain "at" symbol, or @, does not contain a numeric range because it is highly unusual to see numbers on this side of the address.

**Keyword:**   text display, text handling

**See Also:**   awk, egrep, fgrep, find, fmlgrep, gres, sed

### grep "^12-11 " sales.rep returns.rep | cut -d: -f2-

ALL   ALL   SCRIPT POWER

This command extracts all lines from the two files that begin with **12-11** followed by a space. But more, it does away with an annoying charateristic of **grep** when you process multiple files—namely, it removes the filename from the display, thanks to the **cut** command. The - following the **f2** in **cut** does the trick. Without **cut**, a line of output looks like this:

```
sales.rep:12-11 Mighty Max 85
```

Using **cut**, a line of output looks like this:

```
12-11 Mighty Max 85
```

**Keyword:**   text display, text handling

**See Also:**   awk, egrep, fgrep, find, fmlgrep, gres, sed

### grep "^[a-z].*|" /etc/termcap | cut -d´|´ -f2

ALL   ALL   SCRIPT POWER SYSADM

Using **grep** and **cut** lets you manipulate data contained in various system files. In the example, **grep** extracts all lines from **/etc/termcap** that contain the abbreviated names of terminal definitions. Then **cut** reduces the lines to a single field, containing the most common abbreviation for terminals. An excerpt of the output looks like this:

```
vt320
vt330
vt340
vt400
xterm
```

**Keyword:**   text display, text handling

**See Also:**   awk, egrep, fgrep, find, fmlgrep, gres, sed

### grep ´W.*House´ houses.txt

| | | |
|---|---|---|
| ALL | ALL | ALL |

This is yet another way to reel in **White House**. More important is that it requires the .* sequence to form a true wildcard match character. The * alone is not enough, as it is in the shell. The * is defined as being able to match any number of subsequent instances of the preceding character. Thus, because the . character matches any character (just like **?** in the shell), the * also matches any character, any number of times, through the **H** in **House**.

**Keyword:**   text display, text handling

**See Also:**   awk, egrep, fgrep, find, fmlgrep, gres, sed

### grep ´White House$´ houses.txt

| | | |
|---|---|---|
| ALL | ALL | ALL |

This command matches **White House** when it occurs at the end of a line. The **$** is thus the obverse of **^**. The dollar sign, used this way, must be in single quotes or not quoted at all. If you use **$** with a string that requires double quotation marks—such as a string that contains a shell variable—place the **$** outside the quotes, with no spaces between it and the rest of the search expression. To reference a literal **$**, you must escape it with a backslash.

**Keyword:**   text display, text handling

**See Also:**   awk, egrep, fgrep, find, fmlgrep, gres, sed

### grep ´White House´ houses.txt

| | | |
|---|---|---|
| ALL | ALL | ALL |

In this command, there are quotation marks around the search expression. These are necessary when the search expression includes whitespace, special characters, and variables in shell scripts.

**Keyword:**   text display, text handling

**See Also:**   awk, egrep, fgrep, find, fmlgrep, gres, sed

### grep ´[$*!i\^#+-]´ file.lst

| | | |
|---|---|---|
| ALL | ALL | SCRIPT POWER |

Brackets can be quite powerful. Here you can extract any line containing one of the special characters in the regular expression. The **^** character has to be escaped with a backslash because of its special meaning in the context of **grep**.

**Keyword:**   text display, text handling

**See Also:**   awk, egrep, fgrep, find, fmlgrep, gres, sed

ALL ALL SCRIPT POWER

## grep ´[23]\.[1-5]´ report.2 report.3

Depending on how fast and well you type, **grep** can be a real time-saver when you need to extract information from multiple documents. In the example, the use of brackets defines a search expression that will match sections 2.1 through 2.5 and 3.1 through 3.5 in the two files. Also note that **grep** can accept multiple input files and wildcard file patterns.

**Keyword:**  text display, text handling

**See Also:**  awk, egrep, fgrep, find, fmlgrep, gres, sed

ALL ALL ALL

## grep ´[Ww]hite [Hh]ouse´ houses.txt

Just in case one of the junior historians who work on **houses.txt** doesn't know to capitalize **White House**, this command compensates. By using brackets to list permissible matches, you can build some intelligence into your **grep** search expressions (although **egrep** is much more flexible with these kinds of searches).

**Keyword:**  text display, text handling

**See Also:**  awk, egrep, fgrep, find, fmlgrep, gres, sed

ALL OSF ALL

## grep ´[[:digit:][:lower:]].*@[[:lower:]]´ mbox

OSF expedites the matching process with character classes. Your choices are: alpha, upper, lower, digit, alnum, xdigit, space, print, punct, graph, and cntrl.

**Keyword:**  text display, text handling

**See Also:**  awk, egrep, fgrep, find, fmlgrep, gres, sed

ALL OSF SCRIPT POWER

## grep ´^#´ bigscript > bigscript.txt

This command is a handy way of extracting comments from script files. The example makes one assumption: that you regularly place the # comment character at the beginning of the line.

**Keyword:**  text display, text handling

**See Also:**  awk, egrep, fgrep, find, fmlgrep, gres, sed

ALL ALL ALL

## grep ´^..... .....´ houses.txt

To finish up **White House**, how about the most imprecise way to make a match—using the dot character only. Here, two series of five dots with a space between will match any two five-letter words, such as **White House** or **Hyatt hotel**. The dot character can be very useful, however, especially when used with an asterisk.

| | | |
|---|---|---|
| | | |

**Keyword:** text display, text handling
**See Also:** awk, egrep, fgrep, find, fmlgrep, gres, sed

### grep ´^White House´ houses.txt

ALL ALL ALL

This command matches only instances of **White House** that occur at the beginning of a line. That is the function of the ^ symbol, which is a common regular expression device for anchoring a search to the beginning of a line.

**Keyword:** text display, text handling
**See Also:** awk, egrep, fgrep, find, fmlgrep, gres, sed

### grep ´^[^.]´ file.lst

ALL ALL POWER

Instead of displaying all lines that begin with a dot, this command displays all lines that *don't* begin with a dot. And this is exactly what the caret (^) inside the brackets does. It tells **grep** to match anything but the following character(s) in the brackets. At times, you might find this more flexible than the **-h** option to **grep**. The **-h** option also displays all lines except those containing the search string.

**Keyword:** text display, text handling
**See Also:** awk, egrep, fgrep, find, fmlgrep, gres, sed

### grep ´^\.´ files.lst

ALL ALL POWER

This is an example of how to match the real dot character, or period. All you do is escape it, inside either single or double quotation marks. In order to issue the same command without quotation marks, you must escape it twice: **grep ^\\. files.lst**.

**Keyword:** text display, text handling
**See Also:** awk, egrep, fgrep, fmlgrep, gres, sed

### grep -c "See Also:" *.txt

ALL ALL ALL

This command is the method we used to count the number of entries in *The UNIX and X Command Compendium* during the course of the project. When used with a wildcard, as in the example, the output looks like this:

```
a.txt 125
b.txt 134
c.txt 150
```
...

**Keyword:** text display, text handling
**See Also:** awk, egrep, fgrep, find, fmlgrep, gres, sed

### grep -e -font .xinitrc

ALL ALL POWER

The **-e** option to **grep** lets you specify a search string that begins with a hyphen. Without the **-e** option, **grep** complains and exits the search if a hyphen occurs in the first position of the search string.

**Keyword:** text display, text handling
**See Also:** awk, egrep, fgrep, find, fmlgrep, gres, sed

### grep -i "dollar value" db | cut -d´ ´ -f3

ALL ALL SCRIPT POWER

This command uses **grep** as a front end to the **cut** command. The combination of **grep** and **cut** is often faster than **sed** alone.

**Keyword:** text display, text handling
**See Also:** awk, egrep, fgrep, find, fmlgrep, gres, sed

### grep -i "dollar value" db | sed ´s/dollar value: //p´

ALL ALL SCRIPT POWER

For large files, using **grep** as a front end to **sed** can speed up processing time. In the example, **grep** feeds all lines containing **dollar value** to **sed**. If a line looked like the following:

```
Dollar value: $1,000
```

the **sed** command from the entry would print:

```
$1,000
```

**Keyword:** text display, text handling
**See Also:** awk, egrep, fgrep, find, fmlgrep, gres, sed

### grep -i sales report.jul /dev/null

ALL ALL POWER

Normally, if you only use **grep** on one file, it does not print out the filename associated with matched lines. If you specify **/dev/null** as a second file, **grep** does print out the filename. No output or apparent delay results from using **/dev/null** in this way.

**Keyword:** text display, text handling
**See Also:** awk, egrep, fgrep, find, fmlgrep, gres, sed

### grep -i tuxedo `grep -il wedding $HOME/personal/*`

This command performs a double **grep**. Using command substitution, the first **grep** command receives filenames for all files that contain the word **wedding**, whether or not it is capitalized. The first **grep** then searches for **tuxedo** and prints the relevant lines. The example assumes that the **$HOME/personal** directory is not overloaded with files, so **grep** can handle the file list. Very large numbers of files can hang some versions of **grep**.

**Keyword:**    text display, text handling

**See Also:**    awk, egrep, fgrep, find, fmlgrep, gres, sed

### grep -il miscellaneous *.txt

This command searches for the word **miscellaneous** and, because of the **-i** option, matches it whether or not it is capitalized. What's different about this command is that it doesn't display the matching lines. Instead, because of the **-1** option, it prints the names of the files that contain matches.

**Keyword:**    text display, text handling

**See Also:**    awk, egrep, fgrep, find, fmlgrep, gres, sed

### grep -il wedding $HOME/personal/* | grep -i tuxedo

This command processes all lines that contain the word **wedding**. There is a big possibility that many instances of **tuxedo** would never be found using this method. On the other hand, the example is a useful command when you want to narrow output. You won't forget it (unless, that is, you use **egrep**, which can do the same thing in a single stroke).

**Keyword:**    text display, text handling

**See Also:**    awk, egrep, fgrep, find, fmlgrep, gres, sed

### grep -in sales report.1

The **-i** option tells **grep** not to distinguish between uppercase and lowercase letters. The **-n** option causes **grep** to display the line number of each match, as well as the line itself. Here is an example:

```
32:late in the month of July sales began to
45:soon after the big event, sales could be
```

**Keyword:**    text display, text handling

**See Also:**    awk, egrep, fgrep, find, fmlgrep, gres, sed

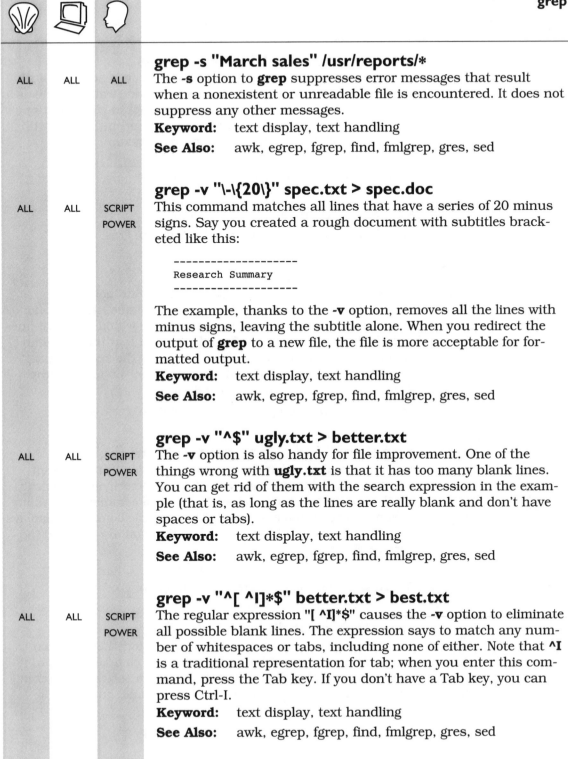

| | | |
|---|---|---|
| ALL | ALL | ALL |

### grep -s "March sales" /usr/reports/*

The **-s** option to **grep** suppresses error messages that result when a nonexistent or unreadable file is encountered. It does not suppress any other messages.

**Keyword:** text display, text handling

**See Also:** awk, egrep, fgrep, find, fmlgrep, gres, sed

| | | |
|---|---|---|
| ALL | ALL | SCRIPT POWER |

### grep -v "\-\{20\}" spec.txt > spec.doc

This command matches all lines that have a series of 20 minus signs. Say you created a rough document with subtitles bracketed like this:

```
--------------------
Research Summary
--------------------
```

The example, thanks to the **-v** option, removes all the lines with minus signs, leaving the subtitle alone. When you redirect the output of **grep** to a new file, the file is more acceptable for formatted output.

**Keyword:** text display, text handling

**See Also:** awk, egrep, fgrep, find, fmlgrep, gres, sed

| | | |
|---|---|---|
| ALL | ALL | SCRIPT POWER |

### grep -v "^$" ugly.txt > better.txt

The **-v** option is also handy for file improvement. One of the things wrong with **ugly.txt** is that it has too many blank lines. You can get rid of them with the search expression in the example (that is, as long as the lines are really blank and don't have spaces or tabs).

**Keyword:** text display, text handling

**See Also:** awk, egrep, fgrep, find, fmlgrep, gres, sed

| | | |
|---|---|---|
| ALL | ALL | SCRIPT POWER |

### grep -v "^[ ^I]*$" better.txt > best.txt

The regular expression "[ ^I]*$" causes the **-v** option to eliminate all possible blank lines. The expression says to match any number of whitespaces or tabs, including none of either. Note that ^I is a traditional representation for tab; when you enter this command, press the Tab key. If you don't have a Tab key, you can press Ctrl-I.

**Keyword:** text display, text handling

**See Also:** awk, egrep, fgrep, find, fmlgrep, gres, sed

### grep -v LUNCHTIME $HOME/.events

ALL   ALL   ALL

The **-v** option is like a command unto itself. Instead of displaying matched lines, it displays all the lines that don't match. This is a handy shell script mechanism to replace data in configuration files. After using **grep -v** on a file, you can append the file with replacement data by using **echo** and redirection:

```
grep -v LUNCHTIME $HOME/.events > /tmp/.events.$$
echo LUNCHTIME:12:30 >> /tmp/.events.$$
mv /tmp/.events $HOME/.events
```

**Keyword:**   text display, text handling

**See Also:**   awk, egrep, fgrep, find, fmlgrep, gres, sed

### grep -w "flash" news.txt

ALL   ALL   ALL

Sometimes you don't want to be bothered with incidental matches to a word you specify. On BSD systems, the **-w** option matches only full words. Thus, the example would not print lines with **flashing**, **flashes**, and **flashlight**. Note that the **-w** option performs the same function as surrounding the search string with **\<** and **\>**, which is available with most versions of **grep**.

**Keyword:**   text display, text handling

**See Also:**   awk, egrep, fgrep, find, fmlgrep, gres, sed

### grep Menu `find . -exec grep -ls Mwm {} \;`

ALL   ALL   POWER

This command searches for a string beginning in the current directory. By using **find**, instead of simply specifying a wildcard for files in the directory, you avoid the **grep** command's inability to handle large numbers of files. The example command displays all lines that contain **Menu** from files that contain **Mwm** in the current directory.

**Keyword:**   text display, text handling

**See Also:**   awk, egrep, fgrep, find, fmlgrep, gres, sed

### grep UNIX pubs.db | sort - dev.db

ALL   ALL   SCRIPT POWER

Another example of **grep** and **sort** working together, this command can be of day-to-day value. The **grep** command outputs lines containing **UNIX** and **sort**. It outputs a sorted list after letting you add text at the keyboard. Try this one. You'll like it.

**Keyword:**   text display, text handling

**See Also:**   awk, egrep, fgrep, find, fmlgrep, gres, sed

### grep UNIX.pubs db | cat - dev.db > UNIX.db

| ALL | ALL | SCRIPT POWER |

The shell - construct is responsible for the added dimension of this **grep** statement. With a relatively short command, **grep** and **cat** can be used to get a combined output which is ultimately redirected to the file **UNIX.db**.

**Keyword:** text display, text handling

**See Also:** awk, egrep, fgrep, find, fmlgrep, gres, sed

### grep White houses.txt

| ALL | ALL | ALL |

Here is the most basic form of **grep**. The example searches a file for **White** and displays all lines with a match. Presumably, the entry is looking for "White House," but this shotgun version of **grep** might find some unrelated instances of **White**.

**Keyword:** text display, text handling

**See Also:** awk, egrep, fgrep, find, fmlgrep, gres, sed

### grep ^415 phone.db | sort

| ALL | ALL | SCRIPT POWER |

This command illustrates one of the most common UNIX pipes. The output from **grep** results from **grep** scanning the file in order, from beginning to end. Therefore, the output is only sorted if it were in alphabetical order to start with. Piping the output through **sort** gives you alphabetical output.

**Keyword:** text display, text handling

**See Also:** awk, egrep, fgrep, find, fmlgrep, gres, sed

### gres September October report.txt > report.new

| ALL | ALL | ALL |

The **gres** command is an MKS-only utility that matches a pattern in a file and then replaces it. Note that you must redirect the output of the command. If you want more flexibility, **gres** can match a conditional string. For example, **gres 'Sept(ember)?' October** matches both **Sept** and **September** and replaces either with **October**.

**Keyword:** DOS, text display, text handling

**See Also:** egrep, fgrep

### groups alans

| ALL | ALL | ALL |

The **groups** command displays the group to which a user belongs. If the user is specified, as in the example, the command returns the group for that user. If no user is specified, the command returns the group for the user invoking the command. A user's group is specified in the **/etc/passwd** file.

**Keyword:**  user environment

**Files:**  /etc/group, /etc/passwd

**See Also:**  users, w, who

## halt

ALL  ALL  SYSADM

This command can be executed only by the superuser. It is used to stop the processor, and therefore should never be run while the system is in multiuser mode.

**Keyword:**  shutdown

**Files:**  /var/adm/wtmp (SVR4), /etc/syslog.conf (BSD)

**See Also:**  fastboot, fasthalt, init, reboot, shutdown

## halt -l

ALL  BSD  SYSADM

This command does not log the system shutdown in the files listed in **/etc/syslog.conf**.

**Keyword:**  shutdown

**Files:**  /etc/syslog.conf

**See Also:**  fastboot, fasthalt, init, reboot, shutdown

## halt -n

ALL  ALL  SYSADM

This command does not allow the disks to be synced before the processor is stopped.

**Keyword:**  shutdown

**Files:**  /var/adm/wtmp (SVR4), /etc/syslog.conf (BSD)

**See Also:**  fastboot, fasthalt, init, reboot, shutdown

## halt -q

ALL  ALL  SYSADM

This command stops the processor quickly. It does not log the shutdown, nor even attempt to kill all the processes, and it doesn't sync the disks.

**Keyword:**  shutdown

**Files:**  /var/adm/wtmp (SVR4), /etc/syslog.con (BSD)

**See Also:**  fastboot, fasthalt, init, reboot, shutdown

## halt -y

ALL  ALL  SYSADM

This command stops the processor, even if it is executed from a dial-up terminal.

**Keyword:**  shutdown

**Files:**    /var/adm/wtmp (SVR4), /etc/syslog.conf (BSD)

**See Also:**    fastboot, fasthalt, init, reboot, shutdown

## haltsys

ALL    SCO    SYSADM

The **haltsys** command flushes disk I/O, marks the filesystems as clean, and shuts down the system. You must be the root user to execute **haltsys**. A single prompt is presented after executing **haltsys**. If other users are working on the system, **haltsys** offers them no chance to save their work. Only the root user sees the confirmation prompt.

**Keyword:**    system shutdown

**See Also:**    init, reboot, shutdown

## haltsys -d

ALL    SCO    SYSADM

The **-d** option to **haltsys** bypasses the normal prompt. Executing **haltsys** this way provides no opportunity for anyone, including the root user, to prevent the system from being shut down. You must be the root user to execute **haltsys**.

**Keyword:**    system shutdown

**See Also:**    init, reboot, shutdown

## hardpaths

CSH    ALL    ALL

When this environment variable is set, the list of paths in the directory are translated to nonsymbolic pathnames.

**Keyword:**    user environment

**Files:**    $HOME/.cshrc

**See Also:**    ls

## hash

ALL    ALL    POWER
              SYSADM

The **hash** command is a Bourne shell built-in. It reports the search path associated with previously executed commands (as well as ones that might be running in the background). The output from **hash** displays *hits* (the number of times that the shell has previously run the command) and *cost* (a relative indicator of the system resources required to remember the path to the command). Here is some sample output:

```
hits   cost    command
0      1       /bin/find
```

**Keyword:**    system information

**Files:**     $HOME/.profile

**See Also:**    cd, ps

## hd -Ao dump.txt

ALL    SCO    POWER    SVR4

This command outputs the **dump.txt** ASCII file as octal codes for all the characters in the file.

**Keyword:**    text display

**See Also:**    cat, more, od, pg

## hd -s 10 -Ad dump.txt

ALL    SCO    POWER    SVR4

This command outputs the **dump.txt** ASCII file as decimal codes for all the characters in the file, except the first ten.

**Keyword:**    text display

**See Also:**    cat, more, od, pg

## hd dump.txt

ALL    SCO    POWER    SVR4

This command displays the **dump.txt** file in hexadecimal format. The default for **hd** is to output file offsets and bytes in hexadecimal and to print characters.

**Keyword:**    binary files

**See Also:**    cat, more, od, pg

## hdeadd

ALL    OSF    SYSADM

The **hdeadd** command prints the list of equipped disks on the system. Only the superuser can execute this command.

**Keyword:**    filesystem, system information

**See Also:**    diskadd, fsck, mkdev, newfs, sysadmsh, sysadmin

## hdeadd -a -B 12 43 52

ALL    OSF    SYSADM

This command adds an error to the hard disk error log for the physical disk block that is located on cylinder 12, track 43, and sector 52.

**Keyword:**    filesystem, system information

**See Also:**    diskadd, fsck, mkdev, newfs, sysadmsh, sysadmin

## hdeadd -a -t 03301135

ALL    OSF    SYSADM

This command enables the superuser to manually add an error report to the hard disk error log, specifying that the error happened on March 30, at 11:35 AM.

**Keyword:**    filesystem, system information

**See Also:**    diskadd, fsck, mkdev, newfs, sysadmsh, sysadmin


## hdeadd -d -D 8 9

ALL    SVR4    SYSADM

This command is used to manually delete an error report in the hard disk error log for the disk specified with **8** as its major device number and **9** as its minor device number.

**Keyword:**    filesystem, system information

**See Also:**    diskadd, fsck, mkdev, newfs, sysadmsh, sysadmin


## hdeadd -d -F 03010000 -T 04010000

ALL    OSF    SYSADM

This command deletes all error reports in the hard disk error log for the entire month of March.

**Keyword:**    filesystem, system information

**See Also:**    diskadd, fsck, mkdev, newfs, sysadmsh, sysadmin


## hdeadd -e -D 8 9

ALL    OSF    SYSADM

This command determines whether **8** and **9** specify the major and minor device numbers of a hard disk on the system.

**Keyword:**    filesystem, system information

**See Also:**    diskadd, fsck, mkdev, newfs, sysadmsh, sysadmin


## hdeadd -f commands.txt

ALL    OSF    SYSADM

This command runs the set of HDE manipulations that are specified in the **commands.txt** file. The format of the file should be one command per line of text.

**Keyword:**    filesystem, system information

**See Also:**    diskadd, fsck, mkdev, newfs, sysadmsh, sysadmin


## hdeadd -r -D 8 9 HDElog.txt

ALL    OSF    SYSADM

This command restores a log that was saved for the specified disk.

**Keyword:**    filesystem, system information

**See Also:**    diskadd, fsck, mkdev, newfs, sysadmsh, sysadmin


## hdeadd -s -D 8 9 HDElog.txt

ALL    OSF    SYSADM

This command saves the HDE log for the disk specified through the major device number **8** and the minor device number **9** to the **HDElog.txt** file.

**Keyword:** filesystem, system information
**See Also:** diskadd, fsck, mkdev, newfs, sysadmsh, sysadmin

## head -24 book.txt

| ALL | ALL | POWER |

This command displays the first 24 lines of the **book.txt** file.
**Keyword:** text handling
**See Also:** cat, less, more, pg, tail

## help

| ALL | SCO SVR4 | POWER |

The **help** command on SCO systems runs an interactive routine that prompts you for a command in the Source Control Control System (SCCS).
**Keyword:** help tools
**See Also:** apropos, catman, man, more, whatis, whereis, xman

## help

| ALL | BSD OSF | END |

This command outputs one page of information that might be useful for new users.
**Keyword:** documentation
**See Also:** man, nroff, troff, whatis

## histchars

| CSH | ALL | SCRIPT |

This is an environment variable containing two characters to replace ! and ^, respectively, in history substitution commands.
**Keyword:** user environment
**See Also:** history

## HISTFILE

| KSH | ALL | POWER |

This environment variable contains the name of the command history file. If this variable is not set, the Korn shell uses **$HOME/.sh_history**.
**Keyword:** user environment
**Files:** $HOME/.sh_history
**See Also:** HISTSIZE, ksh

### history

| | | |
|---|---|---|
| CSH | ALL | ALL |

This environment variable contains the number of command lines that are saved for review. When this variable is not set, only the last command is saved.

**Keyword:** user environment

**See Also:** history (command)

### history

| | | |
|---|---|---|
| CSH KSH | ALL | POWER |

Both the C and Korn shells support a built-in command called **history** that lists recent commands entered at the keyboard. In the C shell, you set the length of the recall list by setting **$history**. In the Korn shell, you set **$HISTSIZE**.

**Keyword:** user environment

**Files:** $HOME/.cshrc, $HOME/.kshrc

**See Also:** history (csh), HISTSIZE (ksh)

### history -h | grep ps > ps_history

| | | |
|---|---|---|
| KSH | ALL | POWER |

The **-h** option to **history** outputs commands in the history list without prepending a number. In the example, **grep** filters all **ps** commands to a file called **ps_history**.

**Keyword:** user environment

**Files:** $HOME/.cshrc, $HOME/.kshrc

**See Also:** history (csh), HISTSIZE (ksh)

### HISTSIZE

| | | |
|---|---|---|
| KSH | ALL | POWER |

This environment variable contains the number of past commands that are accessible.

**Keyword:** user environment

**See Also:** history

### HOME

| | | |
|---|---|---|
| SH KSH | ALL | SCRIPT |

This environment variable contains the user's default location (home directory) for the **cd** command. This directory is represented by ~ in file representation.

**Keyword:** user environment

**See Also:** cd, pwd

## home

| | | |
|---|---|---|
| CSH | ALL | ALL |

The C shell's **$home** environment variable specifies the user's default location (home directory) for the **cd** command. This directory is represented by ~ in file representation.

**Keyword:**    user environment

**Files:**    $HOME/.cshrc

**See Also:**    cd, cwd, pwd

## hostid

| | | |
|---|---|---|
| ALL | ALL | POWER SYSADM |

This command displays a unique hexadecimal number for the local host.

**Keyword:**    Internet, networking, system information

**See Also:**    ftp, hostid, hostname, ping, finger, rcp, rlogin, telnet, rcmd (SCO), rsh, rwho, xhost, uname

## hostid 16.123.208.18

| | | |
|---|---|---|
| ALL | ALL | SYSADM |

You can use **hostid** to set an Internet address, as in the example. The **hostid** command converts the Internet address to hexadecimal for system use. You must be the superuser to run this command.

**Keyword:**    Internet, networking, system information

**See Also:**    ftp, hostid, hostname, ping, finger, rcp, rlogin, telnet, rcmd (SCO), rsh, rwho, xhost, uname

## hostname

| | | |
|---|---|---|
| ALL | ALL | POWER |

The **hostname** command displays the name of the local host. Networks hoppers find it to be a useful command.

**Keyword:**    Internet, networking, system information

**See Also:**    ftp, hostid, hostname, ping, finger, rcp, rlogin, telnet, rcmd (SCO), rsh, rwho, xhost, uname

## hostname alexei

| | | |
|---|---|---|
| ALL | ALL | POWER |

If you are the superuser, you can change the system hostname by providing a name after the **hostname** command. In this example, the computer's new name is **alexei**.

**Keyword:**    Internet, networking, system information

**See Also:**    ftp, hostid, hostname, ping, finger, rcp, rlogin, telnet, rcmd (SCO), rsh, rwho, xhost, uname

### ico -faces

ALL   XWIN   ALL

This command runs the **ico** program, which is a simple graphics demo included with the X Window System. The **ico** object is a polygon that normally appears as wireframe. The **-faces** option in the example fills the object with the background color.

**Keyword:**   X graphics

**See Also:**   maze, puzzle, xeyes

### ico -faces -noedges -r &

ALL   XWIN   ALL

This command causes **ico** to display on the root window. The **-r** option is the root window switch. The **-noedges** option removes the wireframe outline and **faces** fills the object. When you want to stop the **ico** display on the root window, you must either restart the X server or use the **kill** command.

**Keyword:**   root window, X graphics

**See Also:**   kill, xset

### iconedit -Wp 50 50 -Ws 600 100 &

ALL   SunOS   POWER
       Solaris   SYSADM

The **iconedit** program is the Sun bitmap editor tailored to creating icons and cursors for use with the X Window System. You can invoke **iconedit** from the standard root window menu in the Sun OpenWindows environment, or you can execute it from the command line. In the example, the **-Wp** option specifies the display coordinates for **iconedit**, and the **-Ws** option displays the width and height, respectively. The **iconedit** program produces color XPM files, not monochrome X bitmap files.

**Keyword:**   X bitmaps

**See Also:**   bitmap

### iconv -f 88591 -t pc850 book.txt > book.pc

ALL   OSF   POWER

This command converts the **book.txt** file from ISO 8859/1 format (commonly known as Latin 1) to DOS-readable code. The new file is called **book.pc**.

**Keyword:**   DOS, text handling

**See Also:**   doscat

### id

ALL   ALL   ALL

The **id** command prints the user's login name, ID, and group ID. The command is available on both System V and BSD platforms.

If a user's real and effective IDs are not the same, the command prints both IDs. Typical output from **id** looks like this:

```
uid=0(root) gid=1(other)
```

**Keyword:**   user environment

**See Also:**   finger, users, w, who

### id

On systems using the MKS utilities, the **id** command acts slightly differently from its UNIX counterpart. In the MKS version, only the username is significant. A group ID of **0** is displayed, but MKS does not support the concept of groups. You must use the MKS **login** program for **id** to work properly.

**Keyword:**   user environment, DOS

**See Also:**   who

### id -a

The **-a** option to **id** is an SVR4 feature. With it, you can list all the groups to which you belong. Here is typical output for the **root** user:

```
uid=0(root) gid=1(other),0(root),2(bin),3(sys),4(adm),
6(mail),7(tty),8(lp),12(daemon),5(uucp)
```

**Keyword:**   id

**See Also:**   finger, users, w, who

### ident book1.txt book2.txt

This command outputs all the patterns from the **book1.txt** file that are the same as patterns in the **book2.txt** file.

**Keyword:**   text handling

**See Also:**   awk, grep, sed

### if $TERM == xterm then; : ; endif

This command is an example of an **if** statement in a C shell script. The C shell way of using **if** is markedly different from that of the Bourne and Korn shells. For one thing, brackets are not used to surround the test part of the statement (optional parentheses can be used, however). Second, the C shell uses **==** for an equality statement instead of a single **=** as in the Bourne and

| ALL | MKS | ALL |
| ALL | SVR4 | ALL |
| ALL | FSF | POWER |
| CSH | ALL | SCRIPT |

Korn shells. Third, a line return (or semicolon, as in the example) must follow **then**. Last, the C shell uses **endif** instead of **fi** to end an **if** statement.

**Keyword:**    programming

**See Also:**    switch, TERM

### if expr $DBPATH : ".*\/usr\/db\/bin" >/dev/null then : else PATH=${PATH}:${XPATH} fi

SH
KSH    ALL    SCRIPT

This **if** statement checks to see if a given environment variable has been placed in the system path. If not, the **if** statement adds the environment variable. Notice the colon operator. This is the "do nothing" operator, or no-op.

**Keyword:**    programming

**Files:**    /dev/null

**See Also:**    PATH, test

### if test -n "$Term"; then

SH
KSH    ALL    SCRIPT

This **if** command, combined with the **test** facility, determines whether the string is a null string. In the example, if the string is not null, the **if** statement is successful.

**Keyword:**    programming

**See Also:**    case, test

### if test -n "$Term"; then : ; fi

ALL    ALL    SCRIPT

This **if** command, combined with the **test** facility, determines whether the string contains text. If the string does contain text, the **if** statement is successful. The : in the example is the no-op symbol in the shell. Another way of testing for text in a string is with the following statement:

```
if test "$TERM"; then : ; fi
```

You could also write:

```
if [ "$TERM" ]; then : fi
```

The last example is the more traditional way to write an **if** statement. The brackets surrounding the test statement are equivalent to the **test** command. All the following **if** entries use brackets instead of **test**.

**Keyword:**    programming

**See Also:**    case, test

### if test -z "$Term"; then

SH KSH | ALL | SCRIPT

This **if** command, combined with the **test** facility, determines whether the string is empty. If the string contained is null, the **if** statement is successful.

**Keyword:**    programming

**See Also:**    case, test

### if [ ! "$DESKTOP" ]; then : ; fi

SH KSH | ALL | SCRIPT

Here's one command that has significance to all string tests in **if** statements. In many cases, if a variable is not defined, the **if** statement (or more precisely, the **test** command) does not know how to handle the variable. If the script were named **checkvars**, you might see an error message like this:

```
checkvars: test: argument expected
```

The solution is to place double quotes around the variable whenever you suspect the variable is not defined, or defined but equal to null. An environment variable would be equal to null if you ran **setenv** and it appeared similar to **DESKTOP=**.

**Keyword:**    programming

**See Also:**    case, setenv, test

### if [ "`wc -l logfile`" -le 1024 ]; then : ; fi

SH KSH | ALL | SCRIPT

The **-le** operator tests whether the value on the left-hand side is less than or equal to the value on the right-hand side of the **if** statement. In the example, **wc** feeds the line length of **logfile** to the **if** statement. A full routine might look like this:

```
if  [ "`wc -l logfile`" -le 1024 ]; then
    echo Logfile within range
else
    tail -100 logfile >> /tmp/lf.$$
    mv /tmp/lf.$$ logfile
fi
```

The additional set of quotes around the **wc** command is necessary because **wc** returns the filename as well as the line count. The double quotes cause **if** to ignore **logfile** in its evaluation. If you don't like the idea of an unnecessary string in the **if** evaluation, you can change the **wc** command to **cat logfile | wc -l**, which prints only the number of lines.

**Keyword:**    programming

**See Also:**    case, cat, tail, test, wc

### if [ $# -le 2  -a  -s "$1" ]; then : ; fi

SH
KSH

ALL

SCRIPT

This command combines file and numeric operators. The only way the **if** statement is successful is if the number of command line arguments equal **2** or fewer, and the file represented by **$1** exists.

**Keyword:**    programming

**See Also:**    case, test

### if [ $# = argnum ]; then : ; fi

SH
KSH

ALL

SCRIPT

In shell scripts, this command tests for the number of arguments supplied on the command line (or as a result of using the **set** command to fill the shell's argument space with internally specified variables). The **$#** construct, which holds the number of arguments (not the arguments themselves), is frequently used throughout shell scripts.

**Keyword:**    programming

**See Also:**    case, set, test

### if [ $? ]; then : ; fi

SH
KSH

ALL

SCRIPT

In shell scripts, this command tests for the successful completion of the previously executed command. Many UNIX commands return **0** when they complete successfully, and non-**0**, usually **1**, when they fail. Here is an example:

```
grep $word text.doc
if [ $? ]; then
    echo Word Found!
fi
```

**Keyword:**    programming

**See Also:**    case, echo, grep, test

### if [ $a = $d -a $b = $d -a $c = $d ]; then : ; fi

SH
KSH

ALL

SCRIPT

This is another way to use the **-a** operator. The **if** statement is successful only if **$a**, **$b**, and **$c** equal **$d**. There is no limit, within reason, to the number of **-a** tests that you can use in one **if** statement.

**Keyword:**    programming

**See Also:**    case, test

### if [ $a = $z -o \( $b = $z -a $c = $z \) ]; then : ; fi

SH
KSH

ALL

SCRIPT

This command demonstrates the grouping operators for testing in an **if** statement. In the example, the **if** statement is successful if **$a** equals **$z** or if **$b** equals **$z** and **$c** equals **$z**. Note that the parentheses must be escaped; otherwise, the shell complains and issues an error.

**Keyword:**   programming

**See Also:**   case, test

### if [ $DESKTOP ]; then : ; fi

SH KSH   ALL   SCRIPT

With **if**, you can test whether a variable is not null simply by putting the variable in the test brackets. This is a common technique of startup scripts to check whether some environment variables are defined.

**Keyword:**   programming

**See Also:**   case, test

### if [ $SHELL = csh -a $TERM = xterm -o "$DESKTOP" ]; then : ; fi

SH KSH   ALL   SCRIPT

This command combines the use of **-a** and **-o** operators. To be successful, **if** must find that either **$SHELL** equals **csh**, **$TERM** equals **xterm**, or **$DESKTOP** is non-null. Note that **-a** has precedence over **-o**.

**Keyword:**   programming

**See Also:**   case, SHELL, TERM, test

### if [ $SHELL = csh -a $TERM = xterm ]; then : ; fi

SH KSH   ALL   SCRIPT

The **-a** operator for **if** performs a logical AND operation. The statement is only successful if both **$SHELL** equals **csh** and **$TERM** equals **xterm**. Note that you must repeat the initial test variable on the second side of the AND statement.

**Keyword:**   programming

**See Also:**   case, TERM, test, SHELL

### if [ $SHELL = csh -o $SHELL = ksh ]; then : ; fi

SH KSH   ALL   SCRIPT

The **-o** operator performs a logical OR operation. In the example, the **if** statement is successful only if **$SHELL** equals **csh** or **ksh**. If **$SHELL** equals **sh**, or a public domain shell, the test fails.

**Keyword:**   programming

**See Also:**   case, test

### if [ $TERM != xterm ]; then : ; fi

SH
KSH

ALL

SCRIPT

You can test for inequality with **if** by placing the NOT operator, **!**, in front of the equals sign. Note that there is no whitespace between the NOT operator and equals sign. There is whitespace separating all other items in the **if** statement, however.

**Keyword:**    programming

**See Also:**    case, TERM, test

### if [ $TERM = xterm ]; then : ; fi

SH
KSH

ALL

SCRIPT

This example is a straight equality test. If the variable **$TERM** equals **xterm**, the command is successful. Note that double quotes are necessary if the string variable contains whitespace.

**Keyword:**    programming

**See Also:**    case, TERM, test

### if [ -d $HOME/$USER ]; then : ; fi

SH
KSH

ALL

SCRIPT

The **-d** option tests for the existence of a directory. If the directory does not exist, the **if** statement fails.

**Keyword:**    programming

**See Also:**    case, HOME, test, USER

### if [ -r $HOME/.Xdefaults ]; then echo : ; fi

SH
KSH

ALL

SCRIPT

The **-r** option is one of five file-testing options supported by **if** and the **test** command. In the example, the **if** statement checks whether **$HOME/.Xdefaults** is a readable file. If the file is not readable, or the file does not exist, the **if** statement fails.

**Keyword:**    programming

**See Also:**    case, HOME, test

### if [ -s friday.log ]; then : ; fi

SH
KSH

ALL

SCRIPT

The **-s** option tests whether a file exists and whether it contains data. If the test succeeds, the **if** statement is true. To do the obverse of **-s**, use **! -s**. The C shell supports a built-in switch for this operation, but the Bourne shell doesn't.

**Keyword:**    programming

**See Also:**    case, test

| | | |
|---|---|---|
| SH KSH | ALL | SCRIPT |

**if [ -w /etc/exports ]; then echo : ; fi**

The **-w** option tests whether **/etc/exports** is a writable file. If the file is not writable, or the file does not exist, the **if** statement fails.

**Keyword:** programming

**See Also:** case, test

| | | |
|---|---|---|
| SH KSH | ALL | SCRIPT |

**if [ -x "$startup" ]; then; exec $startup $1 else  $term -C; fi**

The first thing **Xsession** does here is check for the failsafe translation. If the user has asked for a failsafe session, **$1** is equal to failsafe. If the tests are successful—that is, if there can be anything successful associated with a failsafe session—an **Xterm** with slightly larger than normal geometry appears.

**Keyword:** programming

**See Also:** case, test

| | | |
|---|---|---|
| SH KSH | ALL | SCRIPT |

**if [ -x $HOME/.xsession ]; then echo : ; fi**

The **-x** option tests whether **$HOME/.xsession** is an executable file. If the file is not executable, or the file does not exist, the **if** statement fails.

**Keyword:** programming

**See Also:** case, HOME, test

| | | |
|---|---|---|
| ALL | ALL | SCRIPT |

**if [ -z "$TERM" ]; then : ; fi**

This **if** command, combined with the bracket representation of the test facility, determines whether the string is null.

**Keyword:** programming

**See Also:** case, test

| | | |
|---|---|---|
| SH KSH | ALL | SCRIPT |

**if [ `date +"%d"` -ge 7 ]; then : ; fi**

The **-ge** operator is another **if** construct that you might want to use to test the date. The example tests whether the day of the month is greater than or equal to **7**.

**Keyword:** programming

**See Also:** case, date, test

| | | |
|---|---|---|
| SH KSH | ALL | SCRIPT |

**if [ `date +"%d"` -gt 7 ]; then : ; fi**

You can use the **date** command with **if** to test whether a certain date has occurred. The example tests whether the current date is greater than the seventh day of the month. The **%d** option to **date** causes **date** to return the day of the month as a number between 0 and 31. The **-gt** operator specifies greater than.

**Keyword:**   programming

**See Also:**   case, date, test

### if [ `df | grep /usr | awk ´{print $4}`` -lt 131072 ]; then : ; fi

SH KSH   ALL   END POWER SCRIPT SYSADM

This example provides another command substitution. The **df** command is piped into **grep** and **awk** in order to obtain the amount of available disk space on the **/usr** partition. The **if** statement then compares the answer to **131072**, or 256 512 K blocks on a BSD system. The **-lt** operator specifies less than.

**Keyword:**   programming

**See Also:**   awk, case, df, grep, test

### if [ `expr $a + $b` -ne $c ]; then : ; fi

SH KSH   ALL   SCRIPT

This **if** statement gets its initial value from the **expr** command. In the example, **expr** sums the script variables **$a** and **$b** and feeds the result to **if**, which tests whether the sum is *not* equal to **$c**.

**Keyword:**   programming

**See Also:**   case, expr, test

### if [ `ps -e | awk ´/calterm/ && ! /awk/ {print $1}`` -eq $pid ]; then : ; fi

SH KSH   ALL   SCRIPT

You can use command substitution in an **if** statement, and if nothing else, it makes scripts more concise. In the example, which demonstrates the first of several integer comparisons, **awk** is used to filter the process ID number for **calterm**, which is a unique instance of an Xterm window. The **-eq** operator is the **if** statement's "equals" operator. Of course, if you don't like **if** statements to be as long as this one, you could write an additional line of code:

```
curpid=`ps -e | awk '/xterm/ && ! /awk/ {print $1}'`
if [ $curpid -eq $pid ]; then
    kill -9 $curpid
fi
```

**Keyword:**   programming

**See Also:**   awk, case, ps, test

**205**

| | | | |
|---|---|---|---|
| SH<br>KSH | ALL | SCRIPT | **IFS**<br>This environment variable specifies the shell's default field separators.<br>**Keyword:** programming<br>**See Also:** ksh, sh |

## ignoreeof

<table>
<tr>
<td>CSH</td>
<td>ALL</td>
<td>SCRIPT</td>
<td>This environment variable bypasses EOF (end of file) characters from terminals.<br>Keyword: user environment<br>See Also: csh</td>
</tr>
</table>

## imake

<table>
<tr>
<td>ALL</td>
<td>XWIN</td>
<td>ALL</td>
<td>The imake command is designed to assist programmers by acting as a C preprocessor interface to the make command in X Window System programming. You use imake to generate a Makefile from a template of *cpp macro functions and an input file called Imakefile. The net result is that machine dependencies, such as compiler options, are maintained in a separate file.<br>Keyword: programming<br>See Also: cc, make, xmkmf</td>
</tr>
</table>

## indent -i6 lister.c lister.fmt

<table>
<tr>
<td>ALL</td>
<td>BSD</td>
<td>POWER</td>
<td>The indent program is designed to reformat C source code files. The program has approximately 50 options and can do such things as add blank lines after procedure bodies, and reformat the arrangement of C statements such as case, if, and else. In the example, the -i option increases the level of indentation from the default four whitespaces to six whitespaces.<br>Keyword: programming<br>See Also: cb, cc</td>
</tr>
</table>

## indxbib book.db

<table>
<tr>
<td>ALL</td>
<td>SVR4<br>SunOS<br>Solaris</td>
<td>POWER</td>
<td>The indxbib utility creates an inverted index file. The utility, which is a shell script, calls two programs that perform formatting chores. The programs are mkey and inv, both of which usually reside in the /usr/ucblib/reftools directory on SVR4 systems. On SunOS systems, these files are located in the /usr/lib/refer directory.<br>Keyword: writing, text handling</td>
</tr>
</table>

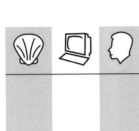

**Files:**     ./*.ia, ./*.ib, ./*.ic, ./*.ig
**See Also:**  addbib, lookbib, refer, roffbib, sortbib

## info

ALL   AIX   POWER

The **info** command on IBM UNIX systems brings up the InfoExplorer application. InfoExplorer is a hypertext help system that uses data stored on disk or a CD-ROM. The application has both an ASCII interface and an X Window/Motif interface. Which of these two versions is invoked when you enter **info** at the command line depends on your system configuration. Command line options for **info** include **-h**, which specifies a help string to search for; **-l**, which specifies a configured database library name; and **-n**, which specifies the default navigation article. For the latter, you can choose **bl** (book contents list), **cl** (commands list), **ed** (education menu), and **ti** (task index).
**Keyword:**   documentation, help
**See Also:**  man

## infocmp

ALL   SCO    POWER
      SVR4   SYSADM

The **infocmp** command is a System V program that lets you compare a binary **terminfo** definition. You can use the command to compare two definitions. By default, the command displays the **terminfo** definition for the calling terminal. The example produces the following output for a generic **ansi** terminal:

```
# Reconstructed via infocmp from file: /usr/share/lib/terminfo/a/ansi
  ansi|generic ansi standard terminal,

     am, xon,
     cols#80, lines#24,
     bel=^G, blink=\E[5m, bold=\E[1m, cbt=\E[Z,
     clear=\E[H\E[J, cr=\r, cub=\E[%p1%dD, cub1=\b,
     cud=\E[%p1%dB, cud1=\n, cuf=\E[%p1%dC, cuf1=\E[C,
     cup=\E[%i%p1%d;%p2%dH, cuu=\E[%p1%dA, cuu1=\E[A,
     dch1=\E[P, dl=\E[%p1%dM, dl1=\E[M, ed=\E[J, el=\E[K,
     home=\E[H, hpa=\E[%p1%{1}%+%dG, ht=\t, hts=\EH,
     ich=\E[%p1%d@, ich1=\E[@, il=\E[%p1%dL, il1=\E[L,
     ind=\n, invis=\E[8m, kbs=\b, kcub1=\E[D, kcud1=\E[B,
     kcuf1=\E[C, kcuu1=\E[A, khome=\E[H,
     rep=%p1%c\E[%p2%{1}%-%db, rev=\E[7m, rmso=\E[m,
     rmul=\E[m,
     sgr=\E[%?%p1%t7;%;%?%p2%t4;%;%?%p3%t7;%;%?%p4%t5;%;%?%p6%t1;%;m,
     sgr0=\E[0m, smso=\E[7m, smul=\E[4m, tbc=\E[2g,
     vpa=\E[%p1%{1}%+%dd,
```

**Keyword:**   system information, terminals

**207**

**Files:**    terminfo
**See Also:**    tic

## infocmp -c ansi vt100

This command compares the **terminfo** definitions for **ansi** and **vt100** terminals. The output displays all definitions *common* to the two terminals specified. Here is some excerpted output:

```
# infocmp -c ansi vt100
   comparing ansi to vt100.
      comparing booleans.
         am= T.
         xon= T.
      comparing numbers.
         cols= 80.
         lines= 24.
      comparing strings.
         bel= '^G'.
         cr= '\r'.
         cub= '\E[%p1%dD'.
         cub1= '\b'.
         cud= '\E[%p1%dB'.
         cud1= '\n'.
         cuf= '\E[%p1%dC'.
         cuu= '\E[%p1%dA'.
         home= '\E[H'.
         ht= '\t'.
         hts= '\EH'.
         ind= '\n'.
         kbs= '\b'.
```

**Keyword:**    system information, terminals
**Files:**    terminfo
**See Also:**    tic

## infocmp -C vt100 > vt100.edit

The **-C** option to **infocmp** lets you convert a terminal definition found in a **termcap** file (usually used on BSD systems) into a **terminfo** definition. The conversion process is not 100 percent accurate, so you must examine and probably make changes to the file in a text editor, which is the reason the example names the output file **vt100.edit**. Questionable parts of the output are commented with the **#** character in the output file.

**Keyword:**    system information, terminals
**Files:**    termcap, terminfo
**See Also:**    captoinfo, tic

ALL    SCO    END
       SVR4   POWER
              SCRIPT
              SYSADM

ALL    SCO    POWER
       SVR4   SYSADM

### infocmp -d vt100 vt100site

The **-d** option to **infocmp** compares two **terminfo** definitions and displays the differences to standard output. This is an easy way to compare similar and customized definitions. The example compares the standard **vt100** definition to a customized **vt100site** definition. (Note that you do not actually have to specify **-d** if you specify two terminal names on the command line.)

**Keyword:**   system information, terminals

**Files:**   terminfo

**See Also:**   tic

ALL   SCO   POWER
SVR4   SYSADM

### infocmp -n vt100site

The **-n** option to **infocmp** compares the specified **terminfo** definition against the list of possible definitions (as defined by the system). Using this option, you can discover what additional capabilities you can add to your **terminfo** definitions.

**Keyword:**   system information, terminals

**Files:**   terminfo

**See Also:**   tic

ALL   SCO   POWER
SVR4   SYSADM

### infocmp vt100 > vt100site

This command redirects the output from **infocmp** to a file that you can use to customize an existing **terminfo** entry. The **tic**, or **terminfo** compiler, is used to compile an ASCII file into a binary file compatible with **terminfo**. If you do not want the compiled file incorporated into the internal database maintained by **terminfo**, change the **TERMINFO** environment variable to a directory other than **/usr/lib/terminfo**.

**Keyword:**   system information, terminals

**Files:**   terminfo

**See Also:**   tic

ALL   SVR4   POWER
SCO   SYSADM

### init

On BSD systems, the **init** program is different: it starts the system, but relies on signals generated by the **kill** command to know when to shut down or adjust run levels.

**Keyword:**   run-level, shutdown, startup

**Files:**   /etc/utmp, /var/adm/wtmp, /etc/rc.local, /etc/ttytab, /usr/etc/getty

**See Also:**   halt, kill, login, reboot, shutdown, stty

ALL   BSD   SYSADM
SunOS

### init 0

ALL OSF SVR4 SYSADM

The **init** command is responsible for resetting the current run level. It can also halt and power-off the system. In all cases, you must have root privileges to use the **init** command. If you run the command without privileges, **init** informs you that you must be the superuser. In the example, the **0** option specifies that the system perform a shutdown and power-off, if possible.

**Keyword:**  run-level, shutdown, startup

**Files:**  /etc/inittab, /var/adm/utmp, /var/adm/wtmp

**See Also:**  halt, kill, login, reboot, stty

### init 1

ALL SVR4 SYSADM

The **1** option to **init** shuts down multiuser mode and puts the system in administration mode. This state is also referred to as run level 1. Typically, a system administrator uses single-user mode when it is necessary to modify the hardware configuration or troubleshoot corrupted system files. No other users can access the system during single-user mode.

**Keyword:**  run-level, shutdown, startup

**Files:**  /etc/inittab, /var/adm/utmp, /var/adm/wtmp

**See Also:**  halt, kill, login, reboot, stty

### init 2

ALL OSF SVR4 SYSADM

The **2** option to **init** puts the system in multiuser mode, or run level 2, which is normal operating mode. All system processes and daemons are activated; all filesystems are accessible.

**Keyword:**  run-level, shutdown, startup

**Files:**  /etc/inittab, /var/adm/utmp, /var/adm/wtmp

**See Also:**  halt, kill, login, reboot, stty

### init 5

ALL SVR4 SYSADM

The **5** option to **init** shuts down the system and enters the hardware operating layer, which is commonly referred to as the ROM monitor or firmware mode. You would use this mode if you needed to perform diagnostics or other hardware-based functions.

**Keyword:**  run-level, shutdown, startup

**Files:**  /etc/inittab, /var/adm/utmp, /var/adm/wtmp

**See Also:**  halt, kill, login, reboot, stty

### init S

ALL SVR4 SYSADM

The **S** option to **init** puts the system in single-user mode. In this mode, a limited number of kernel processes are running. As a rule, only the root filesystem is available. System adminstrators use this mode for maintenance and troubleshooting.

**Keyword:**  run-level, shutdown, startup

**See Also:**  halt, kill, login, reboot, stty

### ipcs

ALL ALL SYSADM

The **ipcs** command displays information on interprocess communications. The command has approximately 10 options and provides information on waiting processes, shared memory segments, and message queues. The default display, as invoked by the example (using no options), shows type (message queue, shared memory segment, or semaphore), associated ID, key, mode, owner, and group.

**Keyword:**  system information

**Files:**  /etc/group, /etc/passwd

**See Also:**  dmesg, group, ps, who

### ismpx

ALL SVR4 SYSADM

The **ismpx** command returns the state of the windowing terminal on System V platforms. A *windowing terminal* is a character-mode window running under the system's *layers* software. If it is running under layers, the command indicates this. Using **-s** with the command causes it to return **0** if the terminal is running under layers; it returns **1** otherwise.

**Keyword:**  terminals, window handling

**See Also:**  jterm, jwin, layers

### jobs

CSH ALL POWER

This command outputs a list of running processes that were started within the current instance of C shell.

**Keyword:**  program execution

**See Also:**  bg, fg, kill, ps

### jobs

KSH ALL POWER

In the Korn shell, the **jobs** command lists information about each job. This shell built-in recognizes three options: **-l**, which lists process IDs (PIDs); **-n**, which displays jobs that have stopped or exited since previous notification to the shell; and **-p**, which simply lists the process group.

**Keyword:**   program execution

**See Also:**   bg, fg, kill, ps

## jobs

In **jsh**, the SVR4 job control version of the Bourne shell, the **jobs** built-in supports the **-l** option, which reports the process ID (PID) of all jobs, and the **-p** option, which displays the group ID (GID) of all jobs. The **jsh** version of **jobs** also supports a **-x** option, which takes one or more arguments. The first argument to **-x** is necessary: It is the name of a previously executed command. The second argument is optional: It is one or more arguments associated with a previously executed job.

**Keyword:**   user environment

**Files:**   $HOME/.profile

**See Also:**   bg, fg, kill, sh, stop, suspend, wait

## join  -o 1.1 2.2 race.start race.finish

This command gives just the name and finish place of the racers, using the data files as above. The **-o** argument produces output lines consisting of the fields specified in one or more **number.field** arguments, where number is **1** for **file1** or **2** for **file2**, and field is a field number. Here is the output:

```
John 2
Keri 1
Phil 3
```

**Keyword:**   text display, text handling

**See Also:**   awk, comm, cut, paste, sed, sort

## join -a1 -e "DNF" -o 1.1 2.2 race.start race.finish

This example adds **DNF** wherever there is an empty output field. Here is the output:

```
John 2
Keri 1
Phil 3
Lynn DNF
```

**Keyword:**   text display, text handling

**See Also:**   awk, comm, cut, paste, sed, sort

ALL   SVR4   POWER SYSADM

ALL   ALL   POWER

ALL   ALL   POWER

### join -a1 -o 1.1 2.2 race.start race.finish

This command produces an output line for each line found in **race.start**. If the argument had been **-a 2**, then the command would have produced an output line for each line found in **race.finish**. Here is the output:

```
John 2
Keri 1
Phil 3
Lynn
```

**Keyword:** text display, text handling

**See Also:** awk, comm, cut, paste, sed, sort

### join race.start race.finish

The **join** command reads **race.start** and **race.finish**, joins lines in the files that contain common fields, and writes the results to standard output. For example, the following input files display the text that concludes the example:

```
#race.start:
John     1       Chevy
Keri     2       Ford
Phil     3       Dodge
Lynn     4       Toyota

#race.finish:
John     2
Keri     1
Phil     3

         #output
         John 1 Chevy 2
         Keri 2 Ford 1
         Phil 3 Dodge 3
```

**Keyword:** text display, text handling

**See Also:** awk, comm, cut, paste, sed, sort

### jsh

In SVR4, you can invoke the Bourne shell with job control features. Instead of executing **sh**, however, you execute **jsh**. The job control features that you get are similar to those in the C and Korn shells. Any active job—either one running in the foreground or one running in the background—can be manipulated in **jsh**. Jobs are tracked by number values assigned by the shell. To refer to a job by number (beginning with 1 for the first job), precede the

ALL ALL POWER

ALL ALL POWER

ALL SVR4 POWER
SYSADM

number with the **%** symbol, as in **%1** and **%5**. To refer to the current job, you can simply enter **%** or **+** in conjunction with a **jsh** command, such as **bg** and **fg**.

**Keyword:**   user environment

**Files:**       $HOME/.profile

**See Also:**   bg, csh, fg, jobs, kill, ksh, sh, stop, suspend, wait

## jterm

ALL   SVR4   POWER

This command resets a layer of a windowing terminal after downloading a terminal program that contains the attributes of the layer. This command is run in conjunction with the **layers** command.

**Keyword:**   terminals, window handling

**See Also:**   ismpx, jwin, layers

## jwin

ALL   SVR4   POWER

This command outputs the size of the window that is associated with the current process, used in conjunction with the **layers** command.

**Keyword:**   terminals, window handling

**See Also:**   ismpx, jterm, layers

## kdb

ALL   ALL   SYSADM

The **kdb** program is a interactive kernel debugger for advanced system administrators on some SVR4 systems. In panic situations, the system automatically enters **kdb** and presents the following prompt:

```
kdb>>
```

With **kdb**, which acts like a Reverse Polish Notation calculator, you can set breakpoints, display kernel structures, show kernel stack traces, perform arithmetic operators, set variables and macros, and perform conditional execution. Only adminstrators experienced with **kdb** should use the tool; otherwise, you could easily corrupt your kernel with the wrong **kdb** command.

**Keyword:**   kernel

**See Also:**   crash, dc

## keylogin

ALL   ALL   POWER
              SYSADM

The **keylogin** command takes no arguments. On both SVR4 and BSD systems, it prompts you for a password, which it then uses to decrypt your secret key stored in the **publickey** database. The key is then made known to the **keyserv** daemon. On many systems, the **login** program automatically handles the **keylogin** process.

**Keyword:** security

**Files:** /etc/publickey

**See Also:** chkey, keylogout, keyserv, publickey, login, newkey

## keyserv

The **keyserv** program runs as a daemon and manages the private encryption keys used for accessing secure networking services. In order to execute **keyserv**, you must have superuser privileges.

**Keyword:** security

**Files:** /etc/.rootkey, /etc/keystore, /etc/publickey

**See Also:** chkey, keylogout, keyserv, publickey, login, newkey

**ALL   ALL   SYSADM**

## kill %1

One of the reasons that the C shell **kill** is built in is that it handles job IDs associated with the C shell mechanism to shift jobs between the foreground and background. In the example, the **kill** command terminates the program with a job ID of **1**.

**Keyword:** job control

**See Also:** bg, fg, init, ps, stop

**CSH   ALL   POWER SYSADM**

## kill %1 %3 %4

Like its **/bin/kill** counterpart, the **kill** used by the C shell takes multiple arguments. All three job numbers refer to programs that have been suspended using the C shell's job control mechanism. For example, you can place **vi** in the background by pressing Ctrl-Shift-Z.

**Keyword:** job control

**See Also:** bg, fg, init, ps, stop

**CSH   ALL   POWER SYSADM**

## kill %vi

If **vi**—and only one copy of **vi**—happens to be running in the background, this command is a sure kill. If more than two instances of **vi** were running in the background, **kill** would not kill either job. Instead, it would report that the command was ambiguous. You can get a listing of suspended C shell programs by running the **jobs** command.

**CSH   ALL   POWER SYSADM**

**Keyword:**  job control
**See Also:**  bg, fg, init, ps, stop

### kill %\?report.txt

CSH    ALL    POWER
SYSADM

If you know that the name of a command is not unique, but that the name of the file being accessed by the command is unique, you can easily kill the job. The C shell built-in **kill** accepts the **?** wildcard character after the **%** job indicator. You must escape the **?** character. You must also supply the full filename associated with the job you want to kill.
**Keyword:**  job control
**See Also:**  bg, fg, init, ps, stop

### kill -9 0

ALL    ALL    POWER
SYSADM

This is another special **kill** command. It terminates all processes belonging to the user who executes it, including the current shell. In effect, it cleanly logs you off the system. This command does not work in the C shell unless you execute it directly, as in **/bin/kill 0**, or alias it to **/bin/kill**.
**Keyword:**  job control
**See Also:**  init, ps

### kill -9 1251

ALL    ALL    POWER
SYSADM

The **-9** option to **kill** successfully kills most processes. Sometimes it is not necessary—for example, when processes don't trap the default SIGTERM (**15**)—but you can rely on **-9** to kill most anything. Don't use **-9**, though, if you can use the default SIGTERM, because the process you are killing will have a chance to shut down gracefully. This command works with both **/bin/kill** and the C shell built-in version of **kill**.
**Keyword:**  job control
**See Also:**  init, ps

### kill -9 `ps -e | awk ´/ vi/ && ! /awk/ {print $1}`

ALL    ALL    POWER
SYSADM

With command substitution, you can create a command that both obtains the process ID and kills the process. The combination of **ps** and **awk** obtains the process ID and **kill -9** takes care of killing the process. This command works with both **/bin/kill** and the C shell built-in version of **kill**.

**Keyword:**   job control
**See Also:**   awk, init, ps

## kill -HUP 1

ALL   ALL   POWER SYSADM

This command sends the hangup signal, or **SIGHUP**, to the modem or network connection. You usually send **HUP** when a process is hung, or someone has left a modem unattended. The second option to the **kill** statement in the example specifies the program group ID. Thus, the example kills all processes with a program group ID of **1**. This command does not work in the C shell unless you execute it directly, as in **/bin/kill 0**, or alias it to **/bin/kill**.

**Keyword:**   job control
**See Also:**   init, ps

## kill -l

ALL   ALL   POWER SYSADM

The **-l** option lists the signals known to **kill**. The listing leaves the SIG prefix off, though it is traditional to refer to signals using this prefix, because it is not recognized by the **kill** command. As an alternative to signal names, you can use numbers associated with the signal. The following diagram presents the signals and their numbers. For more specific information, refer to the **signal** examples in *The UNIX and X Command Compendium*, beginning with **SIGABRT**.

```
HUP 1<TAB>INT 2<TAB>QUIT 3<TAB>ILL 4<TAB>TRAP 5<TAB>
ABRT 6<TAB>EMT7<TAB>FPE 8<TAB>KILL 9<TAB>BUS 10<TAB>SEGV 11
SYS 12<TAB>PIPE 13<TAB>ALRM 14<TAB>TERM 15<TAB>URG 16
STOP 17<TAB>TSTP 18<TAB>CONT 19<TAB>CHLD 20<TAB>TTIN 22
TTOU 23<TAB>IO 24<TAB>XCPU 25<TAB>XFSZ 26<TAB>VTALRM 27
PROF 28<TAB>WINCH 29<TAB>INFO 30<TAB>USR1 32<TAB>USR2 33
```

**Keyword:**   job control
**See Also:**   init, ps

## kill -TERM 1

ALL   ALL   POWER SYSADM

A quick way to bring the system down into single-user mode is to use this command. The **-TERM** signal tells **kill** to terminate all nonessential processes. In this case, **TERM** actually stands for **terminate**. Using this command is a good way to get to single-user mode if you are using the Xdm login facilities under the X Window System. This command does not work in the C shell unless you execute it directly, as in **/bin/kill 0**, or alias it to **/bin/kill**.

**Keyword:**   job control
**See Also:**   init, ps

## kill 0

SH
KSH
ALL
POWER
SYSADM

This is a special **kill** command that terminates all processes belonging to the user who executes it. There is one exception: The current shell is not affected. This command does not work in the C shell unless you execute the **kill** command directly, as in **/bin/kill 0**, or alias it to **/bin/kill**.

**Keyword:** job control

**See Also:** init, ps

## kill 1251

ALL
ALL
POWER
SYSADM

The example is the most basic **kill** command. It terminates the program specified by the process ID, or PID, which you can get by running **ps**. Without arguments, **kill** is its least ruthless. Because programs and scripts can trap the default **kill** signal, SIGTERM, you may or may not be successful with the form of **kill** in this example. Also note that the C shell has a built-in equivalent, also called **kill**, so it supercedes the actual UNIX command. The C shell built-in command works almost identically to the UNIX command, but the C shell version lets you specify processes by *job number* (see **bg** and **fg** for more information). The one drawback to the C shell command is that it does not handle the **0** signal.

**Keyword:** job control

**See Also:** init, ps

## kill 1251 1299 1300 1444

ALL
ALL
POWER
SYSADM

The **kill** command accepts any number of process IDs, and terminates them if possible. Some commands trap the basic **kill** signal, SIGTERM, and prevent **kill** from doing its deed. For a sure kill, use the **-9** or **-KILL** signal.

**Keyword:** job control

**See Also:** init, ps

## killall

ALL
ALL
SYSADM

The **killall** command terminates all active processes except those necessary to maintain the system. Only users with root privileges can execute **killall**.

**Keyword:** job control

**See Also:** init, kill, ps

## ksh

ALL ALL END

The Korn shell was the third of the three standard shells to be incorporated into the standard UNIX environment. It benefited from the existing design of both the Bourne and C shells. It is similar to the C shell in that it offers **alias** and **history** mechanisms. Its major difference from the C shell is that instead of symbolic command line editing, it lets you use a text editor such as **vi** or **emacs** to edit previous commands. New users should note that when you execute **ksh** at the command line, as in the example, a new instance of the Korn shell executes—even if you execute it from the Bourne or C shells.

**Keyword:**  user environment

**Files:**  $HOME/.profile, $HOME/.kshrc

**See Also:**  csh, FCEDIT, sh

## ksh -c kscript

ALL ALL END

The **-c** option to **ksh** tells the Korn shell to execute the command that follows it.

**Keyword:**  user environment

**Files:**  $HOME/.profile, $HOME/.kshrc

**See Also:**  csh, FCEDIT, sh

## ksh -r

ALL ALL SYSADM

The **-r** option executes a restricted shell, which normally prevents the user from performing such operations as changing directories, resetting the system path, and redirecting output.

**Keyword:**  user environment

**Files:**  $HOME/.profile, $HOME/.kshrc

**See Also:**  csh, FCEDIT, sh

## ksh_builtins

ALL ALL SCRIPT

This is the name of a script that the authors used while preparing *The UNIX and X Command Compendium*. It is handy when you need to know quickly whether you are dealing with a Korn shell **builtin** command. Here is the script:

```
#!/bin/sh
echo '
    alias, bg, break, case, cd, continue, do, done, echo,
    elif, else, esac, eval, exec, exit, export, fc, fg,
    fi, for, function, getopts, if, inlib, jobs, kill,
    let, newgrp, print, pwd, read, readonly, return,
```

rmlib, select, set, shift, then, time, trap, typeset,
ulimit, umask, unalias, unset, until, wait, whence, while '

**Keyword:** help

**See Also:** csh, csh_builtins, sh, sh_builtins

## l

This command outputs a long listing of all the nonhidden files in the current directory. The output consists of one file per line; the line starts with the file permissions, number of links, owner, group, size in bytes, and the time of last modification. This command is exactly the same as **ls -l**.

**Keyword:** file handling

**See Also:** lc, lf, lr, ls, lx

## l | awk ´{s += $5} END { print s,"KB in use"}´

This command outputs the amount of disk space that all the nonhidden files in the current directory take up.

**Keyword:** file handling

**See Also:** lc, lf, lr, ls, lx

## l -a | awk ´{s += $5} {print $0} END { print s,"KB in use"}´

This command outputs all the files in the current directory, and includes the total disk space they use.

**Keyword:** file display

**See Also:** lc, lf, lr, ls, lx

## l -a | awk ´{s += $5} END { print s,"KB in use"}´

This command calculates the total number of commands, including hidden files.

**Keyword:** file handling

**See Also:** lc, lf, lr, ls, lx

## l -ap | grep ´/´

This command outputs a long listing of all the subdirectories of the current directory.

**Keyword:** file display

**See Also:** lc, lf, lr, ls, lx

| ALL | SCO | ALL |
| --- | --- | --- |
| ALL | SCO | ALL |
| ALL | SCO | POWER |
| ALL | SCO | ALL |
| ALL | SCO | END POWER |

## labelit -F ufs /dev/dsk/c0d0s6 /u3

ALL  SVR4  SYSADM

This command sets the mounted name of the disk partition represented as **/dev/dsk/c0d0s6** to **/u3**.

**Keyword:** filesystem

**Files:** df, MAKEDEV, mkdev, makefsys

## labelit -F ufs /dev/rmt/ctape1

ALL  SVR4  SYSADM

This command outputs the current values for the tape specified by **/dev/rmt/ctape1**, which is formatted as a **ufs** filesystem.

**Keyword:** filesystem

**Files:** df, MAKEDEV, mkdev, makefsys

## LANG

CSH  BSD  SCRIPT

This is an environment variable that controls the classification of characters in shell commands. If **LC_TYPE** is set, **LANG** does not override it. **LANG**, however, may contain additional information.

**Keyword:** user environment

**See Also:** LC_CTYPE

## last

ALL  ALL  POWER  SYSADM

This command displays a record of all logins and logouts, with the most recent displayed first.

**Keyword:** system information

**Files:** /var/adm/wtmp, /etc/wtmp (SCO)

**See Also:** lastcomm

## last -10

ALL  ALL  POWER  SYSADM

This command shows the 10 most recent logins on the system.

**Keyword:** system information

**Files:** /var/adm/wtmp, /etc/wtmp (SCO)

**See Also:** lastcomm

## last console

ALL  ALL  POWER  SYSADM

This simple version of the **last** command shows the names of everyone who has logged into the system console.

**Keyword:** system information

**Files:** /var/adm/wtmp, /etc/wtmp (SCO)

**See Also:** lastcomm

**221**

### last perkie tty2a

ALL ALL POWER SYSADM

This command shows all the logins and logouts for the user **perkie**, and all the logins and logouts from the terminal **tty2a**. You could substitute **tty2a** for any terminal you want. A good choice might be a dialup terminal, which shows you who is logging in, and when.

**Keyword:** system information

**Files:** /var/adm/wtmp, /etc/wtmp (SCO)

**See Also:** lastcomm

### last root | grep Jan

ALL ALL POWER SYSADM

This command shows all the times that **root** logged in, and where **root** logged in from, for the month of January.

**Keyword:** system information

**Files:** /var/adm/wtmp, /etc/wtmp (SCO)

**See Also:** lastcomm

### last root | grep Jan | lpr

ALL ALL POWER SYSADM

This command prints out to the default printer all the times root logged in, and where root logged in from, for the month of January.

**Keyword:** system information

**Files:** /var/adm/wtmp, /etc/wtmp (SCO)

**See Also:** lastcomm

### last shutdown

ALL ALL POWER SYSADM

This command shows the time between system reboots.

**Keyword:** system information

**Files:** /var/adm/wtmp, /etc/wtmp (SCO)

**See Also:** lastcomm

### last tty2a | grep Feb

ALL ALL POWER SYSADM

This command shows who logged in and out of terminal **tty2a** in the month of February.

**Keyword:** system information

**Files:** /var/adm/wtmp, /etc/wtmp (SCO)

**See Also:** lastcomm

### last | grep ´ :0 ´

ALL  ALL  POWER SYSADM

This command shows the names of everyone who has logged in through the **xdm** program on systems running X11R3 or later versions of the X Window System.

**Keyword:** system information

**Files:** /var/adm/wtmp, /etc/wtmp (SCO)

**See Also:** lastcomm

### last | grep ´tty2A´ | sed y/:/./ | awk ´{if (NF>9) {if ($7>17.00 || $7<7.00) {print $0}} else {if (NF<9) {if ($6>17.00 || $6<7.00) {print $0}}}}´ | sed y/./:/

ALL  ALL  POWER SYSADM

This command examines the **tty2A** serial port. You can substitute any terminal port in place of **tty2A**.

**Keyword:** system information

**Files:** /var/adm/wtmp, /etc/wtmp (SCO)

**See Also:** lastcomm

### last | sed y/:/./ | awk ´{if (NF>9) {if ($7>17.00 || $7<7.00) {print $0}} else {if (NF<9) {if ($6>17.00 || $6<7.00) {print $0}}}}´ | sed y/./:/

ALL  ALL  POWER SYSADM

This command outputs the names of all the users who have ever logged into the system between 5 PM and 7 AM. This is useful for checking if someone has broken into your system. The first **sed** statement formats the output of **last** in a form that **awk** can work with; it changes all the colons to periods so **awk** can treat times as numbers. After converting the times to numbers, the **awk** command checks to see if they are after 5 PM and before 7 AM; if they are, **awk** prints out the line. The last **sed** command is used to format the numbers back into times.

**Keyword:** system information

**Files:** /var/adm/wtmp, /etc/wtmp (SCO)

**See Also:** lastcomm

### lastcomm

ALL  SVR4 BSD  POWER SYSADM

This command shows information on all previously executed commands. It outputs the command that was executed, the user who executed the command, the terminal port from which the command was executed, the execution time of the command, and the date and time the command was executed.

**223**

**Keyword:** system information
**Files:** /var/adm/pacct
**See Also:** last

### lastcomm perkie | awk ´{s += $4} END {print "User", $2, "has spent", s, "seconds executing commands on the system."}´

This command tallies the amount of time that **perkie** has spent actually executing commands on the system.

**Keyword:** system information
**Files:** /var/adm/pacct
**See Also:** last

### lastcomm root

This command shows commands executed by the root user.

**Keyword:** system information
**Files:** /var/adm/pacct
**See Also:** last

### lastcomm tty2A

This command shows all the commands that have been executed from the **tty2A** terminal port. This is a convenient way to monitor activity on this port. If it is world-accessible, via a modem, you can use this command to look for suspicious commands being run, such as **sz /etc/passwd**, or anything having to do with the **/etc/passwd** file.

**Keyword:** system information
**Files:** /var/adm/pacct
**See Also:** fuser, last

### lastcomm xterm

This command shows all the **xterm** programs that have been executed on the system, who executed them, and how long they ran.

**Keyword:** system information
**Files:** /var/adm/pacct
**See Also:** last

ALL | SVR4 BSD | POWER SYSADM

### lastcomm | grep ´ F ´

This command shows all the commands that have performed a **fork**, but not an **exec**.

**Keyword:**   system information

**Files:**       /var/adm/pacct

**See Also:**   last

### lastcomm | grep ´ S ´

This command shows all the commands that have run on the system as a **set-user-id** program.

**Keyword:**   system information

**Files:**       /var/adm/pacct

**See Also:**   last

### lastcomm | grep ´Sep´

This command shows all the commands that were executed in the month of September.

**Keyword:**   system information

**Files:**       /var/adm/pacct

**See Also:**   last

### lastcomm | grep ´Sep´ | lpr

This command prints out to the default printer all the commands that were executed in the month of September.

**Keyword:**   system information

**Files:**       /var/adm/pacct

**See Also:**   acct, last

### lastcomm | grep -v ´__´

This command outputs all the commands that have been executed by users on the system. It doesn't, however, output commands that are run by **cron**, such as **sendmail**.

**Keyword:**   system information

**Files:**       /var/adm/pacct

**See Also:**   last

ALL   SVR4   POWER
      BSD    SYSADM

ALL   SVR4   POWER
      BSD    SYSADM

ALL   SVR4   POWER
      BSD    SYSADM

ALL   SVR4   POWER
      BSD    SYSADM

ALL   SVR4   POWER
      BSD    SYSADM

## lastcomm | grep `date +"%a"`

This command shows all the commands that have been run on the current day of the week. For example, if the day is Sunday, every command that has been run on that day is displayed.

**Keyword:**   system information

**Files:**   /var/adm/pacct

**See Also:**   acct, last

## lastcomm | grep `date +"%b"`

This command shows all the commands that have been executed so far in the current month.

**Keyword:**   system information

**Files:**   /var/adm/pacct

**See Also:**   acct, last

## layers -f .win

The SVR4 implementation of UNIX supports ASCII windowing on most terminal windows. The executable program that starts the ASCII windowing system is **layers**. In the example, **layers** starts the terminal windowing software and calls **.win** for initial window setup information. A simple configuration line looks like this:

```
10 10 510 410 exec $SHELL
```

The example displays an ASCII window that is 500 pixels in width by 400 pixels in height. The first two numbers in the example specify the horizontal and vertical starting positions of the window.

**Keyword:**   ASCII windows

**Files:**   /dev/xt/??[0-7], /usr/lib/layersys/lsys.8;7;3, $DMD/lib/layersys/lsys.8;?;?

**See Also:**   jterm, jwin, sh, write

## lc

On SCO systems, the **lc** command outputs a multicolumn listing of all the files in the current working directory. This command is a system-level alias of the **ls** command. The behavior of **lc** is similar to **ls** on most other versions of UNIX.

**Keyword:**   file display

**See Also:**   chmod, du, find, l, lf, lr, lx, ls

## lc -f

This command outputs the names of all the files in the current directory. The **-f** argument is similar to the **-a** argument, except that the sorting is not alphabetical. The **-f** argument does no sorting at all; the files are output in the order in which entries appear in the directory.

**Keyword:**   file display

**See Also:**   l, lf, lr, ls, lx

## lc -m

This command lists the names of all the files in the current directory across the page, separated by commas.

**Keyword:**   file display

**See Also:**   l, lf, lr, ls, lx

## lc -r

This command outputs a listing of all the files in the current directory, in a multiple-column format. The files are sorted in reverse alphabetical order, Z–A.

**Keyword:**   file display

**See Also:**   l, lf, lr, ls, lx

## lc -s

This command outputs a listing of all the files in the current directory, in a multiple-column format, with the file size, in 512-byte blocks, listed to the left of the filename.

**Keyword:**   file display

**See Also:**   l, lf, lr, ls, lx

## lc -t

This command outputs a listing of all the files in the current directory, in a multiple-column format. The files are sorted by modification time, rather than filename.

**Keyword:**   file display

**See Also:**   l, lf, lr, ls, lx

ALL   SCO   ALL

ALL   SCO   ALL

ALL   SCO   ALL

ALL   SCO   ALL

ALL   SCO   ALL

## lc -tc

ALL SCO ALL

This command outputs a listing of the names of all the files in the current directory, sorting the names by the time of last modification of the inode, with the most recent first.

**Keyword:** file display

**See Also:** l, lf, lr, ls, lx

## lc -u

ALL SCO ALL

This command outputs a listing of all the files in the current directory, in a multiple-column format. The files are sorted by access time, rather than filename.

**Keyword:** file display

**See Also:** l, lf, lr, ls, lx

## LC_CTYPE

ALL ALL ALL

This is an environment variable that controls the classification of characters in shell commands. The default is usually American English.

**Keyword:** user environment

**See Also:** LANG

## LC_MESSAGES

ALL ALL ALL

This environment variable determines the language format of messages. The default is American English.

**Keyword:** user environment

**See Also:** LC_CTYPE

## ld -L /usr/users/perkie/lib

ALL ALL POWER

This command adds the directory **/usr/users/perkie/lib** to the beginning of the list of directories that are searched for object library files when compiling programs.

**Keyword:** programming

**Files:** /usr/ccs/lib*, /usr/lib/lib*, /usr/shlib/lib*.so (OSF)

**See Also:** cc, make, imake, ldd

## ld -L /usr/users/perkie/lib

ALL SVR4 END POWER

This command shows all the pathnames of shared objects that are loaded when the **xwd** program runs.

228

**Keyword:** programming
**Files:** /usr/ccs/lib*, /usr/lib/lib*, /usr/shlib/lib*.so (OSF)
**See Also:** cc, make, imake, ld

### ld file1.o

ALL ALL POWER

This command uses the link editor to create a program from the **file1.o** object file. The name of this program is **a.out**.
**Keyword:** programming
**Files:** /usr/ccs/lib*, /usr/lib/lib*, /usr/shlib/lib*.so (OSF)
**See Also:** cc, make, imake, ldd

### ldd -d xterm

ALL SVR4 END POWER

This command shows the pathnames of shared objects loaded when the **xterm** program is run. It also checks all references to data objects in **xterm**.
**Keyword:** programming
**See Also:** cc, make, imake, ld

### ldd -r w

ALL SVR4 END POWER

This command shows the pathnames of shared objects that **w** uses when it is executed; it also checks the references to data objects and functions.
**Keyword:** programming
**See Also:** cc, make, imake, ld

### ldsysdump -f /dev/rmt/ctape2 /home/temp/dump_file

ALL SVR4 SYSADM

This command it reads the dump image files from **/dev/rmt/ctape2** instead of **/dev/rmt/ctape1**.
**Keyword:** system information
**See Also:** crash

### ldsysdump /home/temp/dump_file

ALL SVR4 SYSADM

This is an interactive command that loads system dump image files from **/dev/rmt/ctape1** and builds them into a single file on the hard disk called **/home/temp/dump_file**.
**Keyword:** system information
**See Also:** crash

## leave

ALL   OSF   ALL

The **leave** command posts a reminder to leave at a certain time. The command is based on a 24-hour clock, but you can only set reminders for hours that remain in the current day. When entered with no options, **leave** prompts:

```
When do you have to leave?
```

Simply enter the time you have to go, and **leave** posts a reminder five minutes before that time. It then posts a second reminder one minute before the specified time. Consider putting the **leave** command in a shell startup file—**.profile** in the Bourne and Korn shells, or **.login** in the C shell.

**Keyword:**   time, user environment

**See Also:**   at, cal, calendar, date

## leave +125

ALL   OSF   ALL

Using **leave** with a numeric value tells it to post a reminder at a later time. The **+** option specifies that the following argument should be interpreted as the number of minutes. The example sets the alarm to go off in **1** hour and **25** minutes.

**Keyword:**   time, user environment

**See Also:**   at, cal, calendar, date

## leave 500

ALL   OSF   ALL

If you use a number directly as an option, **leave** interprets it to specify an exact time of day. The example sets the alarm for 5 PM, assuming that you enter it sometime after midnight and before 5 PM.

**Keyword:**   time, user environment

**See Also:**   at, cal, calendar, date

## less -?

ALL   PD   ALL

This command shows a brief overview of the options that you can use with **less**.

**Keyword:**   text display

**See Also:**   more, pg

## less -a book.txt

ALL   PD   ALL

When searching for a text string in the **book.txt** document, you can use the **-a** option to **less** to start the search after the last line of text is displayed on the screen.

**Keyword:** text display
**See Also:** more, pg

## less -B book.txt

This command disables automatic allocation of buffers, so that only the default number of buffers are used to page through the **book.txt** file.

**Keyword:** text display
**See Also:** more, pg

## less -b50 book.txt

The option **-b50** tells **less** to use 50 1 KB buffers when paging through the **book.txt** file, instead of 10 buffers, which is the default.

**Keyword:** text display
**See Also:** more, pg

## less -c book.txt

This command clears the screen and writes from the top down, rather than the bottom up, which can result in faster screen redraws.

**Keyword:** text display
**See Also:** more, pg

## less -d book.txt

This command is used to suppress error messages output by **less** if the terminal doesn't support some needed type of output. This is useful if you are using **less** with a dumb terminal.

**Keyword:** text display
**See Also:** more, pg

## less -E book.txt

Use this command when you want to exit **less** the first time you reach the end of the file.

**Keyword:** text display
**See Also:** more, pg

ALL PD ALL

### less -e book.txt

ALL    PD    ALL

Use this command when you want to exit **less** the second time you reach the end of the file. By default, the only way you can exit **less** is by typing **q**, **ZZ**, or **Q**, or by hitting the ESC key twice.

**Keyword:**    text display

**See Also:**    more, pg

### less -f /dev/tty00

ALL    PD    ALL

This command shows the input from the serial port **/dev/tty00**. The **-f** argument to **less** is used for opening nonregular files, such as binary and special character files. By default, **less** will not open these files.

**Keyword:**    text display

**See Also:**    more, pg

### less -h35 book.txt

ALL    PD    ALL

This command is used to specify the maximum number of lines to scroll backward in the **book.txt** file.

**Keyword:**    text display

**See Also:**    more, pg

### less -i book.txt

ALL    PD    ALL

Use this command when you are searching through a file, and you want to ignore case. The **-i** option to **less** is used for ignoring case.

**Keyword:**    text display

**See Also:**    more, pg

### less -j12 book.txt

ALL    PD    ALL

Use this command when you want the result of a search through the **book.txt** file to be placed on line 12 of your terminal.

**Keyword:**    text display

**See Also:**    more, pg

### less -M book.txt

ALL    PD    ALL

This command has **less** prompt with the name of the opened file, the line you are at, and the percentage of the file you have already scrolled.

**Keyword:** text display
**See Also:** more, pg

### less -m book.txt

ALL  PD  ALL

This command has a **less** prompt that is similar to **more**. Rather than getting the default colon prompt, **less** tells you the percentage of the file you have already scrolled.
**Keyword:** text display
**See Also:** more, pg

### less -N book.txt

ALL  PD  ALL

This command begins each line of output with line numbers.
**Keyword:** text display
**See Also:** more, pg

### less -Q book.txt

ALL  PD  ALL

The **-Q** option to **less** is used if you never want the terminal bell to be rung.
**Keyword:** text display
**See Also:** more, pg

### less -q book.txt

ALL  PD  ALL

This command tells **less** not to ring the terminal bell when you try to scroll past the end of the file, or before the beginning of the file.
**Keyword:** text display
**See Also:** more, pg

### less -r book.txt

ALL  PD  ALL

This command is used if you want to view raw control characters in the **book.txt** file.
**Keyword:** text display
**See Also:** more, pg

### less -S book.txt

ALL  PD  ALL

This command disables word-wrap in **less**. When viewing the **book.txt** file, any lines longer than the terminal width will be cut off.

| | | |
|---|---|---|

**Keyword:**   text display
**See Also:**   more, pg

### less -s book.txt

ALL   PD   ALL

This command causes consecutive blank lines to be output as a single blank line when viewing the **book.txt** file. The **-s** argument to **less** is useful for viewing **nroff** output.
**Keyword:**   text display
**See Also:**   more, pg

### less -x5 book.txt

ALL   PD   ALL

When viewing the file **book.txt**, **less** sets a tab to equal five spaces. Without the **-x** argument to **less**, a tab would equal eight spaces.
**Keyword:**   text display
**See Also:**   more, pg

### less book.txt

ALL   PD   ALL

This command is similar to **pg** and **more**. It allows you to read through the **book.txt** file, one screenful of text at a time. In addition, you can scroll backward through a file by typing the **b** key.
**Keyword:**   text display
**See Also:**   more, pg

### let ´x = 9 * x´ y=y+7

KSH   ALL   SCRIPT

In this example, the **let** command evaluates two independent expressions. The first expression, **x = 9 * x**,contains spaces and must therefore be quoted. The second expression does not contain spaces and does not require quotes, although you can use them for consistency's sake.
**Keyword:**   math, programming
**See Also:**   awk, bc, dc, expr, xcalc

### let width=columns-offset

KSH   ALL   SCRIPT

The **let** command is a Korn shell built-in. It lets you evaluate arithmetic expressions, without the overhead of calling the **expr** utility as you must do in the Bourne shell. In the example, **width** is set to the value of **columns-offset**.
**Keyword:**   math, programming
**See Also:**   awk, bc, dc, expr, xcalc

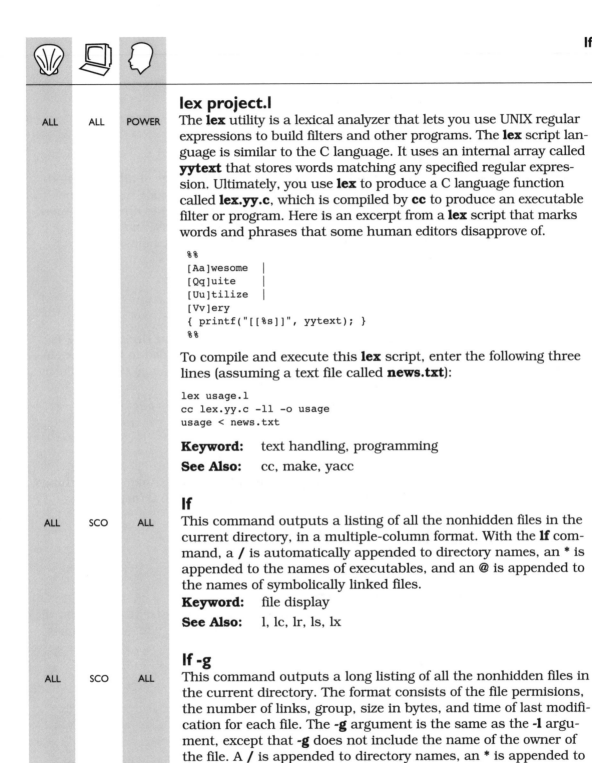

ALL  ALL  POWER

## lex project.l

The **lex** utility is a lexical analyzer that lets you use UNIX regular expressions to build filters and other programs. The **lex** script language is similar to the C language. It uses an internal array called **yytext** that stores words matching any specified regular expression. Ultimately, you use **lex** to produce a C language function called **lex.yy.c**, which is compiled by **cc** to produce an executable filter or program. Here is an excerpt from a **lex** script that marks words and phrases that some human editors disapprove of.

```
%%
[Aa]wesome   |
[Qq]uite     |
[Uu]tilize   |
[Vv]ery
{ printf("[[%s]]", yytext); }
%%
```

To compile and execute this **lex** script, enter the following three lines (assuming a text file called **news.txt**):

```
lex usage.l
cc lex.yy.c -ll -o usage
usage < news.txt
```

**Keyword:**  text handling, programming

**See Also:**  cc, make, yacc

## lf

ALL  SCO  ALL

This command outputs a listing of all the nonhidden files in the current directory, in a multiple-column format. With the **lf** command, a **/** is automatically appended to directory names, an **\*** is appended to the names of executables, and an **@** is appended to the names of symbolically linked files.

**Keyword:**  file display

**See Also:**  l, lc, lr, ls, lx

## lf -g

ALL  SCO  ALL

This command outputs a long listing of all the nonhidden files in the current directory. The format consists of the file permisions, the number of links, group, size in bytes, and time of last modification for each file. The **-g** argument is the same as the **-l** argument, except that **-g** does not include the name of the owner of the file. A **/** is appended to directory names, an **\*** is appended to the names of executables, and an **@** is appended to the names of symbolically linked files.

**235**

**Keyword:** file display
**See Also:** l, lc, lr, ls, lx

## lf -i

ALL    SCO    ALL

This command outputs a listing of the names of all the nonhidden files in the current directory, with the inode number one space to the left of each file. A **/** is appended to directory names, an * is appended to the names of executables, and an @ is appended to the names of symbolically linked files.

**Keyword:** file display
**See Also:** l, lc, lr, ls, lx

## lf -ld /usr

ALL    SCO    ALL

This command outputs the status of the **/usr** directory. A **/** is appended to directory names, an * is appended to the names of executables, and an @ is appended to the names of symbolically linked files.

**Keyword:** file display
**See Also:** l, lc, lr, ls, lx

## limit coredumpsize 0m

CSH    ALL    POWER
SYSADM

The **limit** command is built into the C shell. Among other things, it lets you limit the **size** of **coredump** files to **0** megabytes.

**Keyword:** user environment
**Files:** $HOME/.cshrc
**See Also:** csh

## limit filesize 22m

CSH    ALL    POWER
SYSADM

You can use **limit** to restrict the maximum size of any file on the system. You might consider this as a strategy to guard against runaway files.

**Keyword:** user environment
**Files:** $HOME/.cshrc
**See Also:** csh

## line < phone

ALL    ALL    SCRIPT
POWER

This command outputs the first line of the file called **phone**.

**Keyword:** text handling

**See Also:** cat, head, tail, more, pg

### line > test.txt

This command reads a line of text from standard input, and when you press Return, it writes the line to **test.txt**.

**Keyword:** text handling

**See Also:** cat, head, tail, more, pg, less

### line >> test.txt

This command appends the typed in-line to the end of the **test.txt** file.

**Keyword:** text handling

**See Also:** cat, head, tail, more, pg, less

### line | awk ´{print $1 "::" $7 ":" $8 ":" $2 "," $3 "," $4 ":" $5 ":/bin/" $6}´ >> /etc/passwd

This command adds a user to the system by writing a new line at the end of the **/etc/passwd** file. To use this program, type the command, then supply the user's information in this form:

```
jond JohnDoe Essex 555-1234 /demo/jond ksh 789 625
```

where **jond** is the username, **JohnDoe** is the user's real name, **Essex** is the residence, **555-1234** is the phone number, **/demo/jond** is the home directory, **ksh** is the shell, **789** is the user ID, and **625** is the user's group ID.

NOTE: This is set up so that the new account starts *with no password!*

**Keyword:** text handling

**Files:** /etc/passwd

**See Also:** awk, passwd

### LINENO

This environment variable contains the line number of the command currently executing in a script or function.

**Keyword:** programming

**See Also:** expr

ALL   ALL   SCRIPT POWER

ALL   ALL   END SCRIPT POWER

ALL   ALL   SYSADM

KSH   SVR4 SCO   SCRIPT

| | | | |
|---|---|---|---|
| ALL | ALL | SYSADM | |

## link

Avoid using this command. It is designed to link filenames and directories, but does not have rigorous error checking. It can cause severe system problems if used incorrectly. Use the **ln** command instead.

**Keyword:**   file handling

**See Also:**   ln

| | | |
|---|---|---|
| ALL | ALL | POWER |

## lint -a myprog.c

The **-a** option to **lint** ignores long variable values that are not declared to be long.

**Keyword:**   programming

**See Also:**   cc, dbx, imake, make

| | | |
|---|---|---|
| ALL | ALL | POWER |

## lint -b myprog.c

This command displays the usual **lint** output, but **break** statements that are never reached in the **myprog.c** program are not output as errors because of the **-b** option.

**Keyword:**   programming

**See Also:**   cc, dbx, imake, make

| | | |
|---|---|---|
| ALL | ALL | POWER |

## lint -c myprog.c

This command creates a file called **myprog.ln** that has the same properties as an object file created by the **cc** command.

**Keyword:**   programming

**See Also:**   cc, dbx, imake, make

| | | |
|---|---|---|
| ALL | ALL | POWER |

## lint -h myprog.c

This command outputs any errors or even bad style in the C program **myprog.c**, but it doesn't use heuristic tests to find the errors or determine if the style is bad.

**Keyword:**   programming

**See Also:**   cc, dbx, imake, make

| | | |
|---|---|---|
| ALL | ALL | POWER |

## lint -m myprog.c

The **-m** option to **lint** suppresses outputting errors about external symbols that could be declared static.

**Keyword:**   programming

**See Also:**   cc, dbx, imake, make

**238**

### lint -n myprog.c

| | | |
|---|---|---|
| ALL | ALL | POWER |

The **-n** option tells the **lint** program not to check for compatibility against the standard C **lint** library.

**Keyword:**    programming

**See Also:**    cc, dbx, imake, make

### lint -u subprog1.c

| | | |
|---|---|---|
| ALL | ALL | POWER |

This command is an excellent choice if you want to run **lint** on just a subprogram that is part of a larger program. It does not output errors for undefined or unused functions or variables.

**Keyword:**    programming

**See Also:**    cc, dbx, imake, make

### lint -v myprog.c

| | | |
|---|---|---|
| ALL | ALL | POWER |

This command produces the standard **lint** output, except that it doesn't output an error message if there are unused arguments in some of the functions in **myprog.c**.

**Keyword:**    programming

**See Also:**    cc, dbx, imake, make

### lint -x subprog1.c

| | | |
|---|---|---|
| ALL | ALL | POWER |

This command suppresses error messages for externally declared but unused variables.

**Keyword:**    programming

**See Also:**    cc, dbx, imake, make

### lint myprog.c

| | | |
|---|---|---|
| ALL | ALL | POWER |

This command outputs features of C source code contained in the **myprog.c** file that are likely to have bugs, are nonportable, or are inefficient. It strictly enforces function and variable type checking.

**Keyword:**    programming

**See Also:**    cc, dbx, imake, make

### listdgrp disk

| | | |
|---|---|---|
| ALL | SVR4 | SYSADM |

This command outputs the members of the **disk** device group. The **listdgrp** program gets its information by querying the **/etc/dgroup.tab** file.

**Keyword:** devices

**Files:** /etc/dgroup.tab

**See Also:** df, diskadd, mkfs, mknod, mountall, mountfsys, newfs, smit, sysadmin, sysadmsh

## listres

ALL   XWIN   ALL

The **listres** client program displays a list of widget-based resources in effect for the X Window System. The program is designed mainly for software engineers. Entering **listres** at the command prompt causes all currently active widget resources to be displayed. Here are a few lines of sample output:

```
clock       Object\Rect\Core\Simple\Clock
dialog      Object\Rect\Core\Composite\Constraint\Form\Dialog
scrollbar   Object\Rect\Core\Simple\Scrollbar
wmShell     Object\Rect\Core\Composite\Shell\WMShell
```

**Keyword:** X resources

**See Also:** appres, editres, listres, viewres, xrdb

## listres -all

ALL   XWIN   ALL

This example provides a different form of output for **listres**. In addition to providing the widget class in the first column, the right-hand columns tell you the type of resource. Here is some sample output:

```
WMShell   baseWidth     BaseWidth     Int
Core      borderColor   BorderColor   Pixel
Core      borderPixmap  Pixmap        Pixmap
Rect      x             Position      Position
Rect      y             Position      Position
```

**Keyword:** X resources

**See Also:** appres, editres, listres, viewres, xrdb

## listusers

ALL   SVR4   POWER SYSADM

This command shows a list of the usernames and full names of everyone who has an account on the system.

**Keyword:** user information

**Files:** /etc/passwd

**See Also:** cat, f, finger, passwd, w, who

### listusers -g other,adm

ALL  SVR4  POWER SYSADM

This command is similar to **listusers**, except that two groups are specified after the **-g** argument. This outputs all the users who are in either the **other** group, the **adm** group, or both.

**Keyword:**   user information

**Files:**       /etc/passwd, /etc/groups

**See Also:**   cat, f, finger, passwd, w, who, groups

### listusers -g other,adm -l perkie,alans

ALL  SVR4  SYSADM

This command outputs all the users in the **other** and **adm** groups, and checks whether **perkie** and **alans** are valid usernames.

**Keyword:**   user information

**Files:**       /etc/passwd, /etc/groups

**See Also:**   cat, f, finger, passwd, w, who, groups

### listusers -g wheel

ALL  SVR4  POWER SYSADM

This command lists all the usersnames and full names of everyone who has an account on the system and is a member of the **wheel** group.

**Keyword:**   user information

**Files:**       /etc/passwd, /etc/groups

**See Also:**   cat, f, finger, passwd, w, who, groups

### listusers -l perkie

ALL  SVR4  POWER SYSADM

This command simply checks to see if **perkie** is a valid login username on the system. If it is, **listusers** outputs **perkie**, and then perkie's full name. If **perkie** isn't valid, then **listusers** outputs a message saying, "perkie is not a user login."

**Keyword:**   user information

**Files:**       /etc/passwd, /etc/groups

**See Also:**   cat, f, finger, passwd, w, who, groups

### listusers -l perkie,alans

ALL  SVR4  POWER SYSADM

This command provides the standard **listusers** output, but it checks both **perkie** and **alans** to see if they are valid usernames on the system.

**Keyword:**   user information

**Files:**       /etc/passwd, /etc/groups

**See Also:**   cat, f, finger, passwd, w, who, groups

### ln -f /u1/archive/* /u3/FTP/archive

ALL   SVR4   SYSADM

Unlike the BSD argument, with SVR4, the **-f** argument links files without questioning the user, even if the mode of the target forbids writing.

**Keyword:**   user information

**See Also:**   ls, rm

### ln -f /u1/X11R5/bin /usr/bin/X11

ALL   BSD   SYSADM

This command links directories. The **-f** argument to **ln**, however, hard links the directories, rather than linking them symbolically. This command can be executed only by the superuser.

**Keyword:**   file handling

**See Also:**   awk cat, chmod, cp, cpio, du, find, join, ln, ls, mv, pr, tar, touch, tr

### ln -n /u1/perkie/mbox /u2/alans/mbox

ALL   SVR4   SYSADM

This command creates a link from the **/u1/perkie/mbox** file to a new file, **/u2/alans/mbox**. If **/u2/alans/mbox** already exists, the contents of **/u2/alans/mbox** will not be overwritten.

**Keyword:**   file handling

**See Also:**   ls, rm

### ln -s /home3 H:

ALL   ALL   POWER SYSADM

This example continues the plight of the PC user who needs to enter a drive letter and colon to understand directory hierarchies. Instead of an alias, as presented earlier, this example links the real directory **/home3** to **H:**, which is a symbolic link to **/home3**. After the link is made, you can change directories to **/home3** from anywhere on the system by entering **cd /H:** at the prompt. Also, you might want to see what an **ls -lsd** listing of **H:** looks like:

```
0 lrwxr-xr-x  1 root  system  5 Feb 23 07:23 /H: -> /home3
```

Note that when you actually change directories into **H:**, the **pwd** command outputs the original directory (**/home3**, in the example). If you enter **echo $cwd** in the C shell, however, the symbolic name is output.

**Keyword:**   directories

**See Also:**   cwd, pwd

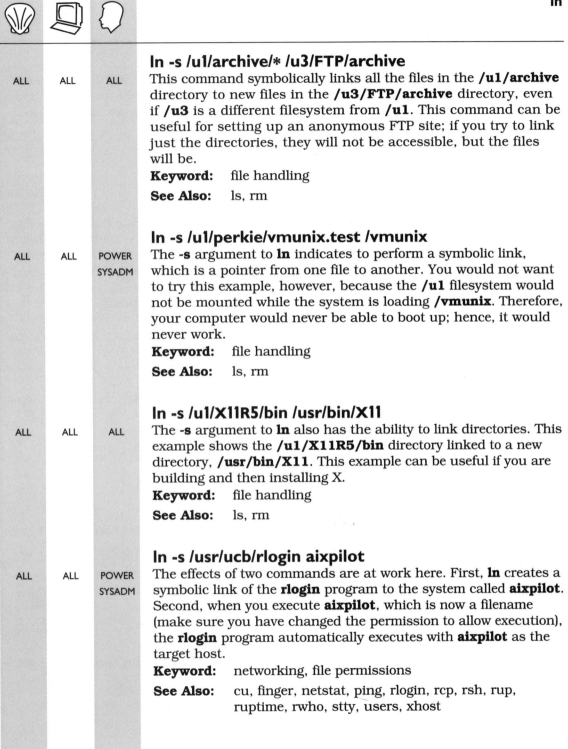

### ln -s /u1/archive/* /u3/FTP/archive

| | | |
|---|---|---|
| ALL | ALL | ALL |

This command symbolically links all the files in the **/u1/archive** directory to new files in the **/u3/FTP/archive** directory, even if **/u3** is a different filesystem from **/u1**. This command can be useful for setting up an anonymous FTP site; if you try to link just the directories, they will not be accessible, but the files will be.

**Keyword:**     file handling

**See Also:**     ls, rm

### ln -s /u1/perkie/vmunix.test /vmunix

| | | |
|---|---|---|
| ALL | ALL | POWER SYSADM |

The **-s** argument to **ln** indicates to perform a symbolic link, which is a pointer from one file to another. You would not want to try this example, however, because the **/u1** filesystem would not be mounted while the system is loading **/vmunix**. Therefore, your computer would never be able to boot up; hence, it would never work.

**Keyword:**     file handling

**See Also:**     ls, rm

### ln -s /u1/X11R5/bin /usr/bin/X11

| | | |
|---|---|---|
| ALL | ALL | ALL |

The **-s** argument to **ln** also has the ability to link directories. This example shows the **/u1/X11R5/bin** directory linked to a new directory, **/usr/bin/X11**. This example can be useful if you are building and then installing X.

**Keyword:**     file handling

**See Also:**     ls, rm

### ln -s /usr/ucb/rlogin aixpilot

| | | |
|---|---|---|
| ALL | ALL | POWER SYSADM |

The effects of two commands are at work here. First, **ln** creates a symbolic link of the **rlogin** program to the system called **aixpilot**. Second, when you execute **aixpilot**, which is now a filename (make sure you have changed the permission to allow execution), the **rlogin** program automatically executes with **aixpilot** as the target host.

**Keyword:**     networking, file permissions

**See Also:**     cu, finger, netstat, ping, rlogin, rcp, rsh, rup, ruptime, rwho, stty, users, xhost

| ALL | ALL | ALL |
| --- | --- | --- |

## ln /u1/perkie/vmunix.test /vmunix

This command results in a message to the effect that you can't make a cross-device link. This means that you are trying to create a hard link between two different filesystems, which is not allowed.

**Keyword:** file handling

**See Also:** ls, rm

| ALL | ALL | ALL |
| --- | --- | --- |

## ln test.c temp.c

This command links the already existing **test.c** file to a new file called **temp.c**. The contents of **temp.c** will be identical to that of **test.c**. If the contents of **temp.c** are changed, with **vi** for example, then the **test.c** file will be changed as well. When executing a long listing of the directory with **ls -l**, both **temp.c** and **test.c** will be the same size and have the same permissions.

**Keyword:** file handling

**See Also:** ls, rm

| ALL | ALL | SYSADM |
| --- | --- | --- |

## logger -f special.conf

This command logs all the lines in the **special.conf** file as a message for the system log file.

**Keyword:** system information

**Files:** /etc/syslog.conf

**See Also:** syslogd

| ALL | ALL | SYSADM |
| --- | --- | --- |

## logger -f special.conf -p 6

This command logs all the lines in the **special.conf** file and gives them a priority of **6**.

**Keyword:** system information

**Files:** /etc/syslog.conf

**See Also:** syslogd

| ALL | ALL | SYSADM |
| --- | --- | --- |

## logger -f special.conf -p info

This command logs all the lines in the **special.conf** file and gives them a priority of **info**.

**Keyword:** system information

**Files:** /etc/syslog.conf

**See Also:** syslogd

## logger -f special.conf -p notice.user

| | | |
|---|---|---|
| ALL | ALL | SYSADM |

This command logs all the lines in the **special.conf** file and gives them a priority of **notice**; the facility is **user**. Example priorities are:

| string | numeric |
|--------|---------|
| panic  | 0 |
| emerg  | 0 |
| alert  | 1 |
| crit   | 2 |
| err    | 3 |
| error  | 3 |

Example facilities are:

| string | numeric |
|--------|---------|
| kern   | 0 |
| user   | 8 |
| mail   | 16 |
| daemon | 24 |
| auth   | 32 |

**Keyword:**   system information

**Files:**   /etc/syslog.conf

**See Also:**   syslogd

## logger -f special.conf -t "test configuration"

This use of **logger** logs all lines to **special.conf,** but each line is logged with **test configuration** because of the **-t** argument to **logger**.

**Keyword:**   system information

**Files:**   /etc/syslog.conf

**See Also:**   syslogd

## logger -i system_reboot

The **-i** argument to **logger** causes the process ID of the process running **logger** to be logged with the message **system reboot**.

**Keyword:**   system information

**Files:**   /etc/syslog.conf

**See Also:**   syslogd

## logger system_reboot

This command is used to log the message **system reboot** to the system log file.

**Keyword:** system information
**Files:** /etc/syslog.conf
**See Also:** syslogd

## login

ALL    ALL    ALL

This command signs the user **perkie** onto the system. You may find this command useful to change from one user to another. You can also use the **login** program to log in as another user from an existing shell session. The shell session, however, must be the original **login** shell. The presence of a **.hushlogin** file in a user's **$HOME** directory suppresses mail and greeting messages at **login**. Another related file is **/etc/nologin**, which the **shutdown** command creates to prevent logins while shutting down the system.

**Keyword:** user environment
**Files:** $HOME/.hushlogin, /etc/nologin, /etc/passwd
**See Also:** rlogin, telnet

## logins

ALL    SVR4    SYSADM

The **logins** command can be useful to administrators. In its basic form, as in the example, it provides a listing of all login accounts, consisting of login ID, user ID, primary group name, primary group ID, and information from the account field in **/etc/passwd**:

```
sys        3        sys        3        0000-Admin(0000)
adm        4        adm        4        0000-Admin(0000)
uucp       5        uucp       5        0000-uucp(0000)
lp         7        lp         8        0000-LP(0000)
nuucp      10                  10       0000-uucp(0000)
listen     37       adm        4        Network Admin
```

**Keyword:** system information
**See Also:** env, login, users, who

## logins -p

ALL    SVR4    SYSADM

The **-p** option to **logins** examines user accounts, and reports which ones do not have a password. System administrators should use this feature, or a similar tool, to perform this activity on a regular basis.

**Keyword:** system information
**See Also:** env, login, users, who

### logins -x

| | | |
|---|---|---|
| ALL | SVR4 | SYSADM |

Using the **-x** option to **logins** provides password aging information about each user. Items include password status, the date a password was last changed, the interval in days between changes, and the allowable interval before the system requires a change.

**Keyword:** system information

**See Also:** env, login, users, who

### logname

| | | |
|---|---|---|
| ALL | ALL | END |

This command displays your username. The output is the same as that of the **whoami** command.

**Keyword:** user information

**Files:** /etc/profile

**See Also:** listusers, w, who, whoami

### look -d apr96

| | | |
|---|---|---|
| ALL | ALL | ALL |

This version of **look** searches a sorted file by letters, digits, tabs, and spaces. Other characters are not compared.

**Keyword:** writing

**Files:** /usr/share/dict/words, /usr/ucblib/dict/words (SVR4)

**See Also:** grep, sort, spell, spellin, spellout

### look -f Apr96

| | | |
|---|---|---|
| ALL | ALL | ALL |

The **-f** argument to **look** causes the command to ignore the case of the search item—in this example, **Apr96**.

**Keyword:** writing

**Files:** /usr/share/dict/words, /usr/ucblib/dict/words (SVR4)

**See Also:** grep, sort, spell, spellin, spellout

### look -to report

| | | |
|---|---|---|
| ALL | ALL | ALL |

This command outputs everything in the system dictionary that has an **r** in it. The **-t** argument has **look** ignore everything after the letter that is specified with the **-t**—in this case, **e**. This command is functionally the same as **look r**.

**Keyword:** writing

**Files:** /usr/share/dict/words, /usr/ucblib/dict/words

**See Also:** grep, sort, spell, spellin, spellout

**247**

## look im

ALL    ALL    END

The **look** command can parse any sorted text file and return matching text strings. You can specify a partial or complete word or phrase if you design your sorted files properly. This example displays all the words in the **/usr/share/dict/words** file that begin with **im**, such as **immodest** and **impassioned**.

**Keyword:**   writing

**Files:**      /usr/share/dict/words (BSD),
              /usr/ucblib/dict/words (SVR4)

**See Also:**   grep, sort, spell, spellin, spellout

## look sed book.txt

ALL    ALL    ALL

This use of **look** searches the sorted database that we built while writing this book. It outputs every command that begins with **sed**.

**Keyword:**   writing, text display

**Files:**      /usr/share/dict/words (BSD),
              /usr/ucblib/dict/words (SVR4)

**See Also:**   grep, sort, spell, spellin, spellout

## lookbib report.bib

ALL    ALL    POWER

This command is used with the **addbib** command. It will interactively search through the bibliography data file called **report.bib**. When prompted by the **>**, enter a search request, and **lookbib** shows everything that matched.

**Keyword:**   writing, text handling

**Files:**      $HOME: x.ia, x.ib, x.ic, x.ig

**See Also:**   addbib, indxbib, refer, roffbib, sortbib

## lp -c test.c

ALL    ALL    POWER
              SYSADM

This command prints the **test.c** file on the default system printer. The **-c** option to **lp** causes it to copy the **test.c** file, rather than create a link. By default, **lp** always makes a link and then prints the link.

**Keyword:**   printing

**Files:**      /etc/printcap (BSD), /var/spool/lp/*

**See Also:**   enable, lpstat, accept, lpadmin, lpfilter, lpforms,
              lpsched, lpsystem, lpusers, lpq, lpr, lprm, lpc, lpd

## lp -d mcc_cnlw test.c

ALL   ALL   POWER SYSADM

This command prints the **test.c** file on the printer called **mcc_cnlw**. The **-d** argument to **lp** is used to identify a specific printer to be used.

**Keyword:**   printing

**Files:**   /etc/printcap (BSD), /var/spool/lp/*

**See Also:**   enable, lpstat, accept, lpadmin, lpfilter, lpforms, lpsched, lpsystem, lpusers, lpq, lpr, lprm, lpc, lpd

## lp -f current-jobs -d mccpr job_status.txt

ALL   SVR4 SCO   END POWER SYSADM

This command prints the **job_status.txt** file on the printer **mccpr**, if it has the forms specified by **current-jobs**. If this form is not loaded in the printer, the print request is rejected.

**Keyword:**   printing

**Files:**   /var/spool/lp/*

**See Also:**   enable, lpstat, accept, lpadmin, lpfilter, lpforms, lpsched, lpsystem, lpusers, lpq, lpr, lprm, lpc, lpd

## lp -H hold book.txt

ALL   SVR4 SCO   SYSADM

This command holds the printing of the **book.txt** file until **lp** is notified that the file should be printed.

**Keyword:**   printing

**Files:**   /var/spool/lp/*

**See Also:**   enable, lpstat, accept, lpadmin, lpfilter, lpforms, lpsched, lpsystem, lpusers, lpq, lpr, lprm, lpc, lpd

## lp -H immediate book.txt

ALL   SVR4 SCO   SYSADM

This command prints the **book.txt** file as soon as the printer finishes the current job, regardless of the numbers of print jobs that were requested prior to the command.

**Keyword:**   printing

**Files:**   /var/spool/lp/*

**See Also:**   enable, lpstat, accept, lpadmin, lpfilter, lpforms, lpsched, lpsystem, lpusers, lpq, lpr, lprm, lpc, lpd

## lp -H resume book.txt

ALL   SVR4 SCO   SYSADM

This command notifies **lp** that it should start printing a job that has been held with the **-H hold** sequence.

**Keyword:** printing

**Files:** /var/spool/lp/*

**See Also:** enable, lpstat, accept, lpadmin, lpfilter, lpforms, lpsched, lpsystem, lpusers, lpq, lpr, lprm, lpc, lpd

### lp -m test.c

ALL    ALL    POWER SYSADM

This command prints out the **test.c** file on the default system printer. When the job has been successfully completed, **lp** will then send email to the user, saying that the job has been completed.

**Keyword:** printing

**Files:** /etc/printcap (BSD), /var/spool/lp/*

**See Also:** enable, lpstat, accept, lpadmin, lpfilter, lpforms, lpsched, lpsystem, lpusers, lpq, lpr, lprm, lpc, lpd

### lp -n 4 test.c

ALL    ALL    POWER SYSADM

This command prints out four copies of the **test.c** file on the default system printer.

**Keyword:** printing

**Files:** /etc/printcap (BSD), /var/spool/lp/*

**See Also:** enable, lpstat, accept, lpadmin, lpfilter, lpforms, lpsched, lpsystem, lpusers, lpq, lpr, lprm, lpc, lpd

### lp -q 0 test.c

ALL    SVR4 SCO    SYSADM

This command requests that the **test.c** file have the highest priority. The priority level is inversely proportional to the number following the **-q** option. The lowest priority setting is 39.

**Keyword:** printing

**Files:** /var/spool/lp/*

**See Also:** enable, lpstat, accept, lpadmin, lpfilter, lpforms, lpsched, lpsystem, lpusers, lpq, lpr, lprm, lpc, lpd

### lp -s test.c

ALL    SVR4 SCO    ALL

This command is similar to using **lp** without options. It prints out the **test.c** file, but doesn't output any messages, unlike the default **lp** command.

**Keyword:** printing

**Files:** /var/spool/lp/*

**See Also:**   enable, lpstat, accept, lpadmin, lpfilter, lpforms, lpsched, lpsystem, lpusers, lpq, lpr, lprm, lpc, lpd

## lp -t "This is the file test.c" test.c

This command prints the title **This is the file test.c** on the first page, the banner page; then, starting with the second page, it prints the **test.c** file.

**Keyword:**   printing

**Files:**   /etc/printcap (BSD), /var/spool/lp/*

**See Also:**   enable, lpstat, accept, lpadmin, lpfilter, lpforms, lpsched, lpsystem, lpusers, lpq, lpr, lprm, lpc, lpd

## lp -w test.c

This command notifies the user after it has completed printing. Unlike the **-m** option, the **-w** option sends a message to the user's terminal, and only if the user is not currently logged in does it send email.

**Keyword:**   printing

**Files:**   /etc/printcap (BSD), /var/spool/lp/*

**See Also:**   enable, lpstat, accept, lpadmin, lpfilter, lpforms, lpsched, lpsystem, lpusers, lpq, lpr, lprm, lpc, lpd, mail, mailx

## lp report.txt

The **lp** command sends files to a line printer for printing. If you do not specify a file, **lp** uses standard input. The example prints the file called **report.txt** on the default system printer.

**Keyword:**   printing

**Files:**   /etc/printcap (BSD), /var/spool/lp/*

**See Also:**   enable, lpstat, accept, lpadmin, lpfilter, lpforms, lpsched, lpsystem, lpusers, lpq, lpr, lprm, lpc, lpd

## lpadmin -p hplj4m -A list

This command outputs a list of the error, or errors, that have caused the printer to stop functioning.

**Keyword:**   printing

**Files:**   /var/spool/lp/*

**See Also:**   enable, lpstat, accept, lpadmin, lpfilter, lpforms, lpsched, lpsystem, lpusers, lpq, lpr, lprm, lpc, lpd

Left margin tags:

- ALL | ALL | ALL
- ALL | ALL | POWER SYSADM
- ALL | ALL | ALL
- ALL | SVR4 SCO | SYSADM

**lpadmin**

### lpadmin -p hplj4m -A mail

ALL  SVR4  SYSADM
SCO

The **lpadmin** is an all-purpose printer management program. The program lets you define and configure new printers, change the characteristics of printers already in use, and remove unwanted printers. In the example, **lpadmin** creates a new printer on the system called **hplj4m** and configures it to send the administrator mail if it detects a printer fault. If the printer **hplj4m** already exists, it is configured to to send the administrator mail if it detects a printer fault.

**Keyword:**   printing

**Files:**   /var/spool/lp/*

**See Also:**   enable, lpstat, accept, lpadmin, lpfilter, lpforms, lpsched, lpsystem, lpusers, lpq, lpr, lprm, lpc, lpd

### lpadmin -p hplj4m -A none

ALL  SVR4  SYSADM
SCO

This command turns off the printer messaging system, but it doesn't automatically turn the system back on like **quiet**. You must run the **lpadmin** program again to get messaging back on.

**Keyword:**   printing

**Files:**   /var/spool/lp/*

**See Also:**   enable, lpstat, accept, lpadmin, lpfilter, lpforms, lpsched, lpsystem, lpusers, lpq, lpr, lprm, lpc, lpd

### lpadmin -p hplj4m -A quiet

ALL  SVR4  SYSADM
SCO

This command turns off the printer messaging system for the current problem. This is a useful command. While trying to fix a printer problem, you don't also have to deal with constantly being told something you already know. After the current problem is fixed, the **quiet** option is automatically shut off.

**Keyword:**   printing

**Files:**   /var/spool/lp/*

**See Also:**   enable, lpstat, accept, lpadmin, lpfilter, lpforms, lpsched, lpsystem, lpusers, lpq, lpr, lprm, lpc, lpd

### lpadmin -p hplj4m -A write

ALL  SVR4  SYSADM
SCO

This use of **lpadmin** creates a new printer or reconfigures an existing one. Instead of sending the administrator mail, however, it sends a message directly to the administrator's terminal screen. If the person is logged into multiple terminals, the computer arbitrarily chooses one.

**Keyword:** printing

**Files:** /var/spool/lp/*

**See Also:** enable, lpstat, accept, lpadmin, lpfilter, lpforms, lpsched, lpsystem, lpusers, lpq, lpr, lprm, lpc, lpd

### lpadmin -p hplj4m -c 600dpi_postscript

This command tells the system the printer's class. If the class doesn't exist, it will be created.

**Keyword:** printing

**Files:** /var/spool/lp/*

**See Also:** enable, lpstat, accept, lpadmin, lpfilter, lpforms, lpsched, lpsystem, lpusers, lpq, lpr, lprm, lpc, lpd

### lpadmin -p hplj4m -D ´Hewlett Packard LaserJet 4M´

This command is used to provide a detailed description of the printer.

**Keyword:** printing

**Files:** /var/spool/lp/*

**See Also:** enable, lpstat, accept, lpadmin, lpfilter, lpforms, lpsched, lpsystem, lpusers, lpq, lpr, lprm, lpc, lpd

### lpadmin -p hplj4m -e hplj3ps

This command copies the interface program associated with the **hplj3ps** printer, and uses it with the new **hplj4m** printer.

**Keyword:** printing

**Files:** /var/spool/lp/*

**See Also:** enable, lpstat, accept, lpadmin, lpfilter, lpforms, lpsched, lpsystem, lpusers, lpq, lpr, lprm, lpc, lpd

### lpadmin -p hplj4m -f allow:paper_types

This command tells the system that the **hplj4m** printer can print on all the forms that are listed in the **paper_types** file.

**Keyword:** printing

**Files:** /var/spool/lp/*

**See Also:** enable, lpstat, accept, lpadmin, lpfilter, lpforms, lpsched, lpsystem, lpusers, lpq, lpr, lprm, lpc, lpd

ALL    SVR4    SYSADM
       SCO

ALL    SVR4    SYSADM
       SCO

ALL    SVR4    SYSADM
       SCO

ALL    SVR4    SYSADM
       SCO

### lpadmin -p hplj4m -f deny:paper_types

**ALL** **SVR4** **SYSADM**
**SCO**

This command tells the system that the **hplj4m** printer cannot print on the forms listed in the **paper_types** file.

**Keyword:** printing

**Files:** /var/spool/lp/*

**See Also:** enable, lpstat, accept, lpadmin, lpfilter, lpforms, lpsched, lpsystem, lpusers, lpq, lpr, lprm, lpc, lpd

### lpadmin -p hplj4m -h

**ALL** **SVR4** **SYSADM**
**SCO**

This command tells the system that the **hplj4m** printer is hard-wired to the computer.

**Keyword:** printing

**Files:** /var/spool/lp/*

**See Also:** enable, lpstat, accept, lpadmin, lpfilter, lpforms, lpsched, lpsystem, lpusers, lpq, lpr, lprm, lpc, lpd

### lpadmin -p hplj4m -i hplj3

**ALL** **SVR4** **SYSADM**
**SCO**

This command tells the system to use a new interface program with an existing printer. The **-i** argument is exactly the same as the **-e** argument, except that where you use **-e** with a new printer, you use **-i** for an existing printer.

**Keyword:** printing

**Files:** /var/spool/lp/*

**See Also:** enable, lpstat, accept, lpadmin, lpfilter, lpforms, lpsched, lpsystem, lpusers, lpq, lpr, lprm, lpc, lpd

### lpadmin -p hplj4m -l

**ALL** **SVR4** **SYSADM**
**SCO**

This command is used to specify that the device to which the printer is attached is a login terminal—for example, **/dev/tty00**.

**Keyword:** printing

**Files:** /var/spool/lp/*

**See Also:** enable, lpstat, accept, lpadmin, lpfilter, lpforms, lpsched, lpsystem, lpusers, lpq, lpr, lprm, lpc, lpd

### lpadmin -p hplj4m -M -f current-jobs

**ALL** **SVR4** **SYSADM**
**SCO**

This command is used to mount the form specified by **current-jobs** onto the **hplj4m** printer, if **current-jobs** is a form type that is supported by **hplj4m**.

**Keyword:** printing

**Files:** /var/spool/lp/*

**See Also:** enable, lpstat, accept, lpadmin, lpfilter, lpforms, lpsched, lpsystem, lpusers, lpq, lpr, lprm, lpc, lpd

### lpadmin -p hplj4m -o banner

ALL    SVR4    SYSADM
       SCO

This forces a banner page at the beginning of every print job, even if the user specified no banner with the print request.

**Keyword:** printing

**Files:** /var/spool/lp/*

**See Also:** enable, lpstat, accept, lpadmin, lpfilter, lpforms, lpsched, lpsystem, lpusers, lpq, lpr, lprm, lpc, lpd

### lpadmin -p hplj4m -o nobanner

ALL    SVR4    SYSADM
       SCO

This command sets up the **hplj4m** printer so that when users print to it, and they specify no banner with their print request, they in fact do not get a banner page.

**Keyword:** printing

**Files:** /var/spool/lp/*

**See Also:** enable, lpstat, accept, lpadmin, lpfilter, lpforms, lpsched, lpsystem, lpusers, lpq, lpr, lprm, lpc, lpd

### lpadmin -p hplj4m -r 600dpi_postscript

ALL    SVR4    SYSADM
       SCO

This command removes the **hplj4m** printer from the **600dpi_postscript** class of printers. If this is the last printer in the class, the entire class is deleted.

**Keyword:** printing

**Files:** /var/spool/lp/*

**See Also:** enable, lpstat, accept, lpadmin, lpfilter, lpforms, lpsched, lpsystem, lpusers, lpq, lpr, lprm, lpc, lpd

### lpadmin -p hplj4m -u allow:all!perkie

ALL    SVR4    SYSADM
       SCO

This command gives **perkie** permission to print on the **hplj4m** printer, regardless of which computer **perkie** is working on.

**Keyword:** printing

**Files:** /var/spool/lp/*, /etc/lp/Systems

**See Also:** enable, lpstat, accept, lpadmin, lpfilter, lpforms, lpsched, lpsystem, lpusers, lpq, lpr, lprm, lpc, lpd

### lpadmin -p hplj4m -u allow:perkie

ALL SVR4 SCO SYSADM

This command gives user **perkie** permission to print on the **hplj4m** printer.

**Keyword:** printing

**Files:** /var/spool/lp/*

**See Also:** enable, lpstat, accept, lpadmin, lpfilter, lpforms, lpsched, lpsystem, lpusers, lpq, lpr, lprm, lpc, lpd

### lpadmin -p hplj4m -u deny:alexei!all

ALL SVR4 SCO SYSADM

This command cuts the access to the **hplj4m** printer for every user on the remote system **alexei**.

**Keyword:** printing

**Files:** /var/spool/lp/*, /etc/lp/Systems

**See Also:** enable, lpstat, accept, lpadmin, lpfilter, lpforms, lpsched, lpsystem, lpusers, lpq, lpr, lprm, lpc, lpd

### lpadmin -p hplj4m -u deny:alexei!perkie

ALL SVR4 SCO SYSADM

This command disallows user **perkie** on the remote computer **alexei** to print on the printer **hplj4m**.

**Keyword:** printing

**Files:** /var/spool/lp/*, /etc/lp/Systems

**See Also:** enable, lpstat, accept, lpadmin, lpfilter, lpforms, lpsched, lpsystem, lpusers, lpq, lpr, lprm, lpc, lpd

### lpadmin -p hplj4m -v /dev/tty00

ALL SVR4 SCO SYSADM

This command tells **lp** to look for the **hplj4m** printer on the **/dev/tty00** device.

**Keyword:** printing

**Files:** /var/spool/lp/*, /etc/lp/Systems

**See Also:** enable, lpstat, accept, lpadmin, lpfilter, lpforms, lpsched, lpsystem, lpusers, lpq, lpr, lprm, lpc, lpd

### lpadmin -p laserwriter -s alexei!mcc_cnlw

ALL SVR4 SCO SYSADM

This command makes the **mcc_cnlw** printer (attached to the computer **alexei**) available to users on the local system. The printer is called **laserwriter** on the local system. The computer **alexei** must be listed in the **/etc/lp/Systems** file for this to work.

**Keyword:** printing

**Files:** /var/spool/lp/*, /etc/lp/Systems

**See Also:** enable, lpstat, accept, lpadmin, lpfilter, lpforms, lpsched, lpsystem, lpusers, lpq, lpr, lprm, lpc, lpd

### lpadmin -p LaserWriter -u allow:all

This command allows every user on every system listed in the **/etc/lp/Systems** file to print on the **LaserWriter** printer.

**Keyword:** printing

**Files:** /var/spool/lp/*, /etc/lp/Systems

**See Also:** enable, lpstat, accept, lpadmin, lpfilter, lpforms, lpsched, lpsystem, lpusers, lpq, lpr, lprm, lpc, lpd

### lpadmin -x hplj4m

This command deletes the entry for the **hplj4m** printer. After the printer entry has been deleted, the printer can no longer be used.

**Keyword:** printing

**Files:** /var/spool/lp/*

**See Also:** enable, lpstat, accept, lpadmin, lpfilter, lpforms, lpsched, lpsystem, lpusers, lpq, lpr, lprm, lpc, lpd

### lpc

The **lpc** command controls the operation of system printers. Commands can be issued with **lpc** to perform the following: start or stop a printer, enable or disable a printer spooling queue, change the order of jobs in a queue, and display the status of the printer, its queue, and the associated daemon. This command, with no arguments, tells **lpc** to run interactively. You get a prompt **lpc>**, from which you can type in any **lpc** command options.

**Keyword:** printing

**Files:** /var/spool/lp/*, /etc/printcap (BSD)

**See Also:** enable, lpstat, accept, lpadmin, lpfilter, lpforms, lpsched, lpsystem, lpusers, lpq, lpr, lprm, lpc, lpd

### lpc ?

This command outputs a list of valid **lpc** command options.

**Keyword:** printing

**Files:** /etc/printcap (BSD), /var/spool/lp/*

**See Also:** enable, lpstat, accept, lpadmin, lpfilter, lpforms, lpsched, lpsystem, lpusers, lpq, lpr, lprm, lpc, lpd

Margin: ALL SVR4 SCO SYSADM; ALL SVR4 SCO SYSADM; ALL SVR4 SCO OSF SunOS SYSADM; ALL SVR4 SCO OSF SunOS SYSADM

## lpc abort all

ALL | SVR4 SCO OSF SunOS | SYSADM

This command kills the spooling daemon for all the printers on the system and disables all printing.

**Keyword:**    printing

**Files:**    /var/spool/lp/*, /etc/printcap (BSD)

**See Also:**    enable, lpstat, accept, lpadmin, lpfilter, lpforms, lpsched, lpsystem, lpusers, lpq, lpr, lprm, lpc, lpd

## lpc abort hplj3

ALL | SVR4 SCO OSF SunOS | SYSADM

This command kills the spooling daemon for the **hplj3** printer and disables printing to that printer.

**Keyword:**    printing

**Files:**    /var/spool/lp/*, /etc/printcap (BSD)

**See Also:**    enable, lpstat, accept, lpadmin, lpfilter, lpforms, lpsched, lpsystem, lpusers, lpq, lpr, lprm, lpc, lpd

## lpc abort hplj4m

ALL | SVR4 SCO OSF SunOS | SYSADM

This command kills the spooling daemon for the **hplj4m** printer and disables printing to that printer.

**Keyword:**    printing

**Files:**    /var/spool/lp/*, /etc/printcap (BSD)

**See Also:**    enable, lpstat, accept, lpadmin, lpfilter, lpforms, lpsched, lpsystem, lpusers, lpq, lpr, lprm, lpc, lpd

## lpc clean hplj4simx

ALL | SVR4 SCO OSF SunOS | SYSADM

This command removes all the files in the spool directory for the **hplj4simx** printer, effectively emptying the print queue.

**Keyword:**    printing

**Files:**    /var/spool/lp/*, /etc/printcap (BSD)

**See Also:**    enable, lpstat, accept, lpadmin, lpfilter, lpforms, lpsched, lpsystem, lpusers, lpq, lpr, lprm, lpc, lpd

## lpc disable all

ALL | SVR4 SCO OSF SunOS | SYSADM

This use of **lpc** turns off the print queues for all the printers on the system. It also prevents new print jobs from being accepted.

**Keyword:**    printing

**Files:**    /var/spool/lp/*, /etc/printcap (BSD)

**See Also:**     enable, lpstat, accept, lpadmin, lpfilter, lpforms,
                  lpsched, lpsystem, lpusers, lpq, lpr, lprm, lpc, lpd

### lpc down laserwriter The printer is out of toner.

This command turns off the print queue, but only for the **laser-writer** printer. The **down** option to **lpc** also leaves a message to users, stating why the printing on **laserwriter** has been stopped.

**Keyword:**    printing

**Files:**      /var/spool/lp/*, /etc/printcap (BSD)

**See Also:**   enable, lpstat, accept, lpadmin, lpfilter, lpforms,
                lpsched, lpsystem, lpusers, lpq, lpr, lprm, lpc, lpd

*ALL   SVR4   SYSADM
       SCO
       OSF
       SunOS*

### lpc enable LaserWriter

This command activates the print queue. When the printer can be brought back on line, use the **enable** option to reactivate it.

**Keyword:**    printing

**Files:**      /var/spool/lp/*, /etc/printcap (BSD)

**See Also:**   enable, lpstat, accept, lpadmin, lpfilter, lpforms,
                lpsched, lpsystem, lpusers, lpq, lpr, lprm, lpc, lpd

*ALL   SVR4   SYSADM
       SCO
       OSF
       SunOS*

### lpc help

This command outputs a list of valid **lpc** command options.

**Keyword:**    printing

**Files:**      /var/spool/lp/*, /etc/printcap (BSD)

**See Also:**   enable, lpstat, accept, lpadmin, lpfilter, lpforms,
                lpsched, lpsystem, lpusers, lpq, lpr, lprm, lpc, lpd

*ALL   SVR4   SYSADM
       SCO
       OSF
       SunOS*

### lpc help abort

This command outputs a description of how to use the **lpc** command argument **abort**. With either **help** or **?** you can get information on any valid command option.

**Keyword:**    printing

**Files:**      /var/spool/lp/*, /etc/printcap (BSD)

**See Also:**   enable, lpstat, accept, lpadmin, lpfilter, lpforms,
                lpsched, lpsystem, lpusers, lpq, lpr, lprm, lpc, lpd

*ALL   SVR4   SYSADM
       SCO
       OSF
       SunOS*

### lpc restart hplj3

ALL  SVR4  END
     SCO   POWER
     OSF   SYSADM
     SunOS

This command is used to attempt to start a new printer daemon for the **hplj3** printer. It is used when the current daemon has died for some reason. A unique feature of this command is that it can be run by any user.

**Keyword:** printing

**Files:** /var/spool/lp/*, /etc/printcap (BSD)

**See Also:** enable, lpstat, accept, lpadmin, lpfilter, lpforms, lpsched, lpsystem, lpusers, lpq, lpr, lprm, lpc, lpd

### lpc start hplj3

ALL  SVR4  SYSADM
     SCO
     OSF
     SunOS

This command starts the printer daemon for the first time.

**Keyword:** printing

**Files:** /var/spool/lp/*, /etc/printcap (BSD)

**See Also:** enable, lpstat, accept, lpadmin, lpfilter, lpforms, lpsched, lpsystem, lpusers, lpq, lpr, lprm, lpc, lpd

### lpc status hplj4m

ALL  SVR4  END
     SCO   POWER
     OSF   SYSADM
     SunOS

This command outputs the status of the printer daemon and print queue for the **hplj4m** printer.

**Keyword:** printing

**Files:** /var/spool/lp/*, /etc/printcap (BSD)

**See Also:** enable, lpstat, accept, lpadmin, lpfilter, lpforms, lpsched, lpsystem, lpusers, lpq, lpr, lprm, lpc, lpd

### lpc stop all

ALL  SVR4  SYSADM
     SCO
     OSF
     SunOS

This use of **lpc** stops the spooling daemon. The command lets any current jobs finish printing, but the next job will not print; no new jobs will be accepted into the queue, either.

**Keyword:** printing

**Files:** /var/spool/lp/*, /etc/printcap (BSD)

**See Also:** enable, lpstat, accept, lpadmin, lpfilter, lpforms, lpsched, lpsystem, lpusers, lpq, lpr, lprm, lpc, lpd

### lpc topq all alans

ALL  SVR4  SYSADM
     SCO
     OSF
     SunOS

This command moves all of the print jobs that user **alans** has queued on the system to the top of the queue. The **all** option specifies that the command apply to all printers.

**Keyword:**    printing

**Files:**    /var/spool/lp/*, /etc/printcap (BSD)

**See Also:**    enable, lpstat, accept, lpadmin, lpfilter, lpforms, lpsched, lpsystem, lpusers, lpq, lpr, lprm, lpc, lpd

## lpc topq hplj3 45

ALL   SVR4   SYSADM   SCO   OSF   SunOS

This command moves print job number **45** to the top of the queue.

**Keyword:**    printing

**Files:**    /var/spool/lp/*, /etc/printcap (BSD)

**See Also:**    enable, lpstat, accept, lpadmin, lpfilter, lpforms, lpsched, lpsystem, lpusers, lpq, lpr, lprm, lpc, lpd

## lpc topq hplj4m perkie

ALL   SVR4   SYSADM   SCO   OSF   SunOS

This command moves all of the print jobs that user **perkie** has queued on the printer **hplj4m** to the top of the queue.

**Keyword:**    printing

**Files:**    /var/spool/lp/*, /etc/printcap (BSD)

**See Also:**    enable, lpstat, accept, lpadmin, lpfilter, lpforms, lpsched, lpsystem, lpusers, lpq, lpr, lprm, lpc, lpd

## lpc up all

ALL   SVR4   SYSADM   SCO   OSF   SunOS

This command activates all the printers on the system and brings them on line. It reactivates a printer that is off line because of the **lpc down** command.

**Keyword:**    printing

**Files:**    /var/spool/lp/*, /etc/printcap (BSD)

**See Also:**    enable, lpstat, accept, lpadmin, lpfilter, lpforms, lpsched, lpsystem, lpusers, lpq, lpr, lprm, lpc, lpd

## lpd

ALL   BSD   SYSADM

The **lpd** line printer daemon, which is responsible for handling the print spooling facilities, is typically executed in a UNIX startup script. It gets printer configuration information from **/etc/printcap**. Additionally, **lpd** only recognizes print requests from printers listed in **/etc/hosts.equiv** or **/etc/hosts.lpd**. Subsequently, **lpd** handles user print requests made with commands such as **lpr** and **lprm**.

**Keyword:**    printing

**Files:** /var/spool/*, /etc/printcap, /etc/hosts.equiv, /etc/hosts.lpd

**See Also:** lpq, lpr, lprm, lpc

## lpfilter -f all  -l

| ALL | SVR4 SCO | SYSADM |

The **lpfilter** command administers filters used with the system print service. You can add, change, and delete filters with **lpfilter**. This example outputs a listing of **lp** filter descriptions. The **-f** option specifies a filter. The **all** argument specifies all filters. The **-l** option displays a list of filters.

**Keyword:** printing

**Files:** /var/spool/lp/*, /etc/printcap (BSD)

**See Also:** enable, lpstat, accept, lpadmin, lpforms, lpsched, lpsystem, lpusers, lpq, lpr, lprm, lpc, lpd

## lpfilter -f all -x

| ALL | SVR4 SCO | SYSADM |

This use of the **lpfilter** command deletes all **lp** filters from the filter table.

**Keyword:** printing

**Files:** /var/spool/lp/*

**See Also:** enable, lpstat, accept, lpadmin, lpforms, lpsched, lpsystem, lpusers, lpq, lpr

## lpfilter -f new_filter -

| ALL | SVR4 SCO | SYSADM |

This command creates a new **lp** filter. The specifications of the filter are then read in from standard input, as indicated by the trailing hyphen.

**Keyword:** printing

**Files:** /var/spool/lp/*

**See Also:** enable, lpstat, accept, lpadmin, lpforms, lpsched, lpsystem, lpusers, lpq, lpr

## lpfilter -f new_filter -F /u1/perkie/filters/filter1

| ALL | SVR4 SCO | SYSADM |

This command creates a new filter, or updates an existing one if **new_filter** already exists. The specifications for this filter are taken from the file **/u1/perkie/filters/filter1**.

**Keyword:** printing

**Files:** /var/spool/lp/*

**See Also:** enable, lpstat, accept, lpadmin, lpforms, lpsched, lpsystem, lpusers, lpq, lpr

### lpfilter -f special_output -i

ALL   SVR4   SYSADM
      SCO

If the **special_output** filter is a standard filter, and you changed it, then realized you shouldn't have, this command restores it to its original settings.

**Keyword:** printing

**Files:** /var/spool/lp/*

**See Also:** enable, lpstat, accept, lpadmin, lpforms, lpsched, lpsystem, lpusers, lpq, lpr

### lpfilter -f special_output -l

ALL   SVR4   SYSADM
      SCO

This command outputs the description of the existing **lp** printer filter called **special_output**.

**Keyword:** printing

**Files:** /var/spool/lp/*, /etc/printcap (BSD)

**See Also:** enable, lpstat, accept, lpadmin, lpforms, lpsched, lpsystem, lpusers, lpq, lpr, lprm, lpc, lpd

### lpfilter -f special_output -x

ALL   SVR4   SYSADM
      SCO

This command deletes the **special_output** filter from the **lp** filter table. The **-x** option specifies deletion.

**Keyword:** printing

**Files:** /var/spool/lp/*

**See Also:** enable, lpstat, accept, lpadmin, lpforms, lpsched, lpsystem, lpusers, lpq, lpr

### lpforms -f faxform -

ALL   SVR4   SYSADM
      SCO

This command creates or modifies the form called **faxform**. The specifications for the form are taken from standard input.

**Keyword:** printing

**Files:** /var/spool/lp/*

**See Also:** enable, lpstat, accept, lpadmin, lpfilter, lpsched, lpsystem, lpusers, lpq, lpr

## lpforms -f faxform -A mail

| | | |
|---|---|---|
| ALL | SVR4 SCO | SYSADM |

This command sets up the **lp** form service to send the administrator email when a print job gets queued that needs the form **faxform** loaded into the printer.

**Keyword:** printing

**Files:** /var/spool/lp/*

**See Also:** enable, lpstat, accept, lpadmin, lpfilter, lpsched, lpsystem, lpusers, lpq, lpr

## lpforms -f faxform -A none

| | | |
|---|---|---|
| ALL | SVR4 SCO | SYSADM |

This use of **lpforms** turns off all notification that the form **faxform** may need to be loaded into a printer.

**Keyword:** printing

**Files:** /var/spool/lp/*

**See Also:** enable, lpstat, accept, lpadmin, lpfilter, lpsched, lpsystem, lpusers, lpq, lpr

## lpforms -f faxform -A quiet

| | | |
|---|---|---|
| ALL | SVR4 SCO | SYSADM |

This command prevents the computer from being an annoyance when informing the administrator of the need to load the form **faxform** into the printer. All messages are halted until the form has been loaded.

**Keyword:** printing

**Files:** /var/spool/lp/*

**See Also:** enable, lpstat, accept, lpadmin, lpfilter, lpsched, lpsystem, lpusers, lpq, lpr

## lpforms -f faxform -A write

| | | |
|---|---|---|
| ALL | SVR4 SCO | SYSADM |

This command notifies the administrator to load a form into the printer. Rather than sending email, though, it writes a message to the administrator's terminal window.

**Keyword:** printing

**Files:** /var/spool/lp/*

**See Also:** enable, lpstat, accept, lpadmin, lpfilter, lpsched, lpsystem, lpusers, lpq, lpr

ALL SVR4 SYSADM
SCO

### lpforms -f faxform -F /u1/perkie/forms/form1

This command creates a new form, or updates an existing one if **faxform** already exists. The specifications for this form are taken from the file **/u1/perkie/forms/form1**.

**Keyword:** printing

**Files:** /var/spool/lp/*

**See Also:** enable, lpstat, accept, lpadmin, lpfilter, lpsched, lpsystem, lpusers, lpq, lpr

ALL SVR4 SYSADM
SCO

### lpforms -f faxform -l

This command outputs the attributes of the print form **faxform**.

**Keyword:** printing

**Files:** /var/spool/lp/*

**See Also:** enable, lpstat, accept, lpadmin, lpfilter, lpsched, lpsystem, lpusers, lpq, lpr

ALL SVR4 SYSADM
SCO

### lpforms -f faxform -x

The **lpforms** command manages special forms, such as business letterhead, invoices, and fax cover sheets. This example deletes the form called **faxform**.

**Keyword:** printing

**Files:** /var/spool/lp/*

**See Also:** enable, lpstat, accept, lpadmin, lpfilter, lpsched, lpsystem, lpusers, lpq, lpr

ALL SVR4 SYSADM
SCO

### lpmove 9 mccpr

The **lpmove** command moves a print job from one print spool to another. The new destination printer must support all options associated with the original print request. The example moves request **9** to the **mccpr** printer.

**Keyword:** printing

**Files:** /var/spool/lp/*

**See Also:** enable, lpstat, accept, lpadmin, lpfilter, lpforms, lpsched, lpsystem, lpusers, lpq, lpr

## lpmove mcc_cnlw mccpr

ALL    SVR4    SYSADM    SCO

This command tries to move all print jobs waiting to print on **mcc_cnlw** to **mccpr**, and then shut down **mcc_cnlw**.

**Keyword:** printing

**Files:** /var/spool/lp/*

**See Also:** enable, lpstat, accept, lpadmin, lpfilter, lpforms, lpsched, lpsystem, lpusers, lpq, lpr

## lpq

ALL    ALL    ALL

This command outputs the queue of printer jobs for the default printer. Information reported by **lpq** includes username, current position in the queue, input filenames, job number, and the size of the job (in bytes).

**Keyword:** printing

**Files:** /etc/printcap (BSD), /var/spool/lp/*

**See Also:** enable, lpstat, accept, lpadmin, lpfilter, lpforms, lpsched, lpsystem, lpusers, lpq, lpr, lprm, lpc, lpd

## lpq +20

ALL    ALL    ALL

This command continuously displays the print queue for the default printer. The update interval is **20** seconds.

**Keyword:** printing

**Files:** /etc/printcap (BSD), /var/spool/lp/*

**See Also:** enable, lpstat, accept, lpadmin, lpfilter, lpforms, lpsched, lpsystem, lpusers, lpq, lpr, lprm, lpc, lpd

## lpq -l

ALL    ALL    ALL

This command outputs a long listing of print jobs that are currently queued on the default printer. It includes information about the host where the print request originated, the job priority, the user who requested the job, the name of the input file, and the size of the file.

**Keyword:** printing

**Files:** /etc/printcap (BSD), /var/spool/lp/*

**See Also:** enable, lpstat, accept, lpadmin, lpfilter, lpforms, lpsched, lpsystem, lpusers, lpq, lpr, lprm, lpc, lpd

## lpq -Pmcc_cnlw

ALL    ALL    ALL

This command outputs all the printer jobs currently in the queue. It is specific to the printer **mcc_cnlw**, however, rather than just the default printer.

**Keyword:**   printing

**Files:**   /etc/printcap (BSD), /var/spool/lp/*

**See Also:**   enable, lpstat, accept, lpadmin, lpfilter, lpforms, lpsched, lpsystem, lpusers, lpq, lpr, lprm, lpc, lpd

## lpq 7

ALL    ALL    ALL

This command outputs only the information about print job number **7** on the default printer.

**Keyword:**   printing

**Files:**   /etc/printcap (BSD), /var/spool/lp/*

**See Also:**   enable, lpstat, accept, lpadmin, lpfilter, lpforms, lpsched, lpsystem, lpusers, lpq, lpr, lprm, lpc, lpd

## lpq perkie

ALL    ALL    ALL

This command outputs all the print jobs that user **perkie** has waiting in the queue for the default printer.

**Keyword:**   printing

**Files:**   /etc/printcap (BSD), /var/spool/lp/*

**See Also:**   enable, lpstat, accept, lpadmin, lpfilter, lpforms, lpsched, lpsystem, lpusers, lpq, lpr, lprm, lpc, lpd

## lpr -

ALL    ALL    POWER

Although terminal users might wonder about the advantages of this command, anyone using an Xterm can easily see the advantages. The - option to **lpr** tells it to accept standard input, which is then piped into the **lpr** command for printing. When you enter the command, the shell drops into its simple edit mode and you can type text. When you finish typing, you press Ctrl-D and all the text is printed. This technique is arduous at best, however, so why mention it? Because X users can cut and paste text into shell edit mode. And presto, the text is printing.

**Keyword:**   printing

**See Also:**   cat, lp, pr

ALL | ALL | ALL

## lpr -#8 report.doc

This command prints out **8** copies of the **report.doc** file on the default printer.

**Keyword:** printing

**Files:** /etc/printcap (BSD), /var/spool/lp/*

**See Also:** enable, lpstat, accept, lpadmin, lpfilter, lpforms, lpsched, lpsystem, lpusers, lpq, lprm, lpc, lpd

ALL | ALL | ALL

## lpr -c results.data

This command prints out files that have been created with the **cifplot** program. In this example, the **results.data** file would be printed on the default printer.

**Keyword:** printing

**Files:** /var/spool/lp/*

**See Also:** enable, lpstat, accept, lpadmin, lpfilter, lpforms, lpsched, lpsystem, lpusers, lpq, lprm, lpc, lpd

ALL | ALL | ALL

## lpr -C "company confidential" report.doc

The **-C** option to **lpr** lets you add a comment to the printer cover page or burst page. The **-C** option actually inserts your short comment in the field normally occupied by the system hostname. The hostname is removed altogether. The example inserts **company confidential** in place of the hostname.

**Keyword:** printing

**Files:** /etc/printcap (BSD), /var/spool/lp/*

**See Also:** enable, lpstat, accept, lpadmin, lpfilter, lpforms, lpsched, lpsystem, lpusers, lpq, lprm, lpc, lpd

ALL | ALL | ALL

## lpr -d report.tex

This command prints out the **report.tex** file, which is in the **tex** output format.

**Keyword:** printing

**Files:** /var/spool/lp/*, /etc/printcap (BSD)

**See Also:** enable, lpstat, accept, lpadmin, lpfilter, lpforms, lpsched, lpsystem, lpusers, lpq, lprm, lpc, lpd

ALL | ALL | END POWER

## lpr -f program.f77

This command prints out the **program.f77** FORTRAN program on the default printer. It interprets the first character of each line as a standard FORTRAN control character.

**Keyword:** printing

**Files:** /etc/printcap (BSD), /var/spool/lp/*

**See Also:** enable, lpstat, accept, lpadmin, lpfilter, lpforms, lpsched, lpsystem, lpusers, lpq, lprm, lpc, lpd

### lpr -g bode1.plot

This command prints out the **bode1.plot** file to the default printer. The **bode1.plot** file is an output file from the **plot** program.

**Keyword:** printing

**Files:** /var/spool/lp/*, /etc/printcap (BSD)

**See Also:** enable, lpstat, accept, lpadmin, lpfilter, lpforms, lpsched, lpsystem, lpusers, lpq, lprm, lpc, lpd

### lpr -h project.c

This command prints out the **project.c** file to the default printer. It doesn't, however, print a burst page.

**Keyword:** printing

**Files:** /var/spool/lp/*, /etc/printcap (BSD)

**See Also:** enable, lpstat, accept, lpadmin, lpfilter, lpforms, lpsched, lpsystem, lpusers, lpq, lprm, lpc, lpd

### lpr -i 5 menu.c

This command prints out the **menu.c** file to the default printer, formatting the output so that it has a 5-character wide left margin.

**Keyword:** printing

**Files:** /var/spool/lp/*, /etc/printcap (BSD)

**See Also:** enable, lpstat, accept, lpadmin, lpfilter, lpforms, lpsched, lpsystem, lpusers, lpq, lprm, lpc, lpd

### lpr -J New_Code menu.c option1.c option2.c

This command prints out **New_Code** as the job name on the burst page, in place of **menu.c**. The command then prints out one copy of **menu.c**, **option1.c**, and **option2.c** after the burst page.

**Keyword:** printing

**Files:** /var/spool/lp/*, /etc/printcap (BSD)

**See Also:** enable, lpstat, accept, lpadmin, lpfilter, lpforms, lpsched, lpsystem, lpusers, lpq, lprm, lpc, lpd

ALL ALL ALL

ALL ALL ALL

ALL ALL ALL

ALL ALL ALL

### lpr -l project.data

ALL   ALL   ALL

This command is used for printing the **project.data** file including all of the control characters; it suppresses the printing of page breaks.

**Keyword:** printing

**Files:** /var/spool/lp/*, /etc/printcap (BSD)

**See Also:** enable, lpstat, accept, lpadmin, lpfilter, lpforms, lpsched, lpsystem, lpusers, lpq, lprm, lpc, lpd

### lpr -m project.c

ALL   ALL   ALL

This command prints out the **project.c** file to the default printer. It then sends email to the user who initiated the print job, announcing that printing is done.

**Keyword:** printing

**Files:** /var/spool/lp/*, /etc/printcap (BSD)

**See Also:** enable, lpstat, accept, lpadmin, lpfilter, lpforms, lpsched, lpsystem, lpusers, lpq, lprm, lpc, lpd

### lpr -n project.ditroff

ALL   ALL   ALL

This command prints out the **project.ditroff** file, which contains **ditroff** binary data.

**Keyword:** printing

**Files:** /var/spool/lp/*, /etc/printcap (BSD)

**See Also:** enable, lpstat, accept, lpadmin, lpfilter, lpforms, lpsched, lpsystem, lpusers, lpq, lprm, lpc, lpd

### lpr -P quickjet review.doc

ALL   ALL   ALL

The **-P** option to **lpr** specifies a printer. The example prints one copy of the **review.doc** file to the printer called **quickjet**.

**Keyword:** printing

**Files:** /etc/printcap (BSD), /var/spool/lp/*

**See Also:** enable, lpstat, accept, lpadmin, lpfilter, lpforms, lpsched, lpsystem, lpusers, lpq, lprm, lpc, lpd

### lpr -p project.data

ALL   ALL   ALL

This command uses the **pr** program to format the **project.data** file; then, it prints the formatted copy on the default printer.

**Keyword:** printing

**Files:**   /var/spool/lp/*, /etc/printcap (BSD)

**See Also:**   enable, lpstat, accept, lpadmin, lpfilter, lpforms, lpsched, lpsystem, lpusers, lpq, lprm, lpc, lpd

### lpr -r temp.txt

This command prints out the **temp.txt** file to the default printer, then it removes the file.

**Keyword:**   printing

**Files:**   /var/spool/lp/*, /etc/printcap (BSD)

**See Also:**   enable, lpstat, accept, lpadmin, lpfilter, lpforms, lpsched, lpsystem, lpusers, lpq, lprm, lpc, lpd

### lpr -s project.data

This command prints out the **project.data** file without first spooling the file. When using this command, you shouldn't modify the file in any way until it has finished printing.

**Keyword:**   printing

**Files:**   /var/spool/lp/*, /etc/printcap (BSD)

**See Also:**   enable, lpstat, accept, lpadmin, lpfilter, lpforms, lpsched, lpsystem, lpusers, lpq, lprm, lpc, lpd

### lpr -T ´Weather for 10/9/93´ wd10993.txt

This command substitutes **Weather for 10/9/93** for **wd10993.txt** as the title that is sent to the **pr** command, then prints the **wd10993.txt** file.

**Keyword:**   printing

**Files:**   /var/spool/lp/*, /etc/printcap (BSD)

**See Also:**   enable, lpstat, accept, lpadmin, lpfilter, lpforms, lpsched, lpsystem, lpusers, lpq, lprm, lpc, lpd

### lpr -t project.troff

This command prints out the **project.troff** file, which consists of **troff** binary data.

**Keyword:**   printing

**Files:**   /var/spool/lp/*, /etc/printcap (BSD)

**See Also:**   enable, lpstat, accept, lpadmin, lpfilter, lpforms, lpsched, lpsystem, lpusers, lpq, lprm, lpc, lpd

ALL   ALL   ALL

| | | |
|---|---|---|
| ALL | ALL | ALL |

## lpr -v world.ras

This command prints out the **world.ras** raster image file to the default printer. This command works only if you have a printer that has some sort of imaging model built into it, such as Post-Script.

| **Keyword:** | printing |
|---|---|
| **Files:** | /var/spool/lp/*, /etc/printcap (BSD) |
| **See Also:** | enable, lpstat, accept, lpadmin, lpfilter, lpforms, lpsched, lpsystem, lpusers, lpq, lprm, lpc, lpd |

| | | |
|---|---|---|
| ALL | ALL | ALL |

## lpr -w 65 project.c

This command prints out the **project.c** file to the default printer, using a page width of **65** characters for the **pr** program.

| **Keyword:** | printing |
|---|---|
| **Files:** | /var/spool/lp/*, /etc/printcap (BSD) |
| **See Also:** | enable, lpstat, accept, lpadmin, lpfilter, lpforms, lpsched, lpsystem, lpusers, lpq, lprm, lpc, lpd |

| | | |
|---|---|---|
| ALL | ALL | ALL |

## lpr report.txt

The **lpr** command is the only interface to UNIX printing that most users need. The command sends a printer job to the print spooler for printing. The job waits in the queue until other jobs have finished printing. If a printer is not currently available, jobs sit in the queue until one becomes available. To examine the print queue, use **lpq** (SVR4 and some BSD environments) or **lpstat** (BSD). In the example, the **report.txt** file is queued for printing.

| **Keyword:** | printing |
|---|---|
| **Files:** | /etc/printcap (BSD), /var/spool/lp/* |
| **See Also:** | enable, lpstat, accept, lpadmin, lpfilter, lpforms, lpsched, lpsystem, lpusers, lpq, lprm, lpc, lpd |

| | | |
|---|---|---|
| ALL | ALL | ALL |

## lprm -Pbigps -

This command deletes all of the invoking user's print jobs queued for the **bigps** printer.

| **Keyword:** | printing |
|---|---|
| **Files:** | /etc/printcap (BSD), /var/spool/lp/* |
| **See Also:** | enable, lpstat, accept, lpadmin, lpfilter, lpforms, lpsched, lpsystem, lpusers, lpq, lpr, lpc, lpd |

| | | |
|---|---|---|
| ALL | ALL | ALL |

## lprm -Pquickjet 1

The **lprm** utility allows users to remove their print jobs from the queue. Without any arguments, **lprm** removes the most recently queued job. In the example, **lprm** deletes print job number **1** from the print queue for the **quickjet** printer.

**Keyword:**   printing

**Files:**   /etc/printcap (BSD), var/spool/lp/*

**See Also:**   enable, lpstat, accept, lpadmin, lpfilter, lpforms, lpsched, lpsystem, lpusers, lpq, lpr, lpc, lpd

| | | |
|---|---|---|
| ALL | ALL | SYSADM |

## lprm perkie

If this command is run by the superuser, it deletes all of user **perkie**'s print jobs queued for the default printer. Other users are disallowed from running this command.

**Keyword:**   printing

**Files:**   /var/spool/lp/*

**See Also:**   enable, lpstat, accept, lpadmin, lpfilter, lpforms, lpsched, lpsystem, lpusers, lpq, lpr, lpc, lpd

| | | |
|---|---|---|
| ALL | SVR4 SCO | SYSADM |

## lpsched

The **lpsched** utility starts the UNIX system print server (referred to as the **lp** print service). The print service is typically started in a UNIX startup file. The **lpshut** and **lpmove** utilities shut down the print service and move requests (something you might want to do before shutting down). The example simply starts the print service.

**Keyword:**   printing

**Files:**   /var/spool/lp/*

**See Also:**   enable, lpstat, accept, lpadmin, lpsched, lp, lpshut, lpmove

| | | |
|---|---|---|
| ALL | SVR4 SCO | SYSADM |

## lpshut

This command is the opposite of **lpsched**. It stops the **lp** print service.

**Keyword:**   printing

**Files:**   /var/spool/lp/*

**See Also:**   enable, lpstat, accept, lpadmin, lp, lpmove

## lpstat

lpstat

**ALL**   SVR4   SYSADM
OSF
SunOS

This command outputs the status of all print jobs made by **lp**.

| | |
|---|---|
| **Keyword:** | printing |
| **Files:** | /var/spool/lp/* |
| **See Also:** | enable, lpstat, accept, lpadmin, lpfilter, lpforms, lpsched, lpsystem, lpusers, lpq, lpr |

## lpstat -a quickjet

**ALL**   SVR4   SYSADM
OSF
SunOS

This command shows whether the **quickjet** printer is accepting requests.

| | |
|---|---|
| **Keyword:** | printing |
| **Files:** | /var/spool/lp/* |
| **See Also:** | enable, lpstat, accept, lpadmin, lpfilter, lpforms, lpsched, lpsystem, lpusers, lpq, lpr |

## lpstat -c

**ALL**   SVR4   SYSADM

This command shows the name of all the printer classes and their members on the system.

| | |
|---|---|
| **Keyword:** | printing |
| **Files:** | /var/spool/lp/* |
| **See Also:** | enable, lpstat, accept, lpadmin, lpfilter, lpforms, lpsched, lpsystem, lpusers, lpq, lpr |

## lpstat -c hplj

**ALL**   SVR4   SYSADM

This command outputs the name of all the members of the printer class **hplj**.

| | |
|---|---|
| **Keyword:** | printing |
| **Files:** | /var/spool/lp/* |
| **See Also:** | enable, lpstat, accept, lpadmin, lpfilter, lpforms, lpsched, lpsystem, lpusers, lpq, lpr |

## lpstat -d

**ALL**   SVR4   SYSADM
OSF
SunOS

This command shows the computer system's default printer destination for all print jobs.

| | |
|---|---|
| **Keyword:** | printing |
| **Files:** | /var/spool/lp/* |
| **See Also:** | enable, lpstat, accept, lpadmin, lpfilter, lpforms, lpsched, lpsystem, lpusers, lpq, lpr |

### lpstat -f -l

| | | |
|---|---|---|
| ALL | SVR4 | SYSADM |

This command is used to verify that the forms set up are recognized by the **lp** print service.

**Keyword:**  printing

**Files:**  /var/spool/lp/*

**See Also:**  enable, lpstat, accept, lpadmin, lpfilter, lpforms, lpsched, lpsystem, lpusers, lpq, lpr

### lpstat -o mccpr

| | | |
|---|---|---|
| ALL | SVR4 | SYSADM |
| | OSF | |
| | SunOS | |

This command shows the status of output requests for the **mccpr** printer. In addition to specifying a printer, you could specify a class of printers, print requests, or a combination of the three.

**Keyword:**  printing

**Files:**  /var/spool/lp/*

**See Also:**  enable, lpstat, accept, lpadmin, lpfilter, lpforms, lpsched, lpsystem, lpusers, lpq, lpr

### lpstat -p mccpr

| | | |
|---|---|---|
| ALL | SVR4 | SYSADM |
| | OSF | |
| | SunOS | |

This command shows the status of the **mccpr** printer.

**Keyword:**  printing

**Files:**  /var/spool/lp/*

**See Also:**  enable, lpstat, accept, lpadmin, lpfilter, lpforms, lpsched, lpsystem, lpusers, lpq, lpr

### lpstat -p mccpr -D

| | | |
|---|---|---|
| ALL | SVR4 | SYSADM |
| | OSF | |
| | SunOS | |

This command shows the status of the **mccpr** printer and a description of the printer.

**Keyword:**  printing

**Files:**  /var/spool/lp/*

**See Also:**  enable, lpstat, accept, lpadmin, lpfilter, lpforms, lpsched, lpsystem, lpusers, lpq, lpr

### lpstat -p mccpr -l

| | | |
|---|---|---|
| ALL | SVR4 | SYSADM |
| | OSF | |
| | SunOS | |

This command shows the status of the **mccpr** printer and a detailed description of the printer. This description contains information about the form currently mounted, acceptable content and printer types, and the interface option used.

**Keyword:**   printing

**Files:**      /var/spool/lp/*

**See Also:**   enable, lpstat, accept, lpadmin, lpfilter, lpforms, lpsched, lpsystem, lpusers, lpq, lpr

## lpstat -R

ALL   SVR4   SYSADM

This command shows a number representing the location of the print job in the print queue.

**Keyword:**   printing

**Files:**      /var/spool/lp/*

**See Also:**   enable, lpstat, accept, lpadmin, lpfilter, lpforms, lpsched, lpsystem, lpusers, lpq, lpr

## lpstat -r

ALL   SVR4
OSF
SunOS

SYSADM

This command simply outputs the status of the **lp** print scheduler, saying whether it is running.

**Keyword:**   printing

**Files:**      /var/spool/lp/*

**See Also:**   enable, lpstat, accept, lpadmin, lpfilter, lpforms, lpsched, lpsystem, lpusers, lpq, lpr

## lpstat -s

ALL   SVR4
OSF
SunOS

SYSADM

This command shows a partial print status summary. The items consist of the status of the **lp** scheduler, the default printer destination, a list of class names and their members, a list of printers and their associated devices, a list of the machines sharing print services, a list of all forms currently mounted, and a list of all recognized character sets and print wheels.

**Keyword:**   printing

**Files:**      /var/spool/lp/*

**See Also:**   enable, lpstat, accept, lpadmin, lpfilter, lpforms, lpsched, lpsystem, lpusers, lpq, lpr

## lpstat -t

ALL   SVR4
OSF
SunOS

SYSADM

This command shows all printer status information. The items consist of the status of the **lp** scheduler, the default printer destination, a list of class names and their members, a list of printers and their associated devices, a list of the machines sharing print services, a list of all forms currently mounted, a list of all recognized character sets and print wheels, and the acceptance and the idle/busy status of all the configured printers on the system.

**Keyword:** printing

**Files:** /var/spool/lp/*

**See Also:** enable, lpstat, accept, lpadmin, lpfilter, lpforms, lpsched, lpsystem, lpusers, lpq, lpr

### lpstat -u alexei!all

ALL    SVR4    SYSADM

This command shows the status of all the print jobs on the remote machine **alexei**.

**Keyword:** printing

**Files:** /var/spool/lp/*

**See Also:** enable, lpstat, accept, lpadmin, lpfilter, lpforms, lpsched, lpsystem, lpusers, lpq, lpr

### lpstat -u alexei!perkie

ALL    SVR4    SYSADM
       OSF
       SunOS

This command shows the status of all of user **perkie**'s print jobs on the remote system **alexei**.

**Keyword:** printing

**Files:** /var/spool/lp/*

**See Also:** enable, lpstat, accept, lpadmin, lpfilter, lpforms, lpsched, lpsystem, lpusers, lpq, lpr

### lpstat -u all

ALL    SVR4    SYSADM
       OSF
       SunOS

This command shows the status of all the print jobs on the local computer system only.

**Keyword:** printing

**Files:** /var/spool/lp/*

**See Also:** enable, lpstat, accept, lpadmin, lpfilter, lpforms, lpsched, lpsystem, lpusers, lpq, lpr

### lpstat -u all!alans

ALL    SVR4    SYSADM
       OSF
       SunOS

This command shows the status of all the print jobs that user **alans** has requested, regardless of what machine he is on.

**Keyword:** printing

**Files:** /var/spool/lp/*

**See Also:** enable, lpstat, accept, lpadmin, lpfilter, lpforms, lpsched, lpsystem, lpusers, lpq, lpr

**277**

## lpstat -u all!all

| ALL | SVR4 | SYSADM |
| --- | OSF | |
| | SunOS | |

This command shows the status of all the print jobs on every computer system, except the local system.

**Keyword:** printing

**Files:** /var/spool/lp/*

**See Also:** enable, lpstat, accept, lpadmin, lpfilter, lpforms, lpsched, lpsystem, lpusers, lpq, lpr

## lpstat -u perkie

| ALL | SVR4 | SYSADM |
| --- | OSF | |
| | SunOS | |

This command shows the status of all of user **perkie**'s print jobs on the system.

**Keyword:** printing

**Files:** /var/spool/lp/*

**See Also:** enable, lpstat, accept, lpadmin, lpfilter, lpforms, lpsched, lpsystem, lpusers, lpq, lpr

## lpstat -v

| ALL | SVR4 | SYSADM |
| --- | OSF | |
| | SunOS | |

This command shows which I/O devices all the printers on the system are connected to.

**Keyword:** printing

**Files:** /var/spool/lp/*

**See Also:** enable, lpstat, accept, lpadmin, lpfilter, lpforms, lpsched, lpsystem, lpusers, lpq, lpr

## lpstat -v laserwriter

| ALL | SVR4 | SYSADM |
| --- | OSF | |
| | SunOS | |

This command shows which I/O devices the **laserwriter** printer is connected to.

**Keyword:** printing

**Files:** /var/spool/lp/*

**See Also:** enable, lpstat, accept, lpadmin, lpfilter, lpforms, lpsched, lpsystem, lpusers, lpq, lpr

## lpsystem -A

| ALL | SVR4 | SYSADM |

The **lpsystem** command handles remote printer configuration. The example outputs the local TCP/IP address for configuring remote print services to and from a SunOS workstation.

**Keyword:** printing, networking

**Files:** /var/spool/lp/*, /etc/lp/*

**See Also:** enable, lpstat, accept, lpadmin, lpfilter, lpforms, lpsched, lpsystem, lpusers, lpq, lpr

### lpsystem -l sparky

ALL   SVR4   SYSADM

This use of the **lpsystem** command shows a description of the printing parameters associated with the remote system named **sparky**. If you use the **-l** option without an argument, **lpsystem** displays information on all remote printers.

**Keyword:** printing, networking

**Files:** /var/spool/lp/*, /etc/lp/*

**See Also:** enable, lpstat, accept, lpadmin, lpfilter, lpforms, lpsched, lpsystem, lpusers, lpq, lpr

### lpsystem -r sparky

ALL   SVR4   SYSADM

This command removes the remote computer **sparky** from the remote printing service.

**Keyword:** printing, networking

**Files:** /var/spool/lp/*, /etc/lp/*

**See Also:** enable, lpstat, accept, lpadmin, lpfilter, lpforms, lpsched, lpsystem, lpusers, lpq, lpr

### lpsystem -t bsd -T n sparky

ALL   SVR4   SYSADM

This command adds the remote computer **sparky** to the remote printing service, and it is used if **sparky** is running BSD UNIX. It also tells the local system never to time out if it loses the connection.

**Keyword:** printing, networking

**Files:** /var/spool/lp/*, /etc/lp/*

**See Also:** enable, lpstat, accept, lpadmin, lpfilter, lpforms, lpsched, lpsystem, lpusers, lpq, lpr

### lpsystem -t bsd sparky

ALL   SVR4   SYSADM

This command is almost the same as **lpsystem sparky**. It adds the remote computer **sparky** to the remote printing service, but is used if **sparky** is running BSD UNIX.

**Keyword:** printing, networking

**Files:** /var/spool/lp/*, /etc/lp/*

**See Also:** enable, lpstat, accept, lpadmin, lpfilter, lpforms, lpsched, lpsystem, lpusers, lpq, lpr

### lpsystem sparky

**ALL**  **SVR4**  **SYSADM**

This command is the opposite of **lpsystem -r sparky**. It adds the remote computer **sparky** to the remote printing service, if **sparky** is running System V UNIX.

**Keyword:**   printing, networking

**Files:**   /var/spool/lp/*, /etc/lp/*

**See Also:**   enable, lpstat, accept, lpadmin, lpfilter, lpforms, lpsched, lpsystem, lpusers, lpq, lpr

### lptest

**ALL**  **SVR4 BSD**  **SYSADM**

This command outputs a test pattern to standard output that consists of 79 ASCII characters that are offset to the right by one column, each row down. It outputs 200 rows of text characters.

**Keyword:**   printing, system information

**See Also:**   lp, lpq, lpr, lpstat

### lptest 50 100

**ALL**  **SVR4 BSD**  **SYSADM**

This command is the same as **lptest**, except that it prints a test pattern that consists of 50 ASCII characters and 100 rows. The display appears on standard output.

**Keyword:**   printing, system information

**See Also:**   lp, lpq, lpr, lpstat

### lptest 50 100 | lp

**ALL**  **SVR4 BSD**  **SYSADM**

This command prints a test pattern to the default printer that consists of 50 ASCII characters and 100 rows. Output is queued to the default printer.

**Keyword:**   printing, system information

**See Also:**   lp, lpq, lpr, lpstat

### lpusers -d 0

**ALL**  **SVR4**  **SYSADM**

The **lpusers** command sets priority levels on the print queue. This command sets a default priority of **0**, which is the highest priority.

**Keyword:**   printing, system setup

**See Also:**   lp, lpadmin, lpstat

### lpusers -d 39

ALL  SVR4  SYSADM

This command sets the local print service to a default priority of **39**, which is the lowest priority.

**Keyword:**    printing, system setup

**See Also:**    lp, lpadmin, lpstat

### lpusers -l

ALL  SVR4  SYSADM

This command shows the local print service default priority.

**Keyword:**    printing, system setup

**See Also:**    lp, lpadmin, lpstat

### lpusers -q 28 -u perkie

ALL  SVR4  SYSADM

This command gives user **perkie** the highest default priority level of **28**.

**Keyword:**    printing, system setup

**See Also:**    lp, lpadmin, lpstat

### lr

ALL  SCO  ALL

On SCO systems, the **lr** command lists the files in the current working directory and every subdirectory of the current one. The format of the **lr** command is to list the files alphabetically and in multiple columns. This system-level alias is based on the **-R** option to the **lc** command.

**Keyword:**    file display

**See Also:**    chmod, du, find, l, lc, lf, lx, ls

### lr -A

ALL  SCO  END

This command lists all files in the current directory, including hidden files. Output is multiple-column.

**Keyword:**    file display

**See Also:**    l, lf, lc, ls, lx

### lr -ld /usr

ALL  SCO  END

This command outputs the status of the **/usr** directory and all its subdirectories.

**Keyword:**    file display

**See Also:**    l, lf, lc, ls, lx

ALL  ALL  ALL

## ls

The **ls** command is ubiquitous. All users employ its talents (even SCO users who are using system-level aliases such as **l** and **lr**). In general, **ls** is roughly similar across all environments, but SVR4, SCO, and BSD versions all have slight differences:

```
BSD:      ls [ -acdfgilqrstulACLFR]    [files]
SVR4      ls [ -1RadCxmnlogrtucpFbqisfL]  [files]
SunOS:    ls [ -aAcCdfFgilLqrRstul]   [files]
Solaris:  ls [ -abcCdfFgilLmnopqrRstux1] [files]
SCO:      ls [ -1ACFLRabcdfgilmnopqrstux]  [files]
OSF1:     ls [ -1ACFLRabcdfgilmnopqrstux]  [files]
AIX       ls [ -AadiLNRrsFpbqCmcultgntx] [files]
MKS       ls [ -1abcCdfFgilmnopqrRsTux ]  [files]
```

The example here is **ls** without options. This is implemented differently depending on the system. If you are working on a BSD or SVR4 derivative system, the default output is a multiple-column listing. On SCO systems, the default display is a single-column format (but SCO users can use **l**, **lc**, **lf**, **lr**, and **lx** for multiple-column displays). Here are some important facts about the way **ls** works:

• Unless you are the root user, hidden files (those beginning with a dot) are listed only when you specify an appropriate option.

• A single dot represents the current directory.

• A double dot represents the parent directory.

• Output from **ls** can appear in single-column, multiple-column, and wide format.

• Multiple-column listings are alphabetized left to right or top to bottom, depending on the option.

**Keyword:**  directories, filename display

**Files:**  /etc/passwd, /etc/group, /usr/share/lib/terminfo?/* (SVR4)

**See Also:**  chmod, du, find, ln (SCO: l, lc, lf, lr, lx)

## ls *

ALL  ALL  ALL

This command lists files in the current directory and one level down.

**Keyword:**  file display

**See Also:**  l, lc, lf, lr, lx

### ls -A

This command lists all the files in the current directory, not just the nonhidden files. The current directory (.) and the parent directory (..) are not shown, however. The output consists of one file per line.

**Keyword:**    file display

**See Also:**    l, lf, lr, lc, lx

### ls -a

This command does the same thing as **ls -A**, except that in addition to showing hidden files, it lists the current directory (.) and the parent directory (..). Files and directories are alphabetized in columns.

**Keyword:**    file display

**See Also:**    l, lf, lr, lc, lx

### ls -al | awk ´{s += $5} END { print s,"kilobytes"}´

The **-a** option in this command takes care of the hidden file problem.

**Keyword:**    file display

**See Also:**    l, lc, lf, lr, lx, awk

### ls -al | awk ´{s+=$5} {print $0} END { print s,"kilobytes"}´

This command outputs all the files in the current directory, and includes the total disk space they use.

**Keyword:**    file display

**See Also:**    awk, l, lc, lf, lr, lx

### ls -alp | grep ´/´

This command outputs a long listing of all the subdirectories of the current directory. Another way to do this is to use only the **-l** option to **ls**, and then pipe the output into **grep ^d**. The advantage of this method in the example is that you can use most **ls** options along with the **-p** option.

**Keyword:**    file display

**See Also:**    grep, l, lc, lf, lr, lx

## ls -altF `find / -type f -perm 777 -print`

ALL  ALL  ALL

This command lists all files that have been found by the **find** command. The method of linking the output from the **find** command to the **ls** command is called UNIX command substitution.

**Keyword:**  file display

**See Also:**  l, lc, lf, lr, lx

## ls -b

ALL  ALL  ALL

This command lists files in the current directory. If a file has nonprintable characters in it, they appear in octal notation. The output consists of one file per line.

**Keyword:**  file display

**See Also:**  l, lf, lr, lc, lx

## ls -F

ALL  ALL  ALL

This command outputs a listing of all the nonhidden files in the current directory, one file per line. The directories have a **/** at the ends of their names, the executables have an **\***, and the symbolically linked files have an **@**.

**Keyword:**  file display

**See Also:**  lf, lr, lc, lx, l

## ls -f

ALL  ALL  ALL

This command outputs the names of all the files in the current directory. The **-f** option is similar to the **-a** option, except that the sorting is not alphabetical. The **-f** option does no sorting at all; the files are output in the order in which they appear in the directory.

**Keyword:**  file display

**See Also:**  l, lf, lr, lc, lx

## ls -g

ALL  ALL  ALL

The listing format of the **-g** option consists of the file permissions, the number of links, group, size in bytes, and time of last modification for each file. The **-g** option is the same as the **-l** option, except that **-g** does not include the owner name.

**Keyword:**  file display

**See Also:**  l, lf, lr, lc, lx

## ls -i

ALL ALL ALL

This command lists files in the current directory; the inode number appears one space to the left of the filename.

**Keyword:** file display

**See Also:** l, lf, lr, lc, lx

## ls -L

ALL ALL ALL

This command lists all nonhidden files in the current directory, one file per line. The option also lists linked files by showing the original file, not the link.

**Keyword:** file display

**See Also:** l, lf, lr, lc, lx

## ls -l

ALL ALL END

The **-l** option to **ls** turns on wide format. Using it without other options alphabetizes the listing. Any filenames beginning with numbers and special characters appear before alphabetical filenames. Here is an example of a directory listing that the authors have in **/usr**:

```
drwxrwxrwx   8 root      bin       2560 Feb 19 18:53 CmdCmp
```

Note that the **-l** option does not list hidden files unless you are the root user.

**Keyword:** directories, filename display

**See Also:** chmod, du, find, ln

## ls -l | awk ´{s += $5} END { print s,"kilobytes"}´

ALL ALL ALL

This command outputs the amount of disk space used by files in the current directory. Note that if you are not the root user, the **ls** output accounts for only nonhidden files.

**Keyword:** file display

**See Also:** l, lc, lf, lr, lx, awk

## ls -l | cut -c0-80

ALL ALL POWER

Sometimes, an **ls** file listing can wrap to the next line. You might not like this, so try using **ls** with **cut**, as in the example.

**Keyword:** directories, filename display

**See Also:** chmod, cut, du, find, ln

## ls -ld /usr

ALL    ALL    ALL

This command displays the listing for the **/usr** directory.

**Keyword:**   file display

**See Also:**   l, lf, lr, lc, lx

## ls -lF | grep "/"

ALL    ALL    ALL

This command is another way to list only directories. The **-l** option tells **ls** to list all files in wide format. The **-F** option specifies that directories be marked with a forward slash (and executable files be marked with an asterisk). The **grep** command does the filtering.

**Keyword:**   file display

**See Also:**   grep, lc, lf, lr, lx, l

## ls -lsd

ALL    ALL    ALL

This command prints a long list of the current directory. The **-s** option adds the file size to the beginning of each listed entry.

**Keyword:**   file display

**See Also:**   l, lf, lr, lc, lx

## ls -lu /dev/ttyp1

ALL    ALL    POWER
SYSADM

This command lists the file associated with **/dev/ttyp1**, which is a terminal device file. The **-u** option is useful because it lets you determine when the terminal was last used.

**Keyword:**   file display

**See Also:**   l, lc, lf, lr, lx

## ls -m

ALL    ALL    POWER

The **-m** option lists the names of files in the current directory across the page, separated by commas. This can be useful when you need to redirect **ls** output to a file for use in a document.

**Keyword:**   file display

**See Also:**   l, lf, lr, lc, lx

## ls -n

ALL    ALL    ALL

The wide format of the **-n** option consists of the permissions, number of links, user ID number, group ID number, size in bytes, and time of last modification for each file.

**Keyword:** file display
**See Also:** l, lf, lr, lc, lx

## ls -o

ALL ALL ALL

The **-o** option lists permissions, number of links, owner, size in bytes, and time of last modification for each file. The **-o** option is the same as the **-l** option, except that **-o** does not include the name of the group to which the file belongs. Note that the **-n** option overrides the **-o** option.

**Keyword:** file display
**See Also:** l, lf, lr, lc, lx

## ls -p

ALL ALL ALL

This command appends a **/** after every entry that is a directory name. Compare it to the **-f** option.

**Keyword:** file display
**See Also:** l, lf, lr, lc, lx

## ls -q

ALL ALL ALL

This command lists files in the current directory. If a filename has any nonprintable characters in it, they are output as **?**.

**Keyword:** file display
**See Also:** l, lf, lr, lc, lx

## ls -R

ALL ALL ALL

The **-R** option tells **ls** to *recursively* list files and directories beginning with the current directory. On SCO systems, the output appears as a single column. Other systems use wide-column format.

**Keyword:** file display
**See Also:** l, lf, lr, lc, lx

## ls -r

ALL ALL ALL

The **-r** option sorts files in reverse alphabetical order, Z–A. If you combine the **-t** option with **-r**, it reverses the order of the sort again, but this time in terms of date of last modification.

**Keyword:** file display
**See Also:** l, lf, lr, lc, lx

## ls -s

ALL ALL ALL

This command lists files in the current directory. The file size, in 512-byte blocks or 1024-byte blocks (BSD), is listed in the space to the left of the filename.

**Keyword:** file display

**See Also:** l, lf, lr, lc, lx

## ls -t

ALL ALL ALL

This command sorts files by modification time, rather than alphabetically. Most recently modified files appear first in the listing.

**Keyword:** file display

**See Also:** l, lf, lr, lc, lx

## ls -tc

ALL ALL ALL

This command lists files in the current directory, sorted by the time of last modification, with the most recent first.

**Keyword:** file display

**See Also:** l, lf, lr, lc, lx

## ls -u

ALL ALL ALL

The **-u** option sorts by access time, rather than filename. The **-u** option is mutually exclusive of the **-t** option.

**Keyword:** file display

**See Also:** l, lf, lr, lc, lx

## ls -x

ALL ALL ALL

The **-x** option sorts files across columns. By default, the sort is alphabetical, but you can combine **-x** with the **-t** or **-u** options.

**Keyword:** file display

**See Also:** l, lf, lr, lc, lx

## lsscreen -n $HOME/dumps/s12.txt

ALL AIX ALL

This command simply copies the contents of the current screen to **$HOME/dumps/s12.txt**. It is useful for an ASCII terminal, but not a graphics display such as an X terminal. If you need a screen dump of an X display, try **xwd**.

**Keyword:** terminal display
**See Also:** cat, echo, xwd

## lx

On SCO systems, the **lx** command lists files in multicolumn format, alphabetized across columns. This system-level alias is based on the **-x** option to **ls** (hence the **x** in **lx**). You can use this alias—and any others in the set of **l**, **lc**, **lf**, **lr**, and **lx**—with many other listing options. Try **lx -F**, which marks directories with a forward slash, executable files with an asterisk, and symbolic links with an at sign.
**Keyword:** file display
**See Also:** chmod, du, find, l, lc, lf, ln, lr, ls

## mach

This command shows you the type of processor your computer has in it.
**Keyword:** system information
**See Also:** arch, machid, machine, uname

## machid m68k

This command returns an exit code of **0** if your computer has a Motorola M68000 series microprocessor in it; otherwise, it returns an exit code of **1**.
**Keyword:** system information, kernel
**See Also:** arch, mach, machine, uname

## machine

This command outputs the processor type of the computer.
**Keyword:** system information, kernel
**See Also:** arch, mach, machid, uname

## MAIL

This environment variable routes incoming mail to the specified file. This occurs only when the **MAILPATH** environment variable is not set. Of course, **MAIL** itself must be set by the user or system administrator.
**Keyword:** email, Internet, user communication
**See Also:** biff, mail, mailx, notify, talk, vacation, write, xbiff

| | | |
|---|---|---|
| ALL | SCO | ALL |
| ALL | BSD SVR4 | POWER SYSADM |
| ALL | SVR4 | POWER SYSADM |
| ALL | OSF | POWER SYSADM |
| SH KSH | ALL | POWER SYSADM |

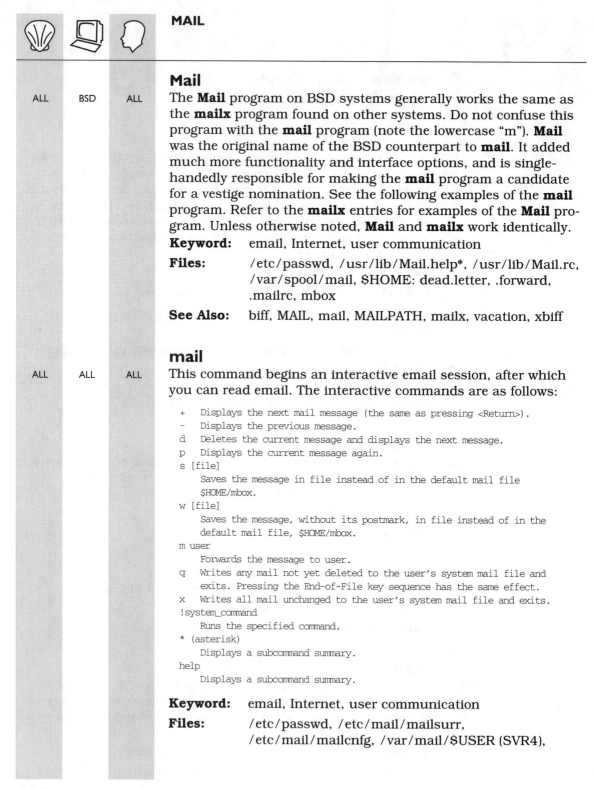

## Mail

ALL  BSD  ALL

The **Mail** program on BSD systems generally works the same as the **mailx** program found on other systems. Do not confuse this program with the **mail** program (note the lowercase "m"). **Mail** was the original name of the BSD counterpart to **mail**. It added much more functionality and interface options, and is single-handedly responsible for making the **mail** program a candidate for a vestige nomination. See the following examples of the **mail** program. Refer to the **mailx** entries for examples of the **Mail** program. Unless otherwise noted, **Mail** and **mailx** work identically.

**Keyword:**  email, Internet, user communication

**Files:**  /etc/passwd, /usr/lib/Mail.help*, /usr/lib/Mail.rc, /var/spool/mail, $HOME: dead.letter, .forward, .mailrc, mbox

**See Also:**  biff, MAIL, mail, MAILPATH, mailx, vacation, xbiff

## mail

ALL  ALL  ALL

This command begins an interactive email session, after which you can read email. The interactive commands are as follows:

```
+    Displays the next mail message (the same as pressing <Return>).
-    Displays the previous message.
d    Deletes the current message and displays the next message.
p    Displays the current message again.
s [file]
     Saves the message in file instead of in the default mail file
     $HOME/mbox.
w [file]
     Saves the message, without its postmark, in file instead of in the
     default mail file, $HOME/mbox.
m user
     Forwards the message to user.
q    Writes any mail not yet deleted to the user's system mail file and
     exits. Pressing the End-of-File key sequence has the same effect.
x    Writes all mail unchanged to the user's system mail file and exits.
!system_command
     Runs the specified command.
* (asterisk)
     Displays a subcommand summary.
help
     Displays a subcommand summary.
```

**Keyword:**  email, Internet, user communication

**Files:**  /etc/passwd, /etc/mail/mailsurr, /etc/mail/mailcnfg, /var/mail/$USER (SVR4),

/var/spool/mail/$USER (SunOS, OSF),
/usr/spool/mail/$USER (BSD), $HOME:
dead.letter, mbox

**See Also:**   biff, binmail, MAIL, MAILPATH, mailx, notify, write, vacation, xbiff

### mail -e

ALL   ALL   END

If you have received email, this command returns an exit code of **0**; if you haven't received any mail, then you get an exit code of **1**.

**Keyword:**   email, Internet, user communication

**Files:**   $HOME/dead.letter, $HOME/mbox

**See Also:**   biff, mailx, notify, write, vacation, xbiff

### mail -F ""

ALL   ALL   END

This command turns off forwarding of email.

**Keyword:**   email, Internet, user communication

**Files:**   $HOME/dead.letter, $HOME/mbox

**See Also:**   biff, mailx, notify, write, vacation, xbiff

### mail -F "emily, alans, perkie, | my_vacation %R"

ALL   ALL   END

This command forwards all your mail to the users **emily**, **alans**, and **perkie** on the local system, and it runs the program **my_vacation**. The return path to the message originator is substituted before **my_vacation** is run.

**Keyword:**   email, Internet, user communication

**Files:**   $HOME/dead.letter, $HOME/mbox

**See Also:**   biff, mailx, notify, write, vacation, xbiff

### mail -F "perkie,jon@newl.com,newl!alans"

ALL   ALL   END

This command forwards all your email to user **perkie** on the local computer; to user **jon** on the computer **newl**, which has Internet access; and to the user **alans**, also on the computer **newl**, but via a UUCP connection.

**Keyword:**   email, Internet, user communication

**Files:**   $HOME/dead.letter, $HOME/mbox

**See Also:**   biff, mailx, notify, write, vacation, xbiff

### mail -F "|/bin/sh -c \"find / -atime +45 -print\""

ALL   ALL   END

This command executes the command **find / -atime +45 -print** in the message recipient's home directory. All the files that have not been accessed in the last **45** days on the recipient's computer system are output.

**Keyword:**   email, Internet, user communication

**Files:**   $HOME/dead.letter, $HOME/mbox

**See Also:**   biff, mailx, notify, write, vacation, xbiff

### mail -F "|cat"

ALL   ALL   END

This command executes the command **cat** in the message recipient's home directory. The message is used as input to the **cat** command.

**Keyword:**   email, Internet, user communication

**Files:**   $HOME/dead.letter, $HOME/mbox

**See Also:**   biff, mailx, notify, write, vacation, xbiff

### mail -F alans@newl.com

ALL   ALL   END

This command forwards all your mail to the user **alans@newl.com**. This is a very convenient command if you have multiple email addresses and you want to consolidate all of your email. Note, however, that you shouldn't use Alan's email address; put in your own.

**Keyword:**   email, Internet, user communication

**Files:**   $HOME/dead.letter, $HOME/mbox

**See Also:**   biff, mailx, notify, write, vacation, xbiff

### mail -f Saved_Mail

ALL   ALL   END

This command checks the file called **Saved_Mail** in the current directory and looks for mail there, rather than your spooling location.

**Keyword:**   email, Internet, user communication

**Files:**   $HOME/dead.letter, $HOME/mbox

**See Also:**   biff, mailx, notify, write, vacation, xbiff

### mail -h

ALL   ALL   END

If you have received email, this command shows the headers on all the mail you have received. It then enters interactive mode.

**Keyword:** email, Internet, user communication
**Files:** $HOME/dead.letter, $HOME/mbox
**See Also:** biff, mailx, notify, write, vacation, xbiff

### mail -m ASCII perkie@mit.edu

ALL    ALL    END

This command starts the **mail** program in send mode. It allows you to write a message; then, when you enter a **.** on a line by itself, it sends the message to **perkie@mit.edu**. A line with **Message-Type: ASCII** is included in the header information.

**Keyword:** email, Internet, user communication
**Files:** $HOME/dead.letter, $HOME/mbox
**See Also:** biff, mailx, notify, write, vacation, xbiff

### mail -P

ALL    ALL    END

This command outputs to standard output all the mail you have received, listing the newest mail first. The output includes all the header information that is contained in the email.

**Keyword:** email, Internet, user communication
**Files:** $HOME/dead.letter, $HOME/mbox
**See Also:** biff, mailx, notify, write, vacation, xbiff

### mail -p

ALL    ALL    END

This command outputs to standard output all the mail you have received, listing the newest mail first.

**Keyword:** email, Internet, user communication
**Files:** $HOME/dead.letter, $HOME/mbox
**See Also:** biff, mailx, notify, write, vacation, xbiff

### mail -q

ALL    ALL    END

This command is used when you want to quit the **mail** program with Ctrl-C.

**Keyword:** email, Internet, user communication
**Files:** $HOME/dead.letter, $HOME/mbox
**See Also:** biff, mailx, notify, write, vacation, xbiff

### mail -r

ALL    ALL    END

This command lists your received mail in the order that it was received. The oldest message is displayed first.

**mail**

**Keyword:**   email, Internet, user communication
**Files:**       $HOME/dead.letter, $HOME/mbox
**See Also:**   biff, mailx, notify, write, vacation, xbiff

### mail -t perkie@mit.edu alans@newl.com

ALL    ALL    END

This command starts the **mail** program in send mode. It allows you to write a message; then, when you enter a **.** on a line by itself, it sends the message to **perkie@mit.edu** and **alans@newl.com**. Included in the message header is a **TO:** line for both **perkie@mit.edu** and **alans@newl.com**.

**Keyword:**   email, Internet, user communication
**Files:**       $HOME/dead.letter, $HOME/mbox
**See Also:**   biff, mailx, notify, write, vacation, xbiff

### mail alpha!perkie < report

ALL    ALL    END

This command sends the file report to the user **perkie** on the remote computer called **alpha**. The **!** is used for UUCP addressing, instead of the **@** used for Internet addressing.

**Keyword:**   email, Internet, user communication
**Files:**       $HOME/dead.letter, $HOME/mbox
**See Also:**   biff, mailx, notify, write, vacation, xbiff

### mail perkie@mit.edu

ALL    ALL    END

This command starts the **mail** program in send mode. It allows you to write a message; then, when you enter a **.** on a line by itself, it sends the message to **perkie@mit.edu**.

**Keyword:**   email, Internet, user communication
**Files:**       $HOME/dead.letter, $HOME/mbox
**See Also:**   biff, mailx, notify, write, vacation, xbiff

### mail perkie@mit.edu < report

ALL    ALL    END

This command sends the file report to the user **perkie@mit.edu**.

**Keyword:**   email, Internet, user communication
**Files:**       $HOME/dead.letter, $HOME/mbox
**See Also:**   biff, mailx, notify, write, vacation, xbiff

## mailalias perkie@mit.edu

| | | |
|---|---|---|
| ALL | SVR4 | END |

The **mailalias** program is specifically designed for the **mail** program. If you do not use **mail** (as opposed to **mailx**), do not concern youself with the **mailalias** program. **mailalias** manages an alias database specifically for **mail**. You can specify one or more *real addresses* to **mailalias**. The **-s** option, if used, causes **mailalias** not to display the real address for multiple aliases. The **mailalias** program searches the following files for aliases: **$HOME/lib/names**, **/etc/mail/namefiles**, and **/etc/mail/names**.

**Keyword:**  email

**Files:**  /etc/mail/namefiles, /etc/mail/names, $HOME/lib/names

**See Also:**  mail

## MAILCHECK

| | | |
|---|---|---|
| ALL | ALL | POWER SYSADM |

This environment variable specifies how often the shell checks for the arrival of new mail. When you set **$MAILCHECK** to **0**, the shell checks after each command you execute.

**Keyword:**  email, Internet, user environment

**See Also:**  biff, mail, mailx, notify, xbiff

## MAILPATH

| | | |
|---|---|---|
| ALL | ALL | POWER SYSADM |

This environment variable informs you of the arrival of mail. It consists of a list of filenames, separated by colons. Whenever any of these files are updated with new mail, the shell alerts you.

**Keyword:**  email, Internet, user environment

**See Also:**  biff, mail, mailx, notify, xbiff

## mailstats

| | | |
|---|---|---|
| ALL | SVR4 BSD | POWER SYSADM |

The **mailstats** command prints a status of mail in the queue as specified by the **sendmail** program, which manages Internet and remote mail. In order for **mailstats** to work, **sendmail** must update the **sendmail.st** file. This file can be renamed using the **S** flag to the **-o** option. Here is an example of output from **mailstat**:

```
Statistics from Feb Aug 16 14:21:34 1994
M      msgsfr    bytes_from    msgsto    bytes_to
1        45         62K          11         8K
4        38         35K          48        79K
```

The output fields in the **mailstats** display tell you the following: **M** specifies the position in **sendmail.cf**, **msgsfr** represents the number of messages received, **bytes_from** specifies the size of the messages received, **msgsto** represents the number of messages sent from the local system, and **bytes_to** specifies the size of the message from the local system.

**Keyword:**    email, Internet, user environment

**See Also:**    mail, mailx, sendmail

## mailstats -S $EMAIL/transfers

ALL    SVR4    POWER
     BSD    SYSADM

If your site uses different configuration files with the **sendmail** program, **mailstats** needs to be informed of the fact. Normally, **mailstats** uses the **sendmail.st** file to obtain transfer information. Use the **-S** option, as in the example, to tell **mailstats** to use a different file.

**Keyword:**    email, Internet, user environment

**See Also:**    mail, mailx, sendmail

## mailx

ALL    ALL    ALL

Invoked without any arguments, **mailx** displays the message headers queued up in your mailbox. You can read messages in sequence by pressing the Return key at the **?** prompt. You can also read messages selectively by entering individual queue numbers at the **?** prompt. Here is a typical **mailx** listing:

```
"/usr/spool/mail/alans": 3 messages 2 new 1 unread
 U  1 root              Wed Aug 18 16:55  13/325
 N  2 perkie@mit.edu    Thu Aug 19 13:01  14/409
 N  3 perkie@mit.edu    Fri Aug 20 13:01  14/409
```

Displaying the queue is the default behavior of **mailx**. The **-H** option also displays the queue (you might need to use this is a shell script if the script always loads mail with some argument). The following examples illustrate other options for reading mail. They are followed by examples for sending mail. Finally, **mailx** subcommands that are used while composing messages are given.

**Keyword:**    email, Internet, user communication

**Files:**    /usr/share/lib/mailx/mailx.help, /var/mail/*
(SVR4), /etc/mail/mailx.rc,
/var/spool/mail/$USER (SunOS, OSF),
/usr/spool/mail/$USER (BSD), $HOME/dead.letter,
$HOME/mbox, $HOME/.mailrc

**See Also:**    biff, binmail, MAIL, MAILPATH, mail, notify, sendmail, write, vacation, xbiff

### mailx -e

ALL    ALL    END

The **-e** option tests for the presence of mail. The option is designed largely for use in shell scripts. With the **-e** option in effect, if **mailx** finds no mail in the queue, it returns a **0** to indicate success.

**Keyword:**    email, Internet, user communication

**Files:**    $HOME/dead.letter, $HOME/mbox, $HOME/.mailrc

**See Also:**    biff, mail, notify, write, vacation, xbiff

### mailx -f

ALL    ALL    END

This command reads your **mbox** file, rather than the file where your new mail is. This is a good way to look through mail you have already received.

**Keyword:**    email, Internet, user communication

**Files:**    $HOME/dead.letter, $HOME/mbox, $HOME/.mailrc

**See Also:**    biff, mail, notify, write, vacation, xbiff

### mailx -f /usr/spool/mail/alans

ALL    ALL    POWER
               SYSADM

If you want to read a different message queue, you can specify the **-f** option. If your system supports Netnews but does not integrate it into **mail**, it is useful for reading Netnews mail that is addressed to you. The example shows the **-f** option being used to read a standard message queue file. For the command to be successful, however, the user executing the command must have both read and write permissions on the file. Because of this, access to mail queues is restricted to the owner and superusers on most systems.

**Keyword:**    email, Internet, user communication

**Files:**    $HOME/dead.letter, $HOME/mbox, $HOME/.mailrc

**See Also:**    biff, mail, notify, write, vacation, xbiff

### mailx -f newsinfo

ALL    ALL    END

This command is used to read through a file that is in the same format as your **mbox** file. In this example, the file is called **newsinfo** in the current directory.

**Keyword:**    email, Internet, user communication

**Files:** $HOME/dead.letter, $HOME/mbox, $HOME/.mailrc
**See Also:** biff, mail, notify, write, vacation, xbiff

## mailx -f newsinfo -I

ALL ALL END

This command is used if the **newsinfo** file is a saved Internet Netnews file. The command includes the newsgroup and article-ID header lines when printing mail messages.
**Keyword:** email, Internet, user communication
**Files:** $HOME/dead.letter, $HOME/mbox, $HOME/.mailrc
**See Also:** biff, mail, notify, write, vacation, xbiff

## mailx -H

ALL ALL END

This command is used to see the mail headers only, not the full message.
**Keyword:** email, Internet, user communication
**Files:** $HOME/dead.letter, $HOME/mbox, $HOME/.mailrc
**See Also:** biff, mail, notify, write, vacation, xbiff

## mailx -i

ALL ALL END

This command starts the **mailx** program and tells it to ignore any interrupts, such as a Ctrl-C.
**Keyword:** email, Internet, user communication
**Files:** $HOME/dead.letter, $HOME/mbox, $HOME/.mailrc
**See Also:** biff, mail, notify, write, vacation, xbiff

## mailx -N

ALL ALL END

The **-N** option tells **mailx** not to print the message header index. When **mailx** executes, you simply get the **?** prompt.
**Keyword:** email, Internet, user communication
**Files:** $HOME/dead.letter, $HOME/mbox, $HOME/.mailrc
**See Also:** biff, mail, notify, write, vacation, xbiff

## mailx -n

ALL ALL END

This command tells **mailx** not to read the configuration information that is in the system default **mailx.rc** file.
**Keyword:** email, Internet, user communication

**Files:**     $HOME/dead.letter, $HOME/mbox, $HOME/.mailrc

**See Also:**     biff, mail, notify, write, vacation, xbiff

## mailx -n -F

ALL     ALL     END

Used together, the **-n** and **-F** options give you significant customizing control over the **mailx** interface. The **-F** option tells **mailx** to save messages to the first recipient's file in your home directory. The **-n** option tells **mailx** to ignore the **/etc/mail/mailx.rc** file, thus allowing your own **$HOME/.mailrc** to have full effect. Here is a **.mailrc** file that is a starter kit of sorts:

```
set sign=Alan                      # Informal signature
set Sign="Alan Southerton"         # Formal signature
set save                           # Save dead messages
set Dead=$HOME/dead.let            # Dead message file
set editheaders                    # For ~e and ~v cmds
set prompt=" [mailx:] "            # Custom prompt
set indentprefix="      >"         # Excerpt marking
set ask                            # Always, a To: line
```

**Keyword:**     email, Internet, user communication

**Files:**     $HOME/dead.letter, $HOME/mbox, $HOME/.mailrc

**See Also:**     biff, mail, notify, write, vacation, xbiff

## mailx -r alans@newl.com perkie@mit.edu

ALL     ALL     END

This command is used to compose and send a message to **perkie@mit.edu**, using **alans@newl.com** as the return address.

**Keyword:**     email, Internet, user communication

**Files:**     $HOME/dead.letter, $HOME/mbox, $HOME/.mailrc

**See Also:**     biff, mail, notify, write, vacation, xbiff

## mailx -s ´Command Compendium´ perkie@mit.edu

ALL     ALL     END

This command is used to compose and send a message to **perkie@mit.edu**. The subject of the message is set to **Command Compendium**.

**Keyword:**     email, Internet, user communication

**Files:**     $HOME/dead.letter, $HOME/mbox, $HOME/.mailrc

**See Also:**     biff, mail, notify, write, vacation, xbiff

### mailx -T newsinfo

| ALL | ALL | END |
|-----|-----|-----|

This command records the message-ID and article-ID header lines in the **newsinfo** file after the message is read.

**Keyword:** email, Internet, user communication

**Files:** $HOME/dead.letter, $HOME/mbox, $HOME/.mailrc

**See Also:** biff, mail, notify, write, vacation, xbiff

### mailx -u alans

| ALL | ALL | END |
|-----|-----|-----|

The **-u** option lets a privileged user read the contents of another user's mail queue. By system default, the mail queue has read and write permissions set to the owner of the file. This means that only the owner and superusers can read another user's mail. On many systems, the mail queue is stored in the **/usr/spool/mail** directory in a file with the user's name. Thus, the entry looks for **/usr/spool/mail/alans**.

**Keyword:** email, Internet, user communication

**Files:** $HOME/dead.letter, $HOME/mbox, $HOME/.mailrc

**See Also:** biff, mail, notify, write, vacation, xbiff

### mailx -U mit.edu!perkie

| ALL | ALL | END |
|-----|-----|-----|

This command is used to compose and send a message to **perkie@mit.edu**. The **-U** argument tells **mailx** to convert the UUCP-style address to Internet style.

**Keyword:** email, Internet, user communication, UUCP

**Files:** $HOME/dead.letter, $HOME/mbox, $HOME/.mailrc

**See Also:** biff, mail, notify, write, vacation, xbiff

### mailx -V

| ALL | ALL | END |
|-----|-----|-----|

This command simply outputs the version number of **mailx**.

**Keyword:** email, Internet, user communication

**Files:** $HOME/dead.letter, $HOME/mbox, $HOME/.mailrc

**See Also:** biff, mail, notify, write, vacation, xbiff

### mailx <--> ~!cat $HOME/.epilog

| ALL | ALL | END |
|-----|-----|-----|

Using the tilde command that performs a shell escape opens the door. One of the more common things to do, for example, is to add a few lines at the end of your mail to act as a commentary on nothing in particular. You'll find famous quotes, homegrown quotes, and drawings on Internet email. You can use the **sign** and **Sign** mail variables (along with the **~s** and **~S** tilde escape commands) to put into signature lines. You can go beyond this by designing an *epilog* file and appending it with **~!cat**, as in the example. In addition to **~!cat**, **mailx** offers **~r** *filename*, **~<** *filename*, and **~-<!** *cmd*, all of which perform the same function.

**Keyword:**    email, Internet, user communication

**Files:**    $HOME/dead.letter, $HOME/mbox, $HOME/.mailrc

**See Also:**    biff, mail, notify, write, vacation, xbiff

## mailx <--> ~?

ALL    ALL    END

The **~?** tilde escape displays a help list defining all the tilde escapes. The help screen subdivides the commands into control commands, heading insertion commands, message insertion commands, and change message commands.

**Keyword:**    email, Internet, user communication

**Files:**    $HOME/dead.letter, $HOME/mbox, $HOME/.mailrc

**See Also:**    biff, mail, notify, write, vacation, xbiff

## mailx <--> !

ALL    ALL    END

If you are in the middle of a **mailx** session and don't want to quit to the shell or use **xi** to exit, you can execute a subshell by entering **!** at the **mailx** prompt. By default, the **mailx** prompt is a **?**.

**Keyword:**    email, Internet, user communication

**Files:**    $HOME/dead.letter, $HOME/mbox, $HOME/.mailrc

**See Also:**    biff, mail, notify, write, vacation, xbiff

## mailx <--> ?

ALL    ALL    END

Don't forget about the **?** when reading mail in **mailx**. It displays a list of important tilde commands. Here is a typical help display:

```
Control Commands:
   q                       Quit - apply mailbox commands entered this session.
   x                       Quit - restore mailbox to original state.
   ! <cmd>                 Start a shell, run <cmd>, and return to mailbox.
   cd [<dir>]              Change directory to <dir> or $HOME.
Display Commands:
   t [<msg_list>]          Display messages in <msg_list> or current message.
   n                       Display next message.
   f [<msg_list>]          Display headings of messages.
   h [<num>]               Display headings of group containing message <num>.
Message Handling:
   e [<num>]               Edit message <num> (default editor is e).
   d [<msg_list>]          Delete messages in <msg_list> or current message.
```

```
u [<msg_list>]              Recall deleted messages.
s [<msg_list>] <file>  Append messages (with headings) to <file>.
w [<msg_list>] <file>  Append messages (text only) to <file>.
pre [<msg_list>]        Keep messages in system mailbox.
Creating New Mail:
m <addrlist>                Create/send new message to addresses in <addrlist>.
r [<msg_list>]              Send reply to senders and recipients of messages.
R [<msg_list>]              Send reply only to senders of messages.
a                           Display list of aliases and their addresses.
```

**Keyword:** email, Internet, user communication

**Files:** $HOME/dead.letter, $HOME/mbox, $HOME/.mailrc

**See Also:** biff, mail, notify, write, vacation, xbiff

## mailx <--> ~!ls

ALL ALL END

The ~!ls sequence is for use in composition mode. (You do not use it, nor many of the following examples, at the command line.) The sequence is called a *tilde escape* command. The important part of the command in the example is ~!, which is the command for executing a shell escape. You can name any UNIX command after ~!. Alternatively, you can execute ~! alone to execute a shell. Here is an example from composition mode:

```
Subject: Testing Shell Escape
This is a listing of my directory. I am sending it to
you to test the shell escape facility in mailx.
~!ls
.Xauthority        .login            DXterm
.Xdefaults         .profile          db
.Xdefaults.old     .sh_history       test.xwd
.cshrc             .xsession-errors  tester
!
Regards,
alans
```

**Keyword:** email, Internet, user communication

**Files:** $HOME/dead.letter, $HOME/mbox, $HOME/.mailrc

**See Also:** biff, ls, mail, notify, write, vacation, xbiff

## mailx <--> ~.

ALL ALL END

The ~. tilde escape sequence puts an immediate end to the message you are creating in composition mode. It is the same as pressing Ctrl-D. If **mailx** is configured to end with a **Cc:** prompt, it is unaffected.

**Keyword:** email, Internet, user communication

**Files:** $HOME/dead.letter, $HOME/mbox, $HOME/.mailrc

**See Also:** biff, mail, notify, write, vacation, xbiff

### mailx <--> ~a

ALL  ALL  END

This tilde escape embeds a signature line into the message that you are composing. The **~a** sequence includes the line of text defined by the **sign** variable in **.mailrc**. There is also a **~A** tilde command that adds a second signature line, if you want one. The **~A** sequence takes its value from the **Sign** variable.

**Keyword:** email, Internet, user communication

**Files:** $HOME/dead.letter, $HOME/mbox, $HOME/.mailrc

**See Also:** biff, mail, notify, write, vacation, xbiff

### mailx <--> ~c perkie

ALL  ALL  END

The **~c** tilde command lets you add another user to the distribution list for the message you are composing. When you enter a sequence like that in the example, **mailx** simply advances the cursor to the next line. The process of adding the user takes place behind the scenes, but you can verify it later by looking at the message header. There is also a **~b** tilde command that adds a user to the blind carbon copy list. The **Bcc:** list does not show the added user in the message header.

**Keyword:** email, Internet, user communication

**Files:** $HOME/dead.letter, $HOME/mbox, $HOME/.mailrc

**See Also:** biff, mail, notify, write, vacation, xbiff

### mailx <--> ~d

ALL  ALL  END

The **~d** tilde command reads **dead.letter** into the message that you are composing. This is an excellent way to resend a message that **mailx** determined has an invalid address. The filename for rejected messages is **$HOME/dead.letter** by default. You can change it in the **.mailrc** file like this:

```
set DEAD=$HOME/.dead
```

**Keyword:** email, Internet, user communication

**Files:** $HOME/dead.letter, $HOME/mbox, $HOME/.mailrc

**See Also:** biff, mail, notify, write, vacation, xbiff

### mailx <--> ~e

The **-e** tilde command invokes the editor defined in the **$EDITOR** shell environment variable. In the C shell, you define **$EDITOR** with the **setenv** command:

```
setenv EDITOR emacs
```

In the Bourne and Korn shells, the process is different:

```
EDITOR=emacs; export EDITOR
```

These types of environment variables are usually included in a shell startup file (**.cshrc** for the C shell or **.profile** for the Bourne and Korn shells). Most other **mailx** variables are defined in the **.mailrc** file. You can define **$EDITOR** in either place.

**Keyword:**  email, Internet, user communication

**Files:**  $HOME/dead.letter, $HOME/mbox, $HOME/.mailrc

**See Also:**  biff, EDITOR, mail, notify, write, vacation, xbiff

### mailx <--> ~f 4

This is one of the most invaluable tilde commands. It applies only when you are in the **mailx** program. The **~f** command forwards any previous message in the queue to the user or users specified in the message header of your current message. If you want to use this capability, but forward messages outside of the **mailx** reply (**r** or **R** formats), use the **mail** subcommand from the **?** prompt, being sure to specify the users on the same command line:

```
? mail perkie@mit.edu  natalie@uworld.com
```

Next, enter a title in the subject line, and you are in composition mode. At this point, enter **~f** followed by the number of the message that you want to forward. The tilde command in the example forwards the message numbered **4** in the queue.

**Keyword:**  email, Internet, user communication

**Files:**  $HOME/dead.letter, $HOME/mbox, $HOME/.mailrc

**See Also:**  biff, mail, notify, write, vacation, xbiff

### mailx <--> ~f 8-12 16 19

Here, the ~f command is used to forward multiple messages. The first reference is **8-12**, which is inclusive, meaning 8, 9, 10, 11, and 12. The next two references send messages **16** and **19**, respectively.

**Keyword:**  email, Internet, user communication

**Files:**     $HOME/dead.letter, $HOME/mbox, $HOME/.mailrc
**See Also:**  biff, mail, notify, write, vacation, xbiff

### mailx <--> ~h

ALL   ALL   END

If you forgot to include a user in the distribution list, or simply made a mistake in the subject line, the **~h** option lets you edit both. Entering **~h** causes **mailx** to prompt you for the following:

```
To: donna
Subject: Annual Report
Cc:
Bcc:
```

After you finish answering the prompts—and you don't have to enter text into all of them, as the example shows—**mailx** acknowledges the new information and puts you back into composition mode. Don't worry: The prompts don't become part of your message.

**Keyword:**   email, Internet, user communication
**Files:**     $HOME/dead.letter, $HOME/mbox, $HOME/.mailrc
**See Also:**  biff, mail, notify, write, vacation, xbiff

### mailx <--> ~m 4-7

ALL   ALL   END

The **~m** tilde command inserts text from the specified messages into the current message. This works only if you are using **mailx** interactively. If you have ever received email from someone who has extensively quoted a previous email message of yours, this is probably how they did it (if they used **mailx**). You can define the **indentprefix** variable in **$HOME/.mailrc** to specify a leading character for the indentation.

**Keyword:**   email, Internet, user communication
**Files:**     $HOME/dead.letter, $HOME/mbox, $HOME/.mailrc
**See Also:**  biff, mail, notify, write, vacation, xbiff

### mailx <--> ~q

ALL   ALL   END

You might want to make a habit of using **~q** to leave composition mode when you have to interrupt writing a message. The **~q** command saves the incomplete message to the file specified by the **DEAD** environment variable. By default, this file is **dead.letter**. You can also exit composition mode by executing **~x**, which does not save the current message.

**Keyword:**   email, Internet, user communication

**Files:** $HOME/dead.letter, $HOME/mbox, $HOME/.mailrc
**See Also:** biff, mail, notify, write, vacation, xbiff

### mailx <--> ~r report.text

ALL    ALL    END

The **~r** tilde command lets you include a text file in the body of a **mail** message. The **~r** sequence is probably the most popular way of doing this, but you can also choose to use **~!cat** *filename*, **~<** *filename*, or **~-<!** *cmd*.

**Keyword:** email, Internet, user communication
**Files:** $HOME/dead.letter, $HOME/mbox, $HOME/.mailrc
**See Also:** biff, mail, notify, write, vacation, xbiff

### mailx <--> ~s Annual Report

ALL    ALL    END

If you have ever pressed Return one extra time by mistake when entering the **mailx** composition mode, you know that it skips you over the **Subject** prompt. With the **~s** tilde command, as shown in the example, you get another chance. Just enter **~s** followed by a whitespace, followed by the subject title.

**Keyword:** email, Internet, user communication
**Files:** $HOME/dead.letter, $HOME/mbox, $HOME/.mailrc
**See Also:** biff, mail, notify, write, vacation, xbiff

### mailx <--> ~t perkie@mit.edu

ALL    ALL    END

The **~t** tilde command lets you add a name to the message distribution list. This is handy if you have inadvertently excluded a name. The command like the one in the example can be entered anywhere in composition mode.

**Keyword:** email, Internet, user communication
**Files:** $HOME/dead.letter, $HOME/mbox, $HOME/.mailrc
**See Also:** biff, mail, notify, write, vacation, xbiff

### mailx <--> ~v

ALL    ALL    END

The **~v** tilde command invokes **vi** within composition mode. This is an excellent way to correct mistakes you have made; or, you might prefer to use **vi** for all your mail editing.

**Keyword:** email, Internet, user communication
**Files:** $HOME/dead.letter, $HOME/mbox, $HOME/.mailrc
**See Also:** biff, mail, notify, write, vacation, xbiff

### mailx <--> ~w report.let

ALL    ALL    END

You can use **mailx** and perhaps never feel the need to learn the tilde commands. But the almost essential **~w** lets you save the current message in composition mode—which is a vital feature, especially if you work in the limited editor of **mailx**.

**Keyword:**    email, Internet, user communication

**Files:**    $HOME/dead.letter, $HOME/mbox, $HOME/.mailrc

**See Also:**    biff, mail, notify, write, vacation, xbiff

### mailx <--> ~| sed ´/Unix/UNIX/g´

ALL    ALL    END

Unlike the **~!** tilde command, this command pipes the current message through the UNIX command. In the example, the message is piped into **sed**, which converts all instances of **Unix** to **UNIX**. Combined with **sed**, the **~|** is a good way to correct spelling mistakes on a global basis.

**Keyword:**    email, Internet, user communication

**Files:**    $HOME/dead.letter, $HOME/mbox, $HOME/.mailrc

**See Also:**    biff, mail, notify, sed, write, vacation, xbiff

### mailx perkie@mit.edu < awk.notes

ALL    ALL    END

You can send an existing file to another user without using the **mailx** composition mode by using the input redirection operator, which appears at the end of the **mailx** command. You can also pipe output into **mailx**, if necessary, as in the following command:

```
cat file1 - file2 | mailx perkie@mit.edu
```

**Keyword:**    email, Internet, user communication

**Files:**    $HOME/dead.letter, $HOME/mbox, $HOME/.mailrc

**See Also:**    biff, mail, notify, write, vacation, xbiff

### mailx perkie@mit.edu natalie@newl.com

ALL    ALL    END

As with the original **mail** program, the default sending behavior of **mailx** is to send mail to the user specified on the command line. When you enter **mailx**, followed by one or more users' email addresses, **mailx** displays the following prompt:

```
Subject:
```

You fill in the subject line, press Return, and **mailx** puts you into composition mode. In this mode, you can create as many lines as you want, but you cannot return to a previous line to edit it. This is the same behavior that results if you enter **cat > note.txt** and begin typing. With **mailx**, however, you can specify that you want to invoke an editor after you enter composition mode. For example, typing **~v** on a line of its own, and then pressing Return, invokes the **vi** editor.

**Keyword:**   email, Internet, user communication

**Files:**   $HOME/dead.letter, $HOME/mbox, $HOME/.mailrc

**See Also:**   biff, mail, notify, write, vacation, vi, xbiff

## mailx `grep users /etc/group | sed ´s/^.*://p`

ALL   ALL   END

Although you might not feel like typing this command, it shows that you can use command substitution to specify a list of users to receive your mail. You might alias this command, or you might want to use something like it in a shell script. In the example, **grep** extracts the line for the group named **users** and pipes it to **sed**, which reduces the line to a list of users separated by commas. A comma-delimited list is acceptable input to **mailx**.

**Keyword:**   email, Internet, user communication

**Files:**   $HOME/dead.letter, $HOME/mbox, $HOME/.mailrc

**See Also:**   biff, grep, mail, notify, sed, write, vacation, xbiff

## make

ALL   ALL   POWER

The **make** command looks for the files **makefile**, **Makefile**, **s.makefile**, or **s.Makefile**, in that order, and executes the command in the first file it finds. This command is used for building large programs that have multiple files. It is usually used by programmers for making applications, but any user can put **make** to work on any large set of files.

**Keyword:**   programming, file handling

**Files:**   makefile, Makefile, s.makefile, s.Makefile

**See Also:**   cc, imake, xmkmf

## make -e all

ALL   ALL   POWER

This command makes all the programs that are addressed in the **makefile**, using the settings of your environment variables instead of the settings in the **makefile**.

**Keyword:**   programming, file handling

**Files:**   makefile, Makefile, s.makefile, s.Makefile

**See Also:**   cc, imake, xmkmf

### make -f test-make

| | | |
|---|---|---|
| ALL | ALL | POWER |

This command executes the command located in the **test-make** file. It is used if your source **make** file isn't called **makefile**, **Makefile**, **s.makefile**, or **s.Makefile**.

**Keyword:** programming, text handling

**Files:** makefile, Makefile, s.makefile, s.Makefile

**See Also:** cc, imake, xmkmf

### make -i all

| | | |
|---|---|---|
| ALL | ALL | POWER |

This command makes all the programs that are addressed in the **makefile**, ignoring any errors returned by invoked commands.

**Keyword:** programming, file handling

**Files:** makefile, Makefile, s.makefile, s.Makefile

**See Also:** cc, imake, xmkmf

### make -k all

| | | |
|---|---|---|
| ALL | ALL | POWER |

This command makes all the programs that are addressed in the **makefile**. If an entry fails, continue working only on entries that don't depend on the failed one.

**Keyword:** programming, file handling

**Files:** makefile, Makefile, s.makefile, s.Makefile

**See Also:** cc, imake, xmkmf

### make -n all

| | | |
|---|---|---|
| ALL | ALL | POWER |

This command outputs all the commands in the **makefile**, without executing any of them.

**Keyword:** programming, file handling

**Files:** makefile, Makefile, s.makefile, s.Makefile

**See Also:** cc, imake, xmkmf

### make -n install

| | | |
|---|---|---|
| ALL | ALL | POWER |

This is a useful **make** command. After a program is compiled, you usually have to install it. This command will show you where the program will be installed, rather than actually installing it.

**Keyword:** programming, file handling

**Files:** makefile, Makefile, s.makefile, s.Makefile

**See Also:** cc, imake, xmkmf

## make -p all

| | | |
|---|---|---|
| ALL | ALL | POWER |

This command is used to output the complete set of macro definitions and target descriptions.

**Keyword:** programming, file handling

**Files:** makefile, Makefile, s.makefile, s.Makefile

**See Also:** cc, imake, xmkmf

## make -pf - 2>/dev/null </dev/null

| | | |
|---|---|---|
| ALL | ALL | POWER |

This command is used to output the rules compiled into **make** on any machine in a form suitable for recompilation.

**Keyword:** programming, file handling

**Files:** makefile, Makefile, s.makefile, s.Makefile

**See Also:** cc, imake, xmkmf

## make -q all

| | | |
|---|---|---|
| ALL | ALL | POWER |

This command tells **make** to return a **0** or **1** exit code, depending on whether the target file has been updated.

**Keyword:** programming, file handling

**Files:** makefile, Makefile, s.makefile, s.Makefile

**See Also:** cc, imake, xmkmf

## make -r all

| | | |
|---|---|---|
| ALL | ALL | POWER |

This command makes all the programs that are addressed in the **makefile**; it doesn't use the built-in rules, however.

**Keyword:** programming, file handling

**Files:** makefile, Makefile, s.makefile, s.Makefile

**See Also:** cc, imake, xmkmf

## make -s all

| | | |
|---|---|---|
| ALL | ALL | POWER |

This command makes all the programs that are addressed in the **makefile**, without outputting the command lines before executing them.

**Keyword:** programming, file handling

**Files:** makefile, Makefile, s.makefile, s.Makefile

**See Also:** cc, imake, xmkmf

## make -t all

This command uses the **touch** command to update the target files, without executing the commands in the **makefile**.

**Keyword:** programming, file handling

**Files:** makefile, Makefile, s.makefile, s.Makefile

**See Also:** cc, imake, xmkmf

ALL ALL POWER

## make all

This command is used to **make all** the programs that are addressed in the **makefile**.

**Keyword:** programming, file handling

**Files:** makefile, Makefile, s.makefile, s.Makefile

**See Also:** cc, imake, xmkmf

ALL ALL POWER

## make World

This is the command to use if you want to build the MIT X11R5 windowing system. If you need to do this, be patient; it will take many hours to build.

**Keyword:** programming, file handling

**Files:** makefile, Makefile, s.makefile, s.Makefile

**See Also:** cc, imake, xmkmf

ALL ALL POWER

## makedbm newdata datafile

This command reads in the data in the **newdata** file and creates two NIS databases, **datafile.pag** and **datafile.dir**.

**Keyword:** networking

**See Also:** ypmake, yppush, ypser, ypxfr, ypfiles

ALL ALL SYSADM

## makedbm -l newdata datafile

This command reads in the data in the **newdata** file and creates two NIS database files, **datafile.pag** and **datafile.dir**. The -l argument to **makedbm** causes it to convert the keys of the map in **newdata** to lowercase, so that NIS will work independently of case.

**Keyword:** networking

**See Also:** ypmake, yppush, ypser, ypxfr, ypfiles

ALL ALL SYSADM

### makedbm -s newdata datafile

ALL    ALL    SYSADM

This command reads in the data in the **newdata** file and creates two NIS database files, **datafile.pag** and **datafile.dir**.

**Keyword:**    networking

**See Also:**    ypmake, yppush, ypser, ypxfr, ypfiles

### makedbm -u datafile

ALL    ALL    SYSADM

This command takes the NIS database file **datafile** and outputs every entry, with a space separating keys from values.

**Keyword:**    networking

**See Also:**    ypmake, yppush, ypser, ypxfr, ypfiles

### makedepend all

ALL    ALL    ALL

The **makedepend** utility creates **makefile** dependencies for X11R5 software development. The utility works similar to a C preprocessor, and it verifies and stipulates which **#include** files should be used in the **make** process.

**Keyword:**    programming

**See Also:**    cc, imake, make, xmkmf

### makedev

ALL    ALL    SYSADM

This command is different for every UNIX system in existence. In general, only system administrators should concern themselves with it. We will include some examples for reference.

**Keyword:**    devices, system setup

**See Also:**    df, diskadd, du, fsck, mount, mkfs, mknod, mountall, mountfsys, umount, mkdev, newfs, smit, sysadmin, sysadmsh

### makedev

ALL    SVR4    SYSADM

This command deletes the generic device names in the **/dev/SA**, **/dev/rSA**, **/dev/term**, **/dev/rmt**, and **/dev/printer** directories. It then creates new device names for attached devices; finally, it creates new generic device names.

**Keyword:**    devices, system setup

**See Also:**    df, diskadd, du, fsck, mount, mkfs, mknod, mountall, mountfsys, umount, mkdev, newfs, smit, sysadmin, sysadmsh

## MAKEDEV DS_5000_100

ALL  OSF  SYSADM

This command creates the standard special device files associated with the Digital Equipment Corp. DECstation 5000. The standard devices are: **klog**, **kmem**, **mem**, **null**, **console**, **tty**, **pty0**, **pty1**, **kbinlog**, **ptm**, **cam pm0**, **xcons**, and **scc0**. This command *must* be executed from the **/dev** directory, and you *must* have superuser authority to execute it.

**Keyword:**   devices, system setup

**See Also:**   df, diskadd, du, fsck, mount, mkfs, mknod, mountall, mountfsys, umount, mkdev, newfs, smit, sysadmin, sysadmsh

## MAKEDEV rz1

ALL  OSF  SYSADM

This command creates a device entry for a SCSI disk that is attached to SCSI bus 0; the disk has a SCSI ID of 1. The number after **rz** is computed by multiplying the SCSI bus number by 8 and adding the SCSI ID number. In this case:

```
(0 x 8) + 1 = 1
```

**Keyword:**   devices, system setup

**See Also:**   df, diskadd, du, fsck, mount, mkfs, mknod, mountall, mountfsys, umount, mkdev, newfs, smit, sysadmin, sysadmsh

## makedev std

ALL  SunOS  SYSADM

This command creates all the standard devices for the system.

**Keyword:**   devices, system setup

**See Also:**   df, diskadd, du, fsck, mount, mkfs, mknod, mountall, mountfsys, umount, mkdev, newfs, smit, sysadmin, sysadmsh

## MAKEDEV tz12

ALL  OSF  SYSADM

This command creates a device entry for a SCSI tape drive that is attached to SCSI bus 1 and has a SCSI ID of 4. The number after **tz** is computed by multiplying the SCSI bus number by 8 and adding the SCSI ID number. In this case:

```
(1 x 8) + 4 = 12
```

**Keyword:**   devices, system setup

| | | | |
|---|---|---|---|

**See Also:**  df, diskadd, du, fsck, mount, mkfs, mknod, mountall, mountfsys, umount, mkdev, newfs, smit, sysadmin, sysadmsh

## makefs

ALL  SVR4  SYSADM

This is an interactive command that allows you to create new filesystems. This command can also be accessed as a menu item to **sysadm**.

**Keyword:**  filesystem, system setup

**See Also:**  df, diskadd, du, fsck, mount, mkfs, mknod, mountall, mountfsys, umount, mkdev, newfs, smit, sysadmin, sysadmsh

## makefsys

ALL  SVR4  SYSADM

The **makefsys** utility provides the administrator with a menu-driven interface for creating a filesystem. The utility is the same one that is available through the **make** task in the **sysadm** shell. You can go directly to the filesystem module by entering **sysadm makefsys** on the command line.

**Keyword:**  filesystem, system setup

**See Also:**  checkfsys, mkfsys, sysadm

## makekey

ALL  SVR4  SCO  SunOS  ALL

If you need an encryption key to enter a program (some sites configure **vi** with an encryption key), try **makekey**. The **makekey** command uses the first eight input bytes as the actual key, and the next two bytes as its salt. The System V documentation suggests that you use ASCII characters for the first eight bytes and a period or slash—or a combination of uppercase and lowercase letters—for the salt.

**Keyword:**  security

**See Also:**  crypt, vi

## man

ALL  ALL  ALL

The **man** command is the ultimate power tool. For all levels of users, it offers online descriptions of commands and utilities in the UNIX system and associated software environments, such as the X Window System, C programming language, and networking. The example command displays a brief help message about

**man**, but if you want to know more, you can always **man man**. As you may already have discovered, the syntax to **man** varies slightly in different environments. Here are the first syntax lines from major versions of UNIX:

```
BSD      man [-] [-M path] [section] title ...
SVR4     man [-] [-t] [-M path] [-T macros] [[sect] title ...] title ...
SunOS    man [-] [-t] [-M path] [-T macros] [[sect] title ...] ...
Solaris  man [-] [-K] [-f] [-altdrF] [-T] [-s sect]
SCO      man [-afbcw] [-tproc] [-ppager] [-ddir] [-Tterm] [sect] [title]
OSF      man [-] [-M pathname] [-t] [section] title ...
AIX      man [-f] [-K] [-M] [-s sect]
MKS      man [-K] [-M] [-WX] [sect]
```

Under all environments, the **man** command makes use of the **MANPATH** and **PAGER** environment variables. If these are not set, **man** looks in **/usr/man/man** for **man** page files, and uses the default pager, **more**.

**Keyword:**   help, system information

**Files:**   /usr/share/man/*, /usr/local/man/*, /usr/man/* (SCO), /usr/ucblib/doctools/tmac/man.macs (SVR4), /usr/lib/tmac/tmac.an (SunOS)

**See Also:**   apropos, catman, col, eqn, eqnchar, more, neqn, nroff, pcat, refer, tbl, troff, whatis, whereis

## man -k X

ALL   ALL   END

This command outputs a one-line summary of all the commands that have **X** in the **whatis** database.

**Keyword:**   help, system information

**Files:**   /usr/share/man/*, /usr/local/man/*, /usr/man/* (SCO)

**See Also:**   apropos, catman, more, whatis, whereis

## man -M /usr/gnu/man emacs

ALL   ALL   END

This command looks for the manual page for the **emacs** command in the directory **/usr/gnu/man/man**. This is useful if you have manual pages in directories other than **/usr/man/man**, and the **MANPATH** environment variable is not set.

**Keyword:**   help, system information

**Files:**   /usr/share/man/*, /usr/local/man/*, /usr/man/* (SCO)

**See Also:**   apropos, catman, more, whatis, whereis

### man -t xterm

ALL ALL END

This command displays the manual page for the command **xterm**. The **-t** argument to **man** is for formatting the manual page with the **troff** command, rather than **nroff**.

**Keyword:** help, system information

**Files:** /usr/share/man/*, /usr/local/man/*, /usr/man/* (SCO)

**See Also:** apropos, catman, more, whatis, whereis

### man 8 shutdown

ALL ALL END

This command displays the manual page for the administrative version of the **shutdown** command. On some systems, you need to include the section number, like the **8** in the example. On systems with **man** pages for system programming functions, the manual page for the shutdown function can appear by default.

**Keyword:** help, system information

**Files:** /usr/share/man/*, /usr/local/man/*, /usr/man/* (SCO)

**See Also:** apropos, catman, more, whatis, whereis

### man csh | grep readonly

ALL ALL USER

From time to time, you may want to know whether a **man** page contains a reference to a command or other item, but you don't want to read through the entire document. Just execute a command similar to the one in the example (which, by the way, comes up empty because **readonly** is supported only in the Korn shell).

**Keyword:** help, system information

**Files:** /usr/share/man*, /usr/local/man/*, /usr/man/* (SCO)

**See Also:** apropos, catman, whatis, whereis

### man vi

ALL ALL END

This command displays the manual page for the program **vi**.

**Keyword:** help, system information

**Files:** /usr/share/man/*, /usr/local/man/*, /usr/man/* (SCO)

**See Also:** apropos, catman, more, whatis, whereis

## maze

ALL · XWIN · ALL

The **maze** client program is simply a graphics demo. You can use **maze** to get an idea of how fast a system operates (especially with regard to graphics display speeds). There are no user options to play **maze**; the system automatically solves the maze as part of the demo.

**Keyword:** X graphics

**See Also:** ico, puzzle, xgc

## merge sales.txt sales.old sales.new

ALL · FSF · ALL

The **merge** command is a product of the Free Software Foundation and is included in some versions of UNIX. The example command writes all changes between **sales.old** and **sales.new** into **sales.txt**.

**Keyword:** text handling

**See Also:** diff, diff3

## mesg -n

ALL · ALL · ALL

This command disables the ability of other users to send you real-time messages via the **write** program.

**Keyword:** user communication

**See Also:** talk, write

## mesg -y

ALL · ALL · ALL

This command is the opposite of **mesg -n**. It enables other users to send you real-time messages via the **write** program.

**Keyword:** user communication

**See Also:** talk, write

## mkdev

ALL · SCO · SYSADM

You can use the **mkdev** command on SCO systems to add hardware devices. Many different devices can be added, including a mouse, hard disk, scanner, and anything else requiring that driver software be linked in the kernel. When called without arguments, as in the example, **mkdev** prints a usage message consisting of allowable arguments, which are shorthand names of device drivers known to the system. There are no options to **mkdev**.

**Keyword:** devices, system setup

**Files:** /usr/lib/mkdev/*, /etc/default/scsihas

**See Also:** divvy, fdisk, mkfs, mknod, mount, sysadmsh

**317**

| | | |
|---|---|---|
| ALL | ALL | ALL |

## mkdir -m 700 /home/perkie/book/chap1

This command creates the **chap1** directory as a subdirectory of **/home/perkie/book**, if **/home/perkie/book** exists. The permission setting of the new directory is **700**, rather than the default of **755**.

**Keyword:** directories

**See Also:** cd, chdir, rm, rmdir

| | | |
|---|---|---|
| ALL | ALL | END POWER |

## mkdir -m+rwx /home/perkie/bin

This command creates the **bin** directory as a subdirectory of **/home/perkie**, if **/home/perkie** exists. The permission setting of the new directory is **777**, rather than the default of **755**.

**Keyword:** directories

**See Also:** cd, chdir, rm, rmdir, umask

| | | |
|---|---|---|
| ALL | ALL | ALL |

## mkdir -p /home/perkie/book/chap1

This command creates a directory that is a subdirectory of another directory. In this case, though, **/home/perkie/book** doesn't have to exist before you execute the command. The entire directory structure is created because of the **-p** argument to **mkdir**.

**Keyword:** directories

**See Also:** cd, chdir, chmod, rm, rmdir, umask

| | | |
|---|---|---|
| ALL | ALL | ALL |

## mkdir /home/perkie/book

This command creates the **book** directory as a subdirectory of **/home/perkie**, if **/home/perkie** exists.

**Keyword:** directories

**See Also:** cd, chdir, chmod, rm, rmdir, umask

| | | |
|---|---|---|
| ALL | ALL | ALL |

## mkdir book

This command creates a subdirectory in the working directory called **book**. The default permissions settings for the new directory are set by the **umask** command.

**Keyword:** directories

**See Also:** cd, chdir, chmod, rm, rmdir, umask

| | | |
|---|---|---|
| ALL | ALL | ALL |

## mkdirhier /usr/u/perkie/programs/kermit

This command creates the directory **kermit** and all parent directories if they do not exist. In essence, **mkdirehier** lets you create an entire structure with a single command. The command is part of the X Window System distribution.

**Keyword:**     filesystem

**See Also:**     mkdir, rm, rmdir

### mkfontdir /home/localfonts

This example tells the X server to recognize **/home/localfonts** as a valid font directory. You must follow this command with the **xset fp rehash** command.

**Keyword:**     X resources

**See Also:**     xset

### mkfs -f DOS /dev/rfd0a

This command creates an MS-DOS filesystem on a formatted diskette.

**Keyword:**     system setup

**See Also:**     df, diskadd, du, fsck, mount, mkfs, mknod, mountall, mountfsys, umount, mkdev, newfs, smit, sysadmin, sysadmsh

### mkfs -F ufs /dev/c0t6d0sa

This command creates a **ufs** filesystem on the device specified as **/dev/c0t6d0sa**.

**Keyword:**     system setup

**See Also:**     df, diskadd, du, fsck, mount, mkfs, mknod, mountall, mountfsys, umount, mkdev, newfs, smit, sysadmin, sysadmsh

### mkfs -F ufs -V /dev/c0t6d0sa

This is used to check your command, without actually executing it.

**Keyword:**     system setup

**See Also:**     df, diskadd, du, fsck, mount, mkfs, mknod, mountall, mountfsys, umount, mkdev, newfs, smit, sysadmin, sysadmsh

### mkfs -f XENIX /dev/rhd1a

This command creates a XENIX filesystem on the disk partition specified **/dev/rhd1a**.

**Keyword:**     system setup

ALL · XWIN · ALL

ALL · SCO · SYSADM

ALL · SVR4 · SYSADM

ALL · SVR4 · SYSADM

ALL · SCO · SYSADM

**See Also:** df, diskadd, du, fsck, mount, mkfs, mknod, mountall, mountfsys, umount, mkdev, newfs, smit, sysadmin, sysadmsh

### mkfs -m /usr

ALL  SVR4  SYSADM

This command shows the command that was used to create the **/usr** filesystem.

**Keyword:** system setup

**See Also:** df, diskadd, du, fsck, mount, mkfs, mknod, mountall, mountfsys, umount, mkdev, newfs, smit, sysadmin, sysadmsh

### mknod /demo/perkie/example b 7 9

ALL  ALL  SYSADM

This command creates a block-oriented device file. This file could be associated with devices such as hard disk drives and tape drives. The **7** is called the major device number, and the **9** is the minor device number. These numbers represent different hardware elements on different machines.

**Keyword:** system setup

**See Also:** mkdev

### mknod /demo/perkie/example c 7 9

ALL  ALL  SYSADM

This command creates a special character file called **example** with a major device number of **7** and a minor device number of **9**.

**Keyword:** system setup

**See Also:** mkdev

### mknod /dev/null c 4 2

ALL  SCO  SYSADM

This command creates the **/dev/null** file used for routing I/O if you want it to "disappear." This command works only for SCO UNIX; other systems would use the **MAKEDEV** or **mkdev** commands.

**Keyword:** system setup

**See Also:** mkdev

### mknod anyname p &

ALL  ALL  POWER

This command creates a named pipe for further use. Options to **mknod** appear after the initial filename, which you supply. The **p** option creates a named pipe, which acts as in-memory FIFO that you can use to quicken data-intensive scripts and programs. Other options to **mknod** allow you to create special files associated with devices such as hard disks.

**Keyword:**   system setup

**See Also:**   mkdev

## more

ALL   ALL   ALL

The **more** command has penetrated UNIX terminals and desktops almost as thoroughly as **ls** and **cat**. It has competition from other system pagers, such as **pg** and **less**, but it is still widely used. Entering **more** without options displays a usage statement, as in any of the following:

```
BSD       more [-dfln] [+line | +/pat] [file...]
SVR4      more [-dflsucrw] [-n] [+line | +/pat] [file...]
SunOS     more [-dfln] [+line | +/pat] [file...]
Solaris SCO    more [-dflsucrwv] [-n] [+line | +/pat] [file...]
OSF1      more [-cdflpsuvwz] [-num] [+line | +[g|G] | +/pat] [file...]
AIX MKS      more [-acefnst] [-n] [-p prompt] [+/pat] [file...]
```

**Keyword:**   text display

**See Also:**   cat, EDITOR, less, page, pg, view

## more +/California states.txt

ALL   ALL   END

This command begins paging through a file at the first occurrence of the specified string. In the example, **more** begins displaying text when it finds the word **California**.

**Keywortd:**   text display

**See Also:**   cat, less, page, view

## more +/^California states.txt

ALL   ALL   END

This command adds the use of regular expressions. In the example, **more** reads through the file and begins displaying text only when it finds **California** at the beginning of a line.

**Keyword:**   text display

**See Also:**   cat, less, page, view

## more +500 report.txt

ALL   ALL   END

With **more**, you don't have to page through a file to get where you are going. If you know the line number, you can go right to the line. In the example, line **500** is the first line displayed.

**Keyword:**   text display
**See Also:**   cat, less ,page, view

### more +g report.txt

ALL   OSF   END

If you have ever wanted to start viewing a file at its end, you'll probably wish you had known about the **+g** option. With **+g**, **more** displays the last screenful of text. You can then page backward through the file using the **b** subcommand or Ctrl-B. You can page forward again using the **s** subcommand or Ctrl-F, which moves in half-screen increments.

**Keyword:**   text display
**See Also:**   cat, less, page, view

### more -c book.txt

ALL   ALL   END

The **-c** option tells **more** to clear the screen before displaying each page of text. This causes **more** to write from the top down, rather than the bottom up, and can result in faster screen redraws.

**Keyword:**   text display
**See Also:**   cat, less, pg, view

### more -d report.txt

ALL   ALL   END

The **-d** option makes **more** a little friendlier. Instead of the usual prompt, you get a reminder to press Space to continue, **q** to quit, and **h** to display a help screen. Here is a typical prompt:

```
--More-- (41%) [Press space to continue, q to quit, h for help]
```

**Keyword:**   text display
**See Also:**   cat, less, page, view

### more -f report.txt

ALL   ALL   END

The **-f** option to **more** displays a file without wrapping lines that don't fit on the terminal; it just cuts them off. In the example, **report.txt** gets this treatment.

**Keyword:**   text display
**See Also:**   cat, less, page, view

### more -l report.txt

ALL   ALL   END

Normally, if **more** encounters a **^L** (end of page), it pauses. The **-l** option causes **more** to ignore a **^L** in a file.

**Keyword:**   text display
**See Also:**   cat, less, page, view

### more -w report.txt

The **-w** option prevents **more** from exiting the file after it reaches the last screen. With this feature in effect, you can use **more** to search forward through a file and then return to the point where you began the search (using the ' subcommand). You can also move forward and backward in a file using the **s** and **b** subcommands, respectively.

**Keyword:**   text display
**See Also:**   cat, less, page, view

### more sales[1-5].txt

The **more** command handles one or more files at a time. In the example, **more** pages through all files (up to five possible) and displays the contents of each file on a screen-by-screen basis. Between files, **more** prompts you to continue or quit.

**Keyword:**   text display
**See Also:**   cat, less, page, view

### mount

The **mount** command, as it appears in the example, displays all filesystems known to the operating system. The **mount** command is a lot more powerful than this: It lets you add filesystems, including diskettes, hard disks, and CD-ROM drives. In order to use **mount**, you require a **mount** point, which is a directory that you typically create in the system's root directory. To track filesystems, **mount** maintains a table in **/etc/mtab** (BSD) or **/etc/mnttab** (SVR4). Additional filesystem information is stored in **/etc/fstab** (BSD) or **/etc/vfstab** (SVR4). Note that some systems, including SVR4 systems, may support multiple versions of **mount**.

**Keyword:**   devices, filesystem, NFS, networking
**Files:**      /etc/mnttab (SVR4, SCO), /etc/vfstab (SVR4),
               /etc/dfs/fstypes (SVR4), /etc/mtab (BSD),
               /etc/fstab (BSD), /etc/fscmd.d/* (SCO),
               /etc/default/filesys (SCO)
**See Also:**   df, du, fsck, mountall, mountfsys, netstat, umount

ALL   ALL   END

ALL   ALL   END

ALL   ALL   POWER
            SYSADM

### mount -F nfs -o hard sparky:/home3 /u3

ALL  SVR4  SYSADM

This command attaches the **NFS** filesystem **/home3** on the computer **sparky** to the local computer system. If the connection is broken between the local computer and the remote system, the local computer continues to try to connect to the remote system until it is successful, because of the **hard** option to **mount**.

**Keyword:**   filesystem

**See Also:**   df, du, umount

### mount -F nfs -r sparky:/home3 /u3

ALL  SVR4  SYSADM

This command is the same as above, in that it attaches the **NFS** filesystem **/home3** on the computer **sparky** to the local computer system. The remote filesystem is read-only; however, no one on the local system can write or change anything on that filesystem, because of the **-r** option to **mount**.

**Keyword:**   filesystem

**See Also:**   df, du, umount

### mount -F nfs sparky:/home3 /u3

ALL  SVR4  SYSADM

This command attaches the NFS filesystem **/home3** on the computer **sparky** to the local computer system. The attached filesystem is called **/u3** on the local system.

**Keyword:**   filesystem

**See Also:**   df, du, umount

### mount -F nfs sun1000:/u1 /export/u1

ALL  SVR4  SYSADM

This command loads the NFS-exported **/u1** filesystem from the computer **sun1000** onto the local **/export/u1** directory.

**Keyword:**   filesystem, NFS, networking

**Files:**   /etc/mnttab, /etc/vfstab

**See Also:**   df, du, mountall, mountfsys, netstat, umount

### mount -f NFS  sun1000:/u1 /export/u1

ALL  SCO  SYSADM

This command loads the NFS-exported **/u1** filesystem from the computer **sun1000** onto the local **/export/u1** directory.

**Keyword:**   filesystem, NFS, networking

**Files:**   /etc/mnttab, /etc/fscmd.d/*

**See Also:**   df, du, netstat, umount

### mount -l

This command outputs all the mounted filesystems that are on the local system. It also lists the **mount** options used and the permissions of the filesystems.

**Keyword:**    filesystem

**Files:**        /etc/fstab, /etc/mtab

**See Also:**    df, du, umount

### mount -o hard sparky:/home2 /home2

This command loads the NFS-exported **/home2** filesystem from the computer **sparky** onto the local **/home2** directory. The mount type is hard, so the local computer will constantly keep in contact with **sparky**. If the connection should break, the local computer will continue to retry contacting **sparky** until it succeeds.

**Keyword:**    filesystem, NFS, networking

**Files:**        /etc/fstab

**See Also:**    df, du, netstat, umount

### mount -p

This command outputs a list of all the attached filesystems. The output of this command is in the same format as the **/etc/fstab** file. You can use this information to set the computer to automatically **mount** the filesystems by entering the information into the **/etc/fstab** file.

**Keyword:**    filesystem

**Files:**        /etc/fstab, /etc/mtab

**See Also:**    df, du, umount

### mount -p > /etc/fstab

This command outputs all the mounted filesystems that are on the local system. It has the same format as the **/etc/fstab** file, so you can redirect output directly to **/etc/fstab**, as in the example. Just make sure you have a backup of **/etc/fstab** first.

**Keyword:**    filesystem, NFS, networking

**Files:**        /etc/fstab, /etc/mtab

**See Also:**    df, du, netstat, umount

| | | |
|---|---|---|
| ALL | OSF | SYSADM |

## mount -t cdfs -o noversion /dev/rz4c /cdrom

This command is used to load an ISO 9660-formatted CD-ROM onto the **/cdrom** directory, if the CD-ROM drive is specified by the **/dev/rz4** device file.

**Keyword:** filesystem

**Files:** /etc/fstab

**See Also:** df, du, umount

| | | |
|---|---|---|
| ALL | SunOS | SYSADM |

## mount -t hsfs -r /dev/rct0 /cdrom

This command loads an ISO 9660-formatted CD-ROM onto the directory **/cdrom**. Once this command has been executed, it is possible to read the information on the CD-ROM disk.

**Keyword:** filesystem

**See Also:** df, du, umount

| | | |
|---|---|---|
| ALL | SunOS | SYSADM |

## mount -t hsfs /dev/sr0 /dev/cdrom

This command loads an ISO 9660 CD-ROM onto the **/dev/cdrom** directory.

**Keyword:** filesystem

**Files:** /etc/fstab

**See Also:** cd, df, eject, umount

| | | |
|---|---|---|
| ALL | BSD | SYSADM |

## mount -t nfs -r sun1000:/u1 /export/u1

This command loads the NFS-exported **/u1** filesystem from the computer **sun1000** onto the local **/export/u1** directory, with read-only rights.

**Keyword:** filesystem, NFS, networking

**Files:** /etc/fstab, /etc/mtab

**See Also:** df, du, netstat, umount

| | | |
|---|---|---|
| ALL | SunOS | SYSADM |

## mount -t nfs aixpilot:/u1 /export/u1

This version of **mount** loads the NFS exported filesystem **/u1** from the system **aixpilot** to the local directory **/export/u1**.

**Keyword:** filesystem

**Files:** /etc/fstab

**See Also:** df, du, umount

## mount /dev/rz1c /u1

ALL  ALL  SYSADM

This command mounts the **/dev/rz1c** filesystem, which usually corresponds to a partition on a disk, to the **/u1** directory.

**Keyword:**  filesystem

**Files:**  /etc/vfstab (SVR4), /etc/fstab (BSD)

**See Also:**  df, mountall, mountfsys, umount

## mount /dev/rz4c /cdrom

ALL  ALL  SYSADM

This command loads a UFS-formatted CD-ROM onto the **/cdrom** directory, if the CD-ROM drive is specified by the **/dev/rz4** device file.

**Keyword:**  devices, filesystem

**Files:**  /etc/vfstab (SVR4), /etc/fstab (BSD)

**See Also:**  df, du, mountall, mountfsys, umount

## mount sparky:/home2 /home2

ALL  BSD  SYSADM

This command loads the NFS-exported **/home2** filesystem from the remote system **sparky** onto the local **/home2** directory.

**Keyword:**  filesystem, NFS, networking

**Files:**  /etc/fstab

**See Also:**  df, du, netstat, umount

## mount | cut -d´ ´ -f1

ALL  ALL  POWER SYSADM

This command parses the output from the **mount** command and displays the device names associated with mounted filesystems.

**Keyword:**  filesystem

**Files:**  /etc/vfstab (SVR4), /etc/fstab (BSD)

**See Also:**  cut, df, mountall, mountfsys, umount

## mountall

ALL  SVR4  SYSADM

If you maintain filesystem mounts in **/etc/vfstab** on SVR4 systems, you can mount them automatically with **mountall**. To use this command, include the **automnt** key value in **/etc/vfstab** for each filesystem that you want to mount.

**Keyword:**  filesystem

**Files:**  /etc/vfstab

**See Also:**  df, du, mount, unmount, umountall

## mountfsys

ALL  SVR4  SYSADM

The **mountfsys** utility provides a menu-driven interface for mounting a filesystem. The utility is also available through **sysadm**. You can go directly to the **mountfsys** module by entering **sysadm mountfsys** on the command line.

**Keyword:**   filesystem

**See Also:**   mount, umountall

## mt -f /dev/rmt0a bsf 20

ALL  BSD  SYSADM

This command moves the tape specified by **/dev/rmt0a** backward by **20** end-of-file marks.

**Keyword:**   backup and restore, devices

**Files:**   /dev/rmt/*

**See Also:**   dd, dump, restore, tar

## mt -f /dev/rmt0a bsr 7

ALL  BSD  SYSADM

This command moves the tape specified by **/dev/rmt0a** backward by **7** records.

**Keyword:**   backup and restore, devices

**Files:**   /dev/rmt/*

**See Also:**   dd, dump, restore, tar

## mt -f /dev/rmt0a eof 15

ALL  BSD  SYSADM

The **mt** command is used to control tape drives on the system. The example writes **15** end-of-file marks at the current position on the tapes specified by **/dev/rmt0a**.

**Keyword:**   backup and restore, devices

**Files:**   /dev/rmt/*

**See Also:**   dd, dump, restore, tar

## mt -f /dev/rmt0a fsf 20

ALL  BSD  SYSADM

This command moves the tape specified by **/dev/rmt0a** forward by **20** end-of-file marks.

**Keyword:**   backup and restore, devices

**Files:**   /dev/rmt/*

**See Also:**   dd, dump, restore, tar

### mt -f /dev/rmt0a fsr 7

**ALL**  **BSD**  **SYSADM**

This command moves the tape specified by **/dev/rmt0a** forward by **7** records.

**Keyword:** backup and restore, devices

**Files:** /dev/rmt/*

**See Also:** dd, dump, restore, tar

### mt -f /dev/rmt0a retension

**ALL**  **BSD**  **SYSADM**

This command completely rewinds the tape specified by **/dev/rmt0a**, then it fast-forwards the tape to the other end, then it rewinds it again.

**Keyword:** backup and restore, devices

**Files:** /dev/rmt/*

**See Also:** dd, dump, restore, tar

### mt -f /dev/rmt0a rewind

**ALL**  **BSD**  **SYSADM**

This command completely rewinds the tape specified by **/dev/rmt0a**.

**Keyword:** backup and restore, devices

**Files:** /dev/rmt/*

**See Also:** dd, dump, restore, tar

### mt -f /dev/rmt0a status

**ALL**  **BSD**  **SYSADM**

This command outputs the status of the tape specified by **/dev/rmt0a**.

**Keyword:** backup and restore, devices

**Files:** /dev/rmt/*

**See Also:** dd, dump, restore, tar

### mv

**ALL**  **ALL**  **ALL**

Entering **mv** at the command line simply displays a usage message, but it is one you might like to check because **mv** can be used in three different ways:

• To change the name of a directory.

• To change the name of a file.

• To move a file or directory to a different directory.

In general, you cannot use **mv** to move directories across remote mounted (NFS) filesystems.

**Keyword:**   file handling, directories

**See Also:**   chmod, cp, cpio, ln, rm, rmdir, tar, umask

### mv -f * /home/perkie/new

ALL   ALL   ALL

This command moves all the nonhidden files in the current directory to the **/home/perkie/new** directory. The **-f** tells **mv** to overwrite any existing files without asking for confirmation.

**Keyword:**   file handling

**See Also:**   cp, rm

### mv -i * /home/perkie/new

ALL   ALL   ALL

This command moves all the nonhidden files in the current directory to the **/home/perkie/new** directory. The **-i** option causes **mv** to ask for confirmation on each file before moving it.

**Keyword:**   file handling

**See Also:**   cp, rm

### mv /usr/home /usr/H:

ALL   ALL   SYSADM

Assuming you implement the **H:** alias, you might want to rename the directory hierarchy that you mount to PCs running DOS. A common name for this hierarchy is **/usr/home**, so we are changing the name to **/usr/H:**. Instead of this approach, you might want to link **H:** to **/usr/home**.

**Keyword:**   file handling

**See Also:**   chmod, cp, ln, rm, umask

### mv report.txt report.jun

ALL   ALL   END

Perhaps the most common use of **mv**, this command renames **report.txt** to **report.jun**. As you can see, **mv** can serve you in archiving old material. And if you have ever used **mv**, you know it is invaluable when you accidentally give a wrong name to a file.

**Keyword:**   file handling

**See Also:**   cp, ln, rm

### mvdir /home/sales/jan /home/93/q1

ALL   SVR4   POWER
      SCO    SYSADM

This command moves the **/home/sales/jan** directory to the **/home/93/q1** directory. You can use it instead of the **mv** command to move directories. This might be helpful in situations where you have aliased **mv** for other reasons.

**Keyword:**    file handling

**See Also:**    cp, rm

## Mwm

This is the resource filename for the **mwm** window manager. The **Mwm** resource file can be located in any of several resource locations. The order of precedence of these locations is **$XENVIRONMENT**, **$HOME/.Xdefaults-*hostname***, **$XAPPLRESDIR**, **$HOME/*app-file***, **$HOME/.Xdefaults**, **/usr/lib/X11/app-defaults/Xdefaults**, and **/usr/lib/X11/app-defaults/app-name**. Note that **.Xdefaults** is a customary name, not mandatory.

**Keyword:**    X resources, window managers

**See Also:**    mwm, xdm, xrdb

## mwm

This is the name of the executable file associated with the Motif window manager. Almost without exception, it is invoked in an X Window System startup file such as **.xinitrc** or **.xsession**. Usually, **mwm** is not run in the background, but if you want to configure your system so that exiting Motif also causes you to exit X, you should run **mwm** in the background.

**Keyword:**    window managers, window handling, user environment

**Files:**    $HOME/.motifbind, $HOME/.mwmrc, $HOME/.Xdefaults

**See Also:**    Mwm, xdm, xrdb

## mwm -display megasun:0

Usually, a particular display (a monitor associated with a hostname) that Motif uses is determined by the **$DISPLAY** variable contained in an X startup file. If, however, you need or want to set the display when you invoke Motif, you can use a command similar to this example.

**Keyword:**    window managers, window handling, user environment

**Files:**    $HOME/.motifbind, $HOME/.mwmrc, $HOME/.Xdefaults

**See Also:**    Mwm, xdm, xrdb

ALL    XWIN    ALL

ALL    XWIN    ALL

ALL    XWIN    ALL

ALL · XWIN · ALL

## mwm -xrm ´clientDecorations all´ -xrm ´clientFunctions all´

If you want to set multiple resources using the **-xrm** option with **mwm**, you must specifiy **-xrm** multiple times. In the example, the resources that control the display of window manager components—such as title bar, minimize box, and window menu—are set through the **clientDecorations** resource. The **all** value tells Motif that all components should be used; because it is being set with the **-xrm** option, you cannot override it from other resource files. This is a handy tactic for system adminstrators and customizers who must contend with other users. The same logic applies for the **clientFunctions** resource in the example.

**Keyword:**   window managers, window handling, user environment

**Files:**   $HOME/.motifbind, $HOME/.mwmrc, $HOME/.Xdefaults

**See Also:**   Mwm, xdm, xrdb

ALL · XWIN · ALL

## mwm -xrm ´mwm*keyboardFocusPolicy: explicit

The **-xrm** option used in this example allows you to set resources when you invoke Motif. The **-xrm** option, which is supported by most X client programs, overrides the same resources set elsewhere, such as in **$XAPPLRESDIR/Mwm** or **$HOME/.Xdefaults**.

**Keyword:**   window managers, window handling, user environment

**Files:**   $HOME/.motifbind, $HOME/.mwmrc, $HOME/.Xdefaults

**See Also:**   Mwm, xdm, xrdb

ALL · SVR4 · ALL

## nawk

This is an enhanced version of **awk**. The **nawk** command has more built-in functions than **awk**, but the syntax of the command is unchanged. Both **nawk** and **awk** are used to search, manipulate, and then output text in a predefined manner.

**Keyword:**   text handling

**See Also:**   awk, gawk, grep, sed

ALL · ALL · END

## nawk ´length < 8´ book.txt

This use of **nawk** displays every line in the **book.txt** file that has fewer than eight characters in it. For additional examples that you can use with **awk**, refer to the **awk** entries.

**Keyword:** text handling
**See Also:** awk, grep, gawk, sed

## nawk ´{print $1," --> " $2}´ /etc/fstab

The **nawk** utility is an enhanced version of **awk**. The example command outputs a graphical representation of which devices get mounted where at boot time. The **print** command in **nawk** first outputs the first record, the device file; next it draws the arrow, then it outputs the second record, the directory. The **nawk** utility is based on the Awk language.

**Keyword:** text handling
**See Also:** awk, df, gawk, sed

## ncheck

The **ncheck** command displays inode and path information on filesystems. Entering **ncheck** without options displays a usage statement on BSD systems; on SVR4 and SCO systems, it executes on **/dev/root**. The following output sample is from an SVR4 Intel-based system:

```
/dev/root:
3        /lost+found/.
768      /etc/.
1536     /stand/.
4        /unix
2304     /dev/.
13824    /usr/.
19968    /sbin/.
20736    /var/.
14684    /tmp/.
14       /.rhosts
```

**Keyword:** filesystem
**Files:** /etc/vfstab (SVR4, SCO), /etc/fstab (BSD)
**See Also:** df, du, fsck, mount

## ncheck -a /dev/rz2c

This command shows names associated with inodes on the filesystem specified by **/dev/rz2c**. The **fsck** command is similar, and recommended over the **ncheck** command.

**Keyword:** filesystem
**Files:** /etc/vfstab (SVR4, SCO), /etc/fstab (BSD)
**See Also:** df, du, fsck, mount

ALL ALL SYSADM

**333**

## ncheck /dev/rz3c | sort +0n | quot -n /dev/rz3c

ALL ALL SYSADM

This command outputs a list of all files and their owners.

**Keyword:** filesystem

**Files:** /etc/vfstab (SVR4, SCO), /etc/fstab (BSD)

**See Also:** df, du, fsck, mount

## neqn formulas | nroff

ALL ALL END

Unless you are a mathematician who uses **nroff**, there is little reason to add **neqn** to your UNIX vocabulary. In brief, **neqn** recognizes a special set of keywords that format mathematical expressions for **nroff** processing. The **eqn** command, you may have noted, does the same thing for **troff**.

**Keyword:** math, text handling

**See Also:** eqn, nroff, tbl

## netconfig

ALL SCO SYSADM

The **netconfig** program is used to set up networking on SCO systems. The application has the following menus: Add a Chain, Remove a Chain, Reconfigure an Element, and Quit. To set up the network, you have to add chains. Chains are built from the top down, so the last item configured is the physical hardware on the system. The **netconfig** program can be used both from the command line and interactively. When it is used from the command line, major options include **-r**, which removes a chain; **-l**, which tells **netconfig** to relink the kernel; and **-a**, which adds a chain to the network setup.

**Keyword:** system setup, system information

**Files:** /etc/hosts, /etc/networks

**See Also:** sysadmsh

## netstat

ALL ALL SYSADM

The **netstat** command displays information about your TCP/IP network. Two items of interest are the Recv-Q and Send-Q fields, which show the activity of the network.

**Keyword:** networking, Internet

**See Also:** finger, nlsadmin, ping, ruptime, rwho

### netstat -a

ALL  ALL  SYSADM

The **-a** option to **netstat** shows the status of all network sockets. The output shows the protocol of each socket, the received and sent packets, the local address, the remote address, and the state of the connection.

**Keyword:**  networking, Internet

**See Also:**  finger, nlsadmin, ping, ruptime, rwho

### netstat -i

ALL  ALL  SYSADM

The **-i** option to **netstat** shows all configured network interfaces. Here is a sample display from an SCO system:

```
Name  Mtu   Network   Address     Ipkts    Ierrs  Opkts   Oerrs  Collis
wdn0  1500  newline   newl        384640   0      164735  0      147
lo0   2048  loopback  localhost   4690     0      4690    0      0
```

**Keyword:**  networking, Internet

**See Also:**  finger, nlsadmin, ping, ruptime, rwho

### netstat -i | grep `hostname` | awk ´{print $1 " has had %"100*($9/$5)" collisions."}´

ALL  ALL  SYSADM

This command shows the percentage of network packet collisions your system has had.

**Keyword:**  networking, Internet

**See Also:**  finger, nlsadmin, ping, ruptime, rwho

### netstat -m

ALL  ALL  SYSADM

The **-m** option to **netstat** outputs information on how much memory the network services are using. Specific information includes the number of buffers allocated, the number of requests for memory, and the number of memory requests denied.

**Keyword:**  networking, Internet

**See Also:**  finger, nlsadmin, ping, ruptime, rwho

### netstat -r

ALL  ALL  SYSADM

This command outputs the routing tables for the local machine.

**Keyword:**  networking, Internet

**See Also:**  finger, nlsadmin, ping, ruptime, rwho

### netstat -s

ALL   ALL   SYSADM

This command shows statistics for each network protocol.

**Keyword:**   networking, Internet

**See Also:**   finger, nlsadmin, ping, ruptime, rwho

### netstat -u

ALL   OSF   SYSADM

The **-u** option on OSF systems tells **netstat** to display information about network domain sockets.

**Keyword:**   networking, Internet

**See Also:**   finger, nlsadmin, ping, ruptime, rwho

### newform -i80 -l80 -e sales.jun >> report.txt

ALL   BSD   SYSADM

The **newform** command changes the formatting of text files. The example reads in the **sales.jun** file and converts all Tab characters to eight spaces, thanks to the **-i8** option. The **-l80** option tells **newform** that the output should be 80 characters. The **-e** option specifies that any characters after the first 80 should be cut.

**Keyword:**   text handling

**See Also:**   awk, cut, csplit, pr, sed

### newfs -N /dev/fd0a

ALL   BSD   SYSADM

This command shows the filesystem parameters, without actually creating the new filesystem on the diskette.

**Keyword:**   filesystem

**See Also:**   df, fsck, makefs, mount, umount

### newfs -n /dev/fd0a

ALL   BSD   SYSADM

This command creates a new filesystem on a formatted diskette, without installing the bootstrap programs.

**Keyword:**   filesystem

**See Also:**   df, fsck, makefs, mount, umount

### newfs -o space /dev/fd0a

ALL   BSD   SYSADM

This command creates a new filesystem on a formatted diskette, and tries to minimize the space fragmentation on the disk.

**Keyword:**   filesystem

**See Also:**   df, fsck, makefs, mount, umount

| | | |
|---|---|---|

### newfs /dev/sd0c

| ALL | BSD | SYSADM |
|---|---|---|

The **newfs** command creates a new filesystem on the device specified by **/dev/sd0c**. After this command has been run, you can mount the filesystem.

**Keyword:**    filesystem

**See Also:**    df, fsck, makefs, mount, umount

### newgrp

| ALL | ALL | POWER SYSADM |
|---|---|---|

This command, with no arguments, causes you to revert to the group ID number listed in the **/etc/passwd** file.

**Keyword:**    file permissions

**See Also:**    chgrp, chmod, chown, passwd

### newgrp wheel

| ALL | ALL | POWER SYSADM |
|---|---|---|

This command logs you into the group called **wheel**. In essence, it changes your real and effective group ID number.

**Keyword:**    file permissions

**See Also:**    chgrp, chmod, chown, passwd

### newkey -h sparky

| ALL | SVR4 | SYSADM |
|---|---|---|

This command is used to build a new public/secret key pair for the computer system **sparky**. When run, this command asks for a password for **sparky**, then the key is created.

**Keyword:**    security

**Files:**    /etc/publickey

**See Also:**    chkey, crypt, passwd

### news

| ALL | SVR4 SCO OSF AIX Solaris | END |
|---|---|---|

The **news** command displays news items stored in the system news directory, which is **/usr/news** on OSF and SCO systems, and **/var/news** on SVR4 systems. To create news items, users copy files into the news directory. When you enter **news**, as in the example, all news messages are displayed (so you should use **more**, as in the next example). To keep track of what you have read, **news** maintains a file in your home directory called **.news_time**. This is a zero-byte file—**news** simply gets the time that you have last read news from the data and date and time stamp on the file.

**Keyword:**    user communication

**Files:**        $HOME/.news_time

**See Also:**    mail, mailx, talk, write

## news -a | grep "lightbulb"

If you don't feel like reading all the news, but like to keep abreast of a favorite subject, pipe **news** into **grep**. In the example, the user might have been looking for **lightbulb** jokes.

**Keyword:**     user communication

**Files:**        $HOME/.news_time

**See Also:**    mail, mailx, talk, write

ALL    SVR4    END
       SCO
       OSF
       AIX
       Solaris

## news -a | more

When you want to read **news** items, it is a good idea to pipe them into **more** or another pager utility. (Otherwise, they scroll off the screen.) Note that the **-a** option in the example tells **news** not to update **$HOME/.news_time**.

**Keyword:**     user communication

**Files:**        $HOME/.news_time

**See Also:**    less, mail, mailx, more, pg, talk, write

ALL    SVR4    END
       SCO
       OSF
       AIX
       Solaris

## news -n

Most of the time you don't want to read the news, but you do like to stay tuned to posted items. The example command takes care of this by displaying the filenames of new postings. Meaningful titles can be created by using long filenames:

```
news: Computer_Bytes_Man
news: News_From_Emily
news: news.ajs
```

**Keyword:**     user communication

**Files:**        $HOME/.news_time

**See Also:**    mail, mailx, talk, write

ALL    SVR4    END
       SCO
       OSF
       AIX
       Solaris

## news -s

This use of the **news** command simply displays the number of items in the news queue.

**Keyword:**     user communication

**Files:**        $HOME/.news_time

**See Also:**    mail, mailx, talk, write

ALL    SVR4    END
       SCO
       OSF
       AIX
       Solaris

| ALL | SVR4<br>SCO<br>OSF<br>AIX<br>Solaris | END |
|-----|------|-----|

## news -s | cut -d´ ´ -f1

The **-s** option to **news** displays the number of items in the queue. There is also a two-word label with the number. The **cut** command in the example eliminates the label. You might want to use this command in **$HOME/.profile** and then test the value with an **if** statement.

**Keyword:** user communication

**Files:** $HOME/.news_time

**See Also:** mail, mailx, talk, write

## news News_From_Emily news.ajs | pg

You can read **news** selectively by specifying one or more items as direct arguments to **news**. Again, the use of a paging utility is desirable.

**Keyword:** user communication

**Files:** $HOME/.news_time

**See Also:** mail, mailx, talk, write

## newvt

The **newvt** command opens a virtual terminal on your system. The virtual terminal inherits the environment of the existing terminal session. Using **newvt**, you can conduct multiple interactive sessions with only one terminal window.

**Keyword:** terminals

**See Also:** jterm, jwin, sh, window, xterm

## nfsstat

For network administrators, the **nfsstat** command displays information about the Network File System (NFS) and Remote Procedure Call (RPC) interface. The **nfsstat** command can also be used to reinitialize NFS and RPC data. Here is a display from the SunOS version of **nfsstat**:

```
Client rpc:
calls  badcalls  retrans  badxid  timeout  wait  newcred  timers
46864  0         7        2       7        0     0        3537

Client nfs:
calls  badcalls  nclget    nclsleep
46864  0         46864     0
null     getattr    setattr    root     lookup    readlink    read
0  0%    106  0%    5  0%      0  0%    41  0%    0  0%      21724 46%
```

339

nice

```
wrcache   write          create   remove   rename   link     symlink
0  0%      24957 53%      13  0%   1  0%    0  0%    0  0%    0  0%
mkdir     rmdir     readdir     fsstat
```

**Keyword:**   networking, NFS

**Files:**   /vmunix

**See Also:**   ping, netstat, nlsadmin

## nice +6 datasort

This is the C shell built-in version of **nice**. It lets regular users increase the **nice** value and therefore set a lower priority on a job. Only the superuser can decrease the **nice** value.

**Keyword:**   program execution

**See Also:**   at, awk, nohup, ps, renice

## nice --15 wall << end
### >System going down in 30 minutes
### >end

This use of the **nice** command is convenient for a system administrator who wants to broadcast a message notifying users of an impending system shutdown. The **<<** notation followed by an arbitrary word (we have used **end** in the example) signifies that subsequent input concludes when it reaches a matching word on a line by itself. This technique is called a "Here document." In the example, **--15** is used, meaning that the existing **nice** value should be increased by 15. Note that the **--** sequence is reserved for the superuser. The first dash is the usual option dash; the second dash indicates a negative number, which actually increases the priority of the process.

**Keyword:**   program execution

**See Also:**   at, nohup, ps, renice, wall

## nice --20 wall << end
### >System going down in 30 minutes
### >end

The example is the superuser version of **nice** on BSD systems. It is similar to the SVR4 version, but the **nice** value yields a value of -20. On an SVR4 system, it would yield a value of 0.

**Keyword:**   program execution

**See Also:**   at, awk, nohup, ps, renice, wall

CSH   SVR4   POWER
      Solaris SYSADM
      SCO
      OSF

SH    SVR4   POWER
KSH   Solaris SYSADM
      SCO
      OSF

SH    BSD    POWER
KSH   SunOS  SYSADM
      AIX

**340**

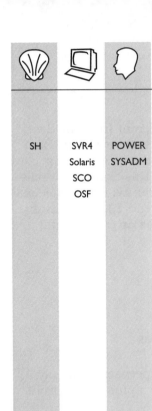

## nice -17 ps -l | awk ´{printf("%s\t%s\t%s\t%s\n", $NF, $4, $7, $8)}´

This command isolates the three fields we need to evaluate the **nice** command. Let's break things down. First we execute **nice** and specify an increment of 10. This should increment by 10 the niceness of the specified program. We have chosen to use **ps** in the example for a reason. The **-l** option to **ps** specifies a verbose display, including niceness (NI) and the system priority (PRI) of the process. If you were to execute the example without the **awk** statement, the output from **ps** would look something like this:

```
 F S UID   PID PPID C PRI NI ADDR1 ADDR2 SZ    WCHAN TTY TIME CMD
20 S 200  1179    1 0  30 20   7f7   7e3 48 f00fadec 2A  0:01 csh
20 S 0    1187 1179 0  30 20   bce   6ec 48 f00fb1f4 2A  0:00 csh
20 S 0    1193 1187 1  30 20   78f   86f 36 f00fb34c 2A  0:00 sh
20 O 0    1205 1193 6  46  3   871   969 72           2A  0:00 ps
```

The **awk** command beautifies. We're only interested in two or three fields, so the **awk** command uses **printf** just to print those:

```
CMD    PID    PRI    NI
csh    1179   30     20
csh    1187   30     20
sh     1193   30     20
awk    1206   26     20
ps     1207   46     3
```

**Keyword:**   program execution

**See Also:**   at, awk, nohup, ps, renice

## nice -19 datasort &

The **nice** command is primarily for UNIX systems with heavy multiuser requirements. In other words, a single user at a workstation has no reason to use **nice**. **nice** executes programs at a different scheduling priority than usual. Its values range from 0 to 39 on System V derivative platforms. The lower the **nice** value, the higher the priority. The argument **-19** in the example is a low-priority request. The default **nice** priority, or **niceness**, is 20. The superuser can specify a high **nice** priority by specifying a negative number.

**Keyword:**   program execution

**See Also:**   at, nohup, ps, renice

### nice -20 datasort

SH    BSD    POWER
KSH   SunOS  SYSADM
      AIX

The BSD version of **nice** is significantly different from the System V version; nevertheless, they work the same way. The BSD version uses a range of -20 to 20 to adjust the niceness of a process. A regular user could have entered this example: It tells the system to run **datasort** at the lowest priority. If you checked the results with a **ps -l**, the NI field would read 19. The reason for this is that the BSD version includes 0 as an incremental value.

**Keyword:**    program execution

**See Also:**    at, awk, nohup, ps, renice

### nice -20 wall << end
### >System going down in 30 minutes
### >end

CSH   BSD    POWER
KSH   SunOS  SYSADM
      AIX

The allowable range is –20 to 20, but the superuser need only use a single dash. For positive values, place a plus sign in front of the **nice** value.

**Keyword:**    program execution

**See Also:**    at, awk, nohup, ps, renice, wall

### nice -3 datasort

CSH   SVR4    POWER
      Solaris  SYSADM
      SCO
      OSF

Using the negative sign in the C shell version of **nice** is reserved for the superuser, who can adjust the niceness through 0. The example sets the niceness to 1.

**Keyword:**    program execution

**See Also:**    at, awk, nohup, ps, renice

### nl -ba sales.db >> sales.nl

ALL   ALL    END

The **nl** command numbers all the lines in the **sales.db** file and writes the output to a new file called **sales.nl**. The -ba notation consists of the option **-b** and the flag **a**. The latter tells **nl** to number all lines.

**Keyword:**    text handling

**See Also:**    sed, awk, pr, cat

### nl -bt report.txt | less

ALL   ALL    END

This use of **nl** outputs **report.txt** to the display, one screen at a time, and numbers each line that contains text.

**Keyword:** text handling

**See Also:** awk, cat, pr, sed

### nl -i10 -v100 write.bas > write2.bas

This command adds line numbers to each line of text contained in **write.bas** and redirects it to **write2.bas**. The **-v** option, with an argument of **100**, tells **nl** to start numbering at 100. The **-i** option, with an argument of **10**, tells **nl** to increment each line by 10.

**Keyword:** text handling

**See Also:** awk, cat, pr, sed

### nl -nln -s´ ´ sales.db

Using the **-s** option to **nl** lets you specify a field separator. In the example, the field separator is a whitespace. The default separator is a tab. To have no separator at all, use **-s** without an argument.

**Keyword:** text handling

**See Also:** awk, cat, pr, sed

### nl -nln sales.db

In this example, the **ln** is an argument to **-n**, and specifies that leading zeros should be suppressed when formatting line numbers.

**Keyword:** text handling

**See Also:** awk, cat, pr, sed

### nl -v1 -i10 -d!+ prog.bas

This command uses the **nl** program to number the file called **prog.bas**, starting at line number **1**, at an increment of **10**. The logical page delimiters are **!+**.

**Keyword:** text handling

**See Also:** awk, cat, pr, sed

### nlsadmin

The **nlsadmin** command is used to set up and maintain the network listener service. When entered at the command line without options, **nlsadmin** displays a usage message.

| ALL | ALL | END |
| ALL | ALL | END |
| ALL | ALL | END |
| ALL | ALL | END |
| ALL | SVR4 | SYSADM |

**Keyword:** networking

**See Also:** ping, netstat, ruptime

## nlsadmin -x

This command outputs the status of all of the listener processes installed on the system.

**Keyword:** networking

**See Also:** ping, netstat, ruptime

## nm a.out

This command outputs the symbol table of the **a.out** object file.

**Keyword:** programming

**See Also:** as, cc, dump, ld

## nobeep

When this C shell environment variable is set, no bell is rung for an ambiguous filename in the C shell file completion facility. The bell sounds if you make an error or there are multiple filenames that match.

**Keyword:** user environment

**See Also:** nonomatch

## noclobber

This C shell environment variable is used for safe redirection processing. Current files cannot be destroyed by inappropriate redirection; **>** can be used only with new files, and **>>** can be used only with existing files.

**Keyword:** user environment

**See Also:** cat, cp, mv

## noglob

This is an environment variable that disables filename substitution.

**Keyword:** user environment

**See Also:** cat, cp, mv

## nohup

The C shell built-in version of **nohup** is similar to the external command. You can use it from the command line with a specific program or add it to **$HOME/.logout**. Here's a suggestion: Create a file called **nohuppers**, and in the file, place the executable filenames of programs that you want to run on a regular basis. You could enhance the approach by testing for a certain day of the week with the **if** and **date** commands. Put the test statement in **$HOME/.logout**.

**Keyword:**   user environment

**See Also:**   at, cron, nice

### nohup datasort &

SH
KSH

ALL

POWER
SYSADM

Using **nohup** enables you to run a command or application and have it continue running after you log off the system. It is a must for administrators and a great convenience for dial-up users. In the example, no arguments are specified, so **nohup** manages all programs that are running after you log off. In the Bourne and Korn shells, **nohup** writes output from any executed commands to **./nohup.out**. If **nohup** cannot write to the current directory, it writes to **$HOME/nohup.out**.

**Keyword:**   user environment

**Files:**       $HOME/nohup.out, $HOME/nohup.out

**See Also:**   at, cron, nice

### nonomatch

CSH

ALL

SCRIPT

This environment variable allows continued processing in a C shell script when filenames are not matched by a substitution pattern. An error is not generated.

**Keyword:**   user environment

**See Also:**   nobeep

### notify -n

ALL

SVR4

END

This command tells the system **mail** program that you do not want to be notified when new email arrives for you.

**Keyword:**   user communication

**See Also:**   biff, xbiff, mail, mailx

### notify -y

ALL

SVR4

END

This command tells the system **mail** program that you want to be notified when new email arrives for you.

**Keyword:**   user communication

**See Also:**   biff, xbiff, mail, mailx

**345**

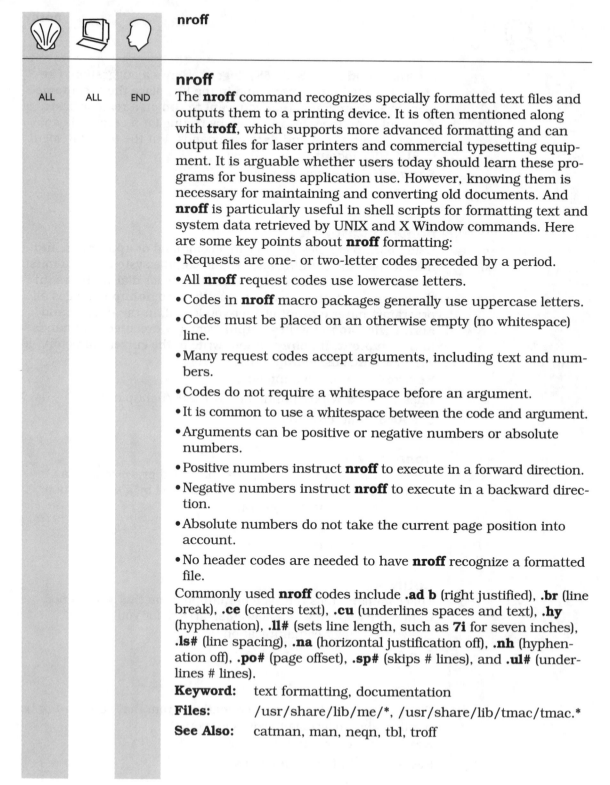

ALL    ALL    END

## nroff

The **nroff** command recognizes specially formatted text files and outputs them to a printing device. It is often mentioned along with **troff**, which supports more advanced formatting and can output files for laser printers and commercial typesetting equipment. It is arguable whether users today should learn these programs for business application use. However, knowing them is necessary for maintaining and converting old documents. And **nroff** is particularly useful in shell scripts for formatting text and system data retrieved by UNIX and X Window commands. Here are some key points about **nroff** formatting:

- Requests are one- or two-letter codes preceded by a period.
- All **nroff** request codes use lowercase letters.
- Codes in **nroff** macro packages generally use uppercase letters.
- Codes must be placed on an otherwise empty (no whitespace) line.
- Many request codes accept arguments, including text and numbers.
- Codes do not require a whitespace before an argument.
- It is common to use a whitespace between the code and argument.
- Arguments can be positive or negative numbers or absolute numbers.
- Positive numbers instruct **nroff** to execute in a forward direction.
- Negative numbers instruct **nroff** to execute in a backward direction.
- Absolute numbers do not take the current page position into account.
- No header codes are needed to have **nroff** recognize a formatted file.

Commonly used **nroff** codes include **.ad b** (right justified), **.br** (line break), **.ce** (centers text), **.cu** (underlines spaces and text), **.hy** (hyphenation), **.ll#** (sets line length, such as **7i** for seven inches), **.ls#** (line spacing), **.na** (horizontal justification off), **.nh** (hyphenation off), **.po#** (page offset), **.sp#** (skips # lines), and **.ul#** (underlines # lines).

**Keyword:**   text formatting, documentation

**Files:**   /usr/share/lib/me/*, /usr/share/lib/tmac/tmac.*

**See Also:**   catman, man, neqn, tbl, troff

| | | |
|---|---|---|
| ALL | ALL | END |

### nroff -e -s8 -h -Tepson -me book.txt

This command formats the **book.txt** file using the **-me** macro package, which spaces words equally in adjusted lines, using Tab characters when possible, and writes the output in a format that is suitable for printing on an Epson FX-80 dot matrix printer.

**Keyword:** text handling, documentation

**Files:** /usr/share/lib/me/*, /usr/share/lib/tmac/tmac.*

**See Also:** catman, man, neqn, tbl, troff

| | | |
|---|---|---|
| ALL | ALL | END |

### nroff -e book.nr

This command outputs the **nroff**-formatted **book.nr** file to the terminal screen, with equally spaced words in adjusted lines.

**Keyword:** text handling, documentation

**Files:** /usr/share/lib/me/*, /usr/share/lib/tmac/tmac.*

**See Also:** catman, man, neqn, tbl, troff

| | | |
|---|---|---|
| ALL | ALL | END |

### nroff -Tepson book.nr

This command formats the output of the **nroff**-formatted **book.nr** file so that it works with an Epson FX-80 dot matrix printer.

**Keyword:** text handling, documentation

**Files:** /usr/share/lib/me/*, /usr/share/lib/tmac/tmac.*

**See Also:** catman, man, neqn, tbl, troff

| | | |
|---|---|---|
| ALL | ALL | SYSADM |

### nslookup -l

This is an interactive command used to get host information from a Domain Name Server. The **-l** argument to **nslookup** is used to query the local system's name server.

**Keyword:** networking, Internet

**See Also:** netstat, nlsadmin, ping

| | | |
|---|---|---|
| ALL | ALL | SYSADM |

### nslookup 18.70.1.0

This is an interactive command used to get host information from the Domain Name Server with the address **18.70.1.0**.

**Keyword:** networking, Internet

**See Also:** netstat, nlsadmin, ping

## oclock &

ALL   XWIN   ALL

The **oclock** client program is one of two clock programs found on most X Window platforms. By default, **oclock** displays as a shapeless window, which means that it has no window frame. If you also want to remove the remaining window components from the clock display, you can insert the following statement in the **$XAPPLRESDIR/Mwm** file (or other applicable resource file):

```
*Mwm*oclock*clientDecoration: none
```

If you take this step, you might also want to add a line to your **.mwmrc** file so that you can invoke a the window menu and exit the clock whenever you want. Here is an example, which should be included in the button bindings section of **.mwmrc**.

```
Alt<Btn3Down> window f.menu DefaultWindowMenu
```

**Keyword:**    time

**Files:**         $HOME/.mwmrc, X resource files

**See Also:**    cal, calendar, date, xclock, xrdb

## oclock -bg green -jewel yellow -minute blue -hour blue -bd green&

ALL   XWIN   ALL

This command beautifies the **oclock** program. You can pick your own colors until you like the results. Note that you do not have to specify a color for the foreground if you use the settings shown in the example. Also, if you do not want to type this long a command—or even include the command in a script file or alias—you can specify resources in the **oclock** resource file. This file should be located in **$XAPPLRESDIR, $HOME**, or other valid location.

**Keyword:**    time

**Files:**         $HOME/.mwmrc, X resource files

**See Also:**    cal, calendar, date, xclock, xrdb

## oclock -geometry 60x60&

ALL   XWIN   ALL

If you do not like the size of the default **oclock**, you can change it with the **-geometry** option. Again, if you prefer, you can set the size in a resource file.

**Keyword:**    time

**Files:**         $HOME/.mwmrc, X resource files

**See Also:**    cal, calendar, date, xclock, xrdb

## od

The **od**, or octal dump, utility converts the byte values in either a binary or ASCII file and displays the conversion. The following table lists the conversion options:

```
-a    ASCII (text)
-b    Octal (byte)
-B    Octal (short)
-c    ASCII (byte)
-C    Extended ASCII
-d    Unsigned decimal (short)
-D    Unsigned decimal (long)
-e    Double-precision floating point
-f    Single-precision floating point
-F    Same as -e
-h    Hexadecimal (short)
-H    Hexadecimal (long)
-i    Signed decimal (short)
-I    Signed decimal (long)
-l    Same as -I
-L    Same as -I
-o    Same a -b
-O    Same as -D
-p    Even partiy
-P    Odd parity
-s    Accepts a string
-v    Shows all data
-x    Same as -h
-X    Same as -H
```

**Keyword:**　binary files, text display

**See Also:**　bc, dc, cat, dd, strings

## od -c data.db | more

Sometimes you want to determine which ASCII escape characters and control codes are being used in a file. The **-c** option does the trick. Don't forget to pipe **od** into a pager; otherwise, the output will run off the screen.

**Keyword:**　binary files, text display

**See Also:**　bc, dc, cat, dd, strings

## od -ch data.db | more

You can combine format requests with **od**. The output for the example, which specifies ASCII and hexadecimal, would look like this for a line that contained the uppercase alphabet and two following blank lines:

**od**

```
0000000   A       B       C       D       E       F       G       H
          2041    2042    2043    2044    2045    2046    2047    2048
0000020   I       J       K       L       M       N       O       P
          2049    204a    204b    204c    204d    204e    204f    2050
0000040   Q       R       S       T       U       V       W       X
          2051    2052    2053    2054    2055    2056    2057    2058
0000060   Y       Z      \n      \n
          2059    0a5a    000a
0000065
```

**Keyword:**    binary files, text display
**See Also:**    bc, dc, cat, dd, strings

### od -hc

This command drops you into shell input mode, where you can enter one or more letters, then press Return and Ctrl-D. To leave, press Ctrl-D a second time. Here's another way to get a quick conversion:

```
echo ABCD | od -hc
```

The output looks like this:

```
0000000    A    B    C    D   \n
           4241      4443      000a
0000005
```

**Keyword:**    binary files, text display
**See Also:**    bc, dc, cat, dd, strings

### od -hoc data.db +500. | more

You can put **od** to work anywhere in a file; you don't have to start at the beginning. Just specify a line number, as in the example. Make sure you use the dot after **500**, so that **od** interprets the number as decimal instead of octal. (Think of ad hoc and you won't forget this command.)

**Keyword:**    binary files, text display
**See Also:**    bc, dc, cat, dd, strings

### open ls -l

This command starts a virtual terminal, and then executes the command **ls -l** in that terminal window. To leave the virtual terminal, press Ctrl-D. To move between virtual terminals, press Alt-Action.

**Keyword:**    terminal display
**See Also:**    newvt, window, xterm

| ALL | SunOS Solaris | ALL |
|---|---|---|

## openwin

On a standard Sun system, the **openwin** command starts the X server and the OpenWindows window manager. Options supported by **openwin** include:

```
-dev       the name of framebuffer device
-display   the display name
-auth      the authentication protocol
-server    the name of the X server
-noauth    host-based authentication
```

You can also specify X servers options when you use **openwin**. The X server options are passed directly to the X server executable.

**Keyword:**    window managers

**See Also:**    mwm, twm, xrdb

| ALL | SunOS Solaris | ALL |
|---|---|---|

## openwin -noauth &

If you use Sun's OpenWindows, you might find that you need to start the X server and window manager when you can't possibly supply an **.Xauthority** file. In other words, the **-noauth** option sets host-based authorization, which means the current host has valid access as well as the hosts permitted by the **xhost** command.

**Keyword:**    window managers

**See Also:**    mwm, twm, xhost, xrdb

| ALL | ALL | SCRIPT |
|---|---|---|

## OPTARG

This environment variable contains the last option argument processed by the **getopts** command.

**Keyword:**    programming

**See Also:**    env, getopts, history, printenv

| ALL | ALL | SCRIPT |
|---|---|---|

## OPTIND

This environment variable contains the index of the last option argument processed by the **getopts** command.

**Keyword:**    programming

**See Also:**    env, getopts, history, printenv

| ALL | ALL | END |
|---|---|---|

## pack

The **pack** command creates a compressed version of the specified file. The compressed file, which replaces the original version, is noticeable by its **.z** extension (compare this to **compress**, which uses a **.Z** extension). File permissions and modification date of the original file remain the same.

**Keyword:** file handling

**See Also:** compress, pcat, uncompress, unpack, zcat

## pack -f report.tar

ALL ALL END

This command compresses the entire **tar** file **report.tar**, even if some of the components individually do not compress. This is helpful if you want all files in a series to carry the **.z** extension.

**Keyword:** file handling

**See Also:** pcat, unpack, compress, zcat, uncompress

## page book.txt

ALL ALL END

The **page** command is a system-level alias for the **more** command. See *The UNIX and X Command Compendium* entries on **more** for more.

**Keyword:** text display

**See Also:** less, more, pg

## pagesize

ALL BSD SCRIPT POWER

This command outputs the page size of system memory. The output is in bytes. There are no options to the command.

**Keyword:** system information

**See Also:** alloc, ipcs, netstat, ps

## passmgmt -a perkie

ALL SVR4 SYSADM

This command creates a new user, **perkie**, on the system. It doesn't create a home directory, and the new user can't log in until a password has been assigned with the **passwd** command.

**Keyword:** user setup

**See Also:** passwd, sysadmsh, useradd, sysadm, smit, su

## passmgmt -m -c "Alan Southerton" alans

ALL SVR4 SYSADM

This command puts the comment **Alan Southerton** into the comment section of the **/etc/passwd** file for user **alans**.

**Keyword:** user setup

**See Also:** passwd, sysadmsh, useradd, sysadm, smit, su

### passmgmt -m -g 235 perkie

ALL   SVR4   SYSADM

This command tells the system that user **perkie**'s group ID number is **235**.

**Keyword:**    user setup

**See Also:**    passwd, sysadmsh, useradd, sysadm, smit, su

### passmgmt -m -h /home/perkie perkie

ALL   SVR4   SYSADM

This command tells the system that user **perkie**'s home directory is **/home/perkie**. It does not create the directory, however.

**Keyword:**    user setup

**See Also:**    passwd, sysadmsh, useradd, sysadm, smit, su

### passmgmt -m -s /bin/ksh perkie

ALL   SVR4   SYSADM

This command sets user **perkie**'s shell to the Korn Shell.

**Keyword:**    user setup

**See Also:**    passwd, sysadmsh, useradd, sysadm, smit, su

### passmgmt -m -u 192 perkie

ALL   SVR4   SYSADM

This command tells the system that user **perkie**'s user ID number is **192**.

**Keyword:**    user setup

**See Also:**    passwd, sysadmsh, useradd, sysadm, smit, su

### passwd

ALL   ALL   END

The **passwd** command lets you change your login password. You are prompted for your old password, and if it is correct, you are asked to type in a new password. After you type in a new password, you are prompted to retype your new password to reduce the chance of a typing error.

**Keyword:**    user environment

**Files:**    /etc/passwd

**See Also:**    finger, login, who

### passwd -d perkie

ALL   SVR4   SYSADM
       SCO

This command deletes the password for **perkie** when **perkie** logs in; no prompting for a password is needed.

**Keyword:**    user environment

**Files:**    /etc/passwd

**See Also:**    sysadm, sysadmsh, passmgmt, userdel

| | | |
|---|---|---|
| ALL | OSF | END |

## passwd -f

This is an interactive command used to change the comment section of the **/etc/passwd** file associated with your account.

**Keyword:** user environment

**See Also:** chfn, finger, login

| | | |
|---|---|---|
| ALL | SVR4 | SYSADM |

## passwd -f perkie

This command is used to force user **perkie** to change his password the next time he logs into the system.

**Keyword:** user environment

**See Also:** sysadmsh, useradd

| | | |
|---|---|---|
| ALL | SVR4 SCO | SYSADM |

## passwd -l perkie

This command locks the password for the user **perkie**. After this command is executed, user **perkie** is locked out of the system.

**Keyword:** user environment

**Files:** /etc/passwd

**See Also:** sysadm, sysadmsh, userdel, passmgmt

| | | |
|---|---|---|
| ALL | SVR4 SCO | END |

## passwd -s

This command is used to output information regarding your password on the system.

**Keyword:** user environment

**Files:** /etc/passwd

**See Also:** passmgmt, sysadmsh, useradd

| | | |
|---|---|---|
| ALL | BSD SunOS OSF | END |

## passwd -s

This interactive command lets you change your login shell.

**Keyword:** user environment

**See Also:** chsh, finger, login

| | | |
|---|---|---|
| ALL | ALL | SYSADM |

## passwd emily

This command makes sense for superusers only. If you perform system administration chores, sooner or later you will need to create a new password for one user or another. The example command does the trick, and you don't need to know the user's existing password to use it.

**Keyword:** user setup, user environment

**See Also:** admintool, sysadm, sysadmsh, smit

### paste -d"\n" data1.txt data2.txt >> data.txt

ALL ALL END

This command merges two files, **data1.txt** and **data2.txt**, to a new file called **data.txt**. **data.txt** contains the first line of **data1.txt** and then the first line of **data2.txt**.

**Keyword:** text handling

**See Also:** awk, cut, grep, join, pr, sed

### paste -s data1.txt >> data.txt

ALL ALL END

This command merges the subsequent lines of the **data1.txt** file, using a tab as a line delimiter, and outputs it to the **data.txt** file.

**Keyword:** text handling

**See Also:** awk, cut, grep, join, pr, sed

### paste data1.txt data2.txt

ALL ALL END

This command replaces the carriage return at the end of every line of the **data1.txt** file with a tab. The corresponding line of **data2.txt** is then pasted after the tab. The results of this merge are then output to the terminal window.

**Keyword:** text handling

**See Also:** awk, cut, grep, join, pr, sed

### PATH

SH
KSH ALL ALL

The **PATH** environment variable defines the system path for the Bourne and Korn shells. As a rule, **PATH** is set at startup time when the shell sources **/etc/profile** and **$HOME/.profile**. Directory names in the **PATH** statement are separated by colons. If you need to customize your system path, do it in **$HOME/.profile**. This is the purpose of **$HOME/.profile**, and even if you are root user, do yourself a favor and refrain from modifying system-level files such as **/etc/profile**. You must also consider the issue of including the current directory in the system path, which is represented by a dot (usually included after the last colon). If you do include the current directory, it can be a security hole. If you don't put it in the path, you can execute scripts and programs in the current directory unless you prepend **./** to the filename.

**Keyword:** user environment, user setup

**Files:** /etc/profile, $HOME/.profile
**See Also:** env, find, path (csh), printenv, set

## path

CSH ALL ALL

In the C shell, directories are separated by spaces and are not acceptably defined if you separate them with a colon. This also applies to the dot character (.), which represents the current directory. Here is an example statement:

```
set path = ( /usr/bin /usr/bin/X11 /home/bin /usr/bin/local . )
```

In most cases, the shell automatically knows when you add executable files to one of the directories in the **path**. If you use the **-c** or **-t** options to start **csh**, you must use the **rehash** command in order to have the shell recognize newly added commands. Last, there are times when you want to update the **path** from the command line or in a shell script. Try this:

```
set path = ($path ~/bin)
```

**Keyword:** user environment, user setup
**Files:** $HOME/.cshrc
**See Also:** env, printenv, set, PATH (sh, ksh)

## PATH=$PATH:$HOME/bin:

SH
KSH ALL ALL

This is an equality command for environment variables (or variables in a shell script). The equals sign is the only operator. In the example, the PATH variable is defined to itself plus **$HOME/bin**. This is an easy way to add directories to your path, without the hassle of editing your original system path.
**Keyword:** user environment
**Files:** /etc/profile, $HOME/.profile
**See Also:** export, env, printenv, set

## pcat report.doc.z | less

ALL ALL ALL

This command outputs the contents of the **report.doc** file, which has been compressed using the **pack** command. With **pcat**, you can view the file as if it were a normal text file, yet save disk space because the file is compressed.
**Keyword:** file handling
**See Also:** compress, pack, unpack, uncompress, zcat

## pg

The **pg** command was introduced as an enhanced pager, and gained an immediate reputation of being more than **more**— because you could scroll forward and backward in **pg**. Years later we still have both pagers, with **less** rivaling **more** and **pg**. In a nutshell, **pg** displays a file, one screenful at a time. It has numerous options to modify the scrolling and move around in the file. Here are the options as available on the operating systems covered:

```
SunOS    pg [-cefns] [-num] [-p string] [+lnum] [+/pat/] [file ...]
SCO      pg [-dflsucrwv] [-n] [+lnum | +/pat] file ...
AIX  Solaris  pg [-num] [-p string] [-cefnrs] [+lnum] [+/pat/] [file ...]
SVR4     pg [-num] [-p string] [-cefnrs] [+lnum] [+/pat/] [file ...]
OSF1     pg [-cefns] [- p string] [+lnum | +/patn/] [-num] [file ...]
MKS      pg [-acefnst] [-n] [-p prompt] [+/pat] [file...]
```

**Keyword:**    text display

**See Also:**    cat, less, more, page, view

### pg -c book.txt

The **-c** argument tells **pg** to clear the screen and output text from the top down. In other words, there is no reading as the text scrolls off.

**Keyword:**    text display

**See Also:**    cat, less, more, page, view

### pg -e *

This command displays the contents of all files in the current directory, one screenful at a time. It doesn't pause between the end of one file and the beginning of another.

**Keyword:**    text display

**See Also:**    cat, less, more, page, view

### pg -f jargon.txt

This command displays the **jargon.txt** file onto the terminal. If any lines are longer than the terminal is wide, they are not wrapped to the next line, they are just cut off.

**Keyword:**    text display

**See Also:**    cat, less, more, page, view

### pg -n book.txt

| | | |
|---|---|---|
| ALL | ALL | END |

This command outputs the **book.txt** file onto the terminal. When you enter a command to **pg**, you don't need to press Return; the command is entered automatically.

**Keyword:**   text display

**See Also:**   cat, less, more, page, view

### pg -p "book" book.txt

| | | |
|---|---|---|
| ALL | ALL | END |

This command outputs the **book.txt** file onto the terminal. The default prompt of **:** for **pg** is replaced with the string **book**.

**Keyword:**   text display

**See Also:**   cat, less, more, page, view

### pg -p "Page %d of file book.txt" book.txt

| | | |
|---|---|---|
| ALL | ALL | END |

This command outputs the **book.txt** file onto the terminal. The default prompt of **:** for **pg** is replaced with a string saying that the current page of the **book.txt** file is being displayed.

**Keyword:**   text display

**See Also:**   cat, less, more, page, view

### pg -r book.txt

| | | |
|---|---|---|
| ALL | ALL | END |

This command outputs the **book.txt** file onto the terminal. The **-r** option to **pg** sets restricted mode on. The shell escape is not allowed; **pg** outputs an error, but doesn't quit.

**Keyword:**   text display

**See Also:**   cat, less, more, page, view

### ping 192.9.200.1

| | | |
|---|---|---|
| ALL | ALL | POWER SYSADM |

This command is used to see whether you have a network connection between your system and the remote system with the IP address **192.9.200.1**.

**Keyword:**   networking

**See Also:**   finger, ping, netstat, nlsadmin, rup, ruptime, rwho

### ping dec1

| | | |
|---|---|---|
| ALL | ALL | POWER SYSADM |

This command is used to determine whether the network connection is working between the local computer and the remote computer **dec1**. If the connection is good, then you will get a response saying either that **dec1** is alive or that the packet loss is 0%. If the connection between the two computers is faulty, you will get a response saying that the packet loss is 100%.

**Keyword:**   networking

**See Also:**   finger, ping, netstat, nlsadmin, rup, ruptime, rwho

### pkgadd -d /dev/rmt0/c0s0 tcp x

This command installs the software **x** and **tcp** off of the tape **/dev/rmt0/c0s0**.

**Keyword:**   system setup

**See Also:**   custom, sysadm, sysadmsh

| ALL | SVR4 SCO | SYSADM |
|---|---|---|

### pkgadd -d ctape1 all

This interactive command installs all the software packages available on the tape specified by **ctape1**.

**Keyword:**   system setup

**See Also:**   sysadm, sysadmsh, custom

### pkgadd -n -d ctape1 all

This command installs noninteractively all the software packages available on the tape specified by **ctape1**.

**Keyword:**   system setup

**See Also:**   sysadm, sysadmsh, custom

### pkgadd -s /tmp/new_package -d ctape1 all

This command puts the new package into the directory **/tmp/new_package** before it installs the package.

**Keyword:**   system setup

**See Also:**   pkgask, pkgchk, pkgmk, pkginfo, pkgparam, pkgproto, pkgtrans, pkgrm

### pkgask -d /dev/rmt/ctape1 -r /u1/pakages/responses/all.1 all

This command generates an answer file in **/u1/pakages/responses** that answers questions asked by **pkgadd** in interactive mode.

**Keyword:**   system setup

**See Also:**   pkgadd, pkgchk, pkgmk, pkginfo, pkgparam, pkgproto, pkgtrans, pkgrm

The left margin for each command entry reads: ALL | SVR4 SCO | SYSADM

## pkgchk

| | | |
|---|---|---|
| ALL | SVR4 SCO | SYSADM |

This command checks the accuracy of all the installed software packages on the system.

**Keyword:** system setup

**See Also:** pkgadd, pkgask, pkgmk, pkginfo, pkgparam, pkgproto, pkgtrans, pkgrm

## pkgchk -a

| | | |
|---|---|---|
| ALL | SVR4 SCO | SYSADM |

This command checks the file attributes of all the installed software packages on the system.

**Keyword:** system setup

**See Also:** pkgadd, pkgask, pkgmk, pkginfo, pkgparam, pkgproto, pkgtrans, pkgrm

## pkgchk -c

| | | |
|---|---|---|
| ALL | SVR4 SCO | SYSADM |

This command checks the file contents of all the installed software packages on the system.

**Keyword:** system setup

**See Also:** sysadm, sysadmsh, tar, cpio, pkgadd, pkgask, pkgmk, pkginfo, pkgparam, pkgproto, pkgtrans, pkgrm

## pkgchk -f

| | | |
|---|---|---|
| ALL | SVR4 SCO | SYSADM |

This command tries to correct the file attributes of all the installed software packages on the system.

**Keyword:** system setup

**See Also:** pkgadd, pkgask, pkgmk, pkginfo, pkgparam, pkgproto, pkgtrans, pkgrm

## pkgchk -l

| | | |
|---|---|---|
| ALL | SVR4 SCO | SYSADM |

This command outputs information on the files that make up all the installed software packages on the system.

**Keyword:** system setup

**See Also:** pkgadd, pkgask, pkgmk, pkginfo, pkgparam, pkgproto, pkgtrans, pkgrm

## pkgchk -q

| | | |
|---|---|---|
| ALL | SVR4 SCO | SYSADM |

This command checks the accuracy of all the installed software packages on the system, without outputting any information.

**Keyword:**   system setup

**See Also:**   pkgadd, pkgask, pkgmk, pkginfo, pkgparam, pkgproto, pkgtrans, pkgrm

## pkgchk -v

ALL   SVR4 SCO   SYSADM

This command checks the accuracy of all the installed software packages on the system, showing each file as it is checked.

**Keyword:**   system setup

**See Also:**   pkgadd, pkgask, pkgmk, pkginfo, pkgparam, pkgproto, pkgtrans, pkgrm

## pkginfo -d /dev/rmt/ctape1 -l

ALL   SVR4 SCO   SYSADM

This command shows a long listing of package information, which includes all available information for the package residing on the tape specified by **/dev/rmt/ctape1**.

**Keyword:**   system setup

**See Also:**   pkgadd, pkgask, pkgmk, pkgchk, pkgparam, pkgproto, pkgtrans, pkgrm

## pkginfo -l -i

ALL   SVR4 SCO   SYSADM

This command shows a long listing of package information, which includes all available information for all packages fully installed.

**Keyword:**   system setup

**See Also:**   pkgadd, pkgask, pkgmk, pkgchk, pkgparam, pkgproto, pkgtrans, pkgrm

## pkginfo -l -p

ALL   SVR4 SCO   SYSADM

This command shows a long listing of package information, which includes all available information for all packages partially installed.

**Keyword:**   system setup

**See Also:**   pkgadd, pkgask, pkgmk, pkgchk, pkgparam, pkgproto, pkgtrans, pkgrm

## pkginfo -l inst.beta

ALL   SVR4 SCO   SYSADM

This command shows a long listing of package information, which includes all available information.

**Keyword:**   system setup

**See Also:** pkgadd, pkgask, pkgmk, pkgchk, pkgparam, pkgproto, pkgtrans, pkgrm

### pkginfo -x inst.beta

ALL    SVR4 SCO    SYSADM

This command shows an extracted listing of package information, containing package abbreviation, name, architecture, and version.

**Keyword:** system setup

**See Also:** pkgadd, pkgask, pkgmk, pkgchk, pkgparam, pkgproto, pkgtrans, pkgrm

### pkgmk -d /dev/rmt/ctape1 -f prototype my_prog.3

ALL    SVR4 SCO    SYSADM

This command creates a new package called **my_prog.3**, using the file called **prototype** as input to the command. The new package is put on the tape specified by **/dev/rmt/ctape1**.

**Keyword:** system setup

**See Also:** pkgadd, pkgask, pkginfo, pkgchk, pkgparam, pkgproto, pkgtrans, pkgrm

### pkgmk -d /dev/rmt/ctape1 -r /home/perkie/my_prog my_prog.3

ALL    SVR4 SCO    SYSADM

This command creates a new package called **my_prog.3** from the code in the directory **/home/perkie/my_prog**, and puts the new package on the tape specified by **/dev/rmt/ctape1**.

**Keyword:** system setup

**See Also:** pkgadd, pkgask, pkginfo, pkgchk, pkgparam, pkgproto, pkgtrans, pkgrm

### pkgparam -v my_prog.3

ALL    SVR4 SCO    SYSADM

This command shows all the parameter values associated with the package **my_prog.3**.

**Keyword:** system setup

**See Also:** pkgadd, pkgask, pkginfo, pkgchk, pkgmk, pkgproto, pkgtrans, pkgrm

### pkgproto /home/perkie/my_prog/bin=bin

ALL    SVR4 SCO    SYSADM

This command creates a prototype file used for creating a new package. It tells **pkgadd** that the directory **/home/perkie/my_prog/bin** should be installed as the **bin** directory.

**Keyword:** system setup

**See Also:** pkgadd, pkgask, pkginfo, pkgchk, pkgmk, pkgparam, pkgtrans, pkgrm

## pkgrm

This is an interactive command used for removing software packages that are installed on the system.

**Keyword:** system setup

**See Also:** pkgadd, custom

## pkgrm -n x

This command removes the software **x** that is installed on the system.

**Keyword:** system setup

**See Also:** pkgadd, custom

## pkgrm my_prog.3

This command removes the software package **my_prog.3** from the system.

**Keyword:** system setup

**See Also:** pkgadd, pkgask, pkginfo, pkgchk, pkgmk, pkgparam, pkgtrans, pkgproto

## pkgtrans /dev/rmt/ctape1 /tmp my_prog.3

This command translates the package **my_prog.3** from a tape format on **/dev/rmt/ctape1** to disk format on **/tmp**.

**Keyword:** system setup

**See Also:** pkgadd, pkgask, pkginfo, pkgchk, pkgmk, pkgparam, pkgrm, pkgproto

## plot -Tcrt plot.dat

This command draws a graph based on the data in the **plot.dat** file and outputs the graph to the terminal window. If no terminal is specified, **plot** uses **$TERM**.

**Keyword:** text handling

**See Also:** ed, lpr, vi

ALL   SVR4 SCO   SYSADM

ALL   SVR4 SCO   SYSADM

ALL   SVR4 SCO   SYSADM

ALL   SVR4 SCO   SYSADM

ALL   SVR4 BSD   END

## popd

ALL · ALL · POWER

The **popd** command is a C shell built-in utility for moving between directories that have been recorded in a shell-maintained directory stack. When you use **popd** (and directories have been recorded to the stack using **pushd** or **dirs**), **popd** pops the top directory off the directory stack. It then changes directories to the new directory occupying the top of the stack. (In other words, when one directory gets popped off, the one beneath it pops up.) The directories in the directory stack are numbered from the top beginning with 0. The **popd** command must be used in conjunction with **dirs** and **pushd**.

**Keyword:**    directories, user environment

**See Also:**    cd, dirs, pushd

## popd +3

CSH · ALL · POWER

This command removes the third entry in the directory stack, but doesn't affect your current working directory.

**Keyword:**    directories, user environment

**See Also:**    cd, dirs, pushd

## powerdown -Y

ALL · SVR4 · SYSADM

This command kills all processes and halts the computer system. There is no delay between the time the computer warns users to log out and the time when the computer halts. This is the quickest way to stop the computer.

**Keyword:**    shutdown

**See Also:**    init, reboot, shutdown

## powerdown -y

ALL · SVR4 · SYSADM

The **powerdown** command kills all processes and halts the computer system. It has a 60-second delay between sending a warning message and halting the system.

**Keyword:**    shutdown

**See Also:**    init, reboot, shutdown

## PPID

KSH · ALL · SCRIPT

This environment variable is set to the process number of the parent shell.

**Keyword:**    program execution

**See Also:**    kill, ps, who

ALL    ALL    END

## pr - | lpr

The **pr** command is useful in different roles, including formatting output for the printer. By itself, however, **pr** (which really stands for "pretty") does not send output to the printer; instead, it sends it to the standard output. If you want, you can also send it along to a printer, terminal, or file. In the example, **pr** receives the standard input (thanks to -) and pipes it to **lpr**. This command is handy if you work in an Xterm window in the X Window System. Just cut and paste to the standard input (a.k.a. shell input mode) and press Ctrl-D when you are finished. Pretty soon, **CUT_BUFFER0** is printing.

**Keyword:**    text formatting, printing

**See Also:**    lp, lpr, nroff, troff

ALL    ALL    END

## pr -2 -w80 -l24 -F book.txt | more

This command is designed for a standard terminal window. It sets the page width to 80 characters and the page length to 24 characters, and it has two columns of text. It also has word-wrap, so a line longer than 40 characters is wrapped to the next line. The **book1.txt** file is output with the above specifications and displayed through **pg**.

**Keyword:**    text formatting

**See Also:**    less, lp, lpr, more, nroff, pg, troff

ALL    ALL    END

## pr -2 -w80 -l24 book1.txt | pg

This command is designed for a standard terminal window. It sets the page width to 80 characters and the page length to 24 characters, and it has two columns of text. The **book1.txt** file is output with the above specifications and displayed through **pg**.

**Keyword:**    text formatting

**See Also:**    less, lp, lpr, more, nroff, pg, troff

ALL    ALL    END

## pr -d book.txt | less

This command doublespaces the **book.txt** file, then outputs it through **less** to the terminal window.

**Keyword:**    text formatting

**See Also:**    less, lp, lpr, more, nroff, pg, troff

### pr -n -t sales.dat

ALL  ALL  POWER

The **pr** command displays the **sale.data** file to the screen, numbers lines, and delimits fields with tabs.

**Keyword:**   text formatting

**See Also:**   cat, nl, xpr

### pr -p -w80 -l24 book1.txt

ALL  ALL  END

This command outputs the **book1.txt** file to the terminal window, rings the bell, and waits for a Return at the end of each page.

**Keyword:**   text formatting

**See Also:**   less, lp, lpr, more, nroff, pg, troff

### pr -r book.txt | lpr

ALL  ALL  END

This command simply prints the **book.txt** file to the default printer. If an error occurs, no diagnostic information is output.

**Keyword:**   text formatting, printing

**See Also:**   lp, lpr, nroff, troff

### pr -t -o6 sales.jun | lpr

ALL  ALL  END

The **-t** option tells **pr** not to print the usual header information. The **-o** option with an argument of **6** tells **pr** to indent six spaces.

**Keyword:**   printing

**See Also:**   lp, lpr, nroff, troff

### pr book.txt | lpr

ALL  ALL  END

This command prints the **book.txt** file to the default printer. Each page is headed by the date, time, filename, and page number.

**Keyword:**   text formatting, printing

**See Also:**   lp, lpr, nroff, troff

### pr chap2 | sed "s/page *[0-9]*$/(&)/" | lpr

ALL  ALL  POWER

This command formats page numbers and prints the **chap2.txt** file onto the local printer.

**Keyword:**   text formatting, printing

**See Also:**   lp, lpr, nroff, troff

### print ´Hello,\a\a\nwelcome to aixpilot.´

KSH  ALL  ALL

This built-in Korn shell displays a message. Its output looks like this:

```
Hello, welcome to aixpilot.
```

It also rings the keyboard bell twice to catch your attention.

**Keyword:**　terminal display

**See Also:**　awk, banner, cat, echo

### printenv

The **printenv** command displays all environment variables and their values. This command works in the C shell, but does not display C shell environment variables.

**Keyword:**　user environment

**See Also:**　env, setenv, set

### printenv HOSTNAME

This command displays the system hostname.

**Keyword:**　user environment

**See Also:**　env, setenv, set

### printenv SHELL

This command displays your command shell.

**Keyword:**　user environment

**See Also:**　env, setenv, set

### printenv TERM

This command displays the current terminal type.

**Keyword:**　user environment

**See Also:**　env, setenv, set

### printf ´%2$s %4$s %1$s %3$s\n´ nice Have day. a

This command outputs the string **Have a nice day.** onto the screen.

**Keyword:**　text display

**See Also:**　cat, echo, print

### printf ´%s %s\n´ Hello World´

The mighty **printf** function from the C language made it to the shell with the release of SVR4. It isn't identical to its C counterpart, but it is close enough. All the conversion characters used

**367**

by the C function are part of the SVR4 command. If you have the **man** pages for the C library, look there for more details; otherwise, we'll have them in a second edition of The UNIX and X Command Compendium. By the way, as the example indicates, **printf** for the shell is not designed for printers.

**Keyword:**   text display

**See Also:**   awk, banner, echo, cat, pr

### prof a.out

ALL    ALL    POWER

The **prof** command profiles C programs. The example outputs statistics about the **a.out** program. The program needs to be compiled with the **-p** option to **cc** for this to work.

**Keyword:**   programming

**See Also:**   cc, make, xmkmf

### PROJECTDIR

ALL    ALL    POWER

This environment variable defines the user's default directory for Source Code Control System (SCCS) files. When setting the variable, note that the directory must be called SCCS. It can be located anywhere you like, including **$HOME**. Here's a C shell example:

```
setenv PROJECTDIR $HOME
```

The example assumes that **$HOME** has been previously defined. It also assumes that the SCCS has been created and is ready for use.

**Keyword:**   file revision, programming, documentation

**Files:**   /usr/sccs/*

**See Also:**   admin, help, sccs

### prompt

CSH    ALL    POWER

The **prompt** environment variable is a helpful C shell feature. It lets you modify your prompt relatively easily. If you know a few things about aliasing, you can insert your current path into the **prompt**. Here are the statements that you should put into your **$HOME/.cshrc** file:

```
set prompt="[`hostname`]<$cwd># "
alias cd 'cd \!*; set prompt="[`hostname`]<$cwd> "'
```

**Keyword:**   user environment

**Files:**   $HOME/.cshrc

**See Also:**   alias, cd, chdir, pwd, set

## ps

The **ps** command displays process information. Without options, **ps** displays information about the current terminal, including process ID, terminal name, cumulative execution time, and the associated command name. Here's how the various versions of **ps** look:

```
SVR4      ps [-edalfcj] [-r sys] [-t tty] [-u user] [-p pid] [-g grp] [-s sess]
Solaris   ps [-edalfcj] [-r sys] [-t tty] [-u user] [-p pid] [-g grp] [- s sess]
SunOS     ps [[-]acCegjklnrSuUvwx][-tx]|[num] [kernel] [core] [swap]
OSF1      ps [-edamjflr] [-oO fmt] [-t tty] [-p pid] [-u usr] [-g grp] [- s sess]
AIX SCO   ps [-edalf] [-n list] [-t ttys] [-p pid] [-u usr] [-g grp]
BSD       ps [aAceglmnstuUvwx] [#] [file]
```

BSD Compatability Syntax

```
OSF1      ps [aexgmlvusjrSUALwhT] [Oo format] [ttty] [process number]
```

**Keyword:**   job control, background processing

**See Also:**   bg, fg, jobs, kill

## ps -a

This command lists the processes currently running, excluding process group leaders and processes not associated with a terminal.

**Keyword:**   job control, background processing

**See Also:**   bg, fg, jobs, kill

## ps -a

This command shows information about processes owned by other users.

**Keyword:**   job control, background processing

**See Also:**   bg, fg, jobs, kill

## ps -al

This command shows information in long format about processes owned by other users.

**Keyword:**   job control, background processing

**See Also:**   bg, fg, jobs, kill

## ps -an

This command shows information in numerical format about processes owned by other users.

| ALL | ALL | SCRIPT POWER SYSADM |
| ALL | SVR4 SCO | POWER |
| ALL | BSD | POWER |
| ALL | BSD | POWER |
| ALL | BSD | POWER |

**Keyword:**   job control, background processing
**See Also:**   bg, fg, jobs, kill

### ps -axl | more
This outputs a listing of all the processes that are running on the system. It also shows the user ID of the person who is running the process, the process ID, and the parent process ID, among many other things.

**Keyword:**   job control, background processing
**See Also:**   bg, fg, jobs, kill

### ps -axlww
This command uses an arbitrarily wide terminal, and lets you view a lot of information about every process that is running.

**Keyword:**   job control, background processing
**See Also:**   bg, fg, jobs, kill

### ps -d
This command lists all the processes currently running, except session leaders.

**Keyword:**   job control, background processing
**See Also:**   bg, fg, jobs, kill

### ps -e
This command lists all the processes currently running.

**Keyword:**   job control, background processing
**See Also:**   bg, fg, jobs, kill

### ps -e
This command shows the entire environment associated with each process that is running on your terminal.

**Keyword:**   job control, background processing
**See Also:**   bg, fg, jobs, kill

### ps -e | awk ´/xterm/ && ! /awk/ {print $1}´
This shows a quicker way to perform the same operation as in the previous example—namely, extract the process IDs for a program, excluding the ID associated with the shell command you

| | | |
|---|---|---|
| ALL | BSD | POWER |
| ALL | BSD | POWER |
| ALL | SVR4 SCO | POWER |
| ALL | SVR4 SCO | POWER |
| ALL | BSD | POWER |
| ALL | SVR4 SCO OSF | POWER |

are using to do the extraction. This command uses **ps** and **awk**. Here, **awk** takes the output from **ps** and prints out all IDs for **xterm**, execept the one associated with the **awk** command, as indicated by the **!/awk/** notation.

**Keyword:**    job control, background processing

**See Also:**    bg, fg, jobs, kill

### ps -e | grep xterm | grep -v "grep xterm"

This command displays **ps** listings for all running Xterms. The first **grep** command extracts all process lines containing **xterm**. The second **grep** command, thanks to the **-v** option, removes the instance of **grep** itself from the pipeline.

**Keyword:**    job control, background processing

**See Also:**    bg, fg, jobs, kill

### ps -e | grep xterm | grep -v "grep xterm" | awk -F´ ´ ´{print $1}´

This command shows the job ID for every Xterm running on the system. The first **grep** extracts all lines containing **xterm**. The second **grep** then extracts all lines not containing **grep xterm**. Last, the **awk** command, using **-F** to establish the field separator as a whitespace character, prints out column **1** of the pipeline, which is the column containing the job ID.

**Keyword:**    job control, background processing

**See Also:**    bg, fg, jobs, kill

### ps -ef | more

This command outputs a full list of all the processes currently running.

**Keyword:**    job control, background processing

**See Also:**    bg, fg, jobs, kill

### ps -efl | more

This outputs a listing of all the processes that are running on the system. It also shows the user ID of the person who is running the process, the process ID, and the parent process ID, among many other things.

**Keyword:**    job control, background processing

**See Also:**    bg, fg, jobs, kill

ALL    ALL    POWER

ALL    SVR4    POWER
       SCO
       OSF

ALL    SVR4    POWER
       SCO
       OSF

ALL    SVR4    POWER

## ps -ej | pg

ALL  SVR4  POWER
SCO

This command lists all the processes currently running. The format consists of the user who owns the process, the process ID, the parent process ID, the process group ID, the session, job, status, time, and name of the process.

**Keyword:**  job control, background processing

**See Also:**  bg, fg, jobs, kill

## ps -el | less

ALL  SVR4  POWER
SCO

This command lists in a long format all the processes currently running.

**Keyword:**  job control, background processing

**See Also:**  bg, fg, jobs, kill

## ps -ft `tty` | awk "/$USER/ && ! /awk/ {print $1}"

ALL  SVR4  POWER
SCO
OSF

This command prints a single line from the normal **ps** listing. The printed line contains system information related to the current terminal for the current user. The command is especially helpful for Xterm users in the X Window System.

**Keyword:**  job control, background processing

**See Also:**  bg, fg, jobs, kill

## ps -g

ALL  BSD  POWER

This command shows processes that are running and doing something, such as **vi** or **man**, but not **lpd** or **inetd**.

**Keyword:**  job control, background processing

**See Also:**  bg, fg, jobs, kill

## ps -jp $$

ALL  SVR4  ALL
SCO
OSF

This command shows the process information for the current process. You can use the **p** option and specify any valid process or processes with it.

**Keyword:**  job control, background processing

**See Also:**  bg, fg, jobs, kill

## ps -jt /dev/ttyp1

ALL  SVR4  POWER
SCO

This command gets the processes associated with the **/dev/ttyp1** pseudo-terminal. You'll find that Xterms have a pseudo-device file, as do multiscreen windows under SCO.

**Keyword:** job control, background processing
**See Also:** bg, fg, jobs, kill

## ps -jt /dev/ttyp1 | tail -1 | cut -d´ ´ -f1

This command gets users of Xterm. It is the same as **whoami**.
**Keyword:** job control, background processing
**See Also:** bg, fg, jobs, kill

## ps -r

This command shows a listing of only running and runnable processes.
**Keyword:** job control, background processing
**See Also:** bg, fg, jobs, kill

## ps -t /dev/ttyp2 | tail -1 | cut -c26-100 | cut -d´ ´ -f2

Although longwinded, this command is useful for Xterm users who want to obtain the name of a text file currently being edited by an editor such as **vi** or **emacs**. Try it. Open two Xterm windows and run **vi** with a file in one window. Then type this command in the other window. You can be sure that the relevant line always occurs last in the **ps** listing, so **tail -1** is appropriate.
**Keyword:** X Window, job control
**See Also:** bg, fg, jobs, kill

## ps -t tty01

This command lists all the processes associated with the terminal **tty01**.
**Keyword:** job control, background processing
**See Also:** bg, fg, jobs, kill

## ps -u

This command shows all the user information associated with your processes, such as the process ID, percentage of CPU use, percentage of real memory usage, the virtual address size of the process, and the real memory size of the process.
**Keyword:** job control, background processing
**See Also:** bg, fg, jobs, kill

Column markers:
- ALL / SVR4 SCO / POWER
- ALL / BSD / POWER
- ALL / SVR4 OSF / POWER
- ALL / ALL / POWER
- ALL / BSD / POWER

| | | |
|---|---|---|

## ps -u $USER

| | | |
|---|---|---|
| ALL | SVR4 | POWER |

This command shows you all the processes that you have currently running.

**Keyword:** job control, background processing

**See Also:** bg, fg, jobs, kill

## ps -v

| | | |
|---|---|---|
| ALL | BSD | POWER |

This command shows a listing of your processes with information about the virtual address size of each process.

**Keyword:** job control, background processing

**See Also:** bg, fg, jobs, kill

## ps eww

| | | |
|---|---|---|
| ALL | BSD | POWER |

This command shows the job status and the entire environment.

**Keyword:** job control, background processing

**See Also:** bg, fg, jobs, kill

## ps | sort -nr | grep -v "PID TT"

| | | |
|---|---|---|
| ALL | SVR4 SCO OSF | POWER |

This command displays jobs in reverse order and removes all header information.

**Keyword:** job control, background processing

**See Also:** bg, fg, jobs, kill

## PS1

| | | |
|---|---|---|
| SH KSH | ALL | ALL |

This environment variable determines the primary prompt string.

**Keyword:** user environment

**See Also:** cd, printenv, set

## PS2

| | | |
|---|---|---|
| SH KSH | ALL | ALL |

This environment variable determines the secondary prompt string.

**Keyword:** user environment

**See Also:** cd, printenv, set

## PS3

| | | |
|---|---|---|
| KSH | ALL | ALL |

This environment variable determines the prompt used inside a Korn shell select loop.

| KSH | ALL | ALL |
| --- | --- | --- |

KSH ALL ALL

**Keyword:** user environment
**See Also:** cd, env, printenv, set

## PS4

This environment variable sets the prompt that appears when you are in debug mode. The **-x** option to the shell, which you can activate with **set**, turns on this type of debugging mode.
**Keyword:** programming
**See Also:** cd, env, printenv, set

## pushd

This command swaps the top two directories on the stack. Your working directory changes to the second directory on the stack.
**Keyword:** directories, user environment
**See Also:** cd, dirs, popd

## pushd +7

Specifying a numeric argument to **pushd** rotates the coinciding directory to the top of the stack. It also changes directories to this directory. Directories are recognized in numerical order beginning with 0 (top of the stack).
**Keyword:** directories, user environment
**See Also:** cd, dir, popd

## pushd /home/bin

The **pushd** command is a C shell built-in, and is used in conjunction with the **dirs** and **popd** commands. When you execute **pushd**, it changes to the specified directory and adds the directory name to the top of the stack.
**Keyword:** directories, user environment
**See Also:** cd, dir, popd

## puzzle

This X client program gives you a chance to relax while playing a game. It is modeled after the children's puzzle games in which you moves tiles until all tiles are numerically arranged. Use the **-geometry** or **-size** options to create a larger puzzle.
**Keyword:** games
**See Also:** ico, maze

## pwck

ALL  OSF  SYSADM

This command checks the **/etc/passwd** file and reports any potential problems to standard output. If you have added a user and not created a home directory, or you haven't given a shell to the user, then these errors are reported.

**Keyword:**   system setup

**Files:**   /etc/passwd

**See Also:**   passwd, sysadm, sysadmsh

## pwconv

ALL  SVR4  SYSADM

This command looks at **/etc/passwd**, and updates the **/etc/shadow** file with any changes that may have been made to **/etc/passwd**. This is useful for adding or removing users by hand, and then having the system recognize the changes. Once you have finished editing the **/etc/passwd** file, you can have your changes take effect on the system by running **pwconv**.

**Keyword:**   system setup

**Files:**   /etc/passwd, /etc/shadow

**See Also:**   passwd, sysadm, sysadmsh

## PWD

KSH  ALL  SCRIPT

This is the environment variable that is set to the current directory.

**Keyword:**   user environment

**See Also:**   cd, printenv, pwd, set

## pwd

ALL  ALL  END

This command outputs the current working directory to your terminal window.

**Keyword:**   user environment

**See Also:**   cd, chdir

## qprt report.doc

ALL  AIX  ALL

This command prints the **report.doc** file on the default printer. If the default printer is busy, your print job is sent to the bottom of the print queue.

**Keyword:**   printing

**Files:**   /etc/qconfig

**See Also:**   lp, lpr, pr

### quot -a

| | | |
|---|---|---|
| ALL | ALL | SYSADM |

This command outputs a listing of how many blocks are owned by each user on the system, for every mounted filesystem.

**Keyword:** system information

**See Also:** df, du, fsck, quota

### quot -c /dev/rz1c

| | | |
|---|---|---|
| ALL | ALL | SYSADM |

This command outputs three columns that show the file size in blocks, the number of files of that size, and cumulative total of blocks in a file of that size or smaller.

**Keyword:** system information

**See Also:** df, du, fsck, quota

### quot -f /dev/rz1c

| | | |
|---|---|---|
| ALL | ALL | SYSADM |

This command outputs the amount of space used and the number of files owned by each user.

**Keyword:** system information

**See Also:** df, du, fsck, quota

### quota

| | | |
|---|---|---|
| ALL | ALL | END |

This command shows your disk quota. Compared to the **quot** command, **quota** is designed for all users.

**Keyword:** system information

**See Also:** df, du, fsck, mount

### quota -v perkie

| | | |
|---|---|---|
| ALL | ALL | POWER SYSADM |

This command shows user **perkie**'s disk quota and disk usage on all the mounted filesystems that have enforced quotas.

**Keyword:** system information

**See Also:** df, du, fsck, quot

### quotacheck -a

| | | |
|---|---|---|
| ALL | BSD | SYSADM |

This command checks the quota consistency of all the filesystems listed in the **/etc/fstab** file.

**Keyword:** system setup

**See Also:** df, du, fsck, mount

## quotacheck -a

| | | |
|---|---|---|
| ALL | SVR4 | SYSADM |

This command checks the quota consistency of all the filesystems listed in the **/etc/mnttab** file as read–write with disk quotas. It also checks all the filesystems in the **/etc/vfstab** file that are marked **rq**.

**Keyword:** system setup

**See Also:** df, du, fsck, mount

## quotacheck -v /dev/rz1c

| | | |
|---|---|---|
| ALL | ALL | SYSADM |

This command is used to show any differences between calculated and recorded disk quotas.

**Keyword:** system setup

**See Also:** df, du, fsck, quota, mount

## quotaon -a

| | | |
|---|---|---|
| ALL | ALL | SYSADM |

This command turns on the quota system for all filesystems marked as read–write with quotas. Filesystems are marked in **/etc/fstab** on BSD systems and **/etc/mnttab** on System V platforms.

**Keyword:** system setup

**See Also:** df, du, fsck, quot, quota, mount

## r

| | | |
|---|---|---|
| KSH | ALL | ALL |

The **r** built-in in the Korn shell reruns the last executed command. The **r** command is actually an alias of **fc -e -**, which is predefined by the shell.

**Keyword:** keyboard shortcuts

**Files:** $HOME/.profile, $HOME/.kshrc

**See Also:** fc, history

## RANDOM

| | | |
|---|---|---|
| KSH | ALL | SCRIPT |

This environment variable stores a random number between 0 and 32767. A new number is generated with each reference.

**Keyword:** math

**See Also:** date, expr, random

## random

| | | |
|---|---|---|
| ALL | SVR4 | SCRIPT |

The **random** command outputs either a 1 or a 0 to the terminal window. Use this command in a shell script as follows:

```
num=`random`
```

**Keyword:**    math
**See Also:**    date, expr, ps

### random -s 97

This command returns a random number between 0 and 97 as an exit value, but not to standard output. Thus, you would not set the RANDOM variable.

**Keyword:**    math
**See Also:**    date, expr, ps

### random 83

This command outputs a random number between 0 and 83 to the terminal window. You can generate random numbers in the range of 0 to 255. Here is how to use **random** with a variable:

```
num=`random 83`
```

**Keyword:**    math
**See Also:**    date, expr, ps

### rcmd megasun ls -altF /home3 \> /home3/emily/dirlist

This command is similar to another example. The difference is that instead of returning the **ls** output to the local system, the output is redirected to a file on the remote system.

**Keyword:**    networking, Internet
**Files:**    $HOME/.rhosts, /etc/hosts.equiv
**See Also:**    rcp, rlogin, telnet, xhost, xterm

### rcmd megasun ls -altF /home3 | more

On SCO systems, you find **rcmd** instead of **rsh**. The two programs work almost identically and have the same goal: to run programs on a remote system and return the output to the local system. In the example, **rcmd** executes **ls** on **megasun** and pipes the output through **more** and back to the local system.

**Keyword:**    networking, Internet
**Files:**    $HOME/.rhosts, /etc/hosts.equiv
**See Also:**    rcp, rlogin, telnet, xhost, xterm

| ALL | SVR4 BSD | POWER |
| --- | --- | --- |

### rcp -p sparky:/home2/report.doc /u1/perkie

This command copies the **report.doc** file from the remote machine **sparky** and puts it on the local computer, maintaining the same modification times, access times, and modes on both systems.

**Keyword:** file handling

**Files:** $HOME/.rhosts, /etc/hosts.equiv

**See Also:** cp, cpio, find, ftp, tar

| ALL | ALL | POWER |
| --- | --- | --- |

### rcp -r /home/perkie aixpilot:/u1/perkie/

This moves the local directory **/home/perkie** and everything in it to the remote computer called **aixpilot**, and puts it in the **/u1/perkie/** directory. For this command to work, an appropriate **$HOME/.rhosts** file must be set up on the remote system.

**Keyword:** file handling

**Files:** $HOME/.rhosts, /etc/hosts.equiv

**See Also:** cp, cpio, find, ftp, tar

| ALL | BSD | POWER |
| --- | --- | --- |

### rcp -r aixpilot:/u1/mail /home/perkie/

This will move the **mail** directory and everything in it that is located on the remote computer called **aixpilot**, and put it in the **/home/perkie/** directory on the local computer. For this command to work, the name of the local computer must be in a file called **.rhosts** in the user's home directory on **aixpilot**. This can be a convenient command, but it can create a security hole.

**Keyword:** networking, file handling

**Files:** $HOME/.rhosts, /etc/hosts.equiv

**See Also:** cp, cpio, find, ftp, tar

| ALL | ALL | ALL |
| --- | --- | --- |

### rcp sales.jun aixpilot:/home/emily

The **rcp** command copies files and directories between systems on the network. This example simply copies **sales.jun** to **/home/alans** on the remote **aixpilot** system. In order for the example to work, the remote system must have a **.rhosts** file in the **home** directory. In the file, on a line by itself, must be the name of the local host followed by the name of the user. For example, for **alans** to copy **sales.jun** from the local computer **alpha**, the line would look like this:

```
alpha alans
```

As an alternative to **$HOME/.rhosts**, you can allow total equivalence between systems by editing the **/etc/hosts.equiv** file. If you choose this method, you need only enter the host-name of each equivalent system (each on its own line in the file). Note that both **/etc/hosts.equiv** and **$HOME/.rhosts** are security holes, so you should use either only in secure environments.

**Keyword:**   networking, file handling

**Files:**   $HOME/.rhosts, /etc/hosts.equiv

**See Also:**   cp, cpio, find, ftp, tar

### rcp sales.jun emily@aixpilot:sales.jun

This example does the same thing as the previous example. You might prefer it, though, because you don't have to specify the home directory on the remote system.

**Keyword:**   networking, file handling

**Files:**   $HOME/.rhosts, /etc/hosts.equiv

**See Also:**   cp, cpio, find, ftp, tar

### rcs report.rcs

This command is used to create the Revision Control System (RCS) management file called **report.rcs**. This file stores a change log and access list of users who work on the report, among other things. After this command has been executed, you can start using RCS.

**Keyword:**   file revision, programming

**See Also:**   rcsintro

### rcsintro

This is actually a **man** page that gives an introduction to the Revision Control System (RCS). The introduction explains RCS and provides command examples. Just enter **man rcsintro**.

**Keyword:**   file revision, programming

**See Also:**   rcs

### rdate

This command checks the network for date and time information. It is usually run at boot time; it checks the network twice, then uses the median of the two results to set the system time.

ALL   ALL   ALL

ALL   FSF   POWER

ALL   FSF   POWER

ALL   ALL   SYSADM

**Keyword:** system setup
**See Also:** cal, calendar, date

## rdist

| | | |
|---|---|---|
| ALL | OSF | POWER SYSADM |

The **rdist** command makes sure that files are consistent on different computer systems. It executes according to an instruction file called **distfile**, which is located in the current directory. Usually **rdist** is run by **cron** so it can automatically update files on different systems. Some systems do not support **rdist**, however, because of security considerations.

**Keyword:** file revision, networking
**See Also:** grep, rcp, sed

## read

| | | |
|---|---|---|
| SH KSH | ALL | SCRIPT |

This shell command is used to read the standard input. It is most useful in writing shell scripts. This command reads only one line of input, and if arguments are provided to **read**, it assigns each word of input to one argument.

**Keyword:** programming
**See Also:** cat, echo, print

## readonly

| | | |
|---|---|---|
| KSH | ALL | ALL |

This command outputs a list of all the environment variables that are set to **readonly** mode. This means that any variables that are shown can't be changed in this session. The only way you can change them is to kill the shell and restart it.

**Keyword:** user environment
**See Also:** echo, env, printenv

## reboot

| | | |
|---|---|---|
| ALL | SCO BSD | SYSADM |

This command halts the system, then automatically reboots it.

**Keyword:** shutdown, startup
**See Also:** fastboot, fasthalt, halt, haltsys (SCO), init, shutdown

## reboot -q

| | | |
|---|---|---|
| ALL | BSD | SYSADM |

This command quickly reboots the system, without killing all the processes or syncing the disks.

**Keyword:** shutdown, startup
**See Also:** fastboot, fasthalt, halt, haltsys (SCO), init, shutdown

### red .cshrc

This command is used to start the interactive editor **red**. This editor is strictly a line editor, similar to **ed**. We can't think of any reason that you would want to use this, but just in case, here it is.

**Keyword:**   text editing

**See Also:**   ed, emacs, vi

### refer report.bib | troff > report.troff

This command reads in the **report.bib** bibliography file and then creates **troff**-formatted output in a file called **report.troff**. Options to **refer** include **-a**, which reverses the author's first and last names, and **-b**, which tells **refer** not to include any flags in the output text.

**Keyword:**   text editing

**See Also:**   addbib, indexbib, lookbib, nroff, troff

### renice +1 987 -u root -p 455

This command changes priorities for the two processes specified by the job IDs 987 and 455, as well as all processes owned by **root**.

**Keyword:**   program execution, job control

**See Also:**   bg, fg, kill, nice, ps

### renice 20 1052

The **renice** command is a BSD contribution. The SVR4 software includes **renice** in its compatibility package. On an SVR4 system, the example command would yield a **nice** value of 39. On a BSD system, it would yield a **nice** value of 19. In both cases, the job identified by PID **1052** would have the lowest possible priority. Additionally, although the **nice** value on SVR4 systems does not match the expected result, **renice** makes the necessary adjustments. For example, if you issued **renice -20 1052** after entering the example, the **nice** value would drop to 0. If you then issued **renice 1 1052**, the **nice** value would jump to 21. The reason for the difference is that SVR4 uses a **nice** range of 0 to 39 and BSD uses a range of -20 to 20. Note that you must be a superuser to increase the priority of a process beyond it normal median, which is 20 on SVR4 systems and 0 on BSD systems.

**Keyword:**   program execution, job control

**See Also:**   bg, fg, kill, nice, ps

**ALL   ALL   ALL**

**ALL   SVR4   POWER**
**Solaris**
**SunOS**

**ALL   BSD   SYSADM**
**SVR4**

**ALL   BSD   SYSADM**
**SVR4**

## repquota -av

ALL  ALL  SYSADM

This command shows the filesystem quotas for all the filesystems that have **rq** in the mount options field of the **/etc/vfstab** file (SVR4), or that are listed in **/etc/fstab** (BSD). The **-v** option includes a header line.

**Keyword:** system information

**Files:** /etc/vfstab (SVR4), /etc/fstab (BSD)

**See Also:** df, du, find

## repquota /dev/rz3c

ALL  ALL  SYSADM

This **repquota** command shows the filesystem quotas and disk usage for the **/dev/rz3c** filesystem.

**Keyword:** system information

**See Also:** df, du, find

## reset

ALL  ALL  END

This command is an alias of **tset**. It is used to reset a terminal to its original line values. When entered without options, **reset** reads the value of the **TERM** environment variable to set the terminal.

**Keyword:** terminals

**Files:** $HOME/.profile, $HOME/.login

**See Also:** set, setenv, tset

## resize

CSH  XWIN  ALL

The **resize** client program is used with windows that cannot inform associated processes of the fact that the window has been resized. You may find that this happens frequently when you use an Xterm window to log in via a modem to another system. C shell users can use the following alias:

```
alias rs 'set noglob; eval `resize`; unset noglob'
```

**Keyword:** X resources

**Files:** /etc/termcap (BSD), /usr/share/lib/terminfo (SVR4)

**See Also:** tset, stty, tic

## resize > tempfile; . tempfile

SH
KSH  XWIN  ALL

These two commands allow Bourne and Korn shell users to use the **resize** client program. Unlike the C shell, which uses **resize** with its alias facility, Bourne and Korn shell users must *source* the output from the **resize** command. The source command for the Bourne and Korn shells is the dot (or period) character. Alternatively, you could use a shell function to automate the two-command sequence:

```
rs() {
resize > /tmp/rs.$$
. /tmp/rs.$$
rm /tmp/rs.$$     return; }
```

The added benefit of using a shell function is that the temporary file is automatically removed. Note that shell functions are usually included in the individual user's **.profile** file.

**Keyword:**   X resources

**Files:**   /etc/termcap (BSD), /usr/share/lib/terminfo (SVR4)

**See Also:**   tset, stty, tic

### restore

ALL   SVR4   SYSADM
      BSD

The **restore** command retrieves individual files, directories, and filesystems from archive diskettes and tapes. It is available on most systems with the notable exception of Solaris, which uses **ufsrestore**. On most other systems, the **restore** command ships in tandem with a backup command (which has various names). In the versions of UNIX covered by *The UNIX and X Command Compendium*, there are essentially three implementations of **restore**: the BSD version, which works with **dump** and appears on SunOS and OSF; the SVR3/4 version, which works with **backup** and and appears on SCO, AIX, and some SVR4 systems (Motorola and NCR systems, for example); and the SVR4 version.

```
SVR4:    restore [-ciot] [-d device] | [pattern]
SVR4.2:  restore [-o targ] [-d date] [-mn] [-sv] [-PSA device]
BSD:     restore [- irRtx] [files]
SunOS:   restore [-irRtx] [files]
Solaris: (uses ufsrestore)
SCO:     restore [-ciotd] [pattern]
OSF1:    restore [-irRtxbcdfFhmNsvyYZ] [argument]
AIX:     restore [-bfpqrstTvxBhimRydMX] [file]
```

In some of the examples that follow, we use the **$TAPE** environment variable. Refer to the example for **$TAPE** for a roundup of popular devices.

**Keyword:**   backup and restore

**See Also:**   backup, cpio, dump, tar, TAPE

### restore -c -d /dev/fd0

ALL · SVR4 SCO · SYSADM

The SVR3/4 **restore** utility is a front end to **cpio**. The example restores from a diskette drive to the current directory on the hard disk. The **-c** option specifies a complete **restore** operation. The **-d** option specifies the device. On an SVR4 system, you might enter the following to **restore** from a diskette backup:

```
restore -c -d /dev/fd/0
```

On an SCO system, which is styled on the SVR3 **/dev** hierarchy, you would use the same command, with a different device name:

```
restore -c -d /dev/rdsk/f0q18d
```

In the example, we use the generic **fd0**. If your system doesn't have a generic **fd0** and you want to create one, use a link like this:

```
ln /dev/fd0 /dev/fd/0
```

**Keyword:**   backup and restore

**See Also:**   backup, cpio, TAPE

### restore -c -o -d /dev/fd0

ALL · SVR4 SCO · SYSADM

The **-o** option in SVR3/4 tells **restore** to overwrite existing files in the **restore** path on the hard disk. The default behavior of **restore** is not to overwrite existing files.

**Keyword:**   backup and restore

**See Also:**   backup, cpio, TAPE

### restore -c -t -d /dev/$TAPE

ALL · SVR4 SCO · SYSADM

The **-t** option to the SVR3/4 version of **restore** specifies a tape device. It must be used in conjunction with the **-d** option.

**Keyword:**   backup and restore

**See Also:**   backup, cpio, TAPE

### restore -i -d /dev/fd0

ALL · SVR4 SCO · SYSADM

The **-i** option in the SVR3/4 version of **restore** orders up a directory listing of the media in the device. The example specifies a diskette drive, but **-i** works the same way for tape drives. Note that the command works only if the archive was created with **backup**.

**Keyword:**   backup and restore

**See Also:**   backup, cpio, TAPE

### restore -if $TAPE

AIX warrants a special entry because it is slightly different in that it can optionally be called from the **smit** interface, works with **backup** instead of **dump**, and has some special instructions. For example, if you must **restore** from an 8mm tape, you need to complement **restore** with other commands. IBM recommends the following:

```
dd if=/dev/rmt0 bs=51200 | restore -xvqf-
restore -xvqf- < /dev/rmt0
`cat /dev/rmt0 | restore -xvqf-`
```

**Keyword:**   backup and restore

**See Also:**   backup, dd, fsck, mkfs, smit

### restore -m -d "10/1/94" -A /dev/rdsk/c0t6d0s0

With the **-d** option, you can specify a deadline for a **restore** operation. This is useful if the restore need not occur immediately, but you still want it to occur by a given date. Also new in this example is the **-A** option, which specifies that an entire disk be restored, rather than just a disk partition (**-P**) or a filesystem (**-S**).

**Keyword:**   backup and restore

**Files:**   /etc/bkup: bkhist.tab, rsstatus.tab, rsnotify.tab

**See Also:**   backup, mail, mailx, rsnotify, rsoper, urestore

### restore -m -o /dev/dsk/c0t6d0sa -P /dev/rdsk/c0t6d0s1

This command restores from the archived partition **/dev/rdsk/c0t6d0s1** to the system disk partition **/dev/dsk/c0t6d0sa**. Again, the **-m** option specifies that mail be sent to the privileged user who made the request. The **-o** option specifies the system partition. The **-P** option specifies the archive partition.

**Keyword:**   backup and restore

**Files:**   /etc/bkup: bkhist.tab, rsstatus.tab, rsnotify.tab

**See Also:**   backup, mail, mailx, rsnotify, rsoper, urestore

### restore -m -o /oldusr -S /usr

This SVR4 **restore** command requests that **/usr** be restored to **/oldusr**. The **-m** option specifies mail. The **-o** option specifies the filesystem on the system disk.

ALL   AIX   SYSADM

ALL   SVR4   SYSADM

ALL   SVR4   SYSADM

ALL   SVR4   SYSADM

**Keyword:** backup and restore
**Files:** /etc/bkup: bkhist.tab, rsstatus.tab, rsnotify.tab
**See Also:** backup, mail, mailx, rsnotify, rsoper, urestore

### restore -m -S /usr

ALL  SVR4  SYSADM

The **restore** utility introduced with SVR4 is part of a suite of tools that lets all users participate in the backup and restore processes. The **restore** program, however, is reserved for privileged users, because it can initiate a **restore** immediately in cases when the archive is available on the system or network. The example command illustrates this approach, and if the **restore** operation cannot occur immediately, **restore** sends mail to the user (this is the role of **-m**).

**Keyword:** backup and restore
**Files:** /etc/bkup: bkhist.tab, rsstatus.tab, rsnotify.tab
**See Also:** backup, mail, mailx, rsnotify, rsoper, urestore

### restore -n -S /home3

ALL  SVR4  SYSADM

This command does not request a **restore** operation. Instead, the **-e** option sends mail to the user containing a directory listing of the archive. With **-n**, the **-m** option is unnecessary.

**Keyword:** backup and restore
**Files:** /etc/bkup: bkhist.tab, rsstatus.tab, rsnotify.tab
**See Also:** backup, mail, mailx, rsnotify, rsoper, urestore

### restore -r -f $TAPE

ALL  BSD  SYSADM
SunOS
OSF
AIX

This command reads **/dev/rst0** and restores all files to the current working directory and any subdirectories, if necessary. The **-r** option is recommended for restoring a level 0 backup to an empty filesystem. You might use **restore -r** in the following manner:

```
newfs /dev/rrz4g
mount /dev/rz4g /mnt
cd /mnt
restore i-r
```

On an AIX system, you would use the following:

```
mkfs /dev/hd1
mount /dev/hd1 /filesys
cd /filesys
restore -r
```

**Keyword:** backup and restore

**Files:** ./restoresymtab, /etc/disktab, /tmp/rstdir*, /tmp/rstmode*

**See Also:** backup (AIX), dump, mkfs, mount, newfs, smit, sysadm, sysadmsh

### restore -T -f $TAPE

ALL    BSD    SYSADM
       SunOS
       OSF
       AIX

You do not have to use interactive mode with **restore** (although many users prefer it). This command line example reads from **/dev/rst0** and displays filenames on the archive. If a filesystem was backed up, it displays the inode numbers as well.

**Keyword:** backup and restore

**Files:** ./restoresymtab, /etc/disktab, /tmp/rstdir*, /tmp/rstmode*

**See Also:** backup (AIX), dump, mkfs, mount, newfs, smit, sysadm, sysadmsh

### restore -t -o -d /dev/$TAPE "/usr/biz/sales/*.jun"

ALL    SVR4    SYSADM
       SCO

To perform a selective **restore** operation, specify the path and filenames that you want to **restore**. The example restores all files with a **.jun** extension from the **/usr/biz/sales** archive path.

**Keyword:** backup and restore

**See Also:** backup, cpio, TAPE

### restore -xf $TAPE /home/sales

ALL    BSD    SYSADM
       SunOS
       OSF
       AIX

This command reads the files in **/home/sales** and restores them to the current directory and any necessary subdirectories on the hard disk.

**Keyword:** backup and restore

**Files:** ./restoresymtab, /etc/disktab, /tmp/rstdir*, /tmp/rstmode*

**See Also:** backup (AIX), dump, mkfs, mount, newfs, smit, sysadm, sysadmsh

### restore -xfs $TAPE 4

ALL    BSD    SYSADM
       SunOS
       OSF
       AIX

The **-s** option tells **restore** to skip the specified number of files when there are several dump files on the same tape. The example begins extracting after it reaches the fourth dump file.

**Keyword:** backup and restore

**Files:**  ./restoresymtab, /etc/disktab, /tmp/rstdir*, /tmp/rstmode*

**See Also:**  backup (AIX), dump, mkfs, mount, newfs, smit, sysadm, sysadmsh

### restore if $TAPE

ALL    BSD    SYSADM    SunOS    OSF    AIX

The BSD **restore** and its derivitives are fairly standard. The OSF version is quite extensive, but it shares the core set of options available on our BSD testbed systems. The example, which uses **$TAPE** to specify the tape drive, initiates interactive mode via a command line. When you see the command line prompt, which is simply **restore** followed by a **>** symbol, you can be sure that **restore** has accessed the tape. If it cannot access the tape, it displays an error and exits. At the prompt, you can enter any of the following:

```
add [file]       Add files/directories to extraction list.
cd dir           Change directories on the archive tape.
delete [file]    Delete files/directories on extraction list.
extract          Extract files/directories on extraction list.
help             Display a help listing of interactive commands.
ls [dir]         List files or current directory on archive.
pwd              Display pathname of current directory on archive.
quit             Exit the program immediately.
verbose          Toggle extended message output on and off.
```

In addition to these commands, OSF supports **setmodes**, which sets owner and file permissions; **what**, which displays the tape header information; and **debug**, which toggles debugging features.

**Keyword:**  backup and restore

**Files:**  ./restoresymtab, /etc/disktab, /tmp/rstdir*, /tmp/rstmode*

**See Also:**  dump, mkfs, mount, newfs, sysadm, sysadmsh

### return

SH    ALL    ALL
KSH

The **return** command is generally used in shell scripts. It signals the end of a function definition. If you enter **return** at the command line, the shell is likely to complain that you "cannot return when not in function." You can, however, define a function at the command line, as in the following:

```
t() { date  +"%r %d %h %y (%a)"; return; }
```

**Keyword:**  programming

**See Also:**  exit

### rev backward.txt

| | | |
|---|---|---|
| ALL | OSF | ALL |

This command reverses the order of the characters in a file and outputs the reversed characters to the screen. If **backward.txt** contained the line, ".og ew ereH," **rev** would output "Here we go."

**Keyword:**　　text handling

**See Also:**　　awk, cat, sed

### rksh

| | | |
|---|---|---|
| KSH | ALL | ALL |

This is one of the names of the restricted Korn shell. It also goes by the name of **krsh** (although we haven't included an entry for **krsh**).

**Keyword:**　　security, user environment

**See Also:**　　ksh, Rsh, rsh, set

### rlogin aixpilot

| | | |
|---|---|---|
| ALL | ALL | END |

This command logs you into the remote system **aixpilot**. If a **$HOME/.rhosts** file exists in the home directory of the remote system, and the file includes a line with the local hostname and your username, you can log in automatically without supplying a password.

**Keyword:**　　networking

**See Also:**　　rcp, rsh, telnet

### rlogin aixpilot -l alans

| | | |
|---|---|---|
| ALL | ALL | END |

This command logs you into the remote system **aixpilot** with the username **alans**. Use this command if you want to log in as **alans** when your current username is something different.

**Keyword:**　　networking

**See Also:**　　rcp, rsh, telnet

### rm old.txt

| | | |
|---|---|---|
| ALL | ALL | END |

This command erases the **old.text** file from the working directory.

**Keyword:**　　file handling

**See Also:**　　cp, mv, rcp

### rm - -weird.txt

| | | |
|---|---|---|
| ALL | ALL | POWER |

Using the hyphen character as an option to **rm** is another way to remove a file that begins with a hyphen. Because this is relatively easy, and because the hyphen has limited uses (other than signifying options), you could use the hyphen to group sets of files.

**Keyword:** file handling

**See Also:** cp, mv, rcp

## rm -e *

ALL   BSD   END

This command erases all the files in the current directory, and displays a message after deleting each file.

**Keyword:** file handling

**See Also:** cp, mv, rcp

## rm -f report.doc

ALL   ALL   END

This command deletes the **report.doc** file, even if it is write-protected. If the **report.doc** file doesn't exist, no error message will be output.

**Keyword:** file handling

**See Also:** cp, mv, rcp

## rm -i *

ALL   ALL   END

This command asks for confirmation before deleting every file in the current directory.

**Keyword:** file handling

**See Also:** cp, mv, rcp

## rm -r /home/perkie/temp

ALL   ALL   END

This command erases the **/home/perkie/temp** directory and all the contents of that directory, including subdirectories.

**Keyword:** file handling

**See Also:** cp, mv, rcp

## rm ./-weird.txt

ALL   ALL   POWER

Here is one way to remove a file that begins with a hyphen. Because the leading hyphen on the filename is not the first character, the file can be deleted.

**Keyword:** file handling

**See Also:** cp, mv, rcp

### rmdir /u1/perkie/stuff

ALL  ALL  END

This command deletes the **/u1/perkie/stuff** directory. This works only if **/u1/perkie/stuff** is already empty.

**Keyword:** file handling

**See Also:** mkdir, mv, rm

### roffbib -e report.bib

ALL  SVR4  POWER
Solaris
SunOS

The **roffbib** command reads the specified file and displays records in bibliographic format. The command is commonly used with **sortbib**, as in the following:

```
sortbib report.bib | roffbib
```

**Keyword:** writing, text handling

**Files:** /usr/share/lib/tmac/tmac.bib

**See Also:** addbib, indxbib, lookbib, refer, sortbib

### rsh (restricted sh)

SH  ALL  SYSADM

This command at first may seem identical to **sh**; most of the functions of **rsh** are identical to those of **sh**. What is different is that you can't change directories in **rsh**, you can't change **$PATH** and **$SHELL**, you can't specify commands or paths with a **/** in them, and you can't redirect output. The **rsh** command is useful for setting up users with limited access to the system. For example, you might use it if you want to grant access only to a single application. Typically, you would have **rsh** start using the **/etc/passwd** file, but it can also be started as **sh -r**.

**Keyword:** user environment

**Files:** /etc/passwd, $HOME/.profile

**See Also:** csh, ksh, sh

### Rsh (restricted sh)

SH  OSF  SYSADM
AIX

On some UNIX systems, the restricted shell is called **Rsh**. The uppercase **R** avoids the naming conflict between the restricted shell and the remote shell execution command, **rsh**. It is interesting to note, too, that this problem exists, even though most versions of **sh** support the **-r** option to invoke the restricted shell.

**Keyword:** user environment

**Files:** /etc/passwd, $HOME/.profile

**See Also:** sh, rsh

### rsh aixpilot -l perkie xterm -ls -n aixpilot -T aixpilot -display sparky:0

ALL  ALL  ALL

This command runs the program **xterm** on the remote computer **aixpilot**, under the username **perkie**. The **xterm** is displayed on the computer **sparky**, and is titled **aixpilot**. The icon for the **xterm** is also called **aixpilot**. For this command to work, you need a proper **$HOME/.rhosts** file.

**Keyword:**   networking

**See Also:**   rlogin, rcmd, telnet

### rsh aixpilot -n /usr/bin/X11/xterm -display alpha:0 &

CSH  XWIN  POWER

This command suppresses job control messages that occur in the C shell if you run the program in the background.

**Keyword:**   Internet, networking, window handling

**Files:**   $HOME/.rhosts, /etc/hosts.equiv

**See Also:**   rcmd (SCO), rcp, rlogin, telnet, xhost, xterm

### rsh aixpilot /usr/bin/X11/xterm -display alpha:0 &

ALL  XWIN  POWER

This **rsh** command executes **xterm** on a remote system named **aixpilot** and displays the Xterm window on the local system named **alpha**. The **:0** notation appended to **alpha** indicates the X Window display screen. In order for this command to work, the home directory of the user logging in must contain a file called **.rhosts**, which in turn must list the local system and username. Also, before executing a remote X Window command, be sure that you have used the xhost client to allow the remote system to access the local system.

**Keyword:**   Internet, networking, window handling

**Files:**   $HOME/.rhosts, /etc/hosts.equiv

**See Also:**   rcmd (SCO), rcp, rlogin, telnet, xhost, xterm

### rsh digital2 /usr/bin/X11/xterm -display alpha:0 -ls </dev/null &

CSH  XWIN  POWER

This is another way to suppress job control messages as described in the previous example.

**Keyword:**   Internet, networking, window handling

**Files:**   $HOME/.rhosts

**See Also:**   rcmd (SCO), rcp, rlogin, telnet, xhost, xterm

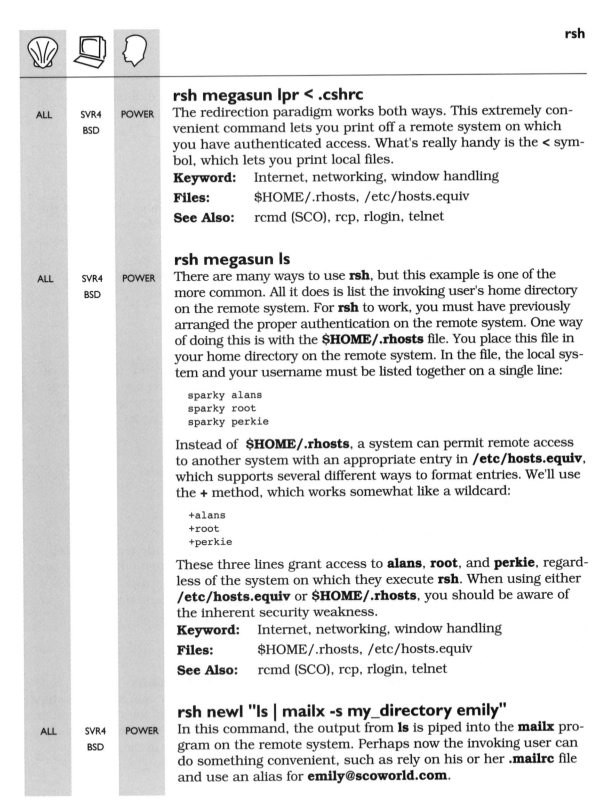

ALL    SVR4   POWER
BSD

## rsh megasun lpr < .cshrc

The redirection paradigm works both ways. This extremely convenient command lets you print off a remote system on which you have authenticated access. What's really handy is the **<** symbol, which lets you print local files.

**Keyword:**    Internet, networking, window handling

**Files:**      $HOME/.rhosts, /etc/hosts.equiv

**See Also:**   rcmd (SCO), rcp, rlogin, telnet

## rsh megasun ls

ALL    SVR4   POWER
BSD

There are many ways to use **rsh**, but this example is one of the more common. All it does is list the invoking user's home directory on the remote system. For **rsh** to work, you must have previously arranged the proper authentication on the remote system. One way of doing this is with the **$HOME/.rhosts** file. You place this file in your home directory on the remote system. In the file, the local system and your username must be listed together on a single line:

```
sparky alans
sparky root
sparky perkie
```

Instead of **$HOME/.rhosts**, a system can permit remote access to another system with an appropriate entry in **/etc/hosts.equiv**, which supports several different ways to format entries. We'll use the **+** method, which works somewhat like a wildcard:

```
+alans
+root
+perkie
```

These three lines grant access to **alans**, **root**, and **perkie**, regardless of the system on which they execute **rsh**. When using either **/etc/hosts.equiv** or **$HOME/.rhosts**, you should be aware of the inherent security weakness.

**Keyword:**    Internet, networking, window handling

**Files:**      $HOME/.rhosts, /etc/hosts.equiv

**See Also:**   rcmd (SCO), rcp, rlogin, telnet

## rsh newl "ls | mailx -s my_directory emily"

ALL    SVR4   POWER
BSD

In this command, the output from **ls** is piped into the **mailx** program on the remote system. Perhaps now the invoking user can do something convenient, such as rely on his or her **.mailrc** file and use an alias for **emily@scoworld.com**.

**Keyword:** Internet, networking, window handling
**Files:** $HOME/.rhosts, /etc/hosts.equiv
**See Also:** rcmd (SCO), rcp, rlogin, telnet

### rsh newl ls ">" dirfile

| | | |
|---|---|---|
| ALL | SVR4 BSD | POWER |

Look familiar? The only difference from the previous command is the use of quotation marks around the **>** symbol. This is all the difference in the world, though, because **dirfile** is saved to the remote system instead of the local system. Again, you can use **>>** the same way.

**Keyword:** Internet, networking, window handling
**Files:** $HOME/.rhosts, /etc/hosts.equiv
**See Also:** rcmd (SCO), rcp, rlogin, telnet

### rsh newl ls 2>/dev/null

| | | |
|---|---|---|
| ALL | SVR4 BSD | POWER |

This command is similar to the previous one, but takes care of any errant output. In some cases, an **stty** command can be generated by an **rsh** command. When the command fails, it generates an error message on the local system. The **2>/dev/null** expression eliminates this problem.

**Keyword:** Internet, networking, window handling
**Files:** $HOME/.rhosts, /etc/hosts.equiv
**See Also:** rcmd (SCO), rcp, rlogin, telnet

### rsh newl ls > dirfile

| | | |
|---|---|---|
| ALL | SVR4 BSD | POWER |

This command performs an **ls** command on the remote system **newl** and redirects the output to **dirfile** located on the local system. You can also use **>>** to append data to a file.

**Keyword:** Internet, networking, window handling
**Files:** $HOME/.rhosts, /etc/hosts.equiv
**See Also:** rcmd (SCO), rcp, rlogin, telnet

### rsh newl ls | mailx emily@scoworld.com

| | | |
|---|---|---|
| ALL | SVR4 BSD | POWER |

Here we are executing an **ls** on the remote system **newl**. This time the output is piped into **mailx**. The important point to remember is that the command uses the local machine's **mailx** system.

**Keyword:** Internet, networking, window handling
**Files:** $HOME/.rhosts, /etc/hosts.equiv
**See Also:** rcmd (SCO), rcp, rlogin, telnet

| | | |
|---|---|---|
| ALL | SVR4 BSD | POWER |

### rsh newl rcp megasun:/home/marky/sales.new .

Here is one of the dangers of the TCP/IP remote programs. In the example, **marky** is a guest on the local system, which unfortunately has another guest lacking scruples, but not lacking the root user password. All it takes is an **su marky** command on the local system, and the guest with no scruples can obtain files from **megasun**, which **marky** thought were "secure enough." By the way, **sales.new** is copied to **newl**, but it can be snapped up from there with another **rcp** command.

**Keyword:**   Internet, networking, window handling

**Files:**   $HOME/.rhosts, /etc/hosts.equiv

**See Also:**   rcmd (SCO), rcp, rlogin, telnet

| | | |
|---|---|---|
| ALL | SVR4 BSD | POWER |

### rsh newl rlogin megasun

If the previous command didn't convince you of the potential security hazards of **$HOME/.rhosts** and **/etc/hosts.equiv**, this one should. All the example does is allow full login access to the unscrupulous guest from the previous example. Of course, in both examples, you can prevent security abuses with proper administrative procedures. An interesting note to this scenario is that when the unscrupulous one logs out of **megasun**, he or she is in an active login session on **newl**.

**Keyword:**   Internet, networking, window handling

**See Also:**   rcmd (SCO), rcp, rlogin, telnet

**Files:**   $HOME/.rhosts, /etc/hosts.equiv

| | | |
|---|---|---|
| ALL | SVR4 | SYSADM |

### rsoper -c rest-883b

The **-c** option causes **rsoper** to cancel a job and mail notification to the user who originated the request.

**Keyword:**   backup and restore

**Files:**   /etc/device.tab, /etc/bkup: bkhist.tab, rsstatus.tab, rsnotify.tab

**See Also:**   backup, mail, mailx, restore, rsnotify, urestore

| | | |
|---|---|---|
| ALL | SVR4 | SYSADM |

### rsoper -d ctape1

The **rsoper** command handles requests to restore an archive. It is an SVR4-only command that interacts with the system restore service. Its purpose is to verify, cancel, or accept **restore** requests made by users and administrators alike. In order to run **rsoper**,

you must have superuser privileges. If you create an entry in
**/etc/device.tab**, you can refer to tape drives by shorthand
names. To create these aliases in **/etc/device.tab**, enter information similar to the following:

```
ctape1:/dev/rmt/c0t3d0s0:::desc="Cartridge Tape Drive - 150 Mb"
volume="cartridge tape" type="ctape" removable="true" mkdtab="true"
capacity="300000" bufsize="20480" norewind="/dev/rmt/c0t3d0s0n"
erasecmd="/sbin/tapecntl -e -d /dev/rmt/c0t3d0s0" display="true"
```

**Keyword:**  backup and restore

**Files:**  /etc/device.tab, /etc/bkup: bkhist.tab, rsstatus.tab,
rsnotify.tab

**See Also:**  backup, mail, mailx, restore, rsnotify, urestore

### rsoper -d ctape1 -u root -v

ALL  SVR4  SYSADM

After specifying **ctape1** as the device on which to service the
**restore** request, this command restricts honoring requests to the
**root** user. The **-v** option then tells **rsoper** to display each file and
directory as it is restored.

**Keyword:**  backup and restore

**Files:**  /etc/device.tab, /etc/bkup: bkhist.tab, rsstatus.tab,
rsnotify.tab

**See Also:**  backup, mail, mailx, restore, rsnotify, urestore

### rsoper -r rest-882b

ALL  SVR4  SYSADM

The **-r** option, which takes a **restore** job ID as an argument,
initiates a response to the user who requested the job. The user
receives mail acknowledging that the job has been marked complete.

**Keyword:**  backup and restore

**Files:**  /etc/device.tab, /etc/bkup: bkhist.tab, rsstatus.tab,
rsnotify.tab

**See Also:**  backup, mail, mailx, restore, rsnotify, urestore

### runacct

ALL  SVR4  OSF  AIX  SYSADM

This command is typically run by **cron** on a daily basis to determine the connection fee, disk usage charges, printer charges,
and other accounting items. It is actually a shell script that runs
other accounting programs, and then creates a report based on
the output of the other programs.

**Keyword:**  system information, security

**Files:**    /etc/passwd, /usr/lib/acct, /var/adm/pacct, /var/adm/wtmp

**See Also:**    acctcms, acctcom, acctcon, acctmerg, acctprc

### rup megasun

ALL    SunOS    POWER

This is a BSD command for displaying information about other hosts on the network. You can either specifically name a host, as in the example, or use **rup** without options, in which case it behaves similarly to the more common **ruptime**.

**Keyword:**    networking, Internet

**See Also:**    finger, netstat, ping, ruptime, rusers, rwho

### ruptime

ALL    ALL    SYSADM

The **ruptime** command outputs a listing of all network hosts running the **rwhod** daemon. Output data consists of hostname, how long each host has been running, how many users on each host, and the load average of each host.

**Keyword:**    networking, Internet

**See Also:**    finger, netstat, ping, rup, rusers, rwho

### rusers

ALL    ALL    SYSADM

This command is similar to **ruptime**, in that it pertains to remote systems. When you execute **rusers**, it outputs a listing of all the users logged into systems running the **rusersd** daemon. Default output consists of hostname and current users.

**Keyword:**    networking, Internet

**See Also:**    finger, netstat, ping, rup, ruptime, rwho, users, who

### rusers -a -l

ALL    ALL    SYSADM

With the **-a** and **-l** options (note that they must each have a hyphen), you can get a better look at network hosts and users. The **-a** option tells **rusers** to report on a host even if no one is logged in. The **-l** option provides a verbose listing:

```
alans    newl:tty2A          Mar  4 22:30              (local)
root     mobius1:tty02       Feb 24 15:56   1922:43    (local)
root     mobius1:ttyp0       Feb 24 15:56   407:19     (remote)
root     sparky:ttyp0        Mar  4 23:14              (newl)
root     next:console        Jan 31 19:36   13952:46
```

**Keyword:**    networking, Internet

**See Also:**    finger, netstat, ping, rup, ruptime, rwho, users, who

### rwall sparky

ALL  ALL  SYSADM

This command is similar to **wall**, which sends a message to all users. In the example, **rwall** sends a message to all users logged into the remote computer **sparky**. After issuing this command, you type a message, and after **rwall** receives an EOF (end-of-file) character, it sends the message.

**Keyword:**   network, Internet

**Files:**       /usr/spool/rwho/*

**See Also:**   mail, mailx, talk, wall, write

### rwho

ALL  ALL  SYSADM

By default, the **rwho** command lists all users who have logged into the network within the last hour. The command only works, however, if the system is running the **rwhod** daemon (see **ruptime**). Many sites feel this is an unnecessary additional burden to place on the network, and thus refrain from using **rwhod**. If you do encounter it, the output is roughly similar to that of the **who** command. Here is an example:

```
alans    scoworld:nty/015 Mar 4 22:59
root     scoworld:nty/017 Mar 4 22:59
perkie      new1:tcp/222 Mar 4 22:59
emily    sparky:inet/034 Mar 4 22:59
```

**Keyword:**   networking, Internet

**Files:**       /usr/spool/rwho/*

**See Also:**   finger, rup, ruptime, rusers, users, who

### rwho -a

ALL  ALL  ALL

This command lists users on network systems that are running the daemon **rwhod**. This command also shows those users who have been idle for over an hour.

**Keyword:**   networking

**See Also:**   finger, w, who

### savehist

CSH  ALL  SCRIPT

This environment variable displays the number of commands that are saved in the **home/.history** history file at the end of a session.

**Keyword:**   user environment

**See Also:**   history, job, ps

## SCCS

ALL    ALL    POWER

The **sccs** program provides the basic interface to the Source Code Control System (SCCS), which is included with the basic UNIX operating system software. Although primarily designed for programmers who need to maintain tight control over source code files, **sccs** can also be used to manage text and document files. The **sccs** program is derived from BSD and is located in **/usr/ucb** on System V platforms. SCO does not include **sccs** in its basic operating system. The program supports the following subcommands: **create**, **enter**, **edit**, **delget**, **deledit**, **fix**, **clean**, **unedit**, **info**, **check**, **tell**, **diffs**, and **print**. In order for **sccs** to work, you must have an SCCS directory defined. It is convenient to create SCCS in a project directory, where other users have equal access to project files. The multiuser aspects of **sccs** enhance document control when applied like this. Commands such as **check** let you easily determine when someone is already working on a file.

**Keyword:**    file revision, programming, documentation

**Files:**        /usr/sccs/*

**See Also:**    admin, help, PROJECTDIR

## sccs check

ALL    ALL    POWER

If you want to find out what files are being edited at any given time, use the **check** subcommand. The example produces output like this:

```
xmenu.jun is being edited: 1.3 1.4 alans 94/02/23 14:06:02
sales.jun is being edited: 1.1.1.2 emily 94/02/23 13:05:41
```

**Keyword:**    file revision, programming, documentation

**Files:**        /usr/sccs/*

**See Also:**    admin, help, PROJECTDIR

## sccs create sales.jun

ALL    ALL    POWER

The **create** subcommand tells **sccs** to create a file in the SCCS directory that duplicates the specified file. The new file is given an **s.** prefix to indicate that it is a SCCS file. The original file is prefixed with a comma. Thus, the example creates two files: **s.sales.jun** located in the SCCS directory, and **,sales.jun** located in the current directory.

**Keyword:**    file revision, programming, documentation

**Files:**        /usr/sccs/*

**See Also:**    admin, help, PROJECTDIR

| | | |
|---|---|---|
| ALL | ALL | POWER |

## sccs info -u emily

The **info** subcommand lets you get specific when you want to check for files being edited by other people. The **-u** argument to **info** causes **sccs** to narrow its checking to files being edited by **emily**.

**Keyword:**   file revision, programming, documentation

**Files:**   /usr/sccs/*

**See Also:**   admin, help, PROJECTDIR

| | | |
|---|---|---|
| ALL | ALL | POWER |

## sccs delget sales.jun

You return a file to the SCCS directory with the **delget** subcommand. Before this occurs, however, you must have created the SCCS version of the file and also used the **sccs edit** command to retrieve it from the SCCS directory (see the **sccs edit** example).

**Keyword:**   file revision, programming, documentation

**Files:**   /usr/sccs/*

**See Also:**   admin, help, PROJECTDIR

| | | |
|---|---|---|
| ALL | ALL | POWER |

## sccs diffs sales.jun

The **diffs** subcommand tells **sccs** to check the current version of the file against the SCCS version. If there are differences in the two files, they are reported in the format of the diff utility. The **diffs** subcommand also accepts most options recognized by **diff**.

**Keyword:**   file revision, programming, documentation

**Files:**   /usr/sccs/*

**See Also:**   admin, diff, help, PROJECTDIR

| | | |
|---|---|---|
| ALL | ALL | POWER |

## sccs edit sales.jun

The **edit** subcommand lets you obtain a file you have already stored in the SCCS directory (using the **create** subcommand). When you invoke a command similar to the example, the specified file appears in your current directory, no matter where it is stored.

**Keyword:**   file revision, programming, documentation

**Files:**   /usr/sccs/*

**See Also:**   admin, help, PROJECTDIR

| | | |
|---|---|---|
| ALL | ALL | POWER |

## sccs unedit

If you need to undo changes made to a file, use the **unedit** subcommand. It tells **sccs** to replace the current version of the file with the previously stored SCCS version. It's handy, but you can lose edits if you use the **unedit** subcommand at the wrong time.

**Keyword:**   file revision, programming, documentation

**Files:**   /usr/sccs/*

**See Also:**   admin, help, PROJECTDIR

### script $HOME/.sh_session

ALL   OSF   END

The **script** command is an OSF utility for making a transcript of a terminal session. In the example, the transcript is sent to the **.sh_session** file in the user's home directory. The **script** command also has a **-a** option to append subsequent sessions to the same file. (Things could get confusing if you use the same session file for multiple Xterm windows. On the other hand, **script** is an excellent tool for documentation writers or anyone else who needs to record commands and program output.)

**Keyword:**   user environment, documentation

**See Also:**   cat, echo, tee

### sdiff -l sales.jun sales.bak

ALL   ALL   POWER

The **-l** option tells **sdiff** to limit the display of matching lines to the left side of the screen or Xterm window. This makes it easier to spot differences in the second file (**sales.bak**).

**Keyword:**   text handling

**See Also:**   bdiff, diff, diff3

### sdiff -s -w 78 -o sales.sdiff sales.jun sales.bak

ALL   ALL   POWER

The **-o** option tells **sdiff** to combine **sales.jun** and **sales.bak**, in the case of the example. The output file, **sales.sdiff**, initially contains all matching lines. Then you get a chance to interactively combine the rest of the files because **sdiff** enters **ed** mode. At this point, you can use the following editing commands to finish combining the file:

```
l       Add left column to output file.
r       Add right column to output file.
s       Suppress printing matching lines.
v       Turn off the s option.
e l     Invoke ed to work on the left column.
e r     Invoke ed to work on the right column.
e b     Invoke ed to work on both columns.
e       Invoke ed with contents in output file.
q       Exit ed and sdiff.
```

**403**

**Keyword:** text handling
**See Also:** bdiff, diff, diff3

## sdiff -s -w 78 sales.jun sales.bak

ALL   ALL   POWER

The **-s** option tells **sdiff** not to display matching lines at all. The **-w** option, which is convenient for ASCII terminal users, tells **sdiff** to narrow the display to a column width of **78**. The default column width is 130 characters.

**Keyword:** text handling
**See Also:** bdiff, diff, diff3

## sdiff sales.jun sales.bak

ALL   ALL   POWER

The **sdiff** command is a so-called beautifier. It takes the output from **diff** and formats its adjacent columns. The format used includes whitespace between identical lines, a separating **<** if a line appears only in the first file (**sales.jun**), a separating **>** if the line appears only in the second file (**sales.bak**), and a separating I for lines that are different.

**Keyword:** text handling
**See Also:** bdiff, diff, diff3

## SECONDS

KSH   ALL   ALL

This environment variable contains the number of seconds the shell has been in operation. You can obtain the value of **$SECONDS** with the following commands:

```
set | grep SECONDS
echo $SECONDS
```

**Keyword:** user environment
**See Also:** date, ksh, set, time

## sed "/$1/ { n; /$2/d; }" sep.txt

ALL   ALL   POWER

You can adapt this example to a script or let it stand alone as a shell function or alias. The only difference between this command and others using the **n** subcommand is the use of double quotes, which are necessary for **sed** to evaluate **$1** and **$2** as shell arguments. If the example were a script unto itself, you would call it like this:

```
foo string1 string2
```

As a result, all lines that contained **string2** and followed a line containing **string1** would be printed to standard output.

**Keyword:**  text display, text formatting, programming

**See Also:**  awk, cat, cut, grep, join, paste

### sed ´$r review.org´ header > review.txt

ALL  ALL  POWER

Instead of inserting **header** at the beginning of the file—and requiring the somewhat artificial introduction of a blank line in the original file—this command tacks **review.org** onto the end of **header**. Of course, you could do the same thing with **cat**, but using **sed**, especially with a script, you can do other things at the same time.

**Keyword:**  text handling, text formatting, programming

**See Also:**  awk, cat, cut, grep, join, paste

### sed ´/--*$/ { n; /^$/d; }´ sep.txt

ALL  ALL  POWER

This example deletes blank lines that follow the first regular expression—which, for example purposes, consists of two or more hyphens. The **n** command tells **sed** to process the line following this regular expression. Next, the regular expression /^$/ specifies that only blank lines should be processed. Finally, the **d** command tells **sed** to delete the blank lines.

**Keyword:**  text display, text formatting, programming

**See Also:**  awk, cat, cut, grep, join, paste

### sed ´/.*/y/abcdefghijklmnopqrstuvwxyz/ ABCDEFGHIJKLMNOPQRSTUVWXYZ/´ l.txt

ALL  ALL  POWER

In **sed**, there's really no other way to change lowercase to uppercase letters and vice versa. The **y** command translates the characters in the first specification to those in the second. There is a one-to-one correspondence, so **a** equals **A**, **b** equals **B**, and **z** equals **Z**. Because it uses **/.*/**, this example matches all characters in the file, and therefore all letters are changed to uppercase. The output in the example is to the screen. You might want to make this an alias and distribute it to uppercase aficionados. You also might want to take a look at **tr,** which presents a much more concise way of changing cases.

**Keyword:**  text handling, text formatting, programming

**See Also:**  awk, cat, cut, grep, join, paste

## sed ´/.*/y/abcdefghijklmnopqrstuvwxyz0123456789/ \
## ZAYBXC9876543210WDVEUFTGSHRIQJPKOLNM/´
## p.txt > c.txt

ALL    ALL    POWER

This example shows the **y** subcommand to **sed** in a homegrown encrypting script. It converts all lowercase letters and the numbers from 0–9 to a mixture of uppercase letters and numbers. Note that existing uppercase lettters, whitespaces, tabs, and punctuation are not affected by the command. To convert these, you could run successive instances of the command, changing the **y** command's transformation sets each time.

**Keyword:**    text handling, text formatting, programming

**See Also:**    awk, cat, cut, grep, join, paste

## sed ´/PC-UNIX/!s/PC/Personal Computer/´ pc.txt > pc.new

ALL    ALL    POWER

Magazine editors could put this command to good use, because it makes it possible to replace a word or phrase, yet specify an exception to the replacement. In the example, because of the **!** operator before **s**, the previously specified word, **PC-UNIX**, is not replaced, while all other instances of **PC** are replaced with **Personal Computer**.

**Keyword:**    text handling, text formatting, programming

**See Also:**    awk, cat, cut, grep, join, paste

## sed ´/PC-UNIX/,/PC Tools/!s/PC/Personal Computer/´
## pc.txt > pc.new

ALL    ALL    POWER

Similar to the previous example, this command also uses the **sed** address space to specify exceptions to the regular expression in the search string. Because the address space supports two addresses, you can specify two exceptions.

**Keyword:**    text handling, text formatting, programming

**See Also:**    awk, cat, cut, grep, join, paste

## sed ´/^$/r header´ review.org > review.txt

ALL    ALL    POWER

If you leave a blank line at the top of a file, you can use the **r** command to insert another file as a header. The output is redirected to a new file.

**Keyword:**    text handling, text formatting, programming

**See Also:**    awk, cat, cut, grep, join, paste

ALL    ALL    POWER

### sed ´/^.*.$/r templ*´ people.lst > people.frm

This **sed** command reads all files in the current directory that begin with **templ** and inserts them after each line in **people.lst**. With this technique, and perhaps conditional logic that you could build in by developing this command into a **sed** script, you could create a routine that assembles forms for different occasions. If you don't choose to write a **sed** script, you could inject some conditional logic with shell metacharacters. For example, think about **r templ[AKL]?**.

**Keyword:**     text handling, text formatting, programming

**See Also:**     awk, cat, cut, grep, join, paste

ALL    ALL    POWER

### sed ´/^.*.$/r template´ people.lst > people.frm

The **sed** read command is interesting. With it, you can do numerous things to incorporate files into your **sed** output. You can't use the **w** command with it to write the output to disk, but you can use redirection, as in the example, which inserts **template** after each line in the file. This is an excellent way to create a personalized form that might takes hours to create in a text editor or word processor. For example, assume that **people.lst** contains the first and last names of individuals, and **template** contains the following lines:

```
Goals:
Desires:
Dreams:
Reality Check:
```

The output of the **sed** command in the example would thus look like this:

```
Donna Smith
Goals:
Desires:
Dreams:
Reality Check:
```

**Keyword:**     text handling, text formatting, programming

**See Also:**     awk, cat, cut, grep, join, paste

ALL    ALL    POWER

### sed ´/^November Sales/,/{}/w sales.nov´ sales.db

The **w** subcommand tells **sed** to write its output to **sales.nov**, minus the normal output. In other words, you don't need the **-n** option to suppress normal output. The reason for this is that **sed** writes its *pattern space* to the file when a match occurs. The pattern space is an internal area in which **sed** places the current line.

**Keyword:**   text search, text handling, programming

**See Also:**   awk, cat, cut, grep, join, paste

### sed ´10,15s/^.*$//´ old.rep > new.rep

ALL   ALL   POWER

This command performs a search and replace operation on the specified range of lines. As with other addresses, you can place a numeric range, such as the **10,15** in the example, inside or outside the single quotes that can bracket the search and replace statement. This example places the address inside the quotes to vary the syntax compared with previous examples.

**Keyword:**   text search, text handling, programming

**See Also:**   awk, cat, cut, grep, join, paste

### sed ´s/ */ /g´ anyfile

ALL   ALL   POWER

This silly command puts a space after every letter in the file.

**Keyword:**   text handling, text formatting, programming

**See Also:**   awk, cat, cut, grep, join, paste

### sed ´s/Mwm\(.*\)foreground:.*/Mwm\1foreground: black/´ .Xdefaults > .Xdefaults.n

ALL   ALL   POWER

This command shows another use for the wildcard replacement pattern in **sed**. Sometimes, as in the example, your replacements affect a given set of lines, but you have no way of specifying an intermediate part of the search string. In these cases, you can use **\(.*\)** in the search specification and **\n** in the replacement string. Here are some sample lines after the command in the example processed them:

```
Mwm*client*foreground: black
Mwm*feedback*foreground: black
Mwm*icon*foreground: black
Mwm*menu*foreground: black
```

**Keyword:**   text handling, text formatting, programming

**See Also:**   awk, cat, cut, grep, join, paste

### sed ´s/[0-9]*-[0-9]*-[0-9]*/(&)/´ old.txt > new.txt

ALL   ALL   POWER

The **&** character in a **sed** command represents the string that has been matched and is about to be replaced. Using **&** in the replacement string lets you reinsert the replacement string (similar to the **\(...\)** wildcard replacement sequence). In the example, the **sed** command looks for telephone numbers and puts parentheses around them.

**Keyword:**   text handling, text formatting, programming

**See Also:**   awk, cat, cut, grep, join, paste

### sed ´s/\(Goterm.background:\).*/\1 grey/p´ .Xdefaults

This example searches for a specific string in the **.Xdefaults** file (one of the X Window System's resource files). After finding the specified string, which you'll notice is enclosed between **\(** and **\)**, it uses the variable **\1** to replace the string. Presumably, the command also changes the color from its previous color to **grey**.

**Keyword:**   text handling, text formatting, programming

**See Also:**   awk, cat, cut, grep, join, paste

### sed ´s/^[0-9]* *\([A-Z]\)/\1/´ lineup.txt

This command removes the leading numbers and subsequent whitespaces up to the first letter falling between **A-Z**. The wildcard replacement feature is used to prevent deletion of the character falling in the **A-Z** range. If you have ever battled with whitespaces while using **sed**, you'll find this to be a handy tool.

**Keyword:**   text handling, text formatting, programming

**See Also:**   awk, cat, cut, grep, join, paste

### sed ´s/^[0-9]*//´ lineup.txt

This command strips leading numbers from a numbered text file. The regular expression **[0-9]\*** matches any number of numbers until a break in the sequence occurs. The only thing inadequate about this command is that it leaves an uneven number of whitespaces when the line numbering moves from 9 to 10 and 99 to 100 and so on.

**Keyword:**   text handling, text formatting, programming

**See Also:**   awk, cat, cut, grep, join, paste

### sed ´s/^\([0-9]\{1,2\}\.\)/Section \1/´ old.rep

This command searches for lines beginning with either one or two digits, followed by a period, such as 1.1 or 10.5. It then

ALL   ALL   POWER

ALL   ALL   POWER

ALL   ALL   POWER

ALL   ALL   POWER

replaces the pattern with **Section** followed by the pattern. Here is a breakdown of the symbols:

```
\(              Begins recording wildcard replacement
[0-9]           Any number from 0-9
\{1,2\}         The previous pattern if it occurs one or two times
\.              The actual period character
\)              Ends recording wildcard replacement
\1              Specifies the first wildcard replacement
```

**Keyword:**   text handling, text formatting, programming

**See Also:**   awk, cat, cut, grep, join, paste

## sed -f app-field *.rec > vendor.db

ALL    ALL    POWER

Assume that you maintain a database of vendors, and that you store each vendor in its own file with an extension of **.rec**. You also combine all the records into **vendor.db** to enter new information (presumably, you also use **sed** to return the updated information to the separate **.rec** files). Next assume that you want to add a new field to each record. The example, which uses a script named **app-field,** uses **a** to add a new field called **Division**:

```
/^Vendor:/a\
Division:
```

The beauty of this approach used with a small database is that you can change records even if they contain user-entered information. You can place this type of command in a plain file and call it something like **app-field**, as in the example, or you can use it in a shell script in order to make the routine reusable:

```
#!/bin/sh
# Name: appf (for append field)
# Syntax: appf pattern item file
re=$1; item=$2; file=$3
sed -e "/^${re}:/a\\
${item}:" < $file
```

In the script example, notice the use of double quotes, which are required if you want to use variables. Also note the double escape sequence at the end of the first line. Last, note that there should not be whitespace to the right of **${item}**.

**Keyword:**   text search, text formatting, programming

**See Also:**   awk, cat, cut, grep, join, paste

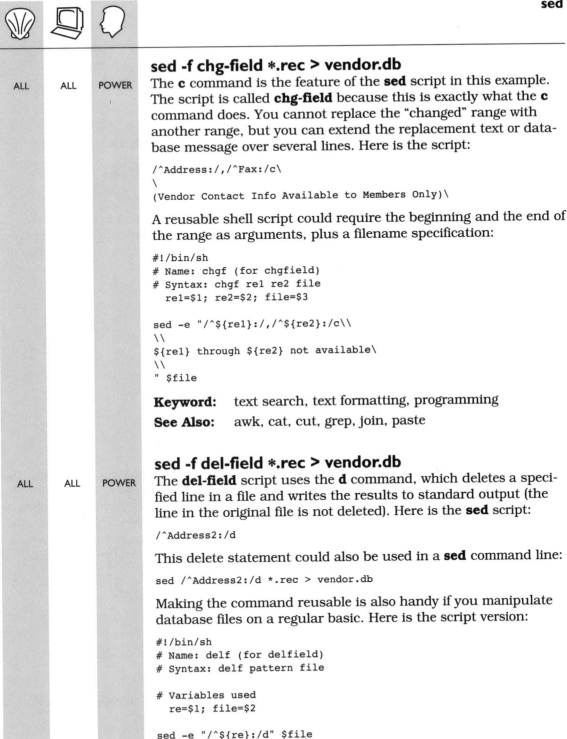

## sed -f chg-field *.rec > vendor.db

The **c** command is the feature of the **sed** script in this example. The script is called **chg-field** because this is exactly what the **c** command does. You cannot replace the "changed" range with another range, but you can extend the replacement text or database message over several lines. Here is the script:

```
/^Address:/,/^Fax:/c\
\
(Vendor Contact Info Available to Members Only)\
```

A reusable shell script could require the beginning and the end of the range as arguments, plus a filename specification:

```
#!/bin/sh
# Name: chgf (for chgfield)
# Syntax: chgf re1 re2 file
  re1=$1; re2=$2; file=$3

sed -e "/^${re1}:/,/^${re2}:/c\\
\\
${re1} through ${re2} not available\
\\
" $file
```

**Keyword:**   text search, text formatting, programming

**See Also:**   awk, cat, cut, grep, join, paste

## sed -f del-field *.rec > vendor.db

The **del-field** script uses the **d** command, which deletes a specified line in a file and writes the results to standard output (the line in the original file is not deleted). Here is the **sed** script:

```
/^Address2:/d
```

This delete statement could also be used in a **sed** command line:

```
sed /^Address2:/d *.rec > vendor.db
```

Making the command reusable is also handy if you manipulate database files on a regular basic. Here is the script version:

```
#!/bin/sh
# Name: delf (for delfield)
# Syntax: delf pattern file

# Variables used
  re=$1; file=$2

sed -e "/^${re}:/d" $file
```

**Keyword:**  text search, text formatting, programming
**See Also:**  awk, cat, cut, grep, join, paste

### sed -f ins-field *.rec > vendor.db

ALL   ALL   POWER

Similar to **sed -f app-field *.rec > vendor.db**, this command
calls a **sed** script that uses the **i** subcommand:

```
/^Address:/i\
Division:
```

The added power of the **i** subcommand lets you insert an item
before the specified line. With the **a** subcommand, the insertion
occurs after the name. If you want to put something at the top of
the file, you are out of luck with **a**, but not with **i**. Here is an
equivalent script:

```
#!/bin/sh
# Name: inf (for insfield)
# Syntax: inf pattern item file

sed -e "/^${1}:/i\\
${2}:" < $3
```

**Keyword:**  text search, text formatting, programming
**See Also:**  awk, cat, cut, grep, join, paste

### sed -f insert sep.txt

ALL   ALL   POWER

The uppercase **N** command in **sed** performs multiline processing. In
most cases, you probably need to use a **sed** script or a shell script to
use the **N** command, because its power only comes into play when
you use it to insert new lines in the replacement pattern. A new line
is inserted by escaping the end of the line in the script file. Here is a
short example **sed** script that inserts codes into a text document:

```
# insert sed script
/<code1>/,/<para2>/{
N
s/<para2>\n/<codeE>\
\
<para2>\
/
}
```

Here is the same command in a shell script:

```
# insert shell script
sed '/<code1>/,/<para2>/{ N; s/<para2>\n/<codeE>\
\
<para2>\
```

```
/
}' db4
```

**Keyword:** text handling, text formatting, programming

**See Also:** awk, cat, cut, grep, join, paste

### sed -n "/APPALOOSA/,/CLYDESDALE/ { /population/p; }" /usr/vet

This is a convenient command for searching a section of a file. In the example, the user assumes that the information he or she wants falls between **APPALOOSA** and **CLYDESDALE**, which denote sections within the text. If a match is found, only lines containing the word **population** are displayed.

**Keyword:** text display, text handling, programming

**See Also:** awk, cat, cut, grep, join, paste

### sed -n ´/--*$/ { n; n; p; }´ sep.txt

When you use multiple **n** subcommands, **sed** skips one line per **n** command and performs any subsequent subcommands on the line equivalent to the last **n**. In the example, **sed** skips one line and prints the line after that—two lines away from the regular expression where it began the procedure.

**Keyword:** text display, text handling, programming

**See Also:** awk, cat, cut, grep, join, paste

### sed -n ´/--*$/ { p; n; n; p; }´ sep.txt

You can combine the **p** and **n** subcommands to print any number of lines processed by **sed**. In the example, the first **p** prints the line matching the regular expression. The two **n** commands then cause **sed** to skip down two lines, and the second **p** command prints that line. Here is an illustration:

```
sep.txt
------------------------------------
    1 This is the first line
    2 This is the second line
    3 This is the third line

output
------------------------------------
    2 This is the second line
```

**Keyword:** text display, text formatting, programming

**See Also:** awk, cat, cut, grep, join, paste

## sed -n ´/Golden Creek/ { n; p; q; }´ database

Suppose you like to keep notes and records in the following form:

```
Estimate: Repairs to Golden Creek Bridge
Slade Bridge Co., $17,500; Brite Construction, $12,900
```

This example does you a favor. If you can't remember the second line, you can **grep** for it. You also know that none of the words in the first line are likely to be unique to the file—but you do know that you keep your estimates in the first section of the file and your miscellaneous notes in the second section. The use of the **q** command suits this situation: It tells **sed** to quit after finding the first match.

**Keyword:**    text search, text handling, programming

**See Also:**    awk, cat, cut, grep, join, paste

## sed -n ´/[A-Z][0-9]..]$/p´ book.txt

The intent of this example is to illustrate how you can anchor a search to the end of a line. But the regular expression in this command also further shows the similarities in **grep** and **sed** regular expressions. The command in the example tells **sed** to search for the following:

```
[A-Z]     A single uppercase character
[0-9]     A single number
..        Any two additional characters, including none
]         A left bracket
$         The end of the line
```

We used a string that fits this description to number the entries in this book. Note that the command in the example does not search for the first bracket, and it assumes that there are no spaces or tabs after the second bracket.

**Keyword:**    text search, text handling, programming

**See Also:**    awk, cat, cut, grep, join, paste

## sed -n ´/[Rr]ed/p´ colors.txt

Although it is more powerful than **grep**, the **sed** command doesn't have an option to tell it to ignore the distinction between uppercase and lowercase letters. If you want to match both cases, you must use a command similar to the example, which uses brackets to list acceptable character matches. If the word you need to match could appear in either all uppercase or lower-case letters, you would write **/[Rr][Ee][Dd]/**. Note that either single or double quotes are required if you use brackets in the C shell. The Bourne and Korn shells do not require any quotation.

**Keyword:**   text handling, text formatting, programming

**See Also:**   awk, cat, cut, grep, join, paste

### sed -n ´/^See Also/ { n; p; }´ book.txt

ALL   ALL   POWER

This command displays the pattern space, which is the line following the line on which the match occurs. This is a handy command for extracting variable text when its follows a line that doesn't vary. Used on the shell database files from which this book was created, the command returned information that varied, but always appeared under the **See Also:** heading. The **n** and **p** options in the example are subcommands, which should be listed in curly brackets and separated by semicolons, including the last subcommand.

**Keyword:**   text search, text handling, programming

**See Also:**   awk, cat, cut, grep, join, paste

### sed -n ´s/Unix/UNIX/gpw os.new´ os.txt

ALL   ALL   POWER

Just when you thought there was never any reason to use the **p** flag with the **g** flag, a reason pops up. And the reason was alluded to in the previous command: Using the **-n** option along with the **w** flag inhibits any **sed** output going to the screen. If you remove the **-n** option, however, all lines in the file are displayed to the screen. But what if you want to see what is being written to the file specified by the **w** option? The answer is, add the **p** command, and the output to the file and the display on the screen will be identical.

**Keyword:**   text handling, text formatting, programming

**See Also:**   awk, cat, cut, grep, join, paste

### sed -n ´s/Unix/UNIX/gw os.new´ os.txt

ALL   ALL   POWER

There are a total of four flags to the substitute command. Here, the **g** and **w** flags are combined. The **g** flag effects global substitution. The **w** flag is new. It writes the output from the substitution routine to the named file. The **-n** option also suppresses normal output, so you don't see anything on screen if you execute this command on the command line. Note that the UNIX system documentation distinguishes the **w** flag from the **w** subcommand, even though they operate identically.

**Keyword:**   text handling, text formatting, programming

**See Also:**   awk, cat, cut, grep, join, paste

### sed -n ´s/\(.*\)   \(.*\)/\2, \1/p´ calendar

ALL  ALL  POWER

Sometimes, formatting ASCII files with the Tab character, instead of a single whitespace, can be handy. This example uses the **\(** and **\)** wildcard replacement notations in **sed** to flip-flop the date and message formatting of the **calendar** file. For example:

```
8/18   T&E meeting for quarter
```

is transposed to

```
T&E meeting for the quarter, 8/18
```

**Keyword:**   text handling, text formatting, programming
**See Also:**   awk, cat, cut, grep, join, paste

### sed -n /red/p colors.txt

ALL  ALL  POWER

This command uses an address formed from a regular expression and imitates a basic **grep** operation. With the **-n** option invoked, the example prints out only lines containing the word **red**. The **p** command is used to print the matched lines.

**Keyword:**   text handling, text formatting, programming
**See Also:**   awk, cat, cut, grep, join, paste

### sed -n /^November Sales/,/{}/p sales.db

ALL  ALL  POWER

This example searches for the first instance of **November Sales** and displays all lines through the {} sequence. If you create and maintain files in some orderly fashion—as in this case, ending each section with the {} sequence—this type of **sed** command can be an invaluable tool. Note that if you decide to use {} as an arbitary code, you must escape each curly brace when using the C shell. Also note the use of **-n**, which suppresses normal **sed** output.

**Keyword:**   text search, text handling, programming
**See Also:**   awk, cat, cut, grep, join, paste

### sed -n /^November Sales/,/{}/p sales.db > sales.nov

ALL  ALL  POWER

This entry takes the previous command and redirects the output to a file. Redirection with **sed** is very common. Again, the **-n** option is crucial for most cases, because getting the normal output of **sed** is usually not what you want.

**Keyword:**   text search, text handling, programming
**See Also:**   awk, cat, cut, grep, join, paste

### sed -n 5p report.txt

ALL ALL POWER

The **-n** option to **sed** tells it to suppress its normal output. As a result, the only output left to display is line **5**, according to the directive of the **p** command. You'll find that the **-n** command is crucial when it comes to extracting small amounts of data with **sed**. It is also excellent for assigning values to variables in shell scripts:

```
repname=`sed -n 1p report.txt
```

The example assumes that the name of the report is contained on a line by itself at the top of the file.

**Keyword:**    text handling, text formatting, programming

**See Also:**    awk, cat, cut, grep, join, paste

### sed -n s/Total:/Total:/2p db

ALL ALL POWER

This command shows a useful aspect to the substitution command's number flag. Namely, you can search for any line with two occurrences of the same regular expression in it. You could also do this in **grep** with a command such as **grep '^.Total:.*Total: db'**, but you would be hard pressed to keep up with the number flag if you want to search for a larger number of regular expressions on the same line.

**Keyword:**    text search, text handling, programming

**See Also:**    awk, cat, cut, grep, join, paste

### sed -n s/Unix/UNIX/p os.txt

ALL ALL POWER

The default behavior of the substitute command in **sed** is to print to the standard output. If you suppress output with the **-n** option, but want to see the lines that have been changed by the command, you must use the **p** (print) option.

**Keyword:**    text handling, text formatting, programming

**See Also:**    awk, cat, cut, grep, join, paste

### sed -n /^Keyword:/p book.txt

ALL ALL POWER

This is another example that performs a task that **grep** could handle. The point of the command is to draw attention to the fact that **sed**, like **grep** and **awk**, uses the ^ symbol to anchor a search to the beginning of a line. Quotation marks are not necessary in any of the three standard shells.

**Keyword:**    text search, text handling, programming

**See Also:**    awk, cat, cut, grep, join, paste

### sed 1p report.txt

| ALL | ALL | POWER |

The **sed** command lets you specify *addresses* by line numbers (as well as regular expressions and the special **$** symbol, which means the last line of the file). In the example, the simple use of the **p**, or print, command causes **sed** to repeat the first line of the file along with the normal output (which would be equivalent to using **cat** on the file, in this case).

**Keyword:**    text handling, text formatting, programming

**See Also:**    awk, cat, cut, grep, join, paste

### sed 8,25!d report.txt

| SH KSH | ALL | POWER |

If you place the NOT operator after the specified range, but before the **d** command, **sed** deletes everything but the range. This is also an alternative way to suppress the normal output of **sed**.

**Keyword:**    text handling, text formatting, programming

**See Also:**    awk, cat, cut, grep, join, paste

### sed 8,25d report.txt

| ALL | ALL | POWER |

This command shows how a range of lines can be deleted with the **d** command. A comma is always the delimiter between the beginning and end numbers.

**Keyword:**    text handling, text formatting, programming

**See Also:**    awk, cat, cut, grep, join, paste

### sed 8,25\!d report.txt

| CSH | ALL | POWER |

The C shell version of the previous example escapes the NOT operator that occurs before the **d** command. From the command line, the C shell interprets the **!** as the command event operator for the shell's history mechanism. If you don't escape the NOT operator, **sed** bails out with a message like "Event not found."

**Keyword:**    text handling, text formatting, programming

**See Also:**    awk, cat, cut, grep, join, paste

### sed 8d report.txt

| ALL | ALL | POWER |

The **-d** command can achieve a very desirable effect without the help of the **-n** option. With **-d**, you can delete any line in a file or any range of lines in a file, as shown in the next example.

**Keyword:**    text handling, text formatting, programming

**See Also:**    awk, cat, cut, grep, join, paste

### sed = report.txt

The = option tells **sed** to print the current line number on a line by itself, followed by the associated line from the file. Here is an example:

```
8
This report should acknowledge that factors in the industry
9
have led to tremendous evolutionary patterns that are now
10
converging with the underlying tension of the market.
```

**Keyword:**   text handling, text formatting, programming

**See Also:**   awk, cat, cut, grep, join, paste

### sed s/Phone:/Fax:/2 phone.db > new.db

The fourth flag to the substitute command is not a letter, but any number in the range of 1 to 512. Think of this flag as always being active. The default is 1, which means **sed** replaces the first occurrence of the regular expression that it finds on each line. When you change the default to another number, **sed** skips to that occurrence. For example, if the **sed** command in the example parsed the following line:

```
John Smith, Dawkins Technology, Phone: 555-1234   Phone: 555-4321
```

it would change it to this:

```
John Smith, Dawkins Technology, Phone: 555-1234   Fax: 555-4321
```

Now, the question is, would you ever want to combine all four substitution flags? The answer is no. The number flag is mutually exclusive with the **g** flag, but you might venture a **2pw**.

**Keyword:**   text handling, text formatting, programming

**See Also:**   awk, cat, cut, grep, join, paste

### sed s/Unix/UNIX/ os.txt > os.new

This command may not be what it seems. The effect of the example is to replace the first occurrence of the specified regular expression in each line in the file. If the word **Unix** occurs twice or more on the same line, the subsequent occurrences are not replaced. The sequence of events in the command establish the basic pattern for the various substitution commands in **sed**. The **s** command always appears before the first forward slash; three forward slashes delineate the regular expression and substitution string. Quotation marks are not required in any of the shells for this particular entry, but if you introduced metacharacters to which the C shell is sensitive, you would need single or double quotes.

**Keyword:**   text handling, text formatting, programming

**See Also:**   awk, cat, cut, grep, join, paste

### sed s/Unix/UNIX/g os.txt > os.new

ALL   ALL   POWER

The **g** (global) flag to the substitution command tells **sed** to replace all occurrences of the regular expression. The **g** appears after the substitution string and its associated forward slash. This is where all flags to the substitute command go.

**Keyword:**   text handling, text formatting, programming

**See Also:**   awk, cat, cut, grep, join, paste

### sendmail

ALL   ALL   POWER

The **sendmail** program is one of the most important software utilities that comes with the UNIX system. The product began as a BSD mail handler and has flourished into a de facto standard in UNIX. In a nutshell, **sendmail** is responsible for forwarding mail between hosts on a network, as well as forwarding it to the Internet. The average UNIX email user rarely comes into contact with **sendmail**. The one important aspect for users is **$HOME/.forward**, in which you can place forwarding addresses for your mail—handy when you relocate, or when you just want to forward mail to your home. The **$HOME/.forward** file simply lists one or more valid email addresses.

**Keyword:**   email, Internet, networking

**Files:**       $HOME/.forward

**See Also:**   biff, binmail, mail, mailx, vacation

### set

ALL   ALL   ALL

All three shells support the built-in **set** command. Entering **set** at the command line in any of the shells prints a display of environment values. Beyond this, each version of **set** performs tasks associated with setting environment concerns. By far, the Korn shell version of **set** is the most extensive, including options to specify a text editor interface for command line entry and revision. Here are the usage statements for the three **set** commands:

```
sh    set [+|-aefhkntuvx-] [arg ...]
csh   set [var[=value]] | var[n]="string"
ksh   set [+|-aefhkmnopstuvx] [+|-o opt ...] [+|-A name] [arg ...]
```

As you can see, **set** in the Bourne and Korn shells shares the same approach as well as several options. In the C shell, **set** sets shell variables. This is not much different from the **setenv** command, but **set** does add the ability to set indexed variables. The following entries provide a sampling of the **set** command; refer to the entries for **csh**, **ksh**, and **sh** for additional examples (that is, you can specify many of the same options when initially invoking the shell).

**Keyword:**   user environment

**Files:**   $HOME/.cshrc, $HOME/.profile

**See Also:**   csh, env, ksh, printenv, sh

### set +o bignice

The **bgnice** argument to the **-o** option in the Korn shell toggles the priority of background jobs. By default, the Korn shell runs background jobs at a lower priority than foreground jobs. You can use the **+** instead of a dash to disable the default value and have jobs run at equal priority. Note that you can use the plus sign with most **set** options.

**Keyword:**   job control

**See Also:**   bg, fg, kill, ps

KSH   ALL   END SCRIPT

### set -au

The Korn shell **-au** options enhance the standard environment. The **-a** option specifies that all shell variables (not those in scripts) be automatically exported. The **-u** option specifies that undefined variables be handled as errors.

**Keyword:**   user environment

**See Also:**   export, if, test

KSH   ALL   END SCRIPT

### set -f

The Bourne and Korn **-f** option disables filename substitution, preventing users from using wildcard matching symbols to manipulate filenames.

**Keyword:**   user environment

**Files:**   $HOME/.profile, /etc/passwd

**See Also:**   env, login, printenv

SH   ALL   ALL

### set -f

| KSH | ALL | END |

This command is used to disable pathname expansion in the Korn shell.

**Keyword:** user environment

**See Also:** env, ksh, printenv

### set -o

| KSH | ALL | END |

This **set** command outputs all of the current settings for the Korn shell options. This is very useful for initially determining how your environment is set up.

**Keyword:** user environment

**See Also:** env, ksh, printev

### set -o emacs

| KSH | ALL | END |

This **set** command tells the Korn shell to use the **emacs** text editing interface for command line entry and revision.

**Keyword:** user environment

**See Also:** emacs, ksh, vi

### set -o vi

| KSH | ALL | END |

This **set** command tells the Korn shell to use the **vi** text editing interface for command line entry and revision.

**Keyword:** user environment

**See Also:** emacs, ksh, vi

### set -xv

| SH | ALL | SCRIPT |
| KSH | | POWER |

The Bourne and Korn **-xv** options let you put the current shell into a debug mode. The **-x** option causes each subsequent command that you enter to be echoed. The **-v** option causes any data replacement in the command to be echoed as well.

**Keyword:** user environment, programming

**Files:** $HOME/.profile

**See Also:** env, login, printenv, sh

### set noclobber

| CSH | ALL | ALL |

This command tells the C shell to check all output redirection to make sure that files are not destroyed by redirecting output over them. An example such as **cat report.doc > status.doc**, where **status.doc** is already a file, will not work if **noclobber** is set.

**Keyword:**    user environment

**Files:**        $HOME/.cshrc

**See Also:**    env, csh, printenv

### set notify

This command tells the C shell to let you know asynchronously if a job running in the background has completed execution. If you don't set this, the C shell will tell you the job's status before it gives you a prompt.

**Keyword:**    user environment

**Files:**        $HOME/.cshrc

**See Also:**    env, csh, printenv

### set prompt = "[`date +%m/%m/%y`] "

This command puts the numerical representation of the date inside your prompt. The whitespace at the end is cosmetic: It prevents the cursor from bumping up against the prompt.

**Keyword:**    user environment, text editing

**Files:**        $HOME/.cshrc

**See Also:**    date, csh, printenv

### set prompt = ´[\!%]´

The C shell's **set** command is similar to the Bourne shell's default equality facility. Competing in this sense with **set** is **setenv**, another C shell built-in, which is designed to set environment variables. But you still use **set** to define the C shell's unique environment variables. In the example, the prompt is set to display the current history number in square brackets.

**Keyword:**    user environment, text editing

**Files:**        $HOME/.cshrc

**See Also:**    csh, history, xterm

### set prompt="[\!][$cwd] "

This style of **prompt** is one of the handiest: In addition to displaying the current history item number, it shows the current

**CSH    ALL    ALL**

**423**

directory. To keep the directory display current, you must also set the following alias:

```
alias cd 'cd \!*; set prompt = "[\\!][$cwd] "'
```

Note that you must escape the **!** twice in order for the shell to correctly evaluate it within double quotes. If your system does not support the **$cwd** environment variable, use the **pwd** command:

```
alias cd 'cd \!*; set prompt = "[\\!][`pwd`] "'
```

**Keyword:**    user environment, text editing
**Files:**    $HOME/.cshrc
**See Also:**    cd, chdir, csh, history


### set `date`; echo $*

SH KSH · ALL · POWER

The **set** command in the Bourne and Korn shells is very flexible. One of the things you can do with it is take the input of a command—using command substitution—and fill the shell's argument space. The **echo $\*** sequence here displays all the arguments set for the shell. In this case, **$\*** is the same as **$1, $2, $3, $4**, and **$5**. The output looks the same as if you entered **date**:

```
Thu Aug 19 14:26:16 EDT 1993
```

**Keyword:**    text search, text formatting, programming
**See Also:**    awk, cat, cut, grep, join, paste


### set `date`; shift; echo $*

SH KSH · ALL · SCRIPT POWER

This command demonstrates that you can shift arguments once you have used **set** to make them known to the shell. The output of the **date** command now looks like this:

```
Aug 19 14:26:16 EDT 1993
```

**Keyword:**    user environment
**See Also:**    alias, ksh, return, sh


### setenv DISPLAY aixpilot:0

CSH · ALL · ALL

This command is used to tell your system to display all X applications on the first display that computer **aixpilot** has running. You can have multiple monitors attached to a single X workstation, but it is unusual outside scientific and engineering sites.

**Keyword:**    user environment
**See Also:**    csh, env, printenv, xprop, xwininfo

**424**

### setenv EXINIT ´set showmode´

| CSH | ALL | ALL |
|-----|-----|-----|

You can set properties for the **vi** editor by specifying **EXINIT** and a value with the **setenv** command. In the example, the **sentenv** command activates **showmode**, which displays an indicator at the bottom of the screen to let you know when you are in insert mode.

**Keyword:**   user environment, text editing

**Files:**     $HOME/.cshrc, $HOME/.exrc

**See Also:**  ed, set, vi

### setenv MORE ´-c´

| CSH | ALL | ALL |
|-----|-----|-----|

If you prefer that the **more** command overwrite the current screen, rather than preserving it with its normal "paging" behavior, set the **MORE** environment variable to **-c**, as in the example.

**Keyword:**   user environment

**Files:**     $HOME/.cshrc

**See Also:**  ed, set, vi

### setenv PROJECTDIR /usr

| CSH | ALL | ALL |
|-----|-----|-----|

This command sets the parent directory for SCCS, which is the project directory for the Source Code Control System. Note that you should not use a trailing forward slash as a directory separator.

**Keyword:**   user environment, programming

**Files:**     $HOME/.cshrc

**See Also:**  printenv, sccs, set

### setenv TERM ´vt100´

| CSH | ALL | ALL |
|-----|-----|-----|

This **setenv** example tells the system that your terminal window supports the commands needed to drive a Digital Equipment Corp. VT100 ASCII terminal.

**Keyword:**   user environment

**See Also:**  stty, tty, tset, env, printenv, csh

### sh

| SH | ALL | ALL |
|----|-----|-----|

The **sh** program is a monument in UNIX. You can enter **sh** at the command line, as you can with most commands in The UNIX and X Command Compendium. But **sh** (pronounced "ess-h") is the Bourne shell, and although many users prefer the C and Korn shells, **sh** will probably outlive them (although the demise of either is not rumored). The reason for the Bourne shell's stature is that it is the preferred shell for UNIX script writing. It is also the common shell for software testing purposes. Implementations of **sh** vary slightly, but not much. Here are representative usage statements:

```
BSD      sh [ -ceiknrstuvx ] [ arg ] ...
SVR4     sh [ -acefhiknprstuvx ] [ args ]
SunOS    sh [ -acefhiknstuvx ] [ args ]
Solaris  sh [ -acefhiknprstuvx ] [ arg ...]
SCO      sh [ -aceiknrstuvx ] [ args ]
OSF      sh [-ir] [+|-aefhkntuvx] [file] [args] [-ccmd|-s]
```

**Keyword:**   user environment

**Files:**   $HOME/.profile, /etc/passwd, /dev/null

**See Also:**   csh, env, ksh, jsh, login, printenv, rsh, set


### sh -c xv_get_sel | lpr

The **-c** option to **sh** lets you specify a command to run as a subshell. When you invoke **sh** from the command line, it automatically starts a new shell. The example is designed for SunOS systems that support the **xv_get_sel** command. The result is that the current X cut buffer selection is printed.

**Keyword:**   user environment

**See Also:**   csh, ksh, rsh


### sh -f

The **-f** option to **sh** disables filename substitution. In other words, it prevents users from incorporating wildcard matching symbols in filenames. This might be a good tactic to use in a restricted environment.

**Keyword:**   user environment.

**Files:**   $HOME/.profile, /etc/passwd

**See Also:**   env, login, printenv


### sh -t

The **-t** option to **sh** creates a shell and lets you execute one command in the new shell. You enter the command interactively, and the shell displays the results, if any, to standard output. After this, you find yourself back in the original shell—or bumped off the system if for some reason this is the login shell. For users of the C and Korn shells, using the **-t** option is an efficient way to

SH    SunOS    POWER

SH    ALL    ALL

SH    ALL    END

test a single command in the Bourne shell and return to the comfort of your preferred shell.

**Keyword:**   user environment

**Files:**   $HOME/.profile, /etc/passwd

**See Also:**   env, login, printenv

## sh -u

The Bourne shell's **-u** option is a handy shell script tool. It tells **sh** to treat any unset variable as an error. Normally, **sh** treats them as null, but sometimes, distinguishing between null and zero-value variables gets tedious.

**Keyword:**   user environment

**Files:**   $HOME/.profile

**See Also:**   env, login, printenv

## sh -vx

If you want to debug shell commands, this example loads the shell so it provides a debug mode. Each command that you enter, thanks to the **-x** option, is echoed. Then, because of the **-v** option, any data replacement in the command is also echoed.

**Keyword:**   user environment, programming

**Files:**   $HOME/.profile

**See Also:**   env, login, printenv

## SHACCT

This is an environment variable that routes accounting records to the named file for the system accounting utilities.

**Keyword:**   system information, security

**Files:**   /etc/passwd, /usr/lib/acct, /var/adm/pacct, /var/adm/wtmp

**See Also:**   acct, acctcms, acctcom, acctcom, acctmerg, acctprc, runacct

## SHELL

All UNIX systems support the **SHELL** environment variable. The most common use is as a storage area for the name of the user's preferred shell. Most systems also support **SHELL** as a way to invoke a restricted shell. It works like this: If you set **SHELL** equal

Sidebar column (left margin) labels:

| | | |
|---|---|---|
| SH | ALL | SCRIPT |
| SH | ALL | SCRIPT POWER |
| ALL | SVR4 OSF AIX | SYSADM |
| ALL | ALL | ALL |

to any pattern that matches **rsh**, the matching restricted shell is invoked. This includes **Rsh**, **rksh**, and **rsh**.

**Keyword:**  user environment

**Files:**  /etc/passwd

**See Also:**  Rsh, rsh, rksh, set, setenv

### showfont -fn ´-schumacher-clean-medium-r-normal--10-100*´

ALL  XWIN  ALL

This X11R5 font utility works with the X font server. It displays the requested font after querying the server. The **-fn** option specifies the font to display. You can use both the * and **?** wildcards, but they must be quoted to prevent the shell from expanding them.

**Keyword:**  X resources

**See Also:**  xfd, xlsfonts, wrdb

### showrgb

ALL  XWIN  ALL

The **showrgb** client program displays color names and values known to the standard X color database. The program uses no options. Here is a sample of its output:

```
112 128 144           slate gray
139  37   0           orangered4
205 140 149           lightpink3
173 216 230           light blue
```

**Keyword:**  X resources

**Files:**  /usr/lib/X11/rgb.txt

**See Also:**  xcol, xcoloredit, xset, xsetroot

### shutdown

ALL  ALL  POWER
SYSADM

The **shutdown** command is ubiquitous, but comes in various forms as the syntax statements show. Primarily used to bring the system down by gracefully killing processes and synchronizing disks, the **shutdown** command also offers a quick way to reboot on some systems. On SunOS and BSD systems, **shutdown** is in **/usr/etc**. On AIX and OSF systems, it is located in **/usr/sbin**. On SVR4 systems, **shutdown** is located in **/sbin**, and the BSD-compatible version is located in **/usr/ucb**. On SCO systems, **shutdown** is located in **/etc**.

```
SunOS shutdown [-fhknr] time [warning-message ...]
BSD   shutdown [-k] [-r] [-h] [-n] [-p] time [msg ...]
```

```
SCO      shutdown [-y] [-ghh:mm] [-i[0156sS]] [-f "msg"] [-f file] [su]
SVR4     shutdown [-y] [-gseconds] [-iinit_state]
Solaris  shutdown [-y] [-gseconds] [-iinit_state]
AIX      shutdown [-c] [-d] [-F] [-h] [-i] [-k] [-m] [-r] [-v] [+ Time [Msg]]
OSF      shutdown [-fhknr] time [warning-message ...]
```

**Keyword:**   shutdown, startup

**Files:**   /etc/nologin, /etc/xtab

**See Also:**   init, fastboot, halt, reboot

### shutdown +5

ALL   ALL   SYSADM

This command is used to bring the system down, but waits five minutes to do it. This command is useful when you want to bring the machine down quickly, yet give people a chance to log out.

**Keyword:**   shutdown, startup

**See Also:**   init, fastboot, halt, reboot

### shutdown -F

ALL   AIX   POWER SYSADM

The **-F** option in AIX is similar to the **-f** option in SunOS and OSF. The difference is that a time value (even **now**) is not required for an immediate shutdown.

**Keyword:**   shutdown, startup

**See Also:**   init, fastboot, halt, reboot

### shutdown -f now

ALL   SunOS OSF   POWER SYSADM

The **-f** option shuts down the system as quickly as possible. As a result, **shutdown** does not notify other users, nor does it synchronize filesystems. You can specify a time, in hh:mm format, instead of **now**, but **now** makes the most sense in the context of the **-f** option.

**Keyword:**   shutdown, startup

**See Also:**   init, fastboot, halt, reboot

### shutdown -h 19:00

ALL   BSD   POWER SYSADM

This form of the **shutdown** command is available on most systems other than SVR4 systems (Solaris, NCR, UnixWare, etc.). Thanks to the **-h** option, the command lets you bypass single-user mode and bring down the system to the point that you can power off.

**Keyword:**   shutdown, startup

**See Also:**   init, fastboot, halt, reboot

### shutdown -m

ALL AIX POWER SYSADM

On AIX systems, this command tells users of the impending event, and then brings down the system to single-user mode.

**Keyword:** shutdown, startup

**See Also:** init, fastboot, halt, reboot

### shutdown -r now

ALL ALL POWER SYSADM

The **-r** option to **shutdown** halts the system and immediately reboots. On systems that lack a fastboot-like command, the example command is a good alternative.

**Keyword:** shutdown, startup

**See Also:** init, fastboot, halt, reboot

### shutdown 19:00

ALL ALL POWER SYSADM

This is a common form of **shutdown**, and it shows how you can halt the system and notify users as the "apocalypse approaches," which is how the SunOS **man** pages phrase it. When you enter the command (you must be root user), a message displays:

```
Shutdown at 20:00 (in 52 minutes) [pid 25252]
```

At this point, you can continue with the shutdown or use the **kill** command to kill the process. The PID number identifies the process. If the shutdown occurs, a message is written in the system log. The message contains the time the system was brought down and who ran the **shutdown** command and for what reason. Finally, **shutdown** sends a terminate signal. In the case of example, the signal is signal 1, which puts the system into single-user mode (also called administrative mode). At this point, the system can be halted so it can be powered down, or it can be reinitialized to a specified run-level.

**Keyword:** shutdown, startup

**Files:** /etc/nologin, /etc/xtab

**See Also:** init, fastboot, halt, reboot

### sh_builtins

SH ALL SCRIPT

This is not a command you will find on your system, unless you create a simple script file as we did. When you create the script, you also have to make it executable (**chmod +x** does the trick). Here is the script:

```
#!/bin/sh
echo '
```

```
case, do, done, elif, else, esac, exec, exit,
export, fi, for, hash, inlib, newgrp, read,
readonly, return, set, shift, then, times, trap,
type, ulimit, umask, unset, while, break, if,
pwd, rmlib, test, until '
```

**Keyword:**   help

**See Also:**   csh, csh_builtins, ksh, ksh_builtins

### sleep 45 ; xv lighthouse.gif

ALL   ALL   ALL

This command causes the system to wait **45** seconds before it executes the command **xv**.

**Keyword:**   program execution

**See Also:**   nice, wait, xv

### ( sleep 45; xv unix2001.gif ) &

ALL   ALL   POWER

This is another way to handle the previous command. By placing the commands in parentheses, however, you can treat them as a grouped command and run both in the background.

**Keyword:**   program execution

**See Also:**   nice, wait, xv

### ( sleep 45; xv unix2001.gif > /dev/null 2>&1 ) &

ALL   ALL   POWER

Here is another refinement on the **sleep** command when paired with **xv** to load an image. Because you have run the command in the background, it is likely that you don't want to see any messages output to your terminal window. Redirecting standard output to **/dev/null**, plus merging standard error with standard output (this is what **2>&1** does), avoids any messages.

**Keyword:**   program execution

**See Also:**   nice, wait, xv

### smit

ALL   AIX   POWER
SYSADM

The **smit** application is IBM's AIX interface to system managment. It is similar in purpose to **sysadm** on SVR4, but more stylized. The **smit** application comes with both an X Window System/Motif interface and an ASCII terminal interface. From the ASCII interface, which can be run in an Xterm window as well as a remote terminal, you can use "fastpath" options that put you into a specified module of the program, such as "Installation and Maintenance" or "Devices." If you are an X Window user, there is a

**smit**

context-sensitive help system to guide you through the different modules.

**Keyword:**   system setup, system information

**See Also:**   sysadm, sysadmsh

### smit arc

ALL   AIX   POWER SYSADM

The **arc** option is a fastpath keyword that displays the **smit** Processes and Subsystems menu. Available submenu options are:

```
Processes
Subsystems
Subservers
```

**Keyword:**   job control, system information

**See Also:**   sysadm, sysadmsh

### smit commo

ALL   AIX   POWER SYSADM

The **commo** option is a fastpath keyword that displays the **smit** Communications Applications and Services menu. Available submenu options are:

```
TCP/IP
NFS
SNA Services
AIX 3270 Host Connection Services/6000 (HCON)
```

**Keyword:**   networking, NFS

**See Also:**   setup, sysadm, sysadmsh

### smit devices

ALL   AIX   POWER SYSADM

The **devices** option is a fastpath keyword that displays the **smit** Devices menu. Available submenu options are:

```
Configure Devices Added After IPL
Printer/Plotter
TTY
PTY
Console
Fixed Disk
CD ROM Drive
Diskette Drive
Tape Drive
Communication
High Function Terminal (HFT)
SCSI Initiator Device
Xstation Configuration
SCSI Adapter
```

```
Asynchronous I/O
Multimedia
List Devices
```

**Keyword:**    devices, system information

**See Also:**    setup, sysadm, sysadmsh

## smit diskless

ALL    AIX    POWER SYSADM

The **diskless** option is a fastpath keyword that displays the **smit** Diskless Workstation Management menu. Available submenu options are:

```
Start Daemons on Server
Manage Shared Product Object Trees (SPOTs)
Install/Maintain Software
Manage Software Inventory
Manage Clients
```

**Keyword:**    networking, applications

**See Also:**    setup, sysadm, sysadmsh

## smit install

ALL    AIX    POWER SYSADM

The **install** option is a fastpath keyword that displays the **smit** Installation and Maintenance menu. Available options are:

```
Software Installation & Maintenance
Diskless Workstation Management
Remote /usr Client Management
```

**Keyword:**    system setup, system information

**See Also:**    setup, sysadm, sysadmsh

## smit performance

ALL    AIX    POWER SYSADM

The **performance** option is a fastpath keyword that displays the **smit** System Environments menu. Available submenu options are:

```
Stop the System
Manage Language Environment
Assign the Console
Change/Show Date, Time, and Time Zone
Change/Show Characteristics of an Operating System
Change Number of Licensed Users
Broadcast Message to All Users
```

**Keyword:**    system setup, system information

**See Also:**    setup, sysadm, sysadmsh

**433**

## smit print

ALL   AIX   POWER SYSADM

The **print** option is a fastpath keyword that displays the **smit** Spooler menu. Available submenu options are:

```
Start a Print Job
Cancel a Print Job
Show the Status of Print Jobs
Prioritize a Print Job
Schedule Jobs
Manage Local Printer Subsystem
Manage Remote Printer Subsystem
```

**Keyword:**   printing

**See Also:**   setup, sysadm, sysadmsh

## smit problem

ALL   AIX   POWER SYSADM

The **problem** option is a fastpath keyword that displays the **smit** Problem Determination menu. Available submenu options are:

```
Error Log
Trace
System Dump
Hardware Diagnostics
Validate Software
Alert Manager
```

**Keyword:**   system information

**See Also:**   setup, sysadm, sysadmsh

## smit security

ALL   AIX   POWER SYSADM

The **security** option is a fastpath keyword that displays the **smit** Security and Users menu. Available submenu options are:

```
Users
Groups
Passwords
```

**Keyword:**   security, user environment

**See Also:**   setup, sysadm, sysadmsh

## smit storage

ALL   AIX   POWER SYSADM

The **storage** option is a fastpath keyword that displays the **smit** Physical and Logical Storage menu. Available submenu options are:

```
File Systems
Paging Space
```

```
Define a Fixed Disk to the Operating System
Logical Volume Manager
```

**Keyword:**  filesystem, system information

**See Also:**  setup, sysadm, sysadmsh

### sort +0f +0u parts.db

What if you want to retain uppercase and lowercase versions as unique items, but still want duplicates removed? The example does the trick by performing two **sorts**: The first, specified by **+0f**, orders the items without considering case; and the second, **+0u**, performs a unique sort.

**Keyword:**  text handling

**See Also:**  awk, comm, grep, join, uniq, sed

### sort +1 -0.1 +2 sales.db

This command compares the first character in field 1 (which we'll say again is actually the second field). The notation **-0.1** after the field specification tells **sort** to stop comparing this field after parsing the first character. The **+2** notation then tells **sort** to finish the comparison based on the value of field 3. Note that we have changed **Smith NH** to **Stevens NH** in the example:

```
01877 Jones CT Pipes     400 $32,231
29742 Stevens NH gravel 4450 $10,001
00456 Smith SD concrete 1000 $20,100
```

**Keyword:**  text handling

**See Also:**  awk, comm, grep, join, uniq, sed

### sort +1 -2 +0n sales.db > sales.sort

You can construct a **sort** command that keys on both numeric and alphabetic data, using the same approach as in the previous example. Note that the example uses the **-n** option by appending it to the secondary **sort** field. Here is the output:

```
01877 Jones CT Pipes     400 $32,231
00456 Smith SD concrete 1000 $20,100
29742 Smith NH gravel   4450 $10,001
```

**Keyword:**  text handling

**See Also:**  awk, comm, grep, join, uniq, sed

ALL   ALL   END

**435**

### sort +1 -2 +3 -f sales.db

ALL ALL END

Note that the **-f** is specified differently in this command. It is good to be aware of both styles.

**Keyword:**  text handling

**See Also:**  awk, comm, grep, join, uniq, sed

### sort +1 -2 +3f sales.db > sales.sort

ALL ALL END

If you have read the other **sort** examples, this looks like a different type of command. It is, in that it specifies a secondary **sort** field, clearing up the problem of having two persons named **Smith** in the list. Before specifying the secondary field, it tells **sort** to stop sorting at field 2. This is what the **-2** represents. At this point, **sort** initiates a second pass through the file. Also, notice that the **-f** option is placed after the number specifying the secondary sort field. Here is the output, with **gravel** appearing in uppercase to prove the point:

```
01877 Jones CT Pipes     400 $32,231
00456 Smith SD concrete 1000 $20,100
29742 Smith NH GRAVEL   4450 $10,001
```

**Keyword:**  text handling

**See Also:**  awk, comm, grep, join, uniq, sed

### sort +1 - m p1 p2 p3

ALL ALL END

The **-m** option to **sort** operates on multiple files and performs a merge operation. The input files, however, must already be sorted. For example, the following three files would result in an alphabetical listing of the planets:

```
file:p1      file:p2      file:p3
Jupiter      Mercury      Earth
Mars         Uranus       Neptune
Pluto        Venus        Saturn
```

**Keyword:**  text handling

**See Also:**  awk, comm, grep, join, uniq, sed

### sort +1 - o sales.sort +1 sales.db

ALL ALL END

Instead of using redirection to create a sorted file, you can specify the **-o** option. Unlike many other UNIX commands, the **-o** and following filename can be specified before the input filename.

**Keyword:**  text handling

**See Also:**  awk, comm, grep, join, uniq, sed

ALL  ALL  END

### sort +1 sales.db -o sales.db

This example is similar to others, but notice that the input and output filenames are the same. This is highly unusual with UNIX commands, but **sort** allows it. Also, note that you can use the **-o** option at the end of the command line if you want.

**Keyword:**   text handling

**See Also:**   awk, comm, grep, join, uniq, sed

ALL  ALL  END

### sort +1 sales.db > sales.sort

Using the **+1** option with **sort** tells it to key its comparison to the second field in the specified file. When using **sort**, remember that it begins counting fields at 0. Here are three lines sorted by the example:

```
01877 Jones CT pipes    400 $32,231
29742 Smith NH gravel   4450 $10,001
00456 Smith SD concrete 1000 $20,100
```

**Keyword:**   text handling

**See Also:**   awk, comm, grep, join, uniq, sed

ALL  ALL  END

### sort +3 sales.db > sales.sort

This command might or might not produce the results that you want. Assuming you want to sort on field 3 (really, field 4), you expect the words to be ordered alphabetically. Instead, they are ordered by their ASCII values, so the line containing **Pipes** comes first:

```
01877 Jones CT Pipes    400 $32,231
00456 Smith SD concrete 1000 $20,100
29742 Smith NH gravel   4450 $10,001
```

**Keyword:**   text handling

**See Also:**   awk, comm, grep, join, uniq, sed

ALL  ALL  END

### sort -b +1 sales.db > sales.sort

Assume that a sample database has unpredictable occurrences of whitespace in it. Normally, after **sort** parses an initial whitespace, it considers all subsequent whitespaces as part of the next string or number. The **-b** option takes care of this problem. Here is the output:

```
01877 Jones CT Pipes    400 $32,231
29742 Smith NH gravel   4450 $10,001
00456 Smith SD concrete 1000 $20,100
```

**Keyword:**    text handling
**See Also:**    awk, comm, grep, join, uniq, sed

## sort -d names.db | sed ´s/,/, /´ > names.sort

The **-d** option tells **sort** to compare only numbers, letters, and whitespace. This is called a dictionary sort, but can be helpful with lists of information that contain punctuation marks, as shown.

```
Jones,Bill
Smith,Alexander
Smith,Brian
```

**Keyword:**    text handling
**See Also:**    awk, comm, grep, join, uniq, sed

## sort -f +3 sales.db > sales.sort

The **-f** option tells **sort** to treat uppercase and lowercase equally:

```
00456 Smith SD concrete 1000 $20,100
29742 Smith NH gravel   4450 $10,001
01877 Jones CT Pipes     400 $32,231
```

**Keyword:**    text handling
**See Also:**    awk, comm, grep, join, uniq, sed

## sort -f p? | sort -umf

Say that the files **p1**, **p2**, and **p3** contain duplicate names of planets, and that some of the duplicates appear in lowercase letters. You want a list with duplicates, however, and you want the list to consist of planet names that are capitalized. This command does the trick.

**Keyword:**    text handling
**See Also:**    awk, comm, grep, join, uniq, sed

## sort -n +0.3 sales.db > sales.sort

You can specify a range of characters or numbers to compare when you use **sort**. The **+0.3** notation tells **sort** to skip the first three digits in the first field and start sorting from there. This is what the output would look like:

ALL    ALL    END

```
29742  Smith NH gravel    4450 $10,001
00456  Smith SD concrete  1000 $20,100
01877  Jones CT Pipes      400 $32,231
```

**Keyword:**    text handling

**See Also:**    awk, comm, grep, join, uniq, sed

### sort -n +4 sales.db > sales.sort

Here again, the **-n** option specifies a numerical sort. This example is important because it shows that **-n** automatically invokes the **-b** option, which tells **sort** that it should ignore leading spaces. In the example output, observe the leading spaces in field **4**, which is the comparison field:

```
01877  Jones CT Pipes      400 $32,231
00456  Smith SD concrete  1000 $20,100
29742  Smith NH gravel    4450 $10,001
```

**Keyword:**    text handling

**See Also:**    awk, comm, grep, join, uniq, sed

### sort -n sales.db > sales.sort

The **-n** option to **sort** specifies a numerical sort. Because no field argument is supplied, **sort** compares the field 0 in the file. The output looks like this:

```
00456  Smith SD concrete  1000 $20,100
01877  Jones CT Pipes      400 $32,231
29742  Smith NH gravel    4450 $10,001
```

**Keyword:**    text handling

**See Also:**    awk, comm, grep, join, uniq, sed

### sort -nr +4 sales.db > sales.sort

This example reverses the order of the sort, thanks to the **-r** option. Here is the output:

```
29742  Smith NH gravel    4450 $10,001
00456  Smith SD concrete  1000 $20,100
01877  Jones CT Pipes      400 $32,231
```

**Keyword:**    text handling

**See Also:**    awk, comm, grep, join, uniq, sed

ALL    ALL    END

ALL    ALL    END

ALL    ALL    END

### sort -t: /etc/passwd

The **-t** option to **sort** lets you change the character that delimits fields on which **sort** operates. In the example, **sort** compares the first field in **/etc/passwd** to display user entries alphabetically by login name. (We're assuming that your users don't capitalize their login names, but if they do, use the **-f** option as well.)

**Keyword:**    text handling

**See Also:**    awk, comm, grep, join, uniq, sed

### sort -u parts.db > parts.db

The **-u** option tells **sort** to remove duplicate lines. To sort, a duplicate line must be an exact match, so output like the following can be expected:

```
Engine
clamps
engine
lights
```

**Keyword:**    text handling

**See Also:**    awk, comm, grep, join, uniq, sed

### sort -uf parts.db > parts.db

This command takes care of the problem with the previous example. The **-f** option tells **sort** to ignore case, so you get a truly unique list of items:

```
clamps
engine
lights
```

(Notice the bias of **sort**: It has discarded the uppercase version of **engine**. See **sort -f p? | sort -umf** for the cure.)

**Keyword:**    text handling

**See Also:**    awk, comm, grep, join, uniq, sed

### sort p1 p2 p3 | sort -m

If the files had not already been sorted by other examples, you could use this command to presort them.

**Keyword:**    text handling

**See Also:**    awk, comm, grep, join, uniq, sed

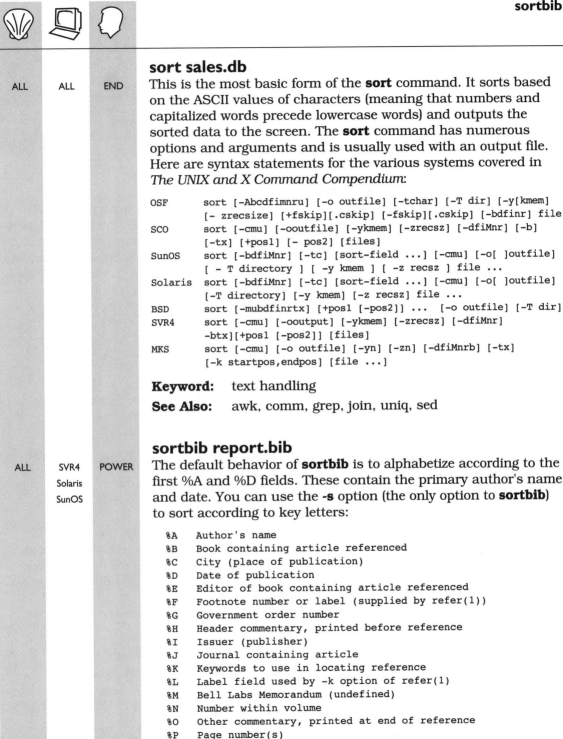

## sort sales.db

| ALL | ALL | END |

This is the most basic form of the **sort** command. It sorts based on the ASCII values of characters (meaning that numbers and capitalized words precede lowercase words) and outputs the sorted data to the screen. The **sort** command has numerous options and arguments and is usually used with an output file. Here are syntax statements for the various systems covered in *The UNIX and X Command Compendium*:

```
OSF       sort [-Abcdfimnru] [-o outfile] [-tchar] [-T dir] [-y[kmem]
          [- zrecsize] [+fskip][.cskip] [-fskip][.cskip] [-bdfinr] file
SCO       sort [-cmu] [-ooutfile] [-ykmem] [-zrecsz] [-dfiMnr] [-b]
          [-tx] [+pos1] [- pos2] [files]
SunOS     sort [-bdfiMnr] [-tc] [sort-field ...] [-cmu] [-o[ ]outfile]
          [ - T directory ] [ -y kmem ] [ -z recsz ] file ...
Solaris   sort [-bdfiMnr] [-tc] [sort-field ...] [-cmu] [-o[ ]outfile]
          [-T directory] [-y kmem] [-z recsz] file ...
BSD       sort [-mubdfinrtx] [+pos1 [-pos2]] ...  [-o outfile] [-T dir]
SVR4      sort [-cmu] [-ooutput] [-ykmem] [-zrecsz] [-dfiMnr]
          -btx][+pos1 [-pos2]] [files]
MKS       sort [-cmu] [-o outfile] [-yn] [-zn] [-dfiMnrb] [-tx]
          [-k startpos,endpos] [file ...]
```

**Keyword:**   text handling

**See Also:**   awk, comm, grep, join, uniq, sed

## sortbib report.bib

| ALL | SVR4 | POWER |
| | Solaris | |
| | SunOS | |

The default behavior of **sortbib** is to alphabetize according to the first %A and %D fields. These contain the primary author's name and date. You can use the **-s** option (the only option to **sortbib**) to sort according to key letters:

```
%A    Author's name
%B    Book containing article referenced
%C    City (place of publication)
%D    Date of publication
%E    Editor of book containing article referenced
%F    Footnote number or label (supplied by refer(1))
%G    Government order number
%H    Header commentary, printed before reference
%I    Issuer (publisher)
%J    Journal containing article
%K    Keywords to use in locating reference
%L    Label field used by -k option of refer(1)
%M    Bell Labs Memorandum (undefined)
%N    Number within volume
%O    Other commentary, printed at end of reference
%P    Page number(s)
%Q    Corporate or Foreign Author (unreversed)
```

**441**

```
%R    Report, paper, or thesis (unpublished)
%S    Series title
%T    Title of article or book
%V    Volume number
```

**Keyword:**   writing, text handling

**See Also:**   addbib, indxbib, lookbib, refer, roffbib

### source .cshrc

CSH  ALL  ALL

We would bet that this is one of the most common commands executed by C shell users. The **source** command lets you execute any commands, including built-in programming commands, and thereby execute any startup file. It is a way to avoid logging out and logging back in again. You can also use **source** in scripts, or simply to execute a special environment or set of commands. In the Bourne and Korn shells, the dot command (**.**) is the equivalent.

**Keyword:**   user environment

**See Also:**   csh, set, setenv, printenv

### spell -b report.txt | more

ALL  ALL  ALL

This command checks British spellings, such as **colour**, **programme**, and **specialise**.

**Keyword:**   writing

**Files:**   /usr/lbin/spell/hlistab, /usr/lib/spell/spellhist

**See Also:**   hashmake, spellin, spellout

### spell -v report.txt > report.spl

ALL  ALL  ALL

The **-v** option to **spell** gives you an idea of how the command makes decisions about whether a word is misspelled. Because **spell** derives correct spellings for different forms of a word contained in the system spelling list, it sometimes adds prefixes, suffixes and inflections to compare a word. The **-v** option displays such matches, after first displaying known misspelled words.

**Keyword:**   writing

**Files:**   /usr/lbin/spell/hlistab, /usr/lib/spell/spellhist

**See Also:**   hashmake, spell, spellin, spellout

### spell book.txt > book.errors

ALL  ALL  ALL

This command checks the **book.txt** file for any spelling errors and writes them to the **book.errors** file.

**Keyword:**  writing

**Files:**  /usr/lbin/spell/hlistab, /usr/lib/spell/spellhist

**See Also:**  hashmake, spellin, spellout

### spellin /usr/lbin/spell/hlista < spell_tmp > spell_lst

The **spellin** command merges one or more words with a spelling list file (in the example, **hlista**) and outputs a revised spelling list used for comparisons by the **spell** command. The revised list is in binary format. Usually, you will want to use **spellin** in conjunction with **hashmake** or **spellout** on OSF systems. You can also use **spellout** in a pipeline to add a single word to the list (see **echo esoteric | spellin**... ).

**Keyword:**  writing

**Files:**  /usr/lbin/spell/hlistab, /usr/lib/spell/spellhist

**See Also:**  hashmake, spell, spellout

### spellout /usr/lbin/spell/hlista < /tmp/spell.$$

The **spellout** command accepts standard input and checks words against those in the system spelling list, which is **hlista** in the example (but you can choose from **hlista** and **hlistb**). The file **/tmp/spell.$$** contains English language words, which **spellout** compares to the words in **hlista** or **hlistb**. When a word doesn't match a word in the system list, **spellout** sends it to standard output. Note that the use of redirection is critical to using **spellout**. An alternative to obtaining input from a file (**/tmp/spell.$$** in the example) is to echo words through a pipeline to **spellout** (see **echo esoteric | spellout**...).

**Keyword:**  writing

**Files:**  /usr/lbin/spell/hlistab, /usr/lib/spell/spellhist

**See Also:**  spell, spellin

### split -100 inventory.jun

When you add a numeric argument to **split**, it breaks files into the specified number of lines. The example again names files **xaa**, **xab**, and **xac**. When you adjust the default in this manner, remember that no more than 676 files can be produced.

**Keyword:**  text handling

**See Also:**  cut, csplit, sed

**443**

| | | |
|---|---|---|
| ALL | ALL | END |

## split -100 inventory.jun invent

When you add a prefix to the **split** command, it names subsequent files using the prefix. In the example, subsequent files would be named **inventaa**, **inventab**, and **inventbc**.

**Keyword:**   text handling

**See Also:**   cut, csplit, sed

| | | |
|---|---|---|
| ALL | ALL | END |

## split inventory.jun

The **split** command is handy for breaking up large files into smaller files. By default, **split** breaks a file into 1,000-line segments. If you do not specify a prefix for these files, **split** names them with an **x** prefix—for example, **xaa**, **xab**, and **xac**.

**Keyword:**   text handling

**See Also:**   cut, csplit, sed

| | | |
|---|---|---|
| CSH | ALL | SCRIPT |

## status

This environment variable indicates the status of the last command. **0** represents successful completion, and **1** represents failure.

**Keyword:**   programming

**See Also:**   if, ps, test

| | | |
|---|---|---|
| ALL | SVR4 | POWER |

## strings -8 core

Normally, **strings** extracts and displays text that is four or more characters in length. Specifying a direct number argument changes this behavior.

**Keyword:**   binary files, programming

**See Also:**   cat, od, print

| | | |
|---|---|---|
| ALL | ALL | POWER |

## strings core

The **strings** command locates and displays ASCII text in a binary file. In the example, **strings** is used with a system core file. The resulting output might help you determine what caused the core dump.

**Keyword:**   system information, programming

**See Also:**   cat, od, print

## stty -a

The **-a** option to **stty** on SVR4 systems displays a report of current terminal settings. Here is an example:

```
speed 19200 baud; intr = DEL; quit = ^|; erase = ^h; kill = @;
eof = ^d; eol = <undef>; eol2 = <undef>; swtch = <undef>;
start = ^q; stop = ^s; susp = ^z; dsusp = ^y; rprnt = ^r;
flush = ^o; werase = ^w; lnext = ^v; parenb -parodd cs7 -cstopb
-hupcl cread clocal -loblk -parext    -ignbrk brkint ignpar -parmrk
-inpck istrip -inlcr -igncr icrnl -iuclc ixon -ixany -ixoff
-imaxbel isig icanon -xcase echo echoe echok -echonl -noflsh -tostop
-echoctl -echoprt -echoke -defecho -flusho -pendin -icxten  opost
-olcuc onlcr -ocrnl -onocr -onlrot -ofill -ofdel tab3
```

**Keyword:**   terminals, devices

**See Also:**   tput, tset, tty

## stty -echo intr ´^a´

You can use this incarnation of **stty** to simulate the way the login process hides what you type when you enter your password. The example properly belongs in a script such as the following:

```
!#/bin/sh
echo "Enter special password: \c"
settings=`stty -g`
stty -echo intr '^a'
read pword
stty $settings
.
.
.
```

The shell script uses **stty -g** to store the current **stty** settings, then turns off character echo while reading a line of input. The stored **stty** values are then restored to the terminal.

**Keyword:**   terminals, devices

**Files:**   /usr/lib/terminfo (SVR4), /etc/termcap (BSD)

**See Also:**   tabs, tset, tput, tty

## stty 19200

This command sets the baud rate of the terminal window to 19200 bps.

**Keyword:**   terminals, devices

**Files:**     /usr/lib/terminfo (SVR4), /etc/termcap (BSD)
**See Also:**  tabs, tset, tput, tty

### stty all

ALL   ALL   POWER SYSADM

Using the **stty** command with the **all** option displays a concise listing of terminal characteristics. The **all** option is available only on BSD-derived systems. Here is an example from a SunOS system:

```
speed 38400 baud, 0 rows, 0 columns; evenp
-inpck imaxbel -tabs
iexten crt
erase  kill  werase  rprnt  flush  lnext  susp    intr  quit  stop   eof
^?     ^U    ^W      ^R     ^O     ^V     ^Z/^Y   ^C    ^\    ^S/^Q  ^D
```

**Keyword:**   terminals, devices
**See Also:**  tput, tset, tty

### stty erase ^H

ALL   ALL   ALL

This useful command tells the system to use the Backspace key for deleting typed characters. On some systems, the default is the Delete key, which can be inconvenient. If **^H** doesn't work, try **'^h'** instead.

**Keyword:**   terminals, devices
**Files:**     /usr/lib/terminfo (SVR4), /etc/termcap (BSD)
**See Also:**  tabs, tput, tset, tty

### stty intr ´^c´; stty erase ´^?´

ALL   ALL   POWER SYSADM

Sometimes it is necessary to perform two **stty** commands in order to attain your goal. The example comes from an SCO system, where the Backspace key is usually defined as the interrupt key. The example first redefines the interrupt key and then redefines the Backspace (erase) key.

**Keyword:**   terminals, devices
**See Also:**  tput, tset, tty

### stty sane

ALL   ALL   POWER SYSADM

The **sane** option resets terminal characteristics. This is convenient if you have been experimenting and your terminal is suddenly being unreasonable (adjective borrowed from AIX documentation).

**Keyword:** terminals, devices
**See Also:** tput, tset, tty

## stty size

ALL  BSD  ALL

This command outputs the size of the terminal window.
**Keyword:** terminals, devices
**Files:** /etc/termcap (BSD)
**See Also:** tabs, tset, tty, xwininfo

## stty speed

ALL  BSD  ALL

This command outputs the baud rate of the terminal window.
**Keyword:** terminals, devices
**Files:** /etc/termcap (BSD)
**See Also:** tabs, tset, tty

## su

ALL  ALL  POWER  SYSADM

By default, the **su** command (for "switch user") lets you become the superuser on the system. Of course, it prompts you for the correct password, which you must enter.
**Keyword:** security, user environment
**See Also:** csh, env, ksh, login, passwd, sh

## su - alans

ALL  ALL  POWER  SYSADM

Specifying the dash option after **su** tells it to execute a full login to the user's environment. This includes sourcing the **.login** file in the C shell or the **.profile** file in the Bourne and Korn shells. If you don't use the - option, your current environment is transferred to the new login.
**Keyword:** security, user environment
**Files:** $HOME/.login, $HOME/.cshrc, $HOME/.profile
**See Also:** csh, env, ksh, login, passwd, sh

## su alans

ALL  ALL  POWER  SYSADM

You can use the **su** command to switch to any user on the system. All you need is the password for that user. If you are superuser, **su** switches you without asking for a password.
**Keyword:** security, user environment
**See Also:** csh, env, ksh, login, passwd, sh

## sum sales.db

The **sum** command displays a 16-bit checksum for the named file. It also displays the number of blocks used by the file. You can use **sum** to check for bad spots in the file, or check whether a file that has been received via modem is okay. In the latter case, the remote site would have to provide a checksum made prior to the modem transmission. The **sum** command supports a **-f** option, which works the same way, but uses a different algorithm.

**Keyword:**    binary files, security

**See Also:**    crypt, wc, uvencode

## sysadm

The **sysadm** command on SVR4 systems invokes a visual interface to system administration. You can assign a password to the **sysadm** command by using the "System Name, Date/Time, and Initial Password Setup" menu. With **sysadm**, you have the option of using the menu interface or entering keyword options at the command line. You can also go directly to a task by entering a task keyword.

**Keyword:**    system setup, system information

**See Also:**    setup, smit (AIX), sysadmsh (SCO)

## sysadm backup_service

The **backup_service** keyword invokes the Backup Service Management menu. Options and task keywords are:

```
Start Backup Jobs                   sysadm backup
Backup History Management           sysadm history
Schedule Backup Reminder            sysadm reminder
Respond to Backup Job Prompts       sysadm respond
Schedule Automatic Backups          sysadm schedule
Backup Control Table Management     sysadm setup
Backup Status Management            sysadm status
```

**Keyword:**    backup and restore

**See Also:**    setup, smit (AIX), sysadmsh (SCO)

## sysadm file_systems

The **file_systems** keyword invokes the Manage File Systems menu. Options and task keywords are:

```
Check a File System                 sysadm check
Manage Defaults                     sysadm defaults
```

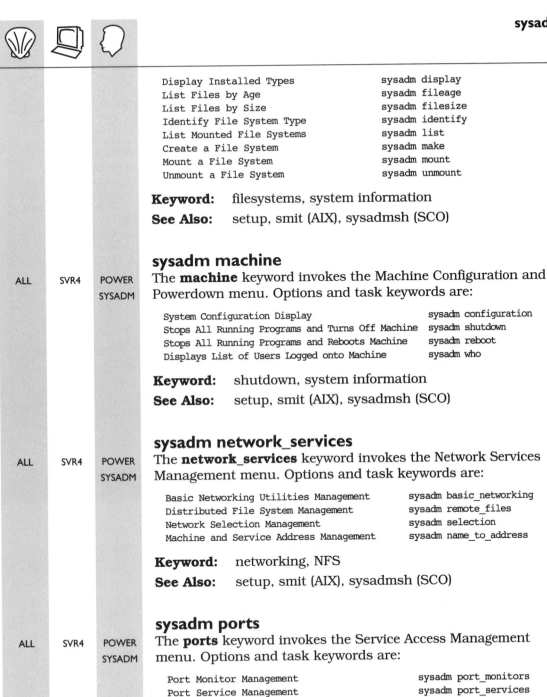

```
Display Installed Types          sysadm display
List Files by Age                sysadm fileage
List Files by Size               sysadm filesize
Identify File System Type        sysadm identify
List Mounted File Systems        sysadm list
Create a File System             sysadm make
Mount a File System              sysadm mount
Unmount a File System            sysadm unmount
```

**Keyword:**   filesystems, system information

**See Also:**   setup, smit (AIX), sysadmsh (SCO)

### sysadm machine

The **machine** keyword invokes the Machine Configuration and Powerdown menu. Options and task keywords are:

```
System Configuration Display                    sysadm configuration
Stops All Running Programs and Turns Off Machine  sysadm shutdown
Stops All Running Programs and Reboots Machine    sysadm reboot
Displays List of Users Logged onto Machine        sysadm who
```

**Keyword:**   shutdown, system information

**See Also:**   setup, smit (AIX), sysadmsh (SCO)

### sysadm network_services

The **network_services** keyword invokes the Network Services Management menu. Options and task keywords are:

```
Basic Networking Utilities Management     sysadm basic_networking
Distributed File System Management        sysadm remote_files
Network Selection Management              sysadm selection
Machine and Service Address Management    sysadm name_to_address
```

**Keyword:**   networking, NFS

**See Also:**   setup, smit (AIX), sysadmsh (SCO)

### sysadm ports

The **ports** keyword invokes the Service Access Management menu. Options and task keywords are:

```
Port Monitor Management           sysadm port_monitors
Port Service Management           sysadm port_services
Quick Terminal Setup              sysadm quick_terminal
Terminal Line Setting Management  sysadm tty_settings
```

**Keyword:**   terminals, devices

**See Also:**   setup, smit (AIX), sysadmsh (SCO)

ALL   SVR4   POWER SYSADM

## sysadm printers

ALL    SVR4    POWER
SYSADM

The **printers** keyword invokes the Line Printer Services Configuration and Operation menu. Options and task keywords are:

```
Manage Classes of Related Printers        sysadm classes
Manage Filters for Special Processing     sysadm filters
Manage Pre-Printed Forms                  sysadm forms
Perform Daily Printer Service Operations  sysadm operations
Configure Printers for the Printer Service sysadm printers
Assign Print Queue Priorities to Users    sysadm priorities
Manage Active Print Requests              sysadm requests
Display Status of Printer Service         sysadm status
Configure Connections to Remote Systems   sysadm systems
```

**Keyword:**    printing, system information

**See Also:**   setup, smit (AIX), sysadmsh (SCO)

## sysadm restore_service

ALL    SVR4    POWER
SYSADM

The **restore_service** keyword invokes the Line Restore Service Management menu. Options and task keywords are:

```
Set/Display the Restore Operator          sysadm operator
Respond to Restore Job Prompts            sysadm respond
Restore from Backup Archives              sysadm restore
Modify/Report Pending Restore Request Status  sysadm status
```

**Keyword:**    backup and restore

**See Also:**   setup, smit (AIX), sysadmsh (SCO)

## sysadm schedule_task

ALL    SVR4    POWER
SYSADM

The **schedule_task** keyword invokes the Schedule Automatic Task menu, which is solely concerned with allowing users to interface with the UNIX **cron** program. Menu options and task keywords are:

```
Add         sysadm add
Change      sysadm change
Delete      sysadm delete
Display     sysadm display
```

**Keyword:**    job control, system information

**See Also:**   setup, smit (AIX), sysadmsh (SCO)

## sysadm software

ALL    SVR4    POWER
SYSADM

The **software** keyword invokes the Software Installation and Removal menu. Options and task keywords are:

```
Checks Accuracy of Installation          sysadm check
Sets Installation Defaults               sysadm defaults
Installs Software Packages               sysadm install
Stores Interactions with Packages        sysadm interact
Displays Information about Packages       sysadm list
Stores Packages Without Installing        sysadm read_in
Removes Packages                         sysadm remove
```

**Keyword:** applications, system setup

**See Also:** setup, smit (AIX), sysadmsh (SCO)

## sysadm storage_devices

ALL   SVR4   POWER
SYSADM

The **storage_devices** keyword invokes the Storage Device Operations and Definitions menu. Options and task keywords are:

```
Device Alias and Attribute Management    sysadm descriptions
Device Group Management                  sysadm groups
```

**Keyword:** devices

**See Also:** setup, smit (AIX), sysadmsh (SCO)

## sysadm system_setup

ALL   SVR4   POWER
SYSADM

The **sytem_setup** keyword invokes the System Name, Date/Time, and Initial Password Setup menu. Options and task keywords are:

```
System Data and Time Information                      sysadm datatime
System Name and Network Note Name of the Machine      sysadm nodename
Assigns Adminstrative Login Passwords                 sysadm password
Sets up System Information for First Time             sysadm setup
```

**Keyword:** system setup, system information, networking

**See Also:** setup, smit (AIX), sysadmsh (SCO)

## sysadm users

ALL   SVR4   POWER
SYSADM

The **users** keyword invokes the User Login and Group Administration menu. Options and task keywords are:

```
Adds Users or Groups                     sysadm add
Defines Dafaults for Adding Users        sysadm defaults
Lists Users or Groups                    sysadm list
Modifies Attributes of Users or Groups   sysadm modify
(Re)defines User Password Information     sysadm password
Removes Users or Groups                  sysadm remove
```

**Keyword:** user environment

**See Also:** setup, smit (AIX), sysadmsh (SCO)

**451**

## sysadmsh

| | | |
|---|---|---|
| ALL | SCO | POWER SYSADM |

The **sysadmsh** program is the SCO visual interface to system adminstration. Unlike **sysadm** (SVR4), it does not provide direct access to modules from the command line. Entering **sysadmsh** at the command line invokes the program. Pressing F1 in the program displays help. Note that you must be the root user to perform many tasks within **sysadmsh**. In some cases, you must also work at the system console and/or run in single-user mode. The **sysadmsh** program also supports the following environment variables:

```
SYSADM, which points to prompt, menu, form, and help files
SA_EDITOR, which defines the sysadmsh editor
SA_MAIL, which  defines the sysadmsh mail program
SA_PRINT, which defines the sysadmsh printer
SA_USERAPPS, which defines a user menu file
```

**Keyword:**   system setup, system information

**See Also:**   setup, smit (AIX), sysadm (SVR4)


## tabs -a

| | | |
|---|---|---|
| ALL | ALL | ALL |

This command sets the tabs for your terminal to positions 1, 10, 16, 36, and 72.

**Keyword:**   terminal display

**See Also:**   set, setenv, stty, tset, tty


## tabs 1,10,15,25 -T /dev/tty01

| | | |
|---|---|---|
| ALL | ALL | ALL |

This command sets tabs to positions 1, 10, 15, and 25 for the terminal **tty01**, as specified by the **-T** option.

**Keyword:**   terminal display

**See Also:**   set, setenv, stty, tset, tty


## tabs 5

| | | |
|---|---|---|
| ALL | ALL | ALL |

This command sets the tabs for your terminal equal to **5** spaces.

**Keyword:**   terminal display

**See Also:**   set, setenv, stty, tset, tty


## tail

| | | |
|---|---|---|
| ALL | ALL | END SCRIPT |

If you know anything about the inside of a file (especially if you have a rough idea about line numbers), **tail** can be quite useful. When you enter **tail** at the prompt with no arguments, it waits for standard input from the shell edit mode. Useful? Not without help, but look what you can do:

```
cat - | tee -a $1 | tail -1 >> ~/daily.log
```

Do we really expect anyone to use this command? Not from the command line (as is obvious from our use of **$1**). But it is good fodder for a script. The command saves your shell input session to a file defined by **$1**, and after this (thanks to **tee**), it pipes the output into **tail**. In turn, **tail** takes the last line of the file and appends it to **daily.log** in the user's home directory. If you use the shell edit mode, you might adopt this command and always make the last line of your editing a summary line such as this:

```
File:sales;important notes;Sep 9,1994
```

**Keyword:**    text display, text handling

**See Also:**    cat, head, less, more, pg, sed


### tail +25c sales.txt

ALL  ALL  END SCRIPT

This command displays everything except the first 25 characters of the **sales.txt** file.

**Keyword:**    text display, text handling

**See Also:**    cat, head, less, more, pg, sed


### tail +50 sales.txt

ALL  ALL  END SCRIPT

This command displays everything except the first 49 lines of the **sales.txt** file.

**Keyword:**    text display, text handling

**See Also:**    cat, head, less, more, pg, sed


### tail -1 -f /var/adm/messages

ALL  ALL  SYSADM

This command is useful for a system administrator to keep running. It shows the contents of the last line of **/var/adm/messages** once every minute.

**Keyword:**    system information

**See Also:**    cat, head, more


### tail -50 sales.txt

ALL  ALL  END SCRIPT

This command displays the last 50 lines of the **sales.txt** file.

**Keyword:**    text display, text handling

**See Also:**    cat, head, less, more, pg, sed

### tail -r ~/daily.log

ALL  ALL  SCRIPT  POWER

If you did adopt a daily log file (see the first **tail** example), you might like to display the latest entries in reverse order. The example displays the default last 20 lines of the file, beginning with the most recent line in **daily.log**.

**Keyword:**   text display, text handling

**See Also:**   cat, head, less, more, pg, sed

### tail sales.txt

ALL  ALL  END  SCRIPT

This command displays the last ten lines of the **sales.txt** file. Ten lines is the default for **tail**.

**Keyword:**   text display, text handling

**See Also:**   cat, head, less, more, pg, sed

### tails() { for f in `ls -1`; do echo "#$f#"; tail $f|pg; done; return; }

ALL  ALL  END  SCRIPT

We couldn't resist including this Bourne shell function. It makes up for one limitation of the **tail** command, namely its inability to handle multiple files.

**Keyword:**   text display, text handling

**See Also:**   cat, head, less, more, pg, sed

### talk emily

ALL  ALL  END

The **talk** command requests a communication session with the specified user. With **talk**, you can initiate conversations across networks as well as on multiuser systems (implied by the example). Here are the different types of addressing:

```
emily@new1.sparky
new1!emily
new1.emily
new1:emily
```

The person contacted by **talk** must respond by starting up **talk**. The **talk** interface consists of a split screen window (either on a terminal or in an Xterm window). Press the Interrupt key to end a **talk** session.

**Keyword:**   user communication, Internet

**See Also:**   mail, mailx, write

### talk emily@newl.sparky /dev/ttyp4

In addition to specifying a system, you can also specify a terminal. In this case, **emily** and the requesting party probably pre-arranged to use **/dev/ttyp4** on **emily**'s system.

**Keyword:** user communication, Internet

**See Also:** mail, mailx, write

ALL ALL END

### TAPE

This can be a very useful environment variable. If you have written scripts to back up your system, and you want them to work on different systems, substituting **TAPE** for the real device file can save you from having to edit the scripts. Here is a list of some common tape device files:

```
AIX:                /dev/rmt0
OSF/1,Ultrix:       /dev/rmt0a
NeXT:               /dev/rxt0
SCO UNIX:           /dev/rmt0
SCO XENIX:          /dev/rct0
SunOS:              /dev/rst0
Solaris:            /dev/rmt/0
SVR4:               /dev/rmt/c0s0
```

**Keyword:** backup and restore, system setup

**See Also:** mkdev, mknod, sysadm, sysadmsh

ALL ALL SYSADM

### tar cf - mytree | compress | uuencode mytree.tar.Z | mail perkie

This command packages a source tree using **tar**, **compress**, and **uuencode**. It then sends it to user **perkie** using the **mail** command.

**Keyword:** backup and restore, devices

**See Also:** compress, uncompress, uuencode

ALL ALL POWER SYSADM

### tar cf /dev/rmt0a /u1

This command copies the entire contents of the **/u1** directory structure to the tape **/dev/rmt0a**. This command formats the tape as it writes data to it. If the tape can't hold everything, another tape is requested.

**Keyword:** backup and restore

**See Also:** cp, cpio, rcp

ALL ALL ALL

| | | | **tar** |
|---|---|---|---|

### tar cf stuff.tar /u2/perkie/stuff ; compress stuff.tar

| ALL | ALL | POWER SYSADM |
|---|---|---|

This command creates a compressed **tar** file called **stuff.tar.Z** containing everything in the **/u2/perkie/stuff** directory.

**Keyword:**   backup and restore, devices

**See Also:**   cp, cpio, rcp, compress, uncompress, zcat

### tar rf /dev/rmt0a /u1/perkie/mail

| ALL | ALL | POWER SYSADM |
|---|---|---|

This command adds the contents of **/u1/perkie/mail** to the end of the **/dev/rmt0a** tape.

**Keyword:**   backup and restore, devices

**See Also:**   cp, cpio, rcp, compress, uncompress, zcat

### tar tvf /dev/rmt0a

| ALL | ALL | POWER SYSADM |
|---|---|---|

This command shows the contents of the **/dev/rmt0a** tape without extracting any information.

**Keyword:**   backup and restore, devices

**See Also:**   cp, cpio, rcp, compress, uncompress, zcat

### tar uf /dev/rmt0a /u1/perkie/mail

| ALL | ALL | ALL |
|---|---|---|

This command updates the contents of the **/dev/rmt0a** tape with any new or modified files in **/u1/perkie/mail**.

**Keyword:**   backup and restore

**See Also:**   cp, cpio, rcp, compress, uncompress, zcat

### tar xf /dev/rmt0a

| ALL | ALL | POWER SYSADM |
|---|---|---|

This command outputs the contents of an archived tape to the current working directory.

**Keyword:**   backup and restore, devices

**See Also:**   cp, cpio, rcp

### tar xf /dev/rmt0a /u1/perkie/mail/alans/54

| ALL | ALL | POWER SYSADM |
|---|---|---|

This command copies the **/u1/perkie/mail/alans/54** file off of the **/dev/rmt0a** tape and writes it to the current working directory in a structure of **/u1/perkie/mail/alans/54**.

**Keyword:**   backup and restore

**See Also:**   cp, cpio, rcp, compress, uncompress, zcat

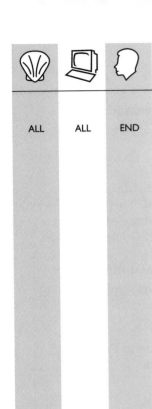

## tbl cmds.tbl | nroff -e | more

Who doesn't have trouble with tables? By the looks of this command, **tbl** isn't promising a rose garden, but you would be surprised at how easily you can make tables with **tbl**. The output, of course, is ASCII, but you can filter it through **nroff** and **troff** for printing. In fact, you have to filter it through one or the other, as the example shows. The **-e** option to **nroff** directs output to your screen, and **more** stops small tables from scrolling completely off screen. Try entering the following file:

```
.TS
center tab(#);
c s s
l l l.
.sp2
DOS-UNIX HELP
.sp2
DOS#UNIX#DESCRIPTION
.sp
DEL#rm#Delete (remove) files
RM#rmdir#Delete empty directory
RMDIR#rmdir#Delete empty directory
DIR#ls -l#Default horizontal directory list
COPY#cp#Copy files
REN#mv#Rename files (but mv moves, too)
.TE
```

In this sample, **.TS** signifies the beginning of the table, and **.TE** signifies the end. On the second line, **center** is a command that tells **tbl** to center the table; **tab(#)** is a command that sets the **#** character to represent a tab. The **c s s** line directs **tbl** to center the first line of text (**s s** indicates blank fields). The **l l l** line indicates that the remaining text in the table is left-justified. The final dot character ends the **tbl** commands section.

**Keyword:**    text formatting, printing, documentation

**See Also:**    eqn, neqn, col, lp, lpr, more, nroff, troff

## tbl man1/ps.1 | neqn | nroff -Ttablpr -man -h | lpr -Plocalhp

This command lets you print **man** pages to the printer. The example assumes that your current working directory is **/usr/share/man**, which is the top of the **man** pages directory hierarchy. The **-T** option specifies an output device file (driver). The device file must be located in the **/usr/share/lib/term** directory. On System V platforms, there is a slight difference: The device file is found in the **/usr/share/lib/nterm** directory.

**Keyword:**   text formatting, printing, documentation

**See Also:**   eqn, neqn, col, lp, lpr, more, nroff, troff

## tbl sales.raw >> sales.tbl

ALL   ALL   END

This command creates an **nroff** table from the data in the **sales.raw** file, and calls the new file **sales.tbl**. The new file is now suitable for use by **nroff**. This is an intermediate step, but you might prefer to save your table files this way. Doing so will let you do final printing without involving **tbl**.

**Keyword:**   text formatting, printing, documentation

**See Also:**   eqn, neqn, col, lp, lpr, more, nroff, troff

## tcopy /dev/rmt0a /dev/rmt1a

ALL   ALL   POWER
SYSADM

This command copies the contents of the tape in drive **/dev/rmt0a** to the tape in drive **/dev/rmt1a**.

**Keyword:**   backup and restore, devices

**See Also:**   cp, cpio, dump, mt, tar

## tee

ALL   ALL   POWER

The **tee** command is used mostly in pipelines. The idea behind **tee** is a plumber's T-connector, which splits the flow through a pipe. Instead of in plumbing, **tee** works in a UNIX pipeline. Here is an example:

```
sort sales.jun | tee -a sales.sort
```

The example sorts the file and then pipes it into **tee**, which displays the text on-screen and appends the text to the named file.

**Keyword:**   program execution, text handling

**See Also:**   cat, echo, script

## tee -a < sales.jun sales.94

ALL   ALL   POWER

There are a few ways to use **tee** and have it begin a command. In the example, text from **sales.jun** is redirected into **tee**, which displays it to the screen and appends it to **sales.94**. The **-a** option is responsible for appending, instead of overwriting, the named file.

**Keyword:**   program execution, text handling

**See Also:**   cat, echo, script

### tee < sales.jun | sort >> sales.sort

ALL  ALL  POWER

Here is a command that combines the two previous examples. In all, three actions are occurring: **tee** displays output to the terminal, **tee** sends the output along the pipeline, and **sort** redirects the text to a file.

**Keyword:**  program execution, text handling

**See Also:**  cat, echo, script

### telnet -l alans aixpilot

ALL  BSD  END

The **-l** option to **telnet** lets you specify a username on the command line. This is useful if you want to log into a remote system under an identity that is different from that on the local system.

**Keyword:**  networking, Internet

**Files:**  $HOME/.telnetrc

**See Also:**  cu, rlogin, rsh, stty

### telnet sunss2

ALL  ALL  ALL

This command starts the communication program **telnet**, which (in the example) connects you to the remote computer called **sunss2**. After you have connected, you can log in and use the remote computer as if it were local.

**Keyword:**  networking, Internet

**Files:**  $HOME/.telnetrc

**See Also:**  cu, rlogin, rsh, stty

### telnet>

ALL  ALL  ALL

This is the standard **telnet** prompt. At the prompt, you can enter commands recognized by **telnet**. These commands do not work at the UNIX prompt. The upcoming examples provide a sampling of commands.

**Keyword:**  networking, Internet

**Files:**  $HOME/.telnetrc

**See Also:**  cu,rcp, rlogin, rsh

### telnet> ?

ALL  ALL  ALL

The question mark displays variables that you can send to change the communication characteristics of your **telnet** session. Here is a sample:

**telnet**

```
close            Close current connection.
display          Display operating parameters.
mode             Try to enter line-by-line or character-at-a-time mode.
open             Connect to a site.
quit             Exit telnet.
send             Transmit special characters ('send ?' for more).
set              Set operating parameters ('set ?' for more).
unset            Unset operating parameters ('unset ?' for more).
status           Print status information.
toggle           Toggle operating parameters ('toggle ?' for more).
slc              Change state of special characters ('slc ?' for more).
z                Suspend telnet.
!                Invoke a subshell.
environ          Change environment variables ('environ ?' for more).
?                Print help information.
```

**Keyword:**  networking, Internet

**Files:**  $HOME/.telnetrc

**See Also:**  cu,rcp, rlogin, rsh

## telnet> close

ALL   ALL   ALL

The **close** command ends a **telnet** session and returns you to the UNIX prompt. The **quit** command does the same thing.

**Keyword:**  networking, Internet

**Files:**  $HOME/.telnetrc

**See Also:**  cu, rcp, rlogin, rsh

## telnet> display

ALL   ALL   ALL

This command lists the **telnet** variables in effect. A typical listing looks like this:

```
echo             [^E]
escape           [^]]
tracefile        "(standard output)"
flushoutput      [^O]
interrupt        [^C]
quit             [^\]
eof              [^D]
erase            [^?]
kill             [^U]
lnext            [^V]
susp             [^Z]
reprint          [^R]
worderase        [^W]
start            [^Q]
stop             [^S]
forw1            [off]
forw2            [off]
```

**Keyword:** networking, Internet
**Files:** $HOME/.telnetrc
**See Also:** cu, rcp, rlogin, rsh

### telnet> open sparky

ALL   ALL   ALL

The **open** command lets you begin a connection from within **telnet**. The hostname, which is **sparky** in the example, can be a local network system or a remote Internet system. The **telnet** program understands both UUCP-style addressing (newl!sparky!emily) and Internet domain addressing (emily@sparky.newl.com).

**Keyword:** networking, Internet
**Files:** $HOME/.telnetrc
**See Also:** cu, rcp, rlogin, rsh

### test

ALL   ALL   END

The **test** command evaluates an expression and returns a zero or nonzero value. One thing to note is that, unlike some other environments, UNIX expects a zero value to equal a true condition and a nonzero value to equal a false condition. See the **if** examples earlier in *The UNIX and X Command Compendium* for typical ways to use **test** (which, in the examples, is represented by square brackets, a system-level alias).

**Keyword:** programming
**See Also:** csh, if, sh

### test -r /usr/spool/mail/alans && mailx

ALL   ALL   END

This example of the **test** command could be used in a script or even at the command line. The **-r** option tests whether the mail file for **alans** exists. The **&&** notation is a logical AND operation. Thus, if the mail file exists, the shell runs **mailx**.

**Keyword:** programming
**See Also:** csh, if, sh

### tftp

ALL   ALL   END

This is an interactive command for transferring files between remote systems. Because no security is associated with it, many sites don't support the application, and we recommend using the **ftp** program instead.

**Keyword:** networking, Internet
**See Also:** ftp, rcp, uucp

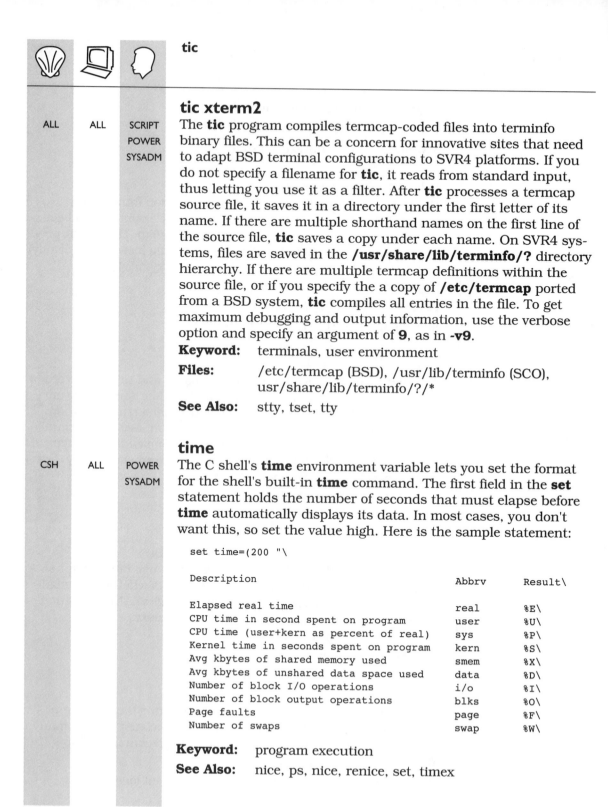

**tic**

## tic xterm2

The **tic** program compiles termcap-coded files into terminfo binary files. This can be a concern for innovative sites that need to adapt BSD terminal configurations to SVR4 platforms. If you do not specify a filename for **tic**, it reads from standard input, thus letting you use it as a filter. After **tic** processes a termcap source file, it saves it in a directory under the first letter of its name. If there are multiple shorthand names on the first line of the source file, **tic** saves a copy under each name. On SVR4 systems, files are saved in the **/usr/share/lib/terminfo/?** directory hierarchy. If there are multiple termcap definitions within the source file, or if you specify the a copy of **/etc/termcap** ported from a BSD system, **tic** compiles all entries in the file. To get maximum debugging and output information, use the verbose option and specify an argument of **9**, as in **-v9**.

**Keyword:** terminals, user environment

**Files:** /etc/termcap (BSD), /usr/lib/terminfo (SCO), usr/share/lib/terminfo/?/*

**See Also:** stty, tset, tty

## time

The C shell's **time** environment variable lets you set the format for the shell's built-in **time** command. The first field in the **set** statement holds the number of seconds that must elapse before **time** automatically displays its data. In most cases, you don't want this, so set the value high. Here is the sample statement:

```
set time=(200 "\
```

| Description | Abbrv | Result\ |
|---|---|---|
| Elapsed real time | real | %E\ |
| CPU time in second spent on program | user | %U\ |
| CPU time (user+kern as percent of real) | sys | %P\ |
| Kernel time in seconds spent on program | kern | %S\ |
| Avg kbytes of shared memory used | smem | %X\ |
| Avg kbytes of unshared data space used | data | %D\ |
| Number of block I/O operations | i/o | %I\ |
| Number of block output operations | blks | %O\ |
| Page faults | page | %F\ |
| Number of swaps | swap | %W\ |

**Keyword:** program execution

**See Also:** nice, ps, nice, renice, set, timex

ALL    ALL    POWER
              SYSADM

## time bmark

The external **time** command can be used in all three shells. It measures the time it takes for the program (in the example, **bmark**) to execute its chores. To use **time**, just place it in front of any program or command. In the C shell, you normally invoke **time** as **/bin/time**. Here is what the output from **time** looks like:

```
real     1:37.5
user        1.1
sys        24.0
```

The output reports time in minutes and seconds. The **real** category represents actual elapsed time, **user** represents the time spent in the user's environment executing the command, and **sys** represents the time spent by the CPU running the command.

**Keyword:**    program execution

**See Also:**    nice, ps, renice

CSH    ALL    POWER
              SYSADM

## time bmark

This is not a duplicate entry. It is the C shell's built-in version of **time**. It works similarly to **/bin/time**, but provides a different data display:

```
1.04u 23.99s 1:40 25% 0+0k 1119+435io 0pf+0w
```

The default fields in the C shell's **time** display correspond to values that you can set using the **time** environment variable. The order of the default display is **%U**, **%S**, **%E**, **%P**, **%X**, **%D**, and **%I**. Here are the definitions for the default display:

```
1.04u          CPU time in seconds spent on program
23.99s         Kernel time in seconds spent on program
1.40           Elapsed real time
25%            Total CPU time (%U + %S as percent of %E)
0+0k           Average kilobytes of shared memory used
1119+435io     Average kilobytes of unshared data space used
0pf+0w         Number of block I/O operations
```

**Keyword:**    program execution

**See Also:**    nice, ps, nice, renice, time, timex

SH    ALL    END

## TIMEOUT

This Bourne shell environment variable sets a limit on the interval between commands entered at the prompt. If the interval elapses before you enter a command, the shell logs you out.

**TIMEOUT** units are in minutes. Setting **TIMEOUT** to 0, however, prevents the shell from automatically logging you out.

**Keyword:** user environment

**Files:** $HOME/.profile

**See Also:** env, login, printenv

### TMOUT

KSH  ALL  END

This is the Korn shell version of the previous example. The major difference is that the Korn shell you are using could have a maximum **TMOUT** value programmed into it, meaning that you can't override it.

**Keyword:** user environment

**Files:** $HOME/.kshrc

**See Also:** env, login, printenv

### touch -a book.txt

ALL  ALL  END

This command changes the access time of the **book.txt** file to the current time.

**Keyword:** file, display, file handling

**See Also:** find, ls, vi

### touch -c book.new

ALL  ALL  END

The **-c** option tells **touch** not to create a file if the target file does not exist.

**Keyword:** file handling

**See Also:** du, find, ls

### touch -m book.txt

ALL  ALL  END

This command changes the modification time of the **book.txt** file to the current time.

**Keyword:** file handling

**See Also:** find, ls, vi

### touch ./123.hlp

ALL  ALL  END

If you try to use **touch** on a filename that begins with a number, **touch** chokes because it thinks it's a date specification. This example sidesteps the problem.

**Keyword:** file handling

**See Also:** du, find, ls

### touch 09231715 deadline

Specifying a numeric data sequence before a filename changes the access and modification dates for the file.

**Keyword:** file handling

**See Also:** du, find, ls

ALL ALL END

### touch book.txt

This is an excellent command if you have a co-author who checks to see if you have done your work by looking at the time-stamp of a file. This command updates both the access and modification times of the **book.txt** file to equal the current time.

**Keyword:** file handling

**See Also:** du, find, ls

ALL ALL END

### tr ´[0-9]´ ´[#*]´ <sales.db >list.db

This command changes all the numbers in the **sales.db** file to #s and writes the resulting file to **list.db**.

**Keyword:** text filters

**See Also:** awk, dd, expand, sed

ALL SVR4 Solaris SunOS SCO OSF AIX MKS POWER

### tr ´[A-Z]´ ´[a-z]´ <raw.db >new.db

This command changes the uppercase letters in the **raw.db** file to lowercase, and writes the output to the **new.db** file.

**Keyword:** text filters

**See Also:** awk, dd, expand, sed

ALL SVR4 Solaris SunOS SCO OSF AIX MKS POWER

### tr ´{}´ ´[]´ < story.txt > story.jun

Editors often use square brackets to note comments in a story. We're sure other people do the same thing, but some of us prefer curly brackets. This command converts the curlies to squares.

**Keyword:** text filters

**See Also:** awk, dd, expand, sed

ALL SVR4 Solaris SunOS SCO OSF AIX MKS POWER

### tr -cs ´[A- Z][a-z][0-9]´ ´[\012*]´ < data.txt > data.db

Using the **-cs** option combination opens up many possibilities with **tr**. This command parses the file and puts each word and number on a line by itself. This can be handy in manipulating data from uneven records and files.

ALL SVR4 Solaris SunOS SCO OSF AIX MKS POWER

**Keyword:** text filters
**See Also:** awk, dd, expand, sed

### tr -cs A- Za-z ´\012´ < data.txt > data.db

ALL · SVR4 SunOS · POWER

The BSD version of **tr** is different from the more common SVR4 version. Vendors tend to support both, however, with a few exceptions. The example parses the file and outputs each word in the file on a line of its own. If numbers or symbols are originally part of the word, they are removed, but the remaining letters are printed as a word.

**Keyword:** text filters
**See Also:** awk, dd, sed

### tr -d ´$´ < sales.dat > sales.wk1

ALL · SVR4 Solaris SunOS SCO OSF AIX MKS · POWER

The **-d** option to **tr** removes the specified character or range of characters from the input text. In the example, text is redirected to **tr** from the **sales.dat** file and output to the **sales.wk1** file.

**Keyword:** text filters
**See Also:** awk, dd, expand, sed

### tr -s " " < notes.txt

ALL · SVR4 Solaris SunOS SCO OSF AIX MKS · POWER

The **-s** option to **tr** reduces a series of the same character to a single instance of the character. The example reduces all successive instances of whitespace characters.

**Keyword:** text filters
**See Also:** awk, dd, expand, sed

### tr -s ´\015´ ´\012´ < apple.txt > unix.txt

ALL · SVR4 Solaris SunOS SCO OSF AIX MKS · POWER

If you are an Apple and UNIX user, or just have to convert an Apple file on occasion, this command does the trick. It converts all Apple carriage returns to newlines. Carriage returns by themselves cause all the text to run together on a UNIX system.

**Keyword:** text filters
**See Also:** awk, dd, sed

### tr -s ´\015´ < report.dos > report.txt

ALL · SVR4 Solaris SunOS · POWER

If you don't have a DOS-to-UNIX file conversion program on your system, use this command to strip the ^M carriage return marker at the end of each line. This is invaluable if you work with DOS files.

**Keyword:** text filters

**See Also:** awk, dd, dos2unix, sed

### trace csh

The **trace** command runs the specified command, intercepts system calls and signals, and displays system calls on the standard output. The command is an excellent way to determine dependencies, including the resource files that a program uses in the X Window System. Here are some sample lines of output from the example:

```
open ("/usr/lib/ld.so", 0, 0442120) = 3
read (3, "".., 32) = 32
mmap (0, 40960, 0x5, 0x80000002, 3, 0) = 0xf77e0000
mmap (0xf77e8000, 8192, 0x7, 0x80000012, 3, 32768) = 0xf77e8000
```

**Keyword:** program execution, programming

**See Also:** truss (SVR4 equivalent)

### trap "" 1 2 3 15

The **trap** command handles the hangup, interrupt, quit, and kill signals. The quotes in the example tell **trap** to *ignore* all signals. The quotes represent the null string. In general, **trap** is used in shell scripts, but it can also be effective at the command line.

**Keyword:** programming, program execution

**See Also:** init, kill, ps

### trap "cat $file | mailx -s ´File Aborted´ $USER" 1 2 3 15

This **trap** command pipes the contents of **$file** into **mailx**, which then forwards it to the user. The **-s** object to **mailx** specifies a subject line.

**Keyword:** programming, program execution

**See Also:** init, kill, ps

### trap ´/bin/echo -n "\nExit(y/n): "; read an; [ "$an" = "y" ] && exit 0´ 2

This **trap** command confirms that you want to exit a shell script after you press Ctrl-C. With additional **if** statements, or a case structure, you can develop extensive exit routines with **trap**.

SCO
OSF
AIX
MKS

ALL    SunOS    SCRIPT
       AIX      POWER
            SYSADM

SH    ALL    SCRIPT
KSH          POWER

SH    ALL    SCRIPT
KSH

SH    ALL    SCRIPT
KSH          POWER

**Keyword:** programming, program execution
**See Also:** init, kill, ps

### trap 2 3

SH
KSH
ALL
SCRIPT
POWER

This command reinstitutes trap processing of signals after they have been turned off.
**Keyword:** programming, program execution
**See Also:** init, kill, ps

### trap : 2

SH
KSH
ALL
SCRIPT
POWER

This command ignores the previously set **trap**. This is useful in shell script programming. By including one **trap** inside a loop and another in the condition that drives the loop, you can have simultaneous traps:

```
while [ 1 ]; echo $prompt; trap exit 2; read $value;
do trap : 2; eval $value; done
```

**Keyword:** programming, program execution
**See Also:** init, kill, ps

### trbsd 0-9 # < sales.db > list.db

ALL
OSF
POWER

This is the OSF version of **tr** for BSD. The example changes all numbers in the **sales.db** file to **list.db**.
**Keyword:** text filters
**See Also:** awk, dd, sed

### troff

ALL
SVR4
Solaris
SunOS
SCO
AIX
BSD
END

The **troff** text formatting program is designed for use with laser printers and professional typesetting equipment, but it is a direct descendent of **nroff**. The major difference is that **troff** can support proportionally spaced fonts, while **nroff** supports only monospaced fonts. In addition to the basic set of **nroff** commands (see **nroff**), **troff** supports **.co** (endmark), **.cs** (constant font character spacing), **.fd** (display available fonts), **.fp** (specify font name), **.fz** (specify point size for **.fp**), **.lf** (load font), **.ps** (set overall point size), **.rb** (read input file), **.ss** (set word spacing), and **.vs** (set vertical spacing). Additionally, special symbols and characters can be used with **troff**.
**Keyword:** text formatting

**Files:**    /usr/ucblib/doctools/tmac/.* (SVR4),
/usr/lib/tmac/* (BSD)

**See Also:**    eqn, lpr, nroff, tbl

## true

ALL   ALL   SCRIPT

The **true** command returns a true value. It has no purpose at the command line, but is used in scripts. Here is a template for a Bourne shell routine that uses **true**:

```
# User input function
getans() {
prompt=$1
lastans=$2
while [ true ]
do
    echo $prompt $lastans | \
        awk '{printf("\n%30s [%s]: ", $1, $2)}'
    read ans
    if [ "$ans" = "" ]; then
        ans=$lastans
        break
    fi
done
return; }
```

**Keyword:**    programming
**See Also:**    false, if, test, while

## truss -f csh

ALL   SVR4   SCRIPT
POWER
SYSADM

The **truss** command runs the specified command, intercepts system calls and signals, and displays system calls on the standard output. This command is an excellent way to determine dependencies. Unlike the **trace** command in SunOS, the **truss** command offers numerous options. The **-f** option in the example is required to track shell activity and shell scripts. Here are a few lines of output:

```
xecve("/usr/bin/csh",0x08047EB8,0x08047EC0) argc=1
open("/dev/zero",O_RDONLY,020000527744)=3
mmap(0x00000000,4096,PROT_READ|PROT_WRITE,MAP_PRIVATE,3,0)=0x8002 D000
```

**Keyword:**    program execution, programming
**See Also:**    trace (SunOS equivalent)

## tset

ALL   ALL   SCRIPT
POWER
SYSADM

The **tset** command is a powerful utility for setting the system interface to terminals and dialup terminals. Designed for use with **termcap**, **tset** lets you set terminal types as well as keyboard

**469**

**tset**

behavior. Without options, **tset** displays the settings for the Erase, Kill, and Interrupt keys:

```
Erase is Delete
Kill is Ctrl-U
Interrupt is Ctrl-C
```

**Keyword:**   terminals, user environment

**See Also:**   set, stty, tty

### tset vt100

**ALL   ALL   SCRIPT**
**POWER**
**SYSADM**

This command sets the terminal type to work with a Digital Equipment Corp. VT100 ASCII terminal.

**Keyword:**   terminals, user environment

**See Also:**   set, stty, tty

### tty

**ALL   ALL   END**

This command shows you the name of the terminal that you are currently working on.

**Keyword:**   terminals

**See Also:**   ps, stty, tset, tput, who

### ttyadm -b -p "login at your own risk here -->" -d /dev/tty2A

**ALL   SVR4   SYSADM**

This command sets the serial port **/dev/tty2A** to be bidirectional, and sets the login prompt to read **login at your own risk here -->**.

**Keyword:**   terminals, devices

**Files:**      /etc/ttydefs

**See Also:**   sysadm, tty, stty

### twm

**ALL   XWIN   ALL**

The **twm** window manager ships with the X Window System. Its full name is Tab Window Manager, and it has been an influential piece of software: It has served as a model for the Motif window manager and the Open Look (Sun OpenWindows) window manager. The most common way to invoke **twm** is to edit your X startup file. If you are currently running Motif or OpenWindows, you should comment out the line that starts either of these window managers. Then, near the commented line, insert **twm**.

**Keyword:**   window managers, user environment

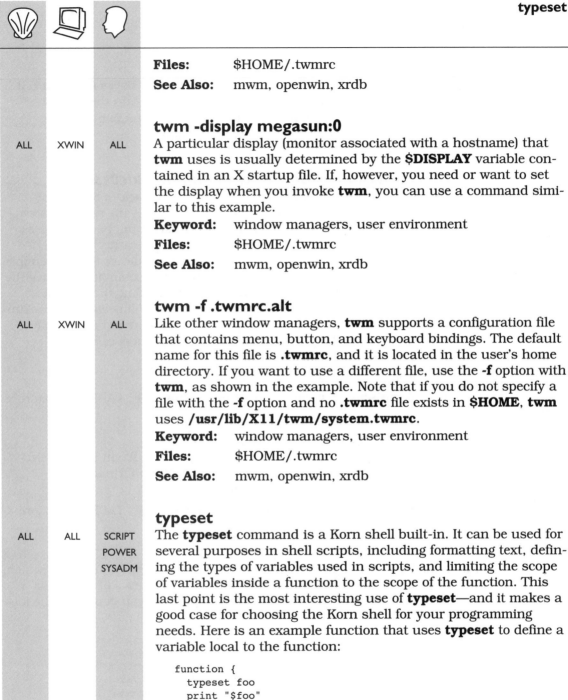

**Files:**     $HOME/.twmrc
**See Also:**   mwm, openwin, xrdb

## twm -display megasun:0

ALL   XWIN   ALL

A particular display (monitor associated with a hostname) that **twm** uses is usually determined by the **$DISPLAY** variable contained in an X startup file. If, however, you need or want to set the display when you invoke **twm**, you can use a command similar to this example.

**Keyword:**   window managers, user environment
**Files:**     $HOME/.twmrc
**See Also:**   mwm, openwin, xrdb

## twm -f .twmrc.alt

ALL   XWIN   ALL

Like other window managers, **twm** supports a configuration file that contains menu, button, and keyboard bindings. The default name for this file is **.twmrc**, and it is located in the user's home directory. If you want to use a different file, use the **-f** option with **twm**, as shown in the example. Note that if you do not specify a file with the **-f** option and no **.twmrc** file exists in **$HOME**, **twm** uses **/usr/lib/X11/twm/system.twmrc**.

**Keyword:**   window managers, user environment
**Files:**     $HOME/.twmrc
**See Also:**   mwm, openwin, xrdb

## typeset

ALL   ALL   SCRIPT
            POWER
            SYSADM

The **typeset** command is a Korn shell built-in. It can be used for several purposes in shell scripts, including formatting text, defining the types of variables used in scripts, and limiting the scope of variables inside a function to the scope of the function. This last point is the most interesting use of **typeset**—and it makes a good case for choosing the Korn shell for your programming needs. Here is an example function that uses **typeset** to define a variable local to the function:

```
function {
  typeset foo
  print "$foo"
}
```

**Keyword:**   programming
**See Also:**   awk, ksh, troff

## u

**ALL**    **OSF**    **ALL**

This command is a system-level alias of the **users** command. It simply outputs a list of all the users logged into the system.

**Keyword:**    system information, user environment

**See Also:**    rusers, rwho, users, w, who

## ufsdump 0cfuov /dev/rmt/0 /dev/rdsk/c0t3d0s0

**ALL**    **Solaris**    **SYSADM**

This **ufsdump** example creates a complete backup of the root filesystem to a QIC-150 1/4-inch tape. This is the most conservative backup method: The **0** option specifies a full backup; the **c** option tells **ufsdump** to use a cartridge tape, rather than a 1/2-inch reel tape; the **f** option specifies a target device (in the example, **/dev/rmt/0**). The **u** option to the **ufsdump** command updates the **/etc/dumpdates** file with information regarding the current backup. The **o** option takes the tape drive off-line after the backup is completed, which is useful, so that tapes are not mistakenly overwritten. The **v** option verifies the contents of each tape.

**Keyword:**    backup and restore

**Files:**    /etc/dumpdates

**See Also:**    backup, cpio, dump, restore, tar, TAPE, ufsrestore

## ufsdump 0D report.txt

**ALL**    **Solaris**    **SYSADM**

This simple command writes the **report.txt** file in the current directory to the diskette. The file is in **dump** format.

**Keyword:**    backup and restore

**See Also:**    backup, cpio, dump, restore, tar, TAPE, ufsrestore

## ufsrestore if /dev/rmt/0

**ALL**    **Solaris**    **SYSADM**

This command invokes the interactive mode of **ufsrestore**, which checks for a valid device and reads the contents of the media before displaying a prompt. At the prompt, you can enter the following:

```
add [filename]      Add [filename] to the extraction list.
cd [directory]      Change to [directory] in the dump file.
delete [filename]   Remove [filename] from the extraction list.
extract             Restore files from the dump file.
help                Show a list of possible commands.
ls                  Show the contents of the dump file.
pwd                 Show the current directory in the dump file.
quit                Exit ufsrestore.
setmodes            To set the file permissions on restored files.
verbose             Set the ls command to display more information.
```

**Keyword:** backup and restore

**See Also:** backup, cpio, dump, restore, tar, TAPE, ufsdump

## ufsrestore xf /dev/fd0 report.txt

**ALL   Solaris   SYSADM**

This command extracts the **report.txt** file from a diskette. For the command to work, the **report.txt** file must have been copied to the disk using the **ufsdump** command.

**Keyword:** backup and restore

**See Also:** backup, cpio, dump, restore, tar, TAPE, ufsdump

## uil

**ALL   XWIN   ALL**

The **uil** command runs the UIL compiler, which adheres to the User Interface Language (UIL) for describing the initial interface state of a Motif application. A UIL file describes objects such as menus, dialog boxes, and push buttons. It also specifies the routines to be called when the interface changes its state as a result of user interaction.

**Keyword:** programming, window managers

**See Also:** cc, make, mwm

## ul -t vt100 book.txt

**ALL   ALL   END**

This command outputs the contents of the **book.txt** file to the terminal window, with support for underlining on a Digital Equipment Corp. VT100 ASCII terminal.

**Keyword:** text formatting, terminals

**Files:** /etc/termcap (BSD), /usr/share/lib/terminfo (SVR4)

**See Also:** cat, col, colcrt, man, more, nroff, pg

## ulimit -a

**KSH   ALL   POWER**
**SYSADM**

The **ulimit** command is a Korn shell built-in. It offers extensive support for limiting system resources. The command uses H and S flags to indicate hard and soft limits. A hard limit cannot be increased. A soft limit can be increased up to the value of the hard limit. The example command lists current limits:

```
time(seconds)        unlimited
file(blocks)         unlimited
data(kbytes)         131072
stack(kbytes)        2048
memory(kbytes)       unlimited
coredump(blocks)     unlimited
nofiles(descriptors) 4096
```

**473**

**Keyword:** user environment, system information

**See Also:** env, printenv, ps, ksh, set

## umask

The **umask** command shows the current file creation mask. The file creation mask determines the default file permissions when you create a new file. If this value is incorrect, the entire world may be able to read and write your files. It is a good idea to put this command in your **.login** file.

**Keyword:** file permissions, user environment

**Files:** $HOME/.login, $HOME/.profile

**See Also:** chown, chmod, ls

## umask 022

This command sets the file creation default permissions so that only you can overwrite a file you create.

**Keyword:** file permissions, user environment

**Files:** $HOME/.login, $HOME/.profile

**See Also:** chown, chmod, ls

## umask 446

This command sets the file creation default permissions so that only you can read and write a file, while the whole world can read the file.

**Keyword:** file permissions, user environment

**Files:** $HOME/.login, $HOME/.profile

**See Also:** chown, chmod, ls

## umount -A

This command unmounts all the filesystems currently mounted on the computer system. If any of the filesystems are in use, this command doesn't work.

**Keyword:** filesystem

**Files:** /etc/fstab

**See Also:** mount, mountall, mountfsys, umountall, umountfsys

ALL   ALL   ALL

ALL   ALL   ALL

ALL   ALL   ALL

ALL   BSD   SYSADM

### umount -a

| | | |
|---|---|---|
| ALL | BSD | SYSADM |

This command **unmounts** all the filesystems listed in the **/etc/fstab** file that are currently mounted on the computer system. If any of the filesystems are in use, this command doesn't work.

**Keyword:** filesystem

**Files:** /etc/fstab

**See Also:** mount, mountall, mountfsys, umountall, umountfsys

### umount /cdrom

| | | |
|---|---|---|
| ALL | ALL | SYSADM |

This command detaches the CD-ROM from the filesystem so that you can eject the CD. If someone is using the CD-ROM, or even has a directory on the CD set as the current directory, the **umount** command doesn't work.

**Keyword:** filesystem

**Files:** /etc/fstab

**See Also:** mount, mountall, mountfsys, umountall, umountfsys

### umountall

| | | |
|---|---|---|
| ALL | SCO | SYSADM |

This command unmounts all the filesystems, except the root filesystem, that are currently mounted on the computer system. If any of the filesystems are in use, this command doesn't work.

**Keyword:** filesystem

**Files:** /etc/default/filesys

**See Also:** mount, mountall, mountfsys, umountall, umountfsys

### unalias dir

| | | |
|---|---|---|
| CSH KSH | ALL | ALL |

The **unalias** command removes an alias created with the **alias** command. To view a list of current aliases, just enter **alias**. Then, if you want to unset one, such as **dir** in this example, use the **unalias** command. Note that the **csh** and **ksh** versions of **alias** act identically (so for once we got to combine different versions into a single example).

**Keyword:** keyboard shortcuts, user environment

**See Also:** alias, env, history

## uname

| ALL | ALL | POWER SYSADM |
|-----|-----|--------------|

This command outputs the name of the type of UNIX you currently have on your system, such as OSF for a Digital Equipment Corp. AXP workstation.

**Keyword:** system information

**See Also:** arch, hostname, hostid, xprop, xwininfo

## uname -a

| ALL | ALL | POWER SYSADM |
|-----|-----|--------------|

This command outputs all available information on the type of system that you have.

**Keyword:** system information

**See Also:** arch, hostname, hostid, xprop, xwininfo

## uname -m

| ALL | ALL | POWER SYSADM |
|-----|-----|--------------|

This command outputs your system's type of hardware, including processor.

**Keyword:** system information

**See Also:** arch, hostname, hostid, xprop, xwininfo

## uncompress - f dir.tar.Z

| ALL | ALL | POWER |
|-----|-----|-------|

The **-f** option to **uncompress** forces it to process a file even though the file may already exist. Try using this approach if you need to process files in the background and don't want **uncompress** to prompt you for permission to overwrite the existing file.

**Keyword:** file handling, Internet, modem communications

**See Also:** compress, tar, uncompress, uuencode, zcat

## uncompress - v dir.tar.Z

| ALL | ALL | POWER |
|-----|-----|-------|

The **-v** option to **uncompress** tells it to display the filename. You might want to take advantage of **-v** in aliases and scripts, because otherwise **uncompress** works quite silently. Of course, the uncompressed filename is always the same as the one specified, minus the **.Z** extension.

**Keyword:** file handling, Internet, modem communications

**See Also:** compress, tar, uncompress, uuencode, zcat

## uncompress < dir.tar.Z | tar tvf -

| ALL | ALL | POWER |
|-----|-----|-------|

Before you uncompress a tarfile (it might contain files that you don't even want, after all), why not take a look at the contents?

That's what this command lets you do: **dir.tar.Z** is redirected into **uncompress**, which then pipes the results in **tar**. The **-t** switch tells **tar** to list the contents of the tarfile.

**Keyword:** file handling, Internet, modem communications

**See Also:** compress, tar, uncompress, uuencode, zcat

### uncompress < dir.tar.Z | tar xfvp -

ALL  ALL  POWER

The beauty of this command is that you can both **uncompress** and un-tar the file at the same time. In order to process the pipe, **tar** looks for standard input, as indicated by the - character.

**Keyword:** file handling, Internet, modem communications

**See Also:** compress, tar, uncompress, uuencode, zcat

### uncompress dir.tar.Z

ALL  ALL  POWER

This command is the opposite of the **compress** command. It reads the **compress** formatted file and expands it to its normal size and content.

**Keyword:** file handling, Internet, modem communications

**See Also:** compress, tar, uncompress, uuencode, zcat

### unexpand -a july.txt > july.mail

ALL  ALL  END
SCRIPT
POWER
SYSADM

This example is designed to compress the original file. It does this by replacing two or more whitespaces with tabs whenever the net result would reduce the size of the file.

**Keyword:** file handling

**See Also:** compress, expand, uncompress

### unexpand july.txt > july.rep

ALL  ALL  END

The **unexpand** command is a direct cousin of **expand**, a BSD-only command that replaces tabs with spaces. Use **unexpand** when you want to reverse the process. These are sometimes extremely useful utilities when you need to convert ASCII text files into documents for word processing and electronic publishing software. As a rule, tabs are easier to reformat, if necessary.

**Keyword:** text formatting

**See Also:** dd, expand, sed, tr

### uniq +25 - d phone.db > phone.2

This example begins comparing lines after the **25**th character. If the rest of characters on adjacent lines are identical, the lines are deemed **uniq**ue. What the **-d** option does, however, is print only the lines that had adjacent duplicates, making this a handy tool.

**Keyword:**    text handling

**See Also:**    awk, comm, grep, sed, sort

### uniq -2 -c phone.db > phone.2

One of the best features about **uniq** is it lets you sort (so to speak) on a field. If the specified field in adjacent lines matches, **uniq** discards the match. The **-c** option in the example adds some extra output, preceding each "**uniq**-ed" line with the number of times it occured in the file.

**Keyword:**    text handling

**See Also:**    awk, comm, grep, sed, sort

### uniq -u phone.db > phone.2

Dare we say that the **-u** option is very unique? It is, in the sense that it only outputs lines that are unique in the first place. In other words, all occurences of duplicate adjacent lines are discarded.

**Keyword:**    text handling

**See Also:**    awk, comm, grep, sed, sort

### uniq phone.db > phone.2

What's the difference between **sort -u** and **uniq**? The answer is simple: **uniq** discards duplicate lines only when they are adjacent, but **sort -u** discards them no matter where they occur in the file.

**Keyword:**    text handling

**See Also:**    awk, comm, grep, sed, sort

### units

The interactive **units** program converts just about anything to anything else. It prompts you for a **unit** measure that you want to convert, followed by the **unit** that you want to convert to. There are more than 500 different types of measures supported by the **units** program. Here is a sample session:

```
you have: dollar
you want: pound
        * 4.353505e-01
        / 2.297000e+00
you have: mi
you want: km
        * 1.609344e+00
        / 6.213712e-01
you have: shippington
you want: ton
conformability
        1.132674e+00 m3
        9.071847e+02 kg
```

**Keyword:**  math, general information

**Files:**  /usr/lib/unittab (SCO), /usr/lib/units (BSD, SunOS), /usr/share/lib/units (OSF), /usr/share/lib/unittab (SVR4, Solaris, AIX)

**See Also:**  awk, bc, dc, expr, xcalc

## unlimit

CSH   ALL   ALL

This command removes all the resource limitations on the system. This is used to undo any **limit** commands that may have been directed toward a process. Typical resources to be limited include: cputime, filesize, datasize, stacksize, coredumpsize, memoryuse, and descriptors. After running the **unlimit** command on one of our test systems, our resources looked like this:

```
cputime         unlimited
filesize        unlimited
datasize        1048576 kbytes
stacksize       32768 kbytes
coredumpsize    unlimited
memoryuse       unlimited
descriptors     4096
```

**Keyword:**  user environment, system information

**See Also:**  limit, nice, ulimit (sh, ksh)

## unpack xtank1.3d.tar.z

ALL   ALL   ALL

This command is used to uncompress a file that has been compressed with the **pack** command. All files that are packed have a **.z** extension on the filename. If you type just the filename without **.z**, the **unpack** command still works.

**Keyword:**  file handling

**See Also:**  compress, pack, unpack, uncompress, zcat

## unset $XAPPLRESDIR

**SH**
**KSH**  ALL  ALL

In the Bourne and Korn shells, this is the way to unset envrionment variables. The example command is helpful to X users who want to take advantage of X's precedence-based resource setting mechanisms. For instance, if the user had a file called XClock in **$XAPPLRESDIR**, the resources in the file would no longer be visible to the X server if you entered the example command. As a result, the X server would look to any of several other resource file locations, including **/usr/lib/X11/app-defaults**, the resource location of last resort (or first resort, depending on how you view X precedence).

**Keyword:**   user environment

**Files:**   $HOME/.profile, $HOME/.kshrc

**See Also:**   echo, set, env

## unset *

**CSH**  ALL  ALL

One big note about the C shell version of **unset** is that you cannot unset a standard shell environment variable. You have to use the **unsetenv** command to do this.

**Keyword:**   user environment

**Files:**   $HOME/.login, $HOME/.cshrc

**See Also:**   echo, set, setenv, unsetenv

## unset prompt

**CSH**  ALL  ALL

In the C shell, this command unsets the **prompt** environment variable. This means that your prompt goes away—not desirable in most cases, but if you want to record from the terminal screen or Xterm window, it might be just the trick. Interestingly, you can achieve the same effect by entering **set prompt**, which is the same as saying **set** the **prompt** to nothing. The same is true of other C shell variables: you can unset them by setting them to their opposite value. Where **unset** is really helpful is when you need to clear all environment variables in the shell's memory.

**Keyword:**   user environment

**Files:**   $HOME/.login, $HOME/.cshrc

**See Also:**   echo, set, setenv, unsetenv

## unsetenv FEELINGBLUE

**CSH**  ALL  ALL

The **FEELINGBLUE** environment variable is a user-defined variable, but it demonstrates another reason that you might want to set and unset variables. For instance, if a startup or shell script checked for **FEELINGBLUE** and found a value of yes, this could kick off another script that sets your desktop colors to blue. This could be used in conjunction with the **$XAPPLRESDIR** environment variable (see **unset $XAPPLRESDIR** for sh and ksh). Of course, at some point the system would have to be told whether you were feeling blue.

**Keyword:**    user environment

**Files:**    $HOME/.login, $HOME/.cshrc

**See Also:**    echo, set, setenv, unsetenv

## uptime

This command outputs system information. It displays the current time, how long the system has been running, the number of current users, and the load average. Here is a typical display:

```
12:06 up 1 day, 2:03, 1 user, load average: 0.00, 0.01, 0.03
```

**Keyword:**    system information

**See Also:**    ruptime, w, who

## useradd -u 132 -g users -d /home/perkie -s /bin/tcsh -m perkie

This command creates a new user named **perkie**. The home directory of **perkie** is **/home/perkie**, the shell is **/bin/tcsh**, and the user ID number is **132**.

**Keyword:**    system setup

**See Also:**    passwd, adduser, sysadmsh, sysadm, admintool

## userdel -r perkie

This command deletes user **perkie** from the system, and deletes **perkie**'s home directory.

**Keyword:**    system setup

**See Also:**    passwd, adduser, sysadmsh, sysadm, admintool

## usermod -u 132 -g users -d /home/perkie -s /bin/tcsh -m perkie

This command modifies the user named **perkie**. The home directory of **perkie** is **/home/perkie**, the shell is **/bin/tcsh**, and the user ID number is **132**.

| | | |
|---|---|---|
| ALL | ALL | ALL |

**Keyword:** system setup

**See Also:** passwd, adduser, sysadmsh, sysadm, admintool

## users

This command shows a list of all the users logged into the system. The output looks like this:

```
alans perkie emily pat
```

**Keyword:** user environment

**See Also:** env, finger, last, rusers, rwho, w, who

| | | |
|---|---|---|
| ALL | ALL | POWER |
| | | SYSADM |

## uucheck -v

The **uucheck** command checks whether the necessary UUCP configuration files exist to implement UUCP communications. The command also does a limited syntax check of the Permissions file. The directory hierarchies and filenames differ between BSD and SVR4 systems. Here is a synopsis of the major UUCP files on different systems:

```
SVR4 Solaris
/etc/uucp/Systems
/etc/uucp/Permissions
/etc/uucp/Devices
/etc/uucp/Limits (SVR4 only)
/var/spool/uucp/*
/var/spool/locks/*
/var/spool/uucppublic/*
```

```
OSF
/usr/lib/uucp/uucheck
/usr/lib/uucp/Devices
/usr/lib/uucp/Maxuuscheds
/usr/lib/uucp/Maxuuxqts
/usr/lib/uucp/Permissions
/usr/lib/uucp/Systems
/usr/spool/uucp/*
/usr/spool/uucppublic/*
/usr/spool/uucp/locks/LCK*
```

```
SunOS AIX
/etc/uucp/Systems
/etc/uucp/Permissions
/etc/uucp/Devices
/etc/uucp/Maxuuscheds
/etc/uucp/Maxuuxqts
/var/spool/uucp/*
/var/spool/locks/LCK*
/var/spool/uucppublic/*
```

```
SCO
/usr/lib/uucp/Systems
/usr/lib/uucp/Permissions
/usr/lib/uucp/Devices
/usr/lib/uucp/Maxuuscheds
/usr/lib/uucp/Maxuuxqts
/usr/spool/uucp/*
/usr/spool/locks/LCK*
/usr/spool/uucppublic/*
```

```
BSD
/etc/uucp/L.sys
/etc/uucp/L.devices
/usr/spool/uucp/*
/usr/spool/uucppublic/*
/usr/spool/uucp/LCK/LCK*
```

**Keyword:** Internet, modem communications

**See Also:** uucp, uulog, uumonitor, uutry

### uucico -r1 - x9 -f -snewl

ALL ALL POWER SYSADM

The **-f** option to **uucico** forces the program to execute whether or not the maximum number of **uucico** processes has been reached. The maximum number is defined in the **/etc/uucp/Limits** file.

**Keyword:** Internet, modem communications

**Files:** (see uucheck)

**See Also:** cron, uucp, uustat, uutry, uuto, uux

### uucico -r1 - x9 -snewl

ALL ALL POWER SYSADM

Except for debugging purposes, you would rarely invoke **uucico** from the command line. It normally runs as a background process and responds to requests from **uucp** and **uux**. If you do use **uucico** at the command line, you must specify **-r1** to tell **uucico** to run in server mode. The **-x** option tells **uucico** to display the maximum debugging information. The **-s** option specifies the system name that you want to contact. Note that there is no whitespace between **-s** and the system name.

**Keyword:** Internet, modem communications

**Files:** (see uucheck)

**See Also:** cron, uucp, uustat, uutry, uuto, uux

### uucleanup

ALL ALL POWER SYSADM

The **uucleanup** command evaluates the various UUCP spool directories for old files. If it finds any, it informs the appropriate user that the pending UUCP request has not been processed. In addition, **uucleanup** removes lock files and returns undeliverable mail to the sender.

**Keyword:** Internet, modem communications

**Files:** (see uucheck)

**See Also:** cron, uucp, uustat, uux

### uucp -C mktg.doc alr!/usr/neala/mktg.doc

ALL ALL POWER SYSADM

This command copies files to the spool directory. From the spool directory—which is a directory under the user's name in **/usr/spool** (OSF, SCO, BSD) or in **/var/spool** (SVR4, SunOS,

Solaris)—the **uucico** program emails the files. When this occurs depends on settings in the Systems files. It also depends on how frequently **uusched** runs. On many systems, **-C** is set by default.

**Keyword:**    Internet, modem communications

**Files:**        (see uucheck)

**See Also:**    ct, cu, mail, mailx, rmail, tip, uucico, uucleanup, uudecode, uuencode, uulog, uuname, uupick, uusched, uusend, uustat, uuto, uux, uuxqt

### uucp -c mktg.doc alr!/usr/neala/mktg.doc

The **-c** option causes **uucp** to bypass the spool directory. When dealing with large files, this lets you avoid clogging up the spool directory and unnecessarily using filesystem space.

**Keyword:**    Internet, modem communications

**Files:**        (see uucheck)

**See Also:**    ct, cu, mail, mailx, rmail, tip, uucico, uucleanup, uudecode, uuencode, uulog, uuname, uupick, uusched  uusend, uustat, uuto, uux, uuxqt

### uucp -m - nroot -nneala mktg.doc newluucp!/usr/neala

This command is similar to other examples, but adds a friendly touch by sending notification of the **uucp** transfer. The **-m** option takes care of notifying the sender when the copy is completed. The **-n** option lets you notify one or more users on the remote system.

**Keyword:**    Internet, modem communications

**Files:**        (see uucheck)

**See Also:**    ct, cu, mail, mailx, rmail, tip, uucico, uucleanup, uudecode, uuencode, uulog, uuname, uupick, uusched, uusend, uustat, uuto, uux, uuxqt

### uucp alr!/usr/neala/mktg.doc $HOME/mktg.doc

Instead of copying a file to the remote system, **uucp** copies a file from **/usr/neala** on the remote system **alr** to the local system.

**Keyword:**    Internet, modem communications

**Files:**        (see uucheck)

**See Also:**    ct, cu, mail, mailx, rmail, tip, uucico, uucleanup, uudecode, uuencode, uulog, uuname, uupick, uusched uusend, uustat, uuto, uux, uuxqt

ALL  ALL  POWER SYSADM

ALL  ALL  POWER SYSADM

ALL  ALL  POWER SYSADM

ALL    ALL    POWER
              SYSADM

### uucp alr!/usr/neala/mktg.doc
###     sparky!/home3/pat/mktg.doc

This **uucp** command introduces a third system into the picture.
The local system is neiether **alr** or **sparky**. Someone is copying
**mktg.doc** from **/usr/neala** on **alr** to **/home3/pat** on **sparky**.
The only requirement of the third system is that it have permissions on both remote systems.

**Keyword:**    Internet, modem communications

**Files:**    (see uucheck)

**See Also:**    ct, cu, mail, mailx, rmail, tip, uucico, uucleanup,
uudecode, uuencode, uulog, uuname, uupick,
uusched, uusend, uustat, uuto, uux, uuxqt

SH     ALL    POWER
KSH           SYSADM

### uucp mktg.doc alr!/usr/neala/mktg.doc

The **uucp** program—as opposed to the UUCP suite of utilities—
copies files between remote systems. Both **uucp** and **UUCP** stand
for UNIX-to-UNIX copy, or **cp**. From this knowledge, you can expect
**uucp** to behave similarly to the **cp** program. It is great way for small
businesses, clubs, and organizations to exchange data, although in
a larger organization, mail-handling software such as **sendmail**
masks the involvement of the UUCP system. In the example,
**mktg.doc** is copied from the local system to **/usr/neala** on the
remote system **alr**. Note that it is necessary to specify the filename
twice (unlike **cp**, but much like the **cu take** and **put** routines).

**Keyword:**    Internet, modem communications

**Files:**    (see uucheck)

**See Also:**    ct, cu, mail, mailx, rmail, tip, uucico, uucleanup,
uudecode, uuencode, uulog, uuname, uupick,
uusched,  uusend, uustat, uuto, uux, uuxqt

CSH    ALL    POWER
              SYSADM

### uucp report.txt alr\!/usr/neala/mktg.doc

This example is a reminder or warning to C shell users: Don't try
using a UUCP address without escaping the exclamation mark. As
noted often in this book, the exclamation point has special meaning
to the C shell. Subsequent examples do not escape the exclamation
mark, but they do apply to all three shells, given the caveat.

**Keyword:**    Internet, modem communications

**Files:**    (see uucheck)

**See Also:**    ct, cu, mail, mailx, rmail, tip, uucico, uucleanup,
uudecode, uuencode, uulog, uuname, uupick,
uusched, uusend, uustat, uuto, uux, uuxqt

**485**

## uucp uunet!~/ls-lR.Z newl!~/alans

ALL  ALL  POWER SYSADM

This command contacts **uunet** and requests the specified file. In the example, the command requests **ls-lR.Z**, which the UUCP system on the remote machine forwards if the return email address is correct.

**Keyword:** Internet, modem communications

**Files:** (see uucheck)

**See Also:** ct, cu, mail, mailx, rmail, tip, uucico, uucleanup, uudecode, uuencode, uulog, uuname, uupick, uusched, uusend, uustat, uuto, uux, uuxqt

## uucp:*:4:4::/usr/spool/uucppublic:/usr/lib/uucp/uucico

ALL  ALL  POWER SYSADM

For UUCP exchanges, the example is as important as knowing any **uucp** command—but it is not a **uucp** command. It is an example of an entry that your system's **/etc/passwd** file must contain in order for remote UUCP sites to dial in.

**Keyword:** Internet, modem communications

**Files:** (see uucheck)

**See Also:** ct, cu, mail, mailx, rmail, tip, uucico, uucleanup, uudecode, uuencode, uulog, uuname, uupick, uusched, uusend, uustat, uuto, uux, uuxqt

## uudecode dir.tar.Z.uu

ALL  ALL  POWER

This **uudecode** command unwinds packaged binary files created by using **uuencode**, **compress**, and **tar**. The example creates the file **dir.tar.Z** based on a similar argument to **uuencode** in the first place:

```
tar cvf - . | compress | uuencode dir.tar.Z > dir.tar.Z.uu
```

After this command, you are ready to uncompress the file:

```
uncompress < dir.tar.Z | tar xfvp -
```

The crypt command is also commonly used with email:

```
tar cvf - . | compress | crypt | uuencode dir.tar.Z .cr | mail alans
```

And this is unwound with:

```
% crypt < dir.tar.Z .cr | uncompress | tar xfvp -
```

**Keyword:** Internet, modem communications, file handling

**See Also:** compress, mail, mailx, tar, uncompress, uuencode

## uuencode dir.tar.Z > dir.tar.Z.uu

ALL  ALL  POWER

This **uuencode** command converts a binary file into an ASCII representation of the binary contents. The file size is expanded about 35 percent, but it is necessary if you want to send the file via email or UUCP. Here are two other ways to use **uuencode**:

```
chdir dir
tar cvf - . | compress | uuencode dir.tar.Z > dir.tar.Z.uu
chdir dir
% tar cvf - . | compress | uuencode dir.tar.Z | mail perkie
```

**Keyword:**  Internet, modem communications, file handling

**See Also:**  compress, mail, mailx, tar, uudecode

## uugetty

ALL  SVR4  SYSADM
SCO
Solaris
OSF

Don't enter **uugetty** at the command line. It runs as a system daemon and respawns itself as necessary. For each modem line your system supports, you need a **uugetty** processor monitoring the line. As an alternative to **uugetty**, you can use the **getty** daemon, which can monitor all **tty** lines. Using **uugetty** is a better approach because it easily supports two-way dialing on the same line. One drawback, however, is that **uugetty** must be active on the remote system as well. The normal place to start **uugetty** is in the **inittab** file. Here is a sample entry:

```
t00:2:off:/usr/lib/uucp/uugetty -r -t 60 tty00 9600
```

**Keyword:**  devices, modem communications

**Files:**  /etc/gettydefs, /etc/uucp/Devices (SVR4, Solaris), /usr/lib/uucp/Devices (SCO, OSF)

**See Also:**  uucico, getty, init, cu, tip, login, stty

## uulog

ALL  ALL  POWER
SYSADM

This command outputs UUCP transactions made by the local system. It also displays the status of those transactions. If you use the **-r** with **uulog**, you can limit the output to a single system.

**Keyword:**  Internet, modem communications

**See Also:**  uucleanup, uustat, uutry

## uuname

ALL  ALL  POWER
SYSADM

This command outputs a list of all the systems that have been set up for your system to call via UUCP. The **uuname** command

**487**

is useful for giving you an idea of who you are networked to through UUCP and how to route email to different systems.

**Keyword:** system information, UUCP

**See Also:** cu, hostname, uucp, uutry

## uupick

ALL SVR4 END
Solaris
SCO
OSF
AIX

After you receive mail notification that new files have arrived in the public directory, **uupick** is a more expedient tool than **ls** for viewing the files. Just enter **uupick**, as in the example, and it displays the following prompt:

```
from system new1: file payroll.db
?
```

If you press * at the prompt, you get a usage message:

```
usage: [d][m dir][a dir][p][q][cntl-d][!cmd][*][new-line]
```

From left to right, **d** deletes the current file, **m** moves the current file to the named directory, **a** moves all files from the other system to a named directory, **p** prints the contents of the file, **q** quits, and **cntl-d** (better represented as Ctrl-D) also quits. **!cmd** lets you run a subshell and execute a command or interactive shell session if you enter **!sh**, * plus any wrong key prints the usage message, and **new-line** advances to the next file in the active list.

**Keyword:** Internet, modem communications

**Files:** (see uucheck)

**See Also:** uucico, uucleanup, uucp, uustat, uuto

## uupick -s

ALL SVR4 END
Solaris
SCO
OSF
AIX

The **-s** option to **uupick** lets you specify that you only want to view files in the public directory that originated at the named system. If you get a lot of files, this is handy.

**Keyword:** Internet, modem communications

**Files:** (see uucheck)

**See Also:** uucico, uucleanup, uucp, uustat, uuto

## uusched

ALL ALL POWER
SYSADM

The **uusched** command manages when to call which systems. As a rule, **uusched** is run by **cron**. In the **uucp crontab** file, you are likely to find an entry to execute either **uudemon.hour** or

**uudemon.poll**. Both of these shell script files invoke **uusched**. Here is an example from a **crontab** file:

```
25,55 * * * * /usr/lib/uucp/uudemon.hour > /dev/null
```

**Keyword:**    devices, modem communications

**Files:**    /var/spool/cron/crontabs (SVR4, Solaris), /usr/spool/cron/crontabs (SunOS, BSD, SCO), /usr/var/spool/cron/crontabs (OSF)

**See Also:**    cron, crontab, uucheck, uucp, uucico

### uusend report.doc alpha!newl!uunet!report.doc

ALL   SCO   END
OSF
SunOS

This command sends the local file **report.doc** to the remote computer **uunet** by way of the remote computer **alpha**, then to the computer **newl**, then finally to **uunet**. When the file reaches **uunet** it is called **report.doc** on that system. As noted elsewhere, UCCP and programs like **uusend** can be effective ways to exchange files between remote sites, but mail handling systems have made the command in the example look arduous. Still, with custom scripts, and no other reason to use the mailer (such as for automated accounting between sites), **uusend** has possibilities.

**Keyword:**    Internet, modem communications

**See Also:**    uucico, uucleanup, uucp, uuto

### uustat

ALL   ALL   END

The **uustat** program displays status information on pending UUCP requests and lets you cancel previous requests. In addition, for administrators and others configuring a UUCP system, **uustat** provides information on remote systems, including performance statistics. When entering **uustat** by itself at the command line, you get a display like this one:

```
newlN7e59 Tue Mar 08 18:52:03 1994 R newl root
/usr/alans/mktg.doc
newlN7e5b Tue Mar 08 18:53:57 1994 S newl root 1037
/usr/alans/sales.db
```

**Keyword:**    Internet, modem communications

**Files:**    (see uucheck)

**See Also:**    cron, cu, ps, stty, uucico, uucleanup, uucp, uusched

### uustat -a

ALL ALL END

This command displays the status of all queued UUCP requests. If you want to cancel a request, you need to know the job number, which appears in the first column of the **uustat** output:

```
newlN7e58 Tue Mar 08 17:10:34 1994 S newl alans 51 /usr/CmdCmp/cpr
newlN7e59 Tue Mar 08 18:52:03 1994 R newl root  /usr/alans/mktg.doc
newlN7e5b Tue Mar 08 18:53:57 1994 S newl root 1037 /usr/alans/sales.db
```

**Keyword:**    Internet, modem communications

**Files:**      (see uucheck)

**See Also:**    cron, cu, ps, stty, uucico, uucleanup, uucp, uusched

### uustat -k newlN7e58

ALL ALL END

The **-k** option to **uustat** lets you cancel a pending request. It is an invaluable option if you are the kind of person who likes to take back your words.

**Keyword:**    Internet, modem communications

**Files:**      (see uucheck)

**See Also:**    cron, cu, ps, stty, uucico, uucleanup, uucp, uusched

### uustat -p

ALL ALL END

The **-p** option displays any lock files currently in effect. Here is some sample output, in which **cu** has a lock on the **tty** line:

```
LCK..tty2a: 2160
  F F     UID   PID  PPID  C PRI NI  ADDR1  ADDR2  SZ
 20 S   perkie 2160    1  2  39 20    4f1    39e  236
          WCHAN   STIME  TTY       TIME CMD
        e0000000 11:30:35  2A      ):02 -tcsh
```

**Keyword:**    Internet, modem communications

**Files:**      (see uucheck)

**See Also:**    cron, cu, ps, stty, uucico, uucleanup, uucp, uusched

### uustat -s newl

ALL ALL END

The **-s** option to **uustat** lets you specify a system on which you want a status report. The output is the same as that of the **-a** option, minus information on other systems.

**Keyword:**    Internet, modem communications

**Files:**      (see uucheck)

**See Also:**    cron, cu, ps, stty, uucico, uucleanup, uucp, uusched

### uustat -u neala - s sparky

| ALL | ALL | END |

You can narrow the output to **uustat** even further by adding **-u** option. The example outputs pending requests to remote system **sparky** from user **neala**.

**Keyword:** Internet, modem communications

**Files:** (see uucheck)

**See Also:** cron, cu, ps, stty, uucico, uucleanup, uucp, uusched

### uuto *.doc alr!neala

| ALL | SVR4 | END |
| | Solaris | |
| | SCO | |
| | OSF | |
| | AIX | |

The **uuto** program spools UUCP requests into a public directory in order to restrict file access. On the remote side, the **uupick** command is used to obtain the delivered files. In the example, all **\*.doc** files from the current directory of the local system are sent to the remote system. Note that **uuto** does not require a destination filename. Also note that on some systems, an environment variable called **$PUBDIR** defines the location of the public directory. By default on SVR4 systems, **uuto**-delivered mail is placed in a directory under the user's name in **/var/spool/uucppublic/receive**. The receive subdirectory is constant across platforms; check your system for the directory hierarchy in which **uucppublic** (also constant) is located.

**Keyword:** Internet, modem communications

**Files:** (see uucheck)

**See Also:** uucico, uucleanup, uucp, uupick, uustat

### uuto -m /home3/alans/mktg.doc alr!neala

| ALL | SVR4 | END |
| | Solaris | |
| | SCO | |
| | OSF | |
| | AIX | |

The **-m** option to **uuto** tells **uuto** to pass along a request to the remote system that it should return a message indicating whether the file was correctly copied.

**Keyword:** Internet, modem communications

**Files:** (see uucheck)

**See Also:** uucico, uucleanup, uucp, uupick, uustat

### uuto .cshrc megasun!perkie

| ALL | SVR4 | END |
| | Solaris | |
| | SCO | |
| | OSF | |
| | AIX | |

This example illuminates a glitch in **uuto**. If you want to send a dot file (any file that begins with a period), you must explicity refer to it on the command line. For example, **uuto** would reject **\*chsrc** and **??shrc**.

**Keyword:** Internet, modem communications

**491**

**Files:** (see uucheck)

**See Also:** uucico, uucleanup, uucp, uupick, uustat

### uuto mktg.doc markb

ALL SVR4 END
Solaris
SCO
OSF
AIX

On OSF systems, the previous example is surefire because you don't have to specify a system name at all. Instead, the OSF version of **uuto** checks the public directory names. If it finds a match, it sends the file; otherwise, it fails.

**Keyword:** Internet, modem communications

**Files:** (see uucheck)

**See Also:** uucico, uucleanup, uucp, uupick, uustat

### uuto mktg.doc newl!pat

ALL SVR4 END
Solaris
SCO
OSF
AIX

This looks like a lot of other **uuto** commands, but it is a little different because the system sending the file is the same as the one receiving it. Why do this? In a secure environment, it is a possible way to exchange files. Also, because users might get accustomed to looking for files in UUCP's public directories, your file might reach its destined user sooner than a simple **cp** to the user's home directory. Try this one. It works on some systems, but is configuration-dependent.

**Keyword:** Internet, modem communications

**Files:** (see uucheck)

**See Also:** uucico, uucleanup, uucp, uupick, uustat

### uutry uunet

ALL ALL POWER
SYSADM

This command is actually a shell script that runs **uucico** and calls the remote system **uunet**, while outputting debugging information for use when first setting up UUCP.

**Keyword:** Internet, modem communications

**Files:** (see uucheck)

**See Also:** uucico, uucleanup, uucp, uutry, uustat, uux

### uux newl!lpr /usr/sales/mktg.doc

ALL ALL POWER
SYSADM

This is a basic example of the **uux** command, which lets you execute a command on a remote system and use a file or standard output from the local system. Related UUCP files are **/usr/lib/uucp/Maxuuxqts** and **/usr/lib/uucp/Permissions**, depending on the platform.

**Keyword:** Internet, modem communications

**Files:** (see uucheck)

**See Also:** uucico, uucleanup, uucp, uutry, uustat, uux

### uux newl!uucp
### sparky!/home3/pat/sales.db\{alr!/usr/neala/sales.db\}

| | | |
|---|---|---|
| ALL | ALL | POWER SYSADM |

This **uux** command involves four systems: the local system, which is not represented in the command line, and the remote systems **newl**, **sparky**, and **alr**. In this example, the local system requested **newl** to transfer a file with **uucp**, but the file resides on **sparky** and its destination is **alr**. Note that escaped curly brackets are required to include the third system in the command line.

**Keyword:** Internet, modem communications

**Files:** (see uucheck)

**See Also:** uucico, uucleanup, uucp, uutry, uustat, uuxqt

### uuxqt -snewl

| | | |
|---|---|---|
| ALL | ALL | POWER SYSADM |

This is another debugging command when started from the command line. In this case, it executes the specified commands on the remote system **newl**. The specified commands are those that have been sent using the **uux** program. Related UUCP files are **/usr/lib/uucp/Maxuuxqts** and **/usr/lib/uucp/Permissions**, depending on the platform.

**Keyword:** Internet, modem communications

**Files:** (see uucheck)

**See Also:** uucico, uucleanup, uucp, uutry, uustat, uux

### vacation -I

| | | |
|---|---|---|
| ALL | BSD SVR4 | POWER |

This command starts the **vacation** email program. It is used when you are not going to have access to your email for some time, and you want an automated reply sent to all incoming email. The **$HOME/.vacation** file is used to store your message.

**Keyword:** Internet, modem communications

**Files:** $HOME/.vacation

**See Also:** uucico, uucleanup, uucp, uutry, uustat, uux

### vedit paper.doc

| | | |
|---|---|---|
| ALL | ALL | END |

The **vedit** command opens the **paper.doc** file for editing. If the file doesn't exist, it is created by **vedit**. The **vedit** program is an alias of **vi**, designed for beginners. Using **vedit** is the same as **vi** with the **novice**, **report**, and **showmode** flags set.

**Keyword:**    text editing, text handling

**See Also:**    e, ed, edit, emacs, ex, vi, view

## vgrind -lc -x -Php4 robot.c

This command formats the **robot.c** program file and prints it on the printer **hp4**. The **vgrind** command is a front end to **troff**, which does the actual formatting of the file. Formatting consists of placing comments in italics and keywords in boldface. Function names are listed down the margin of each page.

**Keyword:**    text formatting, programming

**See Also:**    eqn, neqn, nroff, tbl, troff

## vi

How many times has it been said that **vi** is venerable? Well, it persists in wide use in the UNIX market, and in the DOS market, thanks to the MKS and other implementations. Created in the late 1970s by Bill Joy, who later went on to found Sun Microsystems, the **vi** editor rivals **emacs** in popularity, although its dual mode approach to text editing usually befuddles new users. The authors suggest that if you want to use **vi**, just get in the habit of pressing the Escape key a lot.

**Keyword:**    editors, text handling

**See Also:**    cat, less, more, pg

## vi -R /var/adm/messages

The **-R** option to **vi** turns it into a viewer. In this example, you can look at the **/var/adm/messages** file, but you can save any change you make to the file. In other words, **-R** stands for read-only mode.

**Keyword:**    file display

**See Also:**    cat, less, more, pg

## vi -r install

Little **-r** in **vi** restores a lost file (or at least you thought you lost it when the electricity went out). As a rule, good UNIX editors save such files to an editor buffer. You'll know when it happens because the system sends you the following email message:

A copy of an editor buffer of your file "install" was saved when the editor was killed. This buffer can be retrieved using the "recover" command of the editor. An easy way to do this is to give the command "ex -r install." This works for "edit" and "vi" also.

**Keyword:** editors, text handling

**See Also:** ed, emacs

### vi -x reorg.doc

ALL ALL ALL

This command is used to encrypt the file you are working on. When you are done editing it, **vi** saves and encrypts it. To restore the file to normal format, use the **-x** option a second time. Think of it as a toggle between nonsense and wisdom.

**Keyword:** security, editors, text handling

**See Also:** crypt, emacs

### view report.doc

ALL ALL END

This command is used to open and read the **report.doc** file. You can edit the file, but you can't save any changes made. The **view** command is a system-level alias to **vi -R**.

**Keyword:** text viewing, editors

**See Also:** e, ed, edit, ex, vedit, vi

### viewprint - P epson4 -# 2 11.Audio_Tool

ALL Solaris POWER

This command works with Sun's Answerbook help environment. If you don't want Answerbook running on-screen, open the Answerbook item that you need and print it with **viewprint**.

**Keyword:** help, text viewing

**See Also:** lp, lpr, man

### Viewres

ALL XWIN ALL

This is the resource filename for the **viewres** client program. A client's resource file can be located in any of several places. The order of precedence of these locations is **$XENVIRONMENT**, **$HOME/.Xdefaults-*hostname*, $XAPPLRESDIR**, **$HOME/*app-file*, $HOME/.Xdefaults, /usr/lib/X11/app-defaults/Xdefaults**, and **/usr/lib/X11/app-defaults/app-name**. Note that **.Xdefaults** is a customary name, not mandatory.

**Keyword:** X resources

**See Also:** env, viewres, xrdb

| | | |
|---|---|---|
| ALL | XWIN | ALL |

## viewres

Yet another way to view resources, the **viewres** client program displays a graphical tree of all widget-level resources. In general, **viewres** is designed for use by software engineers, but X customizers and system adminstrators may also find it useful.

**Keyword:**   X resources

**See Also:**   appres, editres, listres, xrdb, Viewres

| | | |
|---|---|---|
| ALL | Solaris OSF | SYSADM |

## vipw

The **vipw** command lets you make changes to **/etc/passwd**. In addition, **vipw** updates the **/etc/shadow** file on SVR4 systems. On BSD, or BSD-influenced systems, it does various things, but usually ensures that no one else can make changes to the file while you are editing it. In order to use **vipw**, you must be the root user. Note that on SVR4 systems, if you edit **/etc/passwd** with a regular text editor, **/etc/shadow** is not updated.

**Keyword:**   system setup, security, user environment

**Files:**       /etc/passwd, /etc/ptmp, /etc/shells, /etc/shadow

**See Also:**   admintool, passwd, sysadm, sysadmsh, smit, vi

| | | |
|---|---|---|
| KSH | ALL | SCRIPT |

## VISUAL

This environment variable actuates the **visual** command line editing option when it ends in **emacs**, **gmacs**, or **vi**.

**Keyword:**   user environment

**See Also:**   ed, emacs, vi

| | | |
|---|---|---|
| ALL | Solaris SCO SunOS OSF | POWER SYSADM |

## vmstat

The command **vmstat** outputs statistics about your system's virtual memory and how it is being used. It shows the number of processes, the amount of RAM and swap available, memory paging information, and disk statistics.

**Keyword:**   system information

**Files:**       /vmunix, /dev/kmem, /kernel/unix

**See Also:**   ps, ruptime, who

| | | |
|---|---|---|
| ALL | SVR4 Solaris | ALL |

## volcancel /vol/dsk/floppy_1

This command cancels the request to have the **floppy_1** disk installed into the drive. This command is useful when you have a system that is shared by many people, and they are not all physically near the computer.

**Keyword:** system setup, devices, system information

**Files:** /vol/dsk/*

**See Also:** volcheck, volcopy

## volcheck

ALL   SVR4   ALL
Solaris

The **volcheck** command checks to see whether a diskette is in the drive. If it is in the drive, the computer opens up the File Manager program with the diskette as the current directory.

**Keyword:** system setup, devices, system information

**Files:** /vol/dsk/*

**See Also:** volcancel, volcopy

## volcheck -i60 -t1200 /dev/diskette &

ALL   SVR4   ALL
Solaris

This command checks to see whether a diskette is in the drive every minute for the next 20 minutes. If it is in the drive, the computer opens up the File Manager program, with the floppy disk as the current directory.

**Keyword:** system setup, devices, system information

**Files:** /vol/dsk/*

**See Also:** volcancel, volcopy

## volcopy /u1 /dev/rdsk/c0t0d0s2 /dev/rmt/0

ALL   SVR4    SYSADM
Solaris
SCO

This command makes an image of the **/u1** filesystem onto the tape in the drive specified by **/dev/rmt/0**.

**Keyword:** backup and restore

**Files:** /etc/fstab

**See Also:** cp, cpio, dd

## w

ALL   ALL   ALL

This short command lists everyone currently logged into the system. It also shows the load on the system and the terminal ports in use.

**Keyword:** system information

**Files:** /var/adm/utmp

**See Also:** last, rwho, who

### wait 1076

ALL   ALL   END

This command locks up your terminal until the background process with the ID number of **1076** is done executing.

**Keyword:**   program execution

**See Also:**   bg, fg, jobs

### wall

ALL   ALL   SYSADM

This command reads in text from the terminal, and when it reaches the end of file marker, it sends the text to all users on the system.

**Keyword:**   user communication

**See Also:**   mail, talk, write

### wall -a

ALL   ALL   SYSADM

The **-a** option to **wall** reads input from your keyboard and sends it to all active terminals. This is an excellent way for the system adminstrator to send messages to Xterm users. When you use **wall** without the **-a** option, it sends the message only to the console window, which most X users keep minimized.

**Keyword:**   terminals

**See Also:**   mail, mailx, talk, write

### wall -a news.doc

ALL   ALL   SYSADM

This command is similar to other examples. The difference is that when you specify a filename with **-a**, it broadcasts the text contained in the file.

**Keyword:**   system information, user communication

**See Also:**   mail, mailx, talk, write

### wc -c book.txt

ALL   ALL   ALL

The **-c** option to **wc** shows the file size in bytes. You can check this command by comparing its output to **ls -l book.txt**.

**Keyword:**   file display

**See Also:**   df, lc, ls

### wc -l book.txt

ALL   ALL   ALL

The **-l** option to **wc** outputs the number of lines in the specified file. Pipe it into **grep** if you want to know how many lines contain an identical string.

**Keyword:** text handling
**See Also:** grep, less, more

## wc -w book.txt

ALL ALL ALL

This command shows the number of words in the **book.txt** file.
**Keyword:** file display
**See Also:** less, more, vi

## wc book.txt

ALL ALL SYSADM

This command returns the number of lines, words, and characters in the **book.txt** file.
**Keyword:** text comparison
**See Also:** grep, less, more

## what .login

ALL ALL END

This command outputs file information for the **.login** file.
**Keyword:** file display
**See Also:** find, ls, touch

## whatis mwm

ALL ALL END

This command outputs a one-line summary about the keyword **mwm**.
**Keyword:** help
**See Also:** man

## whence ps

KSH ALL ALL

This Korn shell example shows the exact location of the **ps** file that executes when you run the command. If you are on an SVR4 system and the location comes back as **/usr/ucb/ps**, you are running the BSD version of the command. This means you are probably running other BSD commands as well.
**Keyword:** file display
**Files:** $HOME/.profile
**See Also:** find, whereis, which

## whereis -b xterm

ALL ALL ALL

This command outputs the location of the **xterm** executable file. This is an excellent command for searching for which program you are actually running when you have multiple copies on your system.

**Keyword:**   file display

**Files:**      $HOME/.login, $HOME/.profile

**See Also:**   find, whence, which

### whereis -m xterm

The **-m** option to **whereis** outputs the locations of the manual page files that correspond to the supplied program name.

**Keyword:**   file display

**Files:**      $HOME/.login, $HOME/.profile

**See Also:**   find, whence, where, which

### whereis mwm

This command returns the location of the **mwm man** page and the **mwm** executable.

**Keyword:**   file listing

**See Also:**   whence, which

### which mwm

This command returns the location of the **mwm** executable.

**Keyword:**   file listing

**See Also:**   whence, whereis

### which xterm

This command is the same as **whereis -b xterm**, in that it outputs the location of the executable file **xterm**. If it comes to a symbolic link, it outputs the link information as well.

**Keyword:**   file display

**Files:**      $HOME/.login, $HOME/.profile

**See Also:**   find, whence, where, whereis

### who

The **who** command outputs a list of all the users currently logged into the system. This command with no options outputs less information than **w**, and you don't get the system load information. The output of the command **who** with no options is:

```
perkie    console    Mar  9 09:23
root      pts/1      Mar  9 09:16
```

**500**

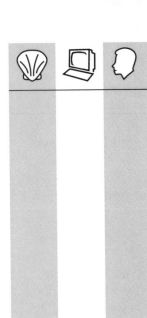

```
perkie     pts/2      Mar  9 09:24
perkie     pts/3      Mar  9 09:24
```

On different systems, the login port may have a different syntax, but this is a good idea of what you can expect to see. Some of the options included with **who** are:

```
-a  This option executes the who command with all options set on.
-b  This option shows when the system was last rebooted.
-d  This option shows killed processes that haven't been respawned by init.
-H  This option shows a header above the output.
-l  This option lists the lines that are available for login.
-p  This option shows active processes started by init.
-q  This option shows only usernames of people on the system.
-r  This option shows the current run level of the system.
-t  This option shows when the system clock was last set.
-u  This option shows only the users currently logged into the system.
```

**Keyword:**   system information

**Files:**   /etc/utmp, /var/adm/utmp, /etc/inittab

**See Also:**   f, finger, init, w

## who | awk ´/^´"$USER"´/ { print $2 }´

The **entry** prints out a list of all **ttys** belonging to the user. The **awk** command is used to extract lines from the **who** pipeline. It is also used to print out the second column of the pipeline—which is where the **tty** numbers are stored. Note the use of double quotation marks around **$USER**. These are not necessary for **user**, which is a single word, but anytime a variable might contain whitespace, you should use them. The alternative in this example would have been to write **'/^'$USER'/**.

**Keyword:**   user environment

**See Also:**   ps, rwho, tty, users, whoami, whodo

## whoami

This command returns your login name on BSD systems. You can get the same results on SVR4 systems by entering **who am i**.

**Keyword:**   user environment

**See Also:**   ps, rwho, tty, users, who, whodo

## whodo

This command shows a list of the users on the system and what they are doing.

**Keyword:**   system information

**See Also:**   ps, rwho, tty, users, who, whodo

ALL   ALL   ALL

ALL   BSD   END

ALL   ALL   END

**501**

### whodo -h

ALL ALL ALL

The **-h** option to **whodo** outputs information about which processes are being run by users currently logged into the system. It doesn't provide a header, however.

**Keyword:** system information

**Files:** /etc/utmp, /var/adm/utmp, /etc/inittab

**See Also:** f, finger, init, ps, w

### whois Southerton

ALL ALL ALL

This command searches the Internet for the name, or handle, **Southerton**. Of course, this command doesn't work if you don't have an Internet connection, but if you do, it is an easy way to try to find someone.

**Keyword:** Internet, user communication

**See Also:** f, finger, who

### write emily

ALL ALL ALL

The **write** command permits two-way communication between any two users. The command provides a split-screen interface. You type **write emily tty01**. This command sends a message to user **emily** on the **tty01** terminal window. Specifying the exact terminal line is handy when you want to communicate with someone who is using an X terminal, or who has multiple Xterm windows open.

**Keyword:** user communication

**See Also:** mail, mailx, talk

### write perkie

ALL ALL END

The **write** command, which is much older and less preferred to **talk**, is used to write a real-time message to another user who is logged in—in this case, user **perkie**.

**Keyword:** user communication

**See Also:** mail, talk, wall

### write perkie tty01

ALL ALL ALL

This command sends a message to user **perkie** on the **tty01** terminal window. Specifying the exact terminal line is handy when you want to communicate with someone who is using an X terminal, or who has multiple Xterm windows open.

**Keyword:** user communication
**See Also:** mail, mailx, talk

## x11perf

The **x11perf** client program is a standard benchmark for X servers and systems. It includes benchmarks for creating and mapping windows, mapping existing windows after restoring from an icon, and rearranging windows. The program also measures graphics performance for operations specific to X. In general, end users have little reason to use **x11perf**, other than to satisfy their curiosity.

**Keyword:** X graphics
**See Also:** x11perfcomp

## x11perfcomp

The **x11perfcomp** client program merges the output from multiple uses of **x11perf** and compiles it into a table. The program shows the objects/second rate of each tested X server. If you use the **-r** or **-ro** options, **x11perfcomp** shows the relative performance of each server to the first server. In general, end users have little reason to use **x11perfcomp**, other than to satisfy their curiosity.

**Keyword:** X graphics
**See Also:** x11perf

## xauth

The **xauth** commands lets you edit and display X authorization data. When you enter **xauth** without arguments, it retrieves the default authority file, which is **$HOME/.Xauthority**, unless the **$XAUTHORITY** environment variable points to a different file. When it executes, **xauth** enters interactive mode and displays a prompt. At this point, you can enter a command such as **list**. Here is some sample output (including prompts):

```
Using authority file /usr/alans/.Xauthority
xauth> list
alpha:0  MIT-MAGIC-COOKIE-1  c0f4359190bc24c38a9b7f0b0db97b4e
alpha:0  MIT-MAGIC-COOKIE-1  c0f4359190bc24c38a9b7f0b0db97b4e
alpha/unix:0  MIT-MAGIC-COOKIE-1  c0f4359190bc24c38a9b7f0b0db97b4e
xauth>
```

**Keyword:** X resources
**See Also:** xdm

ALL    XWIN    SYSADM

ALL    XWIN    SYSADM

ALL    XWIN    SYSADM

| | | |
|---|---|---|
| ALL | XWIN | SYSADM |

## xauth extract - $DISPLAY | rsh aixpilot xauth merge -

The most common way to use **xauth** is to use it to extract authority data from one host and merge it with a second host. This example does this using the **extract** and **merge** options, as well as the **rsh** command.

**Keyword:**  X resources

**See Also:**  rcmd, rsh, telnet

| | | |
|---|---|---|
| ALL | XWIN | ALL |

## XAUTHORITY

This is the X Window System environment variable that specifies the authority file that the **xauth** command accesses by default. If you do not use this variable, the default file is **$HOME/.Xauthority**.

**Keyword:**  X resources

**See Also:**  xauth, xdm

| | | |
|---|---|---|
| ALL | XWIN | ALL |

## XBiff

This is the resource filename for the **xbiff** client program. A client's resource file can be located in any of several resource locations. The order of precedence of these locations is **$XENVIRONMENT**, **$HOME/.Xdefaults-*hostname***, **$XAPPLRESDIR**, **$HOME/*app-file***, **$HOME/.Xdefaults**, **/usr/lib/X11/app-defaults/Xdefaults**, and **/usr/lib/X11/app-defaults/app-name**. Note that **.Xdefaults** is a customary name, not mandatory.

**Keyword:**  X resources

**See Also:**  mail, xbiff, xrdb

| | | |
|---|---|---|
| ALL | XWIN | ALL |

## xbiff &

The **xbiff** program is a neat little program that lets you know when mail has arrived in your mailbox. Most users run **xbiff** from a startup file such as **.xinitrc** or **.xsession**, so that it can be relied on to notify them of all mail. As for appearance, **xbiff** is simply a bitmap picture of a mailbox. When the flag on the mailbox is up, mail has arrived. When the flag is down, it means one of two things: You are up to date on reading your mail, or you have clicked in the window (which puts **xbiff** on alert for the next message). Because of its size, **xbiff** is a good candidate for some window redecorating. It doesn't make much aesthetic sense to have the mailbox wrapped in a window frame, so if you are using Motif, you might want to use the following statement in a valid Motif resource file such as **$XPPLRESDIR/Mwm**:

```
*Mwm*xbiff*clientDecoration: none
```

**Keyword:**    user communication
**See Also:**    mail, mailx

### xbiff -file /usr/spool/mail/root &

If you are a system administrator or someone with root privileges, you might want to run two instances of **xbiff**. By default, **xbiff** reads the mailbox associated with your login. To specify a different file—which you would want to do for the second instance of **xbiff**—specify a mail file, as in the example.

**Keyword:**    user communication, Internet
**See Also:**    biff, mail, mailx

### xbiff -geometry 50x35 -bg black -fg yellow &

This command specifies a custom size for **xbiff** and sets its foreground and background colors (if you need to change a border, use **-bd**, too). If you have turned off the window decorations to **xbiff**, you might consider combining it with the **xclocc -digital** command. Try these resources (place them in **$XAPPLRESDIR** files or **$HOME/.Xdefaults**):

```
!Xbiff section of status bar
xbiff*geometry: 50x35+20+10
xbiff*foreground: yellow
xbiff*background: black
!XClock section of status bar
xclock*analog: False
xclock*geometry: 50x35+70+10
xclock*font: *adobe*times*bold*r*normal*180*
xclock*foreground: yellow
xclock*background: black
```

**Keyword:**    user communication, Internet
**See Also:**    biff, mail, mailx

### xbiff -name newlogin &

When you consider the **checkCommand** resource for **xbiff**, it becomes an even more powerful function. The **checkCommand** resource runs any specified command that could otherwise be executed from the command line. You have to be careful, though, because **xbiff** runs the command each time it polls its specified file (which you can name with the **-f** option or the **file** resource. One way to approach the situation is to build a script that tests whether

ALL    XWIN    ALL

ALL    XWIN    ALL

ALL    XWIN    POWER

**505**

the command has already been executed. The script is up to you, but here are the resources:

```
newlogincheckCommand: /usr/bin/local/script
newlogin*file: $HOME/.xsession errors
newlogin*emptyPixmap: noerror.xbm
newlogin*fullPixmap: newerror.xbm
```

**Keyword:** user environment, programming

**See Also:** if, tail, while

### xbiff -name xerror &

ALL    XWIN    POWER

As with other X client programs, **xbiff** lets you specify a named instance (versus the default instance—which, as a rule, is the name of the executable file). Why do this with **xbiff**? Well, if you think about it, **xbiff** is not a mere mail-checking program—it is a function that checks whether a file has changed size. As a result, you can have it check any file. Not to confuse issues, though, you should designate two different bitmaps when you use **xbiff** for another purpose.

```
xerror*file: $HOME/.xsession errors
xerror*emptyPixmap: noerror.xbm
xerror*fullPixmap: newerror.xbm
```

**Keyword:** user environment, programming

**See Also:** tail, if, while

### xbiff -xrm ´xbiff*emptyPixmap: xlogo32´ &

ALL    XWIN    ALL

If you don't like looking at a picture of a mailbox, you can change one or both of the bitmaps used with **xbiff**. In this command, only the bitmap for the empty mailbox is replaced. The replacement bitmap is **xlogo32**, which is located in **/usr/include/X11/bitmaps**. By default, **xbiff** looks to this directory for a referenced bitmap. You can also specify a path to a bitmap stored elsewhere.

**Keyword:** user communication, Internet

**See Also:** biff, mail, mailx

### xbiff -xrm ´xbiff*onceOnly: true´ &

ALL    XWIN    ALL

Even if you have set up **xbiff** in a resource file, you might want to leave the **onceOnly** resource to command line use. The **onceOnly** resource, as with any resource, can be loaded with the **-xrm** option. What does **onceOnly** do? It tells **xbiff** to check the mailbox once, and not to check it again until you have read your mail. This makes sense if you often get an onslaught of mail.

**Keyword:** user communication, Internet

**See Also:** biff, mail, mailx

## XCalc

ALL XWIN ALL

This is the resource filename for the **xcalc** client program. A client's resource file can be located in any of several resource locations. The order of precedence of these locations is **$XENVIRONMENT**, **$HOME/.Xdefaults-*hostname***, **$XAPPLRESDIR**, **$HOME/*app-file***, **$HOME/.Xdefaults**, **/usr/lib/X11/app-defaults/Xdefaults**, and **/usr/lib/X11/app-defaults/app-name**. Note that **.Xdefaults** is a customary name, not mandatory.

**Keyword:** math, user environment

**See Also:** bc, dc, xcalc, xrdb

## xcalc &

ALL XWIN ALL

The **xcalc** client program is a scientific calculator that can emulate either a Texas Instruments TI-30 or a Hewlett-Packard 10C. In addition to standard toolkit options (such as **-name**, **-fg**, and **-bg**), **xcalc** offers **-stipple** to improve its appearance on monochrome systems, and **-rpn** so it operates in Reverse Polish Notation mode. You'll also find that **xcalc** has an extensive set of keyboard commands. For information on these, read the **man** page, or view **/usr/lib/X11/app-defaults/XCalc**.

**Keyword:** math, user environment

**See Also:** awk, bc, dc, expr, units

## xcalc -name medium &

ALL XWIN ALL

This command uses resources specified by the **medium** resource name. To create named resources for a client program, simply enter them into a custom resource file (which usually has the first letter capitalized, but has the first *two* letters capitalized if it begins with an X). Custom resource files can be located in numerous places. For example, you could store your custom copy of XCalc in **$HOME** or **$XAPPLRESDIR**. It is a good idea not to edit the system-level XCalc, which is located in **/usr/lib/X11/app-defaults**. Here are a few resources you might want to include in your XCalc:

```
medium*Title: Personal Calculator
medium*IconName: pcalc
medium*IconPixmap: calculator
medium*Font: -*-helvetica-bold-r-normal--*-180-*-*-*-*-*-*
medium*bevel.screen.LCD.Font: -*-helvetica-bold-r-normal--*-180-*-*-*-*-*-*
medium*geometry: 350x400
medium*bevel.Background: gray50
medium*bevel.width: 0
medium*bevel.height: 0
medium*background: gray50
medium*DEG.width: 75
medium*INV.horizDistance: 5
medium*INV.width: 75
medium*INV.fromVert: LCD
```

**Keyword:**   math, user environment

**See Also:**   awk, bc, dc, expr, units

## xcalc -xrm ´xcalc*customization: -color´ &

ALL   XWIN   ALL

Another way to get a different version of **xcalc** is to use the **customization** resource. You can use it either via the **-xrm** option or in a resource file. It simply causes **xcalc** to look for a resource file—in the normal places—that has the specified extension, such **-color** in the example.

**Keyword:**   math

**See Also:**   awk, bc, dc

## XClipboard

ALL   XWIN   ALL

This is the resource filename for the **xclipboard** client program. A client's resource file can be located in any of several resource locations. The order of precedence of these locations is **$XENVIRONMENT**, **$HOME/.Xdefaults-*hostname***, **$XAPPLRESDIR**, **$HOME/*app-file***, **$HOME/.Xdefaults**, **/usr/lib/X11/app-defaults/Xdefaults**, and **/usr/lib/X11/app-defaults/app-name**. Note that **.Xdefaults** is a customary name, not mandatory.

**Keyword:**   math, user environment

**See Also:**   awk, bc, dc, expr, units

## xclipboard &

ALL   XWIN   ALL

The **xclipboard** client program is fairly useful, but it must be explicitly supported by an application. The benefit of **xclipboard** is that you can accumulate cut and paste selections in it. The selections remain even after an application has been closed. To

enable an application in a resource file, the application must support key and mouse translations—with functions specifically designed for exchanging data with the clipboard. Here are the proper translations for implementing the **xclipboard** cut and paste feature in an Xterm window:

```
XTerm*VT100.Translations: #override \
Shift <Btn1Up>: select-end(CLIPBOARD) \n\
Shift <Btn2Up>: insert-selection(PRIMARY, CLIPBOARD)
```

**Keyword:** X resources

**See Also:** xcutsel, xterm

### xclipboard -name custom &

As with other X client programs, you can use named resources with **xclipboard**. And, as usual, the resources should be placed in a valid resource file such as **$XAPPLRESDIR/XClipboard**. The following resources make **xclipboard** more appealing to Motif users:

```
custom.geometry: 550x190
custom*form*font: *helvetica-bold-r-normal*140*
custom*Text*Font: *courier-medium-r-normal*140*
custom*ShapeStyle: box
custom*quit.label: Close
custom*quit*borderWidth: 0
custom*quit*background: gray70
custom*delete*borderWidth: 0
custom*delete*background: gray70
custom*new*borderWidth: 0
custom*new*background: gray70
custom*next*borderWidth: 0
custom*next*background: gray70
custom*save*borderWidth: 0
custom*save*background: gray70
custom*prev*borderWidth: 0
custom*prev*background: gray70
custom*index*borderWidth: 0
custom*index*background: gray70
```

**Keyword:** X resources

**See Also:** xprop, xrdb, xcutsel, xterm

### xclipboard -w &

ALL    XWIN    ALL

The **-w** option to **xclipboard** specifies that lines should wrap, so that you can view all cut text without using the horizontal scrollbar. By default, **xclipboard** does not wrap lines.

ALL    XWIN    POWER

**509**

**Keyword:** X resources
**See Also:** xprop, xcutsel, xterm

### xclipboard -xrm ´xclipboard*quit.label: Close´ &

This example makes **xclipboard** a little like Motif, in that it renames the Quit button to Close. You can adjust any resources using the **-xrm** option, excluding Motif-related resources.

**Keyword:** X resources
**See Also:** xprop, xcutsel, xterm

### XClock

This is the resource filename for the **xclock** client program. A client's resource file can be located in any of several resource locations. The order of precedence of these locations is **$XENVIRONMENT**, **$HOME/.Xdefaults-*hostname***, **$XAPPLRESDIR**, **$HOME/*app-file***, **$HOME/.Xdefaults**, **/usr/lib/X11/app-defaults/Xdefaults**, and **/usr/lib/X11/app-defaults/app-name**. Note that **.Xdefaults** is a customary name, not mandatory.

**Keyword:** X resources
**See Also:** cal, xclock, xrdb

### xclock -digital &

If you prefer a digital clock, use this command. For additional options, see the following examples.

**Keyword:** time
**See Also:** cal, date, oclock

### xclock -digital -bg black -fg yellow -update 1 &

This command spiffs up the default display of the analog clock. In addition to providing a running view of seconds (thanks to the **-update 1**) option, the example uses a black background and yellow foreground. To further customize the clock, you could change the font, using the **-xrm** option (standard for all X programs) to load a value for the font resources. Or you could include the following line in the XClock resource files (which can be located in your home directory or **$XAPPLRESDIR**):

```
*font: *adobe*times*bold*r*normal*180*
```

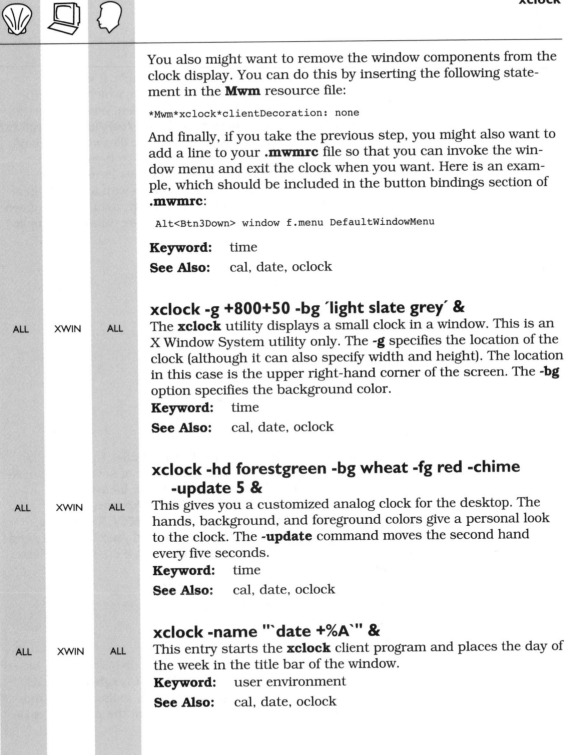

You also might want to remove the window components from the clock display. You can do this by inserting the following statement in the **Mwm** resource file:

```
*Mwm*xclock*clientDecoration: none
```

And finally, if you take the previous step, you might also want to add a line to your **.mwmrc** file so that you can invoke the window menu and exit the clock when you want. Here is an example, which should be included in the button bindings section of **.mwmrc**:

```
Alt<Btn3Down> window f.menu DefaultWindowMenu
```

**Keyword:**     time

**See Also:**     cal, date, oclock

### xclock -g +800+50 -bg ´light slate grey´ &

ALL     XWIN     ALL

The **xclock** utility displays a small clock in a window. This is an X Window System utility only. The **-g** specifies the location of the clock (although it can also specify width and height). The location in this case is the upper right-hand corner of the screen. The **-bg** option specifies the background color.

**Keyword:**     time

**See Also:**     cal, date, oclock

### xclock -hd forestgreen -bg wheat -fg red -chime -update 5 &

ALL     XWIN     ALL

This gives you a customized analog clock for the desktop. The hands, background, and foreground colors give a personal look to the clock. The **-update** command moves the second hand every five seconds.

**Keyword:**     time

**See Also:**     cal, date, oclock

### xclock -name "`date +%A`" &

ALL     XWIN     ALL

This entry starts the **xclock** client program and places the day of the week in the title bar of the window.

**Keyword:**     user environment

**See Also:**     cal, date, oclock

ALL   XWIN   ALL

## XCMS

XCMS is not a command or environment variable. It is the acronymn for the X Color Management System, which was introduced in X11R5. It provides a device-independent method of setting colors rather than using the hexadecimal and **/usr/lib/X11/rgb.txt** approaches in earlier releases of X. In resource files and command line options, you can take advantage of XCMS by using an rgb device specification: **rgb:<red>/<green>/<blue>**. In using this approach, replace **<red>**, **<green>**, and **<blue>** with a hexadecimal number from 0 to 7 corresponding, respectively, to black, red, green, blue, yellow, magenta, cyan, and white. Here are examples supplied by the MIT X Consortium:

```
black          rgb:0/0/0
red            rgb:ffff/0/0
green          rgb:0/ffff/0
blue           rgb:0/0/ffff
yellow         rgb:ffff/ffff/0
magenta        rgb:ffff/0/ffff
cyan           rgb:0/ffff/ffff
white          rgb:ffff/ffff/ffff
```

**Keyword:**   X resources

**See Also:**   xcol, xcoloredit, xrdb

## XCol

ALL   XWIN   ALL

This is the resource filename for the **xcol** client program. A client's resource file can be located in any of several resource locations. The order of precedence of these locations is **$XENVIRONMENT**, **$HOME/.Xdefaults-*hostname***, **$XAPPLRESDIR**, **$HOME/*app-file***, **$HOME/.Xdefaults**, **/usr/lib/X11/app-defaults/Xdefaults**, and **/usr/lib/X11/app-defaults/app-name**. Note that **.Xdefaults** is a customary name, not mandatory.

**Keyword:**   user environment, X resources

**See Also:**   xcol, xcoloredit, xrdb

## xcol &

ALL   XWIN   ALL

This is a public domain client program that displays colors based on the names and values in the **/usr/lib/X11/rgb.txt** file. It solves one of the inadequacies of the basic X tools, namely the lack of a color setting program. The author of the program is Helmut Hoenig (hoenig@informatik.uni-kl.de).

**Keyword:**  user environment, X resources

**See Also:**  xcoloredit, xset, xsetroot

## Xcoloredit

This is the resource filename for the **xcoloredit** client program. A client's resource file can be located in any of several resource locations. The order of precedence of these locations is **$XENVIRONMENT**, **$HOME/.Xdefaults-***hostname*, **$XAPPLRESDIR**, **$HOME/***app-file*, **$HOME/.Xdefaults**, **/usr/lib/X11/app-defaults/Xdefaults**, and **/usr/lib/X11/app-defaults/app-name**. Note that **.Xdefaults** is a customary name, not mandatory.

**Keyword:**  user environment, X resources

**See Also:**  xcoloredit, xrdb, xset

## xcoloredit &

This is another public domain client program that sets colors. The program has three scrollbars that let you set a color. Another three scrollbars let you set the hue, saturation, and value of the color. By default, **xcoloredit** returns a hexadecimal color value to the shell after the user presses the Quit button. The author of the program is Richard Hesketh (rlh2@ukc.ac.uk).

**Keyword:**  user environment, X resources

**See Also:**  xcol, xset, xsetroot

## xcoloredit -title "Custom Color" &

The **xcoloredit** program supports most standard toolkit options. In the example, the **-title** option provides a user-defined text string for the window title bar. Unfortunately, not all versions of **xcoloredit** support the **-name** resource, so you cannot set custom resources via a named set of resources. You can still change resources, however, by editing one of the standard resource files for **xcoloredit**. Note that the resource filename is **Xcoloredit** (it doesn't capitalize the "c"). Here are some resources:

```
xcoloredit.mixingForm.title.label: \ Pick Color via Left
Scrollbars
xcoloredit.height: 280
xcoloredit.width: 410
*Scrollbar.borderWidth: 1
*Scrollbar.height: 255
*quit.label: Select Color and Close
*font: -adobe-times-bold-r-normal--14-140-75-75-p-77-iso8859-1
```

ALL    XWIN    ALL

ALL    XWIN    ALL

ALL    XWIN    POWER

```
*colorMemory.width: 0
*colorMemory.height: 0
*colorMemory.borderWidth: 0
*redLocked.label: R
*greenLocked.label: G
*blueLocked.label: B
```

**Keyword:**   user environment, X resources

**See Also:**   xcol, xset, xsetroot

## XConsole

**ALL   XWIN   ALL**

This is the resource filename for the **xconsole** client program. A client's resource file can be located in any of several resource locations. The order of precedence of these locations is **$XENVIRONMENT**, **$HOME/.Xdefaults-*hostname***, **$XAPPLRESDIR**, **$HOME/*app-file***, **$HOME/.Xdefaults**, **/usr/lib/X11/app-defaults/Xdefaults**, and **/usr/lib/X11/app-defaults/app-name**. Note that **.Xdefaults** is a customary name, not mandatory.

**Keyword:**   X resources

**See Also:**   xrdb

## xconsole -daemon &

**ALL   XWIN   ALL**

This example specifies that **xconsole** run as a background process using the **fork** and **exit** system calls.

**Keyword:**   system information

**See Also:**   xterm

## xconsole -motif -stdin

**ALL   XWIN   ALL**

The **stdin** option tells **xconsole** to read from standard input. It also continues to read from **/dev/console**. You can also have **xconsole** read from an entirely different device by using the **-file** option and specifying the device name (using **/dev/*filename***). Note also that you can write to **/dev/console** by redirecting output from commands, as in the following:

```
echo "Good Morning Xconsole" >> /dev/xconsole
```

**Keyword:**   system information

**See Also:**   xterm

ALL  XWIN  ALL

## xconsole -verbose &

The **xconsole** client program receives and displays console messages (those normally sent to **/dev/console**). This is handy to use in order to avoid having the system splatter messages across the root window. Here are two other points to consider:

- As an alternative to **xconsole**, you can use the **-C** option with an Xterm window. Doing so turns the Xterm window into a psuedo console.
- When you use **Xmd** to start and manage X, you can redirect console and other messages to an error file.

All in all, **xconsole** offers the most flexiblity to handle system messages. In the example, the **-verbose** option tells **xconsole** to display a startup message in the first line of its buffer.

**Keyword:**   system information

**See Also:**   xterm

ALL  XWIN  ALL

## xconsole -verbose -motif -maxSize 16384 &

It would be convenient if all client programs from the MIT X Consortium had Motif interfaces. Well, **xconsole** has one if you use the **-motif** option. The implementation comes complete with Motif-style scrollbars, buttons, and an overall 3D look. The other option in the example, **-maxSize**, sets the maximum buffer size (in bytes) for **xconsole**.

**Keyword:**   system information

**See Also:**   xterm

ALL  XWIN  ALL

## XCutsel

This is the resource filename for the **xcutsel** client program. A client's resource file can be located in any of several resource locations. The order of precedence of these locations is **$XENVIRONMENT**, **$HOME/.Xdefaults-*hostname***, **$XAPPLRESDIR**, **$HOME/*app-file***, **$HOME/.Xdefaults**, **/usr/lib/X11/app-defaults/Xdefaults**, and **/usr/lib/X11/app-defaults/app-name**. Note that **.Xdefaults** is a customary name, not mandatory.

**Keyword:**   X resources

**See Also:**   xrdb

## xcutsel &

| | | |
|---|---|---|
| ALL | XWIN | ALL |

The **xcutsel** client program was designed for applications that could not make use of X Window System cut and paste facilities. The idea behind **xcutsel** is to act as an intermediary in cutting and pasting. The "copy PRIMARY to 0" button copies the current selection into the cut buffer. The "copy 0 to PRIMARY" option converts the current contents of the cut buffer into the selection.

**Keyword:** text handling, X resources

**See Also:** xclipboard, xprop, xterm, xcutsel

## xcutsel -xrm ´*selection: BUFFER4´ &

| | | |
|---|---|---|
| ALL | XWIN | POWER |

To Xterm window users, relegating **xcutsel** to control over a secondary cut buffer is practical. In this way, you can use **xcutsel** to cut and paste to an additional buffer—and still keep **BUFFER0** open for normal cut and paste operations in the Xterm window. In the example, the **-xrm** option loads the **selection** resource to change the default buffer to **BUFFER4**. In all, X supports eight cut buffers, numbered 0 to 7. (You can also change the cut buffer by using the **-cutbuffer** option to **xcutsel**).

**Keyword:** text handling, X resources

**See Also:** xclipboard, xprop, xterm, xcutsel

## xcutsel -xrm ´*selection: CLIPBOARD´ &

| | | |
|---|---|---|
| ALL | XWIN | POWER |

The **xcutsel** client program makes a little more sense when you use it with **xclipboard**. At the least, you have a visual way of tracking what has been cut and what can be pasted. In the example, the **-xrm** loads the **selection** resource and names the **CLIPBOARD** as the location to manipulate. The buttons in **xcutsel** change accordingly.

**Keyword:** text handling, X resources

**See Also:** xclipboard, xprop, xterm, xcutsel

## xdm:23:respawn:/sbin/sh /sbin/xdm.init respawn > /dev/console 2>&1

| | | |
|---|---|---|
| ALL | XWIN | SYSADM |

The **inittab** entry tells the system to execute **xdm** at run levels of **2** and **3**. The third field tells it to be sure that the process is always running, even if you use a **kill -9** on it. The next two fields run the specified processes—in this case, the Bourne shell and **xdm.init**, which is a recursive shell script that starts **xdm** and takes **respawn** as an argument.

**Keyword:** system setup
**Files:** /etc/inittab
**See Also:** init, openwin, xinit

## xdpr

The **xdpr** command makes and prints a standard screen dump to a printer. Without options, **xdpr** uses the default printer. Note that you can use the **-filename** option to print an existing screen dump (made with the **xwd** client), but this is redundant with the **xpr** client program. When you run **xdpr**, a crosshair pointer appears. Use this to select the window you want to dump.

**Keyword:** printing, devices
**See Also:** pr, xpr, xwd

## xdpr -display megasun:0 -root &

As long as you have X authorization to access another host, you can use **xdpr** to make screen dumps across a network. In the example, the **megasun** host is specified, and the **-root** option tells **xdpr** to dump the entire screen.

**Keyword:** printing, devices
**See Also:** lp, lpr, xpr, xwd

## xdpr -Phunchback

The **-P** option to **xdpr** lets you specify a named printer. The printer must have an entry in **/etc/printcap** or another system-wide printer description file. If you do not specify a printer name, **xdpr** sends output to the printer specified by the **$PRINTER** environment variable. Note that there is no whitespace between **-P** and the printer name (which is **hunchback** in the example).

**Keyword:** system information
**See Also:** lp, lpr, xpr, xwd

## xdpyinfo

The **xdpyinfo** command displays information about the X server. Among other items, **xdpyinfo** shows information on predefined values, interclient communication, and screen type.

**Keyword:** system information
**See Also:** xprop, xset, xwininfo

ALL    XWIN    ALL

ALL    XWIN    ALL

ALL    XWIN    ALL

ALL    XWIN    ALL

### xdpyinfo | grep "root window id" | cut -d: -f2

ALL XWIN SCRIPT

Here is a command that you can use in a script when you need to obtain the root window ID. In the script, you will probably want to use command substitution and place the value in a variable.

**Keyword:** system information

**See Also:** xprop, xset, xwininfo

### xdpyinfo | sed -n 30,41p

ALL XWIN ALL

This command provides a quick way to retrieve important information about the display, including the dimensions and resoultion. Here is the output:

```
screen #0:
    dimensions:    1024x768 pixels (333x256 millimeters)
    resolution:    78x76 dots per inch
    depths (2):    1, 8
    root window id:    0x29
    depth of root window:    8 planes
    number of colormaps:    minimum 1, maximum 1
    default colormap:    0x27
    default number of colormap cells:    256
    preallocated pixels:    black 1, white 0
    options:    backing-store YES, save-unders YES
    current input event mask:    0x70003c
```

**Keyword:** system information

**See Also:** xprop, xset, xwininfo

### Xedit

ALL XWIN ALL

This is the resource filename for the **xedit** client program. A client's resource file can be located in any of several resource locations. The order of precedence of these locations is **$XENVIRONMENT**, **$HOME/.Xdefaults-*hostname***, **$XAPPLRESDIR**, **$HOME/*app-file***, **$HOME/.Xdefaults**, **/usr/lib/X11/app-defaults/Xdefaults**, and **/usr/lib/X11/app-defaults/app-name**. Note that **.Xdefaults** is a customary name, not mandatory.

**Keyword:** X resources

**See Also:** vi, xedit, xrdb

### xedit -xrm ´xedit*enableBackups: on´ &

ALL XWIN ALL

As with other client programs, you may not want to use the **-xrm** option from the command line—but it is a convenient way to squirrel away resources in scripts (especially because you can override them from resource files). In the example, backups are enabled. By default, a **.BAK** extension is used on the backup file. You can change this with **backupNameSuffix**. You can also name a backup prefix with the **backupNamePrefix** resource.

**Keyword:**    editors, text handling, xemacs

**See Also:**    e, emacs, vi

### xedit xnotes.doc

ALL    XWIN    ALL

The **xedit** program is X Window System's contribution to system editors. It is described in the **man** pages as a simple editor, and for this reason as well as others, the popular **vi** and **emacs** editors have nothing to worry about. In the example, **xnotes.doc** is a filename that loads into **xedit**. You can also invoke **xedit** without a filename and load and save documents from within the program.

**Keyword:**    editors, text handling

**See Also:**    e, emacs, vi, xemacs

### xemacs -i -wm &

ALL    XWIN    ALL

The two options in this example are unique to **xemacs**. The **-i** option tells **xemacs** to use an internal icon called "Kitchen Sink." The second option inserts a user-specified name in the **xemacs** status line.

**Keyword:**    text handling

**See Also:**    vi, xedit, xterm

### xemacs -rn Xemacs &

ALL    XWIN    ALL

The X version of **emacs** supports resources on a named resource basis. Instead of the otherwise ubiquitous **-name** option, it uses **-rn** to specify the name. Also note that because **xemacs** runs in an Xterm window, it does not support its own resources file. For organization's sake, however, you can use the **#include** directive and have it call call an Xemacs resource file when **$HOME/.Xdefaults** is loaded. Alternatively, you can place Xemacs resources (as the example indicates) in XTerm, which would be located in **$XAPPLRESDIR** or another valid resource file location.

**Keyword:**    editors, text handling

**See Also:**    e, vi, xterm, xedit

**519**

### xemacs -w 80x32 -fg green -bg black -fn 9x15bold &

ALL  XWIN  ALL

As you can see from the example, the **xemacs** program uses many of the same option names as Xterm. The **-w** option is used to indicate the width and height of the window, but **-geometry** could have been used as well.

**Keyword:**  editors, text handling

**See Also:**  e, vi, xterm, xedit

### xev -geometry 150x100 -rv

ALL  XWIN  ALL

In addition to monitoring other windows through the **-id** option, **xev** can also run an "Event Tester" window. All in all, this is a learning tool, and it is one of the most convenient ways to learn about X events.

**Keyword:**  X resources

**See Also:**  xdpyinfo, xprop, xwininfo

### xev -id 37748751

ALL  XWIN  ALL

If you want to monitor a specific window with **xev**, you can supply the value contained in **$WINDOWID**. In a script, you could simply obtain the value from **$WINDOWID**, but for live purposes, you must first obtain the value and then enter it at the command line, as in the example.

**Keyword:**  X resources

**See Also:**  xdpyinfo, xprop, xwininfo

### xeyes -fg red &

ALL  XWIN  ALL

The **xeyes** program is a demonstration program. Two eyes appear on screen (by default, the program's shaped window is not visible) and the pupils follow the mouse pointer. The **-fg** changes the color to that of the author's eyes when he wrote this at a late hour. If you like, you can use an **Xeyes** resource file with **xeyes**.

**Keyword:**  X graphics

**See Also:**  ico, maze, puzzle

### Xfd

ALL  XWIN  ALL

This is the resource filename for the **xfd** client program. A client's resource file can be located in any of several resource locations. The order of precedence of these locations is **$XENVIRONMENT**, **$HOME/.Xdefaults-*hostname***, **$XAPPLRESDIR**, **$HOME/*app-file***, **$HOME/.Xdefaults**, **/usr/lib/X11/app-defaults/Xdefaults**, and **/usr/lib/X11/app-defaults/app-name**. Note that **.Xdefaults** is a customary name, not mandatory.

**Keyword:**   X resources

**See Also:**   xfd, xfontsel, xrdb

### xfd -fn ´*times*bold*r*normal*140*´

The **xfd** client program displays a font that you specify. If you do not specify a font, **xfd** does not execute. One handy use of **xfd** is to confirm a font wildcard pattern, as in the example. When **xfd** evaluates a wildcarded font, it displays the first one that matches in the X server's font database. If your wildcard is not specific enough, the font that displays won't match the font that you want. Thus, you can use **xfd** to sharpen your wild-carding skills.

**Keyword:**   text display, X graphics

**See Also:**   showfont, xfontsel, xlsfonts, xrdb

### xfd -fn 9x15bold &

This command uses a font alias with **xfd** and selects the associated font (another way **xfd** can be used as a learning tool). The X font string appears at the top of the window.

**Keyword:**   text display, X graphics

**See Also:**   showfont, xfontsel, xlsfonts, xrdb

### xfd -fn fixed -box -bc gray60 &

Here, the system default font, **fixed**, is viewed. It is different from the previous **xfd** commands in that a box appears around each character in the font. This is the function of the **-box** option. The **-bc** option specifies the color for the box.

**Keyword:**   text display, X graphics

**See Also:**   showfont, xfontsel, xlsfonts, xrdb

### xfd -fn fixed -xrm ´*grid.gridWidth: 0´ &

Using the **-xrm** option with **xfd** lets you access many resources not available at the command line. In the example, the width of the grid presenting letters is set to **0**, making it invisible.

**Keyword:**   text display, X graphics

**See Also:**   showfont, xfontsel, xlsfonts, xrdb

ALL   XWIN   ALL

ALL   XWIN   ALL

ALL   XWIN   ALL

ALL   XWIN   ALL

## XFontSel

ALL    XWIN    ALL

This is the resource filename for the **xfontsel** client program. A client's resource file can be located in any of several resource locations. The order of precedence of these locations is **$XENVIRONMENT**, **$HOME/.Xdefaults-***hostname*, **$XAPPLRESDIR**, **$HOME/***app-file*, **$HOME/.Xdefaults**, **/usr/lib/X11/app-defaults/Xdefaults**, and **/usr/lib/X11/app-defaults/app-name**. Note that **.Xdefaults** is a customary name, not mandatory.

**Keyword:**    text display, x graphics

**See Also:**    xfd, xfontsel, xrdb

## xfontsel &

ALL    XWIN    ALL

Invoking **xfontsel** without any options is one of the most useful ways to use the program. When you do not specify a font at the command line, for instance, **xfontsel** gives you access to all fonts in the X server font database. You can then select fonts to display by highlighting and selecting them from other windows, or by using any of the 14 main menu items.

**Keyword:**    text display, X graphics

**See Also:**    showfont, xfontsel, xlsfonts, xrdb

## xfontsel -fn 9x15bold -pattern ´*times*´

ALL    XWIN    ALL

This example uses two options to specify fonts. The **-fn** option is the standard X toolkit option used to specify a font for the client to use in its own display. The second option specifies a font pattern for **xfontsel** to load. As a result, only Times fonts are loaded, making it convenient to view your narrowed down font choices.

**Keyword:**    text display, X graphics

**See Also:**    showfont, xfontsel, xlsfonts, xrdb

## xfontsel -name mwmlike &

ALL    XWIN    ALL

You can specify a named set of resources by using the **-name** option with **xfontsel**. Here is a total face-lift:

```
mwmlike.geometry: 700x200
mwmlike*Title: Personal Font Selector
mwmlike*font: *adobe-times-bold-r-normal*140*
mwmlike*fieldBox*font: *adobe-times-bold-r-normal*140*
mwmlike*fieldBox*field11.menu*font:*misc-fixed-medium-r-
normal*7*c*50*
```

```
mwmlike*dash.label: \
mwmlike*showGrip: false
mwmlike*fontName.label.background: gray70
mwmlike*fieldBox*field0.background: gray70
mwmlike*fieldBox*field0.Label: \ Name\
mwmlike*fieldBox*field1.background: gray70
mwmlike*fieldBox*field1.Label: \ Font\
mwmlike*fieldBox*field2.background: gray70
mwmlike*fieldBox*field2.Label: \ Weight\
mwmlike*fieldBox*field3.background: gray70
mwmlike*fieldBox*field3.Label: \ Slant\
mwmlike*fieldBox.field3.menu.r*label: Upright
mwmlike*fieldBox*field4.background: gray70
mwmlike*fieldBox*field4.Label: \ Width\
mwmlike*fieldBox*field5.background: gray70
mwmlike*fieldBox*field5.Label: \ Stroke\
mwmlike*fieldBox*field6.background: gray70
mwmlike*fieldBox*field6.Label: \ Pixels\
mwmlike*fieldBox*field7.background: gray70
mwmlike*fieldBox*field7.Label: \ Size\
mwmlike*fieldBox*field8.background: gray70
mwmlike*fieldBox*field8.Label: \ Horiz\
mwmlike*fieldBox*field9.background: gray70
mwmlike*fieldBox*field9.Label: \ Vertical\
mwmlike*fieldBox*field10.background: gray70
mwmlike*fieldBox*field10.Label: \ Spacing\
mwmlike*fieldBox*field11.background: gray70
mwmlike*fieldBox*field11.Label: \ Average\
mwmlike*fieldBox*field12.background: gray70
mwmlike*fieldBox*field12.Label: \ Id\
mwmlike*fieldBox*field13.background: gray70
mwmlike*fieldBox*field13.Label: \ Code
mwmlike*sampleText: 012345670\n\
abcdefghijklmnopqrstuvwxyz\n\
ABCDEFGHIJKLMNOPQRSTUVWXYZ
mwmlike*quitButton.label: Close
mwmlike*quitButton.borderWidth: 0
mwmlike*quitButton.background: gray70
mwmlike*ownButton.label: Select
mwmlike*ownButton.borderWidth: 0
mwmlike*ownButton.background: gray70
mwmlike*countLabel.background: gray70
```

**Keyword:**  text display, X graphics

**See Also:**  showfont, xfontsel, xlsfonts, xrdb

## xfontsel -noscaled

ALL   XWIN   ALL

This option disables support for scaled fonts available from X11R5 font servers. By using this option, you can be sure that the font you select is a bitmap font.

**Keyword:**   text display, X graphics

**See Also:**   showfont, xfontsel, xlsfonts, xrdb

## xgc

ALL   XWIN   ALL

The **xgc** client program is a graphics demonstration program. According to its authors, it has never been documented (it has a copyright date of 1989). If you experiment with the buttons, however, you will probably get **xgc** to run its graphics routines in its drawing area.

**Keyword:**   X graphics

**See Also:**   ico, maze, puzzle

## xhost +

ALL   XWIN   ALL

If security is not an issue at your site, you might want to grant all systems on the network access to your system. This is easily accomplished by specifying **+** as the only argument to **xhost**.

**Keyword:**   networking

**See Also:**   xauth, xdm, xset

## xhost -

ALL   XWIN   ALL

The **-** option without any additional arguments restricts access to systems listed in the **/etc/X_n.hosts** file. The **n** represents the display number of the remote system.

**Keyword:**   networking

**See Also:**   xauth, xdm, xset

## xhost +`hostname` > /dev/null &

ALL   XWIN   ALL

This example sets the **xhost** status for the local system. It takes the output of **hostname** and adds the system to the allowed list of systems.

**Keyword:**   networking, system information

**See Also:**   ping, xdm, xset

## xhost sparky

ALL   XWIN   ALL

The **xhost** command manages access between different X displays (unless you use the **xauth** method). In the example, the host named **sparky** is added to the local system's access list. For two-way display access, you must run mirror image **xhost** commands. For example, on **sparkplug**, the example suffices; on **sparky**, you would enter **xhost sparkplug**.

**Keyword:**   networking

**See Also:**   xauth, xdm, xset

### xhost -sparky

ALL   XWIN   ALL

The - option to **xhost** gives you an interactive way to remove access permissions from another system. If there are any existing connections to the remote system, they remain intact. Also, be careful not use this - option on the local host. If you do, you must reset the server.

**Keyword:**   networking

**See Also:**   xauth, xdm, xset

### xinit -geometry =80x65 -fn terminal-bold \ -fg ´green´ -bg ´black´

ALL   XWIN   SYSADM

This sets the default Xterm's size, font, and colors. You could also set numerous other resources. The default action of **xinit**, incidentally, is to start an Xterm, thus allowing the user to start other clients from the Xterm.

**Keyword:**   system setup, X resources

**See Also:**   openwin, xdm, mwm

### xinit /usr/bin/scomail ibmpc:0 -display $LOCAL:0

ALL   XWIN   SYSADM

Doing this is a lot different from asking users to execute a remote session, fire up **scomail**, and read their important messages. There's nothing to stop a user from closing **scomail** and breaking the connection to the remote server, but the user won't have a good excuse when you ask why. To complete the tale of the enforced mail reader, you would also have to be sure that local systems allowed the mail server access. This is accomplished with the **xhost** command or by adding the server's name to the **/etc/X.hosts** file; providing access to the server by listing the remote machine in the **/etc/hosts.equiv** or **$HOME/.rhosts** file; or on systems using user-based access, running the **xauth** command.

**Keyword:**   system setup, X resources

**See Also:**   Xserver, xdm, openwin

## xkill

ALL    XWIN    ALL

The **xkill** program allows you to selectively close any X window. The program presents you with a crosshair cursor, which you use to select the window that you want to kill. In most cases, **xkill** is used to kill a window that has hung for some reason. Depending on the nature of the problem, **xkill** may or may not work. Resort to **kill -9** if **xkill** fails.

**Keyword:**    job control

**See Also:**    jobs, kill, ps

## xload &

ALL    XWIN    ALL

The **xload** program posts a small window and, in it, a histogram of system performance. Somewhat a curiosity for many users, **xload** is a convenient tool to visually monitor the effects of running a given application on system resources.

**Keyword:**    system information

**See Also:**    vmstat, xev, who

## xload -name rootbar &

ALL    XWIN    ALL

This command runs **xload** and uses the resources defined for it under the **name** system. The following resources spruce up **xload** a bit, including adding a horizontal line and changing the colors:

```
!Rootbar resources
rootbar*geometry: 34x15+249+0
rootbar*background: #000074
rootbar*foreground: red
rootbar*showLabel: false
rootbar*highlight: white
rootbar*minScale: 3
rootbar*borderWidth: 8
rootbar*borderColor: #000074
```

**Keyword:**    system information

**See Also:**    vmstat, xev, who

## xlogo -name rootbar &

ALL    XWIN    ALL

Normally, all **xlogo** does is display a graphical **X**—you know, like the one on the cover of *The UNIX and X Command Compendium*—and sit around until you get rid of it. The following resources make it a candidate for decoration to the **rootbar** interface mentioned in other examples. Here are some resources:

```
!Rootbar resources
rootbar*geometry: 40x31+0+0
rootbar*background: #000074
rootbar*foreground: white
rootbar*borderWidth: 0
```

**Keyword:**   system information

**See Also:**   ico, xev, maze

## xlsclients

ALL   XWIN   ALL

The **xlsclients** utility reports on all clients currently known to
the X server. Here is the type of output you get when you enter
**xlsclients** from the command line with no options:

```
alpha  xclock -digital -   bg black -fg yellow -update 1
alpha  xload -name rootbar
alpha  xterm -name gold -n Tue -title 'Tue Mar 08'
```

**Keyword:**   system information

**See Also:**   ps, xev, xkill

## xlsclients -l

ALL   XWIN   ALL

The **-1** option to **xlsclients** gives more information about
active clients than the default version of the command. Here
is the equivalent display for the three clients in the previous
example:

```
Window 0x1c00008:
  Machine: alpha
  Name: xclock
  Icon Name: xclock
  Command: xclock -digital -bg black -fg yellow -update 1
  Instance/Class: xclock/XClock
Window 0x2400005:
  Machine: alpha
  Name: rootbar2
  Icon Name: rootbar2
  Command: xload -name rootbar2
  Instance/Class: rootbar2/XLoad
Window 0x200000f:
  Machine: alpha
  Name: Tue Mar 08 13:39:54 EST 1994
  Icon Name: Tue
  Command: xterm -name gold -n Tue -title 'Tue Mar 08'
```

**Keyword:**   system information

**See Also:**   ps, xev, xkill

### xlsclients -l | sed -n ´s/Window //p´ | cut -d: -f1

ALL   XWIN   SCRIPT
POWER

The X Consortium documentation mentions that **xlsclients** can be used to "generate scripts representing a snapshot of the user's current session." That's all it says. This example fills in the details. With it, you can relatively quickly obtain the window IDs of each active client. After you have these, you can use **xwindow** and **xprop** to get more information.

**Keyword:**   system information

**See Also:**   ps, xev, xkill

### xlsfonts -fn ´*fix*bold*140*75*´

ALL   XWIN   ALL

This command narrows a font selection to a single font (if you are using a standard X11 font database). The **-fn** option to **xlsfonts** can search for wildcard patterns and recognizes * and ?, but none of the other shell metacharcters. The * and ? characters must be quoted, using either ' or ". The expression in the example lists the following font:

```
-misc-fixed-bold-r-normal--15-140-75-75-c-90-iso8859-1
```

**Keyword:**   text display, X graphics

**See Also:**   showfont, xfd, xfontsel, xrdb

### xlsfonts | grep ´r-no.*140-75´

ALL   XWIN   ALL

To obtain all 140-point fonts, excluding italic fonts, use this command. The **r** specifies a roman, or straight-up font. The **no** abbreviates part of the word **normal**, which is the width specification. The **140** is the point size in pixels; the **75** is the horizontal resolution. A value of **75** is appropriate for most high-resolution monitors. A value of **100** is appropriate for very high-resolution monitors.

**Keyword:**   text display, X graphics

**See Also:**   showfont, xfd, xfontsel, xrdb

### xlsfonts | grep ´[0-9]\{1,2\}x[0-9]\{1,2\}´

ALL   XWIN   ALL

This command retrieves font aliases from the X Window System font database. X ships with aliases that follow the format of **10x16**, so you can safely search for this style of sequence, as the example does. You could even use a less explicit regular expression than in the example, but it is possible that local modifications to the font database might cause you to match some aliases you don't want.

**Keyword:**   text display, X graphics

**See Also:**   showfont, xfd, xfontsel, xrdb

ALL · XWIN · ALL

## xlsfonts | more
The **xlsfonts** program displays the X Window fonts available on the system. The output is ASCII formatted, one font per line. As a rule, there are more than 1,000 fonts and font aliases, so you don't really need to be advised to use **more** or **pg**.

**Keyword:** fonts, system information

**See Also:** showfont, xfd, xfontsel, xrdb

ALL · XWIN · ALL

## xmag &
The **xmag** program is an image capture utility. When you run **xmag** from the command line, it takes control of the mouse and displays the image capture box, a rectangle that you can move around the screen until you frame your target. When you are ready, press the left mouse button to capture the image.

**Keyword:** images

**See Also:** xv, xwd, xwud

ALL · XWIN · ALL

## xmag -mag 1 - source 150x150
By default, **xmag** uses a magnification level of 5. This command changes the magnification level to **1**, which is normal size. The command also adjusts the size of the source box (also known as a tracking rectangle) to 150 by 150 pixels. These settings make **xmag** appropriate for capturing modest-sized, but meaningful, parts of images.

**Keyword:** images

**See Also:** xv, xwd, xwud

ALL · XWIN · ALL

## Xman
This is the resource filename for the **xman** client program. A client's resource file can be located in any of several resource locations. The order of precedence of these locations is **$XENVIRONMENT**, **$HOME/.Xdefaults-*hostname***, **$XAPPLRESDIR**, **$HOME/*app-file***, **$HOME/.Xdefaults**, **/usr/lib/X11/app-defaults/Xdefaults**, and **/usr/lib/X11/app-defaults/app-name**. Note that **.Xdefaults** is a customary name, not mandatory.

**Keyword:** X resources

**See Also:** man, xman, xrdb

## xman -name button&

If you don't want **xman** to take up screen real-estate, and you don't like a lot of icons, try turning it into a button. The following resources pull this off, and position the **xman** button in the upper left-hand corner of the root window:

```
button*topBox*ShapeStyle: rectangle
button*topBox*geometry: 59x31-17+0
button*manpageButton*borderWidth: 0
button*manpageButton*horizDistance: 0
button*manpageButton*font: *adobe*time*bold*r*normal*240*
button*manpageButton*label: Help
button*manpageButton*vertDistance: -35
button*manpageButton*highlightThickness: 0
button*quitButton*mappedWhenManaged: false
button*helpButton*mappedWhenManaged: false
button*topLabel*mappedWhenManaged: false
```

**Keyword:**    images

**See Also:**    man, whatis, whereis

## xman -notopbox &

The **xman** client **-notopbox** option lets you specify that the program should not display the opening menu. This is handy on a crowded desktop. Xman accepts most standard toolkit options such a **-bg** and **-fg**.

**Keyword:**    help, documentation

**See Also:**    apropos, catman, man, whatis, whereis

## xman -notopbox -bothshown -geometry 500x600&

This command eliminates the opening menu window (see the previous example), and combines the Xman index and command display into one window with **-bothshown**. The **-geometry** option sets the initial size of the window.

**Keyword:**    help, documentation

**See Also:**    apropos, catman, man, whatis, whereis

## xmkmf

The **xmkmf** command creates a Makefile from an Imakefile. You will often find an Imakefile with X programs that require compiling, such as public domain software. When you use **xmkmf** with no arguments in the directory that contains the Imakefile, the **imake** utility is auomatically executed. Because of **xmkmf**, all necessary arguments for compiling on the local system are fed to **imake**. The result is a Makefile. If you use the **-a** option, **xmkmf** creates the Makefile in the current directory and automatically executes **make Makefiles**, **make includes**, and **make depend**.

**Keyword:**    images

**See Also:**    cc, make, vil

### xmodmap $HOME/.keymap.km

This command loads a custom key map for the X server. When loading, **xmodmap** reads all definitions before mapping them, thereby allowing you to refer to **keysyms** defined elsewhere in the file.

**Keyword:**    keyboard definitions, devices

**Files:**    /usr/include/X11/keysymdef.h,
/usr/lib/X11/XKeysymDB

**See Also:**    xev, xset

### xmodmap -e "keysym BackSpace = Delete"

This command binds the **backspace** function to the Delete key. You can specify any number of **keysym** definitions from the command line, as long as you precede each with **-e**.

**Keyword:**    keyboard definitions, devices

**Files:**    /usr/include/X11/keysymdef.h,
/usr/lib/X11/XKeysymDB

**See Also:**    xev, xset

### xmodmap -pk | more

This use of **xmodmap** displays the current set of X key mappings. To have the mappings displayed so that **xmodmap** can resuse them, use the **-pke** option instead of **-pk**.

**Keyword:**    keyboard definitions, devices

**Files:**    /usr/include//X11/keysymdef.h,
/usr/lib/X11/XKeysymDB

**See Also:**    xev, xset

### xon sparky

The **xon** program starts a remote session on the named system. The default session runs in an Xterm window, but you can specify other programs to run with **xon**. In essence, **xon** is a front

ALL    XWIN    POWER

**531**

end to the **rsh** program. Like **rsh**, the **xon** program attempts to log in as the current user, but you specify a different username with the **-user** option.

**Keyword:**    keyboard definitions, devices

**Files:**         /usr/include/X11/keysymdef.h,
                      /usr/lib/X11/XKeysymDB

**See Also:**    xdm, xev, xinit

### xpr -density 180 -width 6.667 xclock.xwd | lpr

ALL    XWIN    ALL

This is the first X Consortium example, because we don't have a Hewlett-Packard ThinkJet in our lives.

**Keyword:**    printing, windows, file conversion, devices

**Files:**         /var/spool/*, /etc/printcap

**See Also:**    lp, lpq, lpr, lprm, xwd, xwpd

### xpr -density 96 -width 6.667 xclock.xwd | lpr

ALL    XWIN    ALL

This command is another one straight from the X Consortium. It shows how you can print to a Hewlett-Packard ThinkJet (HP2225A). It is one of the few commands we didn't test (because ours is a laser-driven existence), but we trust it. In the example, **-density** specifies the printer's dots per inch (dpi) value, and **-width** specifies the maiximum page width.

**Keyword:**    printing, windows, file conversion, devices

**Files:**         /var/spool/*, /etc/printcap

**See Also:**    lp, lpq, lpr, lprm, xwd, xwpd

### xpr -device ljet xclock.xpr | lpr

ALL    XWIN    ALL

If your default printer is not a PostScript printer, you will want to use this command. The **-device** option lets you specify an alternative printer. In the example, **-device** specifies a Hewlett-Packard LaserJet, which must have at least 2 megabytes of memory to print a full-page 300-dpi PostScript file. Here is the X Consortium's description of printer devices:

```
la100
  Digital LA100
ljet
  HP LaserJet series and other monochrome PCL devices such as
  ThinkJet, QuietJet, RuggedWriter, HP2560 series, and HP2930
  series printers
ln03
  Digital LN03
```

```
pjet
  HP PaintJet (color mode)
pjetxl
  HP HP PaintJet XL Color Graphics Printer (color mode)
pp
  IBM PP3812
ps
  PostScript printer
```

**Keyword:**    printing, windows, file conversion, devices

**Files:**    /var/spool/*, /etc/printcap

**See Also:**    lp, lpq, lpr, lprm, xwd, xwpd

### xpr -header "Digital Xclock" -portrait xclock.xwd | lpr

ALL    XWIN    ALL

To add a title to your screen dumps, use the **-header** option, as shown in the example. To ensure that a screen dump prints either in landscape or **portrait** mode, specify either one as an option. Note that if a screen dump is oriented horizontally, even one small enough to fit in portrait mode, **xpr** prints it in landscape mode. This is probably not what you want.

**Keyword:**    printing, windows, file conversion

**Files:**    /var/spool/*, /etc/printcap

**See Also:**    lp, lpq, lpr, lprm, xwd, xwpd

### xpr -rv -trailer "Digital Xclock" xclock.xwd | lpr

ALL    XWIN    ALL

This command does two things: The **-rv** option tells **xpr** to format the screen dump in reverse video, and the **-trailer** option specifies a title that appears underneath the printed image.

**Keyword:**    printing, windows, file conversion, devices

**Files:**    /var/spool/*, /etc/printcap

**See Also:**    lp, lpq, lpr, lprm, xwd, xwpd

### xpr -scale 2 xclock.xwd | lpr

ALL    XWIN    ALL

This command changes the size of the printed image. PostScript, LN03, and Hewlett-Packard printers can translate each pixel in the image into a grid of a specified size. In the example, the **-scale** value of **2** translates each pixel into a 2-by-2 grid. Using this command to make images larger is not necessary; by default, **xpr** prints the screen dump as large as possible for the page size.

**Keyword:**    printing, windows, file conversion, devices

**Files:**    /var/spool/*, /etc/printcap

**See Also:**    lp, lpq, lpr, lprm, xwd, xwpd

**533**

## xpr xclock.xwd -output xclock.ps

ALL    XWIN    ALL

If you don't want to print a screen dump immediately, you can save it in a file. By default, **xpr** formats the file for PostScript output. This is also a handy way to save screen dumps if it suits your needs. Look at the following filesize differences for our example dump, which was of the **xclock** program, which we displayed as a digital clock in an 18-point font:

```
ls -ls xclock.xwd xclock.xpr
 4 -rw-r--r--   1 alans bin    3822 Mar 10 08:34 xclock.xpr
14 -rw-r--r--   1 alans bin   13779 Mar 10 08:26 xclock.xwd
```

**Keyword:**    printing, windows, file conversion, devices

**Files:**       /var/spool/*, /etc/printcap

**See Also:**    lp, lpq, lpr, lprm, xwd, xwpd

## xpr xclock.xwd | lpr

ALL    XWIN    ALL

Here is one common way of printing an X window dump (XWD) file made with the **xwd** utility. Because **xpr** prints to the standard output, which is the terminal window or screen, you can redirect it to a printer by piping it to **lpr**.

**Keyword:**    printing, windows, file conversion, devices

**Files:**       /var/spool/*, /etc/printcap

**See Also:**    lp, lpq, lpr, lprm, xwd, xwpd

## xprop

ALL    XWIN    END

The **xprop** program can be extremely useful for anyone customizing the X Window environment—or for anyone who just happens to need some details on a window. By default, **xprop** is an interactive command. It takes control of the mouse pointer, and you select the window for which you want information. Here is a sample display:

```
WM_STATE(WM_STATE):
                window state: Normal
                icon window: 0x800723
WM_PROTOCOLS(ATOM): protocols  WM_DELETE_WINDOW
WM_CLASS(STRING) = "fenway", "XTerm"
WM_HINTS(WM_HINTS):
                Client accepts input or input focus: True
                Initial state is Normal State.
                bitmap id # to use for icon: 0x1400001
WM_NORMAL_HINTS(WM_SIZE_HINTS):
                program specified size: 500 by 316
                program specified minimum size: 26 by 17
```

```
                         program specified resize increment: 6 by 13
                         program specified base size: 20 by 4
WM_CLIENT_MACHINE(STRING) = "alpha"
WM_COMMAND(STRING) = { "xterm", "-name", "fenway" }
WM_ICON_NAME(STRING) = "fenway"
WM_NAME(STRING) = "fenway"
```

**Keyword:**    windows, user environment

**See Also:**    xev, xlsclients, xwininfo

### xprop -id `printenv WINDOWID`

Instead of using interactive mode, you can specify the window ID of a client, and **xprop** displays the same set of information as in the previous example. We used **printenv** in this example to obtain the window ID—which, as a rule, is defined by the client in the shell environment.

**Keyword:**    windows, user environment

**See Also:**    xev, xlsclients, xwininfo

### xprop -name bworks

Another alternative to using interactive mode is the **-name** option. The name of the program is either the executable file-name, or—if you have used the **-name** option with the client—the argument supplied to **name**.

**Keyword:**    windows, user environment

**See Also:**    xev, xlsclients, xwininfo

### xprop -root

This command serves as the basis for obtaining important information about the X server. You can use it in scripts or enter it at the command line. Here is a sample display:

```
_XSETROOT_ID(PIXMAP): pixmap id # 0x1800004
WM_ICON_SIZE(WM_ICON_SIZE):
                    minimum icon size: 16 by 16
                    maximum icon size: 50 by 50
                    incremental size change: 1 by 1
_MOTIF_WM_INFO(_MOTIF_WM_INFO) = 0x0, 0x800024
RESOURCE_MANAGER(STRING) =
"*Background:\t#9cb6f3\n*Foreground:\t#000000\n
CUT_BUFFER7(STRING) =
CUT_BUFFER6(STRING) =
CUT_BUFFER5(STRING) =
CUT_BUFFER4(STRING) =
CUT_BUFFER3(STRING) =
```

ALL    XWIN    SCRIPT    POWER

ALL    XWIN    SCRIPT    POWER

ALL    XWIN    SCRIPT    POWER

**535**

```
CUT_BUFFER2(STRING) =
CUT_BUFFER1(STRING) =
CUT_BUFFER0(STRING) = "THE COMMAND COMPENDIUM"
```

Above, note that the resource manager string has two resource statements. We reduced our resources for the sample. Normally, all resources that you have loaded using **xrdb** are displayed here.

**Keyword:**   windows, user environment

**See Also:**   xev, xlsclients, xwininfo

### xprop -root -len 100 CUT_BUFFER0

The **-len** option lets you set a limit on the number of characters that you want displayed from the cut buffer.

**Keyword:**   windows, user environment

**See Also:**   xev, xlsclients, xv_get_sel, xwininfo

### xprop -root -len 100 CUT_BUFFER0 | cut -d″″ -f2

This command is similar to the previous one, but the addition of the **cut** command lets you slice off the leading and ending quotation marks in the output.

**Keyword:**   windows, user environment

**See Also:**   cut, xev, xlsclients, xv_get_sel, xwininfo

### xprop -root CUT_BUFFER0

To display a single property with **xprop**, you can specify the property after the name. This is convenient for obtaining information for shell scripts, as well as for interactive use.

**Keyword:**   windows, user environment

**See Also:**   xev, xlsclients, xv_get_sel, xwininfo

### xprop -spy

This command maintains a watchful eye on the root window properties. It can serve as a learning tool, or perhaps you might want to use it in a script. Each time a property in the root window changes, the **-spy** option prints the change and the rest of the properties to standard input.

**Keyword:**   windows, user environment

**See Also:**   xev, xlsclients, xwininfo

ALL   XWIN   SCRIPT   POWER

ALL   XWIN   SCRIPT   POWER

ALL   XWIN   SCRIPT   POWER

ALL   XWIN   SCRIPT   POWER

## xprop WM_NAME

**xprop** requires that you select a target window by clicking on the window. The sample output would look something like this:

```
WM_NAME(STRING) = "Lotus 1-2-3"
```

**Keyword:**    windows, user environment

**See Also:**    xev, xlsclients, xwininfo

## xrdb

The **xrdb** client manages the X resource database, which is maintained in server memory and accessible through several X programs. Of these, however, **xrdb** is reponsible for setting, adding, and deleting resources. It is an extensive interface to the X Window System and deserves careful study by adminstrators and integrators. When you enter **xrdb** on the command line by itself, as in the example, it drops you into shell edit mode (because it fully handles standard input). In shell edit mode, you can set new resources as in the following:

```
$ xrdb
Mwm*menu*DefaultWindowMenu*background:  #004b81
Mwm*menu*DefaultWindowMenu*foreground:  #ffffff
Ctrl-D
```

**Keyword:**    X resources

**See Also:**    mwm, ps, xset

## xrdb $HOME/.Xdefaults

When you specify a filename with **xrdb**, it loads the resources contained in the file and overwrites all existing resources. New resources are only evident the next time you load a related application. No changes are made to currently running programs. If you are changing resources to Motif or another window manager, you must restart the window manager before resource changes take effect.

**Keyword:**    X resources

**See Also:**    mwm, xinit, xset

ALL    XWIN    END

ALL    XWIN    POWER

ALL    XWIN    POWER

### xrdb -load $HOME/.Xdefaults

ALL    XWIN    POWER

If you are using **xrdb** in shell scripts, perhaps it is advisable to use the **-load** option. The reason for this is that the X Consortium, in its documentation, describes the **default** behavior as a bug: "The default for no arguments should be to query, not to overwrite, so that it is consistent with other programs."

**Keyword:**    X resources

**See Also:**    mwm, xinit, xset

### xrdb -load /dev/null

ALL    XWIN    POWER

At times, you might want to clear the resources in server memory. Perhaps you are testing various sets of resources and comparing them to the default behavior. This command does the trick.

**Keyword:**    X resources

**See Also:**    mwm, xinit, xset

### xrdb -load Bworks

ALL    XWIN    POWER

If a resource file is not in the system resource path, you can load it directly if you don't mind temporarily losing your other resources, which can be easily restored with other examples. In the example, an arbitrary file called **Bworks** is loaded. Note that all other **xrdb**-maintained resources are overridden, and only the **Bworks** resources are now available through the X resource database.

**Keyword:**    X resources

**See Also:**    mwm, openwin, xinit

### xrdb -merge ./xrdb

ALL    XWIN    POWER

The use of **xrdb** is most relevant for script writers. The command merges resources in **./xrdb** into the existing server resource database. If you need to use the **-merge** option from the command line, use the **echo** command in a pipeline:

```
echo "licenseLock: true" | xrdb -merge
```

**Keyword:**    X resources

**See Also:**    mwm, openwin, xinit

### xrdb -query

ALL  XWIN  POWER

The **-query** option outputs currently set resources. The option is fully operable with UNIX standard output. As a result, you can use the **xrdb** memory space with most UNIX utilities.

**Keyword:**  X resources

**See Also:**  mwm, openwin, xinit

### xrdb -query | grep -i xterm

ALL  XWIN  POWER

This command queries the X server resource database and displays resources associated with the Xterm terminal emulator. Using the **-i** option to **grep** ensures that you obtain both class and instance name, or in the case of the example, **Xterm** and **xterm**.

**Keyword:**  X resources

**See Also:**  mwm, openwin, xinit

### xrdb -query | grep licenseLock | cut -d: -f2

ALL  XWIN  SCRIPT

There is no such resource as licenseLock (at least, we don't think so, because we made it up). Instead, licenseLock is an arbitrary string paired with a value, but stored in the X resource database, just like any real resource. Thus, as long as you don't abuse it to the point where it slows the system, you can use the resource database as a temporary repository. The example indicates that the technique might work in a rudimentary license management scheme.

**Keyword:**  X resources

**See Also:**  mwm, openwin, xinit

### xrsh -display megabox xterm -fn terminal-bold &

ALL  XWIN  ALL

The **xrsh** command is a contributed client program, which means that you may or may not find it in your default installation of X. The purpose of **xrsh**, as shown in the example, is to start a remote client on your local system.

**Keyword:**  networking

**See Also:**  rsh, rlogin, telnet

### Xserver

ALL  XWIN  ALL

Although you may not run across a program named **Xserver**, this is the generic name for the X server. In fact, some systems have a **man** page entry for Xserver. Otherwise, look in your system

**xset**

documentation for the specific name of your X server. Examples include Xsun, Xdec, and Xsco.

**Keyword:** X resources, security, networking

**See Also:** xauth, xdm, xset, xinit

### "xset +fp /home/altfonts

ALL  XWIN  ALL

This command adds an alternative font directory to the X server's font path. You can set the directory to any direcetory containing valid fonts. It is likely that your server does not support the use of shell metacharacters (wildcards) in the path. To set multiple font directories using a single invocation of **xset +fp**, be sure to separate directories with commas.

**Keyword:** user environment

**See Also:** xfd, xlsfonts, xrdb, Xserver, xsetroot

### "xset -fp /home/altfonts

ALL  XWIN  ALL

This command removes a font directory from the font path used by the X server. Be careful if you use shell metacharacters, which generally are not supported with the **xset** command.

**Keyword:** user environment

**See Also:** xfd, xlsfonts, xrdb, Xserver, xsetroot

### xset -q

ALL  XWIN  ALL

The **xset** command sets, changes, and displays hardware and system values known to the X server. The **-q** option, as used in the example, displays the current state of values associated with **xset**. Here is some sample output:

```
Keyboard Control:
    auto repeat:  on     key click percent:  50
    auto repeating keys:  ffffffffffffffff
                          ffffffffffffffff
                          ffffffffff07f8df
                          ffffffffffffffff
    bell percent:  50     bell pitch:  400     bell duration:  100
Pointer Control:
    acceleration:  7/1    threshold:  3
Screen Saver:
    prefer blanking:  yes     allow exposures:  yes
    timeout:  600     cycle:  600
Colors:
    default colormap:  0x27     BlackPixel:  1     WhitePixel:  0
Font Path:
```

```
/usr/lib/X11/fonts/misc/,/usr/lib/X11/fonts/Speedo/,/usr/lib/X11

/fonts/Type1/,/usr/lib/X11/fonts/75dpi/,/usr/lib/X11/fonts/100dpi/
   Bug Mode: compatibility mode is disabled
```

**Keyword:**  X resources

**See Also:**  set, xrdb, xsetroot

## xset -q | grep -i

ALL  XWIN  ALL

To view the current font path without displaying other **xset** values, this example usually does the trick. It relies on the fact that every font directory usually uses the word "font" somewhere in its hierarchy. The **-i** option to **grep** causes **grep** to consider both uppercase and lowercase letters. Here is the display produced by the example:

```
Font Path:
/usr/lib/X11/fonts/misc/,/usr/lib/X11/fonts/Speedo/,/usr/lib/X11
/fonts/Type1/,/usr/lib/X11/fonts/75dpi/,/usr/lib/X11/fonts/100dpi/
```

If you simply need to get the value the font path, and don't want the "Font Path" title, don't use the **-i** option to **grep**.

**Keyword:**  user environment

**See Also:**  xfd, xlsfonts, xrdb, Xserver, xsetroot

## xset b 95 1500 150

ALL  XWIN  ALL

The **b** option to **xset** specifies the tone of the system bell. The three values correspond to volume, pitch, and duration. You can specify either one, two, or all three of the values at the same time. Simply increasing volume does not produce much tone difference on many systems. To test your settings, use **/bin/echo**, as in **/bin/echo "\07"**.

**Keyword:**  user environment

**See Also:**  set, xprop, xmodmap, xrdb, Xserver, xsetroot, xwininfo

## xset c 60

ALL  XWIN  ALL

If you like to have the system sound a short simulation of a key click, this is the command. The value supplied to the **-c** option is the percentage of the maximum key click.

**Keyword:**  user environment

**See Also:**  set, xprop, xmodmap, xrdb, Xserver, xsetroot, xwininfo

### xset c off

| | | |
|---|---|---|
| ALL | XWIN | ALL |

If you don't like sounding off (you might like typing while talking on the phone), use the **c** option with the **off** parameter. This disables key click tones.

**Keyword:**   user environment

**See Also:**   set, xprop, xmodmap, xrdb, Xserver, xsetroot, xwininfo

### xset fp default

| | | |
|---|---|---|
| ALL | XWIN | ALL |

If you need to reset the font path to the system default, use this command.

**Keyword:**   user environment

**See Also:**   xfd, xlsfonts, xrdb, Xserver, xsetroot

### xset fp rehash

| | | |
|---|---|---|
| ALL | XWIN | ALL |

If you create a new font directory and want to tell the X server about it, use this command. Previously, you would have created the new directory by using the **mkfontdir** command.

**Keyword:**   user environment

**See Also:**   mkfontdir, xfd, xlsfonts, xrdb, Xserver, xsetroot

### xset fp=/usr/lib/X11/fonts/misc/,/usr/lib/X11/fonts/Speedo /,/usr/lib/X11 /fonts/Type1/,/usr/lib/X11/fonts/75dpi/

| | | |
|---|---|---|
| ALL | XWIN | ALL |

This command sets the font path for the X server. Note that each font directory is separated from the previous one by a comma. The directories used in the example comprise the default set, excluding the 100-dpi directory, which is **/usr/lib/X11/fonts/100dpi/**.

**Keyword:**   user environment

**See Also:**   xfd, xlsfonts, xrdb, Xserver, xsetroot

### xset led 3

| | | |
|---|---|---|
| ALL | XWIN | ALL |

To turn on a single LED on the keyboard, you can specify the numeric value associated with the LED. On most servers, the value **3** controls the CapsLock key. You can turn off a single LED by using a hyphen before the option, as in **xset -led 3**. Note that many of the **xset** options use - and + as a convenient method to toggle a given function.

**Keyword:**   user environment, devices

**See Also:**   xrdb, Xserver, xsetroot

### xset led off

ALL    XWIN    ALL

Most users expect the LED lights on the keyboard to react as configured in the hardware. If someone has been using **xset** with the **led** option to change things, you can turn off the lights with this command. If you need to turn them on again, replace the **off** parameter with **on**.

**Keyword:**    user environment, devices

**See Also:**    xrdb, Xserver, xsetroot

### xset m 7 10 &

ALL    XWIN    ALL

The **m** option to **xset** lets you modify how fast the pointer moves when you move the mouse. The **m** option takes two parameters: acceleration, which sets the speed, and threshold, which specifies how many pixels the mouse must move before the pointer moves. This example results in highly accelerated movement. A more typical setting would be **xset m 3 10**. To set pointer speed to its default, use the **default** parameter, as in **xset m default**.

**Keyword:**    user environment, devices

**See Also:**    xrdb, Xserver, xinit

### xset p $pixel $color

ALL    XWIN    ALL

The **p** option to **xset** lets you set the color for a pixel in the system colormap. First, however, the pixel must have been deemed to be writable. Use the following script if you want to check pixel status.

```
#!/bin/sh
#viewpix, check of colormap pixels are writable
#Syntax: viewpix color
#Initial values
  color=$1
  MAP=255
#Exit if arg count is wrong
  [ $# -ne 1 ] && exit 1
#Loop to test pixels
  while [ $pixel -le $MAP ]
  do
     xset p $pixel $color
     pixel=`expr $pixel + 1`
  done
```

**Keyword:**    user environment, X graphics

**See Also:**    xrdb, Xserver, xsetroot, xwininfo

### xset r on

ALL  XWIN  ALL

This command turns on auto-repeat, which means you can repeat characters by holding down the key. The **off** argument turns this feature off. Note that some systems may not support this feature.

**Keyword:**   user environment, devices

**See Also:**   set, xrdb, Xserver, xwininfo

### xset s 1200 s noblank

ALL  XWIN  ALL

The default behavior of the X server screen saver is simply to blank the screen. Using **noblank** displays a pattern instead (usually a large X). The **s 1200** option tells the screen saver to activate after 10 minutes of inactivity.

**Keyword:**   user environment, devices

**See Also:**   set, xrdb, Xserver, xwininfo

### xset s 2400

ALL  XWIN  ALL

When used with a single number, **xset** sets the length of time for the system screen saver. The value is expressed in seconds. Thus, the example tells the X server, if 40 minutes elapse during which the user has not used the keyboard or mouse (or perhaps banged the desk, sending vibrations to the hardware), to activate the screen saver.

**Keyword:**   user environment, devices

**See Also:**   set, xrdb, Xserver, xwininfo

### xset s 300 5 s noblank

ALL  XWIN  ALL

This command sets the screen saver to take effect after five minutes of inactivity. It also tells it to cycle the screen saver pattern every five seconds. The **noblank** command tells the X server to display the pattern.

**Keyword:**   user environment, devices

**See Also:**   set, xrdb, Xserver, xwininfo

### xset s on

ALL  XWIN  ALL

If you like the idea of screen savers, and the X environment isn't using one, try this command. It turns on the screen saver facility. If you don't like screen savers, replace **on** with **off** in the example.

**Keyword:** user environment, devices

**See Also:** set, xrdb, Xserver, xwininfo

### xsetroot -solid ´rgbi:.8/.8/.8´

ALL  XWIN  ALL

This entry sets the root window background to white. It uses the X Color Management System (XCMS) syntax.

**Keyword:** user environment, X graphics

**See Also:** xprop, xrdb, xwininfo

### xsetroot -solid `xcoloredit`

ALL  XWIN  ALL

With UNIX command substitution, you can build a color-setting routine that is easy enough to type from the command line (although you probably will want to create a script, alias, or shell function). In the example, the **xcoloredit** program supplies the color value to **xsetroot** in the form of a hexadecimal color value.

**Keyword:** user environment, X graphics

**See Also:** xprop, xrdb, xwininfo

### XTerm

ALL  XWIN  ALL

This is the resource filename for the **xterm** client program. A client's resource file can be located in any of several resource locations. The order of precedence of these locations is **$XENVIRONMENT**, **$HOME/.Xdefaults-*hostname***, **$XAPPLRESDIR**, **$HOME/*app-file***, **$HOME/.Xdefaults**, **/usr/lib/X11/app-defaults/Xdefaults**, and **/usr/lib/X11/app-defaults/app-name**. Note that **.Xdefaults** is a customary name, not mandatory.

**Keyword:** X resources

**See Also:** sh, xrdb, xterm

### xterm -fn `xfontsel -print` &

ALL  XWIN  ALL

As long as **xfontsel** is in the system path, this is great way to use it as a front end to selecting a font for an Xterm window.

**Keyword:** windows, terminals

**See Also:** xfontsel, stty, tty, xrdb, XTERM, cmdtool, aixterm, scoterm, decterm

## xterm -name getstring -title "Get String" \
### -xrm ´getstring.VT100.geometry: 55x3+365+435´ \
### -e getstring "Your Name" $file

ALL  XWIN  POWER

This is an Xterm window designed to prompt the user and obtain an ASCII text string. Note that the resource name of the program is **getstring,** and so is the actual script it calls with the **-e** option:

```
#!/bin/sh
file=$1
bold=`tput smso`
unbold=`tput rmso`

while [ 1 ]  do
  /bin/echo -n "\n ${bold}Enter $prompt:$unbold"
  /bin/echo -n " "
  read string
  echo "$string" > $file
  [ "$string" != "" ] && exit
done
```

**Keyword:**    windows, terminals

**See Also:**   stty, tty, xrdb, XTerm, cmdtool, aixterm, scoterm, decterm

## xterm -name log1 -T Log -n $USER -l -lf
### "$HOME/log.`date +%m%d%y`" &;

ALL  XWIN  POWER

This command starts an Xterm window that duplicates all text typed and displayed on-screen to a log file. The log filename consists of the word **log** and tailored output from the **date** command. The **-T** switch, instead of **-title**, is used to specify the title bar text string.

**Keyword:**    windows, terminals

**See Also:**   stty, tty, xrdb, XTerm, cmdtool, aixterm, scoterm, decterm

## xterm -name talk -n $USER -title "`eval echo $users`"
### -e talk &

ALL  XWIN  POWER

This Xterm command starts a window with the names of current users in the title bar window. The **-title** option is reponsible for this, and the **-n** option is responsible for putting the invoking user's name in the Xterm's icon. The **-name** option specifies a resource name. The **-e** option specifies the UNIX **talk** program. When the user breaks the connection with **talk**, the Xterm disappears.

**Keyword:** windows, terminals

**See Also:** stty, tty, xrdb, XTerm, cmdtool, aixterm, scoterm, decterm

## xterm -name vi &

ALL  XWIN  ALL

This command invokes the Xterm terminal emulator and specifies that the X server should load the resources associated with **-name**; in this case, the name is **vi**. In the case of the example, you can assume the Xterm window is using a custom set of **vi** resources (most likely special keyboard translations).

**Keyword:** windows, terminals

**See Also:** stty, tty, xrdb, Xterm, cmdtool, aixterm, scoterm, decterm

## xterm -title "`date`" -fn 8x13bold -bg black -fg green -g 58x12+15+40 &

ALL  XWIN  POWER

This Xterm command line puts the output from the **date** command into the title bar of the window. It also sets the font, geometry (using **-g** instead of **-geometry**), and the background and foreground colors.

**Keyword:** windows, terminals

**See Also:** stty, tty, xrdb, XTerm

## xwd | xwud

ALL  ALL  ALL

Using the **xwd** and **xwud** commands together in a pipe allows you to make a screen dump and then immediately display it. The **xwd** command makes the initial screen dump (by default, you can select any window with **xwd**, including the root window); and the **xwud** command displays the results of the screen dump.

**Keyword:** X graphics

**See Also:** xsetroot, xwud, xpr

## yacc -d project.y

ALL  ALL  POWER

**yacc** stands for "yet another compiler-compiler." This is a language that, given certain grammars, creates parsers. The parsers can then recognize syntaxes. When creating applications with **yacc**, it is necessary to also use **lex**. Once **yacc** and **lex** have both been run, two files, **y.tab.c** and **lexx.yy.c**, are output. You want to compile and link these files with your C compiler by typing a command similar to:

```
cc project y.tab.c lex.yy.c -ly -ll
```

The executable program that you have created with **yacc** and **lex** is then called **project**.

**Keyword:**   text handling, programming

**See Also:**   cc, lex, make

## yes

ALL   SVR4   POWER
SCO
BSD

The **yes** command simply outputs a **y** until it encounters an interrupt such as Ctrl-C. By itself, **yes** doesn't have much value. Used in a pipeline, however, you can use **yes** to answer continuous lines of questions. For example, if you are going to run the **fsck** program on an unsynced filesystem, it asks you if you want to repair each block as you come to it. This could take hours, typing **y** each time, but the **yes** program can do it for you.

**Keyword:**   background processing

**See Also:**   fsck, mv, rm

## ypcat -k hosts

ALL   ALL   SYSADM

This command shows the keys associated with the **hosts** NIS maps. Also shown by this command are all the other values associated with the **hosts** NIS maps.

**Keyword:**   networking

**Files:**   /var/yp/*

**See Also:**   ypinit, ypmake, ypmatch, yppasswd, ypset, ypwhich

## ypcat -x

ALL   ALL   SYSADM

This command shows a listing of all the NIS maps on your system. If you aren't sure where to check in your NIS database, the -**x** option to **ypcat** shows you information that may be useful.

**Keyword:**   networking

**Files:**   /var/yp/*

**See Also:**   ypinit, ypmake, ypmatch, yppasswd, ypset, ypwhich

## ypcat passwd

ALL   ALL   SYSADM

The **ypcat passwd** command outputs the data in the NIS map with regard to password information about users who have NIS accounts.

**Keyword:**   networking

**Files:**   /var/yp/*

**See Also:**   ypinit, ypmake, ypmatch, yppasswd, ypset, ypwhich

### ypinit -c

ALL    ALL    SYSADM

The **ypinit -c** command is usually run only once on a system, to set up the computer as an NIS client workstation. If you add new NIS servers, you have to run **ypinit** again so that the client recognizes the new servers.

**Keyword:**    networking

**Files:**    /var/yp/*

**See Also:**    ypcat, ypmake, ypmatch, yppasswd, ypset, ypwhich

### ypmake

ALL    ALL    SYSADM

This command is used to rebuild the yellow pages or NIS database of connected systems. It will update the database with any new system names, as well.

**Keyword:**    networking

**See Also:**    ping

### ypmake

ALL    ALL    SYSADM

This command is used to rebuild the NIS database on the server system. It is the same as **cd /var/yp ; make**. Although **ypmake** is no longer supported under Solaris 2.x, it is still common on many networks.

**Keyword:**    networking

**Files:**    /var/yp/*

**See Also:**    make, ypcat, ypinit, ypmatch, yppasswd, ypset, ypwhich

### ypmatch hosts

ALL    ALL    SYSADM

This command is similar to the **ypcat** command with the **-k** option. The **ypmatch** command shows the value of the keys that are associated with the **hosts** NIS map.

**Keyword:**    networking

**Files:**    /var/yp/*

**See Also:**    ypcat, ypinit, ypmake, yppasswd, ypset, ypwhich

### yppasswd perkie

ALL    ALL    ALL

This command is used to change your NIS network password. When you type this command, you are prompted first for your old NIS password, then for your new NIS password.

**Keyword:**    networking

**Files:** /var/yp/*

**See Also:** ypcat, ypinit, ypmake, ypmatch, ypset, ypwhich

## ypset niserv1

The **ypset niserv1** command is used to bind the client workstation to the NIS server **niserv1**.

**Keyword:** networking

**Files:** /var/yp/*

**See Also:** ypcat, ypinit, ypmake, ypmatch, yppasswd, ypwhich

## ypwhich hosts

This command shows which NIS server is supplying information regarding the **hosts** map in the NIS database.

**Keyword:** networking

**Files:** /var/yp/*

**See Also:** ypcat, ypinit, ypmake, ypmatch, yppasswd, ypset

## zcat dir.tar.Z | tar xvf -

This command uncompresses the **dir.tar.Z** file and pipes it into **tar** so that it can be restored to the hard disk.

**Keyword:** file compression

**See Also:** cat, compress, less, more, pg, uncompress

## zcat report.doc.Z | more

On many systems, disk space is limited. One of the best ways to save space is to compress files. A disadvantage of compressing files is that they are more difficult to work with. This command outputs the **report.doc.Z** file to the display, in exactly the same manner that the **cat** command would.

**Keyword:** text display

**See Also:** cat, compress, less, more, pg, uncompress

## zdump EST

This command outputs the current date and time for the time zone listed. In this example, we chose Eastern Standard Time.

**Keyword:** system information

**See Also:** cal, date, xclock

ALL ALL SYSADM

ALL ALL SYSADM

ALL ALL POWER

ALL ALL ALL

ALL ALL POWER

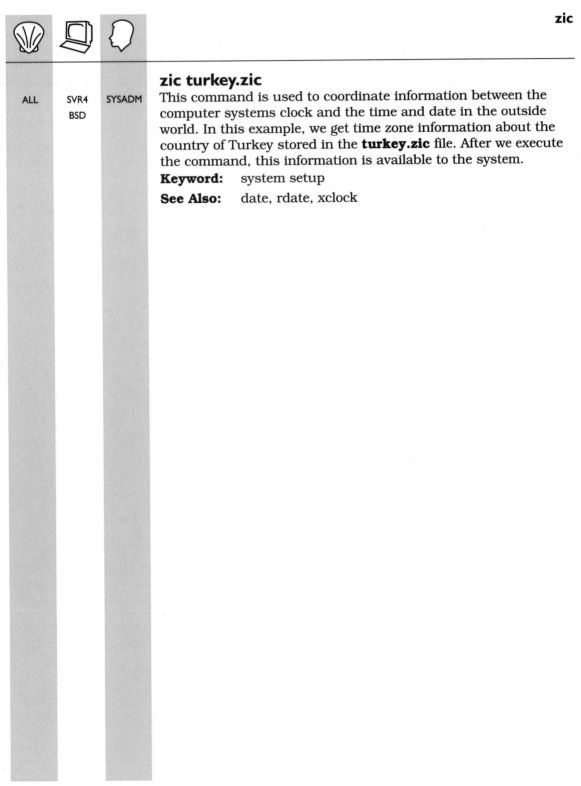

### zic turkey.zic
This command is used to coordinate information between the computer systems clock and the time and date in the outside world. In this example, we get time zone information about the country of Turkey stored in the **turkey.zic** file. After we execute the command, this information is available to the system.

**Keyword:**    system setup

**See Also:**    date, rdate, xclock

# Appendix A:
# vi Reference

Some users like **vi**, and others hate it. Still others users avoid it, but use it when they have to. If you fall into one of these categories, this appendix will be useful, because it provides brief but helpful descriptions of various **vi** commands.

## Operation Modes

| Option | Description |
| --- | --- |
| Esc | Initiates command mode, which lets you issue commands that include deleting, viewing, and saving your text. Command mode does not allow any text insertion. |
| | By default, you are in command mode when you first enter the **vi** editor. If you are in input mode, pressing Esc switches you to command mode. If you are in command mode, pressing Esc cancels your current command. |
| i | Initiates input mode for text insertion by allowing you to insert text before your current cursor position. |
| I | Initiates input mode for text insertion by allowing you to insert text at the *beginning* of the line where your cursor is currently positioned. |
| a | Initiates input mode for text insertion by allowing you to insert text *after* your current cursor position. |
| A | Initiates input mode for text insertion by allowing you to insert text at the *end* of the line where your cursor is currently positioned. |
| o | Initiates input mode for text insertion by opening a blank line *above* the line of existing text where your cursor is currently positioned. The cursor moves to the beginning of the new blank line. |

| Option | Description |
|--------|-------------|
| O | Initiates input mode for text insertion by opening a blank line *below* the line of existing text where your cursor is currently positioned. The cursor moves to the beginning of the new blank line. |
| r | Initiates input mode for text insertion by replacing a single text character at the current cursor position with the new character that you specify after the *r* command option. After entering the new character, the **vi** editor automatically returns to command mode. |
| R | Initiates input mode for text insertion by replacing the text at the current cursor position with as many new characters as you specify until you press Esc. The **vi** editor automatically returns to command mode. |

## Cursor Movement by Characters

| Option | Description |
|--------|-------------|
| l | (ell key) Moves the cursor forward one character at a time without moving past the *end* of the line where your cursor is currently positioned. If you precede this command option with *count n,* the cursor moves forward *n* characters. |
| h | Moves the cursor to the left one character at a time, without moving past the *beginning* of the line where your cursor is currently positioned. If you precede this command option with *count n,* the cursor moves backwards *n* characters. |
| O | Moves the cursor to the first character on the line where your cursor is currently positioned. |
| ^ | Moves the cursor to the first *nonwhite* character on the line where your cursor is currently positioned. (*White* characters are space, end-of-line, tab, and form-feed.) |
| $ | Moves the cursor to the last character on the line where your cursor is currently positioned. |

## Cursor Movement by Words

| Option | Description |
| --- | --- |
| w | Moves the cursor forward to the beginning of the *next* word from the current cursor position. If you precede this command option with *count n*, the cursor moves forward *n* words. |
| b | Moves the cursor back to the beginning of the *previous* word from the current cursor position. If you precede this command option with *count n*, the cursor moves back *n* words. |
| e | Moves the cursor to the last character of the word where your cursor is currently positioned. |
| W | Moves the cursor forward to the beginning of the *next* word from the current cursor position *including punctuation*. If you precede this command option with *count n*, the cursor moves forward *n* words. |
| B | Moves the cursor back to the beginning of the *previous* word from the current cursor position *including punctuation*. If you precede this command option with *count n*, the cursor moves back *n* words. |
| E | Moves the cursor to the last character of the word, *including punctuation*, where your cursor is currently positioned. |

## Cursor Movement by Lines

| Option | Description |
| --- | --- |
| j | Moves the cursor directly *down* one line from the current cursor position. (If there is no character directly below the cursor, the cursor moves to the end of the next line.) |
| k | Moves the cursor directly *up* one line from the current cursor position. |
| H | Moves the cursor to the beginning of the *first* line on the screen window. |
| M | Moves the cursor to the beginning of the *middle* line on the screen window. |
| L | Moves the cursor to the beginning of the *last* line on the screen window. |

## Cursor Movement by Sentences and Paragraphs

| Option | Description |
|---|---|
| ) | Moves the cursor forward to the beginning of the next sentence from the current cursor position. |
| ( | Moves the cursor back to the beginning of the sentence where the cursor is currently positioned. |
| { | Moves the cursor forward to the beginning of the next paragraph from the current cursor position. |
| } | Moves the cursor back to the beginning of the paragraph where the cursor is currently positioned. |

## Cursor File Movement

| Option | Description |
|---|---|
| 1G | Moves the cursor to the first line of your file. If you precede this command option with *count n*, your cursor moves *n* lines in your file. |
| G | Moves the cursor to the last line of your file. |
| Ctrl-G | Displays the status of the line where your cursor rests. Status information includes the name of the file, modifications to the file, the line number on which your cursor rests, and the total number of lines in your file. |

## Deleting Text

| Option | Description |
|---|---|
| x | Deletes the character on which your cursor currently rests. If you precede this command option with *count n*, your cursor deletes *n* characters. |
| dw | Deletes to the *end* of the word from your current cursor position. |
| db | Deletes to the *beginning* of the word from your current cursor position. |
| dd | Deletes the line on which your cursor currently rests. If you precede *dd* with *count n*, *n* lines are deleted from the current cursor position. |

| Option | Description |
|--------|-------------|
| d Return | Deletes the line where your cursor currently rests *and* the line that follows. |
| dO | Deletes to the *beginning* of the line from your current cursor position. |
| d) | Deletes to the *end* of the sentence from your current cursor position. |
| d( | Deletes to the *beginning* of the sentence from your current cursor position. |
| d} | Deletes to the *end* of the paragraph from your current cursor position. |
| d{ | Deletes to the *beginning* of the paragraph from your current cursor position. |

## Changing Existing Text

| Option | Description |
|--------|-------------|
| cw | Changes existing text to the *end* of a word from your current cursor position. |
| cb | Changes existing text to the *beginning* of a word from your current cursor position. |
| cc | Changes existing text on the line where your cursor currently rests. If you precede this command option with *count n, n* lines are deleted beginning with the current line. |
| c) | Changes existing text to the *end* of a sentence from your current cursor position. |
| c( | Changes existing text to the *beginning* of a sentence from your current cursor position. |
| c} | Changes existing text to the *end* of a paragraph from your current cursor position. |
| c{ | Changes existing text to the *beginning* of a paragraph from your current cursor position. |
| . | Repeats the most recent command that made a change. |
| u | Undoes your *last* text change. |

| Option | Description |
|--------|-------------|
| U | Restores the line where your cursor currently rests to its original state before any changes were made. The line will reflect only the original state of your current **vi** edit session. |
| Ctrl-l | (ell) Refreshes your screen display. |

## Searching for Text Patterns

| Option | Description |
|--------|-------------|
| /pattern | Searches forward in your file for the next occurrence of characters specified in a text pattern. |
| ?pattern | Searches backward in your file for the first occurrence of characters specified in a text pattern. |
| n | Repeats the last search command. |
| N | Repeats the last search command in the opposite direction. |

## Replacing Text

| Option | Description |
|--------|-------------|
| r | Replaces the current character. If you precede this command option with *count n*, you can replace the current character *n* times with the same letter. |
| R | Replaces only those characters you type over until you press Esc. If you reach the end of a line, this command option appends the input as new text. |

## Substituting Text

| Option | Description |
|--------|-------------|
| s | In input mode, deletes the character on which your cursor rests and appends the new text. Press Esc to return to command mode. If you precede this command option with *count n*, *n* characters are deleted before the text is appended. |
| S | Replaces all the characters in the line of your current cursor position. |

## Copying Text

| Option | Description |
| --- | --- |
| yw | Yanks the word from where your cursor currently rests and places it in a temporary buffer. If you precede this command option with *count n*, *n* words are yanked. |
| yy | Yanks the line where your cursor currently rests and places it in a temporary buffer. If you precede this command option with *count n*, *n* lines are yanked. |
| y Return | Yanks both the line where your cursor currently rests *and* the line that follows and places them in a temporary buffer. |
| y) | Yanks the sentence (ending with a period, comma, exclamation point, or question mark, followed by either two spaces or a newline) from where your cursor currently rests and places it in a temporary buffer. If you precede this command option with *count n*, *n* sentences are yankeds. |
| y} | Yanks the paragraph (beginning and ending with a blank line) from where your cursor currently rests and places it in a temporary buffer. If you precede this command option with *count n*, *n* paragraphs are yanked. |
| P | Places yanked text *after* the cursor or current line. |
| p | Places yanked text *before* the cursor or current line. |

## Ending a vi editor Session

| Option | Description |
| --- | --- |
| :w | Writes the buffer to a file without quitting the **vi** editor. You can specify a filename after this command option if you wish to save the file under another name. |
| :wq or ZZ | Saves your file and quits the **vi** editor. |
| :q | Quits the vi editor without saving your file. |
| :e | Abandons the current buffer and allows you to begin editing another file. |

# Appendix B:
# emacs Reference

This appendix lists **emacs** keystrokes, followed by a generic sequence when applicable. This appendix is not intended to cover all of **emacs**—which is a rich editor with many additional module functions—but it does provide a reference for for entering text, cursor movement, and editing. You can enter **emacs** commands in different modes. For example, text mode lets you write text, fill mode enables wordwrapping as you enter text, and C mode lets you to write C programs.

**Note:** Keystrokes that appear in the format *Ctrl-x-n* (where *n* represents any character) must be executed by holding down the Ctrl-key while you press both x and *n*, and then releasing Ctrl. Keystrokes that appear in the format *Ctrl-x,n* (where *n* represents any character) must be executed by holding down Ctrl, pressing x, and then releasing Ctrl-x just before pressing *n*.

## Entering emacs

| Keystrokes | Description |
|---|---|
| emacs | Allows you to start emacs without reading a file into the buffer. |
| emacs *filename* | Allows you to start emacs by reading a specific file into the buffer. You can name either an existing file that you wish to edit or a new file that you want to create. |

## Finding and Saving Files

| Keystrokes | Command Name | Description |
|---|---|---|
| Ctrl-x-f | find-file | Prompts you for the name of the file that you want to create or edit. |

| Keystrokes | Command Name | Description |
| --- | --- | --- |
| Ctrl-x,i | insert-file | Inserts a file at the current cursor position into the buffer. |
| Ctrl-x-w | write-file | Saves your file and allows you to specify a different filename. |
| Ctrl-x-s | save-buffer | Saves your file without allowing you to change your filename. If your terminal hangs after using this command, hit Ctrl-q to restart your terminal. |
| Ctrl-x-c | save-buffers-kill-emacs | Exits emacs and gives you the option of saving your file. |

## On-line Help

| Keystrokes | Command Name | Description |
| --- | --- | --- |
| Ctrl-h | help-command | Accesses on-line help in emacs. |
| Ctrl-h,f | describe-function | Accesses on-line help in emacs for a specific command name. |
| Ctrl-h,k | describe-key | Accesses on-line help in emacs for a specific keystroke sequence. |

## Cursor Movement

| Keystrokes | Command Name | Description |
| --- | --- | --- |
| Ctrl-f | forward-char | Moves the cursor one character to the right. |
| Ctrl-b | backward-char | Moves the cursor one character to the left. |
| Esc-f | forward-word | Moves the cursor one word forward. |
| Esc-b | backward-word | Moves the cursor one word backward. |
| Ctrl-a | beginning-of-line | Moves the cursor to the beginning of the line. |
| Ctrl-e | end-of-line | Moves the cursor to the end of the line. |

| Keystrokes | Command Name | Description |
|---|---|---|
| Ctrl-p | previous-line | Moves the cursor up to the previous line. |
| Ctrl-n | next-line | Moves the cursor to the next line. |
| Esc-[ | backward-paragraph | Moves the cursor to the previous paragraph. |
| Ctrl-x,[ | backward-page | Moves to the previous page. |
| Ctrl-x ] | forward-page | Moves to the next page. |
| Ctrl-v | scroll-up | Moves one screen forward. |
| Esc-v | scroll-down | Moves one screen backward. |
| Esc-> | end-of-buffer | Moves the cursor to the end of the file. |
| Esc-< | beginning-of-buffer | Moves the cursor to the beginning of the file. |
| Esc-n | digit-argument | Repeats the next command that you issue $n$ times. |
| Ctrl-l | recenter | Redraws the entire emacs display and places the line of the current cursor position in the center of your screen window. |

## Text Editing

| Keystrokes | Command Name | Description |
|---|---|---|
| Del | backward-delete-char | Deletes the previous character from your cursor position. |
| Ctrl-d | delete-char | Deletes the character on which your cursor rests. |
| Esc-d | kill-word | Deletes the word on which your cursor rests. |
| Esc-Del | backward-kill-word | Deletes the previous word from your cursor position. |
| Ctrl-k | kill-line | Deletes from the current cursor position to the end of the line. |
| Esc-k | kill-sentence | Delete the sentence on which the cursor rests. |

| Keystrokes | Command Name | Description |
| --- | --- | --- |
| Ctrl-@ | set-mark-command | Marks the beginning (or the end) of a text region that you wish to delete, move, or copy. |
| Ctrl-w | kill-region | Deletes a marked text region. |
| Ctrl-y | yank | Restores a delete text region. |
| Ctrl-g | keyboard-quit | Aborts the current command. |
| Ctrl-x-u | advertised-undo | Undoes your last editing change. (You can repeat this command to undo previous changes.) |
| Esc-q | fill-paragraph | Reformats a paragraph. |
| Esc-g | fill-region | Reformats paragraphs in a text region. |
| Esc-c | capitalize-word | Capitalizes the first letter of a word. |
| Esc-u | upcase-word | Capitalizes an entire word. |
| Esc-l | downcase-word | Lowercases an entire word. |
| Ctrl-x-u | upcase-region | Capitalizes an entire text region. |
| Ctrl-x-l | downcase-region | Lowercases an entire text region. |

## Using Buffers and Windows

| Keystrokes | Command Name | Description |
| --- | --- | --- |
| Ctrl-x-b | list-buffer | Displays the names of the buffers that you are using. |
| Ctrl-x,b | switch-to-buffer | Moves to the buffer you specify. |
| Ctrl-x,k | kill-buffer | Deletes the buffer you specify. |
| Ctrl-x,2 | split-window | Divides your current window into two. |
| Ctrl-x,o | other-window | Moves your cursor to the other window. |
| Ctrl-x,O | delete-window | Deletes the window where your cursor is currently positioned. |

# Appendix C:
# Shell Special Characters
# & ASCII Table

## Bourne Shell Special Characters

| Character | Meaning |
| --- | --- |
| .sh | Extension for Bourne shell script. |
| # | Start a comment. |
| ` | Command substitution. |
| " | Weak quotes. |
| ' | Strong quotes. |
| \ | Single-character quote. |
| $var | Variable. |
| ${var} | Same as $var. |
| ${var-default} | If var not set, use default. |
| ${var=default} | If var not set, set it to default and use that value. |
| ${var+instead} | If var set, use instead; otherwise, null string. |
| ${var?message} | If var not set, print message. If var set, use its value. |
| \| | Pipe standard output. |
| & | Run program in background. |
| ? | Match one character. |
| * | Match zero or more characters. |
| ; | Command separator. |
| ;; | End-of-case statement. |
| $# | Number of arguments to script. |
| "#@" | Original arguments to script. |
| $* | Arguments to script. |

| Character | Meaning |
|-----------|---------|
| $- | Flags passed to shell. |
| $? | Status of previous command. |
| $$ | Process identification number. |
| $! | Process identification number of last background job. |
| cmd1 && cmd2 | Execute *cmd2* if *cmd1* succeeds. |
| cmd1 \|\| cmd2 | Execute *cmd2* if *cmd1* fails. |
| . file | Execute commands from file in this shell. |
| : | Evaluate arguments; return true. |
| : | Separate values in paths. |
| [] | Match range of characters. |
| [] | Test. |
| (cmd;cmd) | Run *cmd*; *cmd* in a subshell. |
| {cmd;cmd; } | Like (*cmd;cmd*) without a subshell. |
| >file | Redirect standard output. |
| >>file | Append standard output. |
| <file | Redirect standard input. |
| <<word | Read until word; do command and variable substitution. |
| <<\word | Read until word, no substitution. |
| <<-word | Read until word, ignoring tabs. |
| m> file | Redirect output file descriptor m to file. |
| m>> file | Append output file descriptor m to file. |
| <m file | Redirect input file descriptor m to file. |
| <&m | Make standard input from file descriptor m. |
| <&- | Close standard input. |
| >&m | Use file descriptor m as standard output. |
| >&- | Close standard output. |
| m<&n | Connect input file descriptor n to file descriptor m. |
| m<&- | Close file descriptor m. |
| n>&m | Connect output file descriptor n to file descriptor m |

| Character | Meaning |
|-----------|---------|
| m>&- | Close file descriptor m. |
| prog > file | Send standard output to file. |
| prog 2> file | Send standard error to file. |
| prog > file 2>&1 | Send standard ouput and standard error to file. |
| prog < file | Take standard input from file. |
| prog >> file | Send standard output to end of file. |
| prog 2>> file | Send standard error to end of file. |
| prog >> file2$ >&1 | Send standard output and standard error to end of file. |
| prog <<c | Read standard input from keyboard until c. |
| prog \| prog2 | Pipe standard output to *prog2*. |
| 'xxx' | Disable all special characters in xxx. |
| "xxx" | Disable all special characters except $, `, \. |
| /x | Disable special meaning of character; remove newline. |
| . | Matches any character, except end-of-line character. |
| ^.$ | Matches a line with any single character. |
| * | Matches any line with a *. |
| \* | Matches any line with a *. |
| \\ | Matches any line with a \. |
| ^* | Matches any line starting with a *. |
| ^A* | Matches any line. |
| ^A\* | Matches any line starting with an *A*. |
| ^AA* | Matches any line starting with one *A*. |
| ^AA*B | Matches any line starting one or more A characters followed by a *B*. |
| ^A\{4,8\}B | Matches line starting with 4,5,6,7 or 8 A characters followed by *B*. |
| ^A\{4,\}B | Matches line starting with 4 or more A characters followed by a *B*. |
| ^A\{4\}B | Matches line starting with *AAAAB*. |

| Character | Meaning |
|---|---|
| \\{4,8\\} | Matches any line with a {4,8}. |
| A{4,8} | Matches any line with an A{4,8}. |

## Korn Shell Special Characters

| Character | Meaning |
|---|---|
| # | Start a comment. |
| ` | Command substitution. |
| " | Weak quotes. |
| ' | Strong quotes. |
| \\ | Single-character quote. |
| $var | Variable. |
| ${var} | Same as $var. |
| ${var-default} | If var not set, use default. |
| ${var=default} | If var not set, set it to default and use that value. |
| ${var+instead} | If var set, use instead; otherwise, null string. |
| ${var?message} | If var not set, print message; if set, use its value. |
| ${var#pat} | Value of var with smallest pat deleted from start. |
| ${var##pat} | Value of var with largest pat deleted from start. |
| ${var%pat} | Value of var with smallest pat deleted from end. |
| ${var%%pat} | Value of var with largest pat deleted from end. |
| \| | Pipe standard output. |
| & | Run program in background. |
| ? | Match one character. |
| * | Match zero or more characters. |
| ; | Command separator. |
| ;; | End-of-case statement. |

| Character | Meaning |
|---|---|
| ~ | Home directory. |
| ~user | Home directory of user. |
| $# | Number of arguments to script. |
| "$@" | Original arguments to script. |
| $* | Arguments to script. |
| $- | Flags passed to shell. |
| $? | Status of previous command. |
| $$ | Process identification number. |
| $! | Process identification number of last background job. |
| cmd1 && cmd2 | Execute *cmd2* if *cmd1* succeeds. |
| cmd1 \|\| cmd2 | Execute *cmd2* if *cmd1* fails. |
| $(..$) | Command substitution. |
| ((..)) | Arithmetic evaluation. |
| . file | Execute commands from file in this shell. |
| : | Evaluate arguments; return true. |
| : | Separate values in paths. |
| [] | Match range of characters. |
| [] | Test. |
| (cmd;cmd) | Run *cmd;cmd* in a subshell. |
| {cmd;cmd; } | Like (*cmd;cmd*) without a subshell. |
| >file | Redirect standard output. |
| >>file | Append standard output. |
| <file | Redirect standard input. |
| <<word | Read until *word*; do command and variable substitution. |
| <<\word | Read until *word*, no substitution. |
| <<-word | Read until *word*, ignoring tabs. |
| m> file | Redirect output file descriptor *m* to *file*. |
| m>> file | Append output file descriptor *m* to *file*. |
| <m file | Redirect input file descriptor *m* from *file*. |
| <&m | Close standard input. |

| Character | Meaning |
|---|---|
| >&m | Use file descriptor m as standard output. |
| >&- | Close standard output. |
| $(..$) | Command substitution. |
| m<&n | Connect input file descriptor $n$ to file descriptor $m$. |
| m<&- | Close file descriptor $m$. |
| n>&m | Connect output file descriptor $n$ to file descriptor $m$. |
| m>&- | Close file descriptor $m$. |
| CTRL-b | Move backward one character without deleting. |
| CTRL-f | Move forward one character. |
| CTRL-d | Delete one character forward. |
| CTRL-z | Move to beginning of line. |
| CTRL-e | Move to end of line. |
| CTRL-k | Move ("kill") forward to end of line. |
| CTRL-w | Delete ("wipe") backward to beginning of line. |
| CTRL-y | Retrieve ("yank") last deleted item. |
| CTRL-c | Delete entire line. |
| CTRL-p | Go to previous command. |
| CTRL-n | Go to next command. |
| CTRL-rstring | Search backward for command containing string. |
| prog > file | Send standard output to file. |
| prog 2> file | Send standard error to file. |
| prog > file 2>&1 | Send standard output and standard error to file. |
| prog < file | Take standard input from file. |
| prog >> file | Send standard output to end of file. |
| prog 2>> file | Send standard error to end of file. |
| prog >> file 2>&1 | Send standard output and standard error to end of file. |

| Character | Meaning |
|---|---|
| prog <<c | Read standard input from keyboard until *c*. |
| prog \| prog2 | Pipe standard output to *prog2*. |
| prog 2>&1 \| prog2 | Pipe standard output and standard error to *prog2*. |
| ^A | Anchors an *A* at the beginning of a line. |
| A$ | Anchors an *A* at the end of a line. |
| A^ | Anchors an *A^* anywhere on a line. |
| $A | Anchors a *$A* anywhere on a line. |
| . | Matches any character, except end-of-line character. |
| ^.$ | Matches a line with a single character. |
| * | Matches any line with an *. |
| \* | Matches any line with an *. |
| \\ | Matches any line with a \. |
| ^* | Matches any line with an *. |
| ^A* | Matches any line. |
| ^A\* | Matches any ine starting with an *A*. |
| ^AA* | Matches any line starting with one *A*. |
| ^AA*B | Matches line starting with one or more *A* characters followed by B. |
| ^A\{4,8}B | Matches line starting with 4,5,6,7 or 8 *A* characters followed by B. |
| ^A\{4,\}B | Matches line starting with 4 or more *A* characters followed by B. |
| ^A\{4\}B | Matches line starting with an *AAAAB*. |
| \{4,8\} | Matches any line with a *{4,8}*. |
| A{4,8} | Matches any line with an *A{4,8}*. |
| ?(abc) | Wildcard matches zero or one instance of *abc*. |
| *(abc) | Wildcard matches zero or more instances of *abc*. |
| +(abc) | Wildcard matches one or more instances of *abc*. |
| !(abc) | Wildcard matches anything that doesn't have *abc*. |

## C Shell Special Characters

| Character | Meaning |
|-----------|---------|
| .csh | Extension for C shell script. |
| # | Comment a line. |
| ` | Command substitution. |
| " | Weak quotes. |
| ' | Strong quotes. |
| \ | Single-character quote. |
| () | Group commands. |
| && | Execute next command if previous one was successful. |
| \| \| | Execute next command if previous one fails. |
| < | Redirect standard input. |
| >>&! | Append standard output and standard error. |
| << str | Read input lines until *str* is encountered at beginning of line. |
| [list] | Match any character in list. |
| `cmd` | Execute *cmd* and substitute output. |
| \c | Escape character *c* (taken literally). |
| 'str' | String characters taken literally. |
| "str" | Allow command substitution and variable substitution. |
| *[ ] ? { }~- | File expansion. |
| < > & ! | Redirection. |
| ! ^ | History. |
| $var | Variable. |
| ${var} | Same as *$var*. |
| $#var | Number of words in *var*. |
| $O | Name of script file. |
| $?var | 1 if *var* is defined; 0 if not. |
| $$ | Process ID of parent shell. |
| r | Root name. |

| Character | Meaning |
| --- | --- |
| h | Header name. |
| t | Tail. |
| gr | Extract root names from wordlist. |
| gh | Extract header names from wordlist. |
| gt | Extract tail names from wordlist. |
| q | Quote. |
| x | Quote and expand into separate words. |
| !N | Command *N*. |
| !! | Last command. |
| !str | Last command starting with *str*. |
| !?str? | Last command with *str* anywhere in command. |
| :0 | Command name. |
| :^ | First word. |
| :$ | Last word. |
| :% | Word matched by *?str?* search. |
| ( ) | Change precedence. |
| ~ | Home directory. |
| ~user | Home directory of user. |
| ~ | 1's complement. |
| ! | Command history. |
| ! | Logical negation. |
| * / % | Multiply, divide, module. |
| + - | Add, subtract. |
| << >> | Left shift, right shift. |
| == != | String comparison. |
| & | Run program in background. |
| & | Bitwise "and". |
| ^ | Bitwise "exclusive or". |
| | | Pipe standard output. |
| |& | Pipe standard output and standard error. |
| | | Bitwise "inclusive or". |

| Character | Meaning |
| --- | --- |
| && | Logical "and". |
| \|\| | Logical "or". |
| ++ | Increment. |
| -- | Decrement. |
| = | Assignment. |
| *= | Multiply left side by right side and update left. |
| /= | Divide left side by right side and update left. |
| += | Add left side to right side and update left. |
| -= | Subtract left side from right side and update left. |
| %= | Divide left side by right side and update with remainder. |
| -d | File is a directory. |
| -e | File exists. |
| -f | File is a plain file. |
| -o | User is owner. |
| -r | User has read access. |
| -w | User has write access. |
| -x | User has execute access. |
| -z | File has zero length. |
| ? | Wildcard for one character. |
| * | Wildcard for zero or more characters. |
| ; | Command separator. |
| $# | Number of arguments to script. |
| $* | Arguments to script. |
| $< | Read input from terminal. |
| cmd1 && cmd2 | Execute *cmd2* if *cmd1* succeeds. |
| cmd1 \|\| cmd2 | Execute *cmd2* if *cmd1* fails. |
| : | Variable modifier. |
| [ ] | Match range of characters. |
| %job | Identify job number. |

| Character | Meaning |
|---|---|
| (cmd;cmd) | Run *cmd;cmd* in a subshell. |
| { } | In-line expansion. |
| >file | Redirect standard output. |
| >>file | Append standard output. |
| <<word | Read until *word*; do command and var substitution. |
| <<\word | Read until *word*, no substitution. |
| >>!file | Append to *file*, even if noclobber set/file doesn't exist. |
| >!file | Output to *file*, even if noclobber set and file exists. |
| >&file | Redirect standard output and standard error to *file*. |
| prog>file | Send standard output to *file*. |
| prog>&file | Send standard output and standard error to *file*. |
| prog<file | Take standard input from *file*. |
| prog>>file | Send standard output to end of *file*. |
| prog>>&file | Send standard output and standard error to end of *file*. |
| prog<<c | Read standard input from keyboard until *c*. |
| prog \| prog2 | Pipe standard output to *prog2*. |
| prog \| &prog2 | Pipe standard output and standard error to *prog2*. |
| 'xxx' | Disable all special characters, except !. |
| "xxx" | Disable all special characters, except $, `, !. |
| /x | Disable special meaning of character; treat newline as space. |

## Miscellaneous Commands

| Character | Meaning |
|---|---|
| ? | Wildcard matches single character. |
| * | Wildcard matches any group of zero or more. |

| Character | Meaning |
|-----------|---------|
| [ab] | Wildcard matches either a or b. |
| [a-z] | Wildcard matches any character between a and z. |
| [!ab..z] | Wildcard matches any character that doesn't appear in brackets. |

## Extensions

| Character | Meaning |
|-----------|---------|
| .a | Archive file (library). |
| .c | C program source file. |
| .h | C program header file. |
| .f | FORTRAN program source file. |
| .0 | FORTRAN program source file to pre-process. |
| .s | Assembly language code. |
| .z | Packed file. |
| .Z | Compressed file. |
| .1 to .8 | Online manual source file. |
| .txt | ASCII text file. |
| .tar | Tar archive. |
| .shar | Shell archive. |
| .mm | Text file containing troff's **mm** macros. |
| .ms | Text file containing troff's **ms** macros. |
| .ps | PostScript source file. |
| ^$ | Blank lines. |
| ^.*$ | Entire line. |
| $ | Match end of line. |
| [ ] | Match one from a set. |
| \( \) | Store pattern for later replay. |
| \{ \} | Match a range of instances. |
| \< \> | Match word's beginning or end. |
| + | Match one or more preceding. |

| Character | Meaning |
| --- | --- |
| ? | Match zero or one preceding. |
| \| | Separate choices to match. |
| ( ) | Group expressions to match. |
| \ | Escape character following. |
| \n | Reuse pattern stored in \( \). |
| & | Reuse previous search pattern. |
| ~ | Reuse previous replacement pattern. |
| \u \U | Change character(s) to uppercase. |
| \l \L | Change character(s) to lowercase. |
| \E | Turn off previous \U or \L. |
| \e | Turn off previous \u or \l. |
| . | Match any single character except newline. |
| * | Match any # of single characters preceding. |
| ^ | Match following expression at beginning of line. |
| $ | Match preceding expression at end of the line. |
| [ ] | Match any one of the enclosed characters. |
| \{n,m\} | Match range of occurrences of single character preceding. |
| \ | Turn off the special meaning of the character following. |
| \( \) | Save the pattern enclosed in holding space. |
| \< \> | Match characters at beginnning or end of a word. |
| + | Match one+ instances of preceding regular expression. |
| ? | Match zero/one instance of preceding regular expression. |
| \| | Match regular expression specified before or after. |
| (.) | Apply a match to the enclosed group of regular expressions. |
| \u | Convert first character to uppercase. |

| Character | Meaning |
|-----------|---------|
| \U | Convert replacement pattern to uppercase. |
| \l | Convert first character to lowercase. |
| \L | Convert replacement pattern to lowercase. |
| :s/\<[a-z]\u&/g | Capitalize first character of every beginning word. |
| :%s/\<[a-z]/\u&/g | Capitalize all lines in file. |

## ASCII Table

Decimal-Hexadecimal-Octal-Binary-ASCII Numerical Conversions

| Dex X10 | Hex X16 | Oct X8 | Binary X2 | ASCII | Key |
|---------|---------|--------|-----------|-------|-----|
| 0 | 00 | 00 | 000 0000 | NUL | CTRL/1 |
| 1 | 01 | 01 | 000 0001 | SOH | CTRL/A |
| 2 | 02 | 02 | 000 0010 | STX | CTRL/B |
| 3 | 03 | 03 | 000 0011 | ETX | CTRL/C |
| 4 | 04 | 04 | 000 0100 | EOT | CTRL/D |
| 5 | 05 | 05 | 000 0101 | ENQ | CTRL/E |
| 6 | 06 | 06 | 000 0110 | ACK | CTRL/F |
| 7 | 07 | 07 | 000 0111 | BEL | CTRL/G |
| 8 | 08 | 10 | 000 1000 | BS | CTRL/H or Backspace |
| 9 | 09 | 11 | 000 1001 | HT | CTRL/I or TAB |
| 10 | 0A | 12 | 000 1010 | LF | CTRL/J or Line feed |
| 11 | 0B | 13 | 000 1011 | VT | CTRL/K |
| 12 | 0C | 14 | 000 1100 | FF | CTRL/L |
| 13 | 0D | 15 | 000 1101 | CR | CTRL/M or Return |
| 14 | 0E | 16 | 000 1110 | SO | CTRL/N |
| 15 | 0F | 17 | 000 1111 | SI | CTRL/O |
| 16 | 10 | 20 | 001 0000 | DLE | CTRL/P |
| 17 | 11 | 21 | 001 0001 | DC1 | CTRL/Q |
| 18 | 12 | 22 | 001 0010 | DC2 | CTRL/R |
| 19 | 13 | 23 | 001 0011 | DC3 | CTRL/S |
| 20 | 14 | 24 | 001 0100 | DC4 | CTRL/T |

| Dex X10 | Hex X16 | Oct X8 | Binary X2 | ASCII | Key |
|---|---|---|---|---|---|
| 21 | 15 | 25 | 001 0101 | NAK | CTRL/U |
| 22 | 16 | 26 | 001 0110 | SYN | CTRL/V |
| 23 | 17 | 27 | 001 0111 | ETB | CTRL/W |
| 24 | 18 | 30 | 001 1000 | CAN | CTRL/X |
| 25 | 19 | 31 | 001 1001 | EM | CTRL/Y |
| 26 | 1A | 32 | 001 1010 | SUB | CTRL/Z |
| 27 | 1B | 33 | 001 1011 | ESC | ESC, Escape |
| 28 | 1C | 34 | 001 1100 | FS | CTRL< |
| 29 | 1D | 35 | 001 1101 | GS | CTRL/ |
| 30 | 1E | 36 | 001 1110 | RS | CTRL/= |
| 31 | 1F | 37 | 001 1111 | US | CTRL/- |
| 32 | 20 | 40 | 010 0000 | SP | Spacebar |
| 33 | 21 | 41 | 010 0001 | ! | ! |
| 34 | 22 | 42 | 010 0010 | " | " |
| 35 | 23 | 43 | 010 0011 | # | # |
| 36 | 24 | 44 | 010 0100 | $ | $ |
| 37 | 25 | 45 | 010 0101 | 1/2 | 1/2 |
| 38 | 26 | 46 | 010 0110 | & | & |
| 39 | 27 | 47 | 010 0111 | ' | ' |
| 40 | 28 | 50 | 010 1000 | ( | ( |
| 41 | 29 | 51 | 010 1001 | ) | ) |
| 42 | 2A | 52 | 010 1010 | * | * |
| 43 | 2B | 53 | 010 1011 | + | + |
| 44 | 2C | 54 | 010 1100 | , | , |
| 45 | 2D | 55 | 010 1101 | - | - |
| 46 | 2E | 56 | 010 1110 | . | . |
| 47 | 2F | 57 | 010 1111 | / | / |
| 48 | 30 | 60 | 011 0000 | 0 | 0 |
| 49 | 31 | 61 | 011 0001 | 1 | 1 |
| 50 | 32 | 62 | 011 0010 | 2 | 2 |
| 51 | 33 | 63 | 011 0011 | 3 | 3 |
| 52 | 34 | 64 | 011 0100 | 4 | 4 |
| 53 | 35 | 65 | 011 0101 | 5 | 5 |

| Dex X10 | Hex X16 | Oct X8 | Binary X2 | ASCII | Key |
|---------|---------|--------|-----------|-------|-----|
| 54 | 36 | 66 | 011 0110 | 6 | 6 |
| 55 | 37 | 67 | 011 0111 | 7 | 7 |
| 56 | 38 | 70 | 011 1000 | 8 | 8 |
| 57 | 39 | 71 | 011 1001 | 9 | 9 |
| 58 | 3A | 72 | 011 1010 | : | : |
| 59 | 3B | 73 | 011 1011 | ; | ; |
| 60 | 3C | 74 | 011 1100 | < | < |
| 61 | 3D | 75 | 011 1101 | = | = |
| 62 | 3E | 76 | 011 1110 | > | > |
| 63 | 3F | 77 | 011 1111 | ? | ? |
| 64 | 40 | | 100 0000 | @ | @ |
| 65 | 41 | 101 | 100 0001 | A | A |
| 66 | 42 | 102 | 100 0010 | B | B |
| 67 | 43 | 103 | 100 0011 | C | C |
| 68 | 44 | 104 | 100 0100 | D | D |
| 69 | 45 | 105 | 100 0101 | E | E |
| 70 | 46 | 106 | 100 0110 | F | F |
| 71 | 47 | 107 | 100 0111 | G | G |
| 72 | 48 | 110 | 100 1000 | H | H |
| 73 | 49 | 111 | 100 1001 | I | I |
| 74 | 4A | 112 | 100 1010 | J | J |
| 75 | 4B | 113 | 100 1011 | K | K |
| 76 | 4C | 114 | 100 1100 | L | L |
| 77 | 4D | 115 | 100 1101 | M | M |
| 78 | 4E | 116 | 100 1110 | N | N |
| 79 | 4F | 117 | 100 1111 | O | O |
| 80 | 50 | 120 | 101 0000 | P | P |
| 81 | 51 | 121 | 101 0001 | Q | Q |
| 82 | 52 | 122 | 101 0010 | R | R |
| 83 | 53 | 123 | 101 0011 | S | S |
| 84 | 54 | 124 | 101 0100 | T | T |
| 85 | 55 | 125 | 101 0101 | U | U |
| 86 | 56 | 126 | 101 0110 | V | V |

| Dex X10 | Hex X16 | Oct X8 | Binary X2 | ASCII | Key |
|---------|---------|--------|-----------|-------|-----|
| 87 | 57 | 127 | 101 0111 | W | W |
| 88 | 58 | 130 | 101 1000 | X | X |
| 89 | 59 | 131 | 101 1001 | Y | Y |
| 90 | 5A | 132 | 101 1010 | Z | Z |
| 91 | 5B | 133 | 101 1011 | [ | [ |
| 92 | 5C | 134 | 101 1100 | \ | \ |
| 93 | 5D | 135 | 101 1101 | ] | ] |
| 94 | 5E | 136 | 101 1110 | ^ | ^ |
| 95 | 5F | 137 | 101 1111 | - | - |
| 96 | 60 | 140 | 110 0000 | ` | ` |
| 97 | 61 | 141 | 110 0001 | a | a |
| 98 | 62 | 142 | 110 0010 | b | b |
| 99 | 63 | 143 | 110 0011 | c | c |
| 100 | 64 | 144 | 110 0100 | d | d |
| 101 | 65 | 145 | 110 0101 | e | e |
| 102 | 66 | 146 | 110 0110 | f | f |
| 103 | 67 | 147 | 110 0111 | g | g |
| 104 | 68 | 150 | 110 1000 | h | h |
| 105 | 69 | 151 | 110 1001 | i | i |
| 106 | 6A | 152 | 110 1010 | j | j |
| 107 | 6B | 153 | 110 1011 | k | k |
| 108 | 6C | 154 | 110 1100 | l | l |
| 109 | 6D | 155 | 110 1101 | m | m |
| 110 | 6E | 156 | 110 1110 | n | n |
| 111 | 6F | 157 | 110 1111 | o | o |
| 112 | 70 | 160 | 111 0000 | p | p |
| 113 | 71 | 161 | 111 0001 | q | q |
| 114 | 72 | 162 | 111 0010 | r | r |
| 115 | 73 | 163 | 111 0011 | s | s |
| 116 | 74 | 164 | 111 0100 | t | t |
| 117 | 75 | 165 | 111 0101 | u | u |
| 118 | 76 | 166 | 111 0110 | v | v |
| 119 | 77 | 167 | 111 0111 | w | w |

# Appendix C: Shell Special Characters & ASCII Table

| Dex X10 | Hex X16 | Oct X8 | Binary X2 | ASCII | Key |
|---------|---------|--------|-----------|-------|-----|
| 120 | 78 | 170 | 111 1000 | x | x |
| 121 | 79 | 171 | 111 1001 | y | y |
| 122 | 7A | 172 | 111 1010 | z | z |
| 123 | 7B | 173 | 111 1011 | { | { |
| 124 | 7C | 174 | 111 1100 | \| | \| |
| 125 | 7D | 175 | 111 1101 | } | } |
| 126 | 7E | 176 | 111 1110 | ~ | ~ |
| 127 | 7F | 177 | 111 1111 | DEL | DEL or Rubout |

# Keyword Index

## job control

## NFS

## open look

## printing

## program execution

## text editing

**619**